TEUTONIC MYTHOLOGY

BY JACOB GRIMM

Translated from the Fourth Edition
with Notes and Appendix
by JAMES STEVEN STALLYBRASS

in four volumes   (*Volume I*)

DOVER PUBLICATIONS, INC., NEW YORK

Published in Canada by General Publishing Company, Ltd., 30 Lesmill Road, Don Mills, Toronto, Ontario.

Published in the United Kingdom by Constable and Company, Ltd., 10 Orange Street, London W. C. 2.

This Dover edition, first published in 1966, is an unabridged and unaltered republication of the work first published by George Bell and Sons. Volumes I, II and III were originally published in 1883, and Volume IV was first published in 1888.

The publisher is grateful to the Director of Libraries of Columbia University for making a copy of Volume IV of this work available for purpose of reproduction.

Library of Congress Catalog Card Number: 66-15933

Manufactured in the United States of America
Dover Publications, Inc.
180 Varick Street
New York, N. Y. 10014

TRANSLATOR'S PREFACE.

———◆———

" I THINK Scandinavian Paganism, to us here, is more interesting than any other. It is, for one thing, the latest; it continued in these regions of Europe till the eleventh century; 800 years ago the Norwegians were still worshippers of Odin. It is interesting also as the creed of our fathers; the men whose blood still runs in our veins, whom doubtless we still resemble in so many ways. . . . There is another point of interest in these Scandinavian mythologies, that they have been preserved so well."—CARLYLE'S " HERO-WORSHIP".

What Mr. Carlyle says of the Scandinavian will of course apply to all Teutonic tradition, so far as it can be recovered; and it was the task of Grimm in his *Deutsche Mythologie* to supplement the Scandinavian mythology (of which, thanks to the Icelanders, we happen to know most) with all that can be gleaned from other sources, High-Dutch and Low-Dutch, and build it up into a whole. And indeed to prove that it *was* one connected whole; for, strange as it seems to us, forty years ago it was still considered necessary to prove it.

Jacob Grimm was perhaps the first man who commanded a wide enough view of the whole field of Teutonic languages and literature to be able to bring into a focus the scattered facts which show the prevalence of one system of thought among all the Teutonic nations from Iceland to the Danube. In this he was materially aided by his mastery of the true principles of Philology, which he was the first to establish on a firm scientific basis, and which enabled him to trace a word with certitude through the strangest disguises.

The Comparative Mythology of all nations has made great strides since Grimm first wrote his book; but as a storehouse of facts within his special province of *Teutonic* Mythology, and as a clue to the derivation and significance of the *Names* of persons and things in the various versions of a myth, it has never been superseded and perhaps it never can be. Not that he confines himself to the Teutonic field; he compares it at every point with the classical mythus and the wide circle of Slavic, Lettic and occasionally of Ugric, Celtic, and Oriental tradition. Still, among his *Deutsch* kindred he is most at home; and Etymology is his forte. But then etymology in his hands is transfigured from random guessing into scientific fact.

There is no one to whom Folk-lore is more indebted than to Grimm. Not to mention the loving care with which he hunted up his *Kinder und Haus-märchen* from all over Germany, he delights to detect in many a nursery-tale and popular custom of to-day the beliefs and habits of our forefathers thousands of years ago. It is impossible at times to forbear a smile at the patriotic zeal with which he hunts the trail of his German gods and heroes; the glee with which he bags a new goddess, elf, or swan-maid; and his indignation at any poaching Celt or Slav who has spirited away a mythic being that was German born and bred: "Ye have taken away my gods, and what have I more?"

The present translation of the *Deutsche Mythologie* will, like the last (fourth) edition of the original, be published in three volumes; the first two of which, and part of the third, will contain the translation of Grimm's text, and the remainder of the third volume will consist of his own Appendix and a Supplement.

The author's second and third editions (1844 and 1854) were each published in 2 vols., accompanied by an APPENDIX consisting, first, of a short treatise on the *Anglo-Saxon Genealogies*, and secondly, of a large collection of the *Superstitions* of various Teutonic nations. This Appendix will form a part of our Vol. III. After Grimm's death his heirs entrusted to Prof. E. H. Meyer, of Berlin, the task of bringing out a fourth edition, and including in it such additional matter as the author had collected in his note-books for future use. If Grimm had lived to finish his great Dictionary, which engrossed the latter years of his life,[1] he would, no doubt, have incorporated

---

[1] He used to say, he had a book ready to run out of each of his ten fingers, but he was no longer free.

the pith of these later jottings in the text of his book, rejecting
much that was irrelevant or pleonastic.   The German editor, not
feeling himself at liberty to select and reject, threw the whole of
this posthumous matter into his third volume (where it occupies
370 pages), merely arranging the items according to the order of
subjects in the book, and numbering each by the page which it
illustrates.   This is the SUPPLEMENT so frequently referred to in
the book, under the form (" see Suppl."). I have already introduced
a few extracts from it in the Foot-notes, especially where it appeared
to contradict, or materially to confirm, the author's opinion expressed in the text.   But in the present English edition it is intended
to *digest* this Supplement, selecting the most valuable parts, and
adding original articles by the editor himself and by other gentlemen
who have devoted special attention to individual branches of the
science of Folk-knowledge.   A full classified Bibliography and an
accurate and detailed Index to the whole work will accompany the
book.   It is hoped by this means to render the English Edition as
complete and serviceable as possible.

Grimm's *Preface* to the edition of 1844, giving a vigorous re-
sumé of the book, and of the whole subject, will, as in the German
accompany Vol. II.   There is so much in it, which implies the
reader's acquaintance with every part of the book, that I have felt
bound to keep it where I find it in the original.

The only additions or alterations I have ventured to make in
the text are the following :—

1. The book bristles with quotations in various languages, for
the most part untranslated.   An ordinary German reader might
find the Old and the Middle High German about as intelligible as
an ordinary Englishman does Anglo-Saxon and Chaucer respectively.   But when it comes to making out a word or passage in
Old Norse, Greek, and even Slavic, I must suppose the author to
have written for a much more limited and learned public than that
which, I hope, will find this English edition sufficiently readable.
I have therefore *translated* a great many words and sentences,

where the interest, and even the argument, of the paragraph depended on the reader's understanding the quotations. To have translated *all* that is not English would have swelled the size of the book too much. Apart from such translation, any additions of my own are always placed in square brackets [ ], except a few notes which bear the signature "TRANS.".

2. For the sake of clearness, I have divided some of the chapters (XII. to XVI.) into smaller sections with headings of their own.

3. I have consulted the English reader's convenience by substituting the *w* and *æ*, which he is accustomed to see in Anglo-Saxon words, for Grimm's *v* and *ä*, as 'wæg' instead of 'väg'. I have also used the words 'Dutch, Mid. Dutch' in a wider sense comprehending all the Teutonic dialects of the Netherlands, instead of coining the awkward adjective 'Netherlandish'.

One word on the title of the book. Ought not "*Deutsche* Mythologie" to be translated *German*, rather than *Teutonic* Mythology? I am bound to admit that the author aimed at building up a *Deutsch* mythology, as distinct from the Scandinavian, and that he expressly disclaims the intention of giving a complete account of the latter, because its fulness would have thrown the more meagre remains of the Deutsch into the shade. At the same time he necessarily draws so much upon the richer remains of the Norse mythology, that it forms quite a substantive portion of his book, though not exhaustive as regards the Norse system itself. But what does Grimm mean by *Deutsch?* To translate it by *German* would be at least as misleading in the other direction. It would not amongst us be generally understood to include—what he expressly intends it to include—the Netherlands and England; for the English are simply a branch of the Low German race which happened to cross the sea. I have therefore thought, that for the English ear the more comprehensive title was truer to the facts on the whole than the more limited one would have been.

CONTENTS.

VOL. I.

CHAPTER I.

INTRODUCTION.[1]

From the westernmost shore of Asia, Christianity had turned at once to the opposite one of Europe. The wide soil of the continent which had given it birth could not supply it long with nourishment; neither did it strike deep root in the north of Africa. Europe soon became, and remained, its proper dwelling-place and home.

It is worthy of notice, that the direction in which the new faith worked its way, from South to North, is contrary to the current of migration which was then driving the nations from the East and North to the West and South. As spiritual light penetrated from the one quarter, life itself was to be reinvigorated from the other.

---

[1] In a book that deals so much with Heathenism, the meaning of the term ought not to be passed over. The Greeks and Romans had no special name for nations of another faith (for ἑτερόδοξοι, βάρβαροι were not used in that sense) ; but with the Jews and Christians of the N.T. are contrasted ἔθνος, ἔθνεα, ἐθνικοί, Lat. gentes, gentiles ; Ulphilas uses the pl. thiudôs, and by preference in the gen. after a pronoun, thái thiudô, sumái thiudô (gramm. 4, 441, 457), while thiudiskôs translates ἐθνικῶς Gal. 2, 14. As it was mainly the Greek religion that stood opposed to the Judæo-Christian, the word "Ελλην also assumed the meaning ἐθνικός, and we meet with ἑλληνικῶς = ἐθνικῶς, which the Goth would still have rendered thiudiskôs, as he does render "Ελληνες thiudôs, John 7, 35. 12, 20. 1 Cor. 1, 24. 12, 13 ; only in 1 Cor. 1, 22 he prefers Krêkôs. This "Ελλην = gentilis bears also the meaning of giant, which has developed itself out of more than one national name (Hun, Avar, Tchudi) ; so the Hellenic walls came to be heathenish, gigantic (see ch. XVIII). In Old High German, Notker still uses the pl. diete for gentiles (Graff 5, 128). In the meanwhile pagus had expanded its narrow meaning of κώμη into the wider one of ager, campus, in which sense it still lives on in It. paese, Fr. pays ; while paganus began to push out gentilis, which was lapsing into the sense of nobilis. All the Romance languages have their pagano, payen, &c., nay, it has penetrated into Bohem. pohan, Pol. poganin, Lith. pagonas [but Russ. pogan = unclean]. The Gothic háithi campus early developed an adj. háithns agrestis, campestris = paganus (Ulph. in Mark 7, 26 renders ἑλληνίς by háithnô), the Old H.G. heida an adj. heidan, Mid. H.G. and Dutch heide heiden, A.S. hæð hæðin, Engl. heath heathen, Old Norse heiði heiðinn ; Swed. and Dan. use hedning. The O.H.G word retains its adj. nature, and forms its gen. pl. heidanêro. Our present heide, gen. heiden (for heiden, gen. heidens) is erroneous, but current ever since Luther. Full confirmation is afforded by Mid. Lat. agrestis = paganus, e.g. in the passage quoted in ch. IV from Vita S. Agili ; and the 'wilde heiden' in our Heldenbuch is an evident pleonasm (see Supplement).

The worn out empire of the Romans saw both its interior convulsed, and its frontier overstept. Yet, by the same mighty doctrine which had just overthrown her ancient gods, subjugated Rome was able to subdue her conquerors anew. By this means the flood-tide of invasion was gradually checked, the newly converted lands began to gather strength and to turn their arms against the heathen left in their rear.

Slowly, step by step, Heathendom gave way to Christendom. Five hundred years after Christ, but few nations of Europe believed in him; after a thousand years the majority did, and those the most important, yet not all (see Suppl.).

From Greece and Italy the Christian faith passed into Gaul first of all, in the second and third centuries. About the year 300, or soon after, we find here and there a christian among the Germans on the Rhine, especially the Alamanni; and about the same time or a little earlier[1] among the Goths. The Goths were the first Teutonic people amongst whom christianity gained a firm footing; this occurred in the course of the fourth century, the West-goths leading the way and the East-goths following; and after them the Vandals, Gepidæ and Rugii were converted. All these races held by the Arian doctrine. The Burgundians in Gaul became Catholic at the beginning of the fifth century, then Arian under their Visigoth rulers, and Catholic again at the commencement of the sixth century The Suevi in Spain were at first Catholic, then Arian (about 469), until in the sixth century they, with all the West-goths, went over likewise to the Catholic church. Not till the end of the fifth or the beginning of the sixth did christianity win the Franks, soon after that the Alamanni, and after them the Langobardi. The Bavarians were converted in the seventh and eighth centuries, the Frisians, Hessians and Thuringians in the eighth, the Saxons about the ninth.

Christianity had early found entrance into Britain, but was checked by the irruption of the heathen Anglo-Saxons. Towards the close of the sixth and in the course of the seventh century, they also went over to the new faith.

The Danes became christians in the tenth century, the Norwegians at the beginning of the eleventh, the Swedes not completely

---

[1] Waitz's Ulfila, p. 35.

till the second half of the same century. About the same time christianity made its way to Iceland.

Of the Slavic nations the South Slavs were the first to adopt the christian faith: the Carentani, and under Heraclius (d. 640) the Croatians, then, 150 years after the former, the Moravians in the eighth and ninth centuries. Among the North Slavs, the Obotritæ in the ninth, Bohemians[1] and Poles in the tenth, Sorbs in the eleventh, and Russians at the end of the tenth.

Then the Hungarians at the beginning of the eleventh, Livonians and Lettons in the twelfth, Esthonians and Finns in the twelfth and thirteenth, Lithuanians not even till the commencement of the fifteenth.

All these data are only to be taken as true in the main; they neither exclude some earlier conversions, nor a longer and later adherence to heathenism in limited areas. Remoteness and independence might protect the time-honoured religion of a tribe. Apostates too would often attempt at least a partial reaction. Christianity would sometimes lead captive the minds of the rich and great, by whose example the common people were carried away; sometimes it affected first the poor and lowly.

When Chlodowig (Clovis) received baptism, and the Salian Franks followed his lead, individuals out of all the Frankish tribes had already set the example. Intercourse with Burgundians and West-goths had inclined them to the Arian doctrine, while the Catholic found adherents in other parts of Gaul. Here the two came into collision. One sister of Chlodowig, Lanthild, had become an Arian christian before his conversion, the other, Albofled, had remained a heathen; the latter was now baptized with him, and the former was also won over to the Catholic communion.[2] But even in the sixth and seventh centuries heathenism was not yet uprooted in certain districts of the Frankish kingdom. Neustria

[1] Fourteen Bohemian princes baptized 845; see Palacky 1, 110. The Middle North-slavs—Riaderi, Tolenzi, Kycini, Circipani—still heathen in the latter half of the 11th century; see Helmold 1, 21. 23 (an. 1066). The Rugians not till 1168; Helm. 2, 12. 13.

[2] *baptizata* est Albofledis. . . . Lanthildis *chrismata* est, Greg. Tur. 2, 31. So among the Goths, *chrismation* is administered to Sigibert's wife Brunechild (4, 27), and to Ingund's husband Herminichild (5, 38, who assumes the new name of Joannes. The Arians appear to have *re-baptized* converts from Catholicism; Ingund herself was compelled by her grandmother-mother in law Goisuintha 'ut rebaptizaretur'. Rebaptizare katholicos, Eugippii vita Severini, cap. 8.

had heathen inhabitants on the Loire and Seine, Burgundy in the
Vosges, Austrasia in the Ardennes; and heathens seem still to
have been living in the present Flanders, especially northwards
towards Friesland.[1] Vestiges of heathenism lingered on among the
Frisians into the ninth century, among the Saxons into the tenth,
and in like manner among the Normans and Swedes into the
eleventh and twelfth.[2] Here and there among the northern Slavs
idolatry was not extinct in the twelfth century, and not universally
so among the Finns and Lithuanians in the sixteenth and seven-
teenth[3]; nay, the remotest Laplanders cling to it still.

Christianity was not popular. It came from abroad, it aimed at
supplanting the time-honoured indigenous gods whom the country
revered and loved. These gods and their worship were part and
parcel of the people's traditions, customs and constitution. Their
names had their roots in the people's language, and were hallowed
by antiquity; kings and princes traced their lineage back to
individual gods; forests, mountains, lakes had received a living
consecration from their presence. All this the people was now to
renounce; and what is elsewhere commended as truth and loyalty
was denounced and persecuted by the heralds of the new faith as a
sin and a crime. The source and seat of all sacred lore was
shifted away to far-off regions for ever, and only a fainter borrowed
glory could henceforth be shed on places in one's native land.

The new faith came in escorted by a foreign language, which
the missionaries imparted to their disciples and thus exalted into a
sacred language, which excluded the slighted mother-tongue from
almost all share in public worship. This does not apply to the
Greek-speaking countries, which could follow the original text of
the christian revelation, but it does to the far wider area over
which the Latin church-language was spread, even among
Romance populations, whose ordinary dialect was rapidly emanci-
pating itself from the rules of ancient Latin. Still more violent
was the contrast in the remaining kingdoms.

The converters of the heathen, sternly devout, abstemious,
mortifying the flesh, occasionally peddling, headstrong, and in

[1] Authorities given in Ch. IV.—Conf. lex Frisionum, ed. Gaupp, p. xxiv,
19, 47.   Heathenism lasted the longest between Laubach and the Weser.
[2] Fornmanna sögur 4, 116.   7, 151.
[3] Wedekind's notes 2, 275, 276.   Rhesa dainos, p. 333.   The Lithuanians
proper converted 1387, the Samogits 1413.

slavish subjection to distant Rome, could not fail in many ways to offend the national feeling. Not only the rude bloody sacrifices, but the sensuous pleasure-loving side of heathenism was to them an abomination (see Suppl.). And what their words or their wonder-working gifts could not effect, was often to be executed against obdurate pagans by placing fire and sword in the hands of christian proselytes.

The triumph of Christianity was that of a mild, simple, spiritual doctrine over sensuous, cruel, barbarizing Paganism. In exchange for peace of spirit and the promise of heaven, a man gave his earthly joys and the memory of his ancestors. Many followed the inner prompting of their spirit, others the example of the crowd, and not a few the pressure of irresistible force.

Although expiring heathenism is studiously thrown into the shade by the narrators, there breaks out at times a touching lament over the loss of the ancient gods, or an excusable protest against innovations imposed from without[1] (see Suppl.).

The missionaries did not disdain to work upon the senses of the heathen by anything that could impart a higher dignity to the Christian cultus as compared with the pagan : by white robes for subjects of baptism, by curtains, peals of bells (see Suppl.), the lighting of tapers and the burning of incense.[2] It was also a wise or politic measure to preserve many heathen sites and temples by simply turning them, when suitable, into Christian ones, and assigning to them another and equally sacred meaning. The heathen gods even, though represented as feeble in comparison with the true God, were not always pictured as powerless in themselves ; they were perverted into hostile malignant powers, into demons, sorcerers and giants, who had to be put down, but were nevertheless credited with a certain mischievous activity and influence. Here and there a heathen tradition or a superstitious custom lived on by merely changing the names, and applying to Christ, Mary and the saints what had formerly been related and believed of idols (see Suppl.). On the other hand, the piety of christian priests suppressed and destroyed a multitude of heathen monuments, poems and beliefs, whose annihilation history can hardly cease to

---

[1] Fornmanna sögur 1, 31-35. Laxdæla, p. 170. Kralodworsky rukopis, 72.74.
[2] Greg. Tur. 2, 31. Fornm. sög. 1, 260. 2, 200.

lament, though the sentiment which deprived us of them is not to be blamed. The practice of a pure Christianity, the extinction of all trace of heathenism was of infinitely more concern than the advantage that might some day accrue to history from their longer preservation. Boniface and Willibrord, in felling the sacred oak, in polluting the sacred spring, and the image-breaking Calvinists long after them, thought only of the idolatry that was practised by such means (see Suppl.). As those pioneers 'purged their floor' a first time, it is not to be denied that the Reformation eradicated aftergrowths of heathenism, and loosing the burden of the Romish ban, rendered our faith at once freer, more inward and more domestic. God is near us everywhere, and consecrates for us every country, from which the fixing of our gaze beyond the Alps would alienate us.

Probably some sects and parties, non-conformity here and there among the heathen themselves, nay, in individual minds a precocious elevation of sentiment and morals, came half-way to meet the introduction of Christianity, as afterwards its purification (see Suppl.). It is remarkable that Old Norse legend occasionally mentions certain men who, turning away in utter disgust and doubt from the heathen faith, placed their reliance on their own strength and virtue. Thus in the Sôlar lioð 17 we read of Vêbogi and Râdey 'â sik þau trûðu,' in themselves they trusted; of king Hâkon (Fornm. sög. 1, 35) 'konûngr gerir sem allir aðrir, þeir sem trûa â mâtt sinn ok megin,' the king does like all others who trust in their own might and main; of Barðr (ibid. 2, 151) 'ek trûi ekki â skurðgoð eðr fiandr, hefi ek þvî lengi trûat â mâtt minn ok megin,' I trust not in idols and fiends, I have this long while, &c.; of Hiörleifr 'vildi aldri blôta,' would never sacrifice (Landn. 1, 5.7); of Hallr and Thôrir goðlauss 'vildu eigi blôta, ok trûðu â mâtt sinn' (Landn. 1, 11); of king Hrôlfr (Fornm. sög. 1, 98) 'ekki er þess getit at Hrôlfr konûngr ok kappar hans hafi nokkurn tîma blôtat goð, heldr trûðu â mâtt sinn ok megin,' it is not thought that king H. and his champions have at any time, &c.; of Örvaroddr (Fornald. sög. 2, 165; cf. 505) 'ekki vandist blôtum, þvî hann trûði â mâtt sinn ok megin'; of Finnbogi (p. 272) 'ek trûi â sialfan mik.' This is the mood that still finds utterance in a Danish folk-song (D.V. 4, 27), though without a reference to religion:

Först troer jeg mit gode svärd.
Og saa min gode hest,
Dernäst troer jeg mine dannesvenne,
Jeg troer mig self allerbedst;

and it is Christian sentiment besides, which strives to elevate and consecrate the inner man (see Suppl.).

We may assume, that, even if Paganism could have lived and luxuriated a while longer, and brought out in sharper relief and more spontaneously some characteristics of the nations that obeyed it, yet it bore within itself a germ of disorganisation and disruption, which, even without the intervention of Christian teaching, would have shattered and dissolved it.[1] I liken heathenism to a strange plant whose brilliant fragrant blossom we regard with wonder; Christianity to the crop of nourishing grain that covers wide expanses. To the heathen too was germinating the true God, who to the Christians had matured into fruit.

At the time when Christianity began to press forward, many of the heathen seem to have entertained the notion, which the missionaries did all in their power to resist, of combining the new doctrine with their ancient faith, and even of fusing them into one. Of Norsemen as well as of Anglo-Saxons we are told, that some believed *at the same time* in Christ and in heathen gods, or at least continued to invoke the latter in particular cases in which they

---

[1] Old Norse sagas and songs have remarkable passages in which the gods are coarsely derided. A good deal in Lokasenna and Harbard's song may pass for rough joking, which still leaves the holiest things unshaken (see Suppl.). But faith has certainly grown fainter, when a daring poet can compare Oðinn and Freyja to dogs (Fornm. sög. 2, 207. Islend. sög. 1, 11. ed. nov. 372. Nialss. 160) ; when another calls the gods ràngeyg (squint-eyed, unfair) and rokindusta (Fornm. sög. 2, 154). When we come to Freyr, I shall quote a story manifestly tending to lessen the reverence for him ; but here is a passage from Oswald 2913 : 'dîn got der ist ein junger tôr (fool), ich wil glouben an den alten.'— If we had a list of old and favourite *dogs'-names*, I believe we should find that the designations of several deities were bestowed upon the brute by way of degradation. Vilk. saga, cap. 230. 235, has handed down *Thor* (but cf. ed. nov., cap. 263) and *Paron*, one being the O.N., the other the Slav name in the Slovak form Parom = Perun ch. VIII. With the Saxon herdsmen or hunters *Thunar* was doubtless in use for dogs, as perhaps *Donner* is to this day. One sort of dog is called by the Poles *Grzmilas* (Linde 1, 779a. 2, 798), by the Bohemians *Hřmiles* (Jungm. 1, 759) = Thunder, Forest-thunder. In Helbling 4, 441 seq. I find a dog *Wunsch* (not Wünsch). Similar to this is the transference of national names to dogs : the Bohemian *Bodrok* is a dog's name, but signifies an Obotrite (Jungm. 1, 150) ; *Sámr* in the Nialssaga seems to mean a Same, Sabme=Lapp ; Helbling 4, 458 has a *Frank* (see Suppl.).

had formerly proved helpful to them. So even by christians much later, the old deities seem to have been named and their aid invoked in enchantments and spells. Landnâmabôk 3, 12 says of Helgi: 'hann trûði â Krist, en þô hêt hann â Thôr til sæfara ok harðræða ok alls þess, er honum þôtti mestu varða'; he believed in Christ, and yet he called upon Thor in voyages and difficulties, &c. Hence the poets too transferred heathen epithets to Christ. Beda 1, 15 relates of Redwald, an East-Anglian king in the beginning of the 7th century : 'rediens domum ab uxore sua, a quibusdam perversis doctoribus seductus est, atque a sinceritate fidei depravatus, habuit posteriora pejora prioribus, ita ut in morem antiquorum Samaritanorum, et Christo servire videretur et diis quibus antea serviebat, atque in eodem fano et altare habebat in sacrificium Christi et arulam ad victimas daemoniorum' (see Suppl.). This helps to explain the relapses into paganism.

The history of heathen doctrines and ideas is easier to write, according as particular races remained longer outside the pale of baptism. Our more intimate acquaintance with the Greek and Roman religion rests upon writings which existed before the rise of Christianity ; we are oftener at fault for information as to the altered shape which that religion had assumed among the common people in Greece and Italy during the first centuries of our era. Research has yet to penetrate, even deeper than it has done, into the old Celtic faith ; we must not shrink from recognizing and examining Celtic monuments and customs on ground now occupied by Germans. Leo's important discovery on the real bearings of the Malberg glossary may lead to much. The religion of the Slavs and Lithuanians would be far more accurately known to us, if these nations, in the centuries immediately following their conversion, had more carefully preserved the memory of their antiquities; as it is, much scattered detail only wants collecting, and traditions still alive in many districts afford rich material. On the Finnish mythology we possess somewhat fuller information.

Germany holds a middle place, peculiar to herself and not unfavourable. While the conversion of Gaul and that of Slavland were each as a whole decided and finished in the course of a very few centuries, the Teutonic races forsook the faith of their fathers very gradually and slowly, from the 4th to the 11th century. Remains of their language too have been preserved more fully and from the successive periods. Besides which we possess in the works of Roman writers, and especially Tacitus, accounts of the earlier undisturbed time of Teutonic heathenism, which, though scanty and from a foreign source, are yet exceedingly important, nay invaluable.

The religion of the East and South German races, which were converted first, is more obscure to us than that of the Saxons; about the Saxons again we know incomparably less than about the Scandinavians. What a far different insight we should get into the character and contents of the suppressed doctrine, how vastly the picture we are able to form of it would gain in clearness, if some clerk at Fulda, Regensburg, Reichenau or St. Gall, or one at Bremen, Corvei or Magdeburg, had in the eighth, ninth or tenth century, hit upon the plan of collecting and setting before us, after the manner of Saxo Grammaticus, the still extant traditions of his tribe on the beliefs and superstitions of their forefathers! Let no one tell me, that by that time there was nothing more to be had; here and there a footmark plainly shows that such recollections could not really have died out.[1] And who will show me in Sweden, which clung to heathenism longer and more tenaciously, such a composition as actually appeared in Denmark during the twelfth century? But for this fact, would not the doubters declare such a thing impossible in Sweden? In truth, the first eight books of Saxo are to me the most welcome monument of the Norse mythology, not only for their intrinsic worth, but because they show in what an altered light the ancient faith of the people had to be placed before the recent converts. I especially remark, that Saxo suppresses all mention of some prominent gods; what right have we then to infer from the non-mention of many deities in the far scantier records of inland Germany, that they had never been heard of there?

Then, apart from Saxo, we find a purer authority for the Norse religion preserved for us in the remotest corner of the North, whither it had fled as it were for more perfect safety,—namely, in Iceland. It is preserved not only in the two Eddas, but in a multitude of Sagas of various shape, which, but for that emigration

---

[1] As late as the tenth century the heroic tale of Walther and Hildegund was poetized in Latin at St. Gall, and a relic of heathen poetry was written down in German [deutlich, a misprint for deutsch ?], probably at Merseburg.

coming to the rescue, would probably have perished in Norway, Sweden and Denmark.

To assail the genuineness of the Norse mythology is as much as to cast doubt on the genuineness and independence of the Norse language. That it has been handed down to us both in a clearer and an obscurer shape, through older and more modern authorities, makes it all the easier to study it from many sides and more historically.

Just as little can we fail to perceive the kinship and close connexion of the Norse mythology with the rest of Teutonic mythology. I have undertaken to collect and set forth all that can now be known of German heathenism, and that exclusively of the complete system of Norse mythology. By such limitation I hope to gain clearness and space, and to sharpen our vision for a criticism of the Old German faith, so far as it stands opposed to the Norse, or aloof from it; so that we need only concern ourselves with the latter, where in substance or tendency it coincides with that of inland Germany.

The antiquity, originality and affinity of the German and Norse mythologies rest on the following grounds:

1. The undisputed and very close affinity of speech between the two races, and the now irrefutably demonstrated identity of form in their oldest poetry. It is impossible that nations speaking languages which had sprung from the same stock, whose songs all wore the badge of an alliteration either unknown or quite differently applied by their neighbours, should have differed materially in their religious belief. Alliteration seems to give place to christian rhyme, first in Upper Germany, and then in Saxony, precisely because it had been the characteristic of heathen songs then still existing. Without prejudice to their original affinity, it is quite true that the German and the Norse dialects and poetries have their peculiarities of form and finish; but it would seem incredible that the one race should have had gods and the other none, or that the chief divinities of the two should have been really different from one another. There were marked differences no doubt, but not otherwise than in their language; and as the Gothic, Anglo-Saxon and Old High German dialects have their several points of superiority over the Old Norse, so may the faith of inland Germany have in many points its claims to distinction and individuality.

2. The joint possession, by all Teutonic tongues, of many terms relating to religious worship. If we are able to produce a word used by the Goths in the 4th century, by the Alamanni in the 8th, in exactly the same form and sense as it continues to bear in the Norse authorities of the 12th or 13th century, the affinity of the German faith with the Norse, and the antiquity of the latter, are thereby vindicated.

3. The identity of mythic notions and nomenclature, which ever and anon breaks out: thus the agreement of the O.H.G. muspilli, O. Sax. mudspelli, with the Eddic muspell, of the O.H.G. itis, A. Sax. ides, with the Eddic dîs, or of the A. Sax. brosinga mene with the Eddic brîsînga men, affords perfectly conclusive evidence.

4. The precisely similar way in which both there and here the religious mythus tacks itself on to the heroic legend. As the Gothic, Frankish and Norse genealogies all run into one another, we can scarcely deny the connexion of the veiled myths also which stand in the background.

5. The mingling of the mythic element with names of plants and constellations. This is an uneffaced vestige of the primeval intimate union between religious worship and nature.

6. The gradual transformation of the gods into devils, of the wise women into witches, of the worship into superstitious customs. The names of the gods have found a last lurking-place in disguised ejaculations, oaths, curses, protestations.[1] There is some analogy between this and the transfer of heathen myths from goddesses and gods to Mary and the saints, from elves to angels. Heathen festivals and customs were transformed into christian, spots which heathenism had already consecrated were sometimes retained for churches and courts of justice. The popular religion of the Catholics, particularly in the adoration of saints, includes a good many and often graceful and pleasing relics of paganism (see Suppl.).

7. The evident deposit from god-myths, which is found to this day in various folk-tales, nursery-tales, games, saws, curses, ill-understood names of days and months, and idiomatic phrases.

8. The undeniable intermixture of the old religious doctrine with the system of law; for the latter, even after the adoption of

---

[1] Conf. our 'donner! hammer!' the Serv. 'lele! lado!' the Lat. 'pol! aedepol! me hercle! me castor! mediusfidius,' &c.

the new faith, would not part with certain old forms and usages (see Suppl.).

In unravelling these complex relations, it appears indispensable not to overlook the mythologies of neighbouring nations, especially of the Celts, Slavs, Lithuanians and Finns, wherever they afford confirmation or elucidation. This extension of our scope would find ample reason and justification in the mere contact (so fruitful in many ways) of the languages of those nationalities with Teutonic ones, particularly of the Celtic with Old Frankish, of the Finnish and Lithuanian with Gothic, and of the Slavic with High German. But also the myths and superstitions of these very nations are peculiarly adapted to throw light on the course taken by our domestic heathenism in its duration and decadence.

Against the error which has so frequently done damage to the study of the Norse and Greek mythologies, I mean the mania of foisting metaphysical or astronomical solutions on but half-discovered historical data, I am sufficiently guarded by the incompleteness and loose connexion of all that has been preserved. My object is, faithfully and simply to collect what the distortions early introduced by the nations themselves, and afterwards the scorn and aversion of christians have left remaining of heathenism ; and to enlist fellow-labourers in the slow task of securing a more solid store of facts, without which a general view of the substance and worth of our mythology is not to be attained (see Suppl.).

CHAPTER II.

GOD.

In all Teutonic tongues the Supreme Being has always with one consent been called by the general name God. The dialectic varieties are: Goth. *guð*, A.S., O.S., O. Fris. *god*, O.H.G. *cot*, O. Norse *goð*; Swed. Dan. *gud*, M.H.G. *got*, M.L.G. *god*; and here there is a grammatical remark to make. Though all the dialects, even the Norse, use the word as masculine (hence in O.H.G. the acc. sing. *cotan*; I do not know of a M.H.G. goten), yet in Gothic and O. Norse it lacks the nom. sing. termination (-*s*, -*r*) of a masc. noun, and the Gothic gen. sing. is formed *guðs* without the connecting vowel *i*, agreeing therein with the three irreg. genitives mans, fadrs, brôðrs. Now, as O.H.G. has the same three genitives irreg., man, fatar, pruodar, we should have expected the gen. *cot* to bear them company, and I do not doubt its having existed, though I have nowhere met with it, only with the reg. cotes, as indeed mannes and fateres also occur. It is more likely that the sanctity of the name had preserved the oldest form inviolate, than that frequent use had worn it down.[1] The same reason preserved the O.H.G. spelling *cot* (Gramm. 1, 180), the M. Dut. *god* (1, 486), and perhaps the Lat. vocative deus (1, 1071).[2] Moreover, God and other names of divine beings reject every article (4, 383. 394. 404. 424. 432); they are too firmly established as proper nouns to need any such distinction. The *der got* in MS. 2, 260a. is said of a heathen deity.

On the radical meaning of the word God we have not yet arrived at certainty;[3] it is not immediately connected with the adj.

---

[1] The drift of these remarks seems to be this: The word, though used as a masc., has a neut. form ; is this an archaism, pointing to a time when the word was really neuter; or a mere irregularity due to abtrition, the word having always been masc. ?—TRANS.

[2] Saxo does not inflect Thor; Uhland p. 198.

[3] The Slav. *bôgh* is connected with the Sanskr. bhâga felicitas, bhakta devotus, and bhaj colere; perhaps also with the obscure bahts in the Goth. andbahts minister. cultor; conf. p. 20, note on boghât, dives. Of θεός, deus we shall have to speak in ch. IX.

14   GOD.

good, Goth. gôds, O.N, gôðr, A.S. gôd, O.H.G. cuot, M.H.G., guot, as
the difference of vowel shows ; we should first have to show an
intermediacy of the gradations gida gad, and gada gôd, which
does take place in some other cases ; and certainly God is called the
Good.[1] It is still farther removed from the national name of the
Goths, who called themselves Gutans (O.H.G. Kuzun, O.N. Gotar),
and who must be distinguished from O.N. Gautar (A. S. Geátas,
O.H.G. Kôzâ ; Goth. Gautôs ?).

The word God has long been compared with the Pers. *Khodâ*
(Bopp, comp. gram., p. 35). If the latter be, as has been supposed,
a violent contraction of the Zend qvadâta (a se datus, increatus,
Sanskr. svadâta, conf. Dêvadatta Θεόδοτος, Mitradatta Ἡλιόδοτος,
Srîdatta), then our Teutonic word must have been originally a compound, and one with a very apt meaning, as the Servians also
address God as samozazdâni bôzhe ! self-created God ; Vuk 741.

The O.H.G. *cot* forms the first half of many proper names, as
Cotadio, Cotascalh, Cotafrit, Cotahram, Cotakisal, Cotaperaht,
Cotalint, but not so that we can infer anything as to its meaning ;
they are formed like Irmandio, Hiltiscalh, Sikufrit, and may just as
well carry the general notion of the Divine Being as a more definite
one. When cot forms the last syllable, the compound can only
stand for a god, not a man, as in Irmincot, Hellicot.

In derivatives Ulphilas exchanges the TH for a D, which explains the tenuis in O.H.G. ; thus guda-faurhts (god-fearing) Luke
2, 25, gagudei (godliness) Tit. 1, 1 ; though the dat. sing. is invariably guða.[2] Likewise in speaking of many gods, which to Christians
would mean idols, he spells *guda*, using it as a neuter, John 10,
34-5. The A.S. god has a neut. pl. *godu*, when idols are meant
(cod. exon. 250,2. 254,9. 278,16.). In like manner the O.H.G. and
M.H.G. compound *apcot*, *aptcot* (false god) is commonly neuter, and
forms its pl. apcotir ; whether the M.H.G. '*der* aptgot' in Geo.
3254. 3302 can be correct, is questionable ; we have taken to

---

[1] οὐδεὶς ἀγαθὸς εἰ μὴ εἷς ὁ θεός, Mark 10, 18, Luke 18, 19, which in Gothic
is rendered 'ni hvashun þiuðeigs alja ains Guð', but in A.S, 'nis nân man
gôd buton God âna'. God is the giver of all good, and himself the highest
good, summum bonum. Thus Plato names him τὸ ἀγαθόν.
[2] In Gothic the rule is to change TH into D before a vowel in inflection,
as, faðs, fadis, fada, fað ; haubið, -dis, -da, -ð. The peculiarity of guð is
that it retains TH throughout the sing., guð, guðs, guða, guð ; though in pl.
and in derivatives it falls under rule again.—TRANS.

using *abgott* as a masc. throughout, yet our pl. *götter* itself can only be explained as originally neuter, since the true God is one, and can have no plural; and the O.H.G. cotâ, M.H.G. gote contain so far a contradiction. In Ulph. afguds is only an adj., and denotes impius Sk. 44, 22; afgudei impietas, Rom. 11, 26; εἴδωλα he translates by *galiuga* (figmenta), 1 Cor. 5, 10. 10, 20. 28, or by *galiugaguda*, 1 Cor. 10, 20; and εἰδωλεῖον by galiugê staðs, 1 Cor. 8, 10. Another N.H.G. expression *götze* I have discussed, Gramm. 3, 694; Luther has in Deut. 12, 3 'die *götzen* ihrer *götter*, making götze=idolum. In Er. Alberus fab. 23, the *götz* is a demigod[1] (see Suppl.). The O.N. language distinguished the neut. *goð* idolum from the masc. *guð* deus. Snorri 119 says of Sif 'it hârfagra goð,' the fairhaired god; I do not know if a heathen would have said it.

In curses and exclamations, our people, from fear of desecrating the name of God, resort to some alteration of it:[2] *potz* wetter! *potz* tausend! or, *kotz* tausend! *kotz* wunder! instead of Gottes; but I cannot trace the custom back to our ancient speech. The similar change of the Fr. dieu into *bieu, bleu, guieu*[3] seems to be older (see Suppl.).

Some remarkable uses of the word God in our older speech and that of the common people may also have a connexion with heathen notions.

Thus it is thrown in, as it were, to intensify a personal pronoun (see Suppl.). Poems in M.H.G. have, by way of giving a hearty welcome: *gote* unde *mir* willekomen; Trist. 504. Frîb. Trist. 497.

---

[1] Writers of the 16-17th centuries use *ölgötze* for statue (Stieler says, from an allegorical representation of the apostles asleep on the Mount of Olives, öl = oil). Hans Sachs frequently has 'den ölgötzen tragen' for doing house drudgery, I. 5, 418ᵈ 528ᵈ. III. 3, 24ᵃ 49ᵈ. IV. 3, 37ᵇ 99ᵃ. The O.H.G. coz, simpuvium Numae (Juvenal 6, 343), which Graff 4, 154 would identify with götze, was a vessel, and belongs to giozan=fundere.

[2] Such a fear may arise from two causes: a holy name must not be abused, or an unholy dreaded name, *e.g.*, that of the devil, has to be softened down by modifying its form; see Chap. XXXIII, how the people call formidable animals by another name, and for Donner prefer to say donnerwetter (Dan. tordenveir for Thursday), donnerwettstein (wetterstein or wetzstein?), donnerkeil, donnerwäsche, dummer. In Fornm. sög. 10, 283 we have Oddiner for Oðinn; perhaps Wuotansheer (Woden's host) was purposely changed into Mutesheer; whether Phol into Fàlant, is worth considering.

[3] Sangbieu (sang de Dieu), corbieu (corps de D.) vertubleu (vertu de D.), morbleu (mort de D.), parbleu (par D.), vertuguieu, vertugoi (vertu de D.), morguoi (mort de D.), &c. As early as Renart 18177, por la char bieu. So the Engl. cock's bones, 'od's bones, 'od's wounds, 'zounds, &c. Conf. Weber metr. rom. 3, 284.

gote sult ir willekomen sîn, iurem *lande* unde *mir* (ye shall be welcome to God, your country, and me) ; Trist. 5186. *got* alrêst, dar nâch *mir*, west willekomen ; Parz. 305, 27. wis willekomen *mir* und *got* ; Frauend. 128, 13. sît *mir gote* wilkomen[1] ; Eilh. Trist. 248. rehte *got* wilkomen *mir* ; Dietr. 5200. Nu sît ouch *mir got* wilkomen ; Dietr. 5803. sît willekomen *got* und oueh *mir* ; Dietr. 4619. nu wis *mir got* wilkomen ; Oswalt 208. 406. 1163. 1268. 1393. 2189. du solt grôz willekomen sîn dem rîchen *got* unde *mir* ; Lanz. 1082. wis *mir* unde ouch *got* wilkomen ; Ls. 1, 514. Occasionally gote stands alone : diu naht sî *gote* willekomen ; Iw. 7400, explained in the note, p. 413, as 'devoted to God,' though it only means 'to-night be (thou) welcome'. Upper Germany has to this day retained the greeting 'gottwilche, gottwillkem, gotti-kum, skolkuom' (Stald. 1, 467. Schm. 2, 84). I do not find it in Romance poems ; but the Saxon-Latin song of the 10th century on Otto I. and his brother Heinrich has : sîd wilicomo bêthiu *goda* ende *mi*. The Supreme Being is conceived as omnipresent, and is expected, as much as the host himself, to take the new-comer under his protection ; so the Slovèny say to the arriving guest 'bôgh tè vsprimî, God receive you !'[2] and we to the parting guest 'God guide, keep, bless you !' We call it commending or committing one to God, M.H.G. gote ergeben, Er. 3598. I compare with these the *Hail!* called out to one who arrives or departs (heill ver þu ! Sæm. 67ᵃ 86ᵇ), with which are also associated the names of helpful gods : heill þu farir, heill þu *âsyniom* sêr ! fare thou well, be thou well by (the aid of) the Asynior ; Sæm. 31ᵃ. heill scaltu Agnarr, allz þic heilan biðr vera tŷr vera ! Sæm. 40.

In the same way the name of the omniscient God emphasizes an assurance of knowledge or ignorance : daz weiz *got* unde *ich* ; Trist. 4151. den schatz weiz nu nieman wan (except) *got* unde *mîn* ; Nib. 2308, 3.[3] This comfortable combination of *I* with *God* has for its counterpart the opprobrious one of a *thou* with *devil*, ch. XXXIII. Here too the *got* alone is enough : ingen vet min sorg utan *gud* ; Svenska visor 2, 7. That we are fully justified in

[1] The omission of *and* between the two datives is archaic, conf. Zeitschr. f. d. a. 2, 190.
[2] Buge waz primi, gralva Venus ! Frauend. 192, 20 ; conf. 177, 14.
[3] hie hært uns anders nieman dan *got* unde *diu waltvogellîn* ; Ecke 96. niemen bevinde daz wan er und ich und ein kleinez vogellîn, das mac wol getriuwe sîn ; Walth. 40, 15. Birds play the spy on men's privacy.

referring these modes of speech so far back as to the heathen time, is shown by a remarkable passage in Fornald. sög. 1, 380 : ek hugða engan kunna nema *mik* ok *Oðinn.* By secrets which none can know save Oðinn and to whomsoever he has whispered them, his divinity is at once revealed, Sæm. 38ª, ᵇ, 95ᵇ, Fornald. sög. 1, 487. Not quite parallel are phrases such as : daz geloube *gote* unde *mir* ; Amis 989. *iu* unde *gote* von himile klage ich unser leit ; Nib. 1889, 3. ik klage *gode* unde *iu*; Richtsteig landr. 11. 16. 37. sanc die messe beide *got* u. *in* ; Parz. 378, 25. Wh. 289, 5. neic si *im* unde *gote* ; Iw. 6013. Also in O.Fr., jel te pardoins de *diu* et de *mi* ; Mones untersuch. 245. Sometimes the Evil One is named by the side of the Deity : *got* noch den *tiuvel* loben ; Iw. 1273. in beschirmet der *tiuvel* noch *got* ; Iw. 4635, *i.e.* no one protects him.

Poems of the Middle Ages attribute human passions to God ; especially is He often pictured in a state of complacency and joy (see Suppl.), and again in the contrary state of wrath and vengeance. The former is favourable to the creation of eminent and happily endowed men : got was an einer *süezen zuht*, do'r Parzivâlen worhte (in amiable trim—form, training—when he made Percival) ; Parz. 148, 26. got der was vil *senftes muotes*, dô er geschuof sô reine ein wîp ; MS. 1, 17ᵇ. got der was *in fröiden*, dô er dich als ebene maz (so evenly meted); MS. 1, 22ᵇ. got *in grossen freuden* was, dô er dich schuof (*i.e.*, created wine) ; Altd. bl. 1, 413. got der was *in hôhem werde*,[1] dô er geschuof die reinen fruht, wan ime was gar *wol ze muote* ; MS. 1, 24ᵇ. got si zer werlde brâhte, dô *ze freuden* stuont sîn muot; Wigal. 9282. got der was vil *wol gemuot*, dô er schuof sô reinem wîbe tugent, wünne, schœne an lîbe ; MS. 1, 201ª. got was *gezierde milte*, der si beide schuof nâch lobe ; Troj. 19922. got selb *in rîchen freuden* was, dô er ir lîp als ebene maz ; Misc. 2, 186. ich weiz daz got *in fröiden* was, dô er niht, frouwe, an dir vergaz waz man ze lobe sol schouwen. Ls. 1, 35. So a troubadour sings : belha domna, *de cor y entendia* Dieus, quan formet vostre cors amoros ; Rayn. 1, 117.[2] It is an equally heathen

---

[1] The Gothic gavairthi = peace.
[2] To the creative God rejoicing in his work, the M.H.G. poets especially attribute *diligence* and zeal : an den henden lac der gotes flîz ; Parz. 88, 15. jach, er trüege den gotes flîz ; Parz. 140, 5. got het sînen flîz gar ze wunsche wol an si geleit ; Wigal. 4130. ich wæn got selbe worhte dich mit sîner gotlicher hant ; Wigal. 9723. zwâre got der hât geleit sîne kunst und sîne kraft, sînen flîz und sîne meisterschaft an disen loblîchen lîp ; Iw. 1685. So in

sentiment, that imputes to God a propensity to gaze at human
beauty, or to do whatever men do: got möhte selbe *gerne sehen* die
selben juncfrouwen; Fragm. 22ᵃ. gott möht in (him, *i.e.* the
musician) *gerne hœren* in sinen himelkœren; Trist. 7649. den slac
scolte got selbe haben *gesehen* (should have seen that stroke); Rol.
198, 18. Karl 72. got selbe möht ez *gerne sehen* ; Trist. 6869. ein
puneiz (diadem), daz in got selber *möhte sehen* ; Frauend. 84, 16.
gestrîten dazz d'engel *möhten hœren* in den niun kœren; Willeh.
230, 27. si möhte nâch betwingen mite (might nigh compel
withal) eines engels gedanc, daz er vil lîhte *einen wanc* durch si
von himele tœte (fail from heaven for her); Iw. 6500 (imitated by
Ottocar 166ᵃ). ich weiz daz wol, daz sîn got nicht *verdrüzze* ; MS.
2, 127ᵃ. ir hâr gelîch dem golde, als ez got *wünschen solde;* MS. 2
62ᵇ. sîn swert dat geinc (ging, went) an sîner hant, dat got selve
vrâchde mêre (would ask to know), we der ritter wêre ? dey engele
muosten lachen, dat hey is sus kunde machen ; Haupts zeitschr. 3,
24.   This hilarity of the attendant guardian-angels (ch. XXVIII)
or valkürs must be thought of in connexion with the laughing of
ghosts (ch. XXXI).   In Hartmann's Erec, when Enite's white hands
groomed (begiengen) a horse, it says 355 : und wære, daz got *hien
erde rite*, ich wæn, in genuocte da mite, ob er *solhen marstaller hœte.*
This view of a sympathizing, blithe and gracious god, is particularly
expressed in the subst. *huldi*, O.N. *hylli* : Oðins hylli ; Sæm. 47ᵃ.
Ullar hylli ok allra goða ; Sæm. 45ᵇ.

On the other hand, of the primitive sensuous representation of
an *angry avenging* deity (see Suppl.), the most striking example
will be treated of presently in ch. VIII, under Donar, thunder.[1]
The idea recurs several times in the Edda and elsewhere : *reiðr* er
þer Oðinn, *reiðr* er þer Asabragr ; Sæm. 85ᵇ. Oðinn *ofreiðr* ; Sæm.
228ᵇ. *reið* varð þâ Freyja oc fnasaði ; Sæm. 71ᵇ.—she was wroth,

Chrestien: ja la fist Dex de sa main nue, por nature fere muser, tout le mont i
porroit user, s'ele la voloit contrefere, que ja nen porroit a chief trere; no Dex,
s'il sen voloit pener, mi porroit, ce cuit, assener, que ja une telle feist, por peine
que il i meist (see Suppl.).

[1] Piacula *irœ* deûm, Liv. 22, 9. deos *iratos* habeam ! dii immortales hominibus irasci et succensere consueverunt, Cic. pro Rosc. 16.   And Tacitus on this
very subject of the Germans : propitiine an *irati* dii, Germ. 5.   *ira* dei, Hist. 4,
26.   *infensi* Batavis dii, Hist. 5, 25.   And in the Mid. Ages : tu *odium* Dei
omniumque sanctorum habeas !   Vita Meinwerci, cap. 13 § 95.   crebrescen-
tibus jam jamque cottidie Dei justo judicio in populo diversis calamitatibus et
flagellis . . . .   quid esset in quo Deus offensus esset, vel quibus placari
posset operibus ; Pertz 2, 547.

and snorted or panted, as the angry wolf in Reinh. XLII spirtles out
his beard. guðin *reið* ordin; Fornm. sög. 2, 29. 231. goða *gremi*
(deorum ira) is announced; Egilss. 352. at *gremia* goð (offendere
deos); Fornald. sög. 2, 69. was imo god *âbolgan;* Hel. 157, 19.
than wirdid iu waldand *gram,* mahtig *môdag;* Hel. 41, 16 (elsewhere:
diu Sælde, or the world, earth, is *gram*). ein *zornec* got in daz gebôt
(bade them), daz uns hie suohten mit ir her; Parz. 43, 28. hie ist
geschehen gotes *râche;* Reinh. 975. got wil vervüeren sînen *zorn;*
Osw. 717. ich wæne daz got *ræche* da selbe sînen *anden* (wreak his
vengeance); Gudr. 845, 4. daz *riuwe* got! (God rue it); Trist.
12131. daz ez got immer *riuwe!* Trist. 11704. The Lex Bajuv.
6, 2, in forbidding Sunday labour, says: quia talis causa vitanda
est, quae Deum ad *iracundiam* provocat, et exinde flagellamur in
frugibus et penuriam patimur. How coarse were the expressions
still used in the 17th century! " An abuse that putteth God *on
his mettle,* and maketh him to hold strict and pitiless inquisition,
that verily he shall, for saving of his honour, smite thereinto *with
his fists*"; and again: "to run *upon the spears* of an offended
jealous God ".[1] A wicked man was in the Mid. Ages called *gote leide,*
loathed by God. One form of imprecation was to consign a man
to God's hatred: ûz in *gotes haz!* Trist. 5449. ûz strîchet (sheer
off) balde in *gotes haz!* Trist. 14579. nu vart den *gotes haz* alsam
ein bœswiht von mir hin! Frauend. 109, 12. mich hât der *gotes
haz* bestanden; Kl. 518. iuch hât rehte *gotes haz* (al. foul weather,
the devil, &c.) daher gesendet beide; Iw. 6104. sô müeze ich
haben *gotes hœz;* Altd. w. 3, 212. varet hen an *godes haz!* Wiggert
2, 47. nu mueze er gewinnen *gotes haz;* Roth 611. In like manner
the MLG. *godsat* hebbe! Huyd. op St. 2, 350. Reinaert 3196.[2]
But, what deserves particular notice, this formula ' in gotes haz,' or
in acc. without prepos. ' gotes haz varn, strîchen' has a perfect
parallel in another which substitutes for God the *sun,* and so heigh-
tens the heathenish colouring; ir sult farn der *sunnen haz!* Parz.
247, 26. var der *sunnen haz!* Unprinted poems of Rüediger 46.
hebe dich der *sunnen haz!* Er. 93. nu ziuhe in von mir der *sunnen
haz!* Helmbr. 1799. si hiezen in strîchen in der *sunnen haz;* Eracl.
1100. hiez in der *sunnen haz* hin varn; Frauend. 375, 26. A man
so cursed does not deserve to have the sun shine on him kindly.

---

[1] Hartmann on benedictions, Nürnb. 1680, p. 158, 180.
[2] Serious illness or distress is habitually called ' der *gotes slac,*' stroke.

The Vandal Gizerich steps into his ship, and leaves it to the winds *where* they shall drive it to, or among what people he shall fall that *God is angry* with, ἐφ' οὓς ὁ θεὸς ὤργισται. Procop. de bello Vand. 1, 5.

Such hostile attitude breeds now and then a *rebellious spirit* in men, which breaks out in promethean defiance and threats, or even takes a violent practical turn (see Suppl.). Herodotus 4, 94 says of the Thracians : οὗτοι οἱ αὐτοὶ Θρήϊκες καὶ πρὸς βροντήν τε καὶ ἀστραπὴν τοξεύοντες ἄνω πρὸς τὸν οὐρανὸν, ἀπειλεῦσι τῷ θεῷ. If the god denied the assistance prayed for, his statue was flung into the river by the people, immersed in water, or beaten. In the Carolingian romances we repeatedly come upon the incident of Charles *threatening* the Deity, that if he deny his aid, he will throw down his altars, and make the churches with all their priests to cease from the land of the Franks ; *e.g.* Ferabr. 1211, 1428, &c. So dame Breide too *threatens* to uncover the altar and break the holy relics ; Orendel 2395 ; and Marsilies actually, after losing the battle, has the houses of his gods pulled down ; Rol. 246, 30. If the vintage failed, the statue of Urban was thrown into a bath or the river.[1] The Arcadians would scourge their Pan with squills (σκίλλαις), when they returned bootless from the chase (Theocr. 7, 106). The Greeks imputed to their gods not only anger and hate, but envy, love of mischief, νέμεσις.

EPITHETS OF GOD (see Suppl.). In our modern speech : der *liebe, liebste, gnädige,*[2] *grosse, gute, allmächtige.* In our older tongue : hêrre got der *guote ;* Reinh. 1296. Gute frau, 276. hêrro the *gôdo ;* Hel. 78, 3. 90, 6. frô mîn the *gôdo ;* 143, 7. *gnœdeger* trehtîn ; Reinh. 1309.—Freq. the *rich* God : thie *rîkeo* Christ ; Hel. 1, 2. *rîki* god ; Hel. 195, 9. *rîki* drohtin ; Hel. 114, 22. der *rîche* got von himele ; Roth. 4971. got der *rîche ;* Nib. 1793, 3. Trist. 2492. durch den *rîchen* got von himel , Morolt 3526. der *rîche* got mich ie gesach ; V.d. wîbe list 114.[3]—Cot *almahtico,* cot *heilac ;* Wesso-

---

[1] When lightning strikes, our people say : If God can burn, we can build again ; Ettners hebamme, p. 16.

[2] Where God is, there is grace and peace ; of a solemn spot it is said : Here dwells der liebe Gott ! And, to drive den lieben Gott from a person's room (Lessing 1, 243), means, to disturb a solitary in his sanctum.

[3] OHG. *rîhhi* dives, potens, also beatus ; and dives is near akin to Divus, as Dis, Ditis springs out of divit. From the Slav. *bôgh* is derived *boghát* (dives), Lith. *bagotas ;* compare ops, in-ops (Russ. u-bôghiy), opulentus with Ops, the Bona Dea. Conf. Diefenb. celt. 1, 196.

brunn. Gebet. *mahtig* drohtin ; Hel. 2, 2. freá *ælmihtig ;* Cædm.
1, 9. 10, 1. se *ælmihtiga* wealdend ; Thorpe's anal. 83. mannô
miltisto (largissimus) ; Wessobr. Geb. vil *milter* Christ ; Cod. pal.
350, 56.—The AS. has freq. : *éce* dryhten, æternus ; Cædm. 246,
11. Beow. 3382. 3555. 4655. Also : *witig* god, sapiens ; Beow.
1364, 2105. Cædm. 182, 24. *witig* dryhten ; Beow. 3101. 3679.
Cædm. 179, 8. *witig* wuldorcyning ; Cædm. 242, 30.—*Waltant* got ;
Hild. *waldindinger* got ; Roth. 213. 523. 1009. 2332. 4031.
waltant Krist : OV. 25, 91. Gudr. 2243. (AS.) *wealdend* ; Cædm.
9, 25. wuldres *wealdend ;* Beow. 4. heofnes wealdend ; Cædm.
17, 15. þeoda *wealdend.* fæder *alwealda* ; Beow. 630. (OS.)
waldand ; Hel. 4, 5. 6, 6. *waldand* god 3, 17. *waldand* drohtin
1, 19. *alowaldo* 4, 8. 5, 20. 8, 2. 69, 23. This epithet is not found
in the Edda. The notion of ' wielding ', dominari, regere, is further
applied to the Supreme Being in the phrase *es walten*, Parz. 568, 1.
En. 7299. 10165. 13225. So our *gottwalt's !* M. Dut. *godwouds !*
Huyd. op St. 2, 548. Our acc. in ' *das* walt Gott !' is a blunder ;
Agricola 596. Praet. weltb. 2, 50.—God is occasionally called the
Old : der *alte* Gott lebt noch, *i.e.* the same as ever. A.S. *eald* metod.
MHG. hât got sîn *alt* gemüete ; Wh. 66, 20. der *alde* got ; Roth.
4401. popul. 'der *alte* Vater '. In a Servian song (Vuk 2, 244.
Montenegro 101), bôgh is named ' *stari* krvnik ', the old blood-
shedder, killer ; and in Frauenlob MS. 2, 214[b] der *alte* friedel
(sweetheart). The 13th century poets sometimes use the Lat.
epithet *altissimus*, Wh. 216, 5. 434, 23. Geo. 90, 401 ; with which
may be compared the MHG. *diu hôhste hant*, Parz. 484, 6. 487, 20.
568, 8. Wh. 134, 7. 150, 14. and the OHG. zi waltanteru *henti*,
OV. 25, 91.—The ' all-wielding ' God is at the same time the all-
seeing, all-knowing, all-remembering ; hence it is said of fortunate
men, that God *saw* them, and of unfortunate, that God *forgot* them :
(OHG.) *kesah* tih kot ! = O te felicem ! N. Boeth. 145. (MHG.)
gesach in got !=happy he ! Altd. bl. 1, 347. sô mir got *ergaz ;*
Troj. kr. 14072. sô hât got mîn *vergezzen ;* Nib. 2256, 3. wie gar
iuwer got vergaz (how utterly God forgot you) ; Iw. 6254. got mîn
vergaz ; Ecke 209. got hæte sîn vergezzen ; Trist. 9243. genæde-
licher trehtîn, wie vergæze dû ie mîn sô ? Trist. 12483. For other
examples, see Gramm. 4, 175.—God, by regarding, guards : daz si
got iemer *schouwe !* Iw. 794. O. Engl. God you *see !* God keep
you in his *sight !*

Among substantive epithets are several which God has in common with earthly rulers (see Suppl.):—Gothic *fráuja* OS. *frôho*,
frô, AS. *freâ ;* which name I shall treat of more fully by and by.
—OHG. *truhtín*, MHG. *trehtîn*, OS. *drohtin*, AS. *dryhten*, ON.
dróttinn.—OHG. *hêriro*, MHG. *hêrre*, which however, when used
of God, is never contracted into *her*, any more than Dominus into
the Romance domnus, don.—Conspicuous above all is the name
Father (see Suppl.). In the Edda, *alföðr*. (Sæm. 46ᵇ 88ᵃ 154ᵇ. Sn.
3. 11. 17), *herfaðir, herja faðir, valfaðir* are applied to Oðinn as
the father of all gods, men and created things. Such compounds
are not found in the other dialects, they may have sounded heathenish ; though the AS. could use *fœder* alwealda, Beow. 630, and the
idea of God as Father became more familiar to the christians than
to heathens. The OHG. altfatar = grandfather, O. i. 3, 6. AS.
ealdfæder, Beow. 743. 1883, I have nowhere seen applied to God.
As the Greeks coupled together $Z\epsilon\grave{\upsilon}\varsigma$ $\pi\alpha\tau\acute{\eta}\rho$, esp. in the voc. $Z\epsilon\hat{\upsilon}$
$\pi\acute{\alpha}\tau\epsilon\rho$, and the Romans Jupiter, Diespiter, Dispiter, Mars pater,[1]
as well as $\Delta\eta\mu\acute{\eta}\tau\eta\rho$, $\Delta\alpha\mu\acute{\alpha}\tau\eta\rho$, Terra *mater*, so the Lettons bestow
on almost every goddess the epithet *mahte, mahmina=mater*,
matercula (Büttner 244. Bergmann 142), on which we shall have
more to say hereafter. To all appearance, father Goth. fadr is
connected with faþs lord, as pater $\pi\alpha\tau\acute{\eta}\rho$ is with $\pi\acute{o}\tau\iota\varsigma$, $\pi\acute{o}\sigma\iota\varsigma$, Lith.
pats.—The AS. *meotod, metod*, Cædm. 223, 14. eald metod, Beow.
1883. sôð metod, Beow. 3222. OS. *metod*, Hel. 4, 13. 15, 17. 66, 19,
an expression which likewise appears in the Edda, *miötuðr* Sæm.
226ᵇ 241,ᵇ seems to signify Creator, as verbally it bears the sense of
mensor, moderator, finitor. The full meaning of metod will not be
disclosed, till we have a more exact knowledge of the relation
between the Goth. mitan (to mete) and máitan (to cut), the OHG.
mëzan and meizan ; in the Lat. mētiri and mĕtere, besides there
being no shifting of consonant (d for t), the quantity is inverted.
The ON. *miötuðr* appears to be also sector, messor ; in Snorri 104.
105, the wolf's head with which Heimdall was killed is called
' miötuðr Heimðallar,' and the sword is ' mans miötuðr ' ; so in
Fornald. sög. p. 441, ' manna miötuðr ' (see Suppl.). In MHG.
too, the poets use mezzan of exquisite symmetry in creating : dô
sîn (Wunsch's) gewalt ir bilde *maz ;* Troj. 19626. got selb in

---

[1] Jane pater ! Cato 134 ; but what can Dissunapiter mean in the remarkable conjuring-spell, Cato 160 ?

richen fröuden was, dô er ir lîp als *ebene maz;* Misc. 2, 186. er sol
ze rehte lange *mezzen,* der an si sô *ebene maz,* daz er an si zer werlte
nie nâch vollem wunsche weder des noch des vergaz ; MS. 1, 154ᵇ.
got der was in fröiden, dô er dich als *ebene maz;* MS. 1, 22ᵇ
wer kunde in sô gemezzen, Tit. 130. 1. anders denne got uns
maz, dô er ze werke über mich gesaz, Parz. 518, 21. ' ein bilde
mezzen' is therefore the same thing as ' ein bilde *schaffen* '
to create (Troj. 19805), or *giezen* to cast, mould (Walth. 45,
25. MS. 1, 195ᵇ. 2, 226ᵇ) ; and in Suchenwirt 24, 154 it says :
' got het *gegozzen* ûf ir vel, ir mündel rôt und wîz ir kel'.; which
throws a significant light on the Gothic tribal name *Gáuts,* A.S.
Geát OHG. *Kôz* (see Suppl.).—AS. *scippend,* creator, OHG. *scefo,*
scephio, MHG. *schepfære,* Wh. 1, 3. NHG. *schöpfer.*—Some of
these names can be strung together, or they can be intensified by
composition : *drohtin god,* Hel. 2. 13. *waldand frô* mîn, Hel. 148,
14. 153, 8. *freá dryhten,* Beow. 62. 186. *lîf-freá,* Cædm. 2, 9. 108,
18. 195, 3. 240, 33. Beow. 4. The earthly cuning with a prefix can
be used of God : *wuldorcyning,* king of glory, Cædm. 10, 32. *hevan-*
cuning, Hel. 3, 12, 18. 4, 14. 5, 11. and synonymously with these,
rodora weard, Cædm. 11, 2. or the epic amplification, irmin-got
obana ab hevane, Hild. got *von himele,* Nib. 2090, 4. 2114, 1. 2132, 1.
2136, 1.

Of such *epic formulas* (see Suppl.), beautiful specimens, all of
one tenour, can be cited from the poets, especially the Romance :
they are mostly borrowed from God's dwelling-place, his creative
power, his omnipotence, omniscience and truth :—Dios aquel, que
esta en alto, Cid 800. 2352. 2465. qui la amont el seint cel
maint (abides), Ren. 26018. qui maint el firmament, Berte
129. 149. der hôho sizet unde nideriu sihet, N. ps. 112, 5. qui
haut siet et de loing mire, Ren. 11687. qui haut siet et loins
voit, Berte 44, 181. Guitecl. 2, 139. der über der blauen decke
sitzt, Melander Jocoseria 1, 439. cot almahtico, dû himil inti
erda gaworahtôs (wroughtest heaven and earth), Wessobr. Geb. cel
senhor, qui lo mon a creat, Ferabr. 775. qui tot le mont forma,
Berte 143. que fezit nueyt e dia, Ferabr. 3997. per aycel senhor que
fetz cel e rozada (sky and dew), Ferabr. 2994. 4412. qui fist ciel et
rousee, Berte 28. 66. 111. 139. 171. 188. Aimon 876. qui feis mer
salee, Berte 67. qui fist et mer et onde, Méon 3, 460. des hant
daz mer gesalzen hât, Parz. 514, 15. qui fait courre la nue, Berte

136. 183 (νεφεληγερέτα Ζευς). par celui qui fait toner, Ren.
16658. 17780. par qui li soleus raie, Berte 13. 81. der himel und
erde gebôt und die mergriezen zelt (counts the sea-sands, or pebbles),
Mar. 18. der der sterne zal weiz, Wh. 466, 30. der die sterne hât
gezalt, Parz. 629, 20. der uns gap des mânen (moon's) schin, Wh.
476, 1. qui fait croitre et les vins et les blez, Ferabr. 163ª. der
mir ze lebene geriet (planned), Nib. 2091, 4. Kl. 484. der mir ze
lebene gebôt (bade), Roth. 215. 517. 4552. der uns daz leben
gebôt, Mar. 24. (M. Dut.) bi den here die mi ghebôt (Gramm.
4, 134), die mi ghewrochte, Elegast 345. 451. 996. qui tot
a a baillier (oversee), Berte 35. qui tot a a garder, Berte 7.
que totz nos a jutgier, Ferabr. 308. 694. 1727. the man-
cunnies forwardôt, Hel. 152, 5. qui sor tos homes puet et vaut,
Méon 4, 5. dominus qui omnia potest, Docum. of 1264 in Wenk 3,
no. 151. wider den nieman vermac, A. Heinr. 1355. der aller
wunder hât gewalt, Parz. 43, 9. der gît unde nimt (gives and
takes), Parz. 7 9. der weinen und lachen geschuof, Wh. 258, 19.
der beidiu krump unde sleht gescuof (both crooked and plain),
Parz. 264, 25. der ane sihet alle getougen (secrets), Diut. 3, 52.
der durch elliu herzen siht, Frîd. 355. der in diu herze siht, Wh.
30, 29. der ie daz guote geriet (aye the good devised), Greg. 2993.
ther suntilôso man (sinless), O. iii. 21, 4. dem nie voller genâden
zeran (tear, waste), Er. 2490. qui onques ne menti (nunquam
mentitus), Berte 82. 96. 120. 146. Méon 3, 8. icil dieu qui ne
ment, et qui fist tot quanque mer serre, Ren. 19338. er mik skôp
ok öllu ræðr, Fornm. sög. 1, 3. sâ er öllu ræðr, ibid. 8, 107. er
sôlina hefði skapat, ibid. 1, 242. hêt â þann sem sôlina skapaði,
Landn. p. 139.

If, in some of the preceding names, epithets and phrases descriptive of God, unmistakable traces of Heathenism predominate, while
others have barely an inkling of it, the following expressions are
still more indisputably connected with the heathen way of
thinking.

In the Norse mythology, the notion of a Deus, Divus, if not of
the uppermost and eldest, yet of a secondary rank, which succeeded
to power later, is expressed by the word *âs*, pl. *œsir* (see Suppl.).
Landâs (Egilss. pp. 365-6) is patrium numen, and by it Thor, the
chief god of the North, is designated, though *âs* and *allmâttki âs* is
given to Oðinn (Landn. 4, 7). *âsmegin* is divine power: tha vex

honum âsmegin halfu, Sn. 26. fœraz î âsmegin, Sn. 65. But the
name must at one time have been universal, extending over Upper
Germany and Saxony, under such forms as: Goth. OHG. *ans*, pl.
anseis, ensî, AS. *ôs*, pl. *ês* (conf. our gans, with ON. gâs, pl.
gæss, AS. gôs, pl. gês; and hôse = hansa). It continued to form
a part of proper names: Goth. Ansila, OHG. Anso; the OHG.
Anshelm, Anshilt, Anspald, Ansnôt correspond in sense to Cotahelm,
Cotahilt, &c.; AS. Osweald, Oslâf, Osdæg, Osrêd; ON. Asbiörn,[1]
Asdîs, Asgautr, Aslaug, Asmundr, &c.—Now in Ulphilas Lu. 2,
41-2, *ans* denotes a beam, δοκός, which is also one meaning of the
ON. *âs*, whether because the mighty gods were thought of as joist,
rafter and ceiling of the sky, or that the notions of jugum and
mountain-ridge were associated with them, for *âs* is especially used
of jugum terræ, mountain-ridge, Dan. bierg-aas (dettiâs = sliding
beam, portcullis, Landn. 3, 17). But here we have some other
striking passages and proofs to weigh. An AS. poem couples
together '*êsa* gescot' and '*ylfa* gescot,' the shots of anses and of
elves, jaculum divorum et geniorum, just as the Edda does æsir and
âlfar, Sæm. 8ᵇ 71ᵃ 82ᵃ 83ᵇ. Jornandes says, cap. 13: Tum Gothi,
magna potiti per loca victoria, jam proceres suos quasi qui fortuna
vincebant, non puros homines, sed *semideos*, id est *anses* (which
would be anseis) vocavere. What can be plainer? The Norse æsir
in like manner merge into the race of heroes, and at much the
same distance from an elder dynasty of gods whom they have
dethroned. And here the well-known statement of Suetonius and
Hesychius,[2] that the Etruscans called the gods *æsares* or *æsi*, may
fairly be called to mind, without actually maintaining the affinity
of the Etruscan or Tyrrhenian race with the ancient German,
striking as is the likeness between τυῤῥηνός, τυρσηνός and the ON.
þurs, OHG. durs.[3]

The significance of this analogy, however, is heightened, when

---

[1] Ursus divinus, Asbirna (ursa divina), for which the Waltharius has the
hybrid Ospirn, prop. Anspirn; conf. Reinh. fuchs p. ccxcv. For Asketill,
Oscytel, see end of ch. III.

[2] Suet. Octavian. cap. 97. futurumque, ut inter deos referretur, quod
æsar, id est reliqua pars e Cæsaris nomine, Etrusca lingua *deus* vocaretur.
Hesych. s.v. αἰσοί. θεοὶ ὑπὸ τῶν Τυῤῥηνῶν. Conf. Lanzi 2, 483-4; also Dio
Cass. 56, 29.

[3] Unfortunately þurs means a giant, and durs a demon, which, if they
have anything to do with the τυρσηνοί, would rather imply that these were a
hostile and dreaded people. TRANS.

we observe that the Etruscan religion, and perhaps also the Roman and the Greek, supposed a circle of *twelve* superior beings closely bound together and known by the name of *dii consentes* or *complices* (see Suppl.), exactly as the Edda uses the expressions *höpt* and *bönd*, literally meaning vincula, for those high numina (Sæm. 24ª 89ᵇ. Sn. 176. 204), and also the sing. *hapt* and *band* for an individual god (Sæm. 93ᵇ). Though *haptbandun* in the Merseburg poem cannot with certainty be taken to mean the same thing (the compound seems here to denote mere bodily chains), it is possible that *deus* and δῖος are referable to δέω I bind; that same ' ans ' a yoke, is the same thing as the ' brace and band ' of all things ; neither can we disregard the fact that *twelve* is likewise the number of the Norse æsir ; conf. Sæm. 3ᵇ : ' æsir or þvî liði ' of the set, kindred.

Some other appellations may be added in support. In the earliest period of our language, the neut. *ragin* meant consilium. Now the plural of this, as used in the Edda, denotes in a special manner the plurality of the gods (see Suppl.). *Regin* are the powers that consult together, and direct the world ; and the expressions blið regin,[1] holl regin (kind, merciful gods), uppregin, ginregin (superæ potestates) have entirely this technical meaning. *Ragnarökr* (Goth. raginê riqvis ? dimness, darkness of gods) signifies the end of the world, the setting of the divine luminaries. Sæm. 89ᵇ has "*rögnir* ok *regin*" coupled together, rögnir (cf. 196ª) being used to distinguish the individual *ragineis* (raguneis ?), masc. These ON. regin would be Goth. ragina, as the höpt and bönd are Gothic hafta and banda, all neut.—The same heathen conception peeps out in the OS. *regan*giscapu, *regano*giscapu, Hel. 79, 13. 103, 3, equivalent to fatum, destiny, the decree and counsel of the gods, and synonymous with *wurd*giscapu, Hel. 103, 7, from *wurd*, fatum. And again in *metodo*giscapu, Hel. 66, 19. 147, 11. We have seen that *metod* likewise is a name for the Supreme Being, which the christian poet of the Heliand has ventured to retain from the

[1] The blithe, happy gods : when people stepped along in stately gorgeous attire, men thought that *gods* had appeared : menn hugðu at *æsir* væri þar komnir,' Landn. 3, 10. The Völs. saga c. 26 says of Sigurð : ' þat hygg ec at her *fari einn af goðunum*,' I think that here rides one of the gods. So in Parz. 36, 18 : ' aldâ wîp und man verjach, si ne gesachen nie helt sô wünneclîch, *ir gote im solten sîn gelîch*' (declared, they saw never a hero so winsome, their gods must be like him). The more reason is there for my note on Siegfried (ch. XV), of whom the Nib. 84, 4 says : der dort *sô hêrlîchen gât*' (see Suppl.).

heathen poetry. But these gen. plurals regano, metodo again point
to the plurality of the binding gods.

The collection of Augustine's letters contains (cap. 178), in the
altercatio with Pascentius, a Gothic or perhaps a Vandal formula
sihora armen, the meaning of which is simply κύριε ἐλέησον.[1] Even
if it be an interpolation, and written in the fifth or sixth century,
instead of at the end of the fourth, it is nevertheless remarkable
that *sihora* should be employed in it for God and Lord. Ulphilas
would have said: fráuja armái. The inf. *armén*, if not a mistake
for *armé*, might do duty as an imperative; at the same time there
is a Finn. and Esth. word *armo* signifying gratia, misericordia. But
sihora, it seems, can only be explained as Teutonic, and must have
been already in heathen times an epithet of God derived from his
victorious might (see Suppl.). Goth. *sigis*, ON. *sigr*, OHG. *sigu*,
AS. *sige* victoria, triumphus. Oðinn is styled *sigrgoð*, *sigtýr*,
sigföður; and the Christian poets transfer to God *sigidrohtín*, Hel.
47, 13. 114, 19. 125,6. *sigidryhten*, Cædm. 33, 21. 48, 20.
sigmetod, Beow. 3544. *vígsigor*, Beow. 3108.[2] elsewhere *sigoradryhten*,
sigorafreá, sigorawealdend, sigoragod, sigoracyning. It is even possible that from that ancient *sihora* sprang the title *sira, sire* still
current in Teutonic and Romance languages.[3]

The gods being represented as *superi* and *uppregin*, as dwelling
on high, in the sky, uphimin, up on the mountain height (âs, ans),
it was natural that individual gods should have certain particular
mountains and *abodes* assigned them.

Thus, from a mere consideration of the *general names* for God
and gods, we have obtained results which compel us to accept an
intimate connexion between expressions in our language and conceptions proper to our heathenism. The ' me and God,' the gracious and the angry God, the frôho (lord) and the father, the behold-
ing, creating, measuring, casting, the images of ans, fastening, band,

---

[1] The Tcheremisses also pray 'juma sirlaga,' and the Tchuvashes 'tora
sirlag,' *i.e.*, God have mercy ; G. J. Müllers saml. russ. gesch. 3, 359. The
Morduins say when it thunders ' pashangui Porguini pas,' have mercy, god
Porguini ; Georgi description 1, 64.

[2] den sig hât got in sîner *hant*, MS. 2,16ᵃ.

[3] Gött. anz. 1833, pp. 471-2. Diez however raises doubts, Roman. gram.
1, 41.

and ragin, all lead both individually, and with all the more weight
collectively, into the path to be trod. I shall take up all the threads
again, but I wish first to determine the nature and bearings of the
cultus.

CHAPTER III.

WORSHIP.

The simplest actions by which man expressed his reverence[1] for the gods (see Suppl.), and kept up a permanent connexion with them, were Prayer and Sacrifice. Sacrifice is a prayer offered up with gifts. And wherever there was occasion for prayer, there was also for sacrifice (see Suppl.).

PRAYER.—When we consider the word employed by Ulphilas to express adoration, we at once come upon a correspondence with the Norse phraseology again. For προσκυνέω the Goth. equivalent is *inveita*, inváit, invitum, Matt. 8, 2. 9, 18. Mk. 5, 6. 15, 19. Lu. 4, 7-8. John 9, 38. 12, 20. 1 Cor. 14, 25; and once for ἀσπάζομαι, Mk. 9, 15 (see Suppl.). Whether in using this word the exact sense of προσκύνησις was caught, may be doubted, if only because it is invariably followed by an acc., instead of the Greek dat. In Mod. Greek popular songs, προσκυνεῖν is used of a vanquished enemy's act of falling to the ground in token of surrender. We do not know by what gesture *inveitan* was accompanied, whether a bowing of the head, a motion of the hand, or a bending of the knee. As we read, 1 Cor. 14, 25: driusands ana andavleizn (=antlitz), inveitiđ guđ; a suppliant prostration like προσκύνησις is not at variance with the sense of the word. An OS. giwîtan, AS. gewîtan, means abire; could inveitan also have signified merely *going up to*, approaching? Paul. Diac. 1, 8 twice uses *accedere*. Fraveitan is vindicare. Now let us compare the ON. *vîta inclinare*,[2] which Biörn quotes under veit, and spells, erroneously, I

---

[1] Verehrung, O.H.G. *êra*, Goth. prob. áiza. The O.H.G. *êrôn* is not merely our ehren, to honour, but also verehren, revereri (as reverentia is adoration, cultus); A.S. *weorđian*, O.S. *giwerthôn*. All that comes from the gods or concerns them is *holy*, for which the oldest Teutonic word is Goth. *veihs*. O.H.G. *wîh*; but only a few of the O.H.G. documents use this word, the rest preferring *heilac*, O.S. has only *hêlag*, A.S. *hâlig*, O.N. *heilagr*. On the connexion of wih with the subst. *wih*, more hereafter. *Frôn* denotes holy in the sense of dominicus

[2] Cleasby-Vigfusson gives no meaning like inclinare, either under *vîta* 'to fine,' or under *vita* 'to wit.'—TRANS.

think, vita. From it is derived *veita* (Goth. váitjan ?); veita heiðr, honorem peragere; veita tiðir, sacra peragere; veitsla, epulum, Goth. váitislô ?[1]

The Goth. *bida* preces, *bidjan* precari, rogare, orare, are used both in a secular and a spiritual sense. The same with OHG. *pëta* and *pittan;* but from pëta is derived a *pëtôn* adorare, construed with acc. of the person whom : O.i. 17, 62. ii. 14, 63. nidar-fallan joh *mih bëtôn,* O. ii. 4, 86-9. 97. iii. 11, 25. T. 46, 2. 60, 1. pëtôta inan, Diut. 1, 513ᵇ. But *bëtôn* can also express a spiritual orare, T. 34, 1, 2, 3. *bëto-man* cultores, O. II. 14, 68. In MHG. I find *bëten* always followed by the prep. *an* (see Suppl.) : bëten an diu abgot, Barl. 72, 4. an ein bilde bëten, ibid. 98, 15. sô muoz si iemer mê nâch gote sîn mîn *anebët,* she must after God be my (object of) adoration, Ben. 146. Our *bitten* ask, *beten* pray, *anbeten* adore, are distinct from one another, as *bitte* request is from *gebet* prayer. The OS. *bëdôn* is not followed by acc., but by prep. *te :* bëdôn te minun barma, Hel. 33, 7. 8 ; and this of itself would suggest what I conjectured in my Gramm. 2, 25, that bidjan originally contained the physical notion of jacēre, prosterni, which again is the only explanation of Goth. badi κλινιδιον a bed, and also of the old badu, AS. beado = cædes, strages.[2]—The AS. New Test. translates adorare by *ge-eáð-mêdan, i.e.,* to humble oneself. The MHG. *flêhen,* when it signifies supplicare, governs the dat. : gote flêhen, Aegid. 30. den goten vlêhen, Parz. 21, 6. Wh. 126, 30. Türl. Wh. 71ᵃ ; but in the sense of demulcere, solari, the acc., Parz. 119, 23. 421, 25. Nib. 499, 8 (see Suppl.).[3] It is the Goth *þláihan,* fovere, consolari. An OHG. *flêhôn* vovere I only know from N. cap. 8, Bth. 178, and he spells it *flêhôn :* ten (acc. quem) wir fle-hoton. We say ' zu gott *flehen,*' but ' gott *anflehen*'.—The Goth. *aíhtrôn* προσευχεσθαι, προσαιτειν expresses begging rather than asking or praying. The OHG. *diccan,* OS., *thiggian,* is both precari and impetrare, while AS. *þicgan,* ON., *þiggja,* is invariably

---

[1] Bopp, Comp. gram. p. 128, identifies inveita with the Zend nivaêdhayêmi invoco.

[2] What was the physical meaning of the Slav. moliti rogare, molitise orare, Boh. modliti se, Pol. modlić się ? The Sloven. moliti still means porrigere, conf. Lith. meldziu rogo, inf. melsti, and malda oratio. Pruss. madla, conf. Goth. maþljan loqui, maþleins loquela, which is next door to oratio.

[3] Iw. 3315 vlêgete got ; but in the oldest MS. vlêhete gote.

impetrare, accipere, so that asking has passed over into effectual asking, getting (see Suppl.).

Another expression for prayer is peculiar to the Norse and AS. dialects, and foreign to all the rest: ON. *bón* or *bœn*, Swed. Dan. *bön*, AS. *bén*, gen. bêne f., Cædm. 152, 26, in Chaucer *bone*, Engl. *boon;* from it, *béna* supplex, *bénsian* supplicare. Lastly the Icel. Swed. *dyrka*, Dan. *dyrke*, which like the Lat. colere is used alike of worship and of tillage, seems to be a recent upstart, unknown to the ON. language.

On the form and manner of heathen prayer we lack information ; I merely conjecture that it was accompanied by a *looking up to heaven, bending of the body* (of which bidjan gave a hint), *folding of hands, bowing of knees, uncovering of the head.* These gestures grow out of a crude childlike notion of antiquity, that the human suppliant presents and submits himself to the mighty god, his conqueror, as a *defenceless victim* (see Suppl.). Precari deos *cœlum-que suspicere* is attested by Tacitus himself, Germ. 10. Genuflec-tere is in Gothic *knussjan*, the supplicare of the Romans was flexo corpore adorare. Falling down and bowing were customs of the christians too; thus in Hel. 47, 6. 48, 16. 144, 24 we have: te bedu *hnîgan.* 58, 12: te drohtine hnîgan. 176, 8: te bedu *fallan.* 145, 3: gihnêg an *kniobeda.* In the Sôlarlioð is the remarkable expression: henni ec *laut,* to her (the sun) I bowed, Sæm. 126ᵃ; from *lúta* inclinare. falla â knê ok lúta, Vilk. saga cap. 6. nu *strauk* kongsdôttir *sinn legg,* ok mælti, ok *sér i loptið upp,* (stroked her leg, and spoke, and looks up to the sky), Vilk. saga cap. 61. So the saga of St. Olaf tells how the men bowed before the statue of Thor, *lutu þvî* skrimsli, Fornm. sög. 4, 247. *fell til iardar* fyrir likneski (fell to earth before the likeness). Fornm. sög. 2, 108. The Langobards are stated in the Dial. Gregorii M. 3, 28 to have adored *submissis cervicibus* a divinely honoured goat's head. In the Middle Ages people continued to *bow* to lifeless objects, by way of blessing them, such as a loved country, the road they had traversed, or the day.[1] Latin writers of the time, as Lambert, express urgent entreaty by *pedibus provolvi :* the attitude was used not only to

---

[1] Dem stige nîgen, Iw. 5837. dem wege nîgen, Parz. 375, 26. dem lande nîgen, Trist. 11532. nîgen in daz lant, Wigal. 4018. nîgen in elliu lant, Iw. 7755. in die werlt nîgen, Frauend. 163, 10. den stîgen und wegen segen tuon, Iw. 357 (see Suppl.).

God, but to all whom one wished to honour : neig im ûf den fuoz.
Morolt 41ᵇ. hie viel sie ûf sînen vuoz, Iw. 8130. ouch nîge ich ir
unz ûf den fuoz, MS. 1, 155ᵃ. valle für si (fall before her), und nîge
ûf ir fuoz, MS. 1, 54ᵃ. buten sich (bowed) weinende ûf sînen vuoz,
Greg. 355. neig im nider ûf die hant, Dietr. 55ᵇ. These passages show
that people fell before the feet, and at the feet, of him who was to
be reverenced : wilt fallan te mînun fôtun, bedôs te mînun barma,
Hel. 33, 7. sich bôt ze tal (bowed to the ground) gein sînen füezen
nieder, Wh. 463, 2.[1] An O. Boh. song has : ' sie *klanieti* bohu,' to
bow before God, Königinh. hs. 72 ; but the same has also the un-
Teutonic ' se *biti w čelo* prede bohy,' to beat one's brow before God.[2]
Uncovering the head (see Suppl.) certainly was from of old a token
of respect with our ancestors, which, like bowing, was shown to
deity as well as to kings and chiefs. Perhaps the priests, at least
those of the Goths, formed an exception to this, as their name pileati is thus accounted for by Jornandes, quia *opertis capitibus tiaris*
litabant, while the rest of the people stood uncovered. In a
survival of heathenish harvest-customs we shall find this uncovering further established, ch. VII. In Nicolai Magni de Göw
registrum superstitionum (of 1415) it is said : Insuper hodie
inveniuntur homines, qui cum novilunium primo viderint *flexis
genibus* adorant vel *deposito caputio* vel *pileo*, inclinato capite
honorant alloquendo et suscipiendo.[3] An AS. legend of Cuðberht
relates how that saint was wont to go down to the sea at

[1] Fial *in* sine fuazi, O. III. 10, 27. *an* sîne füeze, Karl 14ᵇ. The Christians in the Mid. Ages called it *venie fallen*, Parz. 460, 10. Karl 104ᵃ. Berth.
173. Ksrchr. 2958. 3055. Kneeling and kissing the ground, to obtain abso-
lution : dâ er ûf sîner venie lac (lay), Barl. 366, 21. den ar.ger maz mit der langen
venie, Frib. Trist. 2095. venien suochen, MS. 1, 23ᵇ. Morolt. 28ᵃ. Troj.
9300. terrae osculationibus, quas *venias* appellant, Pez. bibl. ascet. 8, 440. gie
ze kirchen und banekte (prostrated ?) ze gote sîniu glider mit venien und gebet,
Cod. kolocz. 180.
[2] The tchelo-bîtnaya, beating of the forehead in presenting a petition, was
prohibited in Russia by Catherine II. Conf. pronis vultibus adorare, Helmold
1, 38.
[3] What else I have collected about this practice, may be inserted here :
elevato a capite pileo alloquitur seniorem, Dietm. Merseb. p. 824 (an. 1012).
sublata cydare surgens inclinat honeste, Ruodlieb 2, 93. Odofredus in I.
secundo loco digest. de postulando : Or signori, hic colligimus argumentum,
quod aliquis quando veniet coram magistratu debet ei revereri, quod est contra
Ferrarienses, qui, si essent *coram Deo*, non *extraherent* sibi *capellum* vel *birretum
de capite*, nec flexis genibus postularent. *Pilleus in capite* est, Isengrimus 1139.
oster la chape (in saluting), Méon 4, 261. *gelüpfet* den huot, Ms H. 3, 330.
sînen *huot* er *abenam*, hiemit êret er in alsô, Wigal. 1436. er *zôch* durch sîn
hübscheit den *huot* gezogenlîchen abe, Troj. 1775. dô stuont er ûf geswinde

night, and standing *up to his neck* in the briny breakers, to sing his prayers, and afterwards to *kneel down* on the shingles, with *palms stretched out* to the firmament.[1] *Lifting up* and *folding of the hands* (see Suppl.) was also practised to a master, particularly to a feudal lord. In Ls. 3, 78 we have ' bat mit *zertânen armen,*' prayed with outspread arms. The Old Bavarian stapfsakên (denial of indebtedness) was accompanied by elevation of the hands, RA. 927 (see Suppl.). It is not impossible that the christian converts retained some heathen customs in praying. In a manuscript, probably of the 12th century, the prayers are to be accompanied by some curious actions: sô *miz* (measure) den *ubir dîn herza* in modum crucis, unde *von dem brustleffile zuo demo nabile,* unde *miz* denne *von eime rippe unz an daz andire,* unde sprich alsus. Again: sô *miz* denne *die rehtun hant von deme lengistin vingire unz an daz resti* (wrist), unde *miz* denne von deme dûmin zuo deme minnisten vingire.* One prayer was called ' der vane (flag) des almehtigin gotis'; nine women are to read it nine Sundays, ' sô ez morginet'; the ninth has to read the psalm Domini est terra, in such a posture ' daz ir *lîb niet ruore die erde, wan die ellebogin unde diu chnie,*' that her body touch not the ground, except at the elbows and knees; the others are all to stand till the lighted candle has burnt out; Diut. 2, 292-3.

We cannot now attach any definite meaning to the Gothic *aviliudôn εὐχαριστεῖν;* it is formed from *aviliud χάρις,* which resembles an O. Sax. *alat, olat* gratiae; does it contain liuð cantus, and was there moreover something heathenish about it? (See Suppl.). The old forms of prayer deserve more careful collecting; the Norse, which invoke the help of the gods, mostly contain the

gnuoc, ein *schapel* daz er ûf truoc von gimmen und von golde fîn, daz *nam* er *ab dem houpte* sîn, Troj. 18635. er *zucket* im sîn *keppalî,* Ls. 3, 35. er was gereit, daz er von dem houbt den *huot* liez vliegen und sprach, Kolocz. 101. Festus explains : lucem facere dicuntur Saturno sacrificantes, id est *capita detegere;* again : Saturno fit sacrificium *capite aperto;* conf. Macrob. Sat. 1, 8. Serv. in Virg. 3, 407.

[1] Wæs gewunod þæt he wolde gàn on niht tô sæ, and standan on þam sealtum brimme, oð his swuran, singende his gebedu, and siððan his cneowu on þam ceosle gebygde, ástrehtum handbredum tó heofenlîcum rodere; Thorpe's analecta, pp. 76-7. homil. 2. 138. [I have thought it but fair to rescue the saint from a perilous position in which the German had inadvertently placed him by making him " wade into the sea up to his neck, *and kneel down* to sing his prayers".—Trans.]—In the O.Fr. jeu de saint Nicolas, Tervagant has to be approached on *bare elbows and knees;* Legrand fabl. 1, 343.

verb *duga* with the sense propitium esse: biŏ ec Ottari öll goŏ *duga* (I Ot. pray all, &c.), Sæm. 120ᵇ. biŏja þâ dîsir *duga*, Sæm. 195ᵃ. Duga means to help, conf. Gramm. 4, 687. There is beauty in the ON. prayer: biŏjom herjaföör *î hugom sitja* (rogemus deum in animis sedere nostris), Sæm. 113ᵃ, just as Christians pray the Holy Ghost to descend: *in herzen unsên sâzi*, O. iv. 5, 30 (see Suppl.).

Christians at prayer or confession looked toward the *East*, and lifted up their arms (Bingham lib. xi. cap. 7, ed. hal. 3, 273); and so we read in the Kristinbalkr of the old Gulathing law: ' ver skulun *lûta austr*, oc biŏja til ens helga Krists ârs ok friŏar,' we must bow east, and pray the holy Christ for plenty and peace (conf. Syntagma de baptismo p. 65); in the Waltharius 1159: contra *orientalem* prostratus corpore partem precatur; in AS. formulas: *eástweard* ic stande; and in Troj. 9298. 9642: kêret iuch *gén ôrient*. The heathens, on the contrary, in praying and sacrificing, looked *North-wards*: horfa (turn) *î norŏr*, Fornm. sög. 11, 134. leit (looked) *î norŏr*, Sæm. 94ᵃ. beten gegen *mitternacht*, Keisersperg omeiss 49ᵇ. And the North was looked upon by the christians as the unblessed heathen quarter, on which I have given details in RA. 808; it was unlucky to make a throw toward the north, RA. 57; in the Lombard boundary-treaties the northern tract is styled ' nulla ora,' RA. 544. These opposite views must serve to explain a passage in the Roman de Renart, where the fox prays *christianly*, and the wolf *heathenly*, Reinh. fuchs p. xli.[1]

As the expressions for asking and for obtaining, pp. 30, 31, are identical, a prayer was thought to be the more effectual, the more people it was uttered by:

> got enwolde so manegem munde
> sîn genâde niht versagen. Wigal. 4458.
>
> die juncvrouwen bâten alle got,
> nu ist er sô gnædec unt sô guot
> unt sô reine gemuot,
> daz er niemer kunde
> sô manegem süezen munde
> betelîchiu dinc versagen. Iw. 5351.

---

[1] At the abrenuntiatio one had to face the sunset, with wrinkled brow (fronte caperata), expressing anger and hatred ; but at the confession of faith, to face the sunrise, with eyes and hands raised to heaven ; Bingham lib. xi. cap. 7. § 13.14. Conf. Joh. Olavii synt. de baptismo, pp. 64-5.

in (to the nuns) wâren de mûnde sô royt,
so wes si god bâden,
of syt mit vlîze dâden,
he id in nummer inkûnde
dem rôsenrôten mûnde
bedelicher dinge versagen.

Ged. von der vrouwen sperwere, Cod. berol. 184, 54ᵈ. Hence:
helfen singen, MS. 1, 57ᵃ. 2, 42ᵇ. Conf. cento novelle 61.[1]

SACRIFICE.—The word *opfer*, a sacrifice, was introduced into
German by christianity, being derived from the Lat. *offero. offerre.*[2]
The AS. very properly has only the verb *offrian* and its derivative
offrung (oblatio). In OHG., from *opfarôn, opforôn* there proceeded
also a subst. *opfar*, MHG. *ophern* and *opher* ;[3] and from Germany
the expression seems to have spread to neighbouring nations, ON.
offr, Swed. Dan. *offer*, Lith. *appiera*, Lett. *uppuris*, Esth. *ohwer*, Fin.
uhri, Boh. *ofĕra*, Pol. *ofiara*, Sloven. *ofer*. Everywhere the original
heathen terms disappeared (see Suppl.).

The oldest term, and one universally spread, for the notion 'to
worship (God) by sacrifice,' was *blôtan* (we do not know if the
Goth. pret. was báiblôt or blôtáida) ; I incline to attach to it the
full sense of the Gk. θύειν[4] (see Suppl.). Ulphilas saw as yet no
objection to translating by it σέβεσθαι and λατρεύειν, Mk. 7, 7.

---

[1] Mock-piety, hypocrisy, was branded in the Mid. Ages likewise, by strong
phraseology : er wil *gote die füeze abezzen* (eat the feet off), Ls. 3, 421. Fragm.
28ᵃ. Mones anz. 3, 22. unserm Herrgott die füess abbeissen wollen (bite off),
Schmeller 2, 231. den heiligen die füss abbeten wollen (pray the saints' feet off
them), Simplic. 1. 4, 17. herrgottbeisser, Höfer 2, 48. herrgottfisler (füszler),
Schmid 1, 93. heiligenfresserin, 10 ehen, p. 62. So the Ital. mangiaparadiso,
Fr. mangeur de crucefix, Boh. Pol. liciobrazek (licker of saints). A sham
saint is indifferently termed *kapeltrete, tempeltrete, tempelrinne*, Mones schausp.
p. 123. 137 (see Suppl.).

[2] Not from operari, which in that sense was unknown to the church, the
Romance languages likewise using It. *offerire*, Sp. *ofrecer*, Fr. *offrir*, never
operare, obrar, ouvrer ; the same technical sense adheres to *offerta, ofrenda,
offrande*. From oblata come the Sp. *oblea*, Fr. *oublie*, and perhaps the MHG.
oblei, unless it is from eulogia, oblagia. From offre and offerta are formed the
Wel. *offryd*, Ir. *oifrion, aifrion, offrail*. Lastly, the derivation from ferre,
offerre, is confirmed by the German phrase ' ein opfer *bringen, darbringen*.'

[3] *Ophar, opfer* could hardly be the Goth. áibr δῶρον, in which neither the
vowel nor the consonant agrees. The Wel. *abert*, Gael. *iobairt*, Ir. *iodbairt*,
(sacrificium) probably belong also to offerta.

[4] When Sozomen hist. eccl. 6, 37 in a narrative of Athanaric uses προσκυνεῖν
καὶ θύειν, the Gothic would be *inveitan jah blôtan*.

Lu. 2, 37; he construes it with an acc. of the person: blôtan
fráujan is to him simply Deum colere, with apparently no thought
of a bloody sacrifice. For λατρεία Rom. 12, 1, he puts blôtinassus,
and for θεοσεβής John 9, 31 guðblôstreis. The latter presupposes a
subst. blôstr (cultus, oblatio), of which the S is explained in
Gramm. 2, 208. Usblôteins (παράκλησις) 2 Cor. 8, 4 implies a verb
usblôtjan to implore. Cædmon uses the AS. blôtan pret. blêot,
onblôtan pret. onblêot, of the Jewish sacrifice, and follows them up
with acc. of thing and dat. of person: blôtan sunu (filium sacrificare) 173, 5.   onblêot þæt lâc Gode (obtulit hostiam Deo) 177, 21.
In Ælfred's Orosius we have the same blôtan pret. blôtte.   I derive
from it blêtsian, later blessian, to bless.   The OHG. pluozan, pret.
pliez and pluozta, appears only in glosses, and renders libare, litare,
victimare, immolare, Gl. Hrab. 959ª 960ª 966ᵇ 968ᵇ.   Diut. 1, 245,
258ª.   No case-construction is found, but an acc. of the thing may
be inferred from partic. kaplôzaniu immolata.   A subst. pluostar
sacrificium, bluostar, Is. 382. Gl. emm. 411. Gl. jun. 209.   T. 56, 4.
95, 102 [1]; pluostarhûs idolium, Gl. emm. 402.   ploazhûs fanum,
pluostrari sacrificator, ibid. 405.   It is plain that here the word has
more of a heathen look, and was not at that time used of christian
worship; with the thing, the words for it soon die out.   But its
universal use in Norse heathendom leaves no doubt remaining, that
it was equally in vogue among Goths, Alamanni, Saxons, before
their conversion to christianity.   The ON. verb blôta, pret. blêt and
blôtaði, takes, like the Gothic, an acc. of the object worshipped;
thus, Grâgâs 2, 170, in the formula of the trygdamâl: svâ viða sem
(as widely as) kristnir menn kirkior sœkia, heiðnir menn hof blôta
(fana colunt); and in the Edda: Thôr blôta, mik blôta, blôtaði Oðin.
Sæm. 111ª, 113ᵇ, 141ª, 165ª²: always the meaning is sacrificio venerari.   So that in Goth. and ON. the verb brings out more the idea
of the person, in OHG. and AS. more that of the thing.   But
even the O.Dan. version of the OT. uses blothe immolare, blodhmadh

[1] The Gl. Hrab. 954ª : bacha, plôstar, is incomplete; in Gl. Ker. 45. Diut.
1, 166ª it stands : bacha sacrificat, ploastar ploazit, or zëpar plôzit; so that it is
meant to translate only the Lat. verb, not the subst. bacha (βάκχη).   Or perhaps a better reading is 'bachat' for bacchatur, and the meaning is 'non
sacrificat'.
[2] Landn. 1, 2 : blôtaði hrafna þria, worshipped three ravens, who were
going to show him the road ; so, in Sæm. 141ª, a bird demands that cows be
sacrificed to him ; the victim itself is ON. blôt, and we are told occasionally :
feck at blôti, ak blôti miklu, offered a sacrifice, a great sacrifice, Landn. 2, 29.

libamina, *blotelsä* holocaustum, Molbech's ed. pp. 171. 182. 215. 249. Also the O.Swed. Uplandslag, at the very beginning of the church-balkr has : ængin skal affguðum *blotæ*, with dat. of person, implying an acc. of the thing.—The true derivation of the word I do not know.[1] At all events it is not to be looked for in blôð sanguis, as the dis-agreeing consonants of the two Gothic words plainly show; equally divergent are the OHG. pluozan and pluot from one another; besides, the worship so designated was not necessarily bloody. A remarkable passage in the Livonian rhyming chronicle 4683 tells of the Sameits (Schamaits, Samogits):

> ir *bluotekirl* der warf zuo hant
> sin lôz nâch ir alden site,
> zuo hant er *bluotete* alles mite
> ein quek.

Here, no doubt, an animal is sacrificed. I fancy the poet retained a term which had penetrated from Scandinavia to Lithuania with-out understanding it himself ; for bluotkirl is merely the O.Swed. blôtkarl, heathen priest ; the term is foreign to the Lithuanian language.[2]

A few more of these general terms for sacrifice must be added (see Suppl.).—OHG. *antheiz* (hostia, victima), Diut. 1, 240ᵃ. 246, 258. 278ᵇ ; and as verbs, both *antheizôn* and *inheizan* (immolare), Diut. 1, 246. 258.—OHG. *insakên* (litare), Gl. Hrab. 968ᵇ, *insakêt* pim (delibor), ibid. 959ᵃ 960ᵃ, to which add the Bavarian stapfsakên, RA. 927 ; just so the AS. *onsecgan*, Cod. exon. 171, 32. 257, 23. *onsecgan* tô tibre (devote as sacrifice), Cædm. 172, 30. tiber *onsægde*, 90, 29. 108, 17. tifer *onsecge*, Ps. 65, 12. lâc *onsecge* Cod. exon. 254, 19. 257, 29 ; lâc *onsægde*, Cædm. 107, 21. 113, 15. Cod. exon. 168, 28. gild *onsægde*, Cædm. 172, 11. and *onsægdnes* (oblatio). — As inheizan and onsecgan are formed with the prefix and-, so is apparently the OHG. *ineihan* pim (delibor), Hrab. 960ᵃ, which would yield a Goth. *andáikan* ; it is

---

[1] Letter for letter it agrees with φλοιδόω I light up, burn, which is also ex-pressed in θύω and the Lat. suffio ; but, if the idea of burnt-offering was originally contained in blôtan, it must have got obscured very early.

[2] Even in MHG. the word seems to have already become extinct ; it may survive still in terms referring to place, as *blotz*graben, *blotz*garten in Hessen, conf. the phrase ' *blotzen* müssen,' to have to fork out (sacrifice) money. An old knife or sword also is called *blotz* (see Suppl.).

from this OHG. ineihhan, which I think Graff 1, 128 has misread ireihan, that a later *neihhan* immolare, libare Graff (2, 1015) seems to have risen by aphæresis (Gramm. 2, 810), as nëben from inëben; conf. eichôn (dicare, vindicare), Graff 1, 127. To this place also belongs the OHG. *pifëlahan* (libare, immolare), Diut. 1, 245. 248. —All this strictly denotes only the ' on-saying,' dedication, consecration of the offering; and it follows from the terminology at least that particular objects were selected beforehand for sacrifice.[1] Thus *antheiz* is elsewhere simply a vow, votum, solemn promise, *intheizan* vovere; hence also the AS. onsecgan has determinative substantives added to it.

In the same sense *biudan* (offerre) seems to have been in use very early, AS. lâc *bebeodan*, Cædm. 173, 9. ON. *bodn* (oblatio). From this biudan I derive *biuds* (mensa), ON. *bioðr* (discus), AS. *beod* (mensa, lanx), OHG. *piot*, from its having originally signified the holy table of offerings, the altar.

The Goth. *fullafahjan* (with dat. of pers.) prop. to please, give satisfaction, is used for λατρεύειν, Lu. 4, 8 (see Suppl.).—In Mk. 1, 44. Lu. 5, 14 *atbairan* adferre, προσφέρειν, is used of sacrifice; and in AS. the subst. *bring* by itself means oblatio; so Wolfram in Parz. 45, 1 says: si *brâhten* opfer vil ir goten, and Fundgr. II. 25: ein lam zopphere *brâhte*.—It is remarkable that the Goth. *saljan,* which elsewhere is intransitive and means divertere, manere [put up, lodge, John 1, 39. 40] is in Lu. 1, 9. Mk. 14, 12. 1 Cor. 10, 20. 28 used transitively for θυμιᾶν and θύειν, and hunsla *saljan,* John 16, 2 stands for λατρείαν προσφέρειν, which brings it up to the meaning of OHG. and AS. sellan, ON. selja, tradere, to hand over, possibly because the solemn presentation included a personal approach. The OHG. *pigangan* (obire) is occasionally applied to worship: *piganc* (ritus), Diut. 1, 272[a]. afgoda *begangan,* Lacomblet 1, 11.—*Gildan, këltan,* among its many meanings, has also to do with worship and sacrifice; it was from the old sacrificial banquets that our *guilds* took their name. OS. waldandes (God's) *gëld,* Hel. 3, 11. 6, 1. that *gëld* lêstian, Hel. 16, 5. AS. bryne*gield*, holocaustum, Cædm. 175, 6, 177, 18. *gild* onsecgan, 172, 11. Abel's offering is a *gield*, 60, 5. deofol*gield*, idololatria, Beda 3, 30. Cod.

---

[1] So the O.Boh. *obiecati* obiet (Königinh. hs. 72) is strictly opfer *verheissen,* to promise or devote an offering.

exon. 245, 29. 251, 24. hæðengield, Cod. exon. 243, 23. OHG. heidankëlt sacrilegium: gote ir gelt bringent, Warn. 2906. offeruncghëlstar, sacrificium, Is. 395. dhiu blôstar iro ghëlstro, Is. 382. —Peculiar to the AS. dialect is the general term lác, neut., often rendered more definite by verbs containing the notion of sacrifice: onbléot þæt lác gode, Cædm. 177, 26. dryhtne lác brohton, 60, 2. lác bebeodan, 173, 9. lác onsægde, 107, 21. 113, 15. ongan lác, 90, 19 (see Suppl.). The word seems to be of the same root as the Goth. masc. láiks (saltatio), OHG. leih (ludus, modus), ON. leikr, and to have signified at first the dance and play that accompanied a sacrifice, then gradually the gift itself.[1] That there was playing and singing at sacrifices is shown by the passages quoted further on, from Gregory's dialogues and Adam of Bremen.

The following expressions I regard as more definite (see Suppl.). Ulph. in Rom. 11, 16 renders ἀπαρχή, the offering of firstfruits at a sacrifice, delibatio, by ufarskafts, which I derive not from skapan, but from skaban (shave) · radere, since ἀπαρχαί were the first clippings of hair off the victim's forehead, Odyss. 14, 422. 3, 446. If we explain it from skapan, this word must have passed from its meaning of creare into that of facere, immolare.—The Goth. vitôd is lex, the OHG. wizôt (Graff 1, 1112. Fundgr. 1, 398ᵇ) both lex and eucharistia, the Fris. vitat invariably the latter alone; just as zakón in Serv. has both meanings [but in Russ. only that of lex]. —Ulph. translates θυσία by Goth. hunsl, Matt. 9, 13. Mk. 9, 49. Lu. 2, 24; then again λατρείαν προσφέρειν in John 16, 2 by hunsla saljan, where the reference is expressly to killing. And θυσιαστήριον is called hunslastaðs, Matt. 5, 23-4. Lu. 1, 11. But the corresponding AS. húsel, Engl. housel, allows of being applied to a Christian sacrament, and denotes the eucharist, húselgong the partaking of it, húselfæt the sacred vessel of sacrifice; conf. Cædm. 260, 5 húselfatu hâlegu for the sacred vessels of Jerusalem. Likewise the ON. húsl in the Norw. and Swed. laws is used in a christian, never in a heathen sense. No hunsal is found in OHG.; neither can I guess the root of the word.—Twice, however, Ulph.

---

[1] Serv. prilóg offering, what is laid before, prilozhiti to offer; Sloven. dar, darina, daritva = δῶρον. [Russ. darü sviatüye = δῶρα ἱερα means the eucharist.] The Sloven aldov, bloodless offering, seems not to be Slavic, it resembles Hung. aldozat. θυσία is rendered in O. Slav. by zhrtva (Kopitar's Glagol. 72ᶜ), in Russ. by zhertva [fr. zháriti to roast, burn? or zhráti devour, zhëra glutton?].

renders θυσία by sáuðs, pl. sáudeis, Mk. 12, 33. Rom. 12, 1. I sup-
suppose he thought of the sacrifice as that of an animal slaughtered
and boiled; the root seems to be siuðan to seethe, and the ON. has
sauðr a ram, probably because its flesh is boiled.[1] In Eph. 5, 2 we
have 'hunsl jah sáuð' side by side, for προσφορὰν καὶ θυσίαν, and
in Skeir. 37, 8 gasaljands sik hunsl jah sáuð.—The OHG. zëpar is
also a sacrifice in the sense of hostia, victima, Hymn. 10, 2. 12, 2. 21,
5. Gl. Hrab. 965ᵇ. Diut. 240ᵃ 272ᵃ (see Suppl.). We could match
it with a Goth. tibr, if we might venture on such an emendation of
the unique áibr δῶρον, Matt. 5, 23 (conf. Gramm. 1, 63). My conjecture that our German ungeziefer (vermin), formerly ungeziber,[2]
and the O.Fr. atoivre also belong to this root, has good reasons in
its favour. To this day in Franconia and Thuringia, ziefer, geziefer
(insects) not only designate poultry, but sometimes include even
goats and swine (Reinwald henneb. id. 1, 49. 2, 52, conf. Schm. 4,
228). What seems to make against my view is, that the A.S. tiber
cannot even be restricted to animals at all, Cædm. 90, 29. 108, 5.
172, 31. 175, 3. 204, 6. 301, 1. sigetiber, 203, 12. sigortifer, Cod.
exon. 257, 30; on the contrary, in 60, 9 it is Cain's offering of
grain that is called tiber, in distinction from Abel's gield; and in
Ælfr. gl. 62ᵇ we find wintifer, libatio. But this might be a later
confusion; or our ungeziefer may have extended to weeds, and consequently zëpar itself would include anything fit for sacrifice in
plants and trees.[3] Meanwhile there is also to be considered the
ON. tafn, victima and esca ferarum.—Lastly, I will mention a
term peculiar to the ON. language, and certainly heathen: fôrn,
fem. victima, hostia, fôrna, immolare, or instead of it fôrnfœra,
conf. Fornm, sög. 1, 97 2, 76. this fôrna at the same time, according
to Biörn, meaning elevare, tollere. AS. fôrn porcus, porcaster (?).

---

[1] Rom. 12, 1. 'present your bodies a living sáuð' was scarcely a happy
combination, if sáuðs conveyed the notion of something boiled! Can nothing
be made of sôðjan satiare soothe (Milton's ' the soothest shepherd ' = sweetest,
Goth. sûtista)? Grimm's law of change in mutes has many exceptions: pater
father fæder vater (4 stages instead of 3, so mater); sessel a settle, and sattel
a saddle, both from sit sat; treu true, but trinken drink, &c.—TRANS.

[2] Titur. 5198, ungezibere stands for monster; but what can ungezibele mean
in Lanz. 5028 vor grôzem ungezibele? nibele?

[3] Cædm. 9, 2 : þa seo tíd gewàt ofer tiber sceacan middangeardes. This
passage, whose meaning Thorpe himself did not rightly seize, I understand
thus: As time passed on over (God's) gift of this earth. The inf. sceacan (elabi)
depends on gewàt; so in Judith anal. 140, 5 : gewiton on fleám sceacan, began
to flee; and still more freq. gewiton gangan.

If the ô did not hinder, we could identify it with the adj. *forn* vetus, *forn* sorcerer, *fornœskia* sorcery, and the OHG. *furnir* antiquus, priscus, canus (Graff 3, 628); and in particular, use the same glosses for the illustration of baccha pluostar. *Forn* would then be the term applied by the christians to heathen sacrifices of the *former olden* time, and that would easily glide into sorcery, nay, there would be an actual kinship conceivable between *zëpar* and *zoupar* (zauber, magic), and so an additional link between the notions of sacrifice and sorcery, knowing as we do that the verbs *garawan*, *wîhan* and perhaps *zouwan* [AS. gearwian to prepare, Goth. veihan to consecrate, and taujan to bring about] are applicable to both, though our OHG. *karo, karawi* victima, Graff 4, 241 (Germ. gar, AS. gearw, yare) expresses no more than what is made ready, made holy, consecrated.[1] We shall besides have to separate more exactly the ideas *vow* and *sacrifice*, Mid. Lat. *votum* and *census*, closely as they border on one another: the vow is, as it were, a private sacrifice.

Here then our ancient language had a variety of words at its command, and it may be supposed that they stood for different things; but the difficulty is, to unravel what the differences in the matter were.

Sacrifice rested on the supposition that human food is agreeable to the gods, that intercourse takes place between gods and men The god is invited to eat his share of the sacrifice, and he really enjoys it. Not till later is a separate divine food placed before him (see Suppl.). The motive of sacrifices was everywhere the same: either to render thanks to the gods for their kindnesses, or to appease their anger; the gods were to be kept gracious, or to be made gracious again. Hence the two main kinds of sacrifice: *thank*-offerings and *sin*-offerings.[2] When a meal was eaten, a head of

---

[1] The Skr. *kratu* sacrifice, or accord. to Benfey 2, 307 process, comes from *kri* facere , and in Latin, *facere* (agnis, vitula, Virg. ecl. 3. 77) and *operari* were used of the sacred act of sacrifice ; so in Grk, ῥέζειν = ἔρδειν, Bœot. ῥέδδειν of offering the hecatomb, and ἔρδειν is ἔργειν, our *wirken, work* , ἐπιρρέζειν Od. 17, 211. θύειν, ῥέζειν, δρᾶν, Athenæus 5, 403, as δρᾶν for θύειν, so δρᾶσις = θυσία. The Catholic priest also uses *conficere, perficere* for consecrare (Cæsar. heisterbac. 9, 27) ; compare the ' aliquid plus novi facere ' in Burcard of Worms 10, 16 and p. 193c. The Lat. *agere* signified the slaughtering of the victim.
[2] *Sühn*-opfer. strictly, conciliatory offerings ; but as these were generally identical with *Sünd*-opfer, sin-offerings, I have used the latter expression, as short and familiar.—TRANS.

game killed, the enemy conquered (see Suppl.), a firstling of the cattle born, or grain harvested, the gift-bestowing god had a first right to a part of the food, drink, produce, the spoils of war or of the chase (the same idea on which tithes to the church were afterwards grounded). If on the contrary a famine, a failure of crops, a pestilence had set in among a people, they hastened to present propitiatory gifts (see Suppl.). These sin-offerings have by their nature an occasional and fitful character, while those performed to the propitious deity readily pass into periodically recurring festivals. There is a third species of sacrifice, by which one seeks to know the issue of an enterprise, and to secure the aid of the god to whom it is presented (see Suppl.). Divination however could also be practised without sacrifices. Besides these three, there were special sacrifices for particular occasions, such as coronations, births, weddings and funerals, which were also for the most part coupled with solemn banquets.

As the gods show favour more than anger, and as men are oftener cheerful than oppressed by their sins and errors, thank-offerings were the earliest and commonest, sin-offerings the more rare and impressive. Whatever in the world of plants can be laid before the gods is gay, innocent, but also less imposing and effective than an animal sacrifice. The streaming blood, the life spilt out seems to have a stronger binding and atoning power. Animal sacrifices are natural to the warrior, the hunter, the herdsman, while the husbandman will offer up grain and flowers.

The great anniversaries of the heathen coincide with popular assemblies and assizes.[1] In the Ynglînga saga cap. 8 they are specified thus : þâ skyldi blôta î môti vetri (towards winter) til ârs, enn at miðjum vetri blôta til grôðrar, it þriðja at sumri, þat var sigrblôt (for victory). In the Olafs helga saga cap. 104 (Fornm. sög. 4, 237) . en þat er siðr þeirra (it is their custom) at hafa blôt â haustum (autumn) ok fagna þa vetri, annat blôt hafa þeir at miðjum vetri, en hit þriðja at sumri, þa fagna þeir sumari ; conf. ed. holm. cap. 115 (see Suppl.). The Autumn sacrifice was offered to welcome the winter, and til ârs (pro annonae ubertate) ; the Mid-winter sacrifice til grôðrar (pro feracitate) ; the Summer one to welcome the summer, and til sigrs (pro victoria). Halfdan the Old

---

[1] RA. 245. 745. 821-5.

held a great midwinter sacrifice for the long duration of his life and kingdom, Sn. 190. But the great general blôt held at Upsal every winter included sacrifices 'til ârs ok friðar ok sigrs,' Fornm. sög. 4, 154. The formula sometimes runs 'til ârbôtar' (year's increase), or 'til friðar ok vetrarfars gôðs (good wintertime). In a striking passage of the Gutalagh, p. 108, the great national sacrifices are distinguished from the smaller offerings of cattle, food and drink : 'firi þann tima oc lengi eptir siþan troþu menn â hult oc â hauga, vi ok staf-garþa, oc â haiþin guþ blôtaþu þair *synum* oc *dydrum* sinum, oc *fileþi* miþ *mati* oc *mundgati*, þat gierþu þair eptir vantro sinni. Land alt hafþi sir *hoystu blôtan* miþ *fulki*, ellar hafþi huer þriþiungr sir. En smêri þing hafþu *mindri blôtan* med, *fileþi* mati oc mungati, sum haita *suþnautar:* þi et þair *suþu* allir saman.'

Easter-fires, Mayday-fires, Midsummer-fires, with their numerous ceremonies, carry us back to heathen sacrifices; especially such customs as rubbing the sacred flame, running through the glowing embers, throwing flowers into the fire, baking and distributing large loaves or cakes, and the circular dance. Dances passed into plays and dramatic representations (see ch. XIII, drawing the ship, ch. XXIII, and the witch-dances, ch. XXXIV). Afzelius 1, 3 describes a sacrificial play still performed in parts of Gothland, acted by young fellows in disguise, who blacken and rouge their faces (see ch. XVII, sub fine). One, wrapt in fur, sits in a chair as the *victim,* holding in his mouth a bunch of straw-stalks cut fine, which reach as far as his ears and have the appearance of sow-bristles : by this is meant the boar sacrificed at Yule, which in England is decked with laurel and rosemary (ch. X), just as the devil's offering is with rue, rosemary and orange (ch. XXXIII).—The great sacrificial feast of the ancient Saxons was on Oct. 1, and is traced to a victory gained over the Thuringians in 534 (see ch. VI); in documents of the Mid. Ages this high festival stills bears the name of the *gemeinwoche* or common week (see ch. XIII, Zisa), Würdtwein dipl. magunt. 1 praef. III-V. Scheffers Haltaus p. 142. conf. Höfers östr. wb. 1, 306. Another chronicle places it on Sept. 25 (Ecc. fr. or. 1, 59); Zisa's day was celebrated on Sept. 29, St. Michael's on the 28th; so that the holding of a *harvest-offering* must be intended all through.—In addition to the great festivals, they also sacrificed on special occasions, particularly when famine or

disease was rife; sometimes for long life: 'blôta til lânglifi,' Landn.
3, 4; or for favour (thockasaeld) with the people: ' Grîmr, er
blôtinn var dauðr (sacrificed when dead) für thokkasaeld, ok kallaðr
kamban ', Landn. 1, 14. 3, 16. This epithet *kamban* must refer to
the sacrifice of the dead man's body; I connect it with the OHG.
pichimpida funus, Mid. Dut. *kimban* comere, Diut. 2, 207ª. conf.
note to Andr. 4.

Human Sacrifices are from their nature and origin expiative;
some great disaster, some heinous crime can only be purged and
blotted out by human blood. With all nations of antiquity they
were an old-established custom [1]; the following evidences place it
beyond a doubt for Germany (see Suppl.). Tac. Germ. 9: Deorum
maxime Mercurium colunt, cui certis diebus *humanis* quoque *hostiis*
litare fas habent. Germ. 39: stato tempore in silvam coeunt,
caesoque publice (in the people's name) *homine* celebrant barbari
ritus horrenda primordia. Tac. Ann. 1, 61: lucis propinquis barbarae arae, apud quas *tribunos* ac primorum ordinum *centuriones
mactaverant.* Tac. Ann. 13, 57: sed bellum Hermunduris pros-
perum, Cattis exitiosius fuit, quia victores diversam aciem Marti ac
Mercurio sacravere, quo voto equi, *viri*, cuncta victa *occidioni
dantur.* Isidori chron. Goth., aera 446: quorum (regum Gothi-
corum) unus Radagaisus . . . Italiam belli feritate aggreditur,
promittens *sanguinem* Christianorum *diis suis litare*, si vinceret.
Jornandes cap. 5: quem Martem Gothi semper asperrima placavere
cultura, nam victimae ejus *mortes* fuere *captorum*, opinantes bellorum praesulem aptius *humani sanguinis* effusione placandum.[2]
Orosius 7, 37 of Radagaisus, whom he calls a Scythian, but
makes him lead Goths to Italy: qui (ut mos est barbaris
hujusmodi generis) *sanguinem diis suis propinare devoverat.*[3]

----

[1] Lasaulx die sühnopfer der Griechen u. Römer, Würzburg 1841. pp.
8—13.

[2] Conf. Cæs. de B. Gall. 6, 17 on the worship of Mars among the Gauls;
and Procop. de B. Goth. 3, 14 on the Slavens and Antes : θεὸν μὲν γὰρ ἕνα τὸν
τῆς ἀστραπῆς·δημιουργὸν ἁπάντων κύριον μόνον αὐτὸν νομίζουσιν εἶναι, καὶ θύουσιν
αὐτῷ βόας τε καὶ ἱερεία ἅπαντα. . . . ἀλλ' ἐπειδὰν αὐτοῖς ἐν ποσὶν ἤδη ὁ
θάνατος εἴη, ἢ νόσῳ ἁλοῦσι ἢ ἐς πόλεμον καθισταμένοις, ἐπαγγέλλονται μὲν, ἢν
διαφύγωσι, θυσίαν τῷ θεῷ ἀντὶ τῆς ψυχῆς αὐτίκα ποιήσειν, διαφυγόντες δὲ
θύουσιν ὅπερ ὑπέσχοντο, καὶ οἴονται τὴν σωτηρίαν ταύτης δὴ τῆς θυσίας αὐτοῖς
ἐωνῆσθαι.

[3] Of him Augustine says, in sermo 105, cap. 10: Rhadagaysus rex Gothorum . . . Romae . . . *Jovi sacrificabat* quotidie, nuntiabaturque
ubique, quod a sacrificiis non desisteret.

Procopius de bello Goth. 2, 15 of the Thulites, *i.e.* Scandinavians :
θύουσι δὲ ἐνδελεχέστατα ἱερεῖα πάντα καὶ ἐναγίζουσι. τῶν δὲ
ἱερείων σφίσι τὸ κάλλιστον ἄνθρωπός ἐστιν, ὅνπερ ἂν δοριά-
λωτον ποιήσαιντο πρῶτον. τοῦτον γὰρ τῷ Ἄρει θύουσιν,
ἐπεὶ θεὸν αὐτὸν νομίζουσι μέγιστον εἶναι. Ibid. 2, 14, of the
Heruli : πολύν τινα νομίζοντες θεῶν ὅμιλον, οὓς δὴ καὶ
ἀνθρώπων θυσίαις ἱλάσκεσθαι ὅσιον αὐτοῖς ἐδόκει εἶναι. Ibid.
2, 25, of the already converted Franks at their passage of the Po :
ἐπιλαβόμενοι δὲ τῆς γεφύρας οἱ Φράγγοι, παῖδάς τε καὶ γυναῖ-
κας τῶν Γότθων, οὕσπερ ἐνταῦθα εὗρον ἱερευόν τε καὶ αὐτῶν
τὰ σώματα ἐς τὸν ποταμὸν ἀκροθίνια τοῦ πολέμου ἐρρίπ-
τουν. οἱ βάρβαροι γὰρ οὗτοι, Χριστιανοὶ γεγονότες, τὰ πολλὰ τῆς
παλαιᾶς δόξης φυλάσσουσι, θυσίαις τε χρώμενοι ἀνθρώπων
καὶ ἄλλα οὐχ ὅσια ἱερεύοντες, ταύτῃ τε τὰς μαντείας ποιούμενοι.
Sidonius Apollinaris 8, 6 of the Saxons: mos est remeaturis
decimum quemque captorum per aequales et cruciarias poenas,
plus ob hoc tristi quod superstitioso ritu *necare.* Capitul. de partib.
Saxon. 9: si quis hominem diabolo *sacrificaverit* et *in hostiam, more
paganorum, daemonibus obtulerit.* Lex Frisionum, additio sap. tit.
42 : qui fanum effregerit . . . *immolatur diis,* quorum templa
violavit; the law affected only the Frisians 'trans Laubachi,' who
remained heathens longer. What Strabo relates of the Cimbri, and
Dietmar of the Northmen, will be cited later. Epist. Bonif. 25 (ed.
Würdtw.) : hoc quoque inter alia crimina agi in partibus illis
dixisti, quod quidam ex fidelibus ad *immolandum* paganis sua
venundent mancipia; masters were allowed to sell slaves, and
christians sold them to heathens for sacrifice. The captive prince
Graecus Avar de (a) Suevis *pecudis more* litatus (ch. XIII, the
goddess Zisa).[1] For evidences of human sacrifice among the Norse,
see Müller's sagabibl. 2, 560. 3, 93. As a rule, the victims were
captive enemies, purchased slaves or great criminals ; the sacrifice
of women and children by the Franks on crossing a river reminds
of the Greek διαβατήρια ;[2] the first fruits of war, the first prisoner

---

[1] Adam of Bremen de situ Daniae cap. 24, of the Lithuanians : dracones
adorant cum volucribus, quibus etiam *vivos litant homines,* quos a mercatoribus
emunt, diligenter omnino probatos, ne maculam in corpore habeant.

[2] Hence in our own folk-tales, the first to cross the bridge, the first to
enter the new building or the country, pays with his life, which meant, falls a
sacrifice. Jornandes cap. 25, of the Huns : ad Scythiam properant, et *quantos-
cunque prius in ingressu Scytharum habuere, litavere Victoriae.*

taken, was supposed to bring luck. In folk-tales we find traces of the immolation of *children ;* they are killed as a cure for leprosy, they are walled up in basements (ch. XXXV. XXXVI, end) ; and a feature that particularly points to a primitive sacrificial rite is, that toys and victuals are handed in to the child, while the roofing-in is completed. Among the Greeks and Romans likewise the victims fell amid noise and flute-playing, that their cries might be drowned, and the tears of children are stifled with caresses, ' ne flebilis hostia immoletur '. Extraordinary events might demand the death of kings' sons and daughters, nay, of kings themselves. Thoro offers up *his son* to the gods ; Worm mon. dan. 285. King Oen the Old sacrificed *nine sons* one after the other to Oðin for his long life ; Yngl. saga cap. 29. And the Swedes in a grievous famine, when other great sacrifices proved unavailing, offered up their *own king* Dômaldi ; ibid. cap. 18.

Animal sacrifices were mainly thank-offerings, but sometimes also expiatory, and as such they not seldom, by way of mitigation, took the place of a previous human sacrifice. I will now quote the evidences (see Suppl.). Herculem et Martem *concessis animalibus* placant, Tac. Germ. 9; *i.e.*, with animals suitable for the purpose (Hist. 5, 4), ' concessum ' meaning sacrum as against profanum ; and only those animals were suitable, whose flesh could be eaten by men. It would have been unbecoming to offer food to the god, which the sacrificer himself would have disdained. At the same time these sacrifices appear to be also banquets ; an appointed portion of the slaughtered beast is placed before the god, the rest is cut up, distributed and consumed in the assembly. The people thus became partakers in the holy offering, and the god is regarded as feasting with them at their meal (see Suppl.). At great sacrifices the kings were expected to taste each kind of food, and down to late times the house-spirits and dwarfs had their portion set aside for them by the superstitious people.—Quadraginta rustici a Langobardis capti *carnes immolatitias* comedere compellebantur, Greg. M. dial. 3, 27 ; which means no more than that the heathen Langobards permitted or expected the captive christians to share their sacrificial feast.[1] These 'immolatitiae carnes' and 'hostiae im-

---

[1] I do not know how *compellere* can be softened down to 'permitting or expecting '.—TRANS.

molatitiae, quas stulti homines juxta ecclesias ritu pagano faciunt'
are also mentioned in Bonifacii epist. 25 and 55, ed. Würdtw.

In the earliest period, the *Horse* seems to have been the
favourite animal for sacrifice; there is no doubt that before the
introduction of Christianity its flesh was universally eaten. There
was nothing in the ways of the heathen so offensive to the new
converts, as their not giving up the slaughter of horses *(hrossa-slâtr)*
and the eating of horseflesh; conf. Nialss. cap. 106. The Christian
Northmen reviled the Swedes as *hross-œturnar;* Fornm. sög. 2,
309. Fagrsk. p. 63. King Hâkon, whom his subjects suspected of
Christianity, was called upon 'at ㆍ ᴠnn skyldi eta *hrossaslâtr;*' Saga
Hâk. gôða cap. 18. From Tac. ann. 13, 57 we learn that the Hermunduri sacrificed the *horses* of the defeated Catti. As late as the
time of Boniface (Epist. ed. Würdtw. 25. 87   Serr. 121. 142),[1]
the Thuringians are strictly enjoined to abstain from horseflesh.
Agathias bears witness to the practice of the Alamanni: ἵππους
τε καὶ βόας, καὶ ἄλλα ἄττα μυρία κ α ρ α τ ο μ ο ῦ ν τ ε ς (beheading),
ἐπιθειάζουσι, ed. bonn. 28, 5.—Here we must not overlook the
cutting off of the *head*, which was not consumed with the rest, but
consecrated by way of eminence to the god. When Cæcina, on
approaching the scene of Varus's overthrow, saw *horses' heads*
fastened to the stems of trees (equorum artus, simul *truncis arborum
antefixa ora*, Tac. ann. 1, 61), these were no other than the Roman
horses, which the Germans had seized in the battle and offered up
to their gods[2] (see Suppl.). A similar 'immolati diis *equi abscissum
caput'* meets us in Saxo gram. p. 75; in the North they fixed it on
the neidstange (nîðstöng, stake of envy) which gave the power to
bewitch an enemy, Egilss. p. 389. In a Hessian kindermärchen
(no. 89) we have surviving, but no longer understood, a reminiscence

---

[1] Inter cetera *agrestem caballum* aliquantos comedere adjunxisti, plerosque
et *domesticum.* hoc nequaquam fieri deinceps sinas. And   inprimis de volatili-
bus, id est graculis et corniculis atque ciconiis, quae omnino cavendae sunt ab
esu christianorum. etiam et fibri et lepores et *equi silvatici* multo amplius
vitandi.   Again, Hieronymus adv. Jov. lib. 2 (ed. basil. 1553. 2, 75) · Sar-
matae, Quadi, Vandali et innumerabiles aliae gentes *equorum* et vulpium carnibus
delectantur.   Otto frising. 6, 10 . audiat, quod Pecenati (the wild Peschenære,
Nib. 1280, 2) et hi qui Falones vocantur (the Valwen, Nib. 1279, 2.   Tit.
4097), crudis et immundis carnibus, utpote *equinis* et *catinis* usque hodie
vescuntur.   Rol. 98, 20 of the heathen: sie *ezzent* diu *ros.*   Witches also are
charged with eating horseflesh (see Suppl.).

[2] Also in that passage of Jornandes about Mars: huic *truncis* suspendebantur *exuviae.*

of the mysterious meaning of a suspended *horse's head*.[1]—But on
horse-sacrifices among the heathen Norse we have further information of peculiar value. The St. Olaf's saga, cap. 113 (ed. holm. 2,
181), says: þat fylgði ok þeirri sögn, at þar væri drepit *naut* ok
hross til árbôtar (followed the saying that there were slain neat and
horse for harvest-boot). A tail-piece at the very end of the
Hervararsaga mentions a similar sacrifice offered by the apostate
Swedes at the election of king Svein (second half of 11th century):
var þâ framleidt *hross* eitt â þingit, ok höggvit î sundr, ok *skipt til*
áts, en rioþuðu blôðinu *blôttré*; köstuðu þâ allir Svîar kristni ok
hôfust blôt; then was led forward a horse into the Thing, and hewed
in sunder, and divided for eating, and they reddened with the blood
the blôt-tree, &c. Fornald. sög. 1, 512. Dietmar of Merseburg's
description of the great Norse (strictly Danish) sacrificial rite,
which however was extinct a hundred years before his time,
evidently contains circumstances exaggerated legendwise and distorted; he says 1, 9 : Sed quia ego de hostiis (Northmannorum)
mira audivi, haec indiscussa praeterire nolo. est unus in his
partibus locus, caput istius regni, Lederun nomine, in pago qui
Selon[2] dicitur, ubi post *novem* annos mense Januario, post hoc
tempus quo nos theophaniam domini celebramus, omnes con-
venerunt, et ibi diis suismet lxxxx. et ix. *homines*, et totidem *equos*,
cum canibus et gallis pro accipitribus oblatis, immolant, pro certo,
ut praedixi, putantes hos eisdem erga inferos servituros, et commissa
crimina apud eosdem placaturos. quam bene rex noster (Heinrich I.
an. 931) fecit, qui eos a tam execrando ritu prohibuit !—A grand
festive sacrifice, coming once in nine years, and costing a considerable number of animals—in this there is nothing incredible. Just
as the name hecatomb lived on, when there was nothing like that
number sacrificed, so here the legend was likely to keep to a high-
sounding number; the horror of the human victims perhaps it
threw in bodily. But the reason alleged for the animal sacrifice
is evidently wide of the mark; it mixes up what was done

---

[1] Gregory the Great (epist. 7, 5) admonishes Brunichild to take pre-
cautions with her Franks, ' ut de animalium *capitibus* sacrificia sacrilega non
exhibeant.'

[2] Sêlon for Sêlond, ON. Sælundr, afterwards Sioland, Seeland, *i.e.*, Zealand. Lêderûn, the Sax. dat. of Lêdera, ON. Hleiðra, afterwards Lêthra,
Leire ; conf. Goth. hleiþra tabernaculum.

at funerals [1] with what was done for expiation. It was only the bodies of nobles and rich men that were followed in death by bondsmen and by domestic and hunting animals, so that they might have their services in the other world. Suppose 99 men, we will say prisoners of war, to have been sacrificed to the gods, the animals specified cannot have been intended to escort those enemies, nor yet for the use of the gods, to whom no one ever set apart and slaughtered horses or any beasts of the chase with a view to their making use of them. So whether the ambiguous *eisdem* refers to homines or diis (as eosdem just after stands for the latter), either way there is something inadmissible asserted. At the new year's festival I believe that of all the victims named the horses alone were sacrificed; men, hounds and cocks the legend has added on.[2] How Dietmar's story looks by the side of Adam of Bremen's on the Upsal sacrifice, shall be considered on p. 53.

Among all animal sacrifices, that of the *horse* was preeminent and most solemn. Our ancestors have this in common with several Slavic and Finnish nations, with Persians and Indians: with all of them the horse passed for a specially sacred animal.[3]

Sacrifice of *Oxen* (see Suppl.). The passage from Agathias (ἵππους τε καὶ βόας) proves the Alamannic custom, and that from the Olafssaga (*naut* ok hross) the Norse. A letter to Saint Boniface (Epist. 82, Würdtw.) speaks of ungodly priests ' qui *tauros* et *hircos* diis paganorum immolabant.' And one from Gregory the Great ad Mellitum (Epist. 10, 76 and in Beda's hist. eccl. 1, 30) affirms of the Angles: *boves* solent in sacrificio daemonum *multos* occidere.

---

[1] With Sigurðr *servants* and *hawks* are burnt, Sæm. 225[b]; elsewhere *horses* and *dogs* as well, conf. RA. 344. Asvitus, morbo consumptus, cum *cane* et *equo* terreno mandatur antro; Saxo gram. p. 91, who misinterprets, as though the dead man fed upon them: nec contentus equi vel canis esu, p. 92.

[2] ' Pro accipitribus ' means, that in default of hawks, cocks were used. Some have taken it, as though dogs and cocks were sacrificed *to* deified birds of prey. But the ' pro ' is unmistakable.

[3] Conf. Bopp's Nalas and Damajanti, p. 42, 268. The Hyperboreans sacrificed *asses* to Apollo; Pindar Pyth. 10. Callimach. fr. 187. Anton. Liberal. metam. 20. The same was done at Delphi; Böckh corp. inscr. I, 807. 809. In a Mod. Greek poem Γαδάρου, λύκου καὶ ἀλωποῦς διήγησις vv. 429-434, a similar offering seems to be spoken of; and Hagek's böhm. chron. p. 62 gives an instance among the Slavs. That, I suppose, is why the Silesians are called *ass-eaters* (Zeitvertreiber 1668, p. 153); and if the Göttingers receive the same nickname, these popular jokes must be very old in Germany itself (see Suppl.).

The *black ox* and *black cow*, which are not to be killed for the house-hold (Superst. 887),—were they sacred sacrificial beasts ? Val. Suplit, a free peasant on the Samland coast (Samogitia or Semi-galia), sacrificed a *black bull* with strange ceremonies.[1] I will add a few examples from the Norse. During a famine in Sweden under king Dômaldi : þâ eflðo (instituted) Svîar blôt stôr at Uppsölum, it fyrsta haust (autumn) blôtuðu þeir *yxnum* ; and the oxen proving insufficient, they gradually went up to higher and higher kinds ; Yngl. saga, c. 18. þâ gekk hann til hofs (temple) Freyss, ok leiddi þagat *uxan gamlan* (an old ox), ok mælti svâ : ' Freyr, nû gef ek þer uxa þenna ' ; en uxanum brâ svâ við, at hann qvað við, ok fêll niðr dauðr (dealt the ox such a blow, that he gave a groan and fell down dead) ; Islend. sög. 2, 348. conf. Vigaglumssaga, cap. 9. At a formal duel the victor slew a *bull* with the same weapons that had vanquished his foe: þâ var leiddr fram *grâðúngr mikill* ok *gamall,* var þat kallat *blôtnaut,* þat skyldi sâ höggva er sigr hefði (then was led forth a bull mickle and old, it was called blôt-neat, that should he hew who victory had), Egilss. p. 506. conf. Kormaks-saga p. 214-8.—Sacrifice of *Cows,* Sæm. 141. Fornm. sög. 2, 138. —The Greek ἑκατόμβη (as the name shows, 100 oxen) consisted at first of a large number of neat, but very soon of other beasts also. The Indians too had sacrifices of a hundred ; Holzmann 3, 193.[2]

Boars, Pigs (see Suppl.). In the Salic Law, tit. 2, a higher composition is set on the *majalis sacrivus* or *votivus* than on any other. This seems a relic of the ancient sacrifices of the heathen Franks ; else why the term *sacrivus* ? True, there is no vast differ-ence between 700 and 600 den. (17 and 15 sol.) ; but of animals so set apart for holy use there must have been a great number in heathen times, so that the price per head did not need to be high. Probably they were selected immediately after birth, and marked, and then reared with the rest till the time of sacrificing.—In Frankish and Alamannic documents there often occurs the word *friscing,* usually for porcellus, but sometimes for agnus, occasionally in the more limited sense of porcinus and agninus ; the word may by

---

[1] Berlin. monatschr. 1802. 8, 225. conf. Lucas David 1, 118-122.

[2] In many districts of Germany and France, the butchers at a set time of the year lead through the streets a *fatted ox* decked with flowers and ribbons, accompanied by drum and fife, and collect drink-money. In Holland they call the ox *belder,* and hang gilded apples on his horns, while a butcher walks in front with the axe (beil). All this seems a relic of some old sacrificial rite.

its origin express recens natus, new-born,[1] but it now lives only in the sense of porcellus (frischling). How are we to explain then, that this OHG. *friscing* in several writers translates precisely the Lat. hostia, victima, holocaustum (Notker cap. 8, ps. 15, 4. 26, 6. 33, 1. 39, 8. 41, 10. 43, 12. 22. 50, 21. 115, 17. ôsterfriscing, ps. 20, 3. lamp unkawemmit kakepan erdu friscing, *i.e.* lamb unblemished given to earth a sacrifice, Hymn 7, 10), except as a reminiscence of heathenism? The Jewish paschal lamb would not suggest it, for in friscing the idea of porcellus was predominant.—In the North, the expiatory boar, *sônargöltr*, offered to Freyr, was a periodical sacrifice; and Sweden has continued down to modern times the practice of baking loaves and cakes on Yule-eve in the shape of a boar. This *golden-bristled* boar has left his track in inland Germany too. According to popular belief in Thuringia,[2] whoever on Christmas eve abstains from all food till suppertime, will get sight of a young *golden pig, i.e.* in olden times it was brought up last at the evening banquet. A Lauterbach ordinance (weisthum) of 1589 decreed (3, 369), that unto a court holden the day of the Three-kings, therefore in Yule time, the holders of farm-steads (hübner) should furnish a clean *goldferch* (gold-hog) gelded while yet under milk; it was led round the benches, and no doubt slaughtered afterwards.[3] So among the Welsh, the swine offered to the gods

[1] Ducange sub v. Eccard Fr. or. 2, 677. Dorows denkm. I. 2, 55. Lacom blet 1, 327. Graff 3, 833. Schmeller wtb. 1, 619.

[2] Gutgesells beitr. zur gesch. des deutschen alterthums, Meiningen 1834, p. 138.

[3] This passage from the Lauterb. ordin. I can now match by another from those of Vinkbuch in the Alamann country. It says 1, 436: the provost shall pick out in the convent a *swine worth 7 schilling pfennig*, and as soon as harvest begins, let it into the convent crewyard, where it must be allowed generous fare and free access to the corn; there it is left till the Thursday after St. Adolf's day, when it is slaughtered and divided, half to the farm-bailiff, half to the parish; on the same day there is also a distribution of bread and cheese to the parish.—The price of seven shillings tallies with the seven and a half fixed by the Lauterb. ordin., and is a high one, far exceeding the ordinary value (conf. Gött. anz. 1827, pp. 336-7); it was an arrangement long continued and often employed in these ordinances, and one well suited to a beast selected for sacrifice. The Lauterbach *goldferch*, like that of Vinkbuch, is doled out and consumed at a festive meal; the assize itself is named after it (3, 370); at Vinkbuch the heathenish name only has been forgotten or suppressed. Assuredly such assize-feasts were held in other parts of Germany too. St. Adolf was a bishop of Straszburg, his day falls on August 29 or 30 (Conr. v. Dankr. namenb. p. 117), and the assize therefore in the beginning of September. Swine are slaughtered for the household when winter sets in, in Nov. or Dec.; and as both of these by turns are called *schlacht*monat, there might linger in

became one destined for the King's table. It is the '*swín ealgylden,*
eofor îrenheard' of the Anglo-Saxons, and of its exact relation to
the worship of Frôho (Freyr) we have to treat more in detail by
and by. The Greeks sacrificed swine to Dêmêtêr (Ceres), who as
Nerthus stands very near to Niörðr, Freyr and Freyja.

Rams, Goats (see Suppl.).—As friscing came to mean victima, so
conversely a name for animal sacrifice, Goth. sáuðs, seems to have
given rise to the ON. name for the animal itself, *sauðr*=wether.
This species of sacrifice was therefore not rare, though it is seldom
expressly mentioned, probably as being of small value. Only the
saga Hâkonar gôða cap. 16 informs us : þar var oc drepinn (killed)
allskonar *smali,* ok svâ hross.   Smali (μῆλα) denotes principally
sheep, also more generally the small beasts of the flock as opposed
to oxen and horses, and as 'alls konar (omnis generis) ' is here
added, it seems to include goats. The sacrifice of *he-goats* (hircos)
is spoken of in the above-quoted Epist. Bonif. 82.   In the Swedish
superstition, the water-sprite, before it will teach any one to play
the harp, requires the sacrifice of a *black lamb ;* Svenska folkv. 2,
128.   Gregory the Great speaks once of *she-goats* being sacrificed ;
he says the Langobards offer to the devil, *i.e.,* to one of their gods,
caput caprae, hoc ei, per circuitum currentes, carmine nefando
dedicantes ; Dial. 3, 28.   This head of a she-goat (or he-goat ?) was
reared aloft, and the people bowed before it.   The *hallowing of a
he-goat* among the ancient Prussians is well known (Luc. David 1,
87, 98).   The Slavonian god Triglav is represented with three
goats' heads (Hanka's zbjrka 23).   If that Langobardic 'carmen
nefandum ' had been preserved, we could judge more exactly of the
rite than from the report of the holy father, who viewed it with
hostile eyes.

About other sacrificial beasts we cannot be certain, for of Dietmar's dogs and hawks and cocks, hardly any but the last are to be
depended on (see Suppl.). But even then, what of domestic poultry,
fowls, geese, pigeons ? The dove was a Jewish and christian

---

this also a reference to heathen sacrifices ; an AS. name for Nov. is expressly
*blôt*môneð. The common man at his yearly slaughtering gets up a feast, and
sends meat and sausages to his neighbours (conf. *mäuchli,* Stalder 2, 525),
which may be a survival of the common sacrifice and distribution of flesh.
It is remarkable that in Servia too, at the solemn burning of the badnyak,
which is exactly like the yule-log (ch. XX, Fires), a *whole swine* is roasted, and
often a *sucking pig* along with it ; Vuk's Montenegro, pp. 103-4.

sacrifice, the Greeks offered cocks to Asklepios, and in Touraine a white cock used to be sacrificed to St. Christopher for the cure of a bad finger (Henri Estienne cap. 38, 6). Of game, doubtless only those fit to eat were fit to sacrifice, stags, roes, wild boars, but never bears, wolves or foxes, who themselves possess a ghostly being, and receive a kind of worship. Yet one might suppose that for expiation uneatable beasts, equally with men, might be offered, just as slaves and also hounds and falcons followed the burnt body of their master. Here we must first of all place Adam of Bremen's description (4, 27) of the great sacrifice at Upsala by the side of Dietmar's account of that at Hlethra (see p. 48):—Solet quoque post *novem* annos communis omnium Sveoniae provinciarum solennitas celebrari, ad quam nulli praestatur immunitas ; reges et populi, omnes et singuli sua dona ad Ubsolam transmittunt, et, quod omni poena crudelius est, illi qui jam induerunt christianitatem ab illis ceremoniis se redimunt. Sacrificium itaque tale est : ex *omni animante* quod *masculinum* est, *novem capita* offeruntur ; quorum sanguine deos tales placari mos est. *Corpora* autem suspenduntur in lucum qui proximus est templo. Is enim lucus tam sacer est gentilibus, ut singulae arbores ejus ex morte vel tabo immolatorum divinae credantur. Ibi etiam *canes*, qui pendent cum *hominibus*, quorum corpora mixtim suspensa narravit mihi quidam christian-orum se *septuaginta duo* vidisse. Ceterum naeniae, quae in ejusmodi ritibus libatoriis fieri solent, multiplices sunt et inhonestae, ideoque melius reticendae.—The number nine is prominent in this Swedish sacrificial feast, exactly as in the Danish ; but here also all is conceived in the spirit of legend. First, the *heads* of victims seem the essential thing again, as among the Franks and Langobards; then the dogs come in support of those Hlethra 'hounds and hawks,' but at the same time remind us of the old judicial custom of hanging up wolves or dogs by the side of criminals (RA. 685-6). That only the *male* sex of every living creature is here to be sacrificed, is in striking accord with an episode in the Reinardus, which was composed less than a century after Adam, and in its groundwork might well be contemporary with him. At the wedding of a king, the *males* of all quadrupeds and birds were to have been *slaughtered*, but the cock and gander had made their escape. It looks to me like a legend of the olden time, which still circulated in the 11-12th centuries, and which even a nursery-tale (No. 27, the Townmusicians) knows something of.[1] Anyhow, in heathen times *male animals* seem to be in special demand for sacrifice.[2] As for killing one of every species (and even Agathias's καὶ ἄλλα ἄττα μυρία does not come up to that), it would be such a stupendous affair, that its actual execution could never have been conceivable; it can only have existed in popular tradition. It is something like the old Mirror of Saxony and that of Swabia assuring us that every living creature present at a deed of rapine, whether oxen, horses, cats, dogs, fowls, geese, swine or men, had to be beheaded, as well as the actual delinquent (in real fact, only when they were his property);[3] or like the Edda relating how oaths were exacted of all animals and plants, and all beings were required to weep. The creatures belonging to a man, his domestic animals, have to suffer with him in case of cremation, sacrifice or punishment.

Next to the kind, stress was undoubtedly laid on the colour of the animal, *white* being considered the most favourable. *White* horses are often spoken of (Tac. Germ. 10. Weisth. 3, 301. 311. 831), even so far back as the Persians (Herod. 1, 189). The friscing of sacrifice was probably of a spotless white; and in later law-records *snow-white* pigs are pronounced inviolable.[4] The Votiaks sacrificed a *red* stallion, the Tcheremisses a *white*. When under the old German law *dun* or *pied* cattle were often required in payment of fines and tithes, this might have some connexion with sacrifices[5]; for witchcraft also, animals of a particular hue were requisite. The water-sprite demanded a *black* lamb, and the huldres have a *black* lamb and *black* cat offered up to them (Asb. 1. 159). Saxo Gram. p. 16 says; rem divinam facere *furvis* hostiis; does that mean *black* beasts?—We may suppose that cattle were

---

[1] Or will any one trace this incident in the Reynard to the words of the Vulgate in Matt. 22, 4: tauri mei et altilia occisa sunt, venite ad nuptias; which merely describe the preparations for the wedding-feast? Any hint about males is just what the passage lacks.

[2] The Greeks offered *male* animals to gods, *female* to goddesses, Il. 3, 103: a *white male* lamb to Helios (sun), a *black ewe* lamb to Gê (earth). The Lithuanians sacrificed to their earthgod Zemiennik utriusque sexus domestica animalia; Haupt's zeitschr. 1, 141.

[3] Reyscher and Wilda zeitschr. für deutsches recht 5, 17, 18.

[4] RA. 261. 594. Weisth. 3, 41. 46. 69. conf. Virg. Aen. 8, 82: candida cum fœtu concolor albo sus; and the Umbrian: trif apruf rufru ute peiu (tres apros rubros aut piceos), Aufrecht und Kirchh. umbr. sprachd. 2, 278-9.

[5] RA. 587. 667. Weisth. 1, 498. 3, 430. *White* animals hateful to the gods; Tettau and Temme preuss. sag. 42.

garlanded and *adorned* for sacrifice. A passage in the Edda requires *gold-horned* cows, Sæm. 141ᵃ ; and in the village of Fienstädt in Mansfeld a coal-black ox with a white star and white feet, and a he-goat with *gilded horns* were imposed as dues.[1] There are indications that the animals, before being slaughtered, were led round within the circle of the assembly—that is how I explain the *leading round the benches,* and *per circuitum* currere, pp. 51, 52— perhaps, as among the Greeks and Romans, to give them the appearance of going *voluntarily* to death[2] (see Suppl.). Probably care had to be taken also that the victim should *not* have been used in the *service of man, e.g.,* that the ox had never drawn plough or waggon. For such colts and bullocks are required in our ancient law-records at a formal transfer of land, or the ploughing to death of removers of landmarks.

On the actual procedure in a sacrifice, we have scarcely any information except from Norse authorities. While the animal laid down its life on the sacrificial stone, all the streaming blood (ON. *hlaut*) was caught either in a hollow dug for the purpose, or in vessels. With this gore they smeared the sacred vessels and utensils, and sprinkled the participants.[3] Apparently divination was performed by means of the blood, perhaps a part of it was mixed with ale or mead, and drunk. In the North the blood-bowls (hlaut*bollar,* blôt*bollar*) do not seem to have been large ; some nations had big cauldrons made for the purpose (see Suppl.). The Swedes were taunted by Olafr Tryggvason with sitting at home and licking their sacrificial pots, ' at sitja heima ok sleikja *blôt-bolla* sîna,' Fornm. sög. 2, 309. A cauldron of the Cimbri is noticed in Strabo 7, 2 : ἔθος δέ τι τῶν Κίμβρων διηγοῦνται τοιοῦτον, ὅτι ταῖς γυναιξὶν αὐτῶν συστρατευούσαις παρηκολούθουν προμάντεις ἱερείαι πολιότριχες, λευχείμονες, καρπασίνας ἐφαπτίδας ἐπιπεπορ-

---

[1] Neue mitth. des thür. sächs. vereins V. 2, 131, conf. II. 10, 292. Od. 3, 382 :

σοὶ δ' αὖ ἐγὼ ῥέξω βοῦν ἦνιν, εὐρυμέτωπον,
ἀδμήτην, ἣν οὔπω ὑπὸ ζυγὸν ἤγαγεν ἀνήρ·
τὴν τοι ἐγὼ ῥέξω, χρυσὸν κέρασιν περιχεύας.

[2] Oc eingu skyldi tortŷna hvarki fê ne mönnum, nema siâlft gengi î burt. Eyrb. saga, p. 10. And none should they kill (tortima?) neither beast nor man, unless of itself it ran a-tilt.

[3] Saga Hâkonar gôða, cap. 16. Eyrb. saga p. 10. rauð hörgin, reddened the (stone) altar, Fornald. sög. 1, 413. stalla lâta rioða blôði, 1, 454. 527. Sæm. 114ᵇ *rioðuðu* blôðinu *blôttré,* Fornald. sög. 1, 512. the Grk αἷμα τῷ βωμῷ περιχέειν. conf. Exod. 24, 8.

πημέναι, ζῶσμα χαλκοῦν ἔχουσαι, γυμνόποδες· τοῖς οὖν αἰχμαλώ-
τοις διὰ τοῦ στρατοπέδου συνήντων ξιφήρεις· καταστέψασαι δ'
αὐτοὺς ἦγον ἐπὶ κ ρ α τ ῆ ρ α χαλκοῦν, ὅσον ἀμφορέων εἴκοσι· εἶχον
δὲ ἀναβάθραν, ἣν ἀναβᾶσα (ἡ μάντις) ὑπερπετὴς τοῦ λ έ β η τ ο ς
ἐλαιμοτόμει ἕκαστον μετεωρισθέντα· ἐκ δὲ τοῦ προχεομένου αἵματος
εἰς τὸν κρατῆρα, μαντείαν τινὰ ἐποιοῦντο.[1] Another cauldron of
the Suevi, in the Life of St. Columban : Sunt etenim inibi vicinæ
nationes Suevorum ; quo cum moraretur, et inter habitatores illius
loci progrederetur, reperit eos sacrificium profanum *litare* velle,
vasque magnum, quod vulgo *cupam* vocant, quod viginti et sex
modios amplius minusve capiebat, *cerevisia plenum* in medio habe-
bant positum. Ad quod vir Dei accessit et sciscitatur, quid de illo
fieri vellent ? Illi aiunt : deo suo Wodano, quem Mercurium
vocant alii, se velle *litare.* Jonas Bobbiensis, vita Columb. (from
the first half of the 7th cent. Mabillon ann. Bened. 2, 26). Here
we are expressly told that the cauldron was filled with ale, and not
that the blood of a victim was mixed with it ; unless the narrative
is incomplete, it may have meant only a drink-offering.

Usually the cauldron served to cook, *i.e.* boil, the victim's flesh ;
it never was roasted. Thus Herodotus 4, 61 describes a boiling
(ἕψειν) of the sacrifice in the great cauldron of the Scythians.
From this *seething,* according to my conjecture, the ram was called
saups, and those who took part in the sacrifice *suðnautar* (partakers
of the sodden), Gutalag p. 108 ; the boilings, the cauldrons and pots
of witches in later times may be connected with this.[2] The distribution of the pieces among the people was probably undertaken by
a priest ; on great holidays the feast[3] was held there and then in
the assembly, on other occasions each person might doubtless take

---

[1] ' They say the Cimbri had this custom, that their women marching with
them were accompanied by priestess-prophetesses, gray-haired, white-robed,
with a linen scarf buckled over the shoulder, wearing a brazen girdle, and
bare-footed ; these met the prisoners in the camp, sword in hand, and having
crowned them, led them to a brass *basin* as large as 30 amphoræ (180 gals) ;
and they had a ladder, which the priestess mounted, and standing over the
basin, cut the throat of each as he was handed up. With the blood that gushed
into the basin, they made a prophecy.'

[2] The trolds too, a kind of elves, have a *copper kettle* in the Norw. saga,
Faye 11 ; the christians long believed in a *Saturni dolium,* and in a *large
cauldron* in hell (chaudière, Méon 3, 284-5).

[3] They also ate the strong broth and the fat swimming at the top. The
heathen offer their king Hàkon, on his refusing the flesh, *drecka soðit* and *eta
flotit ;* Saga Hàkonar gôða cap. 18. conf. Fornm. sög. 10, 381.

his share home with him. That priests and people really ate the food, appears from a number of passages (conf. above, p. 46). The Capitularies 7, 405 adopt the statement in Epist. Bonif. cap. 25 (an. 732) of a Christian 'presbyter Jovi mactans, et immolatitias carnes vescens,' only altering it to 'diis mactanti, et immolatitiis carnibus vescenti'. We may suppose that private persons were allowed to offer small gifts to the gods on particular occasions, and consume a part of them; this the Christians called 'more gentilium offerre, et ad honorem daemonum comedere,' Capit. de part. Sax. 20. It is likely also, that certain nobler parts of the animal were assigned to the gods, the *head, liver, heart, tongue*.[1] The head and skin of slaughtered game were suspended on trees in honour of them (see Suppl.).

Whole *burntofferings*, where the animal was converted into ashes on the pile of wood, do not seem to have been in use. The Goth. *allbrunsts* Mk 12, 33 is made merely to translate the Gk. ὁλοκαύτωμα, so the OHG. *albrandopher*, N. ps. 64, 2; and the AS. *brynegield onhreáð* rommes blôðe, Cædm. 175, 6. 177, 18 is meant to express purely a burntoffering in the Jewish sense.[2]

Neither were *incense-offerings* used; the sweet incense of the christians was a new thing to the heathen. Ulphilas retains the Gk. *thymiama* Lu. 1, 10. 11; and our weih-rauch (holy-reek), O. Sax. wîrôc Hel. 3, 22, and the ON. reykelsi, Dan. rögelse are formed according to christian notions (see Suppl.).

While the sacrifice of a slain animal is more sociable, more universal, and is usually offered by the collective nation or community; fruit or flowers, milk or honey is what any household, or even an individual may give. These *Fruit-offerings* are therefore more solitary and paltry; history scarcely mentions them, but they have lingered the longer and more steadfastly in popular customs (see Suppl.).

When the husbandman cuts his corn, he leaves a clump of ears standing for the god who blessed the harvest, and he adorns it with

---

[1] γλῶσσα καὶ κοιλία (tongue and entrails) ἱερείου διαπεπραγμένου, Plutarch, Phoc. 1. γλώσσας τάμνειν and ἐν πυρὶ βάλλειν, Od. 3, 332. 341. conf. De linguæ usu in sacrificiis, Nitzsch ad Hom. Od. 1, 207. In the folk-tales, whoever has to kill a man or beast, is told to bring in proof the tongue or heart, apparently as being eminent portions.

[2] Slav. *páliti* obièt, to kindle an offering, Königinh. hs. 98.

ribbons. To this day, at a fruit-gathering in Holstein, five or six
apples are left hanging on each tree, and then the next crop will thrive.
More striking examples of this custom will be given later, in treating of individual gods. But, just as tame and eatable animals
were especially available for sacrifice, so are *fruit-trees* (frugiferae
arbores, Tac. Germ. 10), and *grains;* and at a formal transfer of
land, boughs covered with leaves, apples or nuts are used as earnest
of the bargain. The MHG. poet (Fundgr. II, 25) describes Cain's
sacrifice in the words : ' eine garb er nam, er wolte sie oppheren mit
eheren joch mit *agenen*,' a sheaf he took, he would offer it with ears
and eke with spikes : a formula expressing at once the upper part
or beard (arista), and the whole ear and stalk (spica) as well.
Under this head we also put the *crowning* of the divine image, of a
sacred tree or a sacrificed animal with *foliage* or *flowers;* not the
faintest trace of this appears in the Norse sagas, and as little in our
oldest documents. From later times and surviving folk-tales I can
bring forward a few things. On Ascension day the girls in more
than one part of Germany twine *garlands* of white and red flowers,
and hang them up in the dwellingroom or over the cattle in the
stable, where they remain till replaced by fresh ones the next year.[1]
At the village of Questenberg in the Harz, on the third day in
Whitsuntide, the lads carry an oak up the castle-hill which
overlooks the whole district, and, when they have set it upright,
fasten to it a large *garland* of branches of trees plaited together,
and as big as a cartwheel. They all shout ' the *queste* (*i.e.* garland)
hangs,' and then they dance round the tree on the hill top ; both
tree and garland are renewed every year.[2] Not far from the
Meisner mountain in Hesse stands a high precipice with a cavern
opening under it, which goes by the name of the Hollow Stone.
Into this cavern every Easter Monday the youths and maidens of
the neighbouring villages carry *nosegays*, and then draw some
cooling water. No one will venture down, unless he has flowers
with him.[3] The lands in some Hessian townships have to pay a
bunch of mayflowers (lilies of the valley) every year for rent.[4] In
all these examples, which can easily be multiplied, a heathen

[1] Bragur VI. 1, 126.
[2] Otmars volkssagen, pp. 128-9. What is told of the origin of the custom
seems to be fiction.
[3] Wigands archiv 6, 317.
[4] Wigands archiv 6, 318. Casselsches wochenbl. 1815, p. 928[b].

practice seems to have been transferred to christian festivals and offerings.[1]

As it was a primitive and widespread custom at a banquet to set aside a part of the *food* for the household gods, and particularly to place a dish of *broth* before Berhta and Hulda, the gods were also invited to share the festive *drink*. The drinker, before taking any himself, would pour some out of his vessel for the god or house-sprite, as the Lithuanians, when they drank beer, spilt some of it on the ground for their earth-goddess Zemynele.[2] Compare with this the Norwegian sagas of Thor, who appears at weddings when invited, and takes up and empties huge casks of ale.—I will now turn once more to that account of the Suevic *ale-tub* (cupa) in Jonas (see p. 56), and use it to explain the heathen practice of *minne-drinking*, which is far from being extinct under christianity. Here also both name and custom appear common to all the Teutonic races.

The Gothic *man* (pl. munum, pret. munda) signified I think; *gaman* (pl. gamunum, pret. gamunda) I bethink me, I remember. From the same verb is derived the OHG. *minna = minia* amor, *minnôn = miniôn* amare, to remember a loved one. In the ON. language we have the same *man, munum,* and also *minni* memoria, *minna* recordari, but the secondary meaning of amor was never developed.

It was customary to honour an absent or deceased one by making mention of him at the assembly or the banquet, and draining a goblet to his memory: this goblet, this draught was called in ON. *erfi dryckja*, or again *minni* (erfi = funeral feast).

At grand sacrifices and banquets the god or the gods were remembered, and their minni drunk: *minnis*-öl (ale), Sæm. 119[b] (opposed to ôminnis öl), *minnis*-horn, *minnis*-full (cupful). fôro *minni* mörg, ok skyldi horn dreckia î *minni* hvert (they gave many a m., and each had to drink a horn to the m.). um gôlf gânga at *minnom* öllum, Egilss. 206. 253. *minniöl signôð* âsom, Olafs helga.

---

[1] Beside cattle and grain, other valuables were offered to particular gods and in special cases, as even in christian times voyagers at sea *e.g.*, would vow a *silver ship* to their church as a votive gift; in Swedish folk-songs, offra en *gryta af malm* (vessel of metal). Arvidss. 2, 116; en gryta af *blankaste malm* (of silver) Ahlqvists Öland II. 1, 214; also articles of clothing, *e.g. red shoes*.

[2] In the Teut. languages I know of no technical term like the Gk. $\sigma\pi\acute{\epsilon}\nu\delta\omega$, $\lambda\epsilon\acute{\iota}\beta\omega$, Lat. libo, for drink-offerings (see Suppl.).

saga (ed. holm.) 113. signa is the German segnen to bless, consecrate. signa full Oðni, Thôr. Oðins full, Niarðar full, Freys full
drecka, Saga Hâkonar gôða cap. 16.18. In the Herrauðs-saga cap.
11, Thôr's, Oðin's and Freya's minne is drunk. At the burial of a
king there was brought up a goblet called Bragafull (funeral toast
cup), before which every one stood up, took a solemn vow, and
emptied it, Yngl. saga cap. 40; other passages have bragarfull,
Sæm. 146ᵃ. Fornald. sög. 1, 345. 417. 515. The goblet was also
called minnisveig (swig, draught), Sæm. 193ᵇ. After conversion
they did not give up the custom, but drank the minne of Christ,
Mary, and the saints: Krists minni, Michaêls minni, Fornm. sög.
1, 162. 7, 148. In the Fornm. sög. 10, 1781, St. Martin demands of
Olaf that his minne be proposed instead of those of Thôr, Oðin, and
the other âses.

The other races were just as little weaned from the practice;
only where the term minne had changed its meaning, it is translated by the Lat. amor instead of memoria;[1] notably as early as in
Liutprand, hist. 6, 7 (Muratori II. 1, 473), and Liutpr. hist. Ott. 12:
diaboli in amorem vinum bibere. Liutpr. antapod. 2, 70 : amoris
salutisque mei causa bibito. Liutpr. leg. 65 : potas in amore beati
Johannis præcursoris. Here the Baptist is meant, not the Evangelist; but in the Fel. Faber evagat. 1, 148 it is distinctly the
latter. In Eckehard casus S. Galli, Pertz 2, 84 : amoreque, ut
moris est, osculato et epoto, laetabundi discedunt. In the Rudlieb
2, 162 :

> post poscit vinum Gerdrudis amore, quod haustum
> participat nos tres, postremo basia fingens,
> quando vale dixit post nos gemit et benedixit.

In the so-called Liber occultus, according to the München MS., at
the description of a scuffle :

> hujus ad edictum nullus plus percutit ictum,
> sed per clamorem poscunt Gertrudis amorem.

In the Peregrinus, a 13th cent. Latin poem, v. 335 (Leyser 2114) :

> et rogat ut potent sanctae Gertrudis amore,
> ut possent omni prosperitate frui.

---

[1] The 12th cent. poem Von dem gelouben 1001 says of the institution of
the Lord's Supper, whose cup is also a drink of remembrance to Christians :
den cof nam er mit dem wîne, unde segente darinne ein vil guote minne. Conf.
loving cup, Thom's Anecd. 82.

At Erek's departure: der wirt neig im an den fuoz, ze hand truog er im dô ze heiles gewinne *sant Gêrtrûde minne*, Er. 4015. The armed champion 'tranc *sant Johannes segen*,' Er. 8651. Hagene, while killing Etzel's child, says, Nib. 1897, 3 :

> nu trinken wir die *minne* unde gelten sküneges wîn,
>
> iz mac anders niht gesîn
>
> wan trinkt und *geltet Ezeln wîn ;* Helbl. 6, 160. 14. 86.

Here the very word *gelten* recalls the meaning it had acquired in connexion with sacrificing; conf. Schm. 2, 40. si dô zucten di suert unde scancten eine *minne* (drew their swords and poured out a m.), Herz. Ernst in Hoffm. fundgr. 1, 230, 35. *minne* schenken, Berthold 276-7. sant *Johannis minne* geben, Oswald 611. 1127. 1225 (see Suppl.). No doubt the same thing that was afterwards called 'einen ehrenwein schenken'; for even in our older speech *êra, êre* denoted verehrung, reverence shown to higher and loved beings.

In the Mid. Ages then, it was two saints in particular that had minne drunk in honour of them, *John* the evangelist and *Gertrude*. John is said to have drunk poisoned wine without hurt, hence a drink consecrated to him prevented all danger of poisoning. Gertrude revered John above all saints, and therefore her memory seems to have been linked with his. But she was also esteemed as a peacemaker, and in the Latinarius metricus of a certain Andreas rector scholarum she is invoked :

> O pia *Gerdrudis*, quae pacis commoda cudis
>
> bellaque concludis, nos caeli mergito ludis !

A clerk prayed her daily, 'dass sie ihm schueffe herberg guot,' to find him lodging good; and in a MS. of the 15th cent. we are informed : aliqui dicunt, quod quando anima egressa est, tunc prima nocte pernoctabit cum beata *Gerdrude*, secunda nocte cum archangelis, sed tertia nocte vadit sicut diffinitum est de ea. This remarkable statement will be found further on to apply to Freya, of whom, as well as of Hulda and Berhta, Gertrude reminds us the more, as she was represented spinning. Both John's and Gertrude's minne used especially to be drunk by parting friends, travellers and lovers of peace, as the passages quoted have shown. I know of no older testimony to Gertrude's minne (which presupposes John's) than that in Rudlieb; in later centuries we find

plenty of them: der brâhte mir sant *Johans* segen, Ls. 3, 336.
sant *Johans segen* trinken, Ls. 2, 262. ich dâht an sant *Johans
minne*, Ls. 2, 264. varn (to fare) mit sant *Gértrûde minne*,
Amgb. 33ᵇ. setz sant *Johans* ze bürgen mir, daz du komest
gesunt herwider schier, Hätzl. 191ᵇ. sant *Johannes namen*
trinken, Altd. bl. 413. sant *Gértrûde minne*, Cod. kolocz. 72.
trinken sant *Johannes segen* und scheiden von dem lande, Morolt.
3103. diz ist sancte *Johans minne*, Cod. pal. 364, 158. S. *Johans
segen* trinken, Anshelm 3, 416. Johans segen, Fischart gesch. kl.
99ᵇ. Simpliciss. 2, 262.[1]

Those Suevi then, whom Columban was approaching, were probably drinking *Wuotan's minne;* Jonas relates how the saint blew
the whole vessel to pieces and spoilt their pleasure : manifesto
datur intelligi, *diabolum* in eo vase fuisse occultatum, qui per profanum litatorem caperet animas sacrificantium. So by Liutprand's
devil, whose minne is drunk, we may suppose a heathen god to
have been meant. *gefa þriggja sálda öl* Oðni (give three tuns of
ale to Oðinn), Fornm. sög. 2, 16. *gefa* Thôr ok Oðni *öl*, ok *signa
full* âsum, ibid. 1, 280. drecka *minni* Thôrs ok Oðins, ibid. 3, 191.
As the North made the sign of Thor's hammer, christians used the
cross for the blessing (segnung) of the cup; conf. *poculum signare*,
Walthar. 225, precisely the Norse *signa full*.

Minne-drinking, even as a religious rite, apparently exists to
this day in some parts of Germany. At Otbergen, a village of
Hildesheim, on Dec. 27 every year a chalice of wine is hallowed by
the priest, and handed to the congregation in the church to drink
as *Johannis segen* (blessing); it is not done in any of the neighbouring places. In Sweden and Norway we find at Candlemas a
dricka eldborgs skål, drinking a toast (see Superst. *k*, Swed. 122).

---

[1] Thomasius de poculo S. Johannis vulgo Johannistrunk, Lips. 1675.
Scheffers Haltaus p. 165. Oberlin s. vb. Johannis minn und trunk. Schmeller
2, 593. Hannov. mag. 1830, 171-6. Ledeburs archiv 2, 189. On Gertrude
espec., Huyd. op St. 2, 343-5. Clignett's bidr. 392-411. Hoffm. horae belg.
2, 41-8. Antiqvariske annaler 1, 313. Hanka's Bohem. glosses 79ᵇ 132ᵃ
render Johannis amor by *swatá mina* (holy m.). And in that Slovenic document, the Freysinger MS. (Kopitar's Glagolita xxxvii, conf. xliii) is the
combination : da klanyamse, i modlimse, im i *tchesti ich piyem*, i obieti nashe
im nesem (ut genuflectamus et precemur eis et honores eorum bibamus et obli-
gationes nostras illis feramus); *tchest* is honor, τιμή, cultus, our old êra ; but
I also find *slava* (fame, glory) used in the sense of minne, and in a Servian
song (Vuk, 1 no. 94) wine is drunk ' za slave bozhye' to the glory of God. In
the Finnish mythology is mentioned an *Ukkon malja*, bowl of Ukko ; malja =
Swed. skål, strictly scutella, potatio in memoriam vel sanitatem.

Now that Suevic *cupa* filled with beer (p. 75) was a hallowed *sacrificial cauldron*, like that which the Cimbri sent to the emperor Augustus.[1] Of the Scythian cauldron we have already spoken, p. 75; and we know what part the cauldron plays in the Hŷmis-qviða and at the god's judgment on the *seizure of the cauldron* (by Thor from giant Hymir). Nor ought we to overlook the ON. proper names *Asketill, Thôrketill* (abbrev. Thorkel) AS. *Oscytel* (Kemble 2, 302); they point to kettles consecrated to the âs and to Thor.

Our knowledge of heathen antiquities will gain both by the study of these drinking usages which have lasted into later times, and also of the shapes given to *baked meats*, which either retained the actual forms of ancient idols, or were accompanied by sacrificial observances. A history of German cakes and bread-rolls might contain some unexpected disclosures. Thus the Indicul. superstit. 26 names *simulacra de consparsa farina*. Baked figures of animals seem to have represented animals that were reverenced, or the attributes of a god.[2] From a striking passage in the Fridthiofssaga (fornald. sög. 2, 86) it appears that the heathen at a dîsa blôt *baked images of gods* and *smeared* them with *oil:* ' sâtu konur við eldinn ok bökuðu goðin, en sumar smurðu ok þerðu með dûkum,' women sat by the fire and baked the gods, while some anointed them with cloths. By Friðþiof's fault a baked Baldr falls into the fire, the fat blazes up, and the house is burnt down. According to Voetius de superstit. 3, 122 on the day of Paul's conversion they placed a figure of straw before the hearth on which they were baking, and if it brought a fine bright day, they anointed it with butter; otherwise they kicked it from the hearth, smeared it with dirt, and threw it in the water.

Much therefore that is not easy to explain in popular offerings and rites, as the colour of animals (p. 54), leading the boar round (p. 51), flowers (p. 58), minne-drinking (p. 59), even the shape of cakes, is a reminiscence of the sacrifices of heathenism (see Suppl.).

---

[1] ἔπεμψαν τῷ Σεβαστῷ δῶρον τὸν ἱερώτατον παρ' αὐτοῖς λέβητα, the most sacred cauldron they had, Strabo VII. 2.

[2] Baking in the shape of a *boar* must have been much more widely spread than in the North alone, see below, Frô's boar; even in France they baked *cochelins* for New Year's day, Mem. de l'ac. celt. 4, 429.

Beside prayers and sacrifices, one essential feature of the heathen cultus remains to be brought out : the *solemn carrying about of divine images*. The divinity was not to remain rooted to one spot, but at various times to bestow its presence on the entire compass of the land (see ch. XIV). So Nerthus rode in state (invehebatur populis), and Berecynthia (ch. XIII), so Frô travelled out in spring, so the sacred ship, the sacred plough was carried round (ch. XIII Isis). The figure of the unknown Gothic god rode in its waggon (ch. VI). Fetching-in the Summer or May, carrying-out Winter and Death, are founded on a similar view. Holda, Berhta and the like beings all make their circuit at stated seasons, to the heathen's joy and the christian's terror ; even the march of Wuotan's host may be so interpreted (conf. ch. XXXI. Frau Gauden). When Frô had ceased to appear, Dietrich with the ber (boar) and Dietrich Bern still showed themselves (ch. X. XXXI), or the sônargöltr (atonement-boar) was conveyed to the heroes' banquet (ch. X), and the boar led round the benches (p. 51). Among public legal observances, the progress of a newly elected king along the highways, the solemn lustration of roads, the beating of bounds, at which in olden times gods' images and priests can hardly have been wanting, are all the same kind of thing. After the conversion, the church permanently sanctioned such processions, except that the Madonna and saints' images were carried, particularly when drought, bad crops, pestilence or war had set in, so as to bring back rain (ch. XX), fertility of soil, healing and victory ; sacred images were even carried to help in putting out a fire. The Indicul. paganiar. XXVIII tells ' de *simulacro* quod *per campos portant,*' on which Eccard 1, 437 gives an important passage from the manuscript Vita Marcsvidis (not Maresvidis) : statuimus ut annuatim secunda feria pentecostes patronum ecclesiae in parochiis vestris *longo ambitu circumferentes* et domos vestras lustrantes, et *pro gentilitio ambarvali* in lacrymis et varia devotione vos ipsos mactetis et ad refectionem pauperum eleemosynam comportetis, et in hac curti pernoctantes super reliquias vigiliis et cantibus solennisetis, ut praedicto mane determinatum a vobis *ambitum* pia lustratione complentes ad monasterium cum honore debito reportetis. Confido autem de patroni hujus misericordia, quod sic *ab ea gyrade terrae semina uberius proveniant,* et *variae aëris inclementiae cessent.* The Roman ambarvalia were purifications of fields, and sacrifices were offered at the terminus publicus ; the *May procession* and the *riding of bounds* and *roads* during the period of German heathenism must have been very similar to them. On the Gabel-heath in Mecklenburg the Wends as late as the 15th century walked round the budding corn with loud cries ; Giesebrecht 1, 87.

CHAPTER IV.

TEMPLES.

In our inquiries on the sacred dwelling-places of the gods, it will be safest to begin, as before, with expressions which preceded the christian terms temple and church, and were supplanted by them.

The Gothic *alhs* fem. translates the Jewish-Christian notions of ναός (Matt. 27, 5. 51. Mk. 14, 58. 15, 29. Lu. 1, 9. 21. 2 Cor. 6, 16) and ἱερόν (Mk. 11, 11. 16. 27. 12, 35. 14, 49. Lu. 2, 27. 46. 4, 9. 18, 10. 19, 45. John 7, 14. 28. 8, 20. 59. 10, 23). To the Goth it would be a time-hallowed word, for it shares the anomaly of several such nouns, forming its gen. *alhs*, dat. *alh*, instead of alháis, alhái. Once only, John 18, 20, *gudhus* stands for ἱερόν ; the simple hus never has the sense of domus, which is rendered razn. Why should Ulphilas disdain to apply the heathen name to the christian thing, when the equally heathen templum and ναός were found quite inoffensive for christian use ?

Possibly the same word appears even earlier ; namely in Tacitus, Germ. 43 : apud Naharvalos antiquae religionis lucus ostenditur ; praesidet sacerdos muliebri ornatu, sed deos interpretatione romana Castorem Pollucemque memorant. Ea vis numini, nomen *Alcis;* nulla simulacra, nullum peregrinae superstitionis vestigium. Ut fratres tamen, ut juvenes venerantur.—This alcis is either itself the nom., or a gen. of *alx* (as falcis of falx), which perfectly corresponds to the Gothic *alhs*. A pair of heroic brothers was worshipped, without any statues, in a sacred grove; the name can hardly be ascribed to *them*,[1] it is the abode of the divinity that is called *alx*. Numen is here the sacred wood, or even some notable tree in it.[2]

---

[1] Unless it were dat. pl. of alcus [or alca ἀλκή]. A Wendicholz, Bohem. holec, which has been adduced, is not to the point, for it means strictly a bald naked wretch, a beggar boy, Pol. golec, Russ. gholiak. Besides, the Naharvali and the other Lygian nations can scarcely have been Slavs.

[2] I am not convinced that numen can refer to the place. The plain sense seems to be : ' the divinity has that virtue (which the Gemini have), and the name Alcis,' or 'of Alx,' or if dat. pl., 'the Alcae, Alci'. May not Alcis be conn. with ἀλκή strength, safeguard, and the dat. ἀλκί pointing to a nom. ἄλξ; *ἄλκω I defend ; or even Caesar's alces and Pausanias's ἄλκαι elks ?—TRANS.

Four or five centuries after Ulphilas, to the tribes of Upper Germany their word *alah* must have had an old-fashioned heathenish sound, but we know it was still there, preserved in composition with proper names of places and persons (see Suppl.) : Alaholf, Alahtac, Alahhilt, Alahgund, Alahtrût; Alahstat in pago Hassorum (A.D. 834), Schannat trad. fuld. no. 404. Alahdorp in Mulahgôwe (A.D. 856), ibid. no. 476. The names *Alahstat, Alahdorf* may have been borne by many places where a heathen temple, a hallowed place of justice, or a house of the king stood. For, not only the fanum, but the folk-mote, and the royal residence were regarded as consecrated, or, in the language of the Mid. Ages, as *frôno* (set apart to the frô, lord). Alstidi, a king's pfalz (palatium) in Thuringia often mentioned in Dietmar of Merseburg, was in OHG. *alahsteti,* nom. alahstat. Among the Saxons, who were converted later, the word kept itself alive longer. The poet of the Heliand uses *alah* masc. exactly as Ulphilas does alhs (3, 20. 22. 6, 2. 14, 9. 32, 14. 115, 9. 15. 129, 22. 130, 19. 157, 16), seldomer *godes hûs* 155, 8. 130, 18, or, that *hêlaga hûs* 3, 19. Cædm. 202, 22 alhn (1. *alh* hâligne =holy temple); 258, 11 *ealhstede* (palatium, aedes regia). In Andr. 1642 I would read ' ealde *ealhstedas* ' (delubra) for ' eolhstedas', conf. the proper names *Ealhstân* in Kemble 1, 288. 296 and *Ealhheard* 1, 292 quasi stone-hard, rock-hard, which possibly leads us to the primary meaning of the word.[1] The word is wanting in ON. documents, else it must have had the form *alr*, gen. *als*.

Of another primitive word the Gothic fragments furnish no example, the OHG. *wih* (nemus), Diut. 1, 492ᵃ ; O. Sax. *wih* masc. (templum), Hel. 3, 15. 17. 19. 14, 8. 115, 4. 119, 17. 127, 10. 129, 23. 130, 17. 154, 22. 169, 1 ; *friduwih,* Hel. 15, 19 ; AS. *wih* wiges, or *weoh* weos, also masc. : wiges (idoli), Cædm. 228, 12. þisne wig wurðigean (hoc idolum colere), Cædm. 228, 24. conf. wigweorðing (cultus idolorum), Beow. 350. weohweorðing Cod. exon. 253, 14. wihgild (cultus idol.), Cædm. 227, 5. weobedd (ara), for weohbedd, wihbedd, Cædm. 127, 8. weos (idola), for weohas, Cod. exon. 341, 28.—The alternation of i and eo in the AS. indicates a short vowel ; and in spite of the reasons I have urged in Gramm. 1, 462, the same seems to be true of the ON. *ve*, which in the sing., as

---

[1] There is however a noun Hard, the name of many landing-places in the south of England, as Cracknor Hard, &c.—TRANS.

Ve, denotes one particular god; but has a double pl., namely, a masc. *vear* dii, idola, and a neut. *ve* loca sacra. Gutalag 6, 108. 111: haita â hult eþa hauga, â *vi* eþa stafgarþa (invocare lucos aut tumulos, idola aut loca palis circumsepta); trûa â hult, â hauga, *vi* oc stafgarþa; han standr î *vi* (stat in loco sacro). In that case we have here, as in alah, a term alternating between nemus, templum, fanum, idolum, numen, its root being doubtless the Gothic veiha (I hallow), váih, váihum, OHG. wîhu, weih, wihum, from which also comes the adj. veihs sacer, OHG. wîh; and we saw on p.41 that wîhan was applied to sacrifices and worship. In Lappish, *vi* is said to mean silva.

Still more decisive is a third heathen word, which becomes specially important to our course of inquiry. The OHG. *haruc* masc., pl. harugâ, stands in the glosses both for fanum, Hrab. 963[b]. for delubrum, Hrab. 959[a]. for lucus, Hrab. 969[a], Jun. 212. Diut. 1, 495[b], and for nemus, Diut. 1, 492[a]. The last gloss, in full, runs thus: ' nemus plantavit=*forst* flanzôta, edo (or) *haruc*, edo *wih*.' So that haruc, like wih, includes on the one hand the notion of templum, fanum, and on the other that of wood, grove, lucus.[1] It is remarkable that the Lex Ripuar. has preserved, evidently from heathen times, *harahus* to designate a place of judgment, which was originally a wood (RA. 794. 903). AS. *hearg* masc., pl. heargas (fanum), Beda 2, 13. 3, 30. Orosius 3, 9, p. 109. *hearg*træf (fani tabulatum), Beow. 349. æt *hearge*, Kemble, 1, 282. ON. *hörgr* masc., pl. hörgar (delubrum, at times idolum, simulacrum), Sæm. 36[a] 42[a] 91[a] 114[b] 141[a]; especially worth notice is Sæm. 114[b]: *hörgr* hlaðinn steinom, griot at gleri orðit, roðit î nyio nauta bloði (h. paven with stones, grit made smooth, reddened anew with neat's blood). Sometimes *hörgr* is coupled with *hof* (fanum, tectum), 36[a] 141[a], in which case the former is the holy place amidst woods and rocks, the built temple, aula; conf. ' *hamarr* ok *hörgr*,' Fornm. sög. 5, 239. To both expressions belongs the notion of the place as well

---

[1] And in one place haragâ=arae. Elsewhere the heathen term for altar, Gk βωμός, was Goth. *biuds*, OHG. *piot*, AS. *beod*, strictly a table (p. 38); likewise the Goth. *badi*, OHG. *petti*, AS. *bed*, *bedd* (lectus, p. 30) gets to mean ara, areola, fanum, conf. AS. *wihbed*, *weohbed*, *weobed*, afterwards distorted into *weofed* (ara, altare), OHG. *kotapetti* (gods'-bed, lectus, pulvinar templi), Graff 3, 51; with which compare Brunhild's *bed* and the like, also the Lat. lectister-nium. 'Ad altare S. Kiliani, quod vulgo *lectus* dicitur,' Lang reg. 1, 239. 255 (A.D. 1160-5); (see Suppl.).

as that of the numen and the image itself (see Suppl.). Haruc seems unconnected with the O. Lat. haruga, aruga, bull of sacrifice, whence haruspex, aruspex. The Gk τέμενος however also means the sacred grove, Il. 8, 48. 23, 148. τέμενος τάμον, Il. 20, 184.

Lastly, synonymous with haruc is the OHG. *paro*, gen. para**wes**, AS. *bearo*, gen. bearwes, which betoken lucus[1] and arbor, a sacred grove or a tree; æt bearwe, Kemble. 1, 255. ON. *barr* (arbor), Sæm. 109[a]; *barri* (nemus) 86[b] 87[a]. qui ad aras sacrificat=de za demo *parawe* (al. za themo we) ploazit, Diut. 1, 150 ; ara, or rather the pl. arae, here stands for templum (see Suppl.).

Temple then means also *wood*. What we figure to ourselves as a built and walled house, resolves itself, the farther back we go, into a holy place untouched by human hand, embowered and shut in by self-grown trees. There dwells the deity, veiling his form in rustling foliage of the boughs ; there is the spot where the hunter has to present to him the game he has killed, and the herdsmen his horses and oxen and rams.

What a writer of the second century says on the cultus of the Celts, will hold good of the Teutonic and all the kindred nations : Κελτοὶ σέβουσι μὲν Δία, ἄγαλμα δὲ Διὸς κελτικὸν ὑψηλὴ δρῦς, Maximus Tyrius (diss. 8, ed. Reiske 1, 142). Compare Lasicz. 46 : deos *nemora* incolere persuasum habent (Samogitae). Habitarunt dî quoque *sylvas* (Haupts zeitschr. 1, 138).

I am not maintaining that this forest-worship exhausts all the conceptions our ancestors had formed of deity and its dwelling-place ; it was only the principal one. Here and there a god may haunt a mountain-top, a cave of the rock, a river ; but the grand general worship of the people has its seat in the *grove*. And no-where could it have found a worthier (see Suppl.).

At a time when rude beginnings were all that there was of the builder's art, the human mind must have been roused to a higher devotion by the sight of lofty trees under an open sky, than it could feel inside the stunted structures reared by unskilful hands. When long afterwards the architecture peculiar to the Teutons reached its

---

[1] To the Lat. *lūcus* would correspond a Goth. láuhs, and this is confirmed by the OHG. *lôh*, AS. *leáh*. The Engl. *lea, ley* has acquired the meaning of meadow, field ; also the Slav. *lug*, Boh. *lutz*, is at once grove, glade, and meadow. Not only the wood, but wooded meadows were sacred to gods (see Suppl.).

perfection, did it not in its boldest creations still aim at reproducing the soaring trees of the forest? Would not the abortion of miserably carved or chiselled images lag far behind the form of the god which the youthful imagination of antiquity pictured to itself, throned on the bowery summit of a sacred tree? In the sweep and under the shade[1] of primeval forests, the soul of man found itself filled with the nearness of sovran deities. The mighty influence that a forest life had from the first on the whole being of our nation, is attested by the 'march-fellowships;' *marka*, the word from which they took their name, denoted first a forest, and afterwards a boundary.

The earliest testimonies to the forest-cultus of the Germans are furnished by Tacitus. Germ. 9: ceterum nec cohibere parietibus deos, neque in ullam humani oris speciem adsimulare ex magnitudine coelestium arbitrantur. *Lucos ac nemora consecrant*, deorumque nominibus adpellant secretum illud quod sola reverentia vident.[2] Germ. 39, of the Semnones; Stato tempore in *silvam* auguriis patrum et *prisca formidine sacram*[3] omnes ejusdem sanguinis populi legationibus coëunt. est et alia *luco reverentia*. nemo nisi vinculo ligatus ingreditur, ut minor et potestatem numinis prae se ferens. si forte prolapsus est, attolli et insurgere haud licitum: per humum evolvuntur.[4] cap. 40: est in insula oceani *castum*

---

[1] Waldes *hleo, hlea* (umbra, umbraculum), Hel. 33, 22. 73, 23. AS. *hleo,* ON. *hlie,* OHG. *liwa,* Graff 2, 296, MHG. *lie, liewe.*

[2] Ruodolf of Fuld († 863) has incorporated the whole passage, with a few alterations, in his treatise De translatione Alexandri (Pertz 2, 675), perhaps from some intermediate source. Tacitus's words must be taken as they stand. In his day Germany possessed no masters who could build temples or chisel statues ; so the grove was the dwelling of the gods, and a sacred symbol did instead of a statue. Möser § 30 takes the passage to mean, that the divinity common to the whole nation was worshipped unseen, so as not to give one district the advantage of possessing the temple ; but that separate gods did have their images made. This view is too political, and also ill-suited to the isolation of tribes in those times. No doubt, a region which included a god's hill would acquire the more renown and sacredness, as spots like Rhetra and Loreto did from containing the Slavic sanctuary or a Madonna : that did not prevent the same worship from obtaining seats elsewhere. With the words of Tacitus compare what he says in Hist. 2, 78 : est Judaeam inter Syriamque Carmelus, ita vocant montem deumque, nec simulacrum deo aut templum, sic tradidere majores, *ara* tantum et *reverentia* ; and in Dial. de Orat. 12 : nemora vero et luci et *secretum* ipsum. In Tacitus secretum = secessus, seclusion, not arcanum.

[3] This hexameter is not a quotation, it is the author's own.

[4] Whoever is engaged in a holy office, and stands in the presence and precincts of the god, must not stumble, and if he falls to the ground, he forfeits his privilege. So he who in holy combat sinks to the earth, may not set

nemus, dicatumque in eo **vehicu**lum **veste** contectum. cap. 43 : apud Naharvalos *antiquae religionis lucus* ostenditur . . . numini nomen *Alcis*, nulla simulacra. cap 7 : effigies et signa (*i.e.* effigiata signa) quaedam detractae *lucis* in proelium ferunt ; with which connect a passage in Hist. 4, 22 : inde depromptæ *silvis lucis*que ferarum imagines, ut cuique genti inire proelium mos est. Ann. **2**, 12 : Caesar transgressus Visurgim indicio perfugae cognoscit delectum ab Arminio locum pugnae, convenisse et alias nationes in *silvam* Herculi *sacram*. Ann. **4**, 73 : mox conpertum a transfugis, nongentos Romanorum apud *lucum*, quem Baduhennae vocant, pugna in posterum extracta confectos ; though it does not appear that this grove was a consecrated one.[1] Ann. **1**, 61 : *lucis* propinquis *barbarae arae*, apud quas tribunos mactaverant ; conf. 2, 25 : propinquo *luco* defossam Varianae legionis aquilam modico praesidio servari. Hist. 4, 14 : Civilis primores gentis . . . *sacrum* in *nemus* vocatos. These expressions can be matched by others from Claudian three centuries later, Cons. Stilich. **1**, 288 :

> Ut procul Hercyniae per vasta silentia silvae
> venari tuto liceat, *luco*sque vetusta
> religione truces, et *robora numinis instar*
> *barbarici* nostrae feriant impune bipennes.

De bello Get. 545 :

> *Hortantes* his adde *deos.* Non somnia nobis,
> nec volucres, sed *clara* palam *vox edita luco est :*
> ' rumpe omnes, Alarice, moras ! '

It is not pure nature-worship that we are told of here ; but Tacitus could have had no eye for the ' mores Germanorum,' if their most essential feature had escaped him. Gods dwell in these groves ; no images (simulacra, in human form) are mentioned by name as being set up, no temple walls are reared.[2] But sacred vessels and altars

---

himself on his legs, but must finish the fight on his knees, Danske viser 1, 115 ; so in certain places a stranger's carriage, if overturned, must not be set upright again, RA. 554. What is fabled of an idol called Sompar at Görlitz (neue lausitz. monatsschr. 1805, p. 1-18) has evidently been spun out of this passage in Tac. ; the Semnones are placed in the Lausitz country, as they had been previously by Aventin (Frankf. 1580, p. 27ᵇ), who only puts a king Schwab in the place of Sompar.

[1] Baduhenna, perhaps the name of a place, like Arduenna. Müllenhoff adds Badvinna, Patunna (Haupts zeitschr. 9, 241).

[2] Brissonius de regno Pers. 2, 28 ; ' Persae diis suis nulla templa vel altaria constituunt, nulla simulacra ' ; after Herodot. 1, 131.

stand in the forest, heads of animals (ferarum imagines) hang on the boughs of trees. There divine worship is performed and sacrifice offered, there is the folk-mote and the assize, everywhere a sacred awe and reminiscence of antiquity. Have not we here *alah, wih, paro, haruc* faithfully portrayed ? How could such technical terms, unless they described an organized national worship presided over by priests, have sprung up in the language, and lived ?

During many centuries, down to the introduction of christianity, this custom endured, of venerating deity in sacred woods and trees.

I will here insert the detailed narrative given by Wilibald († 786) in the Vita Bonifacii (Canisius II. 1, 242. Pertz 2, 343) of the holy oak of Geismar (on the Edder, near Fritzlar in Hesse).[1] The event falls between the years 725 and 731. Is autem (Bonifacius) . . . ad obsessas ante ea Hessorum metas cum consensu Carli ducis (*i.e.* of Charles Martel) rediit. tum vero Hessorum jam multi catholica fide subditi ac septiformis spiritus gratia confirmati manus impositionem acceperunt, et alii quidem, nondum animo confortati, intemeratae fidei documenta integre percipere renuerunt, alii etiam linguis et faucibus clanculo, alii vero aperte *sacrificabant,* alii vero auspicia et divinationes, praestigia atque incantationes occulte, alii quidem manifeste exercebant, alii quippe auspicia et auguria intendebant, diversosque *sacrificandi ritus* incoluerunt, alii etiam, quibus mens sanior inerat, omni abjecta gentilitatis pro-phanatione nihil horum commiserunt. quorum consultu atque consilio *arborem* quandam *mirae magnitudinis,* quae *prisco Pagan-orum vocabulo* appellatur *robur Jovis,* in loco, qui dicitur Gaesmere, servis Dei secum astantibus, succidere tentavit. cumque mentis constantia confortatus arborem succidisset, magna quippe aderat copia Paganorum, qui et inimicum *deorum suorum* intra se diligen-tissime devotabant, sed ad modicum quidem arbore praecisa confestim *immensa roboris moles,* divino desuper flatu exagitata, palmitum confracto culmine, corruit, et quasi superi nutus solatio in quatuor etiam partes disrupta est, et quatuor ingentis magnitu-dinis aequali longitudine trunci, absque fratrum labore astantium apparuerunt. quo viso prius devotantes Pagani etiam versa vice benedictionem Domino, pristina abjecta maledictione, credentes

---

[1] A shorter account of the same in the annalist Saxo, p. 133.

reddiderunt. Tunc autem summae sanctitatis antistes consilio inito cum fratribus ex supradictae arboris materia [1]) oratorium construxit, illudque in honore S. Petri apostoli dedicavit. From that time christianity had in this place a seat in Hesse ; hard by was the ancient capital of the nation, 'Mattium (Marburg), id genti caput,' Tac. Ann. 1, 56 ; which continued in the Mid. Ages to be the chief seat of government. According to Landau, the oak and the church built out of it stood on the site of St. Peter's church at Fritzlar. The whole region is well wooded (see Suppl.).

Not unsimilar are some passages contained in the Vita S. Amandi († 674), on the wood and tree worship of the northern Franks: Acta Bened. sec. 2. p. 714, 715, 718) : Amandus audivit pagum esse, cui vocabulum Gandavum, cujus loci habitatores ini- quitas diaboli eo circumquaque laqueis vehementer irretivit, ut incolae terrae illius, relicto deo, *arbores* et *ligna* pro deo colerent, atque *fana* vel *idola* adorarent.—Ubi *fana* destruebantur, statim monasteria aut ecclesias construebat.—Amandus in pago belvacense verbum domini dum praedicaret, pervenit ad quendam locum, cui vocabulum est Rossonto juxta Aronnam fluvium .   .   . respondit illa, quod non ob aliam causam ei ipsa coecitas evenisset, nisi quod *auguria* vel *idola* semper coluerat. insuper ostendit ei locum, in quo praedictum idolum adorare consueverat, scilicet *arborem, quae erat daemoni dedicata* .   .   . ' nunc igitur accipe securim et hanc *nefandam arborem* quantocius succidere festina'.

Among the Saxons and Frisians the veneration of groves lasted much longer. At the beginning of the 11th century, bishop Unwan of Bremen (conf. Adam. Brem. 2, 33) had all such woods cut down among the remoter inhabitants of his diocese : *lucos* in episcopatu suo, in quibus paludicolae regionis illius *errore veteri* cum profes- sione falsa christianitatis *immolabant*, succidit ; Vita Meinwerci, cap· 22. Of the holy tree in the Old Saxon *Irminsûl* I will treat in ch. VI. Several districts of Lower Saxony and Westphalia have until quite recent times preserved vestiges of *holy oaks*, to which the people paid a half heathen half christian homage. Thus, in the principality of Minden, on Easter Sunday, the young people of both sexes used with loud cries of joy to dance a reigen (rig,

[1] Other MS. have ' mole ' or ' metallo '. A brazen image on the oak is not to be thought of, as such a thing would have been alluded to in what precedes or follows.

circular dance) round an *old oak*.[1]   In a thicket near the village of
Wormeln, Paderborn, stands a *holy oak*, to which the inhabitants
of Wormeln and Calenberg still make a solemn procession every
year.[2]

I am inclined to trace back to heathenism the proper name of
Holy Wood so common in nearly all parts of Germany.   It is not
likely that from a christian church situated in a wood, the wood
itself would be named holy ; and in such forests, as a rule, there is
not a church to be found.   Still less can the name be explained by
the royal ban-forests of the Mid. Ages; on the contrary, these
forests themselves appear to have sprung out of heathen groves,
and the king's right seems to have taken the place of the cultus
which first withdrew the holy wood from the common use of the
people.   In such forests too there used to be sanctuaries for criminals, RA. 886-9.

An old account of a battle between Franks and Saxons at
Notteln in the year 779 (Pertz 2, 377) informs us, that a badly
wounded Saxon had himself secretly conveyed from his castle into a
holy wood : Hic vero (Luibertus) magno cum merore se in castrum
recepit.   Ex quo post aliquot dies mulier egrotum humeris clam in
sylvam Sytheri, *quae fuit thegathon sacra*, nocte portavit.   Vulnera
ibidem lavans, exterrita clamore effugit.   Ubi multa lamentatione
animam expiravit.   The strange expression thegathon is explained
by τ' ἀγαθόν (the good), a name for the highest divinity (summus
et princeps omnium deorum), which the chronicler borrowed from
Macrobius's somn. Scip. 1, 2, and may have chosen purposely, to
avoid naming a well-known heathen god (see Suppl.).   Sytheri,
the name of the wood, seems to be the same as Sunderi (southern),
a name given to forests in more than one district, *e.g.* a Sundernhart
in Franconia (Höfers urk. p. 308).   Did this heathen hope for healing on the sacred soil ? or did he wish to die there ?

The forest called Dat *hillige holt* is mentioned by a document
in Kindlinger's Münst. beitr. 3, 638.   In the county of Hoya there
stood a *Heiligen-loh* (Pertz 2, 362).   A long list of Alsatian
documents in Schöpflin allude to the holy forest near Hagenau; no.
218 (A.D. 1065) : cum foresto *heiligenforst* nominato in comitatu
Gerhardi comitis in pago Nortcowe.   no. 238 (1106): in sylva

[1] Weddigen's westphal. mag. 3, 712.
[2] Spilckers beiträge 2, 121.

heiligeforst. no. 273 (1143) : praedium Loubach in *sacro nemore* situm. no. 297 (1158) : utantur pascuis in *sacra silva.* no. 317 (1175) : in *silva sacra.* no. 402 (1215) : in *sacra silva.* no. 800 (1292) : conventum in königesbrücken in *heiligenforst.* no. 829 (1304) : nemus nostrum et imperii dictum *heiligvorst.* no. 851 (1310) : pecora in foresta nostra, quae dicitur der *heilige forst,* pascere et tenere. no. 1076 (1356) : porcos tempore glandium nutriendos in *silva sacra.* The alternating words ʻforst, silva, nemus,' are enough to show the significance of the term. The name of the well-known *Dreieich* (Drieichahi) is probably to be explained by the heathen worship of three oaks ; a royal ban-forest existed there a long time, and its charter (I, 498) is one of the most primitive.

The express allusion to Thuringia and Saxony is remarkable in the following lines of a poem that seems to have been composed soon after the year 1200, Reinh. F. 302 ; the wolf sees a goat on a tree, and exclaims :

ich sihe ein obez hangen,	I see a fruit hanging,
ez habe hâr ode borst ;	That it has hair or bristles ;
in einem *heiligen vorste*	In any holy forest
ze Düringen noch ze Sachsen	Of Thuringia nor of Saxony
enkunde niht gewahsen	There could not grow
bezzer obez ûf rîse.	Better fruit on bough.

The allusion is surely to sacrificed animals, or firstfruits of the chase, hung up on the trees of a sacred wood ? Either the story is based on a more ancient original, or may not the poet have heard tell from somewhere of heathenish doings going on in his own day among Saxons and Thuringians ? (see Suppl.).

And in other poems of the Mid. Ages the sacredness of the ancient forests still exerts an after-influence. In Alex. 5193 we read ʻ der *edele walt frône* ' ; and we have inklings now and again, if not of sacrifices offered to sacred trees, yet of a lasting indestructible awe, and the fancy that ghostly beings haunt particular trees. Thus, in Ls. 2, 575, misfortune, like a demon, sat on a *tree ;* and in Altd. w. 3, 161 it is said of a *hollow tree :*

dâ sint heiligen inne,	There are saints in there,
die hœrent aller liute bet.[1]	That hear all people's prayers
	(see Suppl.).

---

[1] From the notion of a forest temple the transition is easy to paying divine honours to a single tree. Festus has : *delubrum* fustis delibratus (staff with

Still more unmistakably does this forest cultus prevail in the North, protected by the longer duration of heathenism. The great sacrifice at Lêdera described by Dietmar (see p. 48) was performed in the island which, from its even now magnificent beech-woods, bore the name of *Sœlundr*, sea-grove, and was the finest grove in all Scandinavia. The Swedes in like manner solemnized their festival of sacrifice in a grove near Upsala; Adam of Bremen says of the animals sacrificed: Corpora suspenduntur in *lucum* qui proximus est templo; is enim lucus tam *sacer* est gentibus, ut singulae *arbores* ejus ex morte vel tabo immolatorum *divinae* credantur. Of Hlöðr Heiðreksson we are told in the Hervararsaga cap. 16 (fornald. sög. 1, 491), that he was born with arms and horse in the *holy wood* (â mörk hinni helgu). In the grove *Glasislundr* a bird sits on the boughs and demands *sacrifices*, a temple and gold-horned cows, Sæm. 140-1. The sacred trees of the Edda, *Yggdrasil* and *Mîmameiðr*, Sæm. 109[a], hardly need reminding of.

Lastly, the agreement of the Slav, Prussian, Finnish and Celtic paganisms throws light upon our own, and tends to confirm it. Dietmar of Merseburg (Pertz 5, 812) affirms of the heathen temple at Riedegost: quam undique *sylva* ab incolis *intacta* et *venerabilis* circumdat *magna;* (ibid. 816) he relates how his ancestor Wibert about the .year 1008 rooted up a grove of the Slavs: *lucum* Zutibure dictum, ab accolis *ut deum* in omnibus *honoratum*, et ab aevo antiquo *nunquam violatum*, radicitus eruens, sancto martyri Romano in eo ecclesiam construxit. Zutibure is for Sveti bor = holy forest, from bor (fir), pine-barren; a Merseburg document of 1012 already mentions an 'ecclesia in Scutibure,' Zeitschr. f. archivkunde, 1, 162. An ON. saga (Fornm. sög. 11, 382) names a *blôtlundr* (sacrificial grove) at Stræla, called Böku, Helmold 1, 1 says of the Slavs: usque hodie profecto inter illos, cum cetera

bark peeled off) quem venerabantur pro deo. Names given to particular trees are at the same time names of goddesses, *e.g.* ON. Hlin, Gnâ. It is worthy of notice, that the heathen idea of divine figures on trees has crept into *christian* legends, so deeply rooted was tree worship among the people. I refer doubters to the story of the Tyrolese image of grace, which grew up in a forest tree (Deutsche sagen, no. 348). In Carinthia you find Madonna figures fixed on the trees in gloomy groves (Sartoris reise 2, 165). Of like import seem to be the descriptions of wonderful maidens sitting inside hollow trees, or perched on the boughs (Marienkind, hausmärchen no. 3. Romance de la infantina, see ch. XVI.). Madonna in the wood, Mar. legend. 177. Many oaks with Madonnas in Normandy, Bosquet 196-7.

omnia communia sint cum nostris, solus prohibetur accessus *lucorum* ac fontium, quos autumant pollui christianorum accessu. A song in the Königinhof MS. p. 72 speaks of the grove (*hain*, Boh. hai, hag, Pol. gay, Sloven. gaj; conf. gaius, gahajus, Lex Roth. 324, kaheius, Lex Bajuv. 21, 6) from which the christians scared away the holy sparrow.[1] The Esth. *sallo*, Finn. *salo* means a holy wood, especially a meadow with thick underwood; the national god Tharapila is described by Henry the Letton (ad. ann. 1219): in confinio Wironiae erat *mons* et *silva pulcherrima*, in quo dicebant indigenae magnum deum Osiliensium natum qui Tharapila[2] vocatur, et de loco illo in Osiliam volasse,—in the form of a bird? (see Suppl.). To the Old Prussians, *Romove* was the most sacred spot in the land, and a seat of the gods; there stood their images on a *holy oak* hung with cloths. No unconsecrated person was allowed to set foot in the forest, no tree to be felled, not a bough to be injured, not a beast to be slain. There were many such sacred groves in other parts of Prussia and Lithuania.[3]

The Vita S. Germani Autisiodorensis (b. 378, d. 448) written by Constantius as early as 473 contains a striking narrative of a *peartree* which stood in the middle of Auxerre and was honoured by the heathen.[4] As the Burgundians did not enter Gaul till the beginning of the 5th century, there is not likely to be a mixture in it of German tradition. But even if the story is purely Celtic, it deserves a place here, because it shows how widely the custom prevailed of hanging the heads of sacrificial beasts on trees.[5] Eo tempore (before 400) territorium Autisiodorensis urbis visitatione propria gubernabat Germanus. Cui mos erat tirunculorum potius industriis indulgere, quam christianae religioni operam dare. is ergo assidue venatui invigilans ferarum copiam insidiis atque artis strenuitate frequentissime capiebat. Erat autem *arbor pirus in*

---

[1] Brzetislav burnt down the heathen *groves* and *trees* of the Bohemians in 1093, Pelzel 1, 76. The Poles called a sacred grove *rok* and *uroczysko*, conf. Russ. róshtcha, grove [root *rek rok* = fari, fatum; róshtcha is from rostí, rastí = grow]. On threat of hostile invasion, they cut rods (wicie) from the grove, and sent them round to summon their neighbours. Mickiewicz 1, 56.

[2] Conf. *Turupid* in Fornm. sög. 11, 385; but on Slav nations conf. Schiefner on Castrén 329.

[3] Joh. Voigts gesch. Preussens 1, 595—597.

[4] Acta sanctor. Bolland. July 31. p. 202; conf. Legenda aurea, cap. 102.

[5] Huic (Marti) praedae primordia vovebantur, huic *truncis suspendebantur exuviae*, Jornandes cap. 5

urbe media, amœnitate gratissima : *ad cujus ramusculos ferarum* ab
eo deprehensarum *capita* pro admiratione venationis nimiae *depen-
debant.* Quem celebris ejusdem civitatis Amator episcopus his
frequens compellebat eloquiis : 'desine, quaeso, vir honoratorum
splendidissime, haec jocularia, quae Christianis offensa, Paganis vero
imitanda sunt, exercere. hoc opus *idololatriae* cultura est, non chris-
tianæ elegantissimae disciplinae.' Et licet hoc indesinenter vir deo
dignus perageret, ille tamen nullo modo admonenti se adquiescere
voluit aut obedire. vir autem domini iterum atque iterum eum horta-
batur, ut non solum a consuetudine male arrepta discederet, verum
etiam et ipsam *arborem,* ne Christianis offendiculum esset, radicitus exstirparet. sed ille nullatenus aurem placidam applicare voluit
admonenti. In hujus ergo persuasionis tempore quodam die Germanus ex urbe in praedia sui juris discessit. tunc beatus Amator
opportunitatem opperiens *sacrilegam arborem* cum caudicibus ab-
scidit, et ne aliqua ejus incredulis esset memoria igni concreman-
dam illico deputavit. *oscilla*[1]) vero, quae tanquam trophaea cujus-
dam certaminis umbram dependentia ostentabant, longius a civitatis
terminis projici praecipit. Protinus vero fama gressus suos ad
aures Germani retorquens, dictis animum incendit, atque iram suis
suasionibus exaggerans ferocem effecit, ita ut oblitus sanctae
religionis, cujus jam fuerat ritu atque munere insignitus, mortem
beatissimo viro minitaret.

A poem of Herricus composed about 876 gives a fuller description of the idolatrous peartree :

> altoque et lato stabat gratissima quondam
> urbe *pirus* media, populo spectabilis omni ;
> non quia pendentum flavebat honore pirorum,
> nec quia perpetuae vernabat munere frondis :

---

[1] Virg. Georg. 2, 388 : tibique (Bacche) *oscilla* ex alta suspendunt mollia
pinu. In the story, however, it is not masks that are hung up, but real heads
of beasts ; are the ferarum imagines in Tac. Hist. 4, 22 necessarily images ?
Does oscilla mean capita oscillantia ? It appears that when they hung up the
heads, they propped open the mouth with a stick, conf. Isengr. 645. Reinardus
3, 293 (see Suppl.). Nailing birds of prey *to the gate* of a burg or barn is well
known, and is practised to this day. Hanging up horses' heads was mentioned
on p. 47. The Grîmnismâl 10 tells us, in Oðin's mansion there hung a *wolf
outside the door,* and over that an *eagle ;* were these mere simulacra and insignia ?
Witechind says, the Saxons, when sacrificing, set up an *eagle over the gate* : Ad
orientalem portam ponunt aquilam, aramque Victoriae construentes ; this eagle
seems to have been her emblem. A *dog* hung up over the threshold is also
mentioned. Lex. Alam. 102.

sed deprensarum passim *capita* alta *ferarum*
arboris obscoenae patulis haerentia ramis
praebebant vano plausum spectacula vulgo.
horrebant illic trepidi ramalia *cervi*
et dirum frendentis *apri*, fera spicula, dentes,
acribus exitium meditantes forte molossis.
tunc quoque sic variis arbos induta tropaeis
fundebat rudibus lascivi semina risus.

It was not the laughter of the multitude that offended the christian
priests; they saw in the practice a performance, however degene-
rate and dimmed, of heathen sacrifices.[1]

Thus far we have dwelt on the evidences which go to prove
that the oldest worship of our ancestors was connected with sacred
forests and trees.

At the same time it cannot be doubted, that even in the earliest
times there were temples *built* for single deities, and perhaps rude
images set up inside them. In the lapse of centuries the old forest
worship may have declined and been superseded by the structure
of temples, more with some populations and less with others. In
fact, we come across a good many statements so indefinite or incomplete, that it is impossible to gather from them with any certainty
whether the expressions used betoken the ancient cultus or one
departing from it.

The most weighty and significant passages relating to this part
of the subject seem to be the following (see Suppl.):

Tac. Germ. 40 describes the sacred grove and the worship of
Mother Earth; when the priest in festival time has carried the
goddess round among the people, he restores her to her sanctuary:
satiatam conversatione mortalium deam *templo* reddit.

Tac. ann. 1, 51: Cæsar avidas legiones, quo latior populatio
foret, quatuor in cuneos dispertit, quinquaginta millium spatium
ferro flammisque pervastat; non sexus, non aetas miserationem

---

[1] St. Benedict found at Montecassino vetustissimum fanum, in quo ex
antiquo more gentilium a stulto rusticano populo Apollo colebatur, *circumquaque*
enim in cultum daemoniorum *luci succreverant*, in quibus adhuc eodem tempore
infidelium insana multitudo sacrificiis sacrilegis insudabat. Greg. Mag. dialogi
2, 8. These were not German heathens, but it proves the custom to have been
the more universal.

attulit: profana simul et *sacra*, et *celeberrimum* illis gentibus templum, quod *Tanfanae*[1] vocabant, solo aequantur. The nation to which this temple belonged were the Marsi and perhaps some neighbouring ones (see Suppl.).

Vita S. Eugendi abbatis Jurensis († circ. 510), auctore monacho Condatescensi ipsius discipulo (in Actis sanctor. Bolland. Jan. 1, p. 50, and in Mabillon, acta Ben. sec. 1, p. 570): Sanctus igitur famulus Christi Eugendus, sicut beatorum patrum Romani et Lupicini in religione discipulus, ita etiam natalibus ac provincia extitit indigena atque concivis. ortus nempe est haud longe a vico cui *vetusta paganitas* ob celebritatem clausuramque fortissimam *superstitiosissimi templi* Gallica lingua *Isarnodori*, id est, ferrei ostii indidit nomen: quo nunc quoque in loco, *delubris* ex parte jam dirutis, sacratissime micant coelestis regni culmina dicata Christicolis; atque inibi pater sanctissimae prolis judicio pontificali plebisque testimonio extitit in presbyterii dignitate sacerdos. If Eugendus was born about the middle of the 5th century, and his father already was a priest of the christian church which had been erected on the site of the heathen temple, heathenism can at the latest have lingered there only in the earlier half of that century, at whose commencement the West Goths passed through Italy into Gaul. *Gallica* lingua here seems to be the German spoken by the invading nations, in contradistinction to the Romana; the name of the place is almost pure Gothic, eisarnadaúri, still more exactly it might be Burgundian, îsarnodori.[2] Had either West Goths or Burgundians, or perhaps even some Alamanns that had penetrated so far, founded the temple in the fastnesses and defiles of the Jura?[3] The name is well suited to the strength of the position and of the building, which the christians in part retained (see Suppl.).

A Constitutio Childeberti I of about 554 (Pertz 3, 1) contains the following: Praecipientes, ut quicunque admoniti de agro suo, ubicumque fuerint *simulacra constructa* vel *idola daemoni dedicata*

---

[1] An inscription found in Neapolitan territory, but supposed by Orelli 2053 to have been made by Ligorius, has ' *Tamfanae* sacrum ' (Gudii inscript. antiq. p. lv. 11, de Wal p. 188) ; the word is certainly German, and formed like Hludana, Sigana (Sequana), Liutana (Lugdunum), Râbana (Ravenna), &c.

[2] Yet the Celtic forms also are not far removed, Ir. iaran, Wel. haiarn, Armor. uarn (ferrum) ; Ir. doras, Wel. dor (porta) : haearndor = iron gate, quoted in Davies's Brit. Mythol. pp. 120, 560.

[3] Frontier mountains held sacred and made places of sacrifice by some nations ; Ritters erdkunde 1, aufl. 2, 79. vol. 2, p. 903.

ab hominibus, factum non statim abjecerint vel sacerdotibus haec destruentibus prohibuerint, datis fidejussoribus non aliter discedant nisi in nostris obtutibus praesententur.

Vita S. Radegundis († 587) the wife of Clotaire, composed by a contemporary nun Baudonivia (acta Bened. sec. 1, p. 327): Dum iter ageret (Radegundis) seculari pompa se comitante, interjecta longinquitate terrae ac spatio, *fanum quod a Francis colebatur* in itinere beatae reginae quantum miliario uno proximum erat. hoc illa audiens jussit famulis *fanum* igne comburi, iniquum judicans Deum coeli contemni et diabolica machinamenta venerari. Hoc audientes Franci universa multitudo cum gladiis et fustibus vel omni fremitu conabantur defendere. sancta vero regina immobilis perseverans et Christum in pectore gestans, equum quem sedebat in antea (*i.e.* ulterius) non movit antequam et *fanum* perureretur et ipsa orante inter se populi pacem firmarent. The situation of the temple she destroyed I do not venture to determine; Radegund was journeying from Thuringia to France, and somewhere on that line, not far from the Rhine, the fanum may be looked for.

Greg. Tur. vitae patrum 6 : Eunte rege (Theoderico) in Agrippinam urbem, et ipse (S. Gallus) simul abiit. erat autem ibi *fanum* quoddam diversis ornamentis refertum, in quo barbaris (l. Barbarus) opima *libamina* exhibens usque ad vomitum cibo potuque replebatur. ibi et *simulacra* ut *deum adorans*, membra, secundum quod unumquemque dolor attigisset, sculpebat in ligno. quod ubi S. Gallus audivit, statim illuc cum uno tantum clerico properat, accensoque igne, cum nullus ex stultis Paganis adesset, ad *fanum* applicat et succendit. at illi videntes fumum *delubri* ad coelum usque conscendere, auctorem incendii quaerunt, inventumque evaginatis gladiis prosequuntur ; ille vero in fugam versus aulae se regiae condidit. verum postquam rex quae acta fuerant Paganis minantibus recognovit, blandis eos sermonibus lenivit. This Gallus is distinct from the one who appears in Alamannia half a century later ; he died about 553, and by the king is meant Theoderic I of Austrasia.

Vita S. Lupi Senonensis (Duchesne 1, 562. Bouquet 3, 491) : Rex Chlotarius virum Dei Lupum episcopum retrusit in pago quodam Neustriae nuncupante Vinemaco (le Vimeu), traditum duci pagano (*i.e.* duci terrae), nomine Bosoni Landegisilo (no doubt a Frank) quem ille direxit in villa quae dicitur Andesagina super fluvium

Auciam, ubi erant *templa fanatica* a *decurionibus culta.* (A.D.
614.) Andesagina is Ansenne, Aucia was afterwards called la
Bresle, Briselle.

Beda, hist. eccl. 2, 13, relates how the Northumbrian king
Eadwine, baptized 627, slain 633, resolved after mature consultation
with men of understanding to adopt christianity, and was especially
made to waver in his ancient faith by Coifi (Cœfi) his chief heathen
priest himself: Cumque a praefato pontifice sacrorum suorum
quaereret, quis *aras* et *fana idolorum cum septis quibus erant cir-
cumdata* primus profanare deberet? respondit: ego.   quis enim ea,
quae per stultitiam colui, nunc ad exemplum omnium aptius quam
ipse per sapientiam mihi a Deo vero donatam destruam?   . . .
Accinctus ergo gladio accepit lanceam in manu et ascendens
emissarium regis (all three unlawful and improper things for a
heathen priest), pergebat ad *idola.* quod aspiciens vulgus aesti-
mabat eum insanire.   nec distulit ille.   mox ut appropinquabat ad
fanum, profanare illud, injecta in eo lancea quam tenebat, multum-
que gavisus de agnitione veri Dei cultus, jussit sociis destruere ac
succendere *fanum cum omnibus septis* suis.   ostenditur autem locus
ille quondam *idolorum* non longe ab Eboraco ad orientem ultra
amnem Dorowentionem et vocatur hodie Godmundinga hâm, ubi
pontifex ipse, inspirante Deo vero, polluit ac destruxit eas, quas
ipse sacraverat, aras.[1]

Vita S. Bertuffi Bobbiensis († 640) in Acta Bened. sec. 2, p.
164: Ad quandam villam Iriae fluvio adjacentem accessit, ubi
fanum quoddam *arboribus consitum* videns allatum ignem ei admovit,
congestis in modum pirae lignis.   Id vero cernentes *fani* cultores
Meroveum apprehensum diuque fustibus caesum et ictibus con-
tusum in fluvium illud demergere conantur.—The Iria runs into
the Po; the event occurs among Lombards.

Walafridi Strabonis vita S. Galli († 640) in actis Bened. sec. 2
p. 219, 220: Venerunt (S. Columbanus et Gallus) infra partes
Alemanniae ad fluvium, qui Lindimacus vocatur, juxta quem ad
superiora tendentes pervenerunt Turicinum.   cumque per littus
ambulantes venissent ad caput lacus ipsius, in locum qui Tucconia
dicitur, placuit illis loci qualitas ad inhabitandum.   porro homines

---

[1] The A.S. translation renders arae by *wigbed* (see p.67), fana by *heargas,*
idola by *deofolgild,* septa once by *hegas* (hedges), and the other time by *getymbro.*
The spear hurled at the *hearg* gave the signal for its demolition.

ibidem commanentes crudeles erant et impii, *simulacra colentes, idola sacrificiis venerantes*, observantes auguria et divinationes et multa quae contraria sunt cultui divino superstitiosa sectantes. Sancti igitur homines cum coepissent inter illos habitare, docebant eos adorare Patrem et Filium et Spiritum sanctum, et custodire fidei veritatem. Beatus quoque Gallus sancti viri discipulus zelo pietatis armatus *fana*, in quibus *daemoniis sacrificabant*, igni succendit et quaecumque invenit oblata demersit in lacum.—Here follows an important passage which will be quoted further on ; it says expressly : cumque ejusdem *templi* solemnitas ageretur.

Jonae Bobbiensis vita S. Columbani († 615) cap. 17. in act. Bened. 2, 12. 13 : Cumque jam multorum monachorum societate densaretur, coepit cogitare, ut potiorem locum in eadem eremo (*i.e.* Vosago saltu) quaereret, quo monasterium construeret. invenitque *castrum firmissimo munimine* olim fuisse *cultum*, a supra dicto loco distans plus minus octo millibus, quem prisca tempora Luxovium nuncupabant, ibique *aquae calidae* cultu eximio constructae habebantur. ibi *imaginum lapidearum* densitas vicina saltus densabat,[1] quas *cultu miserabili rituque profano vetusta Paganorum* tempora honorabant.—This Burgundian place then (Luxeuil in Franche Comté, near Vesoul) contained old Roman thermae adorned with statues. Had the Burgundian settlers connected their own worship with these ? The same castrum is spoken of in the

Vita S. Agili Resbacensis († 650), in Acta Ben. sec. 2, p. 317 : *Castrum* namque intra vasta eremi septa, quae Vosagus dicitur, fuerat *fanaticorum cultui* olim *dedicatum*, sed tunc ad solum usque dirutum, quod hujus saltus incolae, quamquam ignoto praesagio, Luxovium [qu. lux ovium ?] nominavere. A church is then built on the heathen site: ut, ubi olim *prophano ritu* veteres *coluerunt fana*, ibi Christi figerentur arae et erigerentur vexilla, habitaculum Deo militantium, quo adversus aërias potestates dimicarent superni Regis tirones. p. 319 : Ingressique (Agilus cum Eustasio) hujus itineris viam, juvante Christo, Warascos praedicatori accelerant, qui *agrestium fanis* decepti, quos vulgi *faunos* vocant, gentilium

---

[1] The multitude of statues *made* the adjoining wood *thicker ?* Must we not supply an acc. copiam or speciem after imag. lapid. ? [vicina saltus densabat evidently means '*crowded* the adjoining part of the wood'. So in Ovid: densae foliis buxi.—TRANS.]

quoque errore seducti, in perfidiam devenerant, Fotini seu Bonosi virus infecti, quos, errore depulso, matri ecclesiae reconciliatos veros Christi fecere servos.

Vita S. Willibrordi († 789), in Acta Bened. sec. 3, p. 609: Pervenit in confinio Fresonum et Danorum ad quandam insulam, quae a quodam deo suo Fosite ab accolis terrae Fositesland appellatur, quia in ea ejusdem dei *fana* fuere constructa. Qui locus a paganis tanta veneratione habebatur, ut nil in eo vel animalium ibi pascentium vel aliarum quarumlibet rerum gentilium quisquam tangere audebat, nec etiam a fonte qui ibi ebulliebat aquam haurire nisi tacens praesumebat.

Vita S. Willehadi († 793), in Pertz 2, 381: Unde contigit, ut quidam discipulorum ejus, divino compuncti ardore, *fana in morem gentilium circumquaque erecta* coepissent evertere et ad nihilum, prout poterant, redigere ; quo facto barbari, qui adhuc forte perstiterant, furore nimio succensi, irruerunt super eos repente cum impetu, volentes eos funditus interimere, ibique Dei famulum fustibus caesum multis admodum plagis affecere.—This happened in the Frisian pagus Thrianta (Drente) before 779.

Vita Ludgeri (beginning of the 9th cent.) 1,8: (In Frisia) Paganos asperrimos . . . mitigavit, ut sua illum *delubra* destruere coram oculis paterentur. Inventum in *fanis* aurum et argentum plurimum Albricus in aerarium regis intulit, accipiens et ipse praecipiente Carolo portionem ex illo.—Conf. the passage cited p. 45 from the Lex Frisionum.

Folcuini gesta abb. Lobiensium (circ. 980), in Pertz 6, 55: Est locus intra terminos pagi, quem veteres, a loco ubi *superstitiosa gentilitas fanum Marti sacraverat, Fanum Martinse* dixeruut.—This is Famars in Hainault, not far from Valenciennes.

In all probability the sanctuary of Tanfana which Germanicus demolished in A.D. 14 was not a mere grove, but a real building, otherwise Tacitus would hardly have called the destruction of it a ' levelling to the ground '. During the next three or four centuries we are without any notices of heathen temples in Germany. In the 5th, 6th, 7th, and 8th centuries, as I have shown, we come upon *castra, templa, fana* among Burgundians, Franks, Lombards, Alamanns, Anglo-Saxons, and Frisians. By *fanum* (whence fanaticus) seems often to have been understood a building of smaller

extent, and by *templum* one of larger; the Indiculus superstit. xxxi.
4 has: 'de *casulis* (huts), *i.e. fanis*' (see Suppl.). I admit that
some of the authorities cited leave it doubtful whether German
heathen temples be intended, they might be Roman ones which
had been left standing; in which case there is room for a twofold
hypothesis : that the dominant German nation had allowed certain
communities in their midst to keep up the Roman-Gallic cultus, or
that they themselves had taken possession of Roman buildings for
the exercise of their own religion[1] (see Suppl.). No thorough
investigation has yet been made of the state of religion among the
Gauls immediately before and after the irruption of the Germans ;
side by side with the converts there were still, no doubt, some
heathen Gauls; it is difficult therefore to pronounce for either
hypothesis, cases of both kinds may have co-existed. So much for
the doubtful authorities ; but it is not *all* of them that leave us in
any doubt. If the Tanfana temple could be built by Germans, we
can suppose the same of the Alamann, the Saxon and the Frisian
temples; and what was done in the first century, is still more likely
to have been done in the 2nd, 3rd, and 4th.

Built Temples must in early times have been named in a variety
of ways (see Suppl.): OHG. AS. OS. ON. *hof*, aula, atrium ;[2]—
OHG. *halla*, templum (Hymn. 24, 8), AS. *heal*, ON. *höll* (conf. hallr,
lapis, Goth. hallus) ;—OHG. *sal*, ON. *salr*, AS. *sele*, OS. *seli*, aula ;—
AS. *reced*, domus, basilica (Cædm. 145, 11. 150, 16. 219, 23), OS.
rakud (Hel. 114, 17. 130, 20. 144, 4. 155, 20), an obscure word not
found in the other dialects ;—OHG. *pëtapûr*, delubrum (Diut. 1,

---

[1] As the vulgar took Roman fortifications for devil's dikes, it was natural
to associate with Roman castella the notion of idolatry. Rupertus Tuitiensis
(† 1135) in his account of the fire of 1128 that levelled such a castellum at
Deuz, which had been adapted to christian worship, informs us that some
thought it was built by Julius Caesar, others by Constantius and Constantine.
In the emperor Otto's time, St. Mary appears by night to archbishop Heribert:
'surge, et Tuitiense castrum petens, locum in eodem mundari praecipe, ibique
monasterium Deo mihique et omnibus sanctis constitue, ut, ubi quondam
habitavit peccatum et *cultus daemonum*, ibi justitia regnet et memoria
sanctorum,' with more of the like, in the Vita Heriberti cap. 15. Conf. the
fanum at Cologne above, p. 81.

[2] The asylum that atrium and temple offered within their precincts is in
ON. *griðastaðr*, OHG. *frîdhof*, OS. *vrîthob*, Hel. 151, 2, 9. MHG. vrône
vrîthof, Nib. 1795, 2 ; not at all our friedhof [but conn. with frei, free], conf.
Goth. freidjan, OS. frîdôn (parcere). That the constitution of the Old
German sanctuaries was still for the most part heathenish, is discussed in RA.
886-92.

195ᵃ)[1];—to which were afterwards added *pëtahús*, minores ecclesiae (Gl. sletst. 21, 32) and *chirihhá*, AS. *cyrice*. The MHG. poets like to use *bëtehús* of a heathen temple as opposed to a christian church (En. 2695. Barl. 339, 11.28. 342,6. Athis D 93. Herb. 952. Wigal. 8308. Pass. 356, 73. Tit. 3329), so in M. Nethl. *bedehús* (Maerl. 1, 326. 3, 125), much as the Catholics in their own countries do not allow to Protestants a church, but only a bethaus, praying-house (see Suppl.). O. iv. 33, 33 has the periphrase *gotes hûs*, and ii. 4, 52 *druhtînes hûs*. Notker cap. 17 makes no scruple of translating the Lat. fanis by *chîlechon*, just as bishop does duty for heathen priest as well. In the earliest times *temple* was retained, Is. 382. 395. T. 15,4. 193,2. 209,1. Diut. 1, 195.ᵃ

The hut which we are to picture to ourselves under the term fanum or pûr (A.S. bûr, bower) was most likely constructed of logs and twigs round the sacred tree ; a wooden temple of the goddess Zisa will find a place in ch. XIII. With halla and some other names we are compelled to think rather of a stone building.

We see all the christian teachers eager to lay the axe to the sacred trees of the heathen, and fire under their temples. It would almost seem that the poor people's consent was never asked, and the rising smoke was the first thing that announced to them the broken power of their gods. But on a closer study of the details in the less high-flown narratives, it comes out that the heathen were not so tame and simple, nor the christians so reckless. Boniface resolved on hewing down the Thunder-oak after taking counsel with the already converted Hessians, and in their presence. So too the Thuringian princess might not have dared to sit so immovable on her palfrey and give the order to fire the Frankish temple, had not her escort been numerous enough to make head against the heathen. That these did make an armed resistance, appears from Radegund's request, after the fane was burnt down, ut inter se populi pacem firmarent.

In most of the cases it is expressly stated that a church was erected on the site of the heathen tree or temple.[2] In this way the

---

[1] Actum in illo *betapûre* (the church at Fulda) publice, Trad. Fuld. ed. Schannat no. 193. in *bedebur*, Lacombl. no. 412 (A.D. 1162). in *bedebure*, Erhard p. 148 (A.D. 1121). *betbur*, Meyer Zürch. ortsn. 917.

[2] Sulp. Severus (ed. Amst. 1665), p. 458 : Nam ubi fana destruxerat (Martinus), *statim ibi* aut *ecclesias* aut *monasteria construebat*. Dietmar of Merseb. 7, 52, p. 859 (speaking of Bishop Reinbern on Slav. territory, A.D. 1015):

people's habits of thinking were consulted, and they could believe that the old sacredness had not departed from the place, but henceforth flowed from the presence of the true God (see Suppl.).

At the same time we here perceive the reason of the almost entire absence of heathen monuments or their remains, not only in Germany proper, but in the North, where certainly such temples existed, and more plentifully ; conf. in chaps. VI. X. XVI. the temple at Sigtûn, baer î Baldrshaga, and the Nornas' temple. Either these were levelled with the ground to make room for a christian church, or their walls and halls were worked into the new building. We may be slow to form any high opinion of the building art among the heathen Germans, yet they must have understood how to arrange considerable masses of stone, and bind them firmly together. We have evidence of this in the grave-mounds and places of sacrifice still preserved in Scandinavia, partly also in Friesland and Saxony, from which some important inferences might be drawn with regard to the old heathen services, but these I exclude from my present investigation.

The results are these : the earliest seat of heathen worship was in groves, whether on mountain or in pleasant mead ; there the first temples were afterwards built, and there also were the tribunals of the nation.

Fana idolorum destruens incendit, et mare daemonibus cultum, immissis quatuor lapidibus sacro chrismate perunctis, et aqua purgans benedicta, novam Domino . . . plantationem eduxit.—On the conversion of the Pantheon into a church, see Massmann's Eradius 476.

CHAPTER V.

PRIESTS.

The most general term for one who is called to the immediate service of deity (minister deorum, Tac. Germ. 10) is one derived from the name of deity itself. From the Goth. guð (deus) is formed the adj. *gaguds* (godly, pius, εὐσεβής), then *gagudei* (pietas, εὐσέβεια). In OHG. and MHG., I find pius translated *érhaft*, strictly reverens, but also used for venerandus ; our *fromm* has only lately acquired this meaning, the MHG. vrum being simply able, excellent. The God-serving, pious man is in Goth. *gudja* (ἱερεύς, Matt. 8, 4, 27, 1. 63. Mk. 10, 34. 11, 27. 14, 61. Lu. 1, 5. 20, 1. Jo. 18, 19. 22. 19, 6. *ufargudja* (ἀρχιερεύς) Mk 10, 33. *gudjinôn* (ἱερατεύειν), Lu. 1, 8. *gudjinassus* (ἱερατεία) Lu. 1, 9. (see Suppl.).

That these were heathen expressions follows from the accordance of the ON. *goði* (pontifex), *hofs goði* (fani antistes), Egilss. 754. Freys *goði*, Nialss. cap. 96. 117. Fornm. sög. 2, 206. *goðord* (sacerdotium). An additional argument is found in the disappearance of the word from the other dialects, just as our alah disappeared, though the Goths had found alhs unobjectionable. Only a faint vestige appears in the OHG. *cotinc* by which tribunus is glossed, Diut. 1, 187 (Goth. gudiggs ?).—Now as Ulphilas[1] associates *gudja* and *sinista* (πρεσβύτερος, elder, man of standing, priest), a remarkable sentence in Amm. Marcell. 28, 5 informs us, that the high priest of the Burgundians was called *sinisto*: Nam *sacerdos omnium maximus* apud Burgundios vocatur *sinistus*, et est perpetuus,[2] obnoxius discriminibus nullis ut reges. The connexion of priests with the nobility I have discussed in RA. 267-8 (see Suppl.).

More decidedly heathen are the OHG. names for a priest *harugari*, Diut. 1, 514[b],[3] and *parawari*, Diut. 1, 150[a], (being derived from haruc and paro, the words for temple given on p. 68-9, and

---

[1] Strictly the Evangelist ; the translator had no choice.—TRANS.

[2] For the sense of perpetuity attaching to *sin-* in composition, see Gramm. 2, 554-5.

[3] If *haruc* meant wood or rock, and *harugari* priest, they are very like the Ir. and Gael. *carn, cairn,* and *cairneac* priest. O'Brien 77[a].

confirming what I have maintained, that these two terms were synonymous). They can hardly have been coined by the glossist to interpret the Lat. aruspex, they must have existed in our ancient speech.—A priest who sacrificed was named *pluostrari* (see p. 36).

The fact that *cotinc* could bear the sense of tribunus shows the close connexion between the offices of priest and judge, which comes out still more clearly in a term peculiar to the High Germ. dialect: *êwa, êa* signified not only the secular, but the divine law, these being closely connected in the olden times, and equally sacred; hence *êowart, êwart* law-ward, administrator of law, νομικός, AS. ǽ-gleaw, ǽ-láreow, Goth. vitôdafasteis, one learned in the law, K. 55ᵃ 56ᵃ,ᵇ. Gl. Hrab. 974ᵃ. N. ps. 50, 9. *êwarto* of the weak decl. in O.I. 4, 2. 18. 72. *gotes êwarto* I. 4, 23. and as late as the 12th century *êwarte*, Mar. 21. and, without the least reference to the Jewish office, but quite synonymous with priest: der heilige *êwarte*, Reinh. 1705. der bâruc und die *êwarten* sîn, Parz. 13, 25. Wh. 217, 23 of Saracen priests (see Suppl.). The very similar *êosago, êsago* stood for judex, legislator, RA. 781.

The poet of the Heliand uses the expression *wihes ward* (templi custos) 150, 24; to avoid the heathen as well as a foreign term, he adopts periphrases: the *giêrôdo man* (geehrte, honoured), 3, 19. the *frôdo man* (frôt, fruot, prudens) 3, 21. 7, 7. *frôdgumo* (gumo, homo) 5, 23. 6, 2. *godcund gumo* 6, 12, which sounds like gudja above, but may convey the peculiar sense in which Wolfram uses ' der *guote man*'.[1] In the Romance expressions *prudens homo, bonus homo* (prudhomme, bonhomme) there lurks a reference to the ancient jurisprudence.—Once Ulphilas renders ἀρχιερεύς by aúhumists *veiha*, John 18, 13, but never ἱερεύς by veiha.

With christianity there came in foreign words (see Suppl.). The Anglo-Saxons adopted the Lat. sacerdos in abbreviated form: *sacerd*, pl. sacerdas; and Ælfred translates Beda's pontifex and summus pontificum (both of them heathen), 2, 13 by *biscop* and *ealdorbiscop*. T. and O. use in the same sense *bisgof, biscof* (from

---

[1] Parz. 457, 2. 458, 25. 460, 19. 476, 23. 487, 23. The gôdo gumo, Hel. 4, 16 is said of John; ther guato man, O. ii. 12, 21. 49 of Nicodemus; in Ulrich's Lanzelot, an abbot is styled der guote man, 4613. 4639. conf. 3857, 4620 êwarte, 4626 priester. But with this is connected *diu guote frouwe* (v. infra), *i.e.* originally bona socia, so that in the good man also there peeps out something heathenish, heretical. In the great Apologue, the cricket is a clergyman, and is called (Ren. 8125) *preudoms* and Frobert = Fruotbert (see Suppl.).

episcopus), O. I. 4, 4. 27. 47; and the Hel. 150, 24 *biscop.* Later on, *priester* (from presbyter, following the idea of elder and superior), and *pfaffe* (papa) came to be the names most generally used; AS. *preost,* Engl. *priest,* Fr. *prestre,* prêtre; in Veldek, prêster rhymes with mêster, En. 9002.

When Cæsar, bell. Gall. 6, 21, says of the Germans: Neque druides habent qui rebus divinis praesint, neque sacrificiis student, —the statement need not be set down as a mistake, or as contradicting what Tacitus tells us of the German priests and sacrifices. Cæsar is all along drawing a contrast between them and the Gauls. He had described the latter 6, 16 as excessively addicted to sacrifices; and his ' non studere sacrificiis ' must in the connexion mean no more than to make a sparing use of sacrifices. As little did there prevail among the Germans the elaborately finished Druid-system of the Gauls; but they did not want for priests or sacrifices of their own.

The German *priests,* as we have already gathered from a cursory review of their titles, were employed in the worship of the gods and in judging the people. In campaigns, discipline is entrusted to them alone, not to the generals, the whole war being carried on as it were in the presence of the deity: Ceterum neque animadvertere neque vincire nec verberare quidem nisi *sacerdotibus* permissum, non quasi in poenam, nec ducis jussu, sed velut *deo* imperante, quem adesse bellantibus credunt, Germ. 7 (see Suppl.). The succeeding words must also refer to the priests, it is they that take the ' effigies et signa ' from the sacred grove and carry them into battle. We learn from cap. 10, that the *sacerdos civitatis* superintends the divination by rods, whenever it is done for the nation. If the occasion be not a public one, the *paterfamilias* himself can direct the matter, and the priest need not be called in :— a remarkable limitation of the priestly power, and a sign how far the rights of the freeman extended in strictly private life; on the same principle, I suppose, that in very early times covenant transactions could be settled between the parties, without the intervention of the *judge* (RA. 201). Again, when the divination was by the neighing of the white steeds maintained by the state, *priests* accompanied the sacred car, and accredited the transaction. The *priest* alone may touch the car of Nerthus, by him her approaching presence is perceived, he attends her full of reverence, and leads her back at last to her sanctuary, cap. 40. Segimund, the son of Segestes, whom Tac. Ann. 1, 57 calls sacerdos, had been not a German but a Roman priest (apud aram Ubiorum), and after tearing up the alien chaplet (vittas ruperat), had fled to his home.

These few incidental notices of priests give us anything but a complete view of their functions (see Suppl.). On them doubtless devolved also the performance of public prayers, the slaying of victims, the consecration of the kings and of corpses, perhaps of marriages too, the administering of oaths, and many other duties. Of their attire, their insignia and gradations, we hear nothing at all; once Tacitus cap. 43 speaks of a sacerdos *muliebri ornatu*, but gives no details. No doubt the priests formed a separate, possibly a hereditary order, though not so powerful and influential as in Gaul. Probably, beside that sacerdos civitatis, there were higher and lower ones. Only one is cited by name, the Cattian, *i.e.* Hessian, Libes in Strabo ($\Lambda i\beta\eta s$ $\tau\hat{\omega}\nu$ $X\acute{a}\tau\tau\omega\nu$ $i\epsilon\rho\epsilon\acute{v}s$), who with other German prisoners was dragged to Rome in the pompa of Germanicus. Of him Tacitus (so far as we still have him) is silent.[1] Jornandes's statement is worthy of notice, that the Gothic priests were termed *pileati* in distinction from the rest of the people, the *capillati*, and that during sacrifice they had the head covered with a hat; conf. RA. 271 (see Suppl.). Oðinn is called Síðhöttr, broadhat.

The succeeding period, down to the introduction of christianity, scarcely yields any information on the condition of the priesthood in continental Germany; their existence we infer from that of temples and sacrifices. A fact of some importance has been preserved by Beda, Hist. eccl. 2, 13: a heathen priest of the Anglo-Saxons was forbidden to carry arms or to ride a male horse: Non enim licuerat, pontificem sacrorum vel *arma ferre*, vel *praeterquam in equa equitare.* Can this have any connexion with the regulation which, it is true, can be equally explained from the Bible, that christian clergymen, when riding about the country, should be mounted on *asses* and *colts*, not horses (RA. 86-88)? Festus also remarks: *Equo vehi* flamini diali non licebat, ne, si longius digrederetur, sacra neglegerentur (see Suppl.). The transmission of such customs, which have impressed themselves on the habits of

[1] Libes might be Leip, Lêb, O.N. Leifr, Goth. Láibs? A var. lect. has $\Lambda i\beta vs$.

life, would seem to have been quite admissible. I shall try elsewhere to show in detail, how a good deal in the gestures and attitudes prescribed for certain legal transactions savours of priestly
ceremony at sacrifice and prayer (see Suppl.). It is not unlikely,
as heathen sacred places were turned into christian ones, that it
was also thought desirable amongst a newly converted people to
attract their former priests to the service of the new religion.
They were the most cultivated portion of the people, the most
capable of comprehending the christian doctrine and recommending
it to their countrymen. From the ranks of the heathen priesthood
would therefore proceed both the bitterest foes and the warmest
partizans of innovation.[1] The collection of the Letters of Boniface
has a passage lamenting the confusion of christian and heathen
rites, into which foolish or reckless and guilty priests had suffered
themselves to fall.[2] This might have been done in blameless ignorance or from deliberate purpose, but scarcely by any men except
such as were previously familiar with heathenism.

Even the Norse priesthood is but very imperfectly delineated in
the Eddas and sagas. A noteworthy passage in the Ynglîngasaga
cap. 2 which regards the Ases altogether as colonists from Asia,
and their residence Asgard as a great place of sacrifice, makes the
twelve principal Ases *sacrificial priests* (hofgoðar) : skyldu þeir râða
fyrir blôtum ok dômum manna î milli (they had to advise about
sacrifices and dooms) ; and it adds, that they had been named *dîar*
(divi) and *drôttnar* (domini). This representation, though it be but
a conjecture of Snorri's, shows the high estimation in which the
priestly order stood, so that gods themselves were placed at the
head of sacrifices and judgments. But we need not therefore confound dîar and drôttnar with real human priests.

---

[1] Just as the Catholic clergy furnished as well the props as the opponents of
the Reformation. The notable example of a heathen priest abjuring his ancient
faith, and even putting forth his hand to destroy the temple he had once held
sacred, has been quoted from Beda on p. 82. This priest was an English, not
a British one, though Beda, evidently for the mere purpose of more exactly
marking his station, designates him by a Gaelic word Coifi (choibi, choibhidh,
cuimhi, see Jamieson, supplement sub. v. coivie, archdruid). Coifi is not a
proper name, even in Gaelic ; and it is incredible that Eadwine king of Nor-
thumbria should have adopted the British religion, and maintained a British
priest.

[2] Ed. Würdtw. 82. Serr. 140 : Pro sacrilegis itaque presbyteris, ut scripsisti,
qui tauros et hircos diis paganorum immolabant, manducantes sacrificia mortuorum. . . . modo vero incognitum esse, utrum baptizantes trinitatem
dixissent an non, &c.—Connect with this the presbyter Jovi mactans, Ep. 25.

I must draw attention to the fact, that certain men who stood nearer to the gods by services and veneration, and priests first of all, are entitled *friends of the gods*[1] (see Suppl.). Hence such names as *Freysvinr*, AS. *Freáwine, Bregowine* for heroes and kings (see ch. X, Frôwin). According to Eyrbygg. pp. 6, 8, 16, 26, Rôlfr was a *Thôrs vinr ;* he had a hof of that god on a meadow, and was therefore named Thôrrôlfr, he dedicated to him his son Steinn and named him Thôrsteinn, who again dedicated his son Grímr to the god and named him Thôrgrímr ; by this dedicating (gefa), was meant the appointing to the office of goði or priest. And (according to Landn. 2, 23) Hallstein gave his son as goði to Thôrr. Here we see the priestly office running on through several generations (see Suppl.). However, Odysseus is also called $Διΐ$ $φίλος$, Il. 10, 527. Also $Αἴολος$ $φίλος$ $ἀθανάτοισι$ $θεοῖσι$, Od. 10, 2 ; but then in Od. 10, 21 he is $ταμίης$ $ἀνέμων$, director of winds, therefore a priest.

How deeply the priestly office in the North encroached on the administration of justice, need not be insisted on here; in their judicial character the priests seem to have exercised a good deal of control over the people, whereas little is said of their political influence at the courts of kings ; on this point it is enough to read the Nialssaga. In Iceland, even under christianity, the *judges* retained the name and several of the functions of heathen *goðar*, Grâgâs 1, 109-113. 130. 165. Convents, and at the same time state-farmers, especially occupiers of old sanctuaries (see p. 85, note) apparently continue in the Mid. Ages to have peculiar privileges, on which I shall enlarge in treating of weisthümer. They have the keeping of the county *cauldron*, or *weights and measures*, and above all, the *brood-animals*, to which great favour is shown everywhere (see Suppl.).

The goði is also called a *blôtmaðr* (sacrificulus), *bliotr* (Egilssaga p. 209), but all blôtmenn need not be priests ; the word denoted rather any participant in sacrifices, and afterwards, among christians, the heathen in general. It tallies with the passage in Tacitus about the paterfamilias, that any iarl or hersir (baron) might perform sacrifice, though he was not a priest. Saxo Gramm. p. 176

---

[1] The MHG. poets still bestow on hermits and monks the epithets *gotes friunt, gotes degen* (þegn, warrior). In the Renner 24587, St. Jost is called heiliger *gotes kneht* (cniht, servant). [See however ' servus dei, famulus dei ' passim in the lives of saints].

relates of Harald after his baptism: Delubra diruit, *victimarios* proscripsit, *flaminium* abrogavit. By victimarii he must mean blôtmenn, by flamens the priests. He tells us on p. 104, that at the great Upsala sacrifices there were enacted effoeminati corporum motus, scenicique mimorum plausus, ac mollia nolarum crepitacula; Greek antiquity has also something to tell of choruses and dances of priests.

On the clothing of the Norse priests, I have not come across any information. Was there a connexion between them and the poets ? Bragi the god of song has nothing to do with sacrifices ; yet the poetic art was thought a sacred hallowed thing : Oðinn spoke in verse, he and his *hofgoðar* are styled *lioðasmiðir* (song-smiths), Yngl. saga cap. 6. Can *skâld* (poeta, but neut.) be the same as the rare OHG. *sgalto* (sacer) ? Diut. 1, 183. Gl. ker. 69, *scaldo*. Even of christian minstrels soon after the conversion one thing and another is told, that has also come down to us about heathen skâlds.

Poetry borders so closely on divination, the Roman vates is alike songster and soothsayer, and soothsaying was certainly a priestly function. Amm. Marcell. 14, 9 mentions Alamannian *auspices*, and Agathias 2, 6 μάντεις or χρησμολόγοι 'Αλαμαννικοί.

Ulphilas avoids using a Gothic word for the frequently occurring προφήτης, he invariably puts praúfêtus, and for the fem. προφῆτις praúfêteis, Lu. 2, 36 ; why not veitaga and veitagô ? The OHG. and AS. versions are bolder for once, and give *wîzago, wîtega*.[1] Was the priest, when conducting auguries and auspices, a veitaga ? conf. inveitan, p. 29. The ON. term is *spâmaðr* (spae-man), and for prophetess *spâkona* (spae-woman, A.S. wîtegestre). Such diviners were Mîmir and Grîpir. In old French poems they are *devin* (divini, divinatores), which occasionally comes to mean poets : uns *devins*, qui de voir dire est esprovez, Méon 4, 145. ce dient li *devin*, Ren. 7383 ; so Tristr. 1229 : li contor dient (see Suppl.).

We have now to speak of the prophetesses and priestesses of antiquity.—The mundium (wardship) in which a daughter, a sister, a wife stood, appears in the old heathen time not to have excluded

---

[1] The î is become ei in our weissager, MHG. wissage for wîzege ; equally erroneous is our verb weissagen, MHG. wîssagen, Iw. 3097 (OHG. wîzagôn, AS. wîtegian).

them from holy offices, such as sacrificing (see Suppl.), or from a good deal of influence over the people. Tacitus, after telling us how mightily the German women wrought upon the valour of their warriors, and that the Romans for greater security demanded noble maidens from particular nations, adds : Inesse quin etiam *sanctum* et *providum* (feminis) putant[1], nec aut *consilia* earum aspernantur, aut *responsa* negligunt. And before that, Caesar 1. 50 : Quod apud Germanos ea consuetudo esset, ut *matres fam.* eorum *sortibus* et *vaticinationibus* declararent, utrum proelium committi ex usu esset, necne ; eas ita dicere : non esse fas Germanos superare, si ante novam lunam proelio contendissent (see Suppl.).

While history has not preserved the name of one German vates, it has those of several prophetesses. Tac. Germ. 8 : Vidimus sub divo Vespasiano *Veledam* (as a prisoner in his triumph) diu apud plerosque *numinis loco* habitam. Hist. 4, 61 : Ea *virgo* nationis Bructerae, *late imperitabat,* vetere apud Germanos more, quo plerasque feminarum *fatidicas,* et augescente superstitione arbitrantur *deas.* Tuncque *Veledae* auctoritas adolevit ; nam ' prosperas Germanis res et excidium legionum ' praedixerat. In 4, 65, when the people of Cologne were making an alliance with the Tencteri they made the offer : Arbitrum habebimus Civilem et *Veledam* apud quos pacta sancientur. Sic lenitis Tencteris, legati ad Civilem et Veledam missi cum donis, cuncta ex voluntate Agrippinensium perpetravere. Sed coram adire, alloquique *Veledam* negatum. Arcebantur aspectu, quo venerationis plus inesset. Ipsa *edita in turre ;* delectus e propinquis *consulta responsaque* ut internuntius *numinis* portabat. 5, 22 : Praetoriam triremem flumine Luppia donum *Veledae* traxere. 5, 25 ; *Veledam* propinquosque monebat. Her captivity was probably related in the lost chapters of the fifth book.[2] This Veleda had been preceded by others : Sed et olim *Auriniam* (hardly a translation of any Teutonic name, such as the ON. Gullveig, gold-cup ; some have guessed Aliruna, Ölrûn, Albruna) et complures alias venerati sunt, non adulatione nec tamquam facerent *deas,* Germ. 8. A later one, named *Ganna,* is

---

[1] A wild force of phantasy, and the state called clairvoyance, have shown themselves preeminently in women.

[2] Statius silv. I. 4, 90 : Captivaeque preces *Veledae* ; he scans the first two syllables as short, which seems more correct than Dio's Βελῆδα. Zeuss 436 thinks Βελέδα, Βελίδα = *Vilida.* Graff has a n. prop. *Wallodu* 1, 800. I would suggest the Gothic fem. name *Valad*amarca in Jornandes cap. 48, and the Thuringian name of a place *Walada* in Pertz I. 308.

cited by Dio Cassius, 67, 5 ;[1] and in the year 577 Gunthcramnus consulted a woman 'habentem *spiritum phitonis*, ut ei quae erant eventura narraret,' Greg. Tur. 5, 14 (in Aimoin 3, 22 she is mulier *phytonissa, i.e.* πυθώνισσα). One much later still, *Thiota*, who had come to Mentz out of Alamannia, is noticed in the Annals of Fulda, anno 847 (Pertz 1, 365).[2] As Cassandra foretold the fall of Troy, our prophetesses predict the end of the world (v. infra) ; and Tacitus Ann. 14, 32 speaks of British druidesses in these words : Feminae in furore turbatae *adesse exitium* canebant ; conf. 14, 30. But we have the sublimest example before us in the Völuspâ (see Suppl.).

Those grayhaired, barefooted Cimbrian priestesses in Strabo (v. supra, p. 55) in white robe and linen doublet, begirt with brazen clasps, slaughtering the prisoners of war and prophesying from

---

[1] Γάννα (al. Γαῦνα) παρθένος μετὰ τὴν Βελῆδαν ἐν τῇ Κελτικῇ θειάζουσα. conf. the masc. name *Gannascus* in Ann. 11, 18. 19 ; the fem. *Ganna,* dat. Gannane, in a Lothr. urk., as late as 709, Don Calmet, ed. 1728, tom. 1. preuves p. 265.

[2] Traditions, which Hubertus Thomas of Lüttich, private secretary to the Elector Palatine, according to his book De Tungris et Eburonibus 1541, professes to have received from an antiquary Joan. Berger out of an old book (libello vetustissimis characteribus descripto), and which he gives in his treatise De Heidelbergae antiquitatibus, relate as follows : Quo tempore Velleda virgo in Bruchteris imperitabat, *vetula* quaedam, cui nomen *Jettha,* eum collem, ubi nunc est arx Heidelbergensis et *Jetthae collis* etiam nunc nomen habet, inhabitabat, vetustissimumque *phanum* incolebat, cujus fragmenta adhuc nuper vidimus, dum comes palatinus Fridericus factus elector egregiam domum construxit, quam novam aulam appellant. Haec mulier *vaticiniis* inclyta, et quo venerabilior foret, raro in conspectum hominum prodiens, volentibus *consilium* ab ea petere, *de fenestra, non prodeunte vultu, respondebat*. Et inter cetera praedixit, ut inconditis versibus canebat, suo colli a fatis esse datum, ut futuris temporibus regiis viris, quos nominatim recensebat, inhabitaretur et templis celeberrimis ornaretur. Sed ut tandem fabulosae antiquitati valedicamus, lubet adscribere quae is liber de infelici morte ipsius *Jetthae* continebat. Egressa quondam amoenissimo tempore *phanum,* ut deambulatione recrearetur, progrediebatur juxta montes, donec pervenit in locum, quo montes intra convallem declinant et multis locis scaturiebant pulcherrimi fontes, quibus vehementer illa coepit delectari, et assidens ex illis bibebat, cum ecce lupa famelica cum catulis e silva prorupit, quae conspectam mulierem nequicquam divos invocantem dilaniat et frustatim discerpsit, quae casu suo fonti nomen dedit, vocaturque quippe in hodiernum diem *fons luporum* ob amoenitatem loci omnibus notus. It is scarcely worth while trying to settle how much in this may be genuine tradition, and how much the erudition of the 16th century foisted in, to the glorification of the new palace at Heidelberg (= Heidberg) ; the very window on the hill would seem to have been copied from Veleda's tower, though Brynhild too resides upon her rock, and has a *high tower* (Völs. saga, cap. 20, 24, 25 ; conf. *Menglöð,* OHG. Maniklata ?) on the rock, with nine virgins at her knees (Saem. 110. 111). If the enchantress's name were *Heida* instead of Jettha, it would suit the locality better, and perhaps be an echo of the ON. *Heiðr.*

their blood in the sacrificial cauldron, appear as frightful witches by the side of the Bructerian Maid; together with divination they exercise the priestly office. Their minutely described apparel, we may suppose, resembled that of the priests.

While in Tac. Germ. 40 it is a *priest* that attends the goddess, and guides the team of kine in her car; in the North conversely, we have *handmaids* waiting upon gods. From a remarkable story in the Olaf Tryggv. saga (Fornm. sög. 2, 73 seq.), which the christian composer evidently presents in an odious light, we at all events gather that in Sweden a *virgin* attended the car of Freyr on its travels among the people: Frey var fengin til þionosto *kona* ung ok friδ (into Frey's service was taken a woman young and fair), and she is called *kona* Freys. Otherwise a priestess is called *gyδja, hofgyδja,* corresponding to goδi, hofgoδi;[1] see Turiδr hofgyδja, Islend. sög. 1, 205. þorlaug gyδja, Landn. 1, 21. Steinvör and Fridgerδr, Sagabibl. 1, 99. 3, 268.

But the Norse authorities likewise dwell less on the priestly functions of women, than on their higher gift, as it seems, of divination: *Perita augurii* femina, Saxo Gram. 121. Valdamarr konûngr âtti môδur miök gamla ok örvasa, svâ at hun lâ î rekkju, en þo var hun framsŷn *af Fitons anda,* sem margir heiδnir menn (King V. had a mother very old and feeble, so that she lay in bed, and there was she seized by a spirit of Python, like many heathen folk), Fornm. sög. 1, 76.—Of like import seems to be a term which borders on the notion of a higher and supernatural being, as in the case of Veleda ; and that is *dîs* (nympha, numen). It may be not accidental, that the spâkona in several instances bears the proper name *Thôrdîs* (Vatnsd. p. 186 seq. Fornm. sög. 1, 255. Islend. sög. 1, 140. Kormakkss. p. 204 seq.) ; *dîs* however, a very early word, which I at one time connected with the Gothic filudeisei (astutia, dolus), appears to be no other than our OHG. *itis,* OS. *idis,* AS. *ides* (femina, nympha).—As famous and as widely spread was the term *völva,*[2] which first denotes any magic-wielding soothsayeress (Vatnsd. p. 44. Fornm. sög. 3, 214. Fornald. sög. 2, 165-6. 506), and is afterwards attached to a particular mythic *Völva,* of whom one of the oldest Eddic songs, the *Völuspâ,* treats. Either völu

---

[1] Can our *götte, gothe, goth* for godmother (taufpathin, susceptrix e sacro fonte) be the survival of an old heathen term? Morolt 3184 has *gode* of the baptized virgin.

[2] The Slavic *volkhv* magus.—TRANS.

stands here for völvu, or the claim of the older form *Vala* may be asserted ; to each of them would correspond an OHG. Walawa or Wala, which suggests the Walada above, being only derived in a different way.   In the saga Eiríks rauða we come upon *Thorbiörg*, the little Vala (Edda Sæm. Hafn. 3, 4).—*Heiðr* is the name not only of the völva in the Edda (Sæm. 4[b], conf. 118[b]) but also of the one in the Orvarodssaga (conf. Sagabibl. 3, 155).—*Hyndla* (canicula) is a prophetess that rides on wolves, and dwells in a cave.—I guess also that the virgins *Thorgerðr* and *Irpa* (Fornm. sög. 2, 108. 3, 100. 11, 134-7. 142. 172), to whom all but divine honours were paid, and the title of hörgabrúðr (nympha lucorum) and even the name of guð (numen) was accorded, Nialss. cap. 89, are not to be excluded from this circle.   So in the *valkyrs*, beside their godhood, there resides somewhat of the priestly, *e.g.* their virginity (see ch. XVI and Suppl.).

We shall return to these 'gleg' and 'wise' women (and they have other names besides), who, in accordance with a deeply marked feature of our mythology, trespass on the superhuman. Here we had to set forth their connexion with sacrifice, divination and the priesthood.

CHAPTER VI.

GODS.

Now, I think, we are fully prepared for the inquiry, whether real gods can be claimed for Germany in the oldest time. All the branches of our language have the same general name for deity and have retained it to the present day; all, or at any rate most of them, so far as the deficiency of documents allows the chain of evidence to be completed, show the same or but slightly varying terms for the heathen notions of worship, sacrifice, temples and priesthood. Above all there shines forth an unmistakable analogy between the Old Norse terminology and the remains, many centuries older, of the other dialects: the Norse æsir, blôta, hörgr, goði were known long before, and with the same meanings, to the Goths, Alamanns, Franks and Saxons. And this identity or similarity extends beyond the words to the customs themselves: in sacred groves the earliest human and animal victims were offered, priests conducted sacrifices and divinations, 'wise women' enjoyed all but divine authority.

The proof furnished by the sameness of language is of itself sufficient and decisive. When the several divisions of a nation speak one and the same language, then, so long as they are left to their own nature and are not exposed to violent influences from without, they always have the same kind of belief and worship.

The Teutonic race lies midway between Celts, Slavs, Lithuanians, Finns, all of them populations that acknowledge gods, and practise a settled worship. The Slav nations, spread over widely distant regions, have their principal gods in common; how should it be otherwise in Teutondom?

As for demanding proofs of the *genuineness* of Norse mythology, we have really got past that now. All criticism cripples and annihilates itself, that sets out with denying or doubting what is treasured up in song and story born alive and propagated amongst an entire people, and which lies before our eyes. Criticism can but collect and arrange it, and unfold the materials in their historical sequence.

Then the only question that can fairly be raised, is : Whether
the gods of the North, no longer disputable, hold good for the rest
of Teutondom ? To say yea to the question as a whole, seems,
from the foregoing results of our inquiry, altogether reasonable
and almost necessary.

A negative answer, if it knew what it was about, would try to
maintain, that the circle of Norse gods, in substance, were formerly
common to all Germany, but by the earlier conversion were extinguished and annihilated here. But a multitude of exceptions and
surviving vestiges would greatly limit the assertion, and materially
alter what might be made out of the remainder.

In the meanwhile a denial has been attempted of quite another
kind, and the opinion upheld, that those divinities have never
existed at all in Germany proper, and that its earliest inhabitants
knew nothing better than a gross *worship of nature without gods*.

This view, drawing a fundamental distinction between German
and Scandinavian heathenism, and misapprehending all the clues
which discover themselves to unprejudiced inquiry as infallible
evidence of the unity of two branches of a nation, lays special stress
upon a few statements on the nature of the heathen faith, dating
from about the sixth century and onwards. These for the most
part proceed from the lips of zealous christians, who did not at all
concern themselves to understand or faithfully portray the paganism
they were assailing, whose purpose was rather to set up a warning
against the grosser manifestations of its cultus as a detestable abomination. It will be desirable to glance over the principal passages
in their uniformity and one-sidedness.

Agathias (✝ before 582), himself a newly converted Greek, who
could only know from christianly coloured reports what he had
heard about the distant Alamanns, thus exhibits the Alamannic
worship as opposed to the Frankish : δένδρα τε γάρ τινα ἱλάσκονται
καὶ ῥεῖθρα ποταμῶν καὶ λόφους καὶ φάραγγας, καὶ τούτοις ὥσπερ
ὅσια δρῶντες 28, 4. Then follow the words quoted on p. 47 about
their equine sacrifices.

But his contrast to the Franks breaks down at once, when
we hear almost exactly the same account of *them* from the lips of
their first historian Gregory : Sed haec generatio fanaticis semper
cultibus visa est obsequium praebuisse, nec prorsus agnovere Deum,
sibique silvarum atque aquarum, avium bestiarumque et aliorum

quoque elementorum finxere formas, ipsasque ut deum colere eisque sacrificia delibare consueti. Greg. Tur. 2, 10.—Similarly, Einhard (Æginhard) in Vita Caroli cap. 7, about the Saxons: Sicut omnes fere Germaniam incolentes nationes et natura feroces et cultui daemonum dediti, nostraeque religioni contrarii.—Ruodolf of Fuld, after quoting Tacitus and Einhard, adds (Pertz 2, 676): Nam et frondosis arboribus fontibusque venerationem exhibebant;[1] and then mentions the Irminsûl, which I shall deal with hereafter (see Suppl.).—Lastly, Helmold 1, 47 affirms of the Holsteiners: Nihil de religione nisi nomen tantum christianitatis habentes; nam lucorum et fontium ceterarumque superstitionum multiplex error apud eos habetur . . . Vicelinus . . . lucos et omnes ritus sacrilegos destruens, &c.'

Conceived in exactly the same spirit are the prohibitions of heathenish and idolatrous rites in decrees of councils and in laws. Concil. Autissiod. anno 586, can. 3: Non licet inter sentes aut ad arbores sacrivos vel ad fontes vota exsolvere; conf. Concil. Turon. II. anno 566, can. 22.—Leges Liutpr. 6, 30: Simili modo et qui ad arborem, quam rustici sanguinum (al. sanctivam, sacrivam) vocant, atque ad fontanas adoraverit.—Capit. de partibus Sax. 20: Si quis ad fontes aut arbores vel lucos votum fecerit, aut aliquid more gentilium obtulerit et ad honorem daemonum comederit. And the converters, the christian clergy, had for centuries to pour out their wrath against the almost ineradicable folly.—It is sufficient merely to allude to the sermons of Caesarius episcopus Arelatensis († 542) ' Contra sacrilegos et aruspices, contra kalendarum quoque paganissimos ritus, contraque augures lignicolas, fonticolas,' Acta Bened. sec. 1, p. 668.

All these passages contain, not an untruth, yet not the whole truth. That German heathenism was destitute of gods, they cannot possibly prove; for one thing, because they all date from periods when heathenism no longer had free and undisturbed sway, but had been hotly assailed by the new doctrine, and was wellnigh overmastered. The general exercise of it had ceased, isolated partizans cherished it timidly in usages kept up by stealth; at the same time there were christians who in simplicity or error continued to practise superstitious ceremonies by the side of christian ones. Such doings, not yet extinct here and there among the

---

[1] Adam of Bremen again copies Ruodolf, Pertz 9, 286.

common people, but withdrawn from all regulating guidance by heathen priests, could not fail soon to become vulgarized, and to appear as the mere dregs of an older faith, which faith we have no right to measure by them. As we do not fail to recognise in the devils and witches of more modern times the higher purer fancies of antiquity disguised, just as little ought we to feel any scruple about tracing back the pagan practices in question to the untroubled fountainhead of the olden time. Prohibitions and preachings kept strictly to the practical side of the matter, and their very purpose was to put down these last hateful remnants of the false religion. A sentence in Cnut's AS. laws (Schmid 1, 50) shows, that fountain and tree worship does not exclude adoration of the gods themselves: Hæðenscipe bið, þæt man deofolgild weorðige, þæt is, þæt man weorðige hæðene godas, and sunnan oððe mônan, fŷre oððe flôðwæter, wyllas oððe stânas oððe æniges cynnes wudutreowa; conf. Homil. 1, 366. Just so it is said of Olaf the Saint, Fornm sög. 5, 239, that he abolished the heathen sacrifices and gods: Ok mörg önnur (many other) blôtskapar skrîmsl, bæði hamra ok hörga, skôga, vötn ok trê ok öll önnur blôt, bæði meiri ok minni.

But we can conceive of another reason too, why on such occasions the heathen gods, perhaps still unforgotten, are passed over in silence: christian priests avoided uttering their names or describing their worship minutely. It was thought advisable to include them all under the general title of demons or devils, and utterly uproot their influence by laying an interdict on whatever yet remained of their worship. The Merseburg poems show how, by way of exception, the names of certain gods were still able to transmit themselves in formulas of conjuring.

Pictures of heathenism in its debasement and decay have no right to be placed on a level with the report of it given by Tacitus from five to eight centuries before, when it was yet in the fulness of its strength. If the adoration of trees and rivers still lingering in the habits of the people no longer bears witness to the existence of gods, is it not loudly enough proclaimed in those imperfect and defective sketches by a Roman stranger? When he expressly tells us of a *deus* terra editus, of heroes and descendants of the god (plures *deo* ortos), of the god who rules in war (velut *deo* imperante), of the names of gods (*deorum* nominibus) which the people transferred to sacred groves, of the priest who cannot begin a divination

without invoking the gods (precatus *deos*) and who regards himself
as a servant of the gods (ministros *deorum*), of a *regnator omnium
deus*, of the gods of Germany (Germaniae *deos* in aspectu, Hist. 5,
17), of the *diis patriis* to whom the captured signa Romana were
hung up (Ann. 1, 59); when he distinguishes between *penetrales*
Germaniae *deos* or *dii penates* (Ann. 2, 10. 11, 16), *communes dii*
(Hist. 4, 64), and *conjugales dii* (Germ. 18); when he even distinguishes individual gods, and tries to suit them with Roman names,
and actually names (interpretatione Romana) a Mars, Mercurius,
Hercules, Castor and Pollux, Isis, nay, has preserved the German
appellations of the deus terra editus and of his son, and of a goddess,
the terra mater; how is it possible to deny that at that time the
Germans worshipped veritable gods? How is it possible, when we
take into account all the rest that we know of the language, the
liberty, the manners, and virtues of the Germani, to maintain the
notion that, sunk in a stolid fetishism, they cast themselves down
before logs and puddles, and paid to them their simple adoration?

The opinion of Cæsar,[1] who knew the Germans more super-
ficially than Tacitus a hundred and fifty years later, cannot be
allowed to derogate from the truth. He wants to contrast our
ancestors with the Gauls, with whom he had had more familiar
converse; but the personifications of the sun, fire, and the moon,
to which he limits the sum total of their gods, will hardly bear even
a forced 'interpretatio Romana'. If in the place of sun and moon
we put Apollo and Diana, they at once contradict that deeply rooted
peculiarity of the Teutonic way of thinking, which conceives of the
sun as a female, and of the moon as a male being, which could not
have escaped the observation of the Roman, if it had penetrated
deeper. And Vulcan, similar to the Norse Loki, but one of those
divinities of whom there is least trace to be found in the rest of
Teutondom, had certainly less foundation than the equally visible
and helpful deities of the nourishing earth, and of the quickening,
fish-teeming, ship-sustaining water. I can only look upon Cæsar's
statements as a half-true and roughcast opinion, which, in the face
of the more detailed testimony of Tacitus, hardly avails to cast a

---

[1] Deorum numero eos solos ducunt, quos cernunt, et quorum opibus aperte
juvantur, *Solem et Vulcanum et Lunam;* reliquos ne fama quidem acceperunt
B.G. 6, 21. Compare with this B.G. 4, 7 where the Usipetes and Tenchtheri
say to Cæsar: Sese unis Suevis concedere, quibus ne *dii* quidem *immortales*
pares esse possint.

doubt on other gods, much less to prove a bare worship of elements among the Germani.

All the accounts that vouch for the early existence of individual gods, necessarily testify at the same time to their great *number* and their mutual relationship. When Procopius ascribes a πολὺς θεῶν ὅμιλος to the Heruli, this 'great host' must also be good for the Goths, just those of whom we know the fewest particulars, and for all the Germans together. Jornandes would have us believe that Diceneus was the first to make the Goths acquainted with gods, cap. 11 : Elegit ex eis tunc nobilissimos prudentiores viros, quos theologiam instruens *numina quaedam* et *sacella* venerari suasit ; here evidently we see the ruler who promoted the service of particular gods. But that Jornandes himself credited his Goths with unmistakably native gods, is plain from cap. 10 : Unde et sacerdotes Gothorum aliqui, illi qui pii vocabantur, subito patefactis portis cum citharis et vestibus candidis obviam sunt egressi *paternis diis*, ut sibi propitii Macedones repellerent voce supplici modulantes. The fact here mentioned may even have been totally alien to the real Goths, but anyhow we gather from it the opinion of Jornandes. And if we also want evidence about a race lying quite at the opposite extremity of Germany, one that clung with great fidelity to their old-established faith, we have it in the Lex Frisionum, addit. tit. 13, where the subject is the penalty on temple-breakers : Immolatur *diis* quorum templa violavit.

We have now arrived at the following result. In the first century of our era the religion of the Germans rested mainly upon gods ; a thousand or twelve hundred years later, among the northern section of the race, which was the last to exchange the faith of its fathers for a new one, the old system of gods is preserved the most perfectly. Linked by language and unbroken tradition to either extremity of heathenism, both its first appearance in history and its fall, stands central Germany from the fifth to the ninth century. During this period the figures of the heathen gods, in the feeble and hostile light thrown upon them by the reports of recent converts, come before us faded and indistinct, but still always as gods.

I must here repeat, that Tacitus knows no *simulacrum* of German gods, no image [1] moulded in human shape ; what he had

---

[1] Grk. ἄγαλμα, signum, statue ; Goth. *manleika*, OHG. *manalîhho*, ON. *líkneski* (see Suppl.) ; can the Sloven. malik, idol, have sprung from manleika?

stated generally in cap. 9, he asserts of a particular case in cap. 43, and we have no ground for disbelieving his assertion. The existence of real statues at that time in Germany, at least in the parts best known to them, would hardly have escaped the researches of the Romans. He knows of nothing but *signa* and *formas*, apparently carved and coloured, which were used in worship as symbols, and on certain occasions carried about; probably they contained some reference to the nature and attributes of the several deities. The model of a boat, *signum* in modum liburnae figuratum (cap. 9), betokened the god of sailing, the *formae* aprorum (cap. 45) the god to whom the boar was consecrated; and in the like sense are to be taken the ferarum imagines on trees and at certain sacrifices (see Suppl.). The vehiculum veste contectum of the goddess Earth will be discussed further on.

The absence of statues and temples, considering the impotence of all artistic skill at the period, is a favourable feature of the German cultus, and pleasing to contemplate. But it by no means follows that in the people's fancy the gods were destitute of a form like the human; without this, gods invested with all human attributes, and brought into daily contact with man, would be simply inconceivable. If there was any German poetry then in existence, which I would sooner assert than deny, how should the poets have depicted their god but with a human aspect?

Attempts to fashion images of gods, and if not to carve them out of wood or stone, at least to draw and paint them, or quite roughly to bake them of dough (p. 63), might nevertheless be made at any period, even the earliest; it is possible too, that the interior parts of Germany, less accessible to the Romans, concealed here and there temples, statues and pictures. In the succeeding centuries, however, when temples were multiplied, images also, to fill their spaces, may with the greatest probability be assumed.

The terminology, except where the words *simulacra*, *imagines*, which leave no room for doubt, are employed, makes use of several

---

Bohem. malik, the little finger, also Thumbkin, Tom Thumb? which may have to do with idol. [In the Slavic languages, màl = little, s-mall]. Other OHG. terms are *avará*; *piladi*, *pilidi* (bild) effigies or imago in general; in the Mid. Ages they said, for making or forming (p. 23), ein *bilde giezen*, eine schœne juncfrouwen *ergiezen*, Cod. Vindob. 428, num. 211, without any reference to metal-casting; ein *bilde mezzen*, Troj. 19626, *mezzen*, Misc. 2, 186. On the Lith. *balwonas*, idolum, statua, conf. Pott de ling. Litth. 2, 51, Russ. *bolván*, Hung. *balvany;* Russ. *kumîr*, idol, both lit. and fig. (object of affection).

terms whose meaning varies, passing from that of temple to that of
image, just as we saw the meaning of grove mixed up with that of
numen.   If, as is possible, that word *alah* originally meant rock or
stone (p. 67), it might easily, like *haruc* and *wih*, melt into the
sense of altar and statue, of ara, fanum, idolum.   In this way the
OHG. *abcut*, *abcuti* (Abgott, false god) does signify both fana and
idola or statuae, Diut. 1, 497^b 513^a 515^a 533^b, just as our *götze* is at
once the false god and his image and his temple (see above, p. 15.
Gramm. 3, 694).   *Idolum* must have had a similar ambiguity,.
where it is not expressly distinguished from delubrum, fanum and
templum.   In general phrases such as idola colere, idola adorare,.
idola destruere, we cannot be sure that images are meant, for just
as often and with the same meaning we have adorare fana, destruere fana.   Look at the following phrases taken from OHG.
glosses : *abcuti* wîhero stetio, fana excelsorum, Diut. 1, 515^a.   *abcut*
in heilagêm stetim, fana in excelsis, Diut. 1, 213^a. *steinînu zeihan*
inti *abcuti*, titulos et statuas, Diut. 1, 497^b.   *altara* inti *manalîhun*
inti haruga, aras et statuas et lucos, Diut. 1, 513^b.   *afgoda* began-
gana, Lacombl. arch. 1, 11.—Saxo Gram. often uses *simulacra* for
idols, pp. 249, 320-1-5-7. The statement in Aribonis vita S.
Emmerammi (Acta sanct. Sept. 6, 483) : ' tradidero te genti
Saxonum, *quae tot idolorum cultor existit*' is undeniable evidence
that the heathen Saxons in the 8th century served *many false gods.*
(Aribo, bishop of Freisingen in the years 764-783).   The vita
Lebuini, written by Hucbald between 918-976, says of the ancient
Saxons (Pertz 2, 361-2) : Inservire *idolorum* cultibus . . .
numinibus suis vota solvens ac sacrificia . . . *simulacra* quae
deos esse putatis, quosque venerando colitis.   Here, no doubt,
statues must be meant (see Suppl.).

In a few instances we find the nobler designation *deus* still
employed, as it had been by Tacitus : Cumque idem rex (Eadwine
in 625) gratias ageret *diis suis* pro nata sibi filia, Beda 2, 9.

The following passages testify to visible representations of gods ;
they do not condescend to describe them, and we are content to
pick up hints by the way.

The very earliest evidence takes us already into the latter half
of the 4th century, but it is one of the most remarkable.   Sozomen,
Hist. eccl. 6, 37, mentions the manifold dangers that beset Ulphilas
among the heathen Goths : While the barbarians were yet heathens

(ἔτι τῶν βαρβάρων ἑλληνικῶς θρησκευόντων)—ἑλληνικῶς here
means in heathen fashion, and θρησκεύειν (to worship) is presently
described more minutely, when the persecution of the Christians
by Athanaric is related—Athanaric, having set the *statue* (evidently
of the Gothic deity) *on a waggon* (ξόανον ἐφ' ἁρμαμάξης ἑστὼς),
ordered it to be carried round to the dwellings of those suspected
of christianity; if they refused to fall down and sacrifice (προσκυνεῖν καὶ θύειν), their houses were to be fired over their heads. By
ἁρμάμαξα is understood a covered carriage; is not this exactly the
vehiculum veste contectum, in which the goddess, herself unseen, was
carried about (Tac. Germ. 40) ? Is it not the *vagn* in which Freyr
and his priestess sat, when in holy days he journeyed round among
the Swedish people (Fornm. sög. 2, 74-5) ? The people used to
carry about *covered images of gods* over the fields, by which fertility
was bestowed upon them.[1] Even the *karrâschen* in our poems of
the Mid. Ages, with Saracen gods in them, and the *carroccio* of the
Lombard cities (RA. 263-5) seem to be nothing but a late reminiscence of these primitive gods'-waggons of heathenism. The Roman,
Greek and Indian gods too were not without such carriages.

What Gregory of Tours tells us (2, 29-31) of the baptism of
Chlodovich (Clovis) and the events that preceded it, is evidently
touched up, and the speeches of the queen especially I take to be
fictitious; yet he would hardly have put them in her mouth, if it
were generally known that the Franks had no gods or statues at all.
Chrothild (Clotilda) speaks thus to her husband, whom she is trying to prepossess in favour of baptism : Nihil sunt *dii quos colitis*,
qui neque sibi neque aliis poterunt subvenire; sunt enim aut ex
lapide aut ex *ligno* aut ex *metallo* aliquo *sculpti*, nomina vero, quae
eis indidistis, homines fuere, non dii. Here she brings up *Saturnus*
and *Jupiter*, with arguments drawn from classical mythology;
and then : Quid *Mars Mercurius*que potuere ? qui potius sunt
magicis artibus praediti quam divini numinis potentiam habuere.
Sed ille magis coli debet qui coelum et terram, mare et omnia quae
in eis sunt, verbo ex non extantibus procreavit, &c. Sed cum haec
regina diceret, nullatenus ad credendum regis animus movebatur,
sed dicebat : *Deorum nostrorum* jussione cuncta creantur ac pro-

---

[1] De *simulacro* quod per campos portant (Indic. superstit. cap. 28) ; one vita
S. Martini cap. 9 (Surius 6, 252) : Quia esset haec Gallorum rusticis consuetudo, *simulacra daemonum, candido tecta velamine*, misera per agros suos cir-
cumferre dementia.

deunt; deus vero vester nihil posse manifestatur,.et quod magis est,
nec *de deorum genere esse probatur* (that sounds German enough!).
When their little boy dies soon after receiving christian baptism,
Chlodovich remarks: Si in nomine *deorum meorum* puer fuisset
dicatus, vixisset utique; nunc autem, quia in nomine dei vestri
baptizatus est, vivere omnino non potuit.—So detailed a report of
Chlodovich's heathenism, scarcely a hundred years after the event,
and from the mouth of a well instructed priest, would be absurd, if
there were no truth at the bottom of it. When once Gregory had
put his Latin names of gods in the place of the Frankish (in which
he simply followed the views and fashion of his time), he would as
a matter of course go on to surround those names with the appropriate Latin myths; and it is not to be overlooked, that the four
·deities named are all gods of the days of the week, the very kind
which it was quite customary to identify with native gods. I
think myself entitled therefore, to quote the passage as proving at
least the existence of images of gods among the Franks (see Suppl.).

The narrative of an incident from the early part of the 7th
century concerns Alamannia. Columban and St. Gallus in 612
came upon a seat of idolatry at Bregenz on the Lake of Constance:
Tres ergo *imagines aereas et deauratas* superstitiosa *gentilitas*
ibi colebat, quibus magis quam Creatori mundi vota reddenda
credebat. So says the Vita S. Galli (Pertz 2, 7) written in the
course of the next (8th) century. A more detailed account is given
by Walafrid Strabo in his Vita S. Galli (acta Bened. sec. 2. p. 233):
Egressi de navicula oratorium in honore S. Aureliae constructum
adierunt. . . . Post orationem, cum per gyrum oculis cuncta
lustrassent, placuit illis qualitas et situs locorum, deinde oratione
praemissa circa oratorium mansiunculas sibi fecerunt. Repererunt
autem in templo *tres imagines aereas deauratas parieti affixas*,[1] quas
populus, dimisso altaris sacri cultu, adorabat, et *oblatis sacrificiis*
·dicere consuevit: isti sunt *dii veteres* et *antiqui hujus loci tutores,*
quorum solatio et nos et nostra perdurant usque in praesens. . . .
Cumque ejusdem templi solemnitas ageretur, venit multitudo non
minima promiscui sexus et aetatis, non tantum propter festivitatis
honorem, verum etiam ad videndos peregrinos, quos cognoverant

---

[1] So then, in a church really christian, these old heathen *gods' images* had
been *let into the wall*, probably to conciliate the people, who were still attached
to them? There are several later instances of this practice, conf. Ledebur's
archiv. 14, 363. 378. Thür. mitth. VI. 2, 13 (see Suppl.).

advenisse. . . . Jussu venerandi abbatis (Columbani) Gallus
coepit viam veritatis ostendere populo. . . . et in conspectu
omnium arripiens *simulacra*, et lapidibus *in frusta comminuens pro-*
jecit in lacum. His visis nonnulli conversi sunt ad dominum.—Here
is a strange jumble of heathen and christian worship. In an
oratory built in honour of St. Aurelia, three heathen statues still
stand against the wall, to which the people continue to sacrifice,
without going near the christian altar: to them, these are still their
old tutelary deities. After the evangelist has knocked the images
to pieces and thrown them into Lake Constance, a part of these
heathen turn to christianity. Probably in more places than one
the earliest christian communities degenerated in like manner,
owing to the preponderance of the heathen multitude and the
supineness of the clergy. A doubt may be raised, however, as to
whether by these heathen gods are to be understood Alamannish, or
possibly Roman gods ? Roman paganism in a district of the old
Helvetia is quite conceivable, and dii tutores loci sounds almost like
the very thing. On the other hand it must be remembered, that
Alamanns had been settled here for three centuries, and any other
worship than theirs could hardly be at that time the popular one. That
sacrifice to Woden on the neighbouring Lake of Zurich[1] (supra, p. 56)
mentioned by Jonas in his older biography of the two saints,
was altogether German. Lastly, the association of *three* divinities to be jointly worshipped stands out a prominent feature in
our domestic heathenism; when the Romans dedicated a temple to
several deities, their images were not placed side by side, but in
separate cellae (chapels).—Ratpert (Casus S. Galli, Pertz 2, 61)
seems to have confounded the two events, that on L. Zurich, and
the subsequent one at Bregenz: Tucconiam (to Tuggen) advenerunt,
quae est ad caput lacus Turicini, ubi cum consistere vellent, popu-
lumque ab errore demonum revocare (nam adhuc *idolis immolabant*),
Gallo *idola vana confringente et in lacum vicinum demergente*, populus
in iram conversus. . . . sanctos exinde pepulerunt. Inde iter
agentes pervenerunt ad castrum quod Arbona nuncupatur, juxta

---

[1] Curiously, Mone (Gesch. des heid. 1, 171-5) tries to put this Woden-
worship at Tuggen upon the Heruli, who had never been heard of there, instead
of the Alamanns, because Jonas says : Sunt inibi *vicinae* nationes Suevorum.
But this means simply those settled thereabouts ; there was no occasion to speak
of distant ones. Columban was staying in a place not agreeable to himself, in
order to convert the heathen inhabitants ; and by Walafrid's description too,
the district lies *infra* partes Alamanniae, where *intra* would do just as well.

lacum potamicum, ibique a Willimaro presbytero honorifice suscepti, septem dies cum gaudio permanserunt. Qui a sanctis interrogatus, si sciret locum in solitudine illorum proposito congruum, ostendit eis locum jocundissimum ad inhabitandum nomine Brigantium. Ibique reperientes *templum* olim christianae religioni dedicatum, nunc autem *demonum imaginibus* pollutum, mundando et consecrando in pristinum restituerunt statum, atque pro statuis quas ejecerunt, sanctae Aureliae reliquias ibidem collocaverunt.—By this account also the temple is first of all christian, and afterwards occupied by the heathen (Alamanns), therefore not an old Roman one. That *Woden's* statue was one of those idola vana that were broken to pieces, may almost be inferred from Jonas's account of the beer-sacrifice offered to him. Ratpert's cantilena S. Galli has only the vague words:

　　　　Castra de Turegum adnavigant Tucconium,

　　　Docent fidem gentem, *Jovem* linquunt *ardentem*.

This Jupiter on fire, from whom the people apostatized, may very well be *Donar* (Thunar, Thor), but his statue is not alluded to. According to Arx (on Pertz 2, 61), Eckehardus IV. quotes '*Jovis et Neptuni* idola,' but I cannot find the passage; conf. p. 122 Ermoldus Nigellus on Neptune. It is plain that the three statues have to do with the idolatry on L. Constance, not with that on L. Zurich; and if Mercury, Jupiter and Neptune stood there together, the first two at all events may be easily applied to German deities. In ch. VII, I will impart my conjecture about Neptune. But I think we may conclude from all this, that our *tres imagines* have a better claim to a German origin, than those *imagines lapideae* of the Luxovian forest, cited on p. 83[1].

---

[1] Two narratives by Gregory of Tours on statues of Diana in the Treves country, and of Mercury and Mars in the south of Gaul, though they exclude all thought of German deities, yet offer striking comparisons. Hist. 8, 15 : Deinde territorium Trevericae urbis expetii, et in quo nunc estis *monte* habitaculum, quod cernitis, proprio labore construxi ; reperi tamen hic *Dianae simulacrum*, quod populus hic incredulus quasi *deum adorabat. columnam* etiam statui, in qua cum grandi cruciatu sine ullo pedum stabam tegmine. . . . Verum ubi ad me multitudo vicinarum civitatum confluere coepit, praedicabam jugiter, nihil esse *Dianam*, nihil *simulacra*, nihilque quae eis videbatur exerceri cultura : indigna etiam esse ipsa, quae inter pocula luxuriasque profluas cantica proferebant, sed potius deo omnipotenti, qui coelum fecit ac terram, dignum sit sacrificium laudis impendere. orabam etiam saepius, ut *simulacro* dominus diruto dignaretur populum ab hoc errore discutere. Flexit domini misericordia mentem rusticam, ut inclinaret aurem suam in verba oris mei, ut scilicet relictis idolis dominum sequeretur, (et) tunc convocatis quibusdam ex eis *simulacrum* hoc *immensum*, quod elidere propria virtute non poteram, cum

The chief authority for images of gods among the Saxons is the famous passage in Widekind of Corvei (1, 12), where he relates their victory over the Thuringians on the R. Unstrut (circ. 530), ‘ut majorum memoria prodit’: Mane autem facto, ad orientalem portam (of castle Schidungen) ponunt aquilam, *aram*que *victoriae* construentes, secundum errorem paternum, sacra sua propria veneratione venerati sunt, nomine *Martem, effigie columnarum* imitantes *Herculem,* loco Solem quem Graeci appellant *Apollinem.*—This important witness will have to be called up again in more than one connexion.

To the Corvei annals, at year 1145, where the Eresburg is spoken of, the following is added by a 12th century hand (Pertz 5, 8 note): Hec eadem Eresburg est corrupto vocabulo dicta, quam et Julius Cesar Romano imperio subegit, quando et Arispolis nomen habuit ab eo qui *Aris* Greca designatione ac *Mars* ipse dictus est Latino famine. *Duobus* siquidem *idolis* hec dedita fuit, id est *Aris,* qui *urbis meniis insertus,* quasi dominator dominantium, et *Ermis,* qui et *Mercurius* mercimoniis insistentibus colebatur in forensibus.—According to this, a statue of Mars seems to have stood on the town-wall.

That the Frisian temples contained images of gods, there seems to be sufficient evidence. It is true, the passage about Fosite (p. 84) mentions only fana dei ; we are told that Wilibrord laid violent hands on the sacred fountain, not that he demolished any image.

eorum adjutorio possem eruere ; jam enim reliqua *sigillorum* (the smaller figures) quae faciliora erant, ipse confregeram. Convenientibus autem multis ad hanc *Dianae statuam,* missis funibus trahere coeperunt, sed nihil labor eorum proficere poterat. Then came prayers ; egressusque post orationem ad operarios veni, adprehensumque funem ut primo ictu trahere coepimus, protinus *simulacrum ruit in terram, confractumque cum malleis ferreis in pulverem redegi.* So images went to the ground, whose contemplation we should think very instructive now. This Diana was probably a mixture of Roman and Gallic worship ; there are inscriptions of a *Diana arduinna* (Bouquet 2, 319).—The second passage stands in Mirac. 2, 5 : Erat autem haud procul a cellula, quam sepulchrum, martyris (Juliani Arvernensis) haec matrona construxerat (in vico Brivatensi), *grande delubrum,* ubi in *columna altissima simulachrum Martis Mercuriique colebatur.* Cumque delubri illius festa a gentilibus agerentur ac mortui mortuis thura deferrent, medio e vulgo commoventur pueri duo in scandalum, nudatoque unus gladio alterum appetit trucidandum. The boy runs to the saint's cell, and is saved. Quarta autem die, cum gentilitas vellet iterum diis exhibere libamina, the christian priests offer a fervent prayer to the martyr, a violent thunderstorm arises, the heathens are terrified : Recedente autem tempestate, gentiles baptizati, *statuas* quas coluerant *confringentes,* in *lacum* vico amnique proximum *projecerunt.*—Soon after this, the Burgundians settled in the district. The statues broken down, crushed to powder, and flung into the lake, every bit the same as in that story of Ratpert's.

On the other hand, the Vita Bonifacii (Pertz 2, 339), in describing
the heathen reaction under King Rêdbod (circ. 716), uses this
language : Jam pars ecclesiarum Christi, quae Francorum prius
subjecta erat imperio, vastata erat ac destructa, *idolorum* quoque
cultura exstructis delubrorum fanis lugubriter renovata.   And if it
should be thought that idolorum here is equivalent to deorum, the
Vita Willehadi (Pertz 2, 380) says more definitely : Insanum esse
et vanum a *lapidibus* auxilium petere et a *simulacris mutis et surdis*
subsidii sperare solatium.   Quo audito, gens fera et idololatriis
nimium dedita stridebant dentibus in eum, dicentes, non debere
profanum longius vivere, imo reum esse mortis, qui tam sacrilegia
contra *deos suos invictissimos* proferre praesumsisset eloquia.—The
event belongs to the middle of the 8th century, and the narrator
Anskar († 865) comes a hundred years later ; still we are not
warranted in looking upon his words as mere flourishes.   And I
am not sure that we have a right to take for empty phrases, what is
said in a Vita S. Goari († 649), which was not written till 839 :
Coepit gentilibus per circuitum (*i.e.* in Ripuaria), *simulacrorum*
cultui deditis et vana *idolorum* superstitionis deceptis, verbum
salutis annuntiare (Acta Bened. sec. 2, p. 282).   Such biographies
are usually based on older memorials.

The Frisians are in every sense the point of transition to the
Scandinavians ; considering the multifarious intercourse between
these two adjoining nations, nothing can be more natural than to
suppose that the Frisians also had in common with their neighbours
the habit of temple and image worship.   Even Fosete's temple in
Heligoland I can hardly imagine destitute of images.

Some facility in carving figures out of wood or chiselling them
out of stone is no more than we should have expected from those
signa and effigies in Tacitus, and the art might go on improving up
to a certain stage.   Stone weapons and other implements that we
find in barrows testify to a not unskilful handling of difficult
materials.   That not a single image of a Teutonic god has escaped
the destructive hand of time and the zeal of the christians, need
surprise us less than the total disappearance of the heathen temples.
Why, even in the North, where the number of images was greater,
and their destruction occurred much later, there is not one preserved;
all the Lethrian, all the Upsalian idols are clean gone.   The technical
term in the Norse was *skurdgoð* (Fornm. sög. 2, 73-5), from skëra

(sculpere), skurd (sculptura) ; in the two passages referred to, it is líkneski af Freyr. Biörn gives *skûrgoð*, idolum, sculptile, from skûr, subgrundium (penthouse), because it had to be placed under cover, in sheds as it were ; with which the OHG. skûrguta (Graff 6, 536) seems to agree. But there is no distinct proof of an ON. skûrgoð.

Dietmar's account is silent about the gods' images at Lethra [1] ; in Adam of Bremen's description of those at Upsal (cap. 233), the most remarkable thing is, that *three statues* are specified, as they were in that temple of the Alamanns : Nunc de superstitione Sveonum pauca dicemus. *Nobilissimum* illa gens *templum* habet, quod Ubsola dicitur, non longe positum a Sictona civitate (Sigtûn) vel Birka. In hoc templo, quod totum ex auro paratum est, *statuas trium deorum* veneratur populus, ita ut potentissimus eorum Thor in medio solium habeat triclinio. Hinc et inde locum possident Wodan et Fricco. The further description we have nothing to do with here, but there occurs in it also the term *sculpere ;* as the whole temple was ex auro paratum, *i.e.*, decorated with gold, he might doubtless have described the figures of the gods above all as *gilded*, just as those in Alamannia were aereae et *deauratae.*—Saxo p. 13 tells of a golden statue of Othin ; Cujus numen Septentrionis reges propensiore cultu prosequi cupientes, effigiem ipsius *aureo* complexi *simulacro, statuam* suae dignationis indicem maxima cum religionis simulatione Byzantium transmiserunt, cujus etiam brachiorum lineamenta confertissimo armillarum pondere per-stringebant. The whole passage, with its continuation, is not only unhistorical, but contrary to the genuine myths ; we can only see in it the view of the gods taken by Saxo and his period, and inasmuch as golden and bedizened images of gods were consonant with such view, we may infer that there still lived in his time a recollection of such figures (see Suppl.). Ermoldus Nigellus, in describing Herold's (Harald's) interview with King Charles, mentions 4, 444 seq. (Pertz 2, 509-10) the *gods' images* (sculpta) of the heathen, and that he was said to have had ploughshares, kettles and water-buckets forged of that metal. According to the Nialssaga cap. 89, in a Norwegian temple (goðahûs) there were to be seen *three figures* again, those of Thor and the two half-goddesses Thorgerðr and Irpa, of human size, and adorned with armlets ;

---

[1] On recently discovered figures of 'Odin,' v. infra, Wôdan.

probably Thor sat *in the middle* on his car. Altogether the portraitures of Thor seem to have been those most in vogue, at least in Norway.[1] One temple in which many skurdgoð were worshipped, but Thor most of all, is described in Fornm. sög. 2, 153 and 159, and his *statue* 1, 295. 302-6; in 2, 44 we read: Thôrr sat *î miðju* ok var mêst tignaðr, hann var mikill ok allr *gulli búinn ok silfri* (ex auro et argento confectus); conf. Olafs helga saga, ed. Holm. cap. 118-9, where a large standing figure of Thor is described; and Fornm. sög. 4, 245, ed. Christ. p. 26. Freyr *giörr af silfri*, Isl. sög. 1, 134. Landn. 3, 2. One man carried a *statuette* of Thor carved in whalebone (líkneski Thôrs af tönn gert) in his pocket, so as to worship him secretly, when living among christians, Fornm. sög. 2, 57. Thôr's *figure* was carved on the öndvegis-pillars, Eyrbygg. p. 8. Landnamab. 2, 12; and on the prows of ships, Fornm. sög. 2, 324. A figure of Thorgerðr hölgabrúðr, with rings of gold round the arm, to which people kneel, Fornm. sög. 2, 108.[2]

---

[1] Finn Magnusen, bidrag til nordisk archaeologie, pp. 113-159.

[2] There is another thing to notice in this passage. The figure of Thorgerðr *bent its hand up*, when some one tried to snatch a ring off its arm, and the goddess was not disposed to let him have it. The same man then brought a lot of money, laid it at the figure's feet, fell on his knees and shed tears, then rose up and once more grasped at the ring, which now *the figure let go*. The same is told in the Fœreyîngasaga, cap. 23, p. 103. I regard it as a genuine trait of heathen antiquity, like others which afterwards passed into christian folk-tales of the Mid. Ages (see Suppl.). Of more than one image of grace we are told that it dropt a *ring off its finger* or a *shoe off its foot* as a gift to those who prayed before it. A figure of Christ gave its shoes to a poor man (Nicolai abbatis peregrinatio, ed. Werlauff p. 20), and a saint's image its gold slippers (Mones anz. 7, 584. Archiv. des Henneb. vereins, pp. 70, 71). A figure of Mary accepts a ring that is presented to it, and bends her finger as a sign that she will keep it (Méon nouv. recueil 2, 296-7. Maerl. 2, 214). The two Virgin-stories in Méon and Maerlant, though one at bottom, have very different turns given them. In the latter, a young man at a game of ball pulls the ring off his finger, and puts it on the hand of a Madonna; in the former, the youth is boxing in the Colosseum at Rome, and puts his ring on the finger of a heathen statue, which bends the finger. Both figures now hold the man to his engagement. But the O. French poem makes the afflicted youth bring an image of Mary to bear on the heathen one, the Mary takes the ring off the other figure, and restores it to the youth. Conf. Kaiserchr. 13142. 13265. 13323. Forduni Scoti chronicon 1, 407 (W. Scott's minstr. 2, 136), relates this fable as an event of the 11th century: a nobleman playing at ball slips his ring on the finger of a broken statue of Venus, and only gets it back with the help of a priest Palumbus who understands magic. We see the story had spread at an early time, but it is old Teutonic in its origin ['*un*deutsch,' evid. a slip for *ur*deutsch]. Even in a painting of Mary, the infant in her lap hands her a casket to give to a suppliant, Cod. pal. 341 fol. 63). Similarly, statues *turn the face away, stretch out the arm to protect*, they *speak, laugh, weep, eat* and *walk*; thus a figure of Christ turns itself away (Ls. 3, 78. 262), another begins to eat and grow bigger (Kinderm. legenden no. 9), to weep, to beckon, to run away

Frey's *statue of silver*, (Freyr markaðr af silfri), Vatnsd. p. 44. 50 ; carried about in a waggon in Sweden, Fornm. sög. 2, 73-7. The Jomsvikîngasaga tells of a temple on Gautland (I. of Gothland), in which were *a hundred gods*, Fornm. sög. 11, 40 ; truly a ' densitas imaginum,' as Jonas has it (see p. 83). Saxo Gram. 327 mentions a simulacrum *quercu factum*, carved in oak ? or an oaktree worshipped as divine ? (see Suppl.).

Not only *three*, but occasionally *two figures* side by side are mentioned, particularly those of *Wuotan and Donar* or of *Mars and Mercurius*, as we see from the passages cited. Figures of Freyr and Thor together, and of Frigg and Freyja, occur in Müller's sagabibl. 1, 92. Names of places also often indicate such joint worship of two divinities, *e.g.* in Hesse the Donnerseiche (Thor's oak) stood close by the Wodansberg; and explorers would do well to attend to the point.

But neither the alleged number of the statues, nor their descriptions in the sagas can pass for historical; what they do prove is, that statues there were. They appear mostly to have been hewn out of wood, some perhaps were painted, clothed, and overlaid with silver or gold; but no doubt stone images were also to be met with, and smaller ones of copper or ivory.[1]

I have put off until now the mention of a peculiar term for statue, with which some striking accounts of heathen idols connect themselves.

OHG. glosses have the word *irmansûlî*, pyramides, Mons. 360. *avarûn, irmansûlî*, pyramides, Doc. 203ᵇ. *irmansûl*, colossus, altissima columna, Florent. 987ᵃ, Blas. 86. colossus est *irminsûl*, Gl. Schletst. 18, 1. 28, 1. The literal meaning seems to be statue, to judge by the synonym *avarâ*, which in Gl. Jun. 226 is used for

(Deutsche sagen, no. 347. Tettaus, preuss. sagen, pp. 211-5-8). In Reinbot's Georg the idol Apollo is flogged with rods by a child, and forced to walk away (3258-69), which reminds one of the god Perûn, whom, according to monk Nestor, Vladîmir the Apostolic caused to be scourged with rods. In an Indian story I find a statue that eats the food set before it, Polier 2, 302-3. Antiquity then did not regard these images altogether as lumps of dead matter, but as penetrated by the life of the divinity. The Greeks too have stories of statues that move, shake the lance, fall on their kness, close their eyes (καταμύσεις), bleed and sweat, which may have been suggested by the attitudes of ancient images ; but of a statue making a movement of the hand, bending a finger, I have nowhere read, significant as the position of the arms in images of gods was held to be. That the gods themselves χεῖρα ὑπερέχουσιν over those whom they wish to protect, occurs as early as in Homer.

[1] Finn Magnusen ibid. 132-7.

statua and imago.   It was not yet extinct in the 12th century, as appears from two places in the Kaiserchronik, near the beginning of the poem, and very likely there are more of them ; it is said of Mercury (Massmann 129) :—

ûf einir *yrmensûle*	Upon an yrmensûl
stuont ein abgot ungehiure,	Stood an idol huge,
den hiezen sie ir koufman.	Him they called their merchant.

Again of Julius Cæsar (Massm. 624) :—

Rômere in ungetrûwelîche sluogen,	Romans him untruly slew, On an yrm. they buried him.
ûf einir *yrmensûl* sie in begruoben.	

And of Simon Magus 24ᶜ (Massm. 4432) :—

ûf eine *yrmensûl* er steic,	On an yrmensul he climbed,
daz lantvolc im allesamt neic.	The land-folk to him all bowed.

That is, worshipped him as a god.   Nay, in Wolfram's Titurel, last chapter, where the great pillars of the (christian) temple of the Grail are described, instead of ' inneren seul' of the printed text (Hahn 6151), the Hanover MS. more correctly reads *irmensûl*.

Further, in the Frankish annals ad ann. 772 it is repeatedly stated, that Charles the Great in his conquest of the Saxons destroyed a chief seat of their heathen superstition, not far from Heresburg[1] in Westphalia, and that it was called *Irminsûl*.   Ann. Petav.: Domnus rex Karolus perrexit in Saxoniam et conquisivit Erisburgo, et pervenit ad locum qui dicitur *Ermensul*, et succendit ea loca (Pertz 1, 16).   Ann. Lauresh.: Fuit rex Carlus hostiliter in Saxonia, et destruxit *fanum* eorum quod vocatur *Irminsul* (Pertz 1, 30).   The same in the Chron. Moissiac., except the spelling *Hirminsul* (Pertz 1, 295), and in Ann. Quedlinb., &c. (Pertz 5, 37).   Ann. Juvavenses: Karolus *idolum* Saxonorum combussit, quod dicebant *Irminsul* (Pertz 1, 88).   Einhardi Fuld. annales: Karolus Saxoniam bello aggressus, Eresburgum castrum cepit, et *idolum* Saxonum quod vocabatur *Irminsul* destruit (Pertz 1, 348).   Ann. Ratisbon.: Carolus in Saxonia conquesivit Eresburc et *Irminsul* (Pertz 1, 92).   Ann. Lauriss.: Karlus in Saxonia castrum Aeresburg expugnat, *fanum* et *lucum* eorum *famosum Irminsul* subvertit (Pertz 1, 117).

---

[1] Now Stadtbergen, conf. the extract from Dietmar ; but strong reasons incline us to push the pillar (seule) some 15 miles deeper into the Osning forest ; Clostermeier Eggesterstein, pp. 26-7 : Eresburg, Horohus in pago Hessi Saxonico Saracho 735. 350. Conf. Massmann's Eggesterst. p. 34.

Ann. Lauriss.: Et inde perrexit partibus Saxoniae prima vice, Aeresburgum castrum cepit, ad *Ermensul* usque pervenit, et ipsum *fanum* destruxit, et aurum et argentum quod ibi repperit abstulit. Et fuit siccitas magna, ita ut aqua deficeret in supradicto loco ubi *Ermensul* stabat, &c. (Pertz 1, 150). Einhardi Ann.: Ferro et igni cuncta depopulatus, Aeresburgum castrum cepit, *idolum* quod *Irminsul* a Saxonibus vocabatur evertit (Pertz 1, 151); repeated in Ann. Tilian., and Chron. Regin., with spelling *Ormensul* (Pertz 1, 220, 557).[1] And Dietmar of Merseburg (Pertz 5, 744) further tells us, in connexion with later events: Sed exercitus capta urbe (Eresburch) ingressus, juvenem praefatum usque in ecclesiam S. Petri, *ubi prius ab antiquis Irminsul colebatur*, bello defatigatum depulit.—Taking all these passages together, Irminsûl passes through the very same gradations of meaning we unfolded in ch. IV, and signifies now *fanum*, now *lucus*, now *idolum* itself. It can scarcely be doubted, that vast woodlands extended over that region: what if *Osning*,[2] the name of the mountain-forest in which the pillar stood, betokened a *holy-wood?* The gold and silver hoard, which Charles was supposed to have seized there, may well be legendary embellishment.[3] Ruodolf of Fuld goes more into detail about the Irminsûl; after his general statement on the heathen Saxons, that 'frondosis arboribus fontibusque venerationem exhibebant' (p.101), he goes on: *Truncum* quoque *ligni* non parvae magnitudinis in altum erectum sub divo colebant, patria eum lingua *Irminsul* appellantes, quod Latine dicitur *universalis columna,* quasi sustinens omnia (Pertz 2, 676),

[1] Poeta Saxo 1, 65 (Bouquet 5, 137):
    Gens eadem coluit simulacrum quod vocitabant
    Irminsûl, cujus factura simulque *columna*
    Non operis parvi fuerat, pariterque decoris.
[2] *ôs* is the Sax. form for *ans* (p. 25), which denoted a god, and also a mountain; in High G. the name would be Ansninc, Ensninc. But, beside this mons *Osnengi* near Theotmelli, *i.e.* Detmold (Pertz 2, 447), there stood also a *silva Osning* not far from Osnabrück (Möser urk. no 2), and a *third* in Ripuaria on the Lower Rhine (Lacomblet no 310. 343. 354), which seems to have extended towards the Ardennes as far as Aachen (Aix la Chap.), mentioned in Vilkinasaga cap. 40; and according to Bärsch on Schannat's Eiflia, illustr. 1, 110, and Hattemer 3, 602ᵃ, the Ardennes itself was called *Osninka, Oseninch.* By the Osnabrück charter above, the forest there appears even to have been modelled on the Osning of Aachen (ad similitudinem foresti Aquisgranum pertinentis). That Osning is met with in several places, speaks for a more general meaning [than that of a mere proper name]; like âs, ans, and faírguni, it is the sacred mountain and forest. Ledebur takes the Teutoburgiensis saltus to be Osning. *Osnabrück, Asnebruggi* (bridge of the âses) seems nearly related.
[3] Is this Ermen-pillar hoard an allusion to the legend of Ermenrich's hoard? (Saxo Gram. 156. Reinh. fuchs CLII.)

(see Suppl.). Here was a great wooden pillar erected, and worshipped under the open sky, its name signifies universal all-sustain-
ing pillar. This interpretation appears faultless, when we take
with it other words in which the meaning is intensified by
composition with *irmin*. In the Hildebrands lied, *irmingot* is the
supreme god, the god of all, not a peculiar one, agreeing in sense
with *thiodgod*, the (whole) people's god, formed by another streng-
thening prefix, Hel. 33, 18. 52, 12. 99, 6. *irminman*, an elevated
expression for man, Hel. 38, 24. 107, 13. 152, 11. *irminthiod*,
the human race, Hel. 87, 13 and in Hildebr.[1] In the same way I
explain proper names compounded with *irman, irmin* (Gramm. 2,
448). And *irmansûl, irminsûl* is the great, high, divinely honoured
statue; that it was dedicated to any one god, is not to be found in
the term itself.—In like manner the AS. has *eormencyn* (genus
humanum), Beow. 309. Cod. Exon. 333, 3. *eormengrund* (terra),
Beow. 1711. (and singularly in an adj. form: ofer ealne *yrmenne*
grund, Cod. Exon. 243, 13). *eormenstrŷnd* (progenies).—ON.
iörmungrund (terra), *iörmungandr* (anguis maximus), *iörmunrekr*
(taurus maximus). From all this may be gathered the high mythic
antiquity of these appellations, and their diffusion among all
branches of the Teutonic race; for neither to the Goths can they
have been strange, as their famous king's name *Ermanaricus*
(Aírmanareiks, ON. Iörmunrekr) shows; and beyond a doubt the
Hermunduri are properly *Ermunduri* (Gramm. 2, 175), the H being
often prefixed to all such forms.

Now whatever may be the probable meaning of the word *irman,
iörmun, eormen*, to which I shall return in due time, one thing is
evident, that the *Irman-pillar* had some connexion, which continued
to be felt down to a late period (p.116), with Mercury or Hermes, to
whom Greek antiquity raised similar posts and pillars, which were
themselves called *Hermae*, a name which suggests our Teutonic one.

The Saxons may have known more about this; the Franks, in
Upper Germany, from the 8th to the 13th century, connected with
irmansûl, irminsûl the general notion of a heathen image set up on
a pillar. Probably Ruodolf associated with his *truncus ligni* the

---

[1] The Slav. ramo, Bohem. ramenso, is with transposition the Lat. armus,
OHG. aram, and means both arm and shoulder; in the Sloven. compound
ramen-velik, valde magnus, it intensifies exactly like irman; does this point to
an affinity between irman and arm? Arminius too is worth considering; conf.
Schaffarik 1, 427.

thought of a choice and hallowed tree-stem (with, or without, a god's image ?), rather than of a pillar hewn into shape by the hand of man; this fits in too with the worshipping sub divo, with the word lucus used by some of the chroniclers, and with the simplicity of the earliest forest-worship. As the image melts into the notion of tree, so does the tree pass into that of image; and our West-phalian Irmen-pillar most naturally suggests the idea of that Thor's-oak in Hesse; the evangelists converted both of them into churches of St. Peter. I suspect an intimate connexion between the Irman-pillars and the *Roland-pillars* erected in the later Mid. Ages, especially in North Germany; there were in Sweden *Thor's-pillars*, and among the Anglo-Saxons *Æthelstán-pillars* (Lappenberg 1, 376). There yet remains to be given an account of a sacred post in Neustria, as contained in the Vita Walarici abbatis Leuconensis (†622), said to have been composed in the 8th century: Et juxta ripam ipsius fluminis *stips* erat *magnus, diversis imaginibus figuratus*, atque ibi in terram magna virtute immissus, qui *nimio cultu morem gentilium* a rusticis colebatur. Walaricus causes the log to be thrown down: et his quidem rusticis habitantibus in locis non parvum tam moerorem quam et stuporem omnibus praebuit. Sed undique illis certatim concurrentibus cum armis et fustibus, indigne hoc ferentes invicem, ut injuriam *dei sui* vindicarent (Acta Bened. sec. 2, pp. 84-5). The place was called Augusta (bourg d' Augst, near the town of Eu), and a church was built on the spot.

I think I have now shown, that in ancient Germany there were gods and statues. It will further be needful to consider, how antiquity went to work in identifying foreign names of gods with German, and conversely German with foreign.

The Romans in their descriptions cared a great deal more to make themselves partially understood by a free translation, than, by preserving barbarous vocables, to do a service to posterity. At the same time they did not go arbitrarily to work, but evidently with care.

Caesar's *Sol, Luna* and *Vulcan* are perhaps what satisfies us least; but Tacitus seems never to use the names of Roman deities, except advisedly and with reflection. Of the gods, he names only *Mercury* and *Mars* (Germ. 9. Ann. 13, 57. Hist. 4, 64); of deified heroes, *Hercules, Castor* and *Pollux* (Germ. 9, 43); of goddesses,

Isis (Germ. 9), the *terra mater* by her German name (Germ. 40),
and the *mater deum* (Germ. 45). Incompatible deities, such as
Apollo or Bacchus, are never compared. What strikes us most, is
the absence of Jupiter, and the distinction given to *Mercury*, who
was but a deity of the second rank with the Romans, a mere god
of merchants, but here stands out the foremost of all: Deorum
maxime Mercurium colunt: to him alone do human sacrifices fall,
while Mars and Hercules content themselves with beasts. This
prominence of Mercury is probably to be explained by the fact,
that ¸this god was worshipped by the Gauls likewise as their chief
divinity, and was the most frequently portrayed (deum *maxime*
Mercurium colunt, hujus sunt plurima simulacra, Caes. B. Gall. 6,
17);[1] and that the looks of the Romans, when directed towards
Germany, still saw Gaul in the foreground; besides, it may have
been Gallic informants that set the German divinity before them in
this light. Observe too the Gaulish juxtaposition of *Mars* and
Mercurius in statues (p.111),precisely as Tacitus names the German
ones together (Ann. 13, 57). The omission of Jupiter is obviously
accounted for, by his worship yielding the precedence to that of
Mercury in those nations which Tacitus knew best: we shall see, as
we go on, that the northern and remoter branches on the contrary
reserved their highest veneration for the thunder-god. On *Isis* and
Hercules I shall express my views further on. Whom we are to
understand by the *Dioscuri*, is hard to guess; most likely two sons
of Woden, and if we go by the statements of the Edda, the brothers
Baldr and Hermôðr would be the most fitting.

This adaptation of classical names to German gods became
universally spread, and is preserved with strict unanimity by the
Latin writers of the succeeding centuries; once set in circulation,
it remained current and intelligible for long ages.

The Gothic historian names but one god after the Roman fashion,
and that is *Mars*: Quem Gothi semper asperrima placavere cultura
(Jornandes cap. 5), with which the Scythian Ares, so early as in
Herodotus 4, 62-3, may be compared.

Paulus Diaconus winds up his account of Wodan with the
express announcement (1, 9): Wodan sane, quem adjecta litera
Gwodan dixerunt, ipse est qui apud Romanos *Mercurius* dicitur, et

---

[1] Schöpflin, Als. ill. 1, 435-60 ; esp. on a fanum of Mercury at Ebermünster
1, 58. Conf. Hummel, bibl. deutsch. alterth. p. 229. Creuzer, altröm. cultur am
Oberrhein, pp. 48, 98.

ab universis Germaniae gentibus ut deus adoratur. Just so his older countryman Jonas of Bobbio, in that account of the sacrificing Alamanns, declares : Illi aiunt, deo suo Vodano, quem *Mercurium* vocant alii, se velle litare ; upon which, a gloss inserted by another hand says less correctly : Qui apud eos Vuotant vocatur, Latini autem *Martem* illum appellant ; though otherwise Woden greatly resembles Mars (v. infra).

Gregory of Tours (supra, p.107) makes *Saturn* and *Jupiter*, and again *Mars Mercurius*que the gods whom the heathen Chlodovich adored. In 1, 34 he expresses himself in more general terms : Privatus, Gabalitanae urbis episcopus. . . . *daemoniis* immolare compellitur a Chroco Alamannorum rege (in the third cent.). Widekind of Corvei names *Mars* and *Hercules* as gods of the Saxons (see p. 111) ; and that little addition to the Corvei Annals (see p.111) couples together the Greek and Latin denominations Aris and Mars, Ermis and Mercurius.

The Indiculus paganiarum reckons up, under 8 : De sacris *Mercurii* vel *Jovis*[1] ; under 20 : De feriis quae faciunt *Jovi* vel *Mercurio*. So that the thunder-god, of whom Tacitus is silent, is in other quarters unforgotten ; and now we can understand Wilibald's narrative of the robur *Jovis* (see p. 72), and in Bonifac. epist. 25 (A.D. 723) the presbyter *Jovi* mactans (see Suppl.).

In the Additamenta operum Matthaei Paris. ed. W. Watts, Paris 1644, pp. 25-6, there is an old account of some books which are said to have been discovered in laying the foundation of a church at Verlamacestre (St Albans) in the tenth century, and to have been burnt. One of them contained ' invocationes et ritus idololatrarum civium Varlamacestrensium, in quibus comperit, quod specialiter *Phoebum deum solis* invocarunt et coluerunt, secundario vero *Mercurium, Voden* anglice appellatum, deum videlicet mercatorum, quia cives et compatriotae . . . fere omnes negotiatores et institores fuerunt.' Evidently the narrator has added somewhat out of his own erudition ; the invocations and rites themselves would have given us far more welcome information.

Passages which appear to speak of a German goddess by the name of *Diana*, will be given later. *Neptune* is mentioned a few times (supra, p. 110).

---

[1] Had these been Roman gods, Jupiter would certainly have been named first, and Mercury after.

Saxo Grammaticus, though he writes in Latin, avoids applying the Roman names of gods, he uses Othinus or Othin, never Mercurius instead; yet once, instead of his usual Thor (pp. 41, 103), he has *Jupiter*, p. 236, and malleus *Jovialis*; *Mars* on p. 36 seems to stand for Othin, not for Tyr, who is never alluded to in Saxo. Ermoldus Nigellus, citing the idols of the Normanni, says 4, 9 (Pertz 2, 501), that for God (the Father) they worshipped *Neptune*, and for Christ *Jupiter;* I suppose Neptune must here mean Oðin, and Jupiter Thor; the same names recur 4, 69. 100. 453-5.

Melis-Stoke, as late as the beginning of the 14th century, still remembers that the heathen Frisians worshipped *Mercury* (1, 16. 17); I cannot indicate the Latin authority from which no doubt he drew this.[1]

If the supposition be allowed, and it seems both a justifiable and almost a necessary one, that, from the first century and during the six or eight succeeding ones, there went on an uninterrupted transfer of the above-mentioned and a few similar Latin names of gods to domestic deities of Gaul and Germany, and was familiar to all the educated; we obtain by this alone the solution of a remarkable phenomenon that has never yet been satisfactorily explained: the early diffusion over half Europe of the heathen nomenclature of the *days of the week*.

These names are a piece of evidence favourable to German heathenism, and not to be disregarded.

The matter seems to me to stand thus.[2]—From Egypt, through the Alexandrians, the week of seven days (ἑβδομάς), which in Western Asia was very ancient, came into vogue among the Romans, but the planetary nomenclature of the days of the week apparently not till later. Under Julius Caesar occurs the earliest mention of 'dies *Saturni*' in connection with the Jewish sabbath, Tibull. 1, 3, 18. Then ἡλίου ἡμέρα in Justin Mart. apolog. 1, 67. Ἑρμοῦ and Ἀφροδίτης ἡμέρα in Clem. Alex. strom. 7, 12. The institution fully carried out, not long before Dio Cassius 37, 18, about the close

---

[1] Our MHG. poets impart no such information; they only trouble their heads about Saracen gods, among whom it is true Jupiter and Apollo make their appearance too. In Rol. 97, 7 are named *Mars, Jovinus, Saturnus*.

[2] I can here use only the beginning, not the conclusion, which would be more useful for my investigation, of a learned paper by Julius Hare on the names of the days of the week (Philolog. Mus., Nov. 1831). Conf. Idelers handb. der chronol. 2, 177-180, and Letronne, observations sur les représentations zodiacales, p. 99.

of the 2nd century.[1] The Romans had previously had a week of nine days, nundinae=novendinae. Christianity had adopted from the Jews the hebdomas, and now it could not easily guard the church against the idolatrous names of days either (see Suppl.).

But these names, together with the institution of the week, had passed on from Rome to Gaul and Germany, sooner than the christian religion did. In all the Romance countries the planetary names have lasted to this day (mostly in a very abridged form), except for the first day and the seventh : instead of dies solis they chose dies *dominica* (Lord's day), It. domenica, Sp. domingo, Fr. dimanche ; and for dies Saturni they kept the Jewish *sabbatum*, It. sabbato, Sp. sabado, Fr. samedi (=sabdedi, sabbati dies). But the heathen names of even these two days continued in popular use long after : Ecce enim *dies solis* adest, sic enim barbaries vocitare diem dominicum consueta est, Greg. Tur. 3, 15.

Unhappily a knowledge of the Gothic names of days is denied us. The *sabbaté* dags, *sabbatô* dags, which alone occurs in Ulphilas, proves nothing, as we have just seen, against a planetary designation of the remaining six or five days. A sunnôns dags, a mênins dags may be guessed ; the other four, for us the most important, I do not venture to suggest. Their preservation would have been of the very highest value to our inquiry.

OLD HIGH GERM.—I. *sunnûn* dag, O. v. 5, 22. Gl. blas. 76ª. Lacombl. arch. 1, 6.—II. *mânin* tac (without authority, for mânitag, mânotag in Graff 2,795. 5, 358 have no reference ; mânetag in Notker, ps. 47, 1).—III. dies Martis, prob. *Ziuwes* tac among Alamanns ; in the 11th cent. *Cies* dac, Gl. blas. 76ª ;[2] prob. different among Bavarians and Lombards.—IV. dies Mercurii, perhaps still *Wuotanes* tac ? our abstract term, diu *mittawecha* already in N. ps. 93, and *mittwocha*, Gl. blas. 76ᵇ.—V. dies Jovis, *Donares* tac, *Toniris* tac, N. ps. 80, 1. *donres*tac, Gl. blas. 76ª. Burcard von Worms 195ᵇ: quintam feriam in honorem *Jovis* honorati.—VI. dies Veneris, *Fria* dag, O. v. 4, 6. *Frije* tag, T. 211, 1.—VII. at last, like the Romance and Gothic, avoiding the heathenish dies Saturni, *sambaztag*, T. 68, 1. N. 91, 1.[3] *samiztag*, N. 88, 40. *sunnûn âband*, our sonnabend,

---

[1] An old hexameter at the end of the editions of Ausonius : Ungues *Mercurio*, barbam *Jove, Cypride* crines (nails on Wednesday, beard on Thursday, hair on Friday).

[2] Cies for Zies, as the same glossist 86ª writes gicimbere and cinnum.

[3] *Sambazolus* n. prop. in Karajan.

already in O. v. 4, 9, prob. abbreviation of sunnûndages âband, feria ante dominicam, for vespera solis cannot have been meant [conf. Engl. Whitsun-eve] ; and occasionally, corresponding to the Romance dies dominica, *frôn*tag, N. ps. 23.

MID. HIGH GERM.—Would any one believe, that the names of the days of the week are not easily to be picked out of the abundant remains of our MHG. literature ? It is true, *sunnen* tac (suntac in Berth. 118) and *mântac* (Parz. 452, 16. mœntac 498, 22. Amis 1648)[1] admit of no doubt. Neither do *Donrestac* (Donerstag, Uolrich 73a. Dunrestac, Berth. 128), spelt *Duristag* in a Semi-Low Germ. urk. of 1300 in Höfer p. 57), and *Dornstag* in one of 1495, Useners femgerichten p. 131 ; nor *Frîtac* (Parz. 448, 7. 470, 1. Walth. 36, 31. Berth. 134), *Vriegtag*, Uolrich 73a ; nor yet *samztac* (Parz. 439, 2. Berth. 138), *sunnen âbent* (Trist. 3880).— But uncertainty hangs about the third and fourth days. The former, by a remarkable variation, was in Bavaria named *Eritac*, *Erctac* (the true form not quite certain, eritag in Adelung's vat. hss. 2, 189. ergetag in Berth. 122 ; see examples collected from urkunden, Schm. 1, 96-7), in Swabia on the contrary *Ziestac*, for Ziewestac. Both of these forms, which have nothing to do with each other, live to this day in the speech of the common people : Bav. *ierte*, Austr. *iärta*, *irita*, Vicentino-Germ. *eörtä*, *ortä*, Alem. *ziestag, zinstag, ziestig, zistig, zienstig, zeinstig, zinstag.* The insertion of the liquid has corrupted the word, and brought in quite irrelevant notions. In central Germany the form *diestag, tiestag* seems to predominate (*diestik* in the Rhön), whence our *dienstag* (less correctly dinstag, there is good reason for the *ie*) ; the spelling dingstag, as if from ding, thing, judicium, is false ; dinstag occurs in Gaupps magdeb. recht p. 272.—The fourth day I have never seen named after the god, either in MHG. or in our modern dialects unless indeed the *gwontig* cited in the note can be justified as standing for Gwuotenstag, Wuotenstag; everywhere that abstraction 'midweek' has carried all before it, but it has itself become

---

[1] *Zuem*tig for Monday, Stald. 2, 470 ought perhaps to be zue mentig, ze mântage ; yet 1, 490 he has guenti, güenti, Tobler 248b has gwontig, guentig, and Zellwegers urk. 1b, 19 guonti, for which Urk. no. 146 has 'an gutem tag,' which seems to be supported by Haltaus jahrzeitb. Or is only this particular Monday after Lent called so ? In the Cod. pal. 372, 103 (ann. 1382) we have 'guotem tag.' The resemblance of this good day to the Westphalian Gudensdag (Woden's day) is purely accidental.

almost unintelligible by being changed into a masculine *mittwoch*, *mittich*, Berth. 24, *mäktig*, Stald. 2, 194, conf. the Gothl. mäjkädag, Almqv. 442ª), 'an der *mitkun*,' fem., is found in the Cod. zaringobad. no. 140 (A.D. 1261). So even for the fifth day, the numeric name *phinztac* (Berth. 128. Ottoc. 144ª. Grätzer urk. of 1338. Schwabenspiegel, p. 196. Schm. 1, 322), or *phingstag*, has made its way into some districts of Upper Germany through Græco-Slavic influences, πέμπτη, petek, piatek, patek, though by these the Slavs mean Friday (see Suppl.).

NEW HIGH GERM.—I. *sonntag*. II. *montag*. III. *Dienstag*. IV. *mittwoch*. V. *Donnerstag*. VI. *Freitag*. VII. *samstag*, *sonnabend*.

OLD SAXON.—The OS. names are wanting, but must have differed in some essential points from the OHG., as the derived dialects prove. We may pretty safely assume *Wôdanes dag* for the fourth day of the week, for in Westphalia it is still called *Godenstag, Gonstag, Gaunstag, Gunstag*, at Aix *Gouesdag*, in Lower Rhen. urkunden *Gudestag*, Günther, 3, 585. 611 (A.D. 1380-7), *Gudenstag*, Kindlinger hörigk. p. 577-8 (A.D. 1448).—The third day was probably *Tiwesdag*, the fifth *Thunaresdag*, the sixth *Friunday*. The most unlike would doubtless be the seventh, was it formed after dies Saturni, *Sâteresdag?* conf. the Westph. *Saterstag, Saiter-staig*, Günter 3, 502 (A.D. 1365). In Sachsensp. 2, 66 one MS. reads for sunavend *Satersdach* (see Suppl.).

MID. DUTCH.—I. *sondach*, Maerl. 2, 159. II. *manendach*, Huyd. op St. 3, 389. *maendach*, Maerl. 2, 139. III. *Disendach*, Maerl. 2, 140. al. *Dicendach, Dissendach,* Cannaert strafrecht, pp. 124, 481 apparently corrupted from Tisdach. IV. *Woensdach*, Maerl. 2, 143. V. *Donresdach*, Maerl. 2, 144. VI. *Vrîdach*, Maerl. 2, 159. gen. *Vrîndaghes*, Maerl. 2, 143. 157. VII. *Saterdach*, Maerl. 2, 114. 120-3. 157-9. 276. 3, 197. 343. also *sonnacht*, Maerl. 2, 164. 3, 240. (see Suppl.).

NEW DUTCH.—I. *zondag*. II. *mândag*. III. *dingsdag*, formerly dinsdag, *Dissendag*. IV. *Wocnsdag*, Belg. Goensdag. V. *Donderdag*. VI. *Vrîdag*. VII. *Zaterdag*.

OLD FRISIAN.—I. *sonnadei*. II. *monadei*. III. *Tysdei*. IV. *Wernsdei*. V. *Thunresdei*, Tornsdei. VI. *Frigendei, Fredei*. VII. *Saterdei* (references for all these forms in Richthofen).

NEW FRISIAN.—I. *sneyn*, abbrev. from sinnedey, sendei, senned (conf. Frêd); the final *n* in sneyn, no doubt, as in OFris. Frigendei, a relic of the old gen. sing. in the weak decl. II. *moandey.* III. *Tyesdey.* IV. *Wânsdey.* V. *Tongersdey.* VI. *Frêd,* abbrev. from Frêdey. VII. *sniuwn, snioun,* abbrev. from sinnejuwn=Sun(day)-even. Conf. tegenwoordige staat van Friesland 1, 121. Wassenbergh's bidraghen 2, 56. Halbertsma naoogst p. 281-2 (see Suppl.).

NORTH FRISIAN.—I. *sennendei.* II. *monnendei.* III. *Tirsdei.* IV. *Winsdei.* V. *Türsdei.* VI. *Fridei.* VII. *sennin (in*=even).

ANGLO-SAXON.—I. *sonnan* dæg. II. *monan* dæg. III. *Tiwes* dæg. IV. *Wôdenes* or *Wôdnes* dæg. V. *Thunores* dæg. VI. *Frige* dæg. VII. *Sœtres* or *Sœternes* dæg.

OLD NORSE.—I. *sunnudagr.*[1] II. *mânadagr.* III. *Tyrsdagr, Tysdagr.* IV. *Oðinsdagr.* V. *Thôrsdagr.* VI. *Friadagr, Frey-judagr.* VII. *laugardagr.*

SWEDISH.—I. *söndag.* II. *måndag.* III. *Tisdag,* whence even Finn. tystai. IV. *Onsdag.* V. *Thorsdag.* VI. *Fredag* VII. *lördag.*

DANISH.—I. *söndag.* II. *mandag.* III. *Tirsdag.* IV. *Onsdag.* V. *Torsdag.* VI. *Fredag.* VII. *löverdag* (see Suppl.).

We see, it is only in the seventh day that the Scandinavian names depart from the Saxon, Frisian and Dutch: laugardagr means bath-day because people bathed at the end of the week. Yet even here there may be some connexion; a Latin poem of the 9th century on the battle of Fontenay (Bouquet 7, 304) has the singular verse: *Sabbatum* non illud fuit, sed *Saturni dolium;* a devil's bath? conf. ch. XII, Saturn. [The Germ. for carnage is blutbad, blood-bath.]

Even if the Germans from the earliest times knew the week of seven days from the four phases of the lunar change,[2] yet the

---

[1] This ON. *sunnudagr* is noticeable, as in other cases sôl is used rather than sunna; sunnudagr seems to have been formed by the christian teachers in imitation of the other Teutonic languages. The Swed. and Dan. *söndag* (instead of soldag) must have been taken bodily from a Plattdeutsch form.

[2] To the Lat. word vix, gen. vicis (change, turn) corresponds, without the usual consonant-change, the Gothic *vikô,* OHG. wêchâ and wêhsal, both referable to the verb veika, váik, OHG. wîchu (I give way), because change is a giving way [in German, ' der wechsel ist ein weichen ']. Ulph. has vikô only once, Lu. 1, 8, where ἐν τῇ τάξει τῆς ἐφημερίας is translated ' in *vikôn* kunjis '; it is evidently something more than τάξις here, it expresses at the same time a part of the gen. ἐφημερίας, therefore lit. ' in *vice* generis ', which the Vulg. renders

naming of the days and the order in which they stand is manifestly an importation from abroad. On the contrary supposition, there would have been variation in details; and Saturn, for whom no Teutonic god seems prepared to stand sponsor, would have been left out in the cold.

But it would be no less absurd to attribute the introduction of the week and the names of the days to the Christians. As they came into vogue among the heathen Romans, they could just as well among heathen Gauls and Germans; nay, considering the lively intercourse between the three nations, a rapid diffusion is altogether natural.[1] Christianity had the Jewish week, and it tolerated names which were a frequent offence to it, but were already too deeply rooted, and could only be partially dislodged. Those words of Gregory reveal the utter aversion of the clergy, which comes out still more plainly in the language (publ. in Syntagma de baptismo, p. 190) of an Icelandic bishop in 1107, who actually did away with them in Iceland, and replaced them by mere numeric names. How should the christian teachers ever have suffered hateful names of idols to be handed over to their recent converts for daily use, unless they had already been long established among the people ? And in Germany, how should the Latin gods have been allowed to get translated into German ones, as if on purpose to put them within easy reach of the people, had they not already been familiar with them for centuries ?

Again, the high antiquity of these translations is fully established by their exact accordance with the terminology used in the first centuries, as soon as people came to turn German gods into Roman. In my opinion, the introduction of the seven days' names

---

by 'in ordine vicis '. Now whether vikô expressed to the Goths the alternation of the moon's quarters, we do not know for certain ; I incline to believe it, as the OHG. wëhâ, wochâ, AS. wice, wuce, ON. vika, Swed. vecka, Dan. uge, are all limited to the one meaning of septimana. The very absence of consonant-change points to a high antiquity in the word. It is remarkable that the Javanese *vuku* means a section of time, the year falling into 30 vukus (Humb. Kawispr. 1, 196). The Finn. wijkko is more likely to have been borrowed from the Norse than from so far back as the Gothic. I remark further, that an observance by the Germani of sections of time must be inferred from the mere fact that *certi dies* were fixed for the sacrifices to Mercury, Tac. Germ. 9.

[1] Jos. Fuchs, gesch. von Mainz 2, 27 seq. (Kupfert 4, no 7) describes a Roman round altar, prob. of the 3rd or 4th century, on which are carved the seven gods of the week (1 Saturn, 2 Apollo, 3 Diana, 4 Mars, 5 Mercury, 6 Jupiter, 7 Venus), and in an 8th place a genius.

amongst us must be placed at latest in the fourth or fifth century ; it may not have taken place simultaneously in all parts of Teutondom.

Our forefathers, caught in a natural delusion, began early to ascribe the origin of the seven days' names to the native gods of their fatherland.—William of Malmesbury, relating the arrival of the Saxons in Britain, says of Hengist and Horsa, that they were sprung from the noblest ancestry: Erant enim abnepotes illius antiquissimi *Voden,* de quo omnium pene barbararum gentium regium genus lineam trahit, quemque gentes Anglorum *deum* esse delirantes, ei *quartum* diem septimanae, et *sextum* uxori ejus *Freae* perpetuo ad hoc tempus consecraverunt sacrilegio (Savile 1601. p. 9).—More circumstantially, Geoffrey of Monmouth (lib. 6. ed. 1587, p. 43) makes Hengist say to Vortigern : Ingressi sumus maria, regnum tuum duce *Mercurio* petivimus. Ad nomen itaque *Mercurii* erecto vultu rex inquirit cujusmodi religionem haberent? cui Hengistus : deos patrios *Saturnum,* atque ceteros, qui mundum gubernant, colimus, maxime *Mercurium* (as in Tac. 9.), quem *Woden* lingua nostra appellamus. Huic veteres nostri dicaverunt *quartam* septimanae feriam, quae usque in hodiernum diem nomen *Wodenesdai* de nomine ipsius sortita est. Post illum colimus *deam* inter ceteras potentissimam, cui et dicaverunt *sextam* feriam, quam de nomine ejus *Fredai* vocamus.—As Matthew of Westminster (Flores, ed. 1601, p. 82) varies in some details, his words may also be inserted here : Cumque tandem in praesentia regis (Vortigerni) essent constituti, quaesivit ab eis, quam fidem, quam religionem patres eorum coluissent ? cui Hengistus : *deos patrios,* scilicet *Saturnum, Jovem* atque ceteros, qui mundum gubernant, colimus, *maxime autem Mercurium,* quem lingua nostra *Voden* appellamus. Huic patres nostri veteres dedicaverunt quartam feriam septimanae, quae in hunc hodiernum diem *Vodenesday* appellatur. Post illum colimus deam inter ceteras potentissimam, vocabulo *Fream,* cujus vocabulo *Friday* appellamus. Frea ut volunt quidam idem est quod *Venus,* et dicitur Frea, quasi Froa a frodos [A-frod-ite = from froth ?] quod est spuma maris, de qua nata est Venus secundum fabulas, unde idem dies appellatur *dies Veneris.*—Anglo-Saxon legend then, unconcerned at the jumbling of foreign and homespun fable, has no doubt at all about the high antiquity of the names among its people.

Saxo Grammaticus, more critical, expresses his opinion (p. 103) of the Norse nomenclature, that it is derived from the native gods, but that these are not the same as the Latin. This he proves by Othin and Thor, after whom the fourth and fifth days of the week are named, as in Latin after Mercury and Jupiter. For Thor, being Othin's son, cannot possibly be identified with Jupiter, who is Mercury's father; consequently, neither can the Norse Othin, Thor's father, with the Roman Mercury, who is Jupiter's son. The discrepancy is certainly strong, but all that it can prove is, that at the time when Othin and Mercury began to be placed on the same pedestal, Mercury was thought of as a Celtic divinity, probably with attributes differing widely from his classical namesake. Saxo is quite right in what he means, and his remark confirms the early heathen origin of these names of days ;[1] yet upon occasion, as we saw on p. 122, he lets himself be carried away after all by the over-powering identity of Thor and Jupiter (see Suppl.).

The variations too in the names of the seven days among the various Teutonic races deserve all attention ; we perceive that they were not adopted altogether cut-and-dry, nor so retained, but that national ideas still exercised some control over them. The later heathenism of Friesland and Saxony caused the old names of Wednesday and Saturday to live on, while in Upper Germany they soon sank into oblivion. But what is especially significant to us, is the deviation of the Alamanns and Bavarians when we come to the third day ; how could it have arisen at a later (christian) time, when the idea of the heathen god that does duty for Mars had already become indistinct ? how came the christian clergy, supposing that from them the naming had proceeded, ever to sanction such a divergence ?

The nations that lie behind us, the Slavs, the Lithuanians, do not know the planetary names of days, they simply count like the Greeks,[2] not because they were converted later, but because they became acquainted with Latin culture later. The Finns and Lapps

---

[1] Conf. Pet. Er. Müller om Saxo, p. 79.
[2] The Indian nations also name their days of the week after planets ; and it seems worth remarking here, that Wednesday is in Sanskrit *Budhuvaras*, Tamil *Budhunkūramei*, because some have identified Buddha with Woden. In reality *Budhas*, the ruler of Mercury and son of the moon, is quite distinct from the prophet *Buddhas* (Schlegel's ind. bibl. 2. 177).

do not count, while the Esthonians again mostly do (see Suppl.).
Even the christianizing influence of Byzantium decided nothing on
this point; Byzantium had no influence over Lithuanians and Finns,
and had it over a part only of the Slavs. These in their counting
begin with Monday, as the first day after rest, consequently Tuesday is their second, and Thursday their fourth,[1] altogether deviating
from the Latin and Icelandic reckoning, which makes Monday second
and Thursday fifth. Hence the Slavic piatek (fifth) means Friday,
and that Up. Germ. pfinztag (fifth) Thursday. Wednesday they
call middle, sreda, sereda, srida (whence Lith. serrada), which may
have acted upon our High German nomenclature; the Finns too
have *keskiwijcko* (half-week, from keski medium). It would be well
worth finding out, when and for what reason the High German and
the Slav first introduced the abstract names mittewoche and sreda
(Boh. středa), while the Low German and the Romance have kept
to Woden and Mercury. Alone of Slavs, the Wends in Lüneburg
show a trace of naming after a god; dies Jovis was with them
Perendan, from Peren, Perun, thunder-god: apparently a mere
imitation of the German, as in all the other days they agree with
the rest of the Slavs.[2]

The nett result of these considerations is, that, in Latin records
dealing with Germany and her gods, we are warranted in interpret-
ing, with the greatest probability, *Mercurius* as Wuotan, *Jupiter* as
Donar, and *Mars* as Ziu. The gods of the days of the week
translated into German are an experiment on Tacitus's 'interpretatio
Romana'.

[1] E.g. in Russian: 1, voskresénie, resurrection (but O.Sl. ne-délia, no-
doing). 2, po-nedél'nik, day after-no-work. 3, vtórnik, second day. 4,
seredá, middle. 5, chetvérg, fourth day. 6, piátnitsa, fifth day. 7, subbóta,
sabbath.—TRANS.

[2] It is striking, that in O. Bohem. glossaries (Hanka 54. 165) Mercury,
Venus and Saturn are quoted in the order of their days of the week ; and that
any Slav deities that have been identified with Latin ones are almost sure to
be of the number of those that preside over the week. And whilst of the Slav
gods, *Svatovit* answers to Mars (Ziu), *Radigast* to Mercury (Wuotan), *Perun* to
Jupiter (Donar), *Lada* (golden dame, zolota baba, in Hanusch 241, 35[b]) to Venus
(Frîa), and perhaps *Sitivrat* to Saturn ; the names of the planets are construed
quite otherwise, Mars by *Smrto-nos* (letifer), Mercury by *Dobro-pan* (good lord,
or rather bonorum dator), Jupiter by *Krale-moc* (rex potens), Venus by *Ctitel*
(cupitor ? venerandus ?), Saturn by *Hlado-let* (famelicus, or annonae caritatem
afferens). Respecting Sitivrat I give details at the end of ch. XII.

CHAPTER VII.

WUOTAN, WODAN (OÐINN).

THE highest, the supreme divinity, universally honoured, as we have a right to assume, among all Teutonic races, would in the Gothic dialect have been called *Vôdans*; he was called in OHG. *Wuotan*, a word which also appears, though rarely, as the name of a man: *Wuotan*, Trad. Fuld. 1, 149. 2, 101-5-8. 128. 158. 161. *Woatan* 2, 146, 152. The Longobards spelt it *Wôdan* or *Guôdan*, the Old Saxons *Wuodan*, *Wôdan*, but in Westphalia again with the *g* prefixed, *Guôdan*, *Gudan*, the Anglo-Saxons *Wôden*, the Frisians *Wêda* from the propensity of their dialect to drop a final *n*, and to modify *ô* even when not followed by an *i*.[1] The Norse form is *Oðinn*, in Saxo *Othinus*, in the Faröe isles *Ouvin*, gen. Ouvans, acc. Ouvan. Up in the Grisons country—and from this we may infer the extent to which the name was diffused in Upper Germany—the Romance dialect has caught the term *Vut* from Alamanns or Burgundians of a very early time, and retained it to this day in the sense of idol, false god, 1 Cor. 8, 4.[2] (see Suppl.).

It can scarcely be doubted that the word is immediately derived from the verb OHG. *watan wuot*, ON. *vaða*, *óð*, signifying meare, transmeare, cum impetu ferri, but not identical with Lat. vadere, as the latter has the *a* long, and is more likely connected with OS. gavîtan, AS. gewîtan. From watan comes the subst. *wuot* (our wuth, fury), as *μένος* and animus properly mean mens, ingenium, and then also impetuosity, wildness; the ON. *óðr* has kept to the

---

[1] A Frisian god *Warns* has simply been invented from the gen. in the compound Warnsdei, Wernsdei (Richth. p. 1142), where Werns plainly stands for Wedens, Wodens, an *r* being put for *d* to avoid collision with the succeeding *sd*; it will be hard to find anywhere a nom. Wern. And the present West Frisians say Wansdey, the North Frisians Winsdei, without such *r*.

[2] Conradis wörterb. 263. Christmann, pp. 30—32.

one meaning of mens or sensus.[1] According to this, *Wuotan*, *Oðinn* would be the all-powerful, all-penetrating being, qui omnia permeat; as Lucan says of Jupiter: Est quodcunque vides, quocunque moveris, the spirit-god[2]; conf. Virg. Georg. 4, 221 : Deum ire per omnes terras, and Ecl. 3, 60 : Jovis omnia plena. In the popular language of Bavaria, *wueteln* is to bestir oneself, to swarm, grow luxuriantly, thrive, Schm. 4, 203 (see Suppl.).

How early this original meaning may have got obscured or extinguished, it is impossible to say. Together with the meaning of wise and mighty god, that of the wild, restless, vehement, must also have prevailed, even in the heathen time. The christians were the better pleased, that they could bring the bad sense into prominence out of the name itself. In the oldest glosses, *wôtan* is put for tyrannus, herus malus, Diut. 1, 276^b. gl. Ker. 270; so *wüeterich*, *wüterich* (Gramm. 2, 516) is used later on, and down to the present day, conf. ein ungestüemer wüeterich, Ben. 431 ; as in Mar. 217. Herod's messengers of murder are wüeterîche, O.i. 19, 18 names the king himself *gotewuoto*. The form *wuotunc* seems not to differ in sense; an unprinted poem of the 13th century says ' Wüetunges her' apparently for 'wütende heer,'[3] the host led as it were by Wuotan; and *Wuotunc* is likewise a man's name in OHG., *Wôdunc*, Trad. patav. no. 19. The former divinity was degraded into an evil, fiendish, bloodthirsty being, and appears to live yet as a form of protestation or cursing in exclamations of the Low German people, as in Westphalia: O Woudan, Woudan! Firmenich 1, 257, 260 ; and in Mecklenburg: Wod, Wod ! (see Suppl.).

Proofs of the general extension of Woden's worship present themselves, for one thing, in the passages collected in the preceding chapter on *Mercurius*, and again in the testimonies of Jonas of Bobbio (pp. 56 and 121) and Paulus Diaconus, and in the Abrenuntiatio, which deserves to be studied more closely, and lastly in the concurrence of a number of isolated facts, which I believe have hitherto been overlooked.

If we are to sum up in brief the attributes of this god, he is the

[1] A word that has never been fully explained, Goth. *vôþis* dulcis, 2 Cor. 2, 15, OHG. *wuodi*, Diut. 2, 304^a, OS. *wuothi*, Hel. 36, 3. 140, 7, AS. *wéðe*, must either be regarded as wholly unconnected, or its meaning be harmonized.

[2] Finn Magnusen comes to the same conclusion, Lex. myth. 621. 636.

[3] The belief, so common in the Mid. Ages, in a 'furious host' or 'wild hunt,' is described in ch. XXXI.—TRANS.

all-pervading creative and formative power, who bestows shape and beauty on men and all things, from whom proceeds the gift of song and the management of war and victory, on whom at the same time depends the fertility of the soil, nay wishing, and all highest gifts and blessings, Sæm. 113[a,b].

To the heathen fancy Wuotan is not only the world-ruling, wise, ingenious god, he is above all the *arranger of wars* and battles.[1] Adam of Bremen cap. 233, ed. 1595 says of the Norse god : Wôdan, id est fortior, bella gerit, hominique ministrat virtutem contra inimicos . . . Wôdanem sculpunt (Sveones) *armatum*, sicut nostri Martem sculpere solent. To the fortior, fortis, would answer his ON. name of *Sviðr, i.e.* the strong, masterful, swift (OS. suîth) : but fortior is, no doubt, a false reading, all the MSS. (conf. Pertz 3, 379) read 'Wôdan, id est *furor*,' which agrees with the conclusion arrived at above. To him, says the Edda, belong all the nobles who *fall* in battle (Sæm. 77[b]). and to Thôr the common folk, but this seems added merely to depreciate the latter; in another passage (Sæm. 42[a]), Freya shares the *fallen* with Oðinn; he is named *valfaðir* and *herfaðir* (val, choice ; her, host). *Oðinn* vildi þiggja mann at hlut-falli at hânga or herinom, Fornald. sög. 3, 31. Eidem prostratorum *manes* muneris loco dedicaturum se pollicetur (Haraldus), Saxo p. 146. Othinus *armipotens*, p. 37, auctor aciei corniculatae, ordinandi agminis disciplinae traditor et repertor, pp. 138-9, 146. When old, he teaches arraying of battle, p. 17, the *hamalt at fylkja, svînfylkja*, Fornald. sög. 1, 380 ; he teaches how to bring down with pebbles those whom sword will not wound, ibid. p. 157 (see Suppl.).

We need not be surprised then to find him confounded with Ziu or Týr, the special god of war, or *Mercurius* coupled with *Mars* (pp. 107, 111), or a gloss on Jonas of Bobbio, who had rightly identified him with Mercury (p. 121), correcting him thus : Qui apud eos (Alamannos) *Vuotant* (part. pres. of wuotan) vocatur, Latini autem *Martem* illum appellant. Are Adam's words also, ' sicut nostri *Martem* sculpere solent,' to be so taken that nostri

---

[1] Got waldes an der *sige kür !* Wh. 425, 24. *sigehafte hende* füege in got ! Dietr. 84[a]. Oðinn, when he sent the people forth to war, laid his *hands on their heads* and blessed, acc. to Yngl. cap. 2, gaf þeim *bianac ;* Ir. beannact, bean-nugad, beandacht, Gael. beannachd, Wel. bianoch (Villemarqué, essai LIX) = benedictio, prob. all from the Lat. word ? conf. Fr. bênir, Ir. beannaigim.

should mean Saxones ? He, it is true, may have meant those acquainted with Roman mythology.

Especially does the remarkable legend preserved by Paulus Diaconus 1, 8 show that it is Wodan who *dispenses victory*, to whom therefore, above all other gods, that antique name *sihora* (p. 27) rightfully belongs, as well as in the Eddas the epithets *Sigtýr* (god of victory), Saem. 248ᵃ, Sn. 94, *Sigföðr* (father of victory), Saem. 68ᵃ ; AS. *vígsigor* (victor in battle), Beow. 3107, *sigmetod* (creator of victory), Beow. 3554 (see Suppl.) :—Refert hoc loco antiquitas ridiculam fabulam, quod accedentes Wandali ad *Wodan, victoriam* de Winilis *postulaverint*, illeque responderit, se illis *victoriam daturum*, quos primum *oriente sole* conspexisset. Tunc accessisse Gambaram ad *Fream*, uxorem *Wodan*, et Winilis *victoriam postulasse, Fream*-que consilium dedisse, Winilorum mulieres solutos crines erga faciem ad barbae similitudinem componerent *mane*que *primo* cum viris adessent, seseque a *Wodan* videndas pariter e regione, qua ille per fenestram orientem versus erat solitus adspicere, collocarent ; atque ita factum fuisse. Quas cum *Wodan* conspiceret oriente sole, dixisse : qui sunt isti Langobardi ? tunc *Fream* subjunxisse, ut quibus nomen tribuerat, *victoriam condonaret*, sicque Winilis *Wodan* victoriam concessisse. Here deacon Paul, as a good christian, drops the remark : Haec risu digna sunt, et pro nihilo habenda : victoria enim non potestati est adtributa hominum, sed e coelo potius ministratur ; and then adds a more exact interpretation of the name Longobard : Certum tamen est Longobardos ab intactae ferro barbae longitudine, cum primitus Winili dicti fuerint, ita postmodum appellatos. Nam juxta illorum linguam lang longam, bart barbam significat. *Wodan* sane, quem adjecta litera *Gwodan* dixerunt, et *ab universis Germaniae gentibus* ut deus adoratur, qui non circa haec tempora, sed longe anterius, nec in Germania, sed in Graecia fuisse perhibetur.[1]

The whole fable bears the stamp of high antiquity ; it has even been related by others before Paul, and with variations, as in the Hist. Francor. epitomata, which has for its author, though not Fredegar, yet some writer of the seventh century. Here Chuni

---

[1] Godfrey of Viterbo (in Pistorius, ed. Struve 2, 305) has the legend out of Paul Diac. with the names corrupted, *Godam* for Wodan, *Feria* for Frea. Godam or Votam sets him thinking of the Germ. word got (deus). The unheard-of ' *Toclacus* historiographus ' has evidently sprung out of ' hoc loco ' in Paul.

(Huns) are named instead of Vandals:—Cum a Chunis (Langobardi) Danubium transeuntes fuissent comperti, eis bellum conati
sunt inferre. Interrogati a Chunis, quare gens eorum terminos
introire praesumeret ? At illi mulieribus suis praecipiunt, comam
capitis ad maxillas et mentum ligare, quo potius virorum habitum
simulantes plurimam multitudinem hostium ostenderent, eo quod
erant mulierum comae circa maxillas et mentum ad instar barbae
valde longae : fertur desuper utraeque phalangae vox dixisse : 'hi
sunt Langobardi!' quod ab his gentibus fertur eorum *deum* fuisse
locutum, quem fanatici nominant *Wodanum* (al. Wisodano, a mere
copyist's or reader's error for Wuodano). Tunc Langobardi cum cla-
massent, qui instituerat nomen, *concederet victoriam,* in hoc praelio
Chunos superant. (Bouquet 2, 406 ; according to Pertz, all the MSS.
read *Wodano.*) In this account, Frea and her advice are nowhere ;
the voice of the god, giving the name, is heard up in the air.

It was the custom for any one who bestowed a name, to follow
it up with a gift.[1] Wodan felt himself bound to confer the victory
on those for whom he had found a new national name. In this
consisted the favour of fortune, for the people, in dressing up their
wives as men, had thought of nothing but swelling the apparent
numbers of their warriors. I need scarcely remind the reader, that
this mythical interpretation of the Lombard name is a false one,
for all the credit it found in the Mid. Ages.[2]

There is one more feature in the legend that must not escape
our notice. Wodan from his heavenly dwelling *looks down on the
earth through a window,* which exactly agrees with ON. descriptions. Oðinn has a throne named *Hliðskialf,* sitting on which he
can survey the whole world, and hear all that goes on among
men : þar er einn staðr er Hliðscialf heitir, oc þaer Oðinn settiz
þar i hâsæti, oc þâ *sâ hann of alla heima,* oc vissi alla luti,
þâ er hann sâ (there is a stead that H. hight, and when O.
sat there on high-seat, then saw he over all countries, and
wist, &c.), Sn. 10. oc þâ er Allföðr sitr î þvî sæti, þâ *ser hann of
allan heim,* Sn. 21. *hlustar* (listens) Oðinn Hliðscialfo î, Sæm. 89[b].

---

[1] Lâta fylgja nafni, Sæm. 142[a]. 150[a]. Fornm. sög. 3, 182. 203. gefa at
nafnfesti (name-feast), Sn. 151. Fornm. sög. 2, 51. 3, 133. 203. Islend. sög.
2, 143. 194. Vocabuli largitionem muneris additione commendare, Saxo
Gram. 71.

[2] Longobardi a longis barbis vocitati, Otto fris. de gest. Frid. 2, 13. But
Oðinn himself was named *Lângbarðr.*

When Loki wanted to hide, it was from this seat that Oðinn espied his whereabouts, Sn. 69. Sometimes also Frigg, his consort, is imagined sitting by his side, and then she enjoys the same prospect : Oðinn ok Frigg *sâto* î Hliðscialfo, ok *sâ um heima alla*, Sæm. 39. The proem to the Grîmnismâl bears a strong resemblance to the legend in Paul; for, just as Frea pulls her favourites the Winili through, in opposition to Wodan's own resolve, so Frigg brings to grief Geirröðr, whom Oðinn favoured.—Sensuous paganism, however, makes the god-like attribute of overseeing all things depend on the position or structure of a particular chair, and as the gift forsakes the god when he does not occupy the seat, others can enjoy the privilege by taking his place. This was the case when Freyr spied the beautiful Gerðr away down in Iötunheim; Freyr *hafði setsc* î Hliðskialf, oc *sâ um heima alla*, Sæm. 81. Sn. 39. The word *hliðscialf* seems to mean literally door-bench, from hlið (ostium, conf. Engl. lid), and skialf (scamnum), AS. scylfe, Cædm. 79, 4. Engl. shelf (see Suppl.). Mark the language in which the OS. poet describes the Ascension of Christ: sôhta imo *thena hêlagon stôl*, sitit imo thar an thea suîdron (right) half Godes, endi *thanan all gisihit* (seeth) waldandeo Crist, sô huat sô (whatso) thius werold behabêt, Hel. 176, 4—7, conf. Cædm. 265, 16.

This idea of a seat in the sky, from which God looks on the earth, is not yet extinct among our people. The sitting on the right hand is in the Bible, but not the looking down. The formulas 'qui haut siet et de loing mire, qui haut siet et loins voit' (supra, p. 23) are not cases in point, for men everywhere have thought of the Deity as throned on high and seeing far around. Zeus also sits on Ida, and looks on at mortal men; he rules from Ida's top, Ἴδηθεν μεδέων, even as Helios, the eye of the sun, surveys and discerns all things, Il. 3, 277. But a widely-circulated märchen tells us of a mortal man, whom St. Peter admitted into heaven, and who, led on by curiosity, ended by climbing into the *chair of the Lord, from which one can look down and see all that is done on the whole earth.* He sees a washerwoman steal two lady's veils, and in his anger seizes the *footstool of the Lord*, which stands before the chair (al. a *chair's leg*), and hurls it down at the thief.[1] To such lengths has the ancient fable travelled.

[1] Kindermärchen no. 35. First in Bebel, ed. 1, Tub. 1506, p. 6. Frey's gartengesellschaft cap. 109, ed. 1556 p. 106, ed. 1590 p. 85. Rollwagenbüchlein 1590, pp. 98-9 (here a golden settle). Mösers vermischte schriften 1, 332. 2,

Can it be alluded to in the MHG. poem, Amgb. 3ᵃ ?

> Der nû den himel hat erkorn,
> der geiselt uns bî unser habe;
> ich vürhte sêre, unt wirt im zorn,
> den *slegel* wirft er uns her abe.[1]

In a Servian song (Vuk 4, 9) the angels descend to earth *out of God's window* (od Bózhieg prozóra; pro-zor (out-look, hence window) reminds one of zora (dawn), prozorie (morning twilight), and of Wodan at early morn looking toward the sunrise. The *dawn* is, so to speak, the opening in heaven, through which God looks into the world.

Also, what Paulus Diac. 1, 20 tells of the *anger of the Lord* (supra, p. 18), whereby the Herulian warriors were smitten before their enemies, I am inclined to trace up to Wuotan : Tanta super eos *coelitus ira respexit ;* and again : Vae tibi, misera Herulia, quae *coelestis Domini* flecteris *ira !* Conf. Egilssaga p. 365 : *reiðr* sê rögn ok Oðinn ! wrathful see the gods and O.; and Fornald. sög. 1, 501 : *gramr* er yðr Oðinn, angry is O. with you.

Victory was in the eyes of our forefathers the first and highest of gifts, but they regarded Wuotan not merely as dispenser of victory ; I have to show next, that in the widest sense he represented to them the god to whose bounty man has to look for every other distinction, who has the giving of all superior blessings ; and in this sense also Hermes (Mercury) was to the Greeks preeminently δώτωρ ἐάων, giver of good things, and I have ventured to guess that the name *Gibika, Kipicho* originally signified the same to us[2].

235. ed. 1842, 4, 5, **39**. H. Sachs (1563) v. 381. According to Greek and O. Norse notions, the gods have a *throne* or *chair* : thâ gengêngo regin öll à rökstóla ginheilög goð, Sæm. 1ᵇ. Compare in the Bible : heaven is God's throne, the earth his footstool, Matt. 5, 34-5 ; and Hel. 45, 11. 12 (see Suppl.).

[1] Also MS. 2, 254ᵇ : ze hûs wirf ich den *slegel* dir. MS. 2, 6ᵇ : mit einem *slegel* er zuo dem kinde warf. This *cudgel-throwing* resembles, what meant so much to our ancestors, the hammer's throw, and the OHG. *slaga* is malleus, *sledge*-hammer (Graff 6, 773). The cudgel thrown from heaven can hardly be other than a thunderbolt ; and the obscure proverb, ' swer irre rite daz der den *slegel* fünde,' whoso astray should ride, that he the s. might find, Parz. 180, 10, may refer to a thunder-stone (see ch. VIII, Donar) which points to hidden treasure and brings deliverance, and which only those can light upon, who have accidentally lost their way in a wood ; for which reason Wolfram calls trunks of trees, from under which peeps out the stone of luck, ' slegels urkünde und zil,' slegel's document and mark (aim).

[2] Haupts zeitschr. 1, 573. Lasicz. 47 names a *Datanus* donator bonorum.

The sum total of well-being and blessedness, the fulness of all graces, seems in our ancient language to have been expressed by a single word, whose meaning has since been narrowed down; it was named *wunsch* (wish). This word is probably derived from wunja, wunnja, our wonne, bliss; wunisc, wunsc, perfection in whatever kind, what we should call the Ideal. Thus, Er. 1699 'der wunsch was an ir garwe,' wish was in her complete; Iw. 3991 'daz mir des wunsches niht gebrast,' nought of wish was wanting; Iw. 6468 'der rât, des der wunsch an wîbe gert,' such store as wish can crave in wife; Gerh. 1754 'an der got wunsches niht vergaz,' in whom God nought of wish forgot (left out); Parz. 742, 15 'der wunsch wirt in beiden' ; Trist. 3710 'dir ist der wunsch gegeben'; Frauend. 87 'der wunsch von edlem obze,' the pick of noble fruit; Parz. 250, 25 'erden wunsches rîche,' rich in all gifts of the earth; 235, 24, 'erden wunsches überwal'; Trist. 4696. 4746 'der wunsch von worten, von bluomen' ; Trist. 1374 'in dem wunsche sweben,' *i.e.,* in perfect satisfaction. And the magic wand, by whose impact treasures are acquired, was a *wunschiligerta*, wishing-rod; conf. Parz. 235, 22 'wurzel unde rîs des wunsches,' root and spray of wish. The (secondary) meaning of 'desiring and longing for' these perfections would seem to have but accidentally attached itself to the *wunsc*, ON. ôsk (see Suppl.).

Among other Eddic names of Oðinn, appears *Osci*, Sæm. 46[b]. Sn. 3, 24, *i.e.* he who makes men partakers of wunsch, of the highest gift. *Osk*, gen. *Oskar*, a woman's name, Fornm. sög. 1, 246. Eyrbyggja saga cap. 7. Laxd. p. 12.

Another thing seems to me to be connected with this, and therefore to be a relic of the heathen religion: the fact that our poets of the 13th century personify *wunsch*, and represent it as a mighty creative being. Instances in proof of this are found chiefly in Hartmann, Rudolf and Conrad:

Got erloubte dem *Wunsche* über in,	About him, God gave to Wish full leave,
daz er lîb unde sin	that he body and mind
meistert nach sîm werde.	fashioned according to his worth.
swâ von ouch ûf der erde	Of whatsoever upon earth,
deheinem man ze loben geschiht,	to any man, praiseworthy falls,
desn gebrast im niht ;	thereof lacked him nought ;
der *Wunsch* het in *gemeistert* sô	Wish had him fashioned so,

daz er *sîn was ze kinde vrô,*
wande er nihts an im vergaz:
er hetn *geschaffet,* kunder, baz.
　　　　　Greg. 1091-1100.

that he was glad of him for child,
for he nought in him forgot:
he had him shapen, if he could,
　　　　　better.

man sagt daz nie kint gewan
ein lîp sô gar dem *Wunsche* glîch.
　　　　　Ex. 330.

They say that never a child won
a body so wholly equal to Wish
　　　　　(or, exactly like Wish).

alsô was ez (daz phert) gestalt,
und ob er (der werltwîse man)
　　danne den *gewalt*
von dem Wunsche hœte,
daz ez belibe stæte

So was it wrought (the horse),
that if he (the wright) had had

the command from Wish,
that (his work) should be left
　　unaltered,

swes er darzuo gedæhte,
und swenne erz volbræhte,
daz erz für sich stalte
und er *von sînem gwalte*
dar abe næme
swaz daran im missezæme,
alsô was ez volkomen
daz er dar abe niht hete geno-
　　men
alse grôz als umb ein hâr.
　　　　　Er. 7375-87.

whatever he attempted thereon,
and when he had completed it,
that he should set it before Him,
and He at his discretion
therefrom should take away
whatever therein misliked him,—
so perfect was it
that he therefrom nought would
　　have taken
so great as a hair.

als ez der *Wunsch gebôt* (bade).　Er. 8213.
was ein *wunschkint* (was a child of wish).　Ex. 8277
Enîte was des *Wunsches* kint,
　der an ir nihtes vergaz.　Er. 8934.
dâ was ir hâr und ir lîch (lyke, lych, body)
so gar dem *Wunsche* gelîch (like).　Iw. 1333.
diz was an ir (zuht, schœne, jugent) und gar der rât (all the store)
des der *Wunsch* (or wunsch?) an wîbe gert (desires.)　Iw. 6468.
wande sie nie gesâhen (for they never had seen)
zwêne riter gestalt (two knights fashioned)
sô gar *in Wunsches gewalt*
an dem lîbe und an den siten (manners).　Iw. 6913.
der *Wunsch vluochet* (curses) im sô.　Iw. 7066.

mir hât der *Wunsch* gevluochet.   Hartm. büchl. 2, 113.

er was schœne und wol gevar (for gefarwet, coloured),

rehte, als in der *Wunsch erkôs* (chose).   Gerh. 771.

mîn herze in (ihnen, to them) des begunde jehen (acknowledge),

in wære des *Wunsches flîz* (zeal, care) bereit.   Gerh. 1599.

an der der *Wunsch* mit kiusche *bar*

sîne süeze lebende fruht.   Gerh. 1660.

daz ich ir schœne krœne

ob allen frouwen schône

mit des *Wunsches krône.*   Gerh. 1668.

ein regen ûz dem wolken vlôz

der ûf des *Wunsches ouwe* gôz

sô heizen regen (?).   Gerh. 2307.

an lobe (praise) des *Wunsches krône.*   Gerh. 2526.

swes ich begunde daz geschach (was accomplished),

der *Wunsch* ie mînen werken jach (ever to my works said yea)

des wunsches als ich wolte

und als ich wünschen solte.   Gerh. 2945.

nach des *Wunsches lére* (lore).   Gerh. 4500.

der *Wunsch mit sîner hende*

vor wandel (change, fault) hete si getwagen (cleansed).   Troj. 1212.

der *Wunsch* hât âne lougen (without lying, undeniably)

erzeiget an ir sîne *kraft,*

und sîner *künste* meisterschaft

mit *vlîze* an ir bewert (carefully evinced in her).   Troj. 7569.

der *Wunsch* hât in *gemachet* wandels vrî (free of fault).   Troj. 3154.

der *Wunsch* der hete an si geleit (gelegt, laid out, spent)

mê *flîzes* denne ûf elliu wip (more pains than on any woman).

    Troj. 19620.

sô daz er niemer wîbes leben

für sie *geschepfen* wolde baz (better) ;

dô *sîn gewalt* ir bilde *maz* (measured),

dô leit (legte) er an sie manec model.   Troj. 19627

und hæte sîn der *Wunsch* gesworn,

er wolde bilden ein schœner wîp,

und *schepfen* alsô klâren lîp

als Hêlenâ mîn frouwe treit (trägt, bears)

er müeste brechen sînen eit (eid, oath)

wan er kunde niemer (for he could never),

und solte *bilden* iemer (were he to shape for ever),
geschepfen wünneclîcher fruht. Troj. 19526-32.
ez hât ze sînem teile der *Wunsch* vergezzen niender.   Engelh. 579.
daz haete an si der *Wunsch* geleit.   Engelh. 4703.
der *Wunsch* der hete niht gespart
an ir die sîne *meisterschaft,*
er hete sîne beste *kraft*
mit ganzem *flîz* an sie geleit.   Der werlde lôn. 84.

Other poets personify too (not, however, Wolfram nor Gotfried):
der zweier kurtêsîe
sich ze dem *Wunsche* het geweten,
si wâre niender ûz getreten.   Wigal. 9246.
an ir schœne was wol schîn,
daz ir der *Wunsch* gedâhte.   Wigal. 9281.
der *Wunsch* het sich *geneiget* in ir gewalt.   ibid. 904.
in was der *Wunsch* bereit.   ib. 10592.
des *Wunsches amîe.*   ib. 7906. 8735.
wen mohte dâ erlangen,
dâ der *Wunsch inne was.*   ib. 10612.
der *Wunsch* het si *gemachet* sô,
und ist ir *ze kinde vrô.*   Amûr 1338. (Pf. 1343).
des *Wunsches ougenweide* (food for the eye)
sit ir und mîner sælden spil (are ye, and the play of my delight).
      Wigal. 8760. Amûr 1068. (Pf. 1072).
si schepfet ûz des *Wunsches heilawâge* (holy water).   Martina, 259.
(diu hant) ist im grôz, lanc unde wiz,
zuo der het sich der *Wunsch gesellet.*   Turl. Wh. 38[a].
hie *stuont* (here stood) der *Wunsch.*   ib. 137[b].
dar an lît (therein lieth) wol des *Wunsches vlîz.*   Tyrol E, 3.
si ist des *Wunsches* hôstez *zil* (highest mark or aim).   Ms. 1, 84[a].
sie ist der *Wunsch* ûf erde.   Ms. 2, 100[b].
sie ist des *Wunsches ingesinde* (one of W.'s household).   Ms. 1, 6[a].
von ir scheitel ûf ir zêhen (from her crown to her toes)
sô ist niht an minneclîchen wîden wan (save, but) des *Wunsches*
      blic. MsH. 3, 493[a].
des *Wunsches blüete* sint entsprungen in mîne herzen.   Fragm. 45[b].
si trage des *Wunsches bilde.* Ms. 1, 191[a].
des *Wunsches krône* tragen.   Docen misc. 2, 186.

sie hât des *Wunsches gewalt.*   Amgb. 31[b]
er was sô gar des *Wunsches kint,*
daz alle man gein (against, before) sîner schœne wâren blint,
und doch menlich gestalt bî clârem velle (complexion) ;
der *Wunsch* im niht gebrechen liez (let nought be lacking)
dâ von man *'s Wunsches kint* den stolzen hiez (should call the
    stately one).   Lohengr. ed. Rückert str. 625.

The following is outside the bounds of MHG. :
an yr yst *Wensches* vlyt geleit.   Haupts zeitschr. 3, 221.
Mid. Dutch poems have no personification Wensch ; nor is there a
Wunsch in the Nibelungen or Gudrun ; but in Wolfdietrich 970 :
des *Wunsches* ein amîe !   There must be many more instances ;
but the earliest one I know of is found in the Entekrist from the
12th century (Hoffm. fundgr. 2, 107) :

mit Wunschis gewalte   With Wish's might
segniti sie der alte.   The old man blessed her.

We see Wish provided with hands, power, looks, diligence, art,
blossom, fruit ; he creates, shapes, produces master-pieces, thinks,
bows, swears, curses, is glad and angry, adopts as child, handmaid,
friend : all such pretty-well stock phrases would scarcely have
sprung up and lived in a poetry, in a language, if they did not
unconsciously relate to a higher being, of whom earlier times had a
livelier image ; on such a basis indeed nearly all the personifications
made use of by MHG. poets seem to me to rest.   In the majority
of our examples we might fairly put the name of God in the place
of Wish, or that of Wish in the phrases quoted on pp. 17-8, which
describe the joyous or the angry God : freudenvoll hât sie *Got*
gegozzen, MS. 1, 226[b] ; der *Wunsch* maz ir bilde, as mezzen is said
of God, p. 23 ; and gebieten, to command, is just as technically
applied to the one as to the other, p. 24.   The 'gramr er yðr Oðinn,'
p. 137, might be rendered in MHG 'der Wunsch zürnet iu, fluochet
iu,' meaning, the world is sick of you.   At times the poet seems to
be in doubt, whether to say God or Wish : in the first passage from
Gregor, Wish is subordinated, as a being of the second rank, so to
speak, as a servant or messenger, to the superior god ; the latter has
to give him leave to assume his creative function, which in other
cases he does of his own might.   Again, when body, figure, hair are
said to be 'like Wish,' it exactly reminds us of Homer's κόμαι

$X\alpha\rho\iota\tau\epsilon\sigma\sigma\iota\nu$ $\dot{o}\mu o\hat{\iota}\alpha\iota$, Il. 17, 51; and $X\dot{\alpha}\rho\iota\tau\epsilon\varsigma$, the Gratiae, creatresses of grace and beauty, play precisely the part of our Wish, even down to the circumstance, that in addition to the personal meaning, there is an abstract $\chi\dot{\alpha}\rho\iota\varsigma$, gratia, as there is a wish.[1] Püterich of Reicherzhausen (Haupts zeitschr. 6, 48) speaks of 'die *wuntsches* füesse' of a princess; the older phrase would have been 'ir füeze wâren dem Wunsche gelîch'. It is a genuine bit of German heathenism to make this creative faculty reside in a god, and not, after the Greek fashion, in a female personage. And there are other features too, that point back to our native heathen eld. Wish's *aue* and *heilwâc* can be matched by Phol's ouwa and brunno, or the meads and holywells of other gods; Wish's *crown* by that worn by gods and kings. And, most remarkable of all, Wish rejoices in his creature as in a *child*; here Woden's self comes upon the scene as patriarch or paterfamilias, before whom created men make their appearance like children, friends, domestics; and 'wunschkint' is also used in the sense of an adopted, *i.e.* wished for, child.[2] Herbort 13330 makes Hecuba exclaim: ich hân einen sun verlorn, er gezæme *gote* ze kinde (would suit God as a child); which does not mean in a christian sense, 'God has doubtless been pleased to take him to Himself,' but in a heathen sense, 'he was so lovely, he might be called Wish's child'. For the Norse Oðinn too has these marvellous children and wish-maidens in his train (see Suppl.)[3]

To the ON. *Oski* ought by rights to correspond an OHG. *Wunsco, Wunscjo,* (weak decl.), which I am not able to produce even as a man's name (see Suppl.).[4] A MHG. *Wunsche* cannot be proved

---

[1] In many places it is doubtful, whether the poet meant *wish* or *Wish*. In Wolfram and Gotfried, who abstain from distinct personification, I always prefer the abstract interpretation, while Hartmann admits of both by turns. When we read in Parz. 102, 30: si was gar ob dem wunsches zil (over wish's goal, beyond all that one could wish), the phrase borders close upon the above-quoted, 'si ist des Wunsches hôstez zil (the highest that Wish ever created)'; and it is but a step from 'mînes wunsches paradîs,' MS. 2, 126ᵃ, to 'des Wunsches paradîs' or 'ouwe'. So, 'dâ ist wunsch, und niender breste (here is one's wish, and nothing wanting),' MS. 1, 88ᵃ = 'der Wunsch liez im niht gebrechen,' W. left him nothing lacking (see Suppl.).

[2] The Germ. an-wünschen verbally translates the Lat. ad-opto.—TRANS.

[3] That Wish was personified, and very boldly, by the christian poets, is abundantly proved. That he was ever believed in as a person, even in heathen times, is, to my thinking, far from clear. I believe some German scholars regard the notion as little better than a mare's nest.—TRANS.

[4] The name does occur later: Johannes dictus de (= der) *Wunsch*, Ch. ann. 1324 (Neue mitth. des thür. vereins I. 4,65). In the Oberhess. wochenblatt, Marburg 1830, p. 420, I read of a Joh. *Wunsch* who is probably alive at this moment.

from Troj. 3154. 7569. 19620. 19726 (Straszb. MS.), both the metre and the strong gen. in -es forbidding. But the whole idea may in the earliest times have taken far stronger root in South Germany than in Scandinavia, since the Edda tells next to nothing of Oski, while our poetry as late as the 15th century has so much to say of Wunsch. That it was not foreign to the North either, is plainly proved by the *Oskmeyjar* = *Wünschelfrauen*, wish-women; by the *Oskasteinn*, a philosopher's stone connected with our *Wünschelrute*, wishing-rod, and Mercury's staff; by *Oskabyrr*, MHG. *Wunschwint*, fair wind; by *Oskabiörn*, wish-bear, a sea-monster; all of which will be discussed more fully by and by. A fem. proper name *Osk* occurs in a few places; what if the unaccountable *Oskopnir*, Sæm. 188[a], were really to be explained as Osk-opnir ? *Opnir, Ofnir*, we know, are epithets of Oðinn. Both word and meaning seem to grow in relevancy to our mythology, it is a stumbling-block indeed, that the AS. remains furnish no contribution, even the simple wûsc (optio, votum) seeming to be rare, and only wŷscan (optare) in common use; yet among the mythic heroes of Deira we meet with a *Wûscfreá*, lord of Wish as it were; and to the Anglo-Saxons too this being may have merely become extinct, though previously well known (see Suppl.).

But to make up for it, their oldest poetry is still dimly conscious of another name of Wuotan, which again the Edda only mentions cursorily, though in Sæm. 46[b] it speaks of *Oski* and *Omi* in a breath, and in 91[b] uses Omi once more for Oðinn. Now this *Omi* stands related to ômr, sonus, fragor, as the AS. wôma to wôm, clamor, sonitus; I have quoted instances in Andr. and El. pp. xxx, xxxi, to which may now be added from the Cod. exon.: heofonwôma 52, 18. 62, 10; dægredwôma 179, 24; hildewôma 250, 32. 282, 15; wîges wôma 277, 5; wintres wôma 292, 22 : in this last, the meaning of hiemis impetus, fragor, furor, is self-evident, and we see ourselves led up to the thought which antiquity connected with Wuotan himself : out of this living god were evolved the abstractions wuot (furor), wunsch (ideal), wôma (impetus, fragor). The gracious and grace-bestowing god was at other times called the stormful, the terror-striking, who sends a thrill through nature ; even so the ON. has both an *Yggr* standing for Oðinn, and an *yggr* for terror. The AS. *wôma* is no longer found as *Wôma*; in OHG. wuomo and Wuomo are alike unknown. Thorpe renders the

'heofonwôman' above in a local sense by 'heaven's corners,' I doubt
if correctly; in both the passages coeli fragores are meant. We
may however imagine *Omi, Wôma* as an air-god, like the Hindu
Indras, whose rush is heard in the sky at break of day, in the din
of battle, and the tramp of the 'furious host' (see Suppl.).

Precisely as the souls of slain warriors arrive at Indra's heaven,[1]
the victory-dispensing god of our ancestors takes up the heroes
that fall in fight, into his fellowship, into his army, into his
heavenly dwelling. Probably it has been the belief of all good
men, that after death they would be admitted to a closer communion with deity. Dying is therefore, even according to the
christian view, called *going to God,* turning home to God: in AS.
metodsceaft seon, Beow. 2360. Cædm. 104,31. Or *seeking, visiting
God:* OS. *god suokian,* Hel. 174,26; *fadar suokion,* Hel. 143, 23;
upôdashêm, lioht ôdar, sinlîf, godes rîki suokian, Hel. 85, 21. 17, 17.
63, 14. 137, 16. 176, 5. In a like sense the Thracians, acc. to
Herodotus 4, 94, said ἰέναι παρὰ Ζάλμοξιν (Γεβελέϊζιν) δαίμονα,
which Zalmoxis or Zamolxes is held by Jornandes to be a deified
king of the Goths (Getae). In the North, *faring to Oðinn, being
guest with Oðinn, visiting Oðinn,* meant simply to die, Fornald.
sög. 1, 118. 422-3. 2, 366. and was synonymous with faring to
Valhöll, being guest at Valhöll, ib. 1, 106. Among the christians,
these were turned into curses: *far þû til Oðins! Oðins eigi þik!*
may Oðin's have thee (see Suppl.). Here is shown the inversion
of the kindly being, with whom one fain would dwell, into an
evil one,[2] whose abode inspires fear and dread. Further on, we shall
exhibit more in detail the way in which Wuotan was pictured
driving through the air at the head of the 'furious (wütende) host'
named after him. *Valhöll* (aula optionis) and *Valkyrja* obviously
express the notion of wish and choice (Germ. wahl, Scotch wale).

Of the peculiarities of figure and outward appearance of this
god, which are brought out in such bold relief in the northern

---

[1] Bopp's Nalas, p. 264.
[2] So Wuotan's name of itself degenerates into the sense of fury (wut) and
anger; the Edda has instances of it. In revenge he pricked Brynhild with
the sleeping-thorn, Sæm. 194[a], and she says: Oðinn þvi veldr, er ek eigi
máttak bregða blunnstöfom. He breeds enmity and strife: einn veldr Oðinn
öllu bölvi, þviat með sifjungom sakrûnar bar, Sæm. 165[b]. inimicitias Othinus
serit, Saxo gram. p. 142, as christians say of the devil, that he sows the seeds
of discord. *gremi* Oðins, Sæm. 151[a] (see Suppl.).

myths, I have found but few traces left among us in Germany. The Norse Oðinn is *one-eyed*, he wears a *broad hat* and *wide mantle*: Grîmnir î *feldi blâm,* blue cloak, Sæm. 40. î *heklu grœnni* ok *blâm brôkum,* green cloak and blue breeks, Fornald. sög. 1, 324. *heklumaðr,* cloaked man, 1, 325. When he desired to drink of Mîmi's fountain, he was obliged to leave one of his eyes in pawn, Sæm. 4ª, Sn. 15.[1] In Saxo, p. 12, he appears as *grandaevus, altero orbus oculo* ; p. 37, armipotens, *uno* semper contentus *ocello* ; p. 138, *senex orbus oculis, hispido amictu.* So in the Sagas : kom þar maðr *gamall,* miök orðspakr, *einsŷnn* ok *augdapr,* ok hafði *hatt sîðan ;* there came an old man, very word-wise, one-eyed and sad-eyed, and had a wide hat, Fornm. sög. 2, 138. hann hafir *heklu flekkôtta* yfir ser, sâ maðr var berfœttr ok hafði knŷtt lînbrôkum at beini, hann var hâr miök (very high), ok eldiligr ok *einsŷnn,* Fornald. sög. 1, 120. þa kom maðr î bardagann með *sîðan hatt* ok *heklu blâ,*[2] hann hafði *eitt auga,* ok geir (spear) î hendi, ib. 1, 145. þetta mun *Oðinn gamli* verit hafa, ok at vîsu var maðrinn *einsŷnn,* ib. 1, 95. sâ hann mann mikinn með *sîðun hetti,* ib. 5, 250. með *hetti* Hângatŷss gânga, cum cidari Odiniana incedere, Vigagl. saga, p. 168. Othinus, *os pileo,* ne cultu proderetur, *obnubens,* Saxo Gram. 44. An Eddic song already names him *Sîðhöttr,* broad-hatted, Sæm. 46ᵇ, and one saga merely *Höttr,* hatted, Fornald. sög. 2, 25-6 ; conf. Müllei sagabibl. 3, 142. Were it not for the name given him in the Grîmnismâl, I should have supposed it was the intention of the christians to degrade the old god by mean clothing, or else that, wrapt in his mantle, he was trying to conceal himself from christians. Have we a right here to bring in the *pileati* of Jornandes ? A saga in Saxo, p. 12, tells prettily, how the *blind old* god takes up a protégé *in his cloak,* and carries him through the air, but Hading, peeping through a hole in the garment, observes that the horse is stepping over the sea-waves. As for that *heklumaðr* of the hat with its rim turned up, he is our *Hakolberend* at the head of the wild host, who can at once be turned into a Gothic

---

[1] Conf. Tritas in the fountain, Kuhn in Höfer 1, 290. Acc. to the popular religion, you must not look into running water, because you look *into God's eye,* Tobler's Appenzel p. 369ᵇ ; neither must you point at the stars with your fingers, for fear of sticking them into the angels' eyes.

[2] There is a Swed. märchen of *Greymantle* (grakappan), Molbech 14, who, like Mary in German tales, *takes one up to heaven* and forbids the opening of a lock, Kinderm. 3, 407.

Hakulabairands, now that hakuls for φελόνης is found in 2 Tim. iv. 13.—Swedish folk-tales picture Odin as *bald-headed*, Iduna 10, 231. In the ancient poetry he is *Harbarðr, Síðgrani, Síðskeggr*, all in allusion to his thick growth of hair and beard. The name Redbeard I have elsewhere understood of Thor, but in Fornald. sög. 2, 239—257 the *Grani* and *Rauðgrani* are expressly Oðinn (see Suppl.).

The Norse myth arms Oðinn with a wonderful *spear* (geir), *Gûngnir* by name, Sæm. 196. Sn. 72 ; which I put on a par with the lance or sword of Mars, not the staff of Mercury. Sigmund's sword breaks, when he hacks at Oðinn's spear, Völs. saga cap. 11. He lends this spear to heroes to win victories with, Sæm. 165. A remarkable passage in the Fornm. sög. 5, 250 says : seldi honum *reyrspióta* (gave him the reeden spear) î hönd, ok bað hann skióta honum yfir lið Styrbiarnar, ok þat skyldi hann mæla : Oðin â yðr alla ! All the enemies over whom the spear he shoots shall fly, are doomed to death, and the shooter obtains the victory. So too the Eyrbyggja saga p. 228 : þâ skaut Steinþôrr spióti at *fornom sið* til heilla ser yfir flock Snorra ; where, it is true, nothing is said of the spear launched over the enemy being the god's. Sæm. 5ᵃ, of Oðinn himself : fleigði ok î fôlk um skaut (see Suppl.).

To the god of victory are attached *two wolves* and *two ravens*, which, as combative courageous animals, follow the fight, and pounce upon the fallen corpses, Andr. and El. xxvi. xxvii. The wolves are named *Geri* and *Freki*, Sn. 42 ; and so late as in Hans Sachs (i. 5, 499), we read in a schwank, that the Lord God has chosen *wolves* for his hounds, that they are his cattle. The two ravens are *Huginn* and *Muninn*, from hugr (animus, cogitatio) and munr (mens) ; they are not only brave, but cunning and wise, they *sit on the shoulders* of Oðinn, and whisper in his ear whatever they see and hear, Sæm. 42ᵇ 88ᵃ. Sn. 42. 56. 322. To the Greek Apollo too the *wolf* and *raven* were sacred ;[1] his messenger the *raven* informed him when Korônis was unfaithful, and Aristeas accompanied him as a *raven*, Herod. 4, 15 ; a *raven* is perched aloft on the mantle of Mithras the sun-god. The Gospels represent the Holy Ghost as a

---

[1] In Marc. Cap. 1, 11, the words : ' augurales vero alites ante currum Delio constiterunt,' are transl. by Notker 37 : tô wâren garo ze Apollinis reito sîne wîzegfogela, *rabena* unde *albisze*. To Oðinn hawks are sometimes given instead of ravens : Oðins *haukar* Sæm. 167ᵇ.

dove descending upon Christ at his baptism, Lu. 3, 22, and resting upon him, ἔμεινεν ἐπ' αὐτόν, mansit super eum, John 1, 32: 'in Krist er sih gisidalta,' says O. i. 25, 24; but Hel. 30, 1 of the dove: *sat im uppan* ûses drohtines *ahslu* (our Lord's shoulder). Is this an echo of heathen thoughts? None of the Fathers have this circumstance, but in the Mid. Ages there is talk enough about doves resting on shoulders;[1] and the dove, though frequently contrasted with the raven (which, like the wolf, the christians applied to the Evil one), may nevertheless be put in the place of it. Oswald's *raven* flies to his *shoulder* and *arm*, 749. 942. Oswald talks to it, 95-6, and kneels before it, 854. Conf. Zingerle, Oswalt p. 67 (see Suppl.).[2]

Now under that figure of the bearded old man, Wuotan is apparently to be regarded as a water-sprite or water-god, answering well to the Latin name of *Neptunus* which some of the earlier writers put upon him (p. 122). In ON. he is *Hnikar, Hnikuðr, Nikarr, Nikuz*, and the hesitation between the two forms which in Sn. 3 are expressly made optional—' Nikarr *eða* (or) Nikuz '—may arise from the diversity of old dialects. Nikarr corresponds to the AS. *Nicor*, and Nikuz to OHG. *Nichus*, the initial Hn seems to be ON. alone. On these I shall have more to say, when treating of water-sprites (see Suppl.)—Another epithet of Oðinn is equally

---

[1] Gregor. Nyssen. encom. Ephraemi relates, that when Basil the Great was preaching, Ephraem saw on his *right shoulder* a *white dove*, which put words of wisdom in his mouth. Of Gregory the Great we read in Paul. Diac., vita p. 14, that when he was expounding the last vision of Ezekiel, a *white dove* sat *upon his head*, and now and then put its beak in his mouth, at which times he, the writer, got nothing for his stylus to put down ; conf. the narrative of a poet of the 12th cent., Hoffm. fundgr. 2, 229 ; also Myst. 1. p. 226-7. Augustine and Thomas Aquinas are portrayed with a *white dove perched on their shoulders* or *hovering over their heads*. A nursery-tale (Kinderm. no. 33) makes *two doves* settle on the pope's *shoulder*, and tell him in his ear all that he has to do. A *white dove* descends singing on the head of St. Devy, and instructs him, Buhez santez Nonn. Paris 1837, p. 117. And on other occasions the dove flies down to make known the will of heaven. No one will trace the story of Wuotan's ravens to these doves, still the coincidence is striking (see Suppl.).

[2] There are said to have been found lately, in Denmark and Sweden, representations of Odin, which, if some rather strange reports are well-founded, ought to be made known without delay. A ploughman at Boeslund in Zealand turned up two golden urns filled with ashes ; on the lids is carved *Odin*, standing up, with two *ravens* on his shoulders, and the two *wolves* at his feet ; Kunstbl. 1843, no. 19, p. 80ᵇ. Gold coins also were discovered near the village of Gömminga in Oeland, one of which represents Odin with the *ravens* on his shoulder ; the reverse has runes ; Kunstbl. 1844, no. 13, p. 52ᵃ.

noticeable for its double form: *Biflði* eða *Biflindi*, Sn. 3; Sæm. 46[b] has *Biblindi*. As bif (Germ. beben) signifies motus, aer, aqua, the quaking element, and the AS. liðe is lenis, OHG. lindi, ON. linr (for linnr); an AS. Biflíðe, Beoflíðe, OHG. Pëpalindi, might be suggested by the soft movement of the air, a very apt name for the all-penetrating god; but these forms, if they gave rise to the Norse term, are no longer found in AS. or OHG. Wuotan's dominion both over the air and over the water explains, how it is that he walks on the waves, and comes rushing on the gale.—It is Oðinn that sends wind to the ships, Fornm. sög. 2, 16, hence a good sailing wind is called *óskabyrr*, Sæm. 165[b], *i.e.,Oskabyrr ;* byrr is from byrja, OHG. purran, to rise, be lifted up. It is in striking accord with this, that the MHG. poets use *wunschwint* in the same sense; Hartmann says, Greg. 615:

> Dô sande in (to them) der süeze Krist
> den vil rehten wunschwint (see Suppl.)

But other attributes of Wuotan point more to *Hermes* and *Apollo.* He resembles the latter, in as much as from him proceed contagious diseases and their cure; any severe illness is the stroke of God, and Apollo's arrows scatter pestilence. The Gauls also imagined that Apollo drove away diseases (Apollinem morbos depellere, Caes. B. G. 6, 17); and Wôdan's magic alone can cure Balder's lamed horse. The raven on the god's shoulder exactly fits Apollo, and still more plainly the circumstance that Oðinn invented the poetic art, and Saga is his divine daughter, just as the Greek Muses, though daughters of Zeus, are under Apollo's protection, and in his train.—On the other hand, writing and the alphabet were not invented by Apollo, but by *Hermes.* The Egyptian priests placed Hermes at the head of all inventions (Iamblich. de myst. Aegypt. 8, 1), and *Theuth* or *Thoth* is said to have first discovered letters (Plato's Phaedr. 1, 96, Bekker), while, acc. to Hygin. fab. 143, Hermes learnt them by watching the flight of cranes. In the AS. dialogue between Saturn and Solomon, we read (Thorpe's anal. p. 100): 'saga me, hwâ ærôst bôcstafas sette?' 'ic the secge, *Mercurius se gygand'*. Another dialogue, entitled Adrian and Epictus (MS. Brit. mus. Arund. no. 351. fol. 39) asks: 'quis primus fecit literas?' and answers 'Seith, which is either a corruption of Theuth, or the Seth of the Bible. Just so the Eddic Rûnatals þâttr seems to ascribe the first teaching of runes to Oðinn, if we may so interpret the words: *nam ec upp rúnar*, Sæm. 28ᵃ. þær ofréð, þær ofreist, þær ofhugði Hroptr, *i.e.*, them Oðinn read out, cut out, thought out, Sæm. 195ᵇ. Also Snorri, Yngl. cap. 7 : allar þessar ídróttir kendi hann með *rúnum* ok *lióðum*. Hincmar of Rheims attributes to Mercury the invention of dice-playing : sicut isti qui de denariis quasi jocari dicuntur, quod omnino diabolicum est, et, sicut legimus, primum *diabolus* hoc *per Mercurium* prodidit, unde et Mercurius inventor illius dicitur, 1, 656. Conf. Schol. to Odyss. 23, 198, and MS. 2, 124ᵇ : der *tiuvel* schuof das würfelspil. Our folk-tales know something about this, they always make the devil play at cards, and entice others to play (see Suppl.).[1] When to this we add, that the wishing-rod, *i.e.*, Wish's staff, recals Mercury's caducēus, and the wish-wives, *i.e.*, oskmeyjar, valkyrior, the occupation of the Psychopompos ; we may fairly recognise an echo of the Gallic[2] or Germanic Mercury in the epithet *Trismegistos* (Lactantius i. 6, 3. vi. 25, 10. *ter maximus Hermes* in Ausonius), which later poets, Romance and German, in the 12th and 13th centuries[3] transferred to a Saracen deity *Termagan*,[4] *Tervagan*, *Tervigant*, *Terviant*. Moreover, when Hermes and Mercury are described as dator bonorum, and the Slavs again call the same god Dobro-pan (p. 130, note), as if mercis dominus ; it is worth noticing, that the Misnere Amgb. 42ᵃ, in enumerating all the planets, singles out Mercury to invoke in the words : Nu *hilf mir*, daz mir sælde wache ! schin er mir ze gelücke, noch sô kum ich wider ûf der sælden phat (pfad). Just so I find Odin invoked in Swedish popular songs : *Hielp nu, Oden* Asagrim ! Svenska fornsångor 1, 11. *hielp mig Othin !* 1, 69. To this god first and foremost the people turned when in distress ; I suppose he is called Asagrim, because among the Ases he bore the name of Grîmnir ?

[1] Reusch, sagen des preuss. Samlands, no. 11. 29.

[2] In the Old British mythology there appears a *Gwydion ab Don*, G. son of Don, whom Davies (Celtic researches pp. 168, 174. Brit. myth. p. 118, 204, 263-4, 353, 429, 504, 541) identifies with Hermes ; he invented writing, practised magic, and built the rainbow ; the milky way was named caer Gwydion, G.'s castle (Owen, sub v.). The British antiquaries say nothing of Wôden, yet *Gwydion* seems near of kin to the above *Gwodan* = Wodan. So the Irish name for dies Mercurii, dia *Geden*, whether modelled on the Engl. Wednesday or not, leads us to the form Goden, Gwoden (see Suppl.).

[3] Even nursery-tales of the present time speak of a *groszmächtige Mercurius*, Kinderm. no. 99. 2, 86.

[4] This *Termagan*, *Termagant* occurs especially in O. Engl. poems, and may have to do with the Irish tormac augmentum, tormacaim augere.

It is therefore not without significance, that also the *wanderings* of the Herald of gods among men, in whose hovels he now and then takes up his lodging, are parallelled especially by those of *Oðinn and Hœnir*, or, in christian guise, of *God and St. Peter*.

Our olden times tell of Wuotan's wanderings, his waggon, his way, his retinue (duce Mercurio, p. 128).—We know that in the very earliest ages the seven stars forming the Bear in the northern sky were thought of as a four-wheeled *waggon*, its pole being formed by the three stars that hang downwards:

῎Αρκτον θ᾿, ἥν καὶ ἄμαξαν ἐπίκλησιν καλέουσιν. Il. 18, 487. Od. 5, 273. So in OHG. glosses: ursa *wagen*, Jun. 304; in MHG. *himelwagen*, Walth. 54, 3.[1] *herwagen* Wackern. lb. 1. 772, 26. The clearest explanation is given by Notker cap. 64 : Selbiu *ursa* ist pî demo norde mannelîchemo zeichenhaftiu fone dien siben glatên sternôn, die allêr der liut *wagen* heizet, unde nâh einemo gloccun joche[2] gescaffen sint, unde ebenmichel sint, âne (except) des mittelôsten. The Anglo-Saxons called the constellation *wœnes þîsl* (waggon's thill, pole), or simply *þîsl*, but *carles wœn* also is quoted in Lye, the Engl. *charles wain*, Dan. *karlsvogn*, Swed. *karlwagn*. Is carl here equivalent to lord, as we have *herrenwagen* in the same sense? or is it a transference to the famous king of christian legend? But, what concerns us here, the constellation appears to have borne in heathen times the full name of *Wuotanes wagan*, after the highest god of heaven. The Dutch language has evidence of this in a MS. of as late as 1470 : ende de poeten in heure fablen heetend (the constell.) ourse, dat is te segghene *Woenswaghen*. And elsewhere : dar dit teekin Arcturus, dat wy heeten *Woonswaghen*, up staet; het sevenstarre ofde *Woenswaghen*; conf. Huydec. proeven 1, 24. I have nowhere met with plaustrum Mercurii, nor with an ON. Oðins vagn ; only *vagn â himnum*.

It is a question, whether the great open highway in heaven—to which people long attached a peculiar sense of sacredness, and perhaps allowed this to eclipse the older fancy of a 'milky way' (caer Gwydion, p. 150)—was not in some districts called *Wuotanes wec* or *strâza* (way or street). *Wôdenesweg*, as the name of a place, stood its ground in Lower Saxony, in the case of a village near Magdeburg, Ch. ad ann. 973 in Zeitschr. für archivk. 2, 349 ; an

---

[1] Septentrion, que nos *char el ciel* apelon ; Roman de Rou.
[2] Crossbeam, such as bells (glocken) are suspended on; conf. ans, âs, p. 125.

older doc. of 937 is said to have *Watanesweg* (conf. Wiggert in the Neu. mitth. des thür. vereins VI. 2, 22). praedium in *Wôdeneswege*, Dietm. Merseb. 2, 14 p. 750. Annal. Saxo 272. Johannes de *Wdenswege*, Heinricus de *Wôdensweghe* (Lenz.) Brandenb. urk. p. 74 (anno 1273), 161 (anno 1301). later, *Wutenswege, Godenschwege, Gutenswegen*, conf. Ledebur n. arch. 2, 165, 170. Gero ex familia *Wodenswegiorum*, Ann. Magdeb. in chron. Marienthal. Meibom 3, 263. I would mention here the lustration der *koninges strate*, RA. 69 ; in the Uplandslag vidherb. balkr 23, 7 the highway is called *karlsveg*, like the heavenly wain above. But we shall have to raise a doubt by and by, whether the notion of *way*, via, is contained at all in Wodensweg.

Plainer, and more to the purpose, appear the names of certain mountains, which in heathen times were sacred to the service of the god. At *Sigtŷs bergi*, Sæm. 248[a]. *Othensberg*, now *Onsberg*, on the Danish I. of Samsöe ; *Odensberg* in Schonen. Godesberg near Bonn, in docs. of Mid. Ages *Gudenesberg*, Günther 1, 211 (anno 1131), 1, 274 (anno 1143), 2, 345 (anno 1265) ; and before that, *Wôdenesberg*, Lacomblet 97. 117, annis 947, 974 So early as in Caesarius heisterb. 8, 46 the two forms are put together : *Gudinsberg* vel, ut alii dicunt, *Wudinsberg*. Near the holy oak in Hesse, which Boniface brought down, there stood a *Wuodenesberg*, still so named in a doc. of 1154 (Schminke beschr. von Cassel, p. 30, conf. Wenk 3, 79), later *Vdenesberg, Gudensberg ;* this hill is not to be confounded with *Gudensberg* by Erkshausen, district Rotenburg (Niederhess. wochenbl. 1830, p. 1296), nor with a *Gudenberg* by Oberelsungen and Zierenberg (ib. p. 1219. Rommel 2, 64. *Gudenburg* by Landau, p. 212); so that three mountains of this name occur in Lower Hesse alone ; conf. ' montem Vodinberg, cum silva eidem monti attinente,' doc. of 1265 in Wenk II, no. 174. In a different neighbourhood, a Henricus comes de *Wôdenesberg* is named in a doc. of 1130, Wedekind's notes 1, 367 ; a curtis *Wôdenesberg* in a doc. of 973, Falke tradit. corb. 534. *Gotansberg* (anno 1275), Langs reg. 3, 471 : vineas duas *gotansberge* vocatas. Mabillon's acta Bened. sec. 5, p. 208 contain the following : ' in loco ubi mons quem dicunt Wonesberth (l. *Wônesberch* = Wôdanesberg) a radicibus astra petit,' said to be situate in pagus Gandavensis, but more correctly Mt. Ardenghen between Boulogne and St. Omer. Comes *Wadanimontis*, aft. Vaudemont in Lorraine (Don Calmet, tome 2, preuves XLVIII. L.), seems to be the same, and to mean *Wodani-mons.*[1] A *Wôdnes beorg* in the Sax. Chron. (Ingram pp. 27. 62), later *Wodnesborough, Wansborough* in Wiltshire; the corruption already in Ethelwerd p. 835: 'facta ruina magna ex utraque parte in loco qui dicitur *Wodnesbyrg*' for Wodnesberg; but Florence, ed. 1592, p. 225, has '*Wodnesbeorh*, id est mons Wodeni'.[2] A *Wôdnes-beorg* in Lappenberg's map near the Bearucwudu, corlf. *Wodnesbury, Wodnesdyke, Wôdanesfeld* in Lappenb. engl. gesch. 1, 131. 258. 354. To this we must add, that about the Hessian Gudensberg the story goes that King Charles lies prisoned in it, that he there won a victory over the Saxons, and opened a well in the wood for his thirsting army, but he will yet come forth of the mountain, he and his host, at the appointed time. The mythus of a victorious army pining for water is already applied to King Carl by the Frankish annalists (Pertz 1, 150. 348), at the very moment when they bring out the destruction of the Irminsûl; but beyond a doubt it is older and heathen: Saxo Gram. 42 has it of the victorious Balder. The agreement of such legends with fixed points in the ancient cultus cannot but heighten and confirm their significance. A people whose faith is falling to pieces, will save here and there a fragment of it, by fixing it on a new and unpersecuted object of veneration. After such numerous instances of ancient Woden-hills, one need not be afraid to claim a *mons Mercurii* when mentioned in Latin annalists, such as Fredegar.

Other names occur, besides those of mountains. The breviarium Lulli, in Wenk II. no. 12, names a place in Thuringia: 'in *Wudaneshusun*,' and again *Woteneshusun* (conf. Schannat no. 84. 105); in Oldenburg there is a *Wodensholt*, now Godensholt, cited in a land-book of 1428, Ehrentraut Fries. arch. 1, 445: 'to Wodensholte Tideke Tammen gut x schillinge'; *Wothenower* (Wô-denôver?), seat of a Brandenburg family, Höfers urk. p. 270, anno 1334; not far from Bergen op Zoom and the Scheldt, towards Antwerp, stands to this day a *Woensdrecht*, as if Wodani trajectum. *Woensel* = Wodenssele, Wodani aula, lies near Eindhoven on the

---

[1] We know of Graisivaudan, a valley near Grenoble in Dauphiné, for which the Titurel has Graswaldane; but there is no ground for connecting it with the god.

[2] Our present -borough, -bury, stands both correctly for *burh, byrig*, castle, town (Germ. burg), and incorrectly for the lost *beorg, beorh*, mountain (Germ. berg).—TRANS.

Dommel in N. Brabant; a remarkable passage on it in Gramaye's
Taxandria, p. 23, was pointed out to me by J. W. Wolf: Imo
amplius supersunt aperte Cymbricorum deorum pagis aliquot, ubi
forte culti erant, indita nomina, nominatim Mercurii in *Woensel*,
honoris in *Eersel*, Martis in *Roysel*. Uti enim Woen Mercurium
eis dictum alias docui, et eer honorem esse omnes sciunt, ita Roy
Martem a colore sanguineo cognominatum ostendunt illi qui tertiam
hebdomadis feriam Roydach indigitant.   In due time I shall
speak of Eersel and Roysel, which lie in the neighbourhood of
Woensel, and all of them in the N. Brabant district of Oirschot.
This Woensel is like the Oðinssalr, Othänsäle, Onsala named on
p. 158.   *Wunstorp*, Wunsdorf, a convent and small town in Lower
Saxony, stands unmutilated as *Wodenstorp* in a doc. of 1179, Falke
tradit. corb. 770.   Near Windbergen in the Ditmar country, an
open space in a wood bears the name of *Wodenslag, Wonslag*.   Near
Hadersleben in Schleswig are the villages of *Wonsbeke, Wonslei,
Woyens* formerly *Wodensyen*.   An AS. doc. of 862 (Kemble 2, 73)
contains in a boundary-settlement the name *Wônstoc = Wôdenesstoc*,
Wodani stipes, and at the same time betrays the influence of the
god on ancient delimitation.   Wuotan, Hermes, Mercury, all seem
to be divinities of measurement and demarcation; conf. *Woedensspanne, Woenslet*, p. 160 (see Suppl.).

As these names, denoting the waggon and the mountain of the
old god, have survived chiefly in Lower Germany, where heathenism
maintained itself longest; a remarkable custom of the people in
Lower Saxony at harvest-time points the same way.   It is usual to
leave a clump of standing corn in a field *to Woden for his horse*.
Oðinn in the Edda rides the eight-footed steed *Sleipnir*, the best of
all horses, Sæm. 46ᵃ 93ᵇ. Sn. 18. 45. 65.   *Sleipnis verðr* (food) is a
poetic name for hay, Yngl. saga cap. 21: other sagas speak of a
tall *white horse*, by which the god of victory might be recognised in
battles (see Suppl.).   Christianity has not entirely rooted out the
harmless practice for the Norse any more than for the Saxon
peasant.   In Schonen and Blekingen it continued for a long time
to be the custom for reapers to leave on the field a gift *for Oden's
horses*.[1]   The usage in Mecklenburg is thus described by Gryse:

[1] Geyers schwed. gesch. 1, 110. orig. 1, 123.   In the Högrumssocken,
Oeland, are some large stones named *Odins flisor*, Odini lamellae, of which the

Ja, im heidendom hebben tor tid der arne (at harvest-tide) de meiers (mowers) dem afgade *Woden* umme god korn angeropen (invoked for good corn), denn wenn de roggenarne geendet, heft men up den lesten platz eins idern (each) veldes einen kleinen ord unde humpel korns unafgemeiet stan laten, datsülve baven (b' oben, a-b'ove) an den aren drevoldigen to samende geschörtet, unde besprenget (ears festooned together three times, and sprinkled). Alle meiers sin darumme her getreden, *ere höde* (their hats) *vam koppe genamen* (v. supra, p. 32), unde ere seisen (scythes) na der sülven wode [mode ?] unde geschrenke (encircling) dem kornbusche upgerichet, und hebben den *Wodendüvel* dremal semplik lud averall also angeropen unde gebeden:

> *Wode*, hale (fetch) *dinem rosse* nu voder,
> nu distil unde dorn,
> tom andern jar beter korn!

welker afgödischer gebruk im Pawestom gebleven. Daher denn ok noch an dissen orden dar heiden gewanet, bi etliken ackerlüden (-leuten, men) solker avergelövischer gebruk in anropinge des *Woden* tor tid der arne gespöret werd, und ok oft desülve *helsche jeger* (the same hellish hunter), sonderliken im winter, des nachtes up dem velde mit sinen jagethunden sik hören let.[1]

David Franck (Meklenb. 1, 56-7), who has heard the same from old people, quotes the rhyme thus :

story is told, that Odin, in turning his horse out to graze, took the bit off him and laid it on a huge block of stone ; the weight of the bit split the stone into two pieces, which were set upright as a memorial. Another story is, that *Oden* was about to fight an adversary, and knew not where to *tie his horse up*. In the hurry he ran to the stone, pierced it with his sword, and tied his horse fast through the hole. But the horse broke loose, the stone burst in pieces and rolled away, and from this arose the deep bog named Högrumsträsk ; people have tied poles together, but never could reach the bottom. Abrah. Ahlquist, Oelands historia, Calmar 1822. 1, 37. 2, 212. There is a picture of the stones in Liliengren och Brunius, no. xviii. In the Högbysocken of Oeland is also a smooth block of granite named *Odinssten*, on which, acc. to the folk-tale, the warriors of old, when marching to battle, used to whet their swords ; Ahlquist 2, 79. These legends confirm the special importance of *Odin's horse* in his mythus. Verelii notae on the Gautrekssaga p. 40 quote from the Clavis computi runici : ' *Odin beter hesta sina* i belg bunden,' which I do not quite understand. In the Fornm. sög. 9, 55-6 Oðinn has his *horse* shod at a blacksmith's, and rides away by enormous leaps to Sweden, where a war breaks out (see Suppl.).

[1] Spegel des antichristischen pawestdoms (popery), dorch Nicolaum Grysen, predigern in Rostock, Rost. 1593. 4, sheet E iiii[b]. With the verses cited by him, conf. the formula in weisthümer : Let it lie fallow one year, and bear *thistle and thorn* the next.

Wode, Wode,
hal dinen rosse nu voder,
nu distel un dorn,
ächter jar beter korn !

He adds, that at the squires' mansions, when the rye is all cut, there is *Wodel-beer* served out to the mowers; no one weeds flax on a *Wodenstag,* lest *Woden's horse* should trample the seeds ; from Christmas to Twelfth-day they will not spin, nor leave any flax on the distaff, and to the question why ? they answer, *Wode* is galloping across.   We are expressly told, this wild hunter *Wode* rides a *white horse.*[1]   Near Sätuna in Vestergötland are some fine meadows called *Onsängarne* (Odens ängar, ings), in which the god's *horses* are said to have *grazed,* Afzelius 1, 4.   In S. Germany they tell of the lord of the castle's *grazing gray* (or white), Mone anz. 3, 259 ; v. infra, the ' wütende heer'.   I have been told, that in the neighbourhood of Kloppenburg in Oldenburg, the harvesters leave a bunch of corn-stalks uncut on the field, and dance round it.   There may be a rhyme sung over it still, no doubt there was formerly.

A custom in Schaumburg I find thus described :[2] the people go out to mow in parties of twelve, sixteen or twenty scythes, but it is so managed, that on the last day of harvest they all finish at the same time, or some leave a strip standing which they can cut down at a stroke the last thing, or they merely pass their scythes over the stubble, pretending there is still some left to mow.   At the last stroke of the scythe they raise their implements aloft, plant them upright, and beat the blades three times with the strop.   Each spills on the field a little of the drink he has, whether beer, brandy, or milk, then drinks himself, while they wave their hats, beat their scythes three times, and cry aloud *Wôld, Wôld, Wôld !* and the women knock all the crumbs out of their baskets on the stubble. They march home shouting and singing.   Fifty years ago a song was in use, which has now died out, but whose first strophe ran thus :

Wôld, Wôld, Wôld !
hävenhüne weit wat schüt,
jümm hei dal van häven süt.

---

[1] Mussäus meklenb. volkssagen no. 5 ; in Lisch meklenb. jahrb. 2, 133 it is spelt *Waud,* and a note is made, that on the Elbe they say *fruh Wod, i.e.* frôho, lord ; conf. infra, fru Gaue and fru Gauden in the 'wütende heer',
[2] By Münchhausen in Bragur VI. 1, 21—34.

Vulle kruken un sangen hät hei,
upen holte wässt (grows) manigerlei :
hei is nig barn un wert nig old.
Wôld, Wôld, Wôld!

If the ceremony be omitted, the next year will bring bad crops of hay and corn.

Probably, beside the libation, there was corn left standing for the venerated being, as the fourth line gives us to understand : ' full crocks and *shocks* hath he '; and the second strophe may have brought in his horse. ' Heaven's giant knows what happens, ever he down from heaven sees,' accords with the old belief in Wuotan's chair (p. 135) ; the sixth line touches off the god that ' ne'er is born and ne'er grows old ' almost too theosophically. *Wôld*, though excused by the rhyme, seems a corruption of *Wôd*, *Wôde*,[1] rather than a contraction from *waldand* (v. supra, p. 21). A Schaumburg man pronounced the name to me as *Wauden*, and related as follows : On the lake of Steinhude, the lads from the village of Steinhude go every autumn after harvest, to a hill named Heidenhügel, light a fire on it, and when it blazes high, wave their hats and cry *Wauden, Wauden!* (see Suppl.).

Such customs reveal to us the generosity of the olden time. Man has no wish to keep all his increase to himself; he gratefully leaves a portion to the gods, who will in future also protect his crops. Avarice increased when sacrificing ceased. Ears of corn are set apart and offered here to Wuotan, as elsewhere to kind spirits and elves, *e.g.*, to the brownies of Scotland (see Suppl. to Elves, pixy-hoarding).

It was not Wuotan exclusively that bestowed fertility on the fields ; Donar, and his mother the Earth, stood in still closer connexion with agriculture. We shall see that goddess put in the place of Wuotan in exactly similar harvest-ceremonies.

In what countries the worship of the god endured the longest, may be learnt from the names of places which are compounded with his name, because the site was sacred to him. It is very unlikely that they should be due to men bearing the same name as the god, instead of to the god himself ; Wuotan, Oðinn, as a man's

---

[1] Conf. Dutch oud, goud for old, gold ; so Woude, which approximates the form Wôde. Have we the latter in ' Theodericus de *Wodestede?* ' Scheidt's mantissa p. 433, aɔno 1205.

name, does occur, but not often; and the meaning of the second
half of the compounds, and their reappearance in various regions,
are altogether in favour of their being attributable to the god.
From Lower Germany and Hesse, I have cited (p. 151) *Wôdenesweg*,
Wôdenesberg, *Wôdenesholt*, *Wôdeneshûsun*, and on the Jutish border
Wonsild; from the Netherlands *Woensdrecht;* in Upper Germany
such names hardly show themselves at all.[1] In England we find:
Woodnesboro' in Kent, near Sandwich : *Wednesbury* and *Wednes-
field* in Staffordshire ; *Wednesham* in Cheshire, called *Wodnesfield*
in Ethelwerd p. 848.[2] But their number is more considerable in
Scandinavia, where heathenism was preserved longer : and if in
Denmark and the Gothland portion of Sweden they occur more
frequently than in Norway and Sweden proper, I infer from this a
preponderance of Odin-worship in South Scandinavia. The chief
town in the I. of Funen (Fion) was named *Odinsve* (Fornm. sög. 11,
266. 281) from *ve*, a sanctuary ; sometimes also *Oðinsey* (ib. 230.
352) from *ey*, island, meadow ; and later again *Odense*, and in
Waldemar's Liber censualis[3] 530. 542 *Othänsö*. In Lower Norway,
close to Frederikstad, a second *Oðinsey* (Heimskr. ed. Havn. 4, 348.
398), aft. called *Onsö*. In Jutland, *Othänshyllä* (-huld, grace,
Wald. lib. cens. 519), aft. *Onsild*. *Othänslef* (Othini reliquiae,
leavings, ib. 526), now *Onslev*. In Halland, *Othänsäle* (-saal, hall,
ib. 533), now *Onsala* (Tuneld's geogr. 2, 492. 504) ; as well as in
Old Norway an *Odhinssalr* (conf. Woensel in Brabant, Woenssele ?).
In Schonen, *Othänshäret* (Wald. lib. cens. 528) ; *Othenshärat* (Bring
2, 62. 138. 142),[4] now *Onsjö* (Tuneld 2, 397) ; *Onslunda* (-grove,
Tuneld 2, 449) ; *Othensvara* (Bring 2, 46-7, Othenvara 39) ;
Othenströö (Bring 2, 48), from vara, foedus, and tro, fides ? In
Småland, *Odensvalahult* (Tuneld 2, 146) and *Odensjö* (2, 109. 147.
Sjöbörg försök p. 61). In Ostergötland, *Odenfors* (Tuneld 2, 72).
In Vestergötland, *Odenskulla* (2, 284) and *Odenskälla* (2, 264), a
medicinal spring ; *Odensåker*, *Onsåker* (-acre, field, 2, 204. 253). In

---

[1] An *Odensberg* in the Mark of Bibelnheim (now Biebesheim below Gerns-
heim in Darmstadt) is named in a doc. of 1403. Chmels reg. Ruperti p. 204 ;
the form Wodensberg would look more trustworthy.

[2] If numbers be an object, I fancy the English contribution might be
swelled by looking up in a gazetteer the names beginning with Wans-, Wens-,
Wadden-, Weddin-, Wad-, Wed-, Wood-, Wam-, Wem-, Wom-.—TRANS.

[3] Langebek script. tom. 7.

[4] Sven Bring, monumenta Scanensia, vol 2, Lond. goth. 1748.

Westmanland, *Odensvi* (1, 266. conf. Grau, p. 427),[1] like the
Odinsve of Fünen; and our Lower Saxon Wodeneswege may have
to do with this *ve* (not with weg, via), and be explained by the old
wig, wih, templum (see p. 67). This becomes the more credible,
as there occurs in the Cod. exon. 341, 28 the remarkable sentence:

> *Wôden* worhte *weos,* wuldor alwealda
> rûme roderas;

i.e., Wôden construxit, creavit fana (idola), Deus omnipotens amplos
coelos; the christian writer had in his recollection the heathen
sanctuaries assigned to Wôden, and contrasts with them the greater
creations of God. The plur. weos is easily justified, as wih is
resolved into weoh, and weohas contracted into weos: so that an
AS. Wôdenesweoh would exactly fit the OS. Wôdanesweg = Wô-
daneswih, and the ON. Oðinsve. Also in Westmanland, an *Odensjö*
(Grau p. 502). In Upland, *Odensala* (Tuneld 1, 56); *Odensfors*
(1, 144); *Onsike* (1, 144). In Nerike, *Odensbacke* (1, 240), (see
Suppl.).

It seemed needful here to group the most important of these
names together, and no doubt there are many others which have
escaped me;[2] in their very multitude, as well as the similarity or
identity of their structure, lies the full proof of their significance.
Few, or isolated, they might have been suspected, and explained
otherwise; taken together, they are incontestable evidence of the
wide diffusion of Odin's worship.

Herbs and plants do not seem to have been named after this
god. In Brun's beitr., p. 54, *wodesterne* is given as the name of a
plant, but we ought first to see it in a distincter form. The Icelanders and Danes however call a small waterfowl (tringa minima,
inquieta, lacustris et natans) *Oðinshani, Odenshane, Odens fugl,*
which fits in with the belief, brought out on p. 147, in birds consecrated to him. An OHG. gloss (Haupts altd. bl. 2, 212) supplies
a doubtful-looking *vtinswaluwe,* fulica (see Suppl.).

Even a part of the human body was named after the god: the

---

[1] Olof Grau, beskrifning öfver Wästmanland. Wästerås 1754. conf. Dybeck
runa I. 3, 41.

[2] There are some in Finn Magnusen's lex. myth. 648; but I do not agree
with him in including the H. Germ. names Odenwald, Odenheim, which lack
the HG. form Wuotan and the -*s* of the genitive; nor the Finn. Odenpä, which
means rather bear's head.

space between the thumb and the forefinger when stretched out, which the Greeks name λιχάς, was called in the Netherlands *Woedensspanne, Woedenspanne, Woenslet.* The thumb was sacred, and even worshipped as thumbkin and Pollux = pollex ; Wodan was the god of play, and lucky men were said to have the game running on their thumb. We must await further disclosures about the name, its purport, and the superstition lying at the bottom of it (see Suppl.).

I started with assuming that the worship of this divinity was common to all the Teutonic races, and foreign to none, just because we must recognise him as the most universal and the supreme one. Wuotan—so far as we have succeeded in gleaning from the relics of the old religion an idea of his being—Wuotan is the most intellectual god of our antiquity, he shines out above all the other gods ; and therefore the Latin writers, when they speak of the German cultus, are always prompted to make mention first of Mercury.

We know that not only the Norsemen, but the Saxons, Thuringians, Alamanns and Langobards worshipped this deity ; why should Franks, Goths, and the rest be excluded from his service ?

At the same time there are plain indications that his worship was not always and everywhere the dominant one. In the South of Germany, although the personification of Wish maintained its ground, Wuotan became extinct sooner than in the North ; neither names of places, nor that of the fourth day of the week, have preserved him there. Among the Scandinavians, the Swedes and Norwegians seem to have been less devoted to him than the Gotlanders and Danes. The ON. sagas several times mention images of Thor, never one of Oðinn ; only Saxo Gram. does so in an altogether mythical way (p. 113) ; Adam of Bremen, though he names Wodan among the Upsala gods, assigns but the second place to him, and the first to Thor. Later still, the worship of Freyr seems to have predominated in Sweden.

An addition to the St. Olaf saga, though made at a later time, furnishes a striking statement about the heathen gods whom the introduction of christianity overthrew. I will quote it here, intending to return to it from time to time : 'Olafr konûngr kristnaði þetta rîki allt, öll blôt braut hann niðr ok öll goð, sem

Thôr Engilsmanna goð, ok *Oðin* Saxa goð, ok Skiöld Skânûnga goð, ok Frey Svîa goð, ok Goðorm Dana goð'; *i.e.* king O. christened all this kingdom, broke down all sacrifices and all gods, as Thor the Englishmen's god, Oðin the Saxons' god, &c., Fornm. sög. 5, 239.—This need not be taken too strictly, but it seems to me to express the still abiding recollections of the old national gods : as the Swedes preferred Freyr, so probably did the Saxons Wôden, to all other deities. Why, I wonder, did the writer, doubtless a Norwegian, omit the favourite god of his own countrymen ? To them he ought to have given Thor, instead of to the English, who, like other Saxons, were votaries of Wôden.

Meanwhile it must not be overlooked, that in the Abrenuntiatio, an 8th century document, not purely Saxon, yet Low German, O. Frankish and perhaps Ripuarian, *Thunar* is named before *Vuodan*, and *Saxnôt* occupies the third place. From this it follows at all events, that the worship of Thunar also prevailed in those regions; may we still vindicate Wuodan's claims to the highest place by supposing that the three gods are here named in the order in which their statues were placed side by side? that Wuodan, as the greatest of them, stood *in the middle ?* as, according to Adam of Bremen, *Thor* did at Upsala, with *Wodan* and *Fricco* on each side of him.

In the ON. sagas, when *two* of these gods are named together, Thôrr usually precedes Oðinn. The Laxdælasaga, p. 174, says of Kiartan : At hann þykist eiga meira traust undir afli sînu ok vâpnum (put more trust in his strength and weapons, conf. pp. 6, 7) heldr enn þar sem er *Thôrr* ok *Oðinn.* The same passage is repeated in Fornm. sög. 2, 34. Again, Eyvindr relates how his parents made a vow before his birth: At sâ maðr skal alt til dauðadags þiona *Thôr* ok *Oðni* (this man shall until death-day serve, &c.), Fornm. sög. 2, 161.[1] But it does not follow from this, that Thôrr was thought the greatest, for Eyvindr was actually dedicated to Oðinn. In Fornm. sög. 5, 249, Styrbiörn sacrifices to Thôrr, and Eirekr to Oðinn, but the former is beaten. *Thôrr* tôk

[1] So in an AS. homily De temporibus Antichristi, in Wheloc's Beda p. 495, are enumerated ' *Thor* aud *Eoðwen*, þe hæðene men heriað swiðe '; and before that, ' *Erculus* se ent (Hercules gigas) and *Apollinis* (Apollo), þe hi mærne god lêton '. The preacher was thinking of the Greek and the Norse deities, not of the Saxon, or he would have said Thunor and Wôden. And in other cases, where distinctly Norse gods are meant, AS. writers use the Norse form of name. F. Magnusens lex. p. 919.

jolaveizlu frâ Haraldi, enn *Oðinn* tôk frâ Hâlfdâni, Fornm. sög.
10, 178. In the popular assembly at Thrândheim, the first
cup is drunk to *Oðinn*, the second to *Thôrr*, ibid. 1, 35. In the
famous Bravalla fight, *Othin* under the name of Bruno acts as
charioteer to the Danish king Harald, and to the latter's destruction;
on the Swedish side there fight descendants of *Freyr*, Saxo Gram.
144-7. Yet the Eddic Harbarzlioð seems to place Oðinn above Thôrr.
A contrast between Oðinn and Thôrr is brought out strongly in the
Gautrekssaga quoted below, ch. XXVIII. But, since Thôrr is represented as Oðin's son, as a rejuvenescence of him, the two must
often resolve into one another.[1]

If the *three* mightiest gods are named, I find Oðinn foremost :
Oðinn, Thôr, Freyr, Sn. edda 131. According to Fornm. sög. 1, 16,
voyagers vow money and three casks of ale to *Freyr*, if a fair wind
shall carry them to Sweden, but to *Thôrr* or *Oðinn*, if it bring them
home to Iceland (see Suppl.).

It is a different thing, when Oðinn in ON. documents is styled
Thridi, the third ;[2] in that case he appears not by the side of Thôrr
and Freyr, but by the side of *Hâr* and *Iafnhâr* (the high and the
even-high or co-equal, OHG. epan hôh) as the *Third High*[3] (see
Suppl.), Sn. 7. Yngl. saga 52. Sæm. 46ᵃ. As we might imagine,
the grade varies : at other times he is *Tveggi* (duplex or secundus).
Again, in a different relation he appears with his brothers *Vili* and
Ve, Sn. 7; with *Hænir* and *Loðr*, Sæm. 3ᵇ, or with *Hænir* and *Loki*
Sæm. 180. Sn. 135 ; all this rests upon older myths, which, as
peculiar to the North, we leave on one side. Yet, with respect to
the trilogy *Oðinn, Vili, Ve*, we must not omit to mention here,
that the OHG. *willo* expresses not only voluntas, but votum,
impetus and spiritus,[4] and the Gothic viljan, velle, is closely connected with valjan, eligere ; whence it is easy to conceive and

---

[1] When Oðinn is called *Thundr* in the songs of the Edda, Sæm. 28ᵇ 47ᵇ,
this may be derived from a lost þynja = AS. þunian, tonare, and so be equivalent
to Donar ; it is true, they explain þundr as loricatus, from þund lorica. But
Wuotan, as Vôma, is the noise of the rushing air, and we saw him hurl the
cudgel, as Thôrr does the hammer.
[2] As Zeus also is τρίτος, from which Τριτογένεια is more easily explained
than by her birth from his head (see Suppl.).
[3] Ælfric's glosses 56ᵃ, *Altanus : Wôden*. Altanus, like Summanus, an
epithet of Jove, the Altissimus ; else Altanus, as the name of a wind, might
also have to do with the storm of the ' wütende heer '.
[4] The Greek μένος would be well adapted to unite the meanings of courage,
fury (mut, wut), wish, will, thought.

believe, how Wuotan, Wish and Will should touch one another (see Suppl.). With the largitor opum may also be connected the AS. wela, OS. welo, OHG. wolo, welo = opes, felicitas [weal, wealth], and Wela comes up several times almost as a personification (conf. Gramm. 4, 752), like the Lat. goddess Ops (conf. infra Sælde, note); there is also a *Vali* among the Norse gods. In the case of *Ve*, gen. vea, the sense may waver between wîho, sanctus (Goth. Ahma sa veiha, Holy Ghost), and wih, idolum. In Sæm. 63, Loki casts in the teeth of Frigg her intrigues with Ve and Vili ; this refers to the story in Yngl. saga cap. 3, from which we clearly gather the identity of the three brothers, so that Frigg could be considered the wife of any one of them.[1]

Lastly, a principal proof of the deeply-rooted worship of this divinity is furnished by Wôdan's being *interwoven with the old Saxon genealogies,* which I shall examine minutely in the Appendix.[2]

Here we see Wôdan invariably in the centre. To him are traced up all the races of heroes and kings ; among his sons and his ancestors, several have divine honours paid them. In parti-

---

[1] According to this story, Oðinn was *abroad* a long time, during which his brothers act for him ; it is worthy of note, that Saxo also makes Othin travel to foreign lands, and *Mithothin* fill his place, p..13 ; this Mithothin's position throws light on that of Vili and Ve. But Saxo, p. 45, represents Othin as once more an exile, and puts *Oller* in his place (see Suppl.). The distant journeys of the god are implied in the Norse by-names *Gângrâðr, Gângleri, Vegtamr,* and *Viðförull,* and in Saxo 45 *viator indefessus.* It is not to be overlooked, that even Paulus Diac. 1, 9 knows of Wodan's residence in *Greece* (qui non circa haec tempora—of the war between Langobards and Vandals—sed longe anterius, nec in Germania, sed in *Graecia* fuisse perhibetur ; while Saxo removes him to *Byzantium,* and Snorri to *Tyrkland*). In the passage in Paul. Diac. : 'Wodan sane, quem adjecta litera Gwodan dixerunt, ipse est qui apud Romanos Mercurius dicitur, et ab universis Germaniae gentibus ut deus adoratur, qui non circa haec tempora, sed longe anterius, nec in Germania, sed in Graecia fuisse perhibetur'—it has been proposed to refer the second 'qui' to Mercurius instead of Wodan (Ad. Schmidt zeitschr. 1, 264), and then the harmony of this account with Snorri and Saxo would disappear. But Paul is dealing with the absurdity of the Langobardic legend related in 1, 8, whose unhistoric basis he lays bare, by pointing out that Wodan at the time of the occurrence between the Wandali and Winili, had not ruled in Germany, but in Greece ; which is the main point here. The notion that Mercury should be confined to Greece, has wider bearings, and would shock the heathen faith not only of the Germans but of the Romans. The heathen gods were supposed to be omnipresent, as may be seen by the mere fact that Woden-hills were admitted to exist in various spots all over the country ; so that the community of this god to Germans, Greeks and Romans raised no difficulty.

[2] This Appendix forms part of the third volume. In the meanwhile, readers may be glad to see for themselves the substance of these pedigrees, which I have extracted from the Appendix, and placed at the end of this chapter.—TRANS.

cular, there appear as sons, *Balder* and that *Saxnôt* who in the 8th century was not yet rooted out of N.W. Germany ; and in the line of his progenitors, *Heremôd* and *Geát*, the latter expressly pronounced a god, or the son of a god, in these legends, while *Wôdan* himself is regarded more as the head of all noble races. But we easily come to see, that from a higher point of view both Geát and Wôdan merge into *one* being, as in fact Oðinn is called 'alda *Gautr*,' Sæm. 93ᵇ 95ᵇ ; conf. infra Goz, Koz.

In these genealogies, which in more than one direction are visibly interwoven with the oldest epic poetry of our nation, the gods, heroes and kings are mixed up together. As heroes become deified, so can gods also come up again as heroes ; amid such reappearances, the order of succession of the individual links varies [in different tables].

Each pedigree ends with real historical kings : but to reckon back from these, and by the number of human generations to get at the *date* of mythical heroes and gods, is preposterous. The earliest Anglo-Saxon kings that are historically certain fall into the fifth, sixth or seventh century ; count four, eight or twelve generations up to Wôden, you cannot push him back farther than the third or fourth century. Such calculations can do nothing to shake our assumption of his far earlier existence. The adoration of Wôden must reach up to immemorial times, a long way beyond the first notices given us by the Romans of Mercury's worship in Germania.

There is one more reflection to which the high place assigned by the Germans to their Wuotan may fairly lead us. Monotheism is a thing so necessary, so natural, that almost all heathens, amidst their motley throng of deities, have consciously or unconsciously ended by acknowledging a supreme god, who has already in him the attributes of all the rest, so that these are only to be regarded as emanations from him, renovations, rejuvenescences of him. This explains how certain characteristics come to be assigned, now to this, now to that particular god, and why one or another of them, according to the difference of nation, comes to be invested with supreme power. Thus our Wuotan resembles Hermes and Mercury, but he stands higher than these two ; contrariwise, the German Donar (Thunor, Thôrr) is a weaker Zeus or Jupiter ; what was added to the one, had to be subtracted from the other ; as for Ziu

(Tîw, Tyr), he hardly does more than administer one of Wuotan's offices, yet is identical in name with the first and highest god of the Greeks and Romans : and so all these god-phenomena keep meeting and crossing one another. The Hellenic Hermes is pictured as a youth, the Teutonic Wuotan as a patriarch : Oðinn hinn *gamli* (the old). Yngl. saga cap. 15, like ' the *old* god ' on p. 21. Ziu and Froho are mere emanations of Wuotan (see Suppl.).

GENEALOGIES OF ANGLO-SAXON KINGS.

Descending Series.

KENT.	EASTANGLIA.	ESSEX.	MERCIA.
Wôden	Wôden	Wôden	Wôden
Wecta	Câsere	Saxneát	Wihtlæg
Witta	Titmon	Gesecg	Wærmund
Wihtgils	Trigel	Andsecg	Offa
Hengest (d. 489)	Hróthmund	Sweppa	Angeltheow
Eoric (Oesc)	Hrippa	Sigefugel	Eomær
Octa	Quichelm	Bedeca	Icel
Eormenrîc	Uffa	Offa	Cnebba
Æthelbeorht (567)	Tidel	Æscwine (527)	Cynewald
	Rædwald (d. 617)	Sledda	Creoda
	Eorpwald (632)	Sæbeorht (604)	Wibba
			Penda (d. 656)

DEIRA.	BERNICIA.	WESSEX.	LINDESFARAN.
Wôden	Wôden	Wôden	Wóden
Wægdæg	Bældæg	Bældæg	Winta
Sigegâr	Brand	Brand	Cretta
Swæfdæg	Beonoc	Fridhogâr	Queldgils
Sigegeát	Aloc	Freáwine	Ceadbed
Sæbald	Angenwit	Wig	Bubba
Sæfugel	Ingwi	Gewis	Bedeca
Westerfalcna	Esa	Esla	Biscop
Wilgisl	Eoppa	Elesa	Eanferth
Uscfreá	Ida (d. 560)	Cerdic (d. 534)	Eatta
Yffe		Cynrîc	Ealdfrith
Ælle (d. 588)		Ceawlin	

According to this, Wôden had *seven* sons (Bældæg being common to two royal lines) ; elsewhere he has only *three, e.g.* Wil. Malm. p. 17 : *tres filii*, Weldegius, Withlegius et Beldegius, from whom the Kentish kings, the Mercian kings, and the West Saxon and Northumbrian kings respectively were descended.

Ascending Series.

Wôden	Finn	Beaw	Hathra (Itermôd)
Fridhuwald	Godwulf (Folcwald)	Sceldwa	Hwala (Hathra)
Freáwine (Freálâf)	Geát	Heremód (Sceáf)	Bedwig (Hwala)
Fridhuwulf	Tætwa	Itermon (Heremôd)	Sceáf (Bedwig)

Some accounts contain only four links, others eight, others sixteen, stopping either at Fridhuwulf, at Geát, or at Sceáf. Sceáf is the oldest heathen name ; but after the conversion the line was connected with Noah, and so with Adam !

CHAPTER VIII.

DONAR, THUNAR, (THORR).

The god who rules over clouds and rain, who makes himself known in the lightning's flash and the rolling thunder, whose bolt cleaves the sky and alights on the earth with deadly aim, was designated in our ancient speech by the word *Donar* itself, OS. *Thunar*, AS. *Thunor*, ON. *Thôrr*.[1] The natural phenomenon is called in ON. þruma, or duna, both fem. like the Gothic þeihvô, which was perhaps adopted from a Finnic language. To the god the Goths would, I suppose, give the name *Thunrs*. The Swed. tordön, Dan. torden (tonitru), which in Harpestreng still keeps the form thordyn, thordun, is compounded of the god's name and that same duna, ON. *Thôrduna?* (see Suppl.). In exactly the same way the Swed. term *åska* (tonitru, fulmen), in the Westgothl. Laws åsikkia,[2] has arisen out of åsaka, the god's waggon or driving, from ås, deus, divus, and aka, vehere, vehi, Swed. åka. In Gothland they say for thunder *Thorsåkan*, Thor's driving; and the ON. *reið* signifies not only vehiculum, but tonitru, and reiðarslag, reiðar-þruma, are thunderclap and lightning. For, a waggon rumbling over a vaulted space comes as near as possible to the rattling and crashing of thunder. The comparison is so natural, that we find it spread among many nations: δοκεῖ ὄχημα τοῦ Διὸς ἡ βροντὴ εἶναι, Hesychius sub. v. ἐλασίβροντα. In Carniola the rolling of thunder is to this day *gottes fahren*. [To the Russian peasant it is the prophet Iliâ driving his chariot, or else grinding his corn.] Thôrr in the Edda, beside his appellation of Asaþôrr, is more minutely described by Ökuþôrr, *i.e.* Waggon-thôrr (Sn. 25); his waggon is drawn by two he-goats (Sn. 26). Other gods have their

---

[1] So even in High German dialects, durstag for donrstag, Engl. Thursday, and Bav. doren, daren for donnern (Schm. 1, 390). In *Thôrr* it is not RR, but only the first R (the second being flectional), that is an abbrev. of NR.; *i.e.* N suffers syncope before R, much as in the M. Dut. ere, mire, for ênre mînre.

[2] Conf. Onsike (Odin's drive ?) supra, p. 159.

waggons too, especially Oðinn and Freyr (see pp. 107, 151), but Thôrr is distinctively thought of as the god who drives ; he never appears riding, like Oðinn, nor is he supposed to own a horse : either he *drives*, or he *walks* on foot. We are expressly told : ' Thôrr *gengr* til dômsins, ok veðr âr,' walks to judgment, and wades the rivers (Sn. 18).[1] The people in Sweden still say, when it thunders : *godgubben* åker, the good old (fellow) is taking a drive, Ihre 696. 740. 926. *gofar* åkar, *goffar* kör, the gaffer, good father, drives (see Suppl.). They no longer liked to utter the god's real name, or they wished to extol his fatherly goodness (v. supra, p. 21, the *old god*, Dan. *vor gamle fader*). The Norwegian calls the lightning *Thors-varme*, -warmth, Faye p. 6.

Thunder, lightning and rain, above all other natural phenomena, proceed directly from God, are looked upon as his doing, his business (see Suppl.).[2] When a great noise and racket is kept up, a common expression is : you could not hear the Lord *thunder* for the uproar ; in France : le bruit est si fort, qu'on n'entend pas Dieu *tonner*. As early as the Roman de Renart 11898 :

> Font une noise si grant
> quen ni oist pas Dieu *tonant*.

> 29143 : Et commença un duel si grant,
> que len ni oist Dieu *tonant*.

> Ogier 10915 : Lor poins deterdent, lor paumes vont batant,
> ni oissiez nis ame Dieu *tonant*.

> Garin 2, 38 : Nes Dieu *tonnant* ni possiez oir.

And in the Roman de Maugis (Lyon 1599, p. 64) : De la noyse quils faisoyent neust lon pas ouy Dieu *tonner*.

But thunder is especially ascribed to an angry and avenging god ; and in this attribute of *anger* and *punishment* again Donar resembles Wuotan (pp. 18, 142). In a thunderstorm the people say to their children : the *gracious God* is angry ; in Westphalia : *use hergot* kift (chides, Strodtm. osnabr. 104) ; in Franconia : *God* is out

---

[1] Scarcely contradicted by his surname *Hlôrriði;* this riði probably points to reið, a waggon ; Hlôrriði seems to me to come by assimilation from hlôðriði, conf. ch. XIII, the goddess Hlôðyn.

[2] A peasant, being requested to kneel at a procession of the Host, said : I don't believe the Lord can be there, 'twas only yesterday I heard him thunder up in heaven ; Weidners apophthegmata, Amst. 1643, p. 277.

there scolding ; in Bavaria : der *himmeltatl* (-daddy) greint (Schm.
1, 462).   In Eckstrom's poem in honour of the county of Honstein
1592, cii[b], it is said :

> *Gott der herr* muss warlich from sein (must be really kind),
> dass er nicht mit *donner* schlegt drein.[1]

The same sentiment appears among the Letton and Finn nations.
Lettic: wezzajs kahjâs, wezzajs tehws barrahs (the old father has
started to his feet, he chides), Stender lett. gramm. 150.   With
dievas (god) and dievaitis (godkin, dear god) the Lithuanians
associate chiefly the idea of the thunderer : dievaitis grauja !
dievaitis ji numusse.   Esthonian : wanna issa hüab, wanna essä
wäljan, mürrisep (the old father growls), Rosenplänters beitr. 8,
116.   'The Lord scolds,' 'heaven wages war,' Joh. Christ. Petris
Ehstland 2, 108 (see Suppl.).

Now with this Donar of the Germani fits in significantly the
Gallic *Taranis* whose name is handed down to us in Lucan 1, 440 ;
all the Celtic tongues retain the word *taran* for thunder, Irish *toran*,
with which one may directly connect the ON. form Thôrr, if one
thinks an assimilation from *rn* the more likely   But an old
inscription gives us also *Tanarus* (Forcellini sub v.) = Taranis.
The Irish name for Thursday, dia *Tordain* (dia ordain, diardaoin)
was perhaps borrowed from a Teutonic one (see Suppl.).

So in the Latin Jupiter (literally, God father, Diespiter) there
predominates the idea of the thunderer ; in the poets *Tonans* is
equivalent to Jupiter (*e.g.*, Martial vi. 10, 9. 13, 7.   Ovid Heroid.
9, 7.   Fasti 2, 69.   Metam. 1, 170.   Claudian's Stilicho 2, 439) ;
and Latin poets of the Mid. Ages are not at all unwilling to apply
the name to the christian God (*e.g.*,Dracontius de deo 1, 1. satisfact.
149.   Ven. Fortunat. p. 212-9. 258).   And expressions in the
lingua vulgaris coincide with this : celui qui fait *toner*, qui fait
courre la nue (p. 23-4).   An inscription, Jovi *tonanti*, in Gruter 21,
6.   The Greek Zeus who sends thunder and lightning (κεραυνός) is
styled κεραύνειος.   Ζεὺς ἔκτυπε, Il. 8, 75. 170.   17, 595.   Διὸς
κτύπος, Il. 15, 379.[2]   And because he sends them down from the

---

[1] In a poem made up of the first lines of hymns and songs : Ach gott vom
himmel sieh darein, und werfe einen donnerstein, es ist gewislich an der zeit,
dass schwelgerei und üppigkeit zerschmettert werden mausetodt ! sonst schrein
wir bald aus tiefer noth.

[2] One might be tempted to connect the Etruscan Tina = Jupiter with
Tonans and Donar ; it belongs more immediately to Ζήν (v. infra, Zio).

height of heaven, he also bears the name ἄκριος, and is pictured dwelling on the mountain-top (ἄκρις). Zeus is enthroned on Olympus, on Athos, Lycaeus, Casius, and other mountains of Greece and Asia Minor.

And here I must lay stress on the fact, that the thundering god is conceived as emphatically a *fatherly* one, as Jupiter and Diespiter, as far and tatl. For it is in close connexion with this, that the mountains sacred to him also received in many parts such names as *Etzel, Altvater, Grossvater*.[1] Thôrr himself was likewise called *Atli, i.e.* grandfather.

A high mountain, along which, from the earliest times, the main road to Italy has lain, in the chain between the Graian and Pennine Alps, what we now call the St. Bernard, was in the early Mid. Ages named *mons Jovis*. This name occurs frequently in the Frankish annals (Pertz 1, 150. 295. 453. 498. 512. 570. 606. 2, 82), in Otto fris. de gest. Frid. 2, 24, in Radevicus 1, 25, who designates it via Julii Caesaris, modo *mons Jovis;* in AS. writers *munt Jofes* (Lye sub. v.), in Ælfr. Boët. p. 150 *muntgiow;* in our Kaiserchronik 88ᵈ *monte job.*—The name and the worship carry us back to the time of the Romans ; the inhabitants of the Alps worshipped a *Peninus* deus, or a *Penina* dea: Neque montibus his ab transitu Poenorum ullo Veragri, incolae jugi ejus norunt nomen inditum, sed ab eo (al. deo) quem in summo sacratum vertice *peninum* montani adpellant; Livy 31, 38. Quamvis legatur a *poenina* dea quae ibi colitur Alpes ipsas vocari ; Servius on Virg. Aen. 10, 13. An inscription found on the St Bernard (Jac. Spon miscellanea antiq. Lugd. 1685, p. 85) says expressly: Lucius Lucilius deo *Penino opt. max.* donum dedit ; from which it follows, that this god was understood to be no other than Jupiter. Conf. *Jupiter apenninus,* Micali storia 131-5. Ζεὺς καραιός occurs in Hesych. [κάρα means head, and so does the Celtic *pen, ben*]. The classic writers never use *mons Jovis,* and the tabula Antonini names only the summus Penninus and the Penni lucus; but between the 4th and 7th centuries *Jovis mons* seems to have taken the place of these,

---

[1] Zeitschr. des hess. vereins 2, 139-142. Altd. blätt. 1, 288. Haupts zeitschr. 1, 26. Finnish : *isäinen* panee (Renval. 118ᵃ), the father thunders. To the Finns *ukko* signifies proavus, senex, and is a surname of the gods Wäinäsnöinen and Ilmarinen. But also *Ukko* of itself denotes the thundergod (v. infra). Among the Swedish Lapps *aija* is both avus and tonitrus (see Suppl.).

perhaps with reference [not so much to the old Roman, as] to the
Gallic or even German sense which had then come to be attached
to the god's name. Remember that German îsarnodori on the Jura
mountains not far off (p. 80).[1]

Such names of mountains in Germany itself we may with
perfect safety ascribe to the worship of the native deity. Every
one knows the *Donnersberg* (mont Tonnerre) in the Rhine palatinate
on the borders of the old county of Falkenstein, between Worms,
Kaiserslautern and Kreuznach; it stands as *Thoneresberg* in a doc.
of 869, Schannat hist. wormat. probat. p. 9. Another *Thuneresberg*
situate on the Diemel, in Westphalia, not far from Warburg, and
surrounded by the villages of Wormeln, Germete and Welda, is
first mentioned in a doc. of 1100, Schaten mon. paderb. 1, 649;
in the Mid. Ages it was still the seat of a great popular assize,
originally due, no doubt, to the sacredness of the spot : ' comes ad
Thuneresberhc' (anno 1123), Wigands feme 222. comitia de *Dunris-*
berg (1105), Wigands arch. I. 1, 56. a judicio nostro *Thonresberch*
(1239), ib. 58. Precisely in the vicinity of this mountain stands the
holy oak mentioned on p. 72-4, just as the *robur Jovis* by Geismar
in Hesse is near a *Wuotansberg*, p. 152. To all appearance the two
deities could be worshipped close to one another. The Knüllge-
birge in Hesse includes a *Donnerkaute*. In the Bernerland is a
Donnerbühel (doc. of 1303, Joh. Müller 1, 619), called *Tonrbül* in
Justingers Berner chron. p. 50. Probably more Donnersbergs are
to be found in other parts of Germany. One in the Regensburg
country is given in a doc. of 882 under the name of *Tuniesberg*,
Ried, cod. dipl. num. 60. A Sifridus marschalcus de *Donnersperch*
is named in a doc. of 1300, MB. 33, pars 1, p. 289; an Otto de
Donersperg, MB. 4, 94 (in 1194), but Duonesberc, 4, 528 (in 1153),
and Tunniesberg 11, 432. In the Thüringer wald, between Stein-

---

[1] This *mons Jovis* must be distinguished from *mons gaudii*, by which the
Mid. Ages meant a height near Rome : Otto frising 1. c. 2, 22 ; the Kaiserchr.
88[d] translates it verbally *mendelberc*. In Romance poems of the 12-13th
centuries, *monjoie* is the French battle-cry, generally with the addition of St
Denis, *e.g. monjoya, monjoya* sant Denis ! Ferabras 365. *monjoie* enseigne S.
Denis ! Garin 108. Ducange in his 11th dissertation on Joinville declares
monjoie inadmissible as a mere diminutive of mont, since in other passages
(Roquefort 2, 207) it denotes any place of joy and bliss, a paradise, so that we
can fairly keep to the literal sense ; and there must have been mountains of
this name in more than one region. It is quite possible that monjoie itself
came from an earlier *monjove* (mons Jovis), that with the god's hill there
associated itself the idea of a mansion of bliss (see Suppl.).

bach and Oberhof, at the 'rennsteig' is a Donershauk (see Suppl.).
—A *Donares eih*, a *robur Jovis*, was a tree specially sacred to the
god of lightning, and of these there grew an endless abundance in
the German forests.

Neither does Scandinavia lack mountains and rocks bearing the
name of Thôrr : *Thors klint* in East Gothland (conf. Wildegren's
Östergötland 1, 17); *Thorsborg* in Gothland, Molbech tidskr. 4, 189.
From Norway, where this god was pre-eminently honoured, I have
nevertheless heard of none. The peasant in Vermland calls the
south-west corner of the sky, whence the summer tempests mostly
rise, *Thorshåla* (-hole, cave, Geijer's Svearikes häfder 1, 268).

And the Thunder-mountains of the Slavs are not to be overlooked. Near Milleschau in Bohemia stands a *Hromolan*, from
hrom, thunder, in other dialects grom. One of the steepest mountains in the Styrian Alps (see Suppl.) is *Grimming, i.e.*, Sl. germnik,
OSl. gr"mnik, thunder-hill (Sloven. gr'mi, it thunders, Serv. grmi,
Russ. grom gremit, quasi βρόμος βρέμει) ; and not far from it is a
rivulet named *Donnersbach*.[1] The Slavs then have two different
words to express the phenomenon and the god: the latter is in OSl.
Perûn, Pol. *Piorun*, Boh. *Peraun* ;[2] among the Southern Slavs it
seems to have died out at an earlier time, though it is still found in
derivatives and names of places. Dobrowsky (inst. 289) traces the
word to the verb peru, ferio, quatio [general meaning rather pello,
to push]. and this tolerably apt signification may have contributed
to twist the word out of its genuine form.[3] I think it has dropt a
k : the Lithuanian, Lettish and OPrussian thundergod is *Perkunas*,
Pehrkons, *Perkunos*, and a great many names of places are compounded with it. Lith., Perkunas grauja (P. thunders), Perkunas
musza (P. strikes, ferit) ; Lett., Pehrkons sperr (the lightning
strikes, see Suppl.). The Slav. *perun* is now seldom applied
personally, it is used chiefly of the lightning's flash. Procopius (de
Bello Goth. 3, 14) says of the Sclaveni and Antes : θεὸν μὲν γὰρ
ἕνα τὸν τῆς ἀ σ τ ρ α π ῆ ς δημιουργὸν ἁπάντων κύριον μόνον αὐτὸν

[1] Kindermann, abriss von Steiermark pp. 66, 67, 70, 81.
[2] The Slovaks say *Parom*, and *paromova* strela (P.'s bolt) for perunova ;
phrases about Parom, from Kollar, in Hanusch 259, 260.
[3] Might *perun* be connected with κεραυνός = περαυνός ? Still nearer to
Perun would seem to be the Sansk. *Parjanyas*, a name borne by Indra as
Jupiter pluvius, literally, fertilizing rain, thunder-cloud, thunder. A hymn to
this rain-god in Rosen's Vedae specimen p. 23. Conf. Hitzig Philist. 296, and
Holtzmann 1, 112, 118.

νομίζουσιν εἶναι, καὶ θύουσιν αὐτῷ βόας τε καὶ ἱερεῖα ἅπαντα.
Again, the oak was consecrated to Perun, and old documents define
boundaries by it (do *perunova duba*, as far as P.'s oak); and the
Romans called the the acorn *juglans*, *i.e.*,joviglans, *Jovis glans*, the
fruit of the fatherly god.   Lightning is supposed to strike oaks by
preference (see Suppl.).

Now *Perkun* suggests that thundergod of the Morduins, *Porguini*
(p. 27), and, what is more worthy of note, a Gothic word also,
which (I grant), as used by Ulphilas, was already stript of all personification.   The neut. noun *fairguni* (Gramm. 2, 175. 453)
means ὄρος, mountain.[1]   What if it were once especially the
Thunder-mountain, and a lost *Fairguns* the name of the god (see
Suppl.) ?   Or, starting with fairguni with its simple meaning of
mons unaltered, may we not put into that masc.   Fairguns or Fairguneis, and consequently into Perkunas, the sense of the above-
mentioned ἄκριος, he of the mountain top ? a fitting surname for
the thundergod.   *Fergunna*, ending like Patunna, p. 71, signifies
in the Chron. moissiac. anno 805 (Pertz 1, 308) not any particular
spot, but the metal-mountains (erzgebirge); and *Virgunnia* (Vir-
gundia, Virgunda, conf. Zeuss p. 10) the tract of wooded mountains
between Ansbach and Ellwangen.   Wolfram, Wh. 390, 2, says of
his walt-swenden (wood-wasting ?) : der Swarzwalt und *Virgunt*
müesen dâ von œde ligen, Black Forest and V. must lie waste
thereby.   In the compounds, without which it would have perished
altogether, the OHG. *virgun*, AS. *firgen* may either bear the simple
sense of mountainous, woody, or conceal the name of a god.—Be that
as it may, we find fairguni, virgun, firgen connected with divinely-
honoured beings, as appears plainly from the ON. *Fiörgyn*, gen.
Fiörgynjar, which in the Edda means Thôr's mother, the goddess
Earth : Thôrr *Jarðar burr*, Sæm. 70[a] 68[a]. *Oðins son*, Sæm. 73[a] 74[b].
And beside her, a male *Fiörgynn*, gen. Fiörgyns, Fiörgvins, appears
as the father of Oðin's wife Frigg, Sn. 10, 118. Sæm. 63[a].   In all
these words we must take fairg, firg, fiörg as the root, and not divide
them as fair-guni, fir-gun, fiör-gyn.   Now it is true that all the Anzeis,
all the Aesir are enthroned on mountains (p. 25), and Firgun might
have been used of more than one of them; but that we have a right
to claim it specially for *Donar and his mother*, is shewn by Perun,

---

[1] Matt. 8, 1. Mk 5, 5. 11. 9, 2. 11, 1.   Lu. 3, 5. 4, 29. 9, 37. 19, 29. 37.
1 Cor. 13, 2.   Baírgahei (ἡ ὀρεινή) in Lu. 1, 39, 65 ; never the simple baírgs.

Perkun, and will be confirmed presently by the meaning of mount and rock which lies in the word hamar. As Zeus is called ἐνάκριος, so is his daughter Pallas ἀκρία, and his mother ὀρεστέρα Γᾶ, μᾶτερ αὐτοῦ Διός (Sophocl. Philoct. 389); the myth transfers from him to his mother and daughter. Of Donar's *mother* our very märchen have things to tell (Pentam. 5, 4); and beyond a doubt, the stories of the devil and his bath and his grandmother are but a vulgarization of heathen notions about the thundergod. Lasicz 47 tells us : Percuna tete mater est fulminis atque tonitrui quae solem fessum ac pulverolentum balneo excipit, deinde lotum et nitidum postera die emittit. It is just matertera, and not mater, that is meant by teta elsewhere.

Christian mythology among the Slav and certain Asiatic nations has handed over the thunderer's business to the prophet Elijah, who drives to heaven *in the tempest*, whom a *chariot and horses of fire* receive, 2 Kings 2, 11. In the Servian songs 2, 1. 2, 2 he is expressly called *gromovnik Iliya*,[1] lightning and thunder (munya and grom) are given into his hand, and to sinful men he shuts up the clouds of heaven, so that they let no rain fall on the earth (see Suppl.). This last agrees with the O.T. too, 1 Kings 17, 1. 18, 41-5, conf. Lu. 4, 25, Jam. 5, 17; and the same view is taken in the OHG. poem, O. iii. 12, 13 :

Quedent sum giwâro, *Helias* sîs ther *mâro*,
ther thiz lant sô *tharta*, then *himil* sô *bisparta*,
ther iu *ni liaz* in nôtin *regonon* then liutin,
thuangta si giwâro harto filu suâro.[2]

But what we have to note especially is, that in the story of Antichrist's appearance a little before the end of the world, which was current throughout the Mid. Ages (and whose striking points of agreement with the ON. mythus of Surtr and Muspellsheim I shall speak of later), *Helias* again occupies the place of the northern *thundergod*. *Thôrr* overcomes the great serpent, but he has scarcely moved nine paces from it, when he is touched by its venomous breath, and sinks to the ground dead, Sn. 73. In the

[1] Udrí gromom, *gromovit Iliya!* smite with thunder, thunderer Elias, 1, 77.

[2] Greg. tur., pref. to bk 2 : Meminerit (lector) sub *Heliae* tempore, qui *pluvias* cum voluit *abstulit*, et cum libuit arentibus terris *infudit*, &c.

OHG. poem of Muspilli 48—54, Antichrist and the devil do indeed fall, but Elias also is grievously wounded in the fight :

> Doh wanit des vilu gotmanno[1]
> daz *Elias* in demo wîge arwartit :
> sâr sô daz *Eliases* pluot
> in erda kitriufit,
> sô inprinnant die perga ;

his blood dripping on the earth sets the mountains on fire, and the Judgment-day is heralded by other signs as well. Without knowing in their completeness the notions of the devil, Antichrist, Elias and Enoch, which were current about the 7th or 8th century,[2] we cannot fully appreciate this analogy between Elias and the Donar of the heathens. There was nothing in christian tradition to warrant the supposition of Elias receiving a wound, and that a deadly one. The comparison becomes still more suggestive by the fact that even half-christian races in the Caucasus worship *Elias* as a god of thunder. The Ossetes think a man lucky who is *struck by lightning*, they believe *Ilia* has taken him to himself ; survivors raise a cry of joy, and sing and dance around the body, the people flock together, form a ring for dancing, and sing : *O Ellai, Ellai*, eldaer tchoppei ! (O Elias, Elias, lord of the rocky summits). By the cairn over the grave they set up a long pole supporting the skin of a black he-goat, which is their usual manner of sacrificing to Elias (see Suppl.). They implore Elias to make their fields fruitful, and keep the *hail* away from them.[3] Olearius already had put it upon record, that the Circassians on the Caspian sacrificed a goat on *Elias's day*, and stretched the skin on a pole with prayers.[4] Even the Muhammadans, in praying that a thunderstorm may be averted, name the name of *Ilya*.[5]

Now, the Servian songs put by the side of Elias the Virgin *Mary ;* and it was she especially that in the Mid. Ages was invoked for rain. The chroniclers mention a rain-procession in the Liège

---

[1] *Gotman,* a divine, a priest ?   Conf. supra, pp. 88-9.

[2] The Rabbinical legend likewise assumes that *Elias* will return and slay the malignant Sammael ; Eisenmenger 2, 696. 851.

[3] Klaproth's travels in the Caucasus 2, 606. 601.

[4] Erman's archiv für Russland 1841, 429.

[5] Ad. Olearius reiseschr. 1647, pp. 522-3.

country about the year 1240 or 1244;[1] three times did priests and people march round (nudis pedibus et in laneis), but all in vain, because in calling upon all the saints they had forgotten the Mother of God; so, when the saintly choir laid the petition before God, *Mary opposed.* In a new procession a solemn 'salve regina' was sung : Et cum serenum tempus ante fuisset, tanta inundatio pluviae facta est, ut fere omnes qui in processione aderant, hac illacque dispergerentur. With the Lithuanians, the holy goddess (dievaite sventa) is a rain-goddess. Heathendom probably addressed the petition for rain to the thundergod, instead of to Elias and Mary.[2] Yet I cannot call to mind a sir $_{\circ}$ ¹ ⌐ passage, even in ON. legend, where Thôrr is said to have bestowed *rain* when it was *asked for ;* we are only told that he sends *stormy weather* when he is angry, Olafs Tryggv. saga 1, 302-6 (see Suppl.). But we may fairly take into account his general resemblance to Zeus and Jupiter (who are expressly ὑέτιος, *pluvius,* Il. 12, 25 : ὗε Ζεὺς συνεχές), and the pre-valence of *votis imbrem vocare* among all the neighbouring nations (see Suppl.).

A description by Petronius cap. 44, of a Roman procession for rain, agrees closely with that given above from the Mid. Ages : Antea stolatae ibant nudis pedibus in clivum, passis capillis, menti-bus puris, et *Jovem aquam exorabant ;* itaque statim urceatim (in bucketfuls) pluebat, aut tunc aut nunquam, et omnes ridebant, uvidi tanquam mures. M. Antoninus (εἰς ἑαυτόν 5, 7) has preserved the beautifully simple prayer of the Athenians for rain : εὐχὴ Ἀθηναίων, ὗσον, ὗσον, ὦ φίλε Ζεῦ, κατὰ τῆς ἀρούρας τῆς Ἀθηναίων καὶ τῶν πεδίων (see Suppl.). According to Lasicz, the Lithuanian prayer ran thus : *Percune devaite* niemuski und mana dirvu (so I emend dievu), melsu tavi, palti miessu. Cohibe te, Percune, neve in meum agrum calamitatem immittas (more simply, strike not), ego vero tibi hanc succidiam dabo. The Old Prussian formula is said to have been : *Dievas Perkunos,* absolo mus! spare us, = Lith. apsaugok mus ! To all this I will add a more extended petition in Esthonian, as Gutslaff[3] heard an old peasant say it as late as the

---

[1] Aegidius aureae vallis cap. 135 (Chapeauville 2, 267-8). Chron. belg. magn. ad ann. 1244 (Pistorius 3, 263).

[2] Other saints also grant rain in answer to prayer, as St Mansuetus in Pertz 6, 512ᵇ. 513ᵇ ; the body of St Lupus carried about at Sens in 1097, Pertz 1, 106-7. Conf. infra, Rain-making.

[3] Joh. Gutslaff, kurzer bericht und unterricht von der falsch heilig ge-

17th century : ' Dear *Thunder* (woda Picker), we offer to thee an ox that hath two horns and four cloven hoofs, we would pray thee for our ploughing and sowing, that our straw be copper-red, our grain be golden-yellow. *Push elsewhither* all the *thick black clouds,* over great fens, high forests, and wildernesses. But unto us ploughers and sowers give a fruitful season and *sweet rain.* Holy *Thunder* (pöha Picken), guard our seedfield, that it bear good straw below, good ears above, and good grain within.' Picker or Picken would in modern Esthonian be called *Pitkne,* which comes near the Finnic *pitkäinen* = thunder, perhaps even Thunder ; Hüpel's Esth. Dict. however gives both *pikkenne* and *pikne* simply as thunder (impersonal). The Finns usually give their thundergod the name *Ukko* only, the Esthonians that of *Turris* as well, evidently from the Norse Thôrr (see Suppl.).[1]

As the fertility of the land depends on thunderstorms and rains, *Pitkäinen* and *Zeus* appear as the oldest divinity of agricultural nations, to whose bounty they look for the thriving of their cornfields and fruits (see Suppl.). Adam of Bremen too attributes thunder and lightning to Thor expressly in connexion with dominion over weather and fruits : Thor, inquiunt, praesidet in aëre, qui tonitrua et fulmina, ventos imbresque, *serena* et *fruges gubernat.* Here then the worship of Thor coincides with that of Wuotan, to whom likewise the reapers paid homage (pp. 154—7), as on the other hand Thor as well as Oðinn guides the events of war, and receives his share of the spoils (p. 133). To the Norse mind indeed, Thor's victories and his battles with the giants have thrown his peaceful office quite into the shade. Nevertheless to Wuotan's mightiest son, whose mother is Earth herself, and who is also named Perkunos, we must, if only for his lineage sake, allow a direct relation to Agriculture.[2] He clears up the atmosphere, he sends fertilizing

---

nandten bäche in Liefland Wöhhanda. Dorpt. 1644, pp. 362-4. Even in his time the language of the prayer was hard to understand ; it is given, corrected, in Peterson's Finn. mythol. p. 17, and Rosenplänter's beitr., heft 5, p. 157.

[1] *Ukko* is, next to *Yumala* (whom I connect with Wuotan), the highest Finnish god. Pitkäinen literally means the long, tall, high one.

[2] Uhland in his essay on Thôrr, has penetrated to the heart of the ON. myths, and ingeniously worked out the thought, that the very conflict of the summer-god with the winter-giants, itself signifies the business of bringing land under cultivation, that the crushing rock-splitting force of the thunderbolt prepares the hard stony soil. This is most happily expounded of the Hrûngnir and Örvandill sagas ; in some of the others it seems not to answer so well.

showers, and his sacred tree supplies the nutritious acorn. Thôr's minni was drunk to the prosperity of cornfields.

The German thundergod was no doubt represented, like Zeus and Jupiter, with a *long beard*. A Danish rhyme still calls him ' Thor med sit *lange skiäg* ' (F. Magnusen's lex. 957). But the ON. sagas everywhere define him more narrowly as *red-bearded*, of course in allusion to the fiery phenomenon of lightning : when the god is angry, he blows in his red beard, and thunder peals through the clouds. In the Fornm. sög. 2, 182 and 10, 329 he is a tall, handsome, red-bearded youth : Mikill vexti (in growth), ok ûngligr, friðr sŷnum (fair to see), ok *rauðskeggjaðr; in* 5, 249 maðr *rauð-skeggjaðr*. Men in distress invoked his red beard : Landsmenn tôko þat râð (adopted the plan) at heita þetta hit *rauða skegg,* 2, 183. When in wrath, he shakes his beard : Reiðr var þâ, *scegg nam at hrísta, scör nam at dŷja* (wroth was he then, beard he took to bristling, hair to tossing), Sæm. 70ª. More general is the phrase : lêt sîga brŷnnar ofan fyrir augun (let sink the brows over his eyes), Sn. 50. His divine rage (âsmôðr) is often mentioned : Thôrr varð reiðr, Sn. 52. Especially interesting is the story of Thôr's meeting with King Olaf 1, 303 ; his power seems half broken by this time, giving way to the new doctrine ; when the christians approach, a follower of Thôrr exhorts him to a brave resistance : *þeyt* þû î mot þeim *skeggrödd* þîna (raise thou against them thy beard's voice). þâ gengu þeir ût, ok *blês* Thôrr fast *î kampana,* ok *þeytti skeggraustina* (then went they out, and Th. blew hard into his beard, and raised his beard's voice). kom þâ þegar andviðri môti konûngi svâ styrkt, at ekki mâtti við halda (immediately there came ill-weather against the king so strong, that he might not hold out, *i.e.*, at sea).—This red beard of the thunderer is still remembered in curses, and that among the Frisian folk, without any visible connex-ion with Norse ideas: 'diis *ruadhiiret donner* regiir !' (let red-haired thunder see to that) is to this day an exclamation of the North Fris-ians.[1] And when the Icelanders call a fox *holtaþôrr*, Thôrr of the holt,[2] it is probably in allusion to his red fur (see Suppl.).

The ancient languages distinguish three acts in the natural

---

[1] Der geizhalz auf Silt, Flensburg 1809, p. 123 ; 2nd ed. Sonderburg 1833, p. 113.

[2] Nucleus lat. in usum scholae schalholtinae. Hafniae 1738, p. 2088.

phenomenon: the flash, *fulgur*, ἀστραπή, the sound, *tonitrus*, βροντή,
and the stroke, *fulmen*, κεραυνός (see Suppl.).

The lightning's flash, which we name *blitz*, was expressed in our
older speech both by the simple *plih*, Graff 3, 244, MHG. *blic*, Iw.
649. Wigal. 7284, and by *plechazunga* (coruscatio), derived from
plechazan,[1] a frequentative of *plechén* (fulgere), Diut. 1, 222-4;
they also used *plechunga*, Diut. 1, 222. *Pleccateshém*, Pertz 2, 383,
the name of a place, now Blexen; the MHG. has *blikze* (fulgur) '
die *blikzen* und die donerslege sint mit gewalte in sîner pflege, MS
2, 166ᵇ.—Again *lôhazan* (micare, coruscare), Goth. láuhatjan, presupposes a lôhên, Goth. láuhan. From the same root the Gotl
forms his *láuhmuni* (ἀστραπή), while the Saxon from blic made a
blicsmo (fulgur). AS. *leoma* (jubar, fulgur), ON. *liomi*, Swed.
ljungeld, Dan. *lyn*.—A Prussian folk-tale has an expressive phrase
for the lightning : ' *He with the blue whip* chases the devil,' *i.e.* the
giants; for a *blue* flame was held specially sacred, and people
swear by it, North Fris. ' donners *blöskén* (blue sheen) help !' in
Hansens geizhals p 123 ; and Schärtlin's curse was *blau feuer !*
(see Suppl.).

Beside *donar*, the OHG. would have at its command *caprëh*
(fragor) from prëhhan (frangere), Gl. hrab. 963ᵇ, for which the
MHG. often has *klac*, Troj. 12231. 14693, and *krach* from krachen,
(crepare) : mit krache gap der doner duz, Parz. 104, 5 ; and as
krachen is synonymous with rîzen (strictly to burst with a crash)
we also find wolkenrîz fem. for thunder, Parz. 378, 11. Wh. 38§
18 ; gegenrîz, Wartb. kr. jen.. 57 ; reht als der wilde dunrslac von
himel kam *gerizzen*, Ecke 105. der *chlafondo* doner, N. Cap. 114 ;
der *chlafleih* heizet toner ; der doner stet *gespannen*, Apollon. 879.
I connect the Gothic *þeihvô* fem. with the Finnic teuhaan (strepo),
teuhaus (strepitus, tumultus), so that it would mean the noisy,
uproarious. Some L. Germ. dialects call thunder *grummel*, Strodtm.
Osnabr. 77, agreeing with the Slav. grom, hrom (see Suppl.).

For the notion of fulmen we possess only compounds, except

---

[1] While writing plechazan, I remember pleckan, plahta (patere, nudari ;
bleak), MHG. blecken, blacte, Wigal. 4890 ; which, when used of the sky,
means : the clouds open, heaven opens, as we still say of forked and sheet
lightning ; conf. Lohengr. p. 125 : reht alsam des himmels bliz von doner sich
erblecket. If this plechan is akin to plih (fulgur), we must suppose two verbs
plîhhan pleih, and plëhhan plah, the second derived from the first. Slav. *blesk*,
blisk, but Boh. bozhi posel, god's messenger, lightning-flash. Russ. *molniya*,
Serv. *munya*, fem. (see Suppl.).

when the simple donner is used in that sense : sluoc alse ein *doner*,
Roth. 1747. hiure hât der *schûr* (shower, storm) erslagen, MS. 3,
223ᵃ ; commonly *donnerschlag, blitzschlag*. OHG. *blig-scuz* (-shot,
fulgurum jactus), N. cap. 13; MHG. *blickeschoz*, Barl. 2, 26. 253, 27,
and *blicschoz*, Martina 205ᵃ ; fiurin *donerstrâle*, Parz. 104, 1 ; *don-
reslac*, Iw. 651; ter *scuz* tero fiurentûn *donerstrâlo* (ardentis fulminis),
erscozen mit tien *donerstrâlôn*, N. Bth. 18. 175; MHG. *wetterstrahl,
blitzstrahl, donnerstrahl*. MHG. *wilder* donerslac, Geo. 751, as
lightning is called *wild fire*, Rab. 412, Schm. 1, 553, and so in ON.
villi-eldr, Sn. 60 (see Suppl.).

So then, as the god who lightens has red hair ascribed to him,
and he who thunders a waggon, he who smites has some weapon
that he shoots. But here I judge that the notion of *arrows* being
shot (*wilder pfîl* der ûz′dem donre snellet, Troj. 7673. doners *pfîle*,
Turnei von Nantheiz 35. 150) was merely imitated from the κῆλα
Διός, tela Jovis ; the true Teutonic Donar throws wedge-shaped
stones from the sky : ' ez wart nie *stein* geworfen dar er enkæme von
der *schûre*,' there was never stone thrown there (into the castle
high), unless it came from the storm, Ecke 203. ein *vlins* (flint)
von donrestrâlen, Wolfram 9, 32. ein herze daz von *vlinse ime donre*
gewahsen wære (a heart made of the flint in thunder), Wh. 12, 16.
schûrestein, Bit. 10332. *schawerstein*, Suchenw. 33, 83. sô slahe
mich ein *donerstein* ! Ms. H. 3, 202ᵃ. We now call it donner*keil*,
Swed. åsk-*vigg* (-wedge) ; and in popular belief, there darts out of
the cloud together with the flash a *black wedge*, which buries itself
in the earth as deep as the highest church-tower is high.[1] But every
time it thunders again, it begins to rise nearer to the surface, and
after *seven years* you may find it above ground. Any house in
which it is preserved, is proof against damage by lightning ; when
a thunder-storm is coming on, it begins to sweat.[2] Such stones are
also called *donneräxte* (-axes) *donnersteine, donnerhammer, albschosse*
(elfshots), *strahlsteine, teufelsfinger*, Engl. *thunder-bolts*, Swed. *Thors
vigge*, Dan. *tordenkile, tordenstraale* (v. infra, ch. XXXVII),[3] and stone
hammers and knives found in ancient tombs bear the same name.
Saxo Gram. p. 236 : Inusitati ponderis *malleos*, quos *Joviales* voca-

---

[1] This *depth* is variously expressed in curses, &c. *e.g.* May the thunder strike
you into the earth as far as a hare can run in a hundred years !
[2] Weddigens westfäl. mag. 3, 713. Wigands archiv 2, 320, has *nine* years
instead of seven.
[3] The Grk name for the stone is βελεμνίτης a missile.

bant, . . . prisca virorum religione cultos ; . . . cupiens
enim antiquitas tonitruorum causas usitata rerum similitudine com-
prehendere, *malleos*, quibus coeli fragores cieri credebat, ingenti aere
complexa fuerat (see Suppl.). To Jupiter too the *silex* (flins) was
sacred, and it was held by those taking an oath. From the mention
of ' elf-shots ' above, I would infer a connexion of the elf-sprites
with the thundergod, in whose service they seem to be employed.

The Norse mythology provides Thôrr with a wonderful *hammer*
named *Miölnir* (mauler, tudes, contundens), which he hurls at the
giants, Sæm. 57ᵇ 67ᵇ 68ᵇ; it is also called *þruðhamar*, strong
hammer, Sæm. 67ᵇ 68ᵇ, and has the property of returning into the
god's hand of itself, after being thrown, Sn. 132. As this hammer
flies through the air (er hann kemr â lopt, Sn. 16), the giants know
it, lightning and thunder precede the throwing of it : þvî næst sâ
hann (next saw he, giant Hrûngnir) *eldîngar* oc heyrði *þrumur*
stôrar, sâ hann þâ Thôr î âsmôði, fôr hann âkaflega, oc *reiddi hamarin
oc kastaði*, Sn. 109. This is obviously the crushing thunderbolt,
which descends after lightning and thunder, which was nevertheless
regarded as the god's permanent weapon ; hence perhaps that
rising of the bolt out of the earth. Saxo, p. 41, represents it as a
club (clava) *without a handle*, but informs us that *Hother* in a battle
with Thor had *knocked off* the manubium clavae; this agrees with
the Eddic narrative of the manufacture of the hammer, when it
was accounted a fault in it that the handle was too short (at
forskeptit var heldr skamt), Sn. 131. It was forged by cunning
dwarfs,[1] and in spite of that defect, it was their masterpiece. In
Saxo p. 163, Thor is armed with a *torrida chalybs*.[2] It is noticeable,
how Frauenlob MS. 2, 214ᵇ expresses himself about God the Father:
der *smit ûz Oberlande* warf *sînen hamer* in mîne schôz. The hammer, as a divine tool, was considered sacred, brides and the bodies
of the dead were *consecrated* with it, Sæm. 74ᵇ. Sn. 49. 66 ; men
blessed with the *sign of the hammer*,[3] as christians did with the sign
of the cross, and a stroke of lightning was long regarded in the

---

[1] As Zeus's lightning was by the Curetes or Cyclopes.
[2] That in ancient statues of the thundergod the *hammer* had not been forgotten, seems to be proved by pretty late evidence, *e.g.* the statue of a *dorper*
mentioned in connexion with the giants (ch. XVIII, quotation from Fergût).
And in the AS. Solomon and Saturn, *Thunor* wields a *fiery axe* (ch. XXV, Muspilli).
[3] In the Old Germ. law, the *throwing of a hammer* ratifies the acquisition
of property.

Mid. Ages as a happy initiatory omen to any undertaking. Thôrr with his hammer hallows dead bones, and makes them alive again, Sn. 49 (see Suppl.).—But most important of all, as vouching for the wide extension of one and the same heathen faith, appears to me that beautiful poem in the Edda, the Hamars heimt (hammer's homing, mallei recuperatio),[1] whose action is motived by Thôr's hammer being stolen by a giant, and buried *eight miles underground*: ' ek hefi Hlôrriða hamar umfôlginn âtta röstom for iörð nedan,' Sæm. 71ª. This unmistakably hangs together with the popular belief I have quoted, that the thunderbolt dives into the earth and takes *seven* or nine *years* to get up to the surface again, mounting as it were a mile every year. At bottom *Thrymr*, þursa drôttinn, lord of the durses or giants, who has only got his own hammer back again, seems identical with Thôrr, being an older nature-god, in whose keeping the thunder had been before the coming of the âses ; this is shown by his name, which must be derived from þruma, tonitru. The compound þrumketill (which Biörn explains as aes tinniens) is in the same case as the better-known þôrketill (see Suppl.).

Another proof that this myth of the thundergod is a joint pos-session of Scandinavia and the rest of Teutondom, is supplied by the word hammer itself. *Hamar* means in the first place a hard stone or rock,[2] and secondly the tool fashioned out of it ; the ON. hamarr still keeps both meanings, rupes and malleus (and *sahs, seax* again is a stone knife, the Lat. saxum). Such a name is particularly well-suited for an instrument with which the mountain-god Donar, our 'Faírguneis,' achieves all his deeds. Now as the god's hammer strikes dead, and the curses '*thunder* strike you' and '*hammer* strike you' meant the same thing, there sprang up in some parts, especially of Lower Gemany, after the fall of the god Donar, a personification of the word *Hamar* in the sense of Death or Devil : ' dat die de *Hamer!* i vor den *Hamer!* de *Hamer* sla!' are phrases still

---

[1] No other lay of the Edda shows itself so intergrown with the people's poetry of the North ; its plot survives in Swedish, Danish and Norwegian songs, which bear the same relation to that in the Edda as our folk-song of Hilde-brand and Alebrand does to our ancient poesy. Thor no longer appears as a god, but as *Thorkar* (Thorkarl) or *Thord af Hafsgaard*, who is robbed of his golden hammer, conf. Iduna 8, 122. Nyerups udvalg 2, 188. Arvidsson 1, 3. Schade's beskrivelse over öen Mors, Aalborg 1811, p. 93. Also the remarkable legend of Thor með tungum hamri in Faye's norske sagn. Arendal 1833, p. 5, wnere also he loses and seeks his hammer.

[2] Slav. *kamen* gen. kamnia, stone ; Lith. *akmů* gen. akmens ; *kam* = *ham*.

current among the people, in which you can exchange Hamer for
Düvel, but which, one and all, can only be traced back to the god
that strikes with the hammer. In the same way: 'dat is en
Hamer, en *hamersken* kerl,' a rascally impudent cheat.[1] de *Hamer*
kennt se all! the devil may know them all, Schütze 2, 96. *Hem-
merlein, meister Hämmerlein,* signified the evil spirit. Consider also
the curses which couple the two names; *donner* und *teufel*! both
of which stood for the ancient god. By *gammel Thor,* old Thor, the
common people in Denmark mean the devil; in Sweden they long
protested by *Thore gud.* The Lithuanians worshipped an *enormous
hammer,* Seb. Frankes weltbuch 55[b] (see Suppl.).

It must have been at an earlier stage that certain attributes
and titles of the Saviour, and some Judeo-christian legends, were
transferred to the heathen god, and particularly the myth of Leviathan
to Iörmungandr. As Christ by his death overmastered the monster
serpent (Barl. 78, 39 to 79, 14), so Thôrr overcomes the miðgarðs-
orm (-worm, snake that encircles the world), and similar epithets
are given to both.[2] Taking into account the resemblance between
the sign of the cross and that of the hammer, it need not seem
surprising that the newly converted Germans should under the
name of *Christ* still have the lord of thunder and the giver of rain
present to their minds; and so a connexion with *Mary* the Mother
of God (p. 174) could be the more easily established. The earliest
troubadour (Diez p. 15. Raynouard 4, 83) actually names Christ
still as the *lord of thunder,* Jhesus del tro.

A Neapolitan fairy-tale in the Pentamerone 5, 4 personifies
thunder and lightning (*truone e lampe*) as a beautiful youth, brother
of seven spinning virgins, and son of a wicked old mother who
knows no higher oath than 'pe *truone e lampe*'. Without assert-
ing any external connexion between this tradition and the German

---

[1] Brem. wtb. 2, 575. dat di de *hamer* sla! Strodtm. p. 80, conf. Schm. 2, 192.
the hammer, or a great hammer strike you! Abeles künstl. unordn. 4, 3.   Ge-
richtsh. 1, 673. 2, 79. 299. 382. *verhamert* dür, kolt, Schütze 2, 96 = verdonnert,
verteufelt, blasted, cursed, &c. How deeply the worship of the god had taken
root among the people, is proved by these almost ineradicable curses, once
solemn protestations: *donner! donnerwetter!* heiliges *gewitter* (holy thunder-
storm)! And, adding the christian symbol: *kreuz donnerwetter!* Then,
euphemistically disguised: bim (by the) dummer, potz dummer! dummer
auch! Slutz 1, 123. 2, 161-2. 3, 56. bim dummer hammer 3, 51. bim *dumstig,
dunnstig!* as in Hesse: *donnerstag!* bim *hamer!* In Flanders: bi Vids morkel
hamer! Willem's vloeken, p. 12.

[2] Finn Magnusen lex. 484-5.

one,[1] we discover in it the same idea of a kind and beneficent, not a hostile and fiendish god of thunder.

The large beetle, which we call stag-beetle or fire-beetle, lucanus cervus, taurus (ch. XXI, beetles), is in some districts of South Germany named *donnergueg, donnerguge, donnerpuppe* (gueg, guegi, beetle), perhaps because he likes to live in oak-trees, the tree sacred to thunder. For he also bears the name eichochs, Swed. ekoxe (oak-ox); but then again feuerschröter, fürböter (fire-beeter, *i.e.* kindler),[2] börner or haus-brenner (-burner), which indicates his relation to thunder and lightning. It is a saying, that on his horns he carries redhot coals into a roof, and sets it alight; more definite is the belief mentioned in Aberglaube, p. xcvi, that lightning will strike a house into which this beetle is carried. In Swed. a beetle is still named horntroll (see Suppl.).

Among herbs and plants, the following are to be specially noted: the *donnerbart*, stonecrop or houseleek, sempervivum tectorum, which, planted on the roof, protects from the lightning's stroke[3]: *barba Jovis* vulgari more vocatur (Macer Floridus 741), Fr. *Joubarbe* (conf. Append. p. lviii);—the *donnerbesen* (-besom), a shaggy tangled nest-like growth on boughs, of which superstition ascribes the generation to lightning; otherwise called *alpruthe*;—the *donnerkraut*, sedum;—the *donnerflug*, fumaria bulbosa;—the *donnerdistel*, eryngium campestre;—the Dan. *tordenskreppe*, burdock.—The South Slavs call the iris *perunik*, Perun's flower, while the Lettons call our

---

[1] How comes the Ital. to have a *trono* (Neap. *truono*, Span. *trueno*) by the side of *tuono*? and the Provençal a *trons* with the same meaning? Has the R slipt in from our donar, or still better from the Goth. drunjus, sonus, Rom. 10, 18 (conf. drönen, 'cymbal's droning sound' of Dryden)? or did the Lat. *thronus* pass into the sense of sky and thunder? 'förchst nicht, wanns tonnert, ein *tron* werd vom himmel fallen?' Garg. 181[b]. The troubadour's 'Jhesus del *tro*' might then simply mean lord of the firmament.

[2] 'I wol don sacrifice, and fyres *beete*,' Chaucer. Hence beetle itself? AS. bytel.—TRANS.

[3] A Provençal troubadour, quoted by Raynouard sub v. *barbajol*, says: e da-quel erba tenon pro li vilan sobra lur maiso. Beside this hauswurz (hauswurzel, Superst. 60), the *hawthorn*, albaspina, is a safeguard against lightning (Mém. de l' acad. celt. 2, 212), as the *laurel* was among the ancient Romans, or the *white vine* planted round a house; conf. *brennessel* (Superst. 336); '*palm branches* laid upon coals, lighted candles, a fire made on the hearth, are good for a thunderstorm,' Braunschw. anz. 1760, p. 1392. The *crossbill* too is a protector (Superst. 335); because his beak forms the sign of the cross or hammer? but the nest-making *redbreast* or *redstart* appears to attract lightning (ch. XXI, redbreast; Superst. 629. 704); was he, because of his red plumage, sacred to the redbearded god? (see Suppl.).

hederich (ground-ivy? hedge-mustard?) *pehrkones*; Perunika is also, like Iris, a woman's name. The oak above all trees was dedicated to the Thunderer (pp. 67, 72): *quercus Jovi* placuit, Phaedr. 3, 17; *magna Jovis antiquo robore quercus*, Virg. Georg. 3, 332. At Dodona stood the δρῦς ὑψίκομος Διός, Od. 14, 327. 19, 297, but at Troy the *beech* often named in the Iliad: φηγὸς ὑψηλὴ Διὸς αἰγιόχοιο, 5, 693. 7, 60. A particular kind of oak is in Servian *grm*, and *grmik* is quercetum, no doubt in close connexion with grom (tonitrus), grmiti or grmlieti (tonare). The acorn is spoken of above, p. 177.

Apparently some names of the snipe (scolopax gallinago) have to do with this subject : *donnerziege* (-goat), *donnerstagspferd* (Thursday horse), *himmelsziege* (capella coelestis) ; because he seems to bleat or whinny in the sky ? But he is also the *weatherbird*, stormbird, rainbird, and his flight betokens an approaching thunder-storm. Dan. *myrehest*, Swed. *horsgjök*, Icel. *hrossagaukr*, horsegowk or cuckoo, from his neighing; the first time he is heard in the year, he prognosticates to men their fate (Biörn sub v.) ; evidently superstitious fancies cling to the bird. His Lettish name *pehrkona kasa*, *pehrkona ahsis* (thunder's she-goat and he-goat) agrees exactly with the German. In Lithuanian too, Mielcke 1, 294. 2, 271 gives *Perkuno ozhys* as heaven's goat, for which another name is tikkutis.—Kannes, pantheum p. 439, thinks the name *donners-tagspferd* belongs to the goat itself, not to the bird ; this would be welcome, if it can be made good. Some confirmation is found in the AS. *firgengæt* (ibex, rupicapra, chamois), and *firginbucca* (capri-cornus), to which would correspond an OHG. virgungeiz, virgun-pocch ; so that in these the analogy of faírguni to Donar holds good. The wild creature that leaps over rocks would better become the god of rocks than the tame goat. In the Edda, Thôrr has *he-goats* yoked to his thunder-car : between these, and the weather-fowl described by turns as goat and horse (always a car-drawing beast), there might exist some half-obscured link of connexion (see Suppl.). It is significant also, that the devil, the modern repre-sentative of the thunder god, has the credit of having created goats, both he and she ; and as Thôrr puts away the bones of his goats after they have been picked, that he may bring them to life again (Sn. 49. 50),[1] so the Swiss shepherds believe that the goat has

---

[1] The myth of the *slaughtered goats brought to life again* by hammer-conse-

something of the devil in her, she was made by him, and her feet especially smack of their origin, and are not eaten, Tobler 214ᵃ. Did the German thundergod in particular have *he-goats and she-goats* sacrificed to him (supra, p. 52) ? The Old Roman or Etruscan *bidental* (from bidens, lamb) signifies the place where lightning had struck and killed a man : there a lamb had to be sacrificed to Jupiter, and the man's body was not burned, but buried (Plin. 2, 54). If the Ossetes and Circassians in exactly the same way offer a *goat* over the body killed by lightning, and *elevate the hide on a pole* (supra, p. 174), it becomes the more likely by a great deal that the goat-offering of the Langobards was intended for no other than Donar. For *hanging up hides* was a Langobardish rite, and was practised on other occasions also, as will presently be shown. In Carinthia, cattle struck by lightning are considered sacred to God ; no one, not even the poorest, dares to eat of them (Sartoris reise 2, 158).

Other names of places compounded with that of the thundergod, besides the numerous Donnersbergs already cited, are forthcoming in Germany. Near Oldenburg lies a village named *Donnerschwee*,

---

cration, and of the *boar* Sæhrîmnir (Sn. 42) being boiled and eaten every day and *coming whole* again every evening, seems to re-appear in more than one shape. In Wolf's Wodana, p. xxviii, the following passage on witches in Ferrara is quoted from Barthol. de Spina († 1546), quaestio de strigibus : Dicunt etiam, quod postquam comederunt aliquem pinguem bovem vel aliquam vegetem, vino vel arcam seu cophinum panibus evacuarunt et consumpserunt ea vorantes, domina illa *percutit aurea virga* quam manu gestat ea vasa vel loca, et statim ut prius plena sunt vini vel panis ac si nihil inde fuisset assumptum. Similiter *congeri jubet ossa mortui bovis super corium ejus extensum,* ipsumque per quatuor partes super ossa revolvens *virgaque percutiens, vivum bovem reddit* ut prius, ac reducendum jubet ad locum suum. The diabolical witches' meal very well matches that of the thundergod. But we are also told in legends, that the saint, after *eating up a cock*, reanimated it out of the bones ; and so early as parson Amis, we find the belief made use of in playing-off a deception (l. 969 seq.). Folk-tales relate how a magician, after a *fish had been eaten,* threw the *bones* into water, and the fish came alive again. As with these eatable creatures, so in other tales there occurs the reanimation of persons who have been cut to pieces : in the märchen vom Machandelbom (juniper-tree) ; in the myth of Zeus and Tantalus, where the shoulder of Pelops being devoured by Demeter (Ovid 6, 406) reminds us of the he-goat's leg-bone being split for the marrow, and remaining lame after he came to life again ; in the myth of Osiris and St Adalbert (Temme p. 33) ; conf. DS. no. 62, and Ezekiel 37. Then in the eighth Finnish rune, Lemminkäimen's mother gathers all the limbs of his dismembered body, and makes them live again. The fastening of heads that have been chopped off to their trunks, in Waltharius 1157 (conf. p. 93) seems to imply a belief in their reanimation, and agrees with a circumstance in Norske eventyr pp. 199, 201.

formerly Donerswe,[1] Donnerswehe, Donnerswede (Kohli handb. von Oldenb. 2, 55), which reminds us of Oðinsve, Wodeneswege (p. 151), and leaves us equally in doubt whether to understand wih a temple, or weg a way. The Norwegian folk-tale tells us of an actual *Thors vej* (way, Faye p. 5). A village *Donnersreut* is to be found in Franconia towards Bohemia, a *Donnersted* in Thedinghausen bailiwick, Brunswick, a *Thunresfeld* [Thurfield] in AS. documents, Kemble 2, 115. 195. 272, &c. &c.—Many in Scandinavia, *e.g.*, in Denmark, *Torslunde* (Thôrs lundr, grove), *Tosingo* (Thôrs engi, ing) ;[2] several in Sweden, *Tors mâse* (gurges) in a boundary-deed of Östergötland, Broocman 1, 15, *Thorsborg* in Gothland, Gutalag p. 107. 260. *Thôrsbiörg* (mountain) and *Thôrshöfn* (haven) in Norway, Fornm. sög. 4, 12. 343 ; *Thôrsmörk* (wood, a holy one ?), Nialss. cap. 149. 150.[3] *Thôrs nes* (nose, cape), Sæm. 155a and Eyrb. saga cap. 4 (see Suppl.). *Thors bro* (Thôrs brû, bridge) in Schonen, like the Norwegian Thor's-way, leads us to that prevalent belief in devil's bridges and other buildings, which is the popular way of accounting for peculiarly shaped rocks, precipices and steep mountain paths : only God or the devil could have burst them so.

As a man's name, *Donar* in its simple form is rarely found ; one noble family on the Rhine was named *Donner* von Lorheim, Siebmach. 5, 144. Its derivatives and compounds are not common in any High Germ. dialect ; a Carolingian doc. in the Cod. lauresh. no. 464 has *Donarad*, which I take to be the ON. *Thôrðr ;* and the Trad. fuld. 2, 23 *Albthonar*, which is the ON. *Thôrâlfr* inverted. Such name-formations are far more frequent in the North, where the service of the god prevailed so long : Thôrarr (OHG. Donarari ?), *Thôrir, Thôrðr, Thôrhallr, Thôrôlfr* (OS. Thunerulf in Calend. merseb. Septemb.), *Thôroddr*, and the feminines *Thôra, Thôrun, Thôrarna* (formed like diorna, Gramm. 2, 336), *Thôrkatla, Thôrhildr, Thôrdîs*, &c. I cannot see why the editors of the Fornmanna sögur deprive such proper names as *Thôrgeirr, Thôrbiörn,*

---

[1] 'to *Donerswe*, dar heft de herscup den tegenden (teind, tithe),' Landregister of 1428.

[2] Others specified in Suhm, krit. hist. 2, 651.

[3] The settlers in Iceland, when they consecrated a district to Thôrr, named it *Thôrsmörk*, Landn. 5, 2. ed. nova p. 343. From *Donnersmark* (Zschötör tökely) in the Hungarian county of Zips, comes the Silesian family of Henkel von Donnersmark. Walach. manura : die Donnersmark*t*.

Thôrsteinn, Thôrketill, Thôrvaldr, Thôrfinnr, Thôrgerðr, &c. of their
long vowel; it is not the abstract þor, audacia, that they are compounded with, and the Nialssaga, *e.g.* cap. 65, spells *Thôr*geirr,
*Thôr*katla.—The frequent name *Thôrketill*, abbrev. Thôrkell, Dan.
Torkild, AS. Turketulus, Thurkytel (Kemble 2, 286, 349. v. supra,
p. 63), if it signifies a kettle, a vessel, of the thundergod, resembles
Wuotan's sacrificial cauldron (p. 56). The Hymisqviða sings of
Thôrr fetching a huge cauldron for the âses to brew ale with, and
wearing it on his head, Sæm. 57; which is very like the strong
man Hans (ans, âs?) in the nursery-tale clapping the church bell
on his head for a cap.—The coupling of *Alp* (elf) with *Donar* in
Albthonar and Thôrâlfr is worthy of notice, for *alpgeschoss* (elf-shot)
is a synonym for the thunderbolt, and *Alpruthe* (elf-rod) for the
donnerkraut [donnerbesen? see p. 183]. An intimate relation must
subsist between the gods and the elves (p. 180), though on the part
of the latter a subordinate one (see Suppl.).[1]

It is observable that in different lays of the Edda Thôrr goes
by different names. In Lokaglepsa and Harbardslioð he is ' Thôrr,
Asaþôrr,' but in Hamarsheimt 'Vingþôrr, Hlôrriði' (yet Thôrr as well),
in Alvismâl always 'Vingþôrr,' in Hymisqviða 'Veorr, Hlôrriði,' not
to mention the periphrases vagna verr (curruum dominus), Sifjar verr,
Oðins sonr. *Hlôrriði* was touched upon in p. 167, note. *Vingthôrr*
they derive from vængr, ala; as if Wing-thunder, the winged one,
aëra quatiens? This appears to be far from certain, as he is elsewhere called fôstri *Vingnis*, Sn. 101, and in the genealogies this
Vingnir appears by the side of him. Especially important is
Veorr, which outside of Hymisqviða is only found once, Sæm. 9[a],
and never except in the nom. sing.; it belongs doubtless to ve,
wih, and so betokens a holy consecrated being, distinct from the
Ve, gen. Vea on p. 163; the OHG. form must have been Wihor,
Wihar? (see Suppl.).

As Oðinn was represented journeying abroad, to the Eastern land
(p. 163), so is Thôrr engaged in eastward travels: Thôrr var î
austrvegi, Sæm. 59, â *austrvega* 68[a]; fôr or *austrvegi*, 75; ec var
austr, 78[a,b]; *austrförom* þînom scaltu aldregi segja seggjom frâ, 68[a].
In these journeys he fought with and slew the giants: var hann

---

[1] To the Boriât Mongols beyond L. Baikal, fairy-rings in grass are "where
the *sons of the lightning* have danced."—TRANS.

farinn î austerveg at berja tröll, Sn. 46. And this again points to
the ancient and at that time still unforgotten connexion of the
Teutonic nations with Asia ; this ' faring east-ways ' is told of
other heroes too, Sn. 190. 363 ; *e.g.*, the race of the Skilfíngar is
expressly placed in that eastern region (sû kynslôð er î austrve-
gum), Sn. 193 ; and Iötunheim, the world of the giants, was there
situated.

Thôrr was considered, next to Oðinn, the mightiest and strongest
of all the gods ; the Edda makes him Oðin's *son*, therein differing
entirely from the Roman view, which takes Jupiter to be Mercury's
father ; in pedigrees, it is true, Thôrr does appear as an ancestor of
Oðinn.   Thôrr is usually named immediately after Oðinn, sometimes before him, possibly he was feared more than Oðinn (see
Suppl.).   In Saxo Gramm., Regner confesses : Se, *Thor deo excepto,*
nullam monstrigenae virtutis potentiam expavere, cujus (sc. Thor)
virium magnitudini nihil humanarum divinarumque rerum digna
possit aequalitate conferri.   He is the true national god of the
Norwegians, *landâs* (patrium numen), Egilss. p. 365-6, and when
âss stands alone, it means especially him, *e.g.*, Sæm. 70ᵃ, as indeed
the very meaning of ans (jugum montis) agrees with that of Faírguneis.   His temples and statues were the most numerous in
Norway and Sweden, and *âsmegin*, divine strength, is understood
chiefly of him.   Hence the heathen religion in general is so
frequently expressed by the simple *Thôr blôta*, Sæm. 113ᵇ, *hêt*
(called) *â Thôr*, Landn. 1, 12, *trúði* (believed) *â Thôr*, Landn. 2, 12.
He assigns to emigrants their new place of abode : *Thôrr vísaði*
honum (shewed him), Landn. 3, 7. 3, 12.   From the Landnâmabôk
we could quote many things about the worship of Thôrr : þar
stendr enn *Thôrs steinn*, 2, 12. gânga til frêtta við *Thôr*, 3, 12.
Thôrr is worshipped most, and *Freyr* next, which agrees with the
names *Thôrviðr* and *Freyviðr* occurring in one family line 2, 6 ;
viðr is wood, does it here mean tree, and imply a priestly function ?
Oðinviðr does not occur, but *Týviðr* is the name of a plant, ch.
XXXVII.   It is Thôr's hammer that hallows a mark, a marriage,
and the runes, as we find plainly stated on the stones.   I show in
ch. XXXIII how Thôrr under various aspects passed into the
devil of the christians, and it is not surprising if he acquired
some of the clumsy boorish nature of the giant in the process, for
the giants likewise were turned into fiends.   The foe and pursuer

of all giants in the time of the Ases, he himself appeared a lubber to the christians; he throws stones for a wager with giants (conf. ch. XVIII). But even in the Eddic Thrymsqviða, he eats and drinks immoderately like a giant, and the Norwegian folk-tale makes him take up cask after cask of ale at the wedding, Faye p. 4; conf. the proverb: mundi enginn Asathôr afdrecka (outdrink). Conversely, the good-natured old giant *Thrymr* is by his very name a Donar (conf. ch. XVIII). The delightful story of the hobergs-gubbe (old man of the mountain, giant) was known far and wide in the North: a poor man invites him to stand godfather to his child, but he refuses to come on hearing that *Thor* or *Tordenveir* is also a bidden guest (conf. ch. XVIII); he sends however a handsome present (conf. Afzelius 2, 158. Molbech's eventyr no. 62, F. Magn. p. 935). In spite of all divergences, there appears in the structure of this fable a certain similarity to that of Gossip Death, ch. XXVII, for death also is a devil, and consequently a giant; conf. Müllen-hoff, schl. holst. p. 289. That is why some of the old tales which still stood their ground in the christian times try to saddle him with all that is odious, and to make him out a diabolic being of a worse kind than Oðinn; conf. Gautrekssaga p. 13. Finnr drags the statue of Thôrr to King Olafr, splits and burns it up, then mixes the ashes in furmety and gives it to dogs to devour: ''tis meet that hounds eat Thôrr, who his own sons did eat,' Fornm. sög. 2, 163. This is a calumny, the Edda knows of no such thing, it relates on the contrary that Môði and Magni outlived their father (see Suppl.). Several revived sagas, like that of the creation of wolves and goats, transform Wuotan into the good God, and Donar into the devil.

From the time they became acquainted with the Roman theogony, the writers identify the German thundergod with Jupiter. Not only is dies Jovis called in AS. *Thunres*dæg, but Latona Jovis mater is *Thunres* môdur, and capitolium is trans-lated *Thôrs*hof by the Icelanders. Conversely, Saxo Gram. p. 236 means by his 'Jupiter' the Teutonic Thor, the *Jupiter ardens* above (p. 110); did that mean *Donar?* As for that Thôrr devouring his children, it seems [a mere importation, aggravated by] a down-right confusion of Jupiter with his father Saturn, just as the Norse genealogy made Thôrr an ancestor of Oðinn. The ' presbyter *Jovi*

mactans,' and the 'sacra' and 'feriae Jovis' (in Indicul. pagan.)
have been dealt with above, p. 121.

Letzner (hist. Caroli magni, Hildesh. 1603, cap. 18 end) relates:
The Saturday after Laetare, year by year, cometh to the little
cathedral-close of Hildesheim a farmer thereunto specially appointed, and bringeth *two logs* of a fathom long, and therewith two
lesser logs pointed in the manner of skittles. The two greater he
planteth in the ground one against the other, and a-top of them
the skittles. Soon there come hastily together all manner of lads
and youth of the meaner sort, and with stones or staves do pelt the
skittles down from the logs ; other do set the same up again, and
the pelting beginneth a-new. By these skittles are to be understood the devilish gods of the heathen, that were thrown down by
the Saxon-folk when they became christian.

Here the names of the gods are suppressed,[1] but one of them
must have been *Jupiter* then, as we find it was afterwards.[2] Among
the farmer's dues at Hildesheim there occurs down to our own
times a *Jupitergeld*. Under this name the village of Grossen-
Algermissen had to pay 12 g. grosch. 4 pfen. yearly to the sexton
of the cathedral; an Algermissen farmer had every year to bring to
the cathedral close an eight-cornered log, a foot thick and four
feet long, hidden in a sack. The schoolboys dressed it in a cloak
and crown, and attacked the *Jupiter* as they then called it, by
throwing stones first from one side, then from the other, and at
last they burnt it. This popular festivity was often attended with
disorder, and was more than once interdicted, pickets were set to
carry the prohibition into effect; at length the royal treasury
remitted the Jupiter's geld. Possibly the village of Algermissen
had incurred the penalty of the due at the introduction of Christianity, by its attachment to the old religion.[3] Was the pelting of

---

[1] In the Corbei chron., Hamb. 1590, cap. 18, Letzner thinks it was the god
of the Irmensûl. He refers to MS. accounts by Con. Fontanus, a Helmers-
haus Benedictine of the 13th century.

[2] A Hildesheim register drawn up at the end of the 14th century or
beginn. of the 15th cent. says : ' De *abgotter* (idols), so sunnabends vor laetare
(Letzn. ' sonnab. *nach* laet.') von einem hausmann von Algermissen gesetzet,
davor (for which) ihm eine hofe (hufe, hide) landes gehört zur sankmeisterie
(chantry ?), und wie solches von dem hausmann nicht gesetzt worden, gehort
Cantori de hove landes.' Hannoversche landesblätter 1833, p. 30.

[3] Lüntzel on farmers' burdens in Hildesheim 1830, p. 205. Hannov. mag.
1833, p. 693. Protocols of 1742-3 in an article ' On the Stoning of Jupiter,'
Hannov. landesbl., ubi supra.

the logs to express contempt ? In Switzerland the well-known throwing of stones on the water is called *Heiden werfen*, heathen-pelting ; otherwise : ' den Herrgott lösen, vater und mutter lösen,' releasing, ransoming ? Tobler 174ᵃ (see Suppl.).

I do not pretend to think it at all established, that this *Jupiter* can be traced back to the *Thunar* of the Old Saxons. The custom is only vouched for by protocols of the last century, and clear evidence of it before that time is not forthcoming; but even Letzner's account, differing as it does, suggests a very primitive practice of the people, which is worth noting, even if Jupiter has nothing to do with it. The definite date ' laetare ' reminds one of the custom universal in Germany of ' driving out Death,' of which I shall treat hereafter, and in which Death is likewise set up to be pelted. Did the skittle represent the sacred hammer ?

An unmistakable relic of the worship paid to the thunder-god is the special observance of *Thursday*, which was not extinct among the people till quite recent times. It is spoken of in quite early documents of the Mid. Ages : ' nullus *diem Jovis* in otio observet,' Aberglaube p. xxx. ' de *feriis* quae faciunt *Jovi* vel Mercurio,' p. xxxii. quintam feriam in honorem *Jovis* honorasti, p. xxxvii. On Thursday evening one must neither spin nor hew ; Superst., Swed. 55. 110. and Germ. 517. 703. The Esthonians think Thursday holier than Sunday.[1] What punishment overtook the transgressor, may be gathered from another superstition, which, it is true, substituted the hallowed day of Christ for that of Donar : He that shall work on Trinity Sunday (the next after Pentecost), or shall wear anything sewed or knitted (on that day), shall be *stricken by thunder* ; Scheffer's Haltaus, p. 225 (see Suppl.).

If *Jupiter* had these honours paid him in the 8th century, if the Capitulare of 743 thought it needful expressly to enjoin an ' ec forsacho *Thunare*,' and much that related to his service remained uneradicated a long time after ; it cannot well be doubted, that at a still earlier time he was held by our forefathers to be a real god, and one of their greatest.

If we compare him with Wuotan, though the latter is more intellectual and elevated, Donar has the advantage of a sturdy material strength, which was the very thing to recommend him to

---

[1] Etwas über die Ehsten, pp. 13-4.

the peculiar veneration of certain races; prayers, oaths, curses retained his memory oftener and longer than that of any other god. But only a part of the Greek Zeus is included in him.

CHAPTER IX.

ZIO, (TIW, TYR).

The ON. name for dies Martis, Týsdagr, has the name of the
Eddic god *Týr* (gen. Týs, acc. Tý) to account for it. The AS.
Tiwesdæg and OHG. Ziestac scarcely have the simple name of the
god left to keep them company, but it may be safely inferred from
them : it must have been in AS. *Tiw*,[1] in OHG. *Zio*. The runic
letter *Ti, Ziu,* will be discussed further on. The Gothic name for the
day of the week is nowhere to be found ; according to all analogy
it would be Tivisdags, and then the god himself can only have been
called *Tius*. These forms, *Tiu-s, Tiw, Tý-r, Zio* make a series like
the similar þiu-s, þeow (þiw), þý-r, dio = puer, servus.

If the idea of our thundergod had somewhat narrow limits, that
of Zio lands us in a measureless expanse. The non-Teutonic
cognate [Aryan] languages confront us with a multitude of terms
belonging to the root div, which, while enabling us to make up
a fuller formula *div, tiv, zio,* yield the meanings ' brightness, sky,
day, god '. Of Sanskrit words, dyaus (coelum) stands the closest
to the Greek and German gods' names Ζεύς, Tius.

	SANSKRIT.	GREEK.	GOTHIC.
Nom.	dyaus	Ζεύς	Tius
Voc.	dyaus	Ζεῦ	Tiu
Acc.	divam	Δίϝα, Δία	Tiu
Gen.	divas	Διϝός, Διός	Tivis
Dat.	divê	Διϝί, Διΐ	Tiva

To the digammated and older form of the Greek oblique cases
there corresponds also the Latin Jovem, Jovis, Jovi, for which we

---

[1] It might have been Teow, from the analogy of þeow to þýr. Lye quotes,
without references : *Tiig*, Mars, Tiiges- vel Tiis-dæg, dies Martis. The Epinal
glosses brought to light by Mone actually furnish, no. 520 (Anzeiger 1838, p.
145), *Tiig*, Mars ; also Oehler p. 351. The change of letters is like that of briig,
jusculum, for bríw ; and we may at least infer from it, that the vowel is long,
Tîg.

must assume a nom. Ju, Jus, though it has survived only in the compound Jupiter = Jus pater, $Z\epsilon\grave{\upsilon}\varsigma$ $\pi\alpha\tau\acute{\eta}\rho$. For, the initial in Jus, Jovis [pronounce j as y] seems to be a mere softening of the fuller dj in Djus, Djovis, which has preserved itself in Dijovis, just as $Z\epsilon\acute{\upsilon}\varsigma$ presupposes an older $\varDelta\epsilon\acute{\upsilon}\varsigma$ which was actually preserved in the Æolic dialect. These Greek and Latin words likewise contain the idea of the heavenly god, *i.e.*, a personification of the sky. Dium, divum is the vault of heaven, and Zeus is the son of heaven, $O\grave{\upsilon}\rho\alpha\nu o\hat{\upsilon}$ $\upsilon\acute{\iota}\acute{o}\varsigma$, $o\grave{\upsilon}\rho\acute{\alpha}\nu\iota o\varsigma$, $Z\epsilon\grave{\upsilon}\varsigma$ $\alpha\grave{\iota}\theta\acute{\epsilon}\rho\iota$ $\nu\alpha\acute{\iota}\omega\nu$ (see Suppl.).

But apart from 'dyaus, Zeus and Jupiter,' the three common nouns *dêvas* (Sansk.), $\theta\epsilon\acute{o}\varsigma$ and *deus* express the general notion of a divinity ; they are related to the first three, yet distinct from them. The Lat. deus might seem to come nearest to our Tius, Zio; but its u, like the *o* in $\theta\epsilon\acute{o}\varsigma$, belongs to the flexion, not to the root, and therefore answers to the a in dêvas.[1] Nevertheless deus too must have sprung from devus, and $\theta\epsilon\acute{o}\varsigma$ from $\theta\epsilon Fo\varsigma$, because the very θ instead of δ in the Greek word is accounted for by the reaction of the digamma on the initial. In the shortness of their e they both differ from dêvas, whose ê (=ai) grew by guna out of i, so that the Lith. dievas comes nearer to it.[2] But the adjectives $\delta\hat{\iota}o\varsigma$ (not from $\delta\acute{\iota}\ddot{o}\varsigma$, but rather for $\delta\acute{\iota}Fo\varsigma$) and *dívus* correspond to dêvas as *díves* dîvitis (p. 20) to dêvatas (deus). This approximation between dîvus and deus serves to confirm the origin of deus out of devus or divus with short i (see Suppl.)[3] Still more helpful to us is the fact that the Edda has a plur. *tívar* meaning gods or heroes, Sæm. 30[a] 41[a] ; rîkir tîvar (conf. rich god, p. 20), Sæm. 72[a] 93[a]; valtîvar, 52[a] ; sigtîvar, 189[a] 248[a] ; the sing. is not in use. This tîvar, though not immediately related to Týr, yet seems related to it as $\delta\hat{\iota}o\varsigma$, $\theta\epsilon\acute{o}\varsigma$, $\theta\epsilon\hat{\iota}o\varsigma$ are to $Z\epsilon\acute{\upsilon}\varsigma$; its î is established by the fact that the ON. dialect contracts a short iv into y ; thus we obtain by the side of tiv a tîv, in Sanskrit by the side of div a dêv, and in Latin by the side of deus a divus, these being strengthened or guna forms of the

---

[1] Kuhn, in Zeitschr. f. d. alt. 2, 231, has rightly pointed out, that Zio can be immediately related only to dyaus and $Z\epsilon\acute{\upsilon}\varsigma$, not to deus and $\theta\epsilon\acute{o}\varsigma$; but he ought to have admitted that mediately it must be related to these last also. That div was the root of Zeus, had already been shown by O. Müller in Gött. anz. 1834, pp. 795-6.

[2] Conf. piemu $\pi o\iota\mu\acute{\eta}\nu$, and kiemas $\kappa\acute{\omega}\mu\eta$ háims.

[3] If, as hinted on p. 26, $\delta\hat{\iota}o\varsigma$ deus were conn. with $\delta\acute{\epsilon}\omega$, the notion of binding must have arisen first out of the divine band, which is hardly conceivable.

root div, tiv (splendere).[1] If the earthborn Tuisco, the ancestral god of our nation, stands (as Zeuss p. 72 has acutely suggested) for *Tivisco, Tiusco*, it shews on its very face the meaning of a divine heavenly being, leaving it an open question whether we will choose to understand it of Wuotan or any other god, barring always Tius himself, from whom it is derived (see Suppl.).

The light of day is a notion that borders on that of heaven, and it was likewise honoured with personification as a god : Lucetium Jovem appellabant, quod eum lucis esse causam credebant ; Festus sub v. To begin with, *dies* (conf. interdiu, dio) is itself connected with deus and divus ; Jupiter was called Diespiter, *i.e.*, diei pater, for the old gen. was dies. Then the word in the sing. fluctuates between the masc. and fem. genders; and as the masc. Ju, Dju with the suffix n, is shaped into the fem. forms Jûno for Jovino, Djovino, and Diana, just so the Lith. name for day, *diena*, is fem., while the Slav. *den,* dzien, dan, is masc. The Teutonic tongues have no word for sky or day taken from this root, but we can point to one in Greek : Cretenses Δία τὴν ἡμέραν vocant (call the day Zeus), ipsi quoque Romani Diespitrem appellant, ut diei patrem ; Macrob. Sat. 1, 15. The poetic and Doric forms Ζῆνα, Ζηνός, Ζηνί, and Ζᾶνα, Ζανός, Ζανί, for Δία, Διός, Διΐ, correspond to the above formations ;[2] and the Etruscans called Jupiter *Tina,* i.e. Dina ; O. Müller 2, 43 (see Suppl.).

A derivative from the same root with another suffix seems to present itself in the ON. *tivor* (deus ?),[3] Sæm. 6ᵇ, AS. *tîr*, gen. tîres (tiir, Cod. exon. 331, 18 gloria, splendor), and OS. *tîr,* gen. tîras, tîreas; with which I connect the OHG. *ziori,* ziari, zieri (splendidus), and the Lat. *decus,* decor, decorus. The AS. poets use the word tîr only to intensify other words: tîrmetod (deus gloriae, summus deus), Cædm. 143, 7 ; æsctîr wera (hasta gloriosa virorum), 124, 27 ; æsca tîr, 127, 10 ; tîrwine, Boëth. metr. 25, 41 ; tîrfruma, Cod. exon. 13, 21 ; tîrmeahtig (potentissimus), 72, 1 ; tîreádig (felicissimus), Cædm. 189, 13. 192, 16 ; tîrfæst (firmissimus), 64, 2. 189, 19 ;

---

[1] Sometimes, though rarely, we find another ON. *diar,* Sæm. 91ᵃ. Sn. 176. Yngl. saga cap. 2 ; it agrees with θεός more than with δῖος.

[2] We know to what shifts Socrates is driven in trying to explain the forms Ζῆνα and Δία (Plato's Cratylus p. 29, Bekker) ; θεός he derives from θεῖν, currere (p. 32).

[3] Or must we read it *tivor,* and connect it with the AS. tifer, tiber, OHG. zepar ?

much in the same way as the AS. eormen, OHG. irman is prefixed.
Now when a similar prefix *tŷ* meets us in the ON. writings, *e.g.*
tŷhraustr (fortissimus), tŷspâkr (sapientissimus), Sn. 29, it confirms
the affinity between tîr and *Tŷ-r*.

These intricate etymologies were not to be avoided : they
entitle us to claim a sphere for the Teutonic god Zio, Tiw, Tŷr,
which places him on a level with the loftiest deities of antiquity.
Represented in the Edda as Oðin's son, he may seem inferior to
him in power and moment ; but the two really fall into one, inasmuch as both are directors of war and battle, and the fame of
victory proceeds from each of them alike. For the olden time
resolved all glory into military glory, and not content with Wuotan
and Zio, it felt the need of a third war-god Hadu ; the finer distinctions in their cultus are hidden from us now.—It is not to be overlooked, that Oðinn is often named Sigtŷr, Hrôptatŷr, Gautatŷr,
hângatŷr, farmatŷr (Sæm. 30. 47. 248ª. Sn. 94-6), bödvartŷr, quasi
pugnae deus, geirtŷr (Fornm. sög. 9, 515-8) ; and that even Thôrr,
to whom Jupiter's lightning has been handed over, appears as
Reiðartŷr, Reiditŷr (Sn. 94), *i.e.* god of the waggon.[1] In all these
poetical terms, we see that *tŷr* bears that more general sense which
makes it suitable for all divinities, especially the higher ones. Tŷr
has a perfect right to a name identical with Zeus. Add moreover,
that the epithet of *father* was in a special degree accorded, not
only to Jupiter, Diespiter, but to victory's patron *Marspiter*.[2]

Further, this lofty position is claimed for Zio by the oldest
accounts that have reached us. *Mars* is singled out as a chief god

---

[1] I do not reckon *Angantŷr* among this set of words. It occurs frequently,
both in the Hervararsaga and in Sæm. 114ª 119ᵇ 9ª ; this last passage calls
Oðinn 'Friggjar ângantŷr'. The true form is doubtless *Anganþŷr*, as appears
from the OHG. *Angandeo* (Trad. fuld. 1, 57), and the AS. *Ongenþeow, Ongenþio*
(Beow. 4770. 4945-67. 5843-97. 5917-67) ; -tŷr would have been in AS. -teow, in
OHG. -zio. Graff gives an Agandeo 1, 132. 5, 87, which seems to be a mis-
spelling, though the Trad. wizenb. no. 20 have a woman's name Agathiu (for
Anganthiu), to which add the acc. Agathien, Agacien (Walthar. 629). The
meaning of angan, ongen, is doubtful ; 'ângan illrar brûdhar' is said to be
'deliciae malae mulieris,' but Biörn interprets it pedisequa, and Oðinn might
fitly be called Friggae pedisequus. That some proper names in the Edda are
corrupt, is plain from Hamdir, which ought everywhere to be Hamþŷr, OHG.
Hamadio, Hamideo (Schannat no. 576. Cod. lauresh. 2529), MHG. Hamdie
(MsH 3, 213ᵇ). This much I am sure of, that neither Anganþŷr nor Hamþŷr
can contain a tŷr, which is almost always compounded with genitives in a
figurative sense.
[2] Gellius 5, 12.

of all the Germanic nations, and mentioned side by side with Mercury. The evidence is collected on p. 44.[1] Tacitus, in Hist. 4, 64, makes the Tencteri say right out: Communibus deis, et *prae-cipuo deorum Marti* grates agimus; we have no occasion to apply the passage to Wuotan, to whom the highest place usually belongs, as particular races may have assigned that to Zio. The still clearer testimony of Procopius 12, 15 to the worship of *Ares* among the dwellers in the North,[2] which says expressly : ἐπεὶ θεὸν αὐτὸν νομίζουσι μέγιστον εἶναι, ought to be compared with the statements of Jornandes on the Gothic *Mars*; in both places human sacrifices are the subject, and therefore Zeuss, p. 22, is for understanding it of Wuotan again, because to him Tacitus says that men were sacrificed ; but he does not say to him alone,—on the contrary, anent the Hermundurian offering, Ann. 13, 57, where ' viri ' were also slain, *Mars* stands mentioned before Mercury. And Jornandes, who identifies the ' Gradivus pater ' of the Getae in Virg. Aen. 3, 35 with the *Mars* of the Goths, must have been thinking of the special god of war, not of a higher and more general one, intimately as they interpenetrate one another in name and nature. All in favour of this view are the Scythian and Alanic legends of the war-sword, which will be examined by and by : if the Getic, Scythian and Gothic traditions meet anywhere, it is on this of *Mars*-worship. Neither can we disregard Widukind's representation at a later time (Pertz 5, 423) of the Saxon *Mars* set up on high. Donar and Wuotan, with whom at other times he is combined in a significant trilogy, appear, like Jupiter and Mercury, to retire before him. But it is quite conceivable how the glossist quoted on p. 133 could render Wuotan by Mars, and Widukind glide easily from Mars to Hermes, *i.e.*, Wodan, particularly if he had in his mind the analogy of those prefixes irman- (of which he is speaking) and tîr-. The ON. writers, while they recognise Oðin's influence on war and victory, speak no less distinctly of *Týr*, who is em-

---

[1] A passage in Florus 2, 4: 'mox Ariovisto duce vovere de nostrorum militum praeda *Marti suo* torquem : intercepit Jupiter votum, nam de torquibus eorum aureum tropaeum Jovi Flaminius erexit,' speaks of the Insubrian Gauls, who were beaten in the consulship of Flaminius B.C. 225. But these Galli are both in other respects very like Germani, and the name of their leader is that of the Suevic (Swabian) king in Caesar.

[2] Θουλῖται (men of Thule) is their generic name, but he expressly includes among them the Γαυτοί, whom he rightly regards as a different people from the Γότθοι, conf. Gött. anz. 1828, p. 553.

phatically their *Vîgaguð* (deus proeliorum), Sn. 105, and again : hann er diarfastr ok best hugaðr, ok hann *rœðr* miöc *sigri î orostom*, Sn. 29 (see Suppl.).

No doubt there were mountains hallowed to Zio, as well as to Wuotan and Donar ; the only difficulty is, to know which god, Wuotan or Zio, was meant by a particular name. May we place to his credit the name of the abbey of Siegburg in the Lower Rhine, which was founded in 1064 on a mountain where the ancient assize of the people was held? From that time the mountain was to have been called Mons sancti Michaelis after the christian conqueror, but the heathen *Sigeberg* could not be dislodged, it was only distorted into Siegburg ;[1] or are we to explain the name by the river Sieg, which flows through the district ? The ON. *Sigtŷsberg* (OS. Sigu-tiwis-berag?), Sæm. 348[a] might belong to Oðinn or to Tŷr. The Weimar map has in section 38 a *Tisdorf*, and in section 48 a *Ziesberg*, both in Lower Saxon districts on the Elbe. A place in Zealand, about which there are folk-tales, is *Tybierg* (Thiele 2, 20) ; also in Zealand are *Tisvelde* (Ti's well), *Tysting* ; in Jutland, *Tystathe*, *Tiislunde*. In Sweden : *Tistad*, *Tisby*, *Tisjö*, *Tyved*. *Zierberg* in Bavaria (Cirberg, Zirberc, MB. 11, 71-3-5-6) and *Zierenberg* in Lower Hesse may be derived from the collateral form (see Suppl.). The *mons Martis* at Paris (Montmartre), of which even Abbo de bell. Par. 2, 196 makes mention, has to do with the Gallic Mars, whom some take to be Belus, others Hesus. With far better right than the Parisian mons Martis (yet conf. Waitz's Salic law, p. 52), we may assign to Zio the *fanum Martis*, now Famars in Hainault (p. 84), according to Herm. Müller the Old Frankish ' *Disbargum* (or Disbargus) in termino Toringorum ' of Greg. tur. 2, 9, Chlodio's castellum. Dis- would be a Latinized form of Tis = Tives, perhaps recalling Dispiter, Diespiter ; there is no Gallic word like it looking towards Mars, and the district is thoroughly Frankish, with Liphtinae close by, where we have Saxnôt named by the side of Thunar and Wôdan. As for *Eresberg* and *Mersberg* (3 or 4 pp. on), I have compared the oldest documents in Seibertz: no. 11 (anno 962) gives us Eresburg; no. 25 (1030) already Mersburg ; 1, 98 (1043) mons Eresburg ; no. 51 (1150) mons Eresberg; no. 70 (1176) mons Eresberch ; no. 85 (1184) Heresburg ;

---

[1] Docum. in Lacomblet, no. 203-4.

no. 115 (1201) mons Martis; no. 153 (1219 Mersberch; no. 167 (1222) Eresberch; no. 179 (1228) mons Martis; no. 186 (1229) mons Heresberg; no. 189 (1230) mons Martis and Mersberg. Mons Martis was the learned name, Mersberg the popular, and Eresberg the oldest. As mons and castellum are used by turns, berg and burg are equally right. Widukind 2, 11 and Dietmar 2, 1 spell *Heresburg* and *Eresburch*, when they describe the taking of the place in 938. According to the Ann. Corb. (Pertz 5, 8), they are sacred to both Ares and Hermes (Mars and Mercury).

The names of plants also confess the god : ON. *Týsfiola*, I daresay after the Lat. viola Martis, march-violet; *Týrhialm* (aconitum), otherwise Thorhialm, Thorhat (helmet, hat), conf. Germ. sturmhut, eisenhut, Dan. troldhat, a herb endowed with magic power, whose helmet-like shape might suggest either of those warlike gods Týr and Thôrr; *Týviðr*, Tý's wood, Dan. *Tyved*, *Tysved* (daphne mezereum), in the Helsing. dial. *tis*, *tistbast*, the mezereon, a beautiful poison-flower (see Suppl.).

While these names of places and plants sufficiently vouch for the wide-spread worship of the god, we must lay particular stress on one thing, that the name for the third day of the week, which is what we started with, bears living witness to him at this moment, not only in Scandinavia and England (ON. Tysdagr, Swed. Tisdag, Dan. Tirsdag, AS. Tiwesdæg), but among the common people in Swabia and Switzerland (Ziestag, Tiestag, diestik, beside our universal Dienstag); Schm. 4, 214 brings all the forms together. And there is yet one more testimony to the high antiquity of Zio-worship in Swabia, which we may gather from an old Wessobrunn gloss 'Cyuvari = Suâpa,' MB. 7, 375 and Diut. 2, 370; which I take to be not Teutonoari, as Zeuss does, pp. 146-9, but *Ziowari* Martem colentes, warian expressing, like Lat. colere, both habitare and θεραπεύειν, so that the Suevi are θεράποντες Ἄρηος.

But that is not all : further and weighty disclosures on the name and nature of the war-god await us at the hands of the Runic alphabet.

It is known that each separate rune has a name to itself, and these names vary more or less according to the nations that use them, but they are mostly very ancient words. The OHG. runes having to bestow the name dorn on D, and tac on T, require for their aspirate Z which closes the alphabet the name of Zio. In the ON.

and AS. alphabets, dag stood for D, *Tŷr* and *Tiw* for T, þorn for þ, being the same three words, only in different places; occasionally the Anglo-Saxons wrote Tir or Tis. Whenever a list of runes keeps thorn for Th, and dag for D, it is sure to have *Ti* for T (as the Cod. Isidori paris. and bruxell.); so it is in the St Gall cod. 260 and the Brussels 9565, except that dorn is improperly put for thorn, and tag for dag, but Ti stands correctly opposite T. The Paris cod. 5239 has dhron (dhorn), tac, Ziu, that of Salzburg dhorn, Ti, daeg: everywhere the form *Ziu* shows the High Germ. acceptation, and the form *Ti* (once, in Cod. vatic. Christinae 338, spelt Tu, perh. Tii) the Low Germ., the Saxon. The *u* in *Ziu* seems to be more archaic than the *o* of *Zio*, which has kept pace with the regular progress of the OHG. dialect, and follows the analogy of dio, servus; this relation between u and o may perhaps be seen still more in its true light, as we go on. But what is very remarkable, is that in the Vienna cod. 140 the name *Tyz* is given to T in an alphabet which uses the Gothic letters, for Tyz comes very near to our conjectural Goth. *Tius*. As well the retention as the unavoidable alterations of this divine name in the runes of the various races, may be taken as proofs of the antiquity and extent of Zio-worship.

How comes it that no rune has taken its name from Wuotan or Oðinn, the inventor of writing itself? ' R = reið, râd,' *i.e.*, waggon, may indirectly at least be referred to the god of the Thunder-car; and F according to one interpretation signifies Freyr. Anyhow, 'T=Tyr' appears to have been a supremely honoured symbol, and the name of this god to have been specially sacred: in scratching the runes of victory on the sword, the name of Tŷr had to be twice inserted, Sæm. 194[b]. The shape of the rune ↑ has an obvious resemblance to the old-established symbol of the planet Mars when set upright ⚦, and an AS. poem on the runes expressly says: *tîr bið tâcna* sum (tîr is one of the tokens, is a certain sign); where again the derivative form tîr is employed to explain the the simple Tiw or Tî. Occasionally the poets speak of 'tîre tâcnian,' to mark with tîr (El. 753. Jud. 137, 18), and'tîres to tâcne,' as mark of tîr (Beow. 3306); we may expound it as ' gloria, decore insignire, in gloriae signum,' and still think of the heathen symbol of the god, pretty much as we saw it done at the solemn blessing of the ale-cups (see Suppl.).[1]

---

[1] Conf. note to Elene 155-6.

Thus far we have dealt with the runic name Týr, Tiw, Zio, and no other. But here the same alphabets come out with a sharp distinction between two names of the selfsame god. First, in the AS. lists, in addition to ↑ Tir, we come upon a similar arrow with two barbs added ⤊ and the name *Ear* attached to it.[1] Then the OHG. alphabets, after using ↑ for tac, find a use for that very symbol ⤊ to which some of them give the name Zio, others again *Eo, Eor, Aer*. And there are AS. alphabets that actually set down by ⤊ the two names Tir and Ear, though Tir had already been given to ↑. It is evident then, that *Tir* and *Ear—Zio* and *Eo, Eor*—were two names for one god, and both must have been current among the several races, both Low German and High.

Evidence as regards Low Germany is found both in the rune *Ear* occurring in Anglo-Saxon, and in the remarkable name of *Eresburg, Aeresburg* being given to a notable seat of pagan worship in a district of Westphalia, in the immediate neighbourhood of the Irmansûl (v. supra, p. 116). That it was strictly Eres*berg* (as Siegburg was originally Sigberg, p. 198), follows both from the Latin rendering *mons Martis*, and from its later name *Mersberg*,[2] whose initial M could be explained by the contraction of the words ' in dem Eresberge, Aresberge,'[3] or it may be an imitation of the Latin name. There was a downright *Marsberg* in another district of Westphalia.[4] This *Eresberc* then is a *Ziesberc*, a Sig-tiwes-berg, and yet more closely an Areopagus, Mars' hill, Ἀρειόπαγος, πέτρα πάγος τ' Ἄρειος (Aeschyl. Eum. 690).

Still more plainly are High German races, especially the Bavarian (Marcomannic) pointed to by that singular name for the third day of the week, *Ertag, Iertag, Irtag, Eritag, Erchtag, Erichtag*, which answers to the rune *Eor*, and up to this moment lives to part off the Bavarians, Austrians and Tyrolese from the Swabians and Swiss (who, as former Ziowari, stick to Ziestag); along the boundary-line of these races must also have run formerly the frontier between Eor-worship and Zio-worship. True, the compound Ertac lacks

---

[1] In one poem, Cod. exon. 481, 18, the rune contains simply the vowel sound *ea*.

[2] This Eresburg or Mersberg stands in the pagus Hessi saxonicus (registr. Sarachonis p. 42, 735) ; conf. Wigands archiv I. 1, 36-7. II. 143. 268.

[3] So : Motgers = in dem Otgêrs hove [and, the nonce = then once, &c.].

[4] In the pagus Marstem, Marshem, Marsem (close to the Weser, near Marklô), reg. Sarachonis 42, 727.

the genitive ending -*s* which is preserved in Ziestac, and I have not been so fortunate as to hunt up an Erestac[1] in the older records of the 13-14th centuries; nevertheless the coincidence of the double names for the day and for the rune should be conclusive here, and we must suppose an OHG. Erestac, to match the Eresberg. One might be led to imagine that in *Ertag* the *Earth* (Erde according to the forms given at the beginning of ch. XIII) was meant. But the ancient way of thinking placed the earth in the centre of the world, not among the planets; she cannot therefore have given name to a day of the week, and there is no such day found in any nation, unless we turn Venus and Freyja into the earth.—To bear this Ertag company, there is that name of a place *Eersel*, quoted p. 154 from Gramaye, in which neither êra honor, nor its personification Era (ch. XVI, XXIX) is to be thought of, but solely a god of the week. It is worth noticing, that *Ertac* and *Erdag* occur as men's names; also, that the Taxandrian Eersel was but a little way off the Tisberg or Fanmars in Hainault (see Suppl.).—Now comes something far more important. As Zio is identical with Zeus as director of wars, we see at a glance that *Eor, Er, Ear*, is one with "Ἄρης the son of Zeus; and as the Germans had given the rank of Zeus to their Wuotan, Tŷr and consequently Eor appears as the son of the highest god. Have we any means now left of getting at the sense of this obscure root *Eor*?

The description of the rune in the AS. poem gives only a slight hint, it runs thus:

> *Ear* biᵭ egle eorla gehwilcum,
> þonne fæstlîce flæsc onginneᵭ
> hræw côlian, hrusan ceosan
> blâc tô gebeddan.   blæda gedreosaᵭ,
> wynna gewîtaᵭ, wera geswîcaᵭ;

i.e., Ear fit importunus hominum cuicumque, quum caro incipit refrigescere, pallidumque corpus terram eligere conjugem. tunc enim gloriae dilabuntur, gaudia evanescunt, foedera cessant. The description is of death coming on, and earthly joys dropping off; but who can that be, that at such a time is burdensome (egle, ail-some) to men? The ordinary meaning of *ear*, spica, arista, can be of no use here; I suppose that approaching dissolution, a personified death

---

[1] In a passage from Keisersberg quoted by Schm. 1, 97, it is spelt Eristag, apparently to favour the derivation from 'dies aeris.'

is to be understood, from which a transition to the destructive god of battles, the βροτολοιγός, μιαιφόνος Ἄρης is easy to conceive.[1] Ἄρης itself is used abstractly by the Greeks for destruction, murder, pestilence, just as our Wuotan is for furor and belli impetus,[2] and the Latin Mars for bellum, exitus pugnae, furor bellicus, conf. 'Mars =cafeht,' gefecht, fight, in Gl. Hrab. 969ᵃ; as conversely the OHG. *wîg* pugna, bellum (Graff 1, 740) seems occasionally to denote the personal god of war. 'Wicgch quoque Mars est' says Ermoldus Nigellus (Pertz 2, 468), and he is said to farneman, AS. forniman, carry off, as Hild (Bellona) does elsewhere : dat inan wîc fornam, Hildebr. lied ; in AS. : *wîg* ealle fornam, Beow. 2155 ; wîg fornom, Cod. exon. 291, 11. Do we not still say, war or battle snatched them all away ? A remarkable gloss in the old Cod. sangall. 913, p. 193, has 'turbines = *ziu* ' (we have no business to write zui), which may mean the storm of war, the Mars trux, saevus, or possibly the literal whirlwind, on which mythical names are sometimes bestowed; so it is either *Zio* himself, or a synonymous female personification *Ziu*, bearing the same relation to Zio as diu (ancilla) to dio (servus).

Here comes in another string of explanations, overbold as some of them may seem. As *Eresburg* is just as often spelt *Heresburg* by the Frankish annalists, we may fairly bring in the Goth. *haírus*, AS. *heor*, OS. *heru*, ON. *hiörr*, ensis, cardo, although the names of the rune and the day of the week always appear without the aspirate. For in Greek we already have the two unaspirated words Ἄρης and ἄορ, sword, weapon, to compare with one another, and these point to a god of the sword. Then again the famous Abrenuntiatio names three heathen gods, *Thunar, Wôden, Saxnôt*, of whom the third can have been but little inferior to the other two in power and holiness. *Sahsnôt* is word for word gladii consors, ensifer [Germ. genoss, sharer]; who else but *Zio* or *Eor* and the Greek *Ares?*[3] The AS. genealogies preserve the name of *Saxneát*

---

[1] Or, without the need of any transition, Ear might at once be Ares : ' war is burdensome in old age '.—TRANSL.

[2] The notions of raving (wüten) and insanire are suitable to the blustering stormful god of war. Homer calls Ares θοῦρος the wild, and ἄφρων the insensate, ὃς οὔτινα οἶδε θέμιστα, Il. 5, 761. But μαίνεται is said of other gods too, particularly Zeus (8, 360) and Dionysos or Bacchus (6, 132).

[3] One might think of Frô, Freyr (ch. X), but of course glittering swords were attributed to more than one god ; thus Poseidon (Neptune) wields a δεινὸν ἄορ, Il. 14, 385, and Apollo is called χρυσάορος, 5, 509. 15, 256.

as the son of Wôden, and it is in perfect accordance with it, that
Týr was the son of Oðinn, and Ares the son of Zeus (see Suppl.).
But further, as the *Saxons* were so called, either because they
wielded the sword of stone (saxum), or placed this god at the head
of their race, so I think the *Cheruscans* of Tacitus, a people
synonymous, nay identical with them, were named after *Cheru*,
Heru = Eor, from whom their name can be derived.[1]   After this
weighty consonance of facts, which opens to us the meaning of the
old national name, and at the same time teaches that 'heru' was
first of all pronounced 'cheru,' and last of all 'eru, er,' I think we
may also bring in the Gallic war-god *Hesus* or *Esus* (Lucan 1, 440),
and state, that the metal iron is indicated by the planetary sign of
Mars, the AS. 'tîres tâcen,' and consequently that the rune of Zio
and Eor may be the picture of a sword with its handle, or of a
spear.[2]   The Scythian and Alanic legends dwell still more emphatically on the god's sword, and their agreement with Teutonic ways
of thinking may safely be assumed, as Mars was equally prominent
in the faith of the Scythians and that of the Goths.

The impressive personification of the sword matches well with
that of the hammer, and to my thinking each confirms the other.
Both idea and name of two of the greatest gods pass over into the
instrument by which they display their might.

Herodotus 4, 62 informs us, that the Scythians worshipped
Ares under the semblance or symbol of an ancient iron sword
(ἀκινάκης), which was elevated on an enormous stack of brushwood
['three furlongs in length and breadth, but less in height']: ἐπὶ
τούτου δὴ τοῦ ὄγκου ἀκινάκης σιδήρεος ἵδρυται ἀρχαῖος
ἑκάστοισι· καὶ τοῦτ' ἔστι τοῦ "Αρηος τὸ ἄγαλμα.   Ammianus
Marcellinus 31, 2 says of the Alani : Nec templum apud eos visitur
aut delubrum, ne tugurium quidem culmo tectum cerni usquam
potest, sed *gladius barbarico ritu humi figitur nudus, eumque ut
Martem*, regionum quas circumcircant praesulem, verecundius
colunt.   And he had previously asserted of the Quadi also, a
decidedly German people, 17, 12 (A.D. 358): Eductis *mucronibus, quos
pro numinibus colunt*, juravere se permansuros in fide.   Perhaps all

---

[1] The suffix -sk would hardly fit with the material sense of heru, far better
with a personal Heru.

[2] Does the author overlook, or deliberately reject, the ON. *ör*, gen. *örvar*,
AS. *arwe*, arrow ?   Among the forms for Tuesday occur *Erig*tag, *Erge*tag ; erge
is to arwe, as sorge to sorwe, morgen to morwen, &c.—TRANS.

the Teutonic nations swore by their weapons, with a touching of the weapon,[1] just as the Scythians and Romans did *per Martis frameam*, Juvenal 13, 79. So Arnobius 6, 11 : Ridetis temporibus priscis coluisse *acinacem* Scythiae nationes, . . . *pro Marte* Romanos hastam, ut Varronis indicant Musae ; this framea and hasta of the Romans is altogether like the Scythian sword.[2] Jornandes, following Priscus 201, 17, tells of the Scythian sword, how it came into the hands of Attila, cap. 35 : Qui (Attila), quamvis hujus esset naturae ut semper confideret, addebat ei tamen confidentiam *gladius Martis* inventus, apud Scytharum reges semper habitus. Quem Priscus historicus tali refert occasione detectum, quum pastor, inquiens, quidam gregis unam buculam conspiceret claudicantem (noticed one heifer walking lame), nec causam tanti vulneris inveniret, sollicitus vestigia cruoris insequitur, tandemque venit ad gladium, quem depascens herbas bucula incaute calcaverat, effossumque protinus ad Attilam defert. Quo ille munere gratulatus, ut erat magnanimus, arbitratur se totius mundi principem constitutum, et per *Martis gladium* potestatem sibi concessam esse bellorum.—But the sword degenerated into an unlucky one, like some far-famed northern swords. Lambert relates, that a queen, Solomon of Hungary's mother, made a present of it to Otto, duke of Bavaria, that from this Otto's hands it came by way of loan to the younger Dedi, margrave Dedi's son, then to Henry IV., and lastly to Lupold of Mersburg, who, being thrown by his horse, and by the same sword transpierced, was buried at Mertenefeld. It is a question whether these local names Mersburg and Mertenefeld can have any reference to the sword of Mars. A great while after, the duke of Alba is said to have dug it out of the earth again after the battle of Mühlberg (Deutsche heldensage p. 311). We see through what lengthened periods popular tradition could go on nourishing itself on this world-old worship (see Suppl.).

With the word "Αρης the Lat. *Mars* appears to have nothing to do, being a contraction of Mavors, and the indispensable initial being even reduplicated in *Mamers;* so the fancied connexion between Eresburg and Marsberg will not hold.

In the Old Roman worship of Mars a prominent place is given

---

[1] Conf. RA. 896 ; and so late as Wigal. 6517: 'Swert, ûf dînem knopfe ich des swer,' Sword, on thy pommel I swear it.

[2] Juro per Dianam et *Martem*, Plaut. Mil. glor. 5, 21.

to the legend of Picus, a son of Saturn, a wood-spirit who helped to nurse the babes Remus and Romulus; certain features in our antiquities seem to recall him, as will be shown later. Romulus consecrated the third month of the year to Mars, his progenitor; our ancestors also named it after a deity who may perhaps be identified with Mars. That is to say, the Anglo-Saxons called March *Hréðemônað*, which Beda without hesitation traces to a goddess *Hréðe*; possibly other races might explain it by a god *Hréða*? These names would come from hröð gloria, fama, ON. hröðr, OHG. hruod, OFrank. chrôd, which helped to form many ancient words, *e.g.* OHG. Hruodgang, Hruodhilt, OFrank. Chrôdo-gang, Chrôdhild; did *Hruodo, Chrôdo* express to certain races the shining god of fame?[1] The Edda knows of no such epithet for Týr as Hröðr or Hrœði (see Suppl.).

To these discoveries or conjectures we have been guided simply by the several surviving names of one of the greatest gods of our olden time, to whose attributes and surroundings we have scarcely any other clue left. But now we may fairly apply to him in the main, what the poetry of other nations supplies. Zio is sure to have been valiant and fond of war, like Ares, lavish of glory, but stern and bloodthirsty (αἵματος ἆσαι Ἄρηα, Il. 5, 289. 20, 78. 22, 267); he raves and rages like Zeus and Wuotan, he is that 'old blood-shedder' of the Servian song, he gladdens the hearts of ravens and wolves, who follow him to fields of battle, although these creatures again must be assigned more to Wuotan (p. 147); the Greek phrase makes them οἰωνοί and κύνες (birds and dogs), and

---

[1] In this connexion one might try to rescue the suspicious and discredited legend of a Saxon divinity *Krodo;* there is authority for it in the 15th century, none whatever in the earlier Mid. Ages. Bothe's Sassenchronik (Leibn. 3, 286) relates under the year 780, that King Charles, during his conquest of the East Saxons, overthrew on the Hartesburg an idol similar to Saturn, which the people called *Krodo.* If such an event had really happened, it would most likely have been mentioned by the annalists, like the overthrow of the Irmansûl. For all that, the tradition need not be groundless, if other things would only correspond. Unfortunately the form Crôdo for Chrôdo, Hrôdo, Rôdo [like Catti, afterw. Chatti, Hatti, Hessen] is rather *too* ancient, and I can find no support for it in the Saxon speech. A doc. of 1284 (Langs reg. 4, 247) has a Waltherus dictus *Krode,* and a song in Nithart's MsH. 3, 208ᵇ a *Krotolf,* which however has no business to remind us of Hruodolf, Ruodolf, being not a proper name, but a nickname, and so to be derived from krote, a toad, to which must be referred many names of places, Krotenpful, &c., which have been mistakenly ascribed to the idol. The true form for Upper Germany would not tolerate a Kr, but only Hr or R (see Suppl.).

the fields of the slain, where the hounds hold revel, are called κυνῶν μέλπηθρα, Il. 13, 233. 17, 255. 18, 179. Battle-songs were also sure to be tuned to the praises of Zio, and perhaps war-dances executed (μέλπεσθαι Ἄρηϊ, Il. 7, 241), from which I derive the persistent and widely prevalent custom of the solemn sword-dance, exactly the thing for the god of the sword. The Edda nowhere lays particular stress on the sword of war, it knows nothing of Sahsnôt, indeed its sverðâs is another god, Heimðallr;[1] but it sets Týr before us as *one-handed*, because the wolf, within whose jaws he laid his right hand as a pledge, bit it off at the joint, whence the wrist was called ûlfliðr, wolf-lith, Sæm. 65[a]. Sn. 35-6. This incident must have been well-known and characteristic of him, for the ON. exposition of runes likewise says, under letter T : Týr er *einhendr* Asa ; conf. Sn. 105. The rest of Teutonic legend has no trace of it,[2] unless we are to look for it in Walther's *onehandedness*, and find in his name the mighty ' wielder of hosts '. I prefer to adopt the happy explanation,[3] that the reason why Týr appears *one-handed* is, because he can only give victory to one part of the combatants, as Hadu, another god who dispenses the fortune of war, and Plutos and Fortuna among the Greeks and Romans, are painted blind, because they deal out their gifts at random (see Suppl.). Now, as victory was esteemed the highest of all fortune, the god of victory shares to the full the prominent characteristics of luck in general, partiality and fickleness. And a remoter period of our nation may have used names which bore upon this.[4]

Amongst the train of Ares and Mars there appear certain mythic beings who personify the notions of fear and horror. Δεῖμος and Φόβος (Il. 4, 440. 11, 317. 15, 119) answer to the Latin *Pallor*

---

[1] Conf. Apollo χρυσάορος above, p. 203, note.

[2] Cod. pal. 361, 65[a] tells of Julian, that he was forced to put his hand into the mouth of Mercury's statue : Die hant stiez er im in den munt dar, darinne uobte sich der vâlant (devil), er clemmete im die hant, und gehabete sie im sô vaste, daz er sich niht irlôsen mohte (could not get loose). Besides, the wolf's limb has a likeness to the Wuotan's limb, Woens-let, p. 160.

[3] Wackernagel's, in the Schweiz. mus. 1, 107.

[4] The Greek epos expresses the changefulness of victory (νίκη ἑτεραλκής, Il. 8, 171. 16, 362 ; νίκη ἐπαμείβεται ἄνδρας, 6, 339) by an epithet of Ares, Ἀλλοπρόσαλλος 5, 831. 889. A certain many-shaped and all-transforming being, with a name almost exactly the same, *Vilanders* (Ls. 1, 369-92), *Baldanderst, Baldander* (H. Sachs 1, 537. Simpliciss. bk 6, c. 9), has indeed no visible connexion with the god of war, but it may have been the name of a god. The similarity of this *Vilanders* to the name of a place in the Tyrol, Villanders near Brixen (Velunutris, Vulunuturusa, acc. to Steub. p. 79. 178) is merely accidental.

and *Pavor*; it is the two former that harness the steeds of Ares,
Φόβος is called his son (13, 299), and in Aeschylus he is provided
with a dwelling (μέλαθρον tectum), out of which he suddenly leaps.
So in the old Bohemian songs, *Třas* (tremor) and *Strakh* (terror)
burst out of forest shades on the enemy's bands, chase them, press
on their necks and squeeze out of their throats a loud cry (Königinh.
hs. 84. 104) ; they are ghostly and spectral. This borders upon
Vôma, *Omi* and *Yggr* (pp. 119, 120), terms which designate the
god himself, not his companions, sons or servants, yet they again
bear witness to the community there was between Wuotan and
Zio. Thôrr was called *ótti iötna*, terror gigantum. When in our
modern phraseology fear 'surprises, seizes, shakes, deprives of sense,'
personification is not far off; in the Iliad also 17, 67 χλωρὸν δέος
(neut.) αἱρεῖ, pale fear seizes ; but masculine embodiments like
δεῖμος, φόβος, pallor, pavor, třas, strakh, bring it more vividly before
us, and pavor was weakened by passing into the fem. paura, peur
of the Romance. AS. þâ hine se brôga ongeat (terror eum invasit),
Beow. 2583. OHG. forhta cham mih ana, N. ps. 54, 5 ; forhta
anafiel ubar inan, T. 2, 4 ; conf. MHG. diu sorge im was sô verre
entriten, sie möhte erreichen niht ein sper, fear was fled so far from
him, a spear could not reach it, Wh. 280, 10 (see Suppl.). But
further on, we shall get acquainted with a female Hilta, comparable
to the Lat. Bellona and the Gr. Enyo and Eris, who is really one
with war and the war-god.

Týr is described in Sn. 105 as a son of Oðinn, but in the
Hymisqviða as a kinsman of the giants. His mother, whose name
is not found, but whose beauty is indicated by the epithet all-gullin,
all-golden, Sæm. 53ᵃ, must have been a giant's daughter, who bore
to Oðinn this immortal son (see Suppl.).

CHAPTER X.

FRO, (FREYR).

The god that stands next in power and glory, is in the Norse mythology *Freyr* (Landn. 4, 7) ; with the Swedes he seems even to have occupied the third place. His name of itself proclaims how widely his worship prevailed among the other Teutonic races, a name sacred enough to be given to the Supreme Being even in christian times. There must have been a broad pregnant sense underlying the word, which made it equally fit for the individuality of one god, and for the comprehensive notion of dominion, whether sacred or secular : to some nations it signified the particular god, to others the soverain deity in general, pretty much as we found, connected with the proper names Zio, Zeus, the more general term deus, θεός. While the names of other heathen gods became an abomination to the christians, and a Gothic Vôdans or Thunrs would have grated harshly on the ear; this one expression, like the primitive guþ itself, could remain yet a long time without offence, and signify by turns the heavenly lord and an earthly one.

It is true, the names do not correspond quite exactly. The ON. *Freyr* gen. Freys, which Saxo gives quite correctly in its Danish form as *Frö* gen. Frös (whence Frösö, Fro's island), the Swed. likewise *Frö*, ought to be in Gothic Fráus or Fravis,[1] instead of which, every page of Ulphilas shows *fráuja* gen. fráujins, translating κυριος; on the other hand, the ON. dialect lacks both the weak form (Freyi, Freyja), and the meaning of lord. The remaining languages all hold with the Gothic. In OHG. the full form frouwo was already lost, the writers preferring truhtîn; it is only in the form of address '*frô* mîn !' (O. i. 5, 35. ii. 14, 27. v. 7, 35. Ludw. lied) that the

---

[1] Frey = Fravi, as hey = havi (hay), mey = mavi (maid), ey = avi (isle), &c.

word for a divine or earthly lord was preserved, just as that antique
sihora and sire (p. 27) lasted longest in addresses.   In the Heliand
too, when the word is used in addressing, it is always in the shortened form *frô* mîn ! 123, 13. 140, 23.   *frô* mîn the gôdo ! 131, 6.
134, 15. 138, 1. 7.   waldand *frô* mîn ! 153, 8.   drohtîn *frô* mîn !
15, 3 ; but in other cases we do find the complete *frôho* gen. frôhon
3, 24 ; *frâho* 119, 14, gen. frâhon 122, 9, frâon 3, 24. 5, 23 ; *frôio*
93, 1. 107, 21.   Still the OS. poet uses the word seldomer than the
synonyms drohtîn and hêrro, and he always puts a possessive with
it, never an adjective (like mâri drohtîn, rîki drohtîn, craftag drohtîn,
liob hêrro), still less does he make compounds with it (like sigi-
drohtîn) : all symptoms that the word was freezing up.   The AS.
freá gen. freán (for freâan, freâwan) has a wider sweep, it not only
admits adjectives (freá ælmihtig, Cædm. 1, 9. 10, 1), but also forms
compounds: âgendfreá, Cædm. 135, 4.   aldorfreá 218, 29.   folcfreá
111, 7 ; and even combines with dryhten : freádryhten, Cædm. 54,
29, gen. freahdrihtnes, Beow. 1585, dat. freodryhtne 5150.—But
now by the side of our OHG. frô there is found a rigid (indecl.)
frôno, which, placed before or after substantives, imparts the notion
of lordly, high and holy ; out of this was gradually developed a
more flexible adj. of like meaning *frôn*, and again an adj. *frônisc*
(pulcher, mundus, inclytus, arcanus), OS. *frônisk, frânisk.*   In
MHG. and even modern German we have a good many compounds
with *vrôn*, as also the adj. in the above sense, while *frohnen, fröhnen* is
to do service to one's lord, to dedicate.   The Frisian dialect contri-
butes a *frân*, dominicus, and *frâna*, minister publicus.   The added
-*n* in all these derivatives can be explained by the Gothic *fráujinon*
dominari, though there was probably no Gothic fráujinisks, as
frônisc seems not to have been formed till after the contraction frô
and frôno had set in.

But even the Gothic *fráuja* does not present to us the simple
stem, I look for it in a lost adj. fravis (like navis νεκρός, Rom. 7, 2),
the same as the OHG. *frô* gen. frouwes, OS. *fra* gen. frahes, MHG.
vrô, and our *froh* [fröhlich, frolic, &c.], and signifying mitis, laetus,
blandus ; whence the same dialects derive frouwî, gaudium, frouwan,
laetum reddere, frouwida, laetitia, &c. (see Suppl.).

I do not mean to assert that a god Fráuja, Frouwo, Fraho was
as distinctly worshipped by the Goths, Alamanns, Franks and
Saxons in the first centuries of our era, as Freyr was long after in

Scandinavia, it is even possible that the form fráuja already
harboured a generalization of the more vividly concrete Fravis =
Freyr, and therefore seemed less offensive to the christians. But
in both words, the reference to a higher being is unmistakable, and
in the Mid. ages there still seems to hang about the compounds
with *vrôn* something weird, unearthly, a sense of old sacredness; this
may account for the rare occurrence and the early disappearance
of the OHG. frô, and even for the grammatical immobility of
frôno; it is as though an echo of heathenism could be still detected
in them.

A worship of Frô may be inferred even from the use of certain
proper names and poetic epithets, especially by the Anglo-Saxons.
The Goths even of later times use *Fráuja* as a man's name, to which
we can hardly attribute the sense of lord simply: an envoy from
king Hadafus to Charles the Great is called *Froia* (Pertz 1, 184.
2, 223), perhaps *Froila* (Fráujila); an OHG. *Frewilo* occurs in a
document in Neugart no. 162. The AS. genealogies contain
Wûscfreá; the name is often found elsewhere (Beda 138, 19. 153,
5), and seems suitable to Wôden the god or lord of wishing (p. 144).
Equally to the point is the poetic *freáwine* (freáwine folca) in
Beow. 4708. 4853. 4871, where it is a mere epithet of divine or god-
loved heroes and kings. But the Wessex pedigree can produce its
Freáwine, whom Saxo Gram. calls *Frowinus* (better Fröwinus);
OHG. documents likewise have the proper name *Frôwin* (Trad.
juvav. p. 302, Cod. lauresh. 712, but *Friowini* 722), and in several
noble families, *e.g.*, the distinguished one of the Von Huttens, it has
been kept up till modern times. What is remarkable, the Edda
uses of a hero *Freys vinr* (Sæm. 219[b]), like the AS. freáwine, only
uncompounded: Sigurðr is Frey's friend and protégé, or perhaps
his votary and servant, in the way shown on p. 93. Here again freá,
frô, freyr, cannot have merely the general meaning of lord, any lord.
The Swedish heroes in the Bravalla fight, who boast their descent
from Frö, are in Saxo, p. 144, called *Frö* dei *necessarii,* which is
exactly our *Freys vinar.* In the same way the AS. and ON. poetries,
and consequently the myths, have in common the expression
freá Ingwina (gen. pl.), Beow. 2638, Ingvinar (gen. sing.) *freyr*,
Ingunnar *freyr*, Sæm. 65[b], Ingi*freyr* (Thorlac. obs. bor. spec. 6, p. 43),
by which is to be understood a hero or god, not 'junior dominus,'
as Thorlacius, p. 68, supposes. Yngvi*freyr* is called Oðin's son, Sn.

211ᵃ. I shall come back to this mysterious combination of two mythical names, when I come to speak of the hero Ingo. The ON. skalds append this freyr to other names and to common nouns, *e.g.*, in Kormakssaga, pp. 104. 122, ' fiörnis *freyr*, myrði*freyr* ' mean no more than hero or man in the heightened general sense which we noticed in the words irmin, tîr and tŷr. In the same way the fem. *freyja* means frau, woman, lady, Kormakss. p. 317.

All that I have made out thus far on the name and idea of the god, will receive new light and confirmation when we come to examine his divine sister Freyja. The brother and sister are made alike in all their attributes, and each can stand for the other.

Frô does not appear in the series of gods of the week, because there was no room for him there ; if we must translate him by a Roman name, it can scarcely be any other than that of *Liber*, whose association with Libera is extremely like that of Frô with Frôwa (Freyr with Freyja). As Liber and Libera are devoted to the service of Ceres or Dêmêtêr, Frô and Frôwa stand in close union with Nerthus. Frô's godhead seems to hold a middle place between the notion of the supreme lord and that of a being who brings about love and fruitfulness. He has Wuotan's creative quality, but performs no deeds of war ; horse and sword he gives away, when consumed with longing for the fair Gerðr, as is sung in one of the most glorious lays of the Edda. Snorri says, *rain* and *sunshine* are in the gift of Freyr (as elsewhere of Wuotan and Donar, pp. 157. 175) ; he is invoked for *fertility* of the soil and for *peace* (*til árs oc friðar*, Sn. 28 ; conf. Yngl. saga cap. 12). The Swedes revered him as one of their chief gods, and Adam of Bremen says that at Upsal his statue stood by those of Thôr and Wôdan (see Suppl.). Also in Sæm. 85ᵇ he is named next to Oðinn and Thôrr (âsabragr) as the third god. Adam calls him *Fricco*,[1] which is precisely parallel to the frequent confusion of the two goddesses Freyja and Frigg, which I shall deal with at a future time. But he paints him as a god of *peace* and *love* : Tertius est *Fricco*, pacem voluptatemque largiens mortalibus, cujus etiam simulachrum fingunt *ingenti*

---

[1] Which occurs elsewhere as a man's name, *e.g.*, *Friccheo* in Schannat, Trad. fuld. 386.

priapo ;[1] si nuptiae celebrandae sunt, (sacrificia offerunt) *Fricconi*. Then there is the story, harmonizing with this, though related from the christian point of view and to the heathen god's detriment, of *Frey's statue* being carried round the country *in a waggon*, and of his beautiful young priestess, Fornm. sög. 2, 73-8. This progress takes place, 'þâ er hann skal gera mönnum *ârbôt*,' when he shall make for men year's boot; the people flock to meet the car, and bring their offerings, then the weather clears up and men look for a fruitful year. The offerings are those which Saxo, p. 15, names *Fröblôt;* live animals were presented, particularly oxen (Vigagl. saga, p. 56. Islend. sög. 2, 348), which seems to explain why *Freyr* is reckoned among the poetic names for an ox, Sn. 221[a]; in like manner, horses were consecrated to him, such a one was called *Freyfaxi* and accounted holy, Vatnsd. p. 140 ; and human victims fell to him in Sweden, Saxo Gram. 42. Freyr possessed a *boar* named *Gullinbursti*, whose ' golden bristles ' lighted up the night like day, who ran with the speed of a horse and drew the deity's car, Sn. 66. 132. It is therefore in Frey's worship that the *atonement-boar* is sacrificed (p. 51) ;[2] in Sweden cakes in the *shape of a boar* are baked on Yule-eve.—And here we come upon a good many relics of the service once done to the god, even outside of Scandinavia. We hear of the *clean gold-hog* (*-ferch*, whence dimin. farrow) in the popular customs of the Wetterau and Thuringia (p. 51). In the Mid. Dutch poem of Lantslôt ende Sandrîn, v. 374, a knight says to his maiden : ' ic heb u liever dan ên *everswîn*, al waert *van finen goude ghewracht*,' I hold you dearer than a boar-swine, all were it of fine gold y-wrought ; were they still in the habit of making gold jewels in the shape of boars ? at least the remembrance of such a thing was not yet lost. Frô and his boar may also have had a hand in a superstition of Gelderland, which however puts a famous hero in the place of the god : *Derk met den*

---

[1] With priapus πρίαπος I would identify the ON. friof semen, friofr foecundus; conf. Goth. fráiv, seed. The statement of Adamus Bremensis looks better, since Wolf in his Wodana xxi. xxii. xxiii brought to light the festivals and images of *Priapus* or *Ters* at a late period in the Netherlands. This *ters* is the AS. *teors*, OHG. *zers*, and Herbort 4054 is shy of uttering the name Xerses. Phallus-worship, so widely spread among the nations of antiquity, must have arisen out of an innocent veneration of the generative principle, which a later age, conscious of its sins, prudishly avoided. After all is said, there is an inkling of the same in Phol too and the avoidance of his name (ch. XI), though I do not venture exactly to identify him with φαλλός.

[2] Not only Demeter, but Zeus received *boar-offerings*, Il. 19, 197. 251.

beer (Theoderic, Derrick with the boar) goes his round on Christmas-
eve night, and people are careful to get all *implements of husbandry*
within doors, else the boar will trample them about, and make
them unfit for use.[1]   In the same Christmas season, dame Holda or
Berhta sallied out, and looked after the *ploughs* and *spindles*,
motherly goddesses instead of the god, Frouwa instead of Frô.
With this again are connected the *formae aprorum* worn as charms
by the remote Aestyans, who yet have the 'ritus habitusque
Suevorum'. Tacitus Germ. 45 says, these figures represent the
worship of the 'mater deûm,' of a female Frô, *i.e.*, of Freyja ; and,
what is conclusive on this point, the Edda (Saem. 114[a]) assigns the
Gullinbursti to Freyja, though elsewhere he belongs to Freyr (see
Suppl.).—Anglo-Saxon poetry, above all, makes mention of these
boar-badges, these *gold swine*.   When Constantine sees a vision in
his sleep, he is said to be *eoforcumble* beþeaht (apri signo tectus)
El. 76 ; it must have been fastened as an auspicious omen over the
head of the bed.   Afterwards again, in the description of Elene's
stately progress to the east : þær wæs on eorle êðgesŷne grîmhelm
manig, *ænlîc eoforcumbul* (tunc in duce apparuit horrida cassis, ex-
cellens apri forma), El. 260.   The poet is describing a decoration of
the old heathen time, cumbul is the helmet's crest, and the king's
helmet appears to be adorned with the image of a boar.   Several
passages in Beowulf place the matter beyond a doubt : *eoforlîc*
scionon ofer hleor beran gehroden golde, fâh and fŷrheard ferhwearde
heold (apri formam videbantur supra genas gerere auro comptam,
quae varia igneque durata vitam tuebatur), 605 ; hêt þa inberan
eofor heáfodsegn, heaðosteápne helm (jussit afferri aprum, capitis
signum, galeam in pugna prominentem), 4300 ; *swîn* ofer helme
(sus supra galea), 2574 ; *swîn ealgylden, eofor* îrenheard (sus aureus,
aper instar ferri durus), 2216, *i.e.*, a helmet placed on the funeral
pile as a costly jewel ; helm befongen *Freáwrâsnum* (= OHG. Frô-
reisanum), swâ hine fyrndagum worhte wæpna smið, besette *swin-
lîcum,* þæt hine sîðþan no brond ne beadomêcas bîtan ne meahtan
(galea ornata Frohonis signis, sicut eam olim fabricaverat armorum
faber, circumdederat eam apri formis, ne gladius ensesve laedere
eam possent), 2905 ; as a sacred divine symbol, it was to protect in

---

[1] Staring, in the journal Mnemosyne, Leyden 1829. 1, 323 ; quoted thence
in Westendorp's Noordsche mythologie, Dordrecht 1830. p. 495.

battle and affright the foe.[1]   The OHG. proper name *Epurhelm*, *Eparhelm* (eber, eofor, aper), placed by the side of *Frôhelm* (both occur in the Trad. patav. no. 20; MB. 28ᵇ, 18) acquires thus a special and appropriate meaning.   Such boar-crests might still serve as ornaments even to christian heroes, after the memory of Frô was obliterated, and long continue to be wrought simply as jewels (see Suppl.).—Some other traces of boar consecration have lasted still later, especially in England.   The custom of the *boar-vow* I have explained in RA. 900-1.   As even at the present day on festive occasions a wild boar's head is seen among the other dishes as a show-dish, they used in the Mid. Ages to serve it up at banquets, garnished with laurel and rosemary, to carry it about and play all manner of pranks with it: ' Where stood a *boar's head* garnishëd With bayes and rosemarye,' says one ballad about Arthur's Table ; when three strokes have been given with a rod over it, it is only the knife of a virtuous man that can carve the first slice.   At other times, even a live boar makes its appearance in the hall, and a bold hero chops its head off.   At Oxford they exhibit a *boar's head* on Christmas day, carry it solemnly round, singing: Caput apri defero, Reddens laudes Domino (see Suppl.).   Those Aestyans may prove a link of fellowship between the Germanic nations and the Finnish and Asiatic ; it is well worth noticing, that the Tcherkass (Circassians) worship a god of woods and hunting, *Mesitch* by name, who rides a wild *boar with golden bristles*.[2]   To most of the other gods tame animals are sacred, to Frô the daring dauntless boar, as well befits a god of the chase.   Perhaps also a huge *boar* with white tusks,[3] who in Slavic legend rises foaming out of a lake, is that of a kindred deity.

The Edda attributes to Freyr a *sword* of surpassing virtue, which could put itself into motion against the brood of giants, Sæm. 82. His giving it away when in straits, proved his ruin afterwards ; it was held to be the cause of his death, when at the Ragnarökr he had to stand single combat with Surtr (swart), and missed his

---

[1] On this point again, the statement of Tacitus about the Aestyans agrees so exactly, that it seems worth quoting in full : Aestyorum gentes.   .   .   . quibus ritus habitusque Suevorum.   .   .   Matrem deûm venerantur : insigne superstitionis, formas aprorum gestant ; id pro armis omniumque tutela securum deae cultorem etiam inter hostes praestat.—TRANS.

[2] Erman's archiv für wissenschaftl. kunde Russlands 1842, heft 1, p. 118.

[3] Λευκὸν ὀδόντα, Il. 11, 416.   σῦς λευκῷ ὀδόντι, Od. 19. 465.

trusty blade. Sn. 73. There appear to have been other traditions also afloat about this sword ;[1] and it would not seem far-fetched, if on the strength of it we placed the well-known trilogy of ' Thunar, Wôdan, Saxnôt' beside Adam of Bremen's 'Wodan, Thor and Fricco' or the Eddic ' Oðinn, Asabragr, Freyr,'[2] that is to say, if we took *Freyr, Fricco = Frô* to be the same as *Sahsnôt* the sword-possessor. Add to this, that the Edda never mentions the sword of Týr. Nevertheless there are stronger reasons in favour of Sahsnôz being Zio : this for one, that he was a son of Wuotan, whereas Freyr comes of Niörðr, though some genealogies to be presently mentioned bring him into connexion with Wôden.

For the brilliant Freyr, the beneficent son of Niörðr, the dwarfs had constructed a wonderful *ship* Skiðblaðnir, which could fold up like a cloth, Sæm. 45[b]. Sn. 48. Yngl. saga cap. 7 (see Suppl.).[3]

Besides the Swedes, the Thrændir in Norway were devoted to Freyr above all other gods, Fornm. sög. 10, 312. Occasionally priests of his are named, as Thorðr *Freys goði* (of the 10th century), Landn. 4, 10 and Nialss. cap. 96 ; Flosi appears to have succeeded his father in the office; other *Freysgyðlingar* are cited in Landn. 4, 13. The Vigaglumssaga cap. 19 mentions *Freys hof* at Upsala, and cap. 26 his statue at Thverâ in Iceland, though only in a night-vision : he is pictured sitting on a chair, giving short and surly (stutt ok reiðuliga) answers to his supplicants, so that Glûmr, who in cap. 9 had sacrificed an old ox to him, now on awaking from his dream neglected his service. In the Landn. 3, 2 and Vatnsd. pp. 44. 50 we are told of a *Freyr giörr af silfri* (made of silver), which was used in drawing lots ; conf. Verlauff's note, p. 362. In the Landn. 4, 7 is preserved the usual formula for an oath : Hiâlpi mer svâ *Freyr* ok *Niörðr* ok hinn *almâttki âs* (so help me F. and N. and that almighty *âs*)! by which last is to be understood Thôrr rather

---

[1] In old French poetry I find a famous sword wrought by Galant himself (Wielant, Wayland), and named *Froberge* or Floberge (Garin 1, 263. 2, 30-8) ; the latter reading has no discoverable sense, though our later Flamberge seems to have sprung from it. *Froberge* might very well be either a mere frô-bergende (lord-protecting) weapon, or a reminiscence of the god Frô's sword ; conf. the word-formations quoted in my Gramm. 2, 486. There are townships called in OHG. Helidberga, Marahaberga (horse-stable). The ON. has no Freybiörg that I know of, though it has Thôrbiörg fem., and Thôrbergr masc.

[2] Also in Sn. 131, Oðinn, Thôrr, Freyr are speakers of doom.

[3] Pliny N. H. 5, 9 mentions Ethiopian ' naves plicatiles humeris translatas.'

than Oðinn, for in the Egilssaga p. 365, *Freyr, Niörðr* and the *landâs* (Thôrr) are likewise mentioned together. In the same Egilss. p. 672, *Freyr* ok *Niörðr* are again placed side by side. The story of the Brîsînga-men (-monile; append. to Sn. 354) says, Oðinn had appointed both *Freyr* and *Niörðr* to be sacrificial gods. Hall-freðr sang (Fornm. sög. 2, 53, conf. 12, 49):

> Mer skyli *Freyr* oc *Freyja*, fiarð læt ek aðul Niarðar,
> lîknist gröm við *Grimni* gramr ok *Thôrr enn rammi !*

That Freyr in these passages should be brought forward with Freyja and Niörðr, is easy to understand (see Suppl.).

Of *Niörðr* our German mythology would have nothing to tell, any more than Saxo Gram. ever mentions him by that name, had not Tacitus put in for us that happy touch of a goddess *Nerthus*, whose identity with the god is as obvious as that of Frô with Frouwa. The Gothic form *Naírþus* would do for either or even for both sexes; possibly Fráuja was considered the son of the goddess Naírþus, as Freyr is of the god Niörðr, and in the circuit which the goddess makes in her car, publishing peace and fertility to mortals, we can recognise that of Freyr or of his father Niörðr. According to Yngl. saga cap. 11, these very bless-ings were believed to proceed from Niörðr also: ' auðigr sem Niörðr ' (rich as N.) was a proverbial saying for a wealthy man, Vatnsd. p. 202. Snorri, in Formâli 10, identifies him with Saturn, for he instructed mankind in vine-dressing and husbandry; it would be nearer the mark to think of him and Freyr in connexion with Dionysus or Liber, or even with Noah, if any stress is to be laid on Niörð's abode being in Nôatûn. As ' freyr ' was affixed to other names of heroes (p. 211-2), I find *geirniörðr* used for a hero in general, Sæm. 266[b]; conf. geirmîmir, geirniflûngr, &c. The name itself is hard to explain; is it akin to north, AS. norð, ON. norðr, Goth. naúrþs? In Sæm. 109[b] there is niarðlâs for sera firma, or pensilis ? I have met with no Nirdu, Nerd, Nird among OHG. proper names, nor with a Neorð in the AS. writings. Irminon's polyptych 222[a] has Narthildis (see Suppl.).

Niörðr appears to have been greatly honoured: hofum oc hörgum hann ræðr hundmörgum, Sæm. 36[a]; especially, no doubt, among people that lived on the sea coast. The Edda makes him rule over wind, sea and fire, he loves waters and lakes, as Nerthus in Tacitus bathes in the lake (Sn. 27); from the mountains of the

midland he longs to be away where the swans sing on the cool
shore; a water-plant, the spongia marina, bears the name of *Niarðar
vöttr*, Niörð's glove, which elsewhere was very likely passed on to
his daughter Freyja, and so to Mary, for some kinds of orchis
too, from their hand-shaped root, are called Mary's hand, lady-hand,
god's hand (Dan. gudshaand).

As Dionysus stands outside the ring of the twelve Olympian
gods, so Niörðr, Freyr and Freyja seem by rights not to have been
reckoned among the Ases, though they are marshalled among
them in Sn. 27-8. They were *Vanir*, and therefore, according to
the view of the elder Edda, different from Ases; as these dwelt in
Asgarð, so did the Vanir in Vanaheim, the Alfar in Alfheim, the
Iötnar in Iötunheim. Freyr is called *Vaningi*, Sæm. 86[b]. The
Vanir were regarded as intelligent and wise, Sæm. 36[a]; and they
entered into intimate fellowship with the Asen, while the
Alfs and Iötuns always remained opposed to them. Some have
fancied that the Alfs and Iötuns stand for Celtic races, and the
Vanir for Slav; and building chiefly on an attempt in the Yngl.
saga cap. 1 to find the name of the Tanais in Tanaqvîsl (or Vana-
qvîsl!), they have drawn by inference an actual boundary-line
between Aesir and Vanir = Germani and Slavi in the regions
formerly occupied by them (see Suppl.). And sure enough a
Russian is to this day called in Finnish Wenäiläinen, in Esth.
Wennelane; even the name of the Wends might be dragged in,
though the Vandili of Tacitus point the other way. Granting that
there may be some foundation for these views, still to my mind
the conceptions of Aesir, Vanir, Alfar in the Edda are sketched on
a ground altogether too mythical for any historical meaning to be
got out of them; as regards the contrast between Ases and Vanir,
I am aware of no essential difference in the cultus of the several
gods; and, whatever stress it may be right to lay on the fact that
Frouwa, Freyja answers to a Slavic goddess Priye, it does not at
all follow that Frô, Frouwa and Nerthus were in a less degree
Germanic deities than the rest. Tacitus is silent on the German
Liber, as he is on our Jupiter, yet we are entitled to assume a
universal veneration of Donar, even though the Gothic faírguni is
better represented in Perkunas or Perûn; so also, to judge by what
clues we have, Fráuja, Frô, Freyr appears so firmly established,
that, considering the scanty information we have about our

antiquities, no German race can be denied a share in him, though some nations may have worshipped him more than others; and even that is not easy to ascertain, except in Scandinavia.[1]

It is worthy of notice, that the AS. and ON. genealogies bring *Freá* into kinship with *Wôden*, making Finn the father of a Freálâf (Friðleifr), and him again of Wôden; some of them insert two more links, Friðuwulf and Friðuwald, so that the complete pedigree stands thus: *Finn, Friðuwulf, Freálâf, Friðuwald, Wôden* (or, in the place of Freálâf, our old acquaintance Freáwine). Here evidently Friðuwulf, Freálâf, Friðuwald are all the same thing, a mere expansion of the simple Freá. This follows even from a quite different ON. genealogy, Fornald. sög. 2, 12, which makes Burr (= Finn; conf. Rask, afh. 1, 107-8) the immediate progenitor of Oðinn, and him of Freyr, Niörðr and a second Freyr. The double Freyr corresponds to the AS. Friðuwulf and Friðuwald, as the words here expressing glad, free and fair are near of kin to one another. Lastly, when the same AS. genealogies by turns call Finn's father *Godwulf* and *Folcwald*, this last name is supported by the 'Fin Folcwalding' (-ing = son) of Cod. exon. 320, 10 and of Beow. 2172, where again the reference must be to Freá and his race, for the Edda (Sæm. 87[a], conf. 10[a]) designates Freyr '*folcvaldi* (al. folcvaldr) goða'. Now this folkvaldi means no other than dominator, princeps, *i.e.* the same as freá, frô, and seems, like it, to pass into a proper name. On the linking of Freyr and Niörðr with Oðinn, there will be more to say in ch. XV (see Suppl.). If Snorri's comparison of Niörðr with Kronos (Saturn) have any justification, evidently Poseidôn (Neptune) the son of Kronos would come nearer to our Teutonic sea-god; and Ποσειδῶν might be referred to πόσις (lord, Lith. pats, Sansk. patis, Goth. faþs), which means the same as Frô. Only then both Frô and Nirðu would again belong to the eldest race of gods.

---

[1] Wh. Müller, Nibelungensage pp. 136—148, wishes to extend the Vanir gods only to the Sueves and Goths, not to the western Germans, and to draw a distinction between the worship of Freyr and that of Wuotan, which to me looks very doubtful. As little can I give up the point, that Niörðr and Nerthus were *brother and sister*, and joint parents of Freyr and Freyja ; this is grounded not only on a later representation of Snorri in the Yngl. saga cap. 4, where yet the female Niörð is nowhere named, as Tacitus conversely knows only a female Nerthus and no god of that name ; but also on Sæm. 65[a] : 'við systor thinni gaztu slíkan mög,' with thy sister begattest thou such brood, though here again the sister is left unnamed.

CHAPTER XI.

PALTAR (BALDER).

The myth of Balder, one of the most ingenious and beautiful in the Edda, has happily for us been also handed down in a later form with variations : and there is no better example of fluctuations in a god-myth. The Edda sets forth, how the pure blameless deity is struck with Mistiltein by the blind Höðr, and must go down to the nether world, bewailed by all ; nothing can fetch him back, and Nanna the true wife follows him in death. In Saxo, all is pitched in a lower key : Balder and Hother are rival suitors, both wooing Nanna, and Hother the favoured one manages to procure a magic sword, by which alone his enemy is vulnerable ; when the fortune of war has wavered long between them, Hother is at last victorious and slays the demigod, to whom Hel, glad at the near prospect of possessing him, shews herself beforehand. But here the grand funeral pile is prepared for Gelder, a companion of Balder, of whom the account in the Edda knows nothing whatever. The worship of the god is attested chiefly by the Friðþiofssaga, v. Fornald. sög. 2, 63 seq. (see Suppl.).

Baldr, gen. Baldrs, reappears in the OHG. proper name *Paltar* (in Meichelbeck no. 450. 460. 611) ;[1] and in the AS. *bealdor, baldor*, signifying a lord, prince, king, and seemingly used only with a gen. pl. before it : gumena baldor, Cædm. 163, 4. wîgena baldor, Jud. 132, 47. sinca bealdor, Beow. 4852. winia bealdor 5130. It is remarkable that in the Cod. exon. 276, 18 mægða bealdor (virginum princeps) is said even of a maiden. I know of only a few examples in the ON. : baldur î brynju, Sæm. 272[b], and herbaldr 218[b] are used for a hero in general ; atgeirs baldr (lanceae vir), Fornm. sög. 5, 307. This conversion from a proper name to a noun appellative

---

[1] Graff 1, 432 thinks this name stands for Paltaro, and is a compound of aro (aar, aquila), but this is unsupported by analogy ; in the ninth and tenth centuries, weak forms are not yet curtailed, and we always find Epuraro (eberaar, boar-eagle), never Epurar.

exactly reminds us of fráuja, frô, freá, and the ON. týr. As bealdor
is already extinct in AS. prose, our proper name Paltar seems
likewise to have died out early ; heathen songs in OHG. may have
known a paltar = princeps. Such Gothic forms as Baldrs, gen.
Baldris, and baldrs (princeps), may fairly be assumed.[1]

This Baldrs would in strictness appear to have no connexion
with the Goth. balþs (bold, audax), nor Paltar with the OHG. pald,
nor Baldr with the ON. ballr. As a rule, the Gothic ld is represented
by ON. ld and OHG. lt: the Gothic lþ by ON. ll and OHG. ld.[2]
But the OS. and AS. have ld in both cases, and even in Gothic, ON. and
OHG. a root will sometimes appear in both forms in the same language;[3] so that a close connexion between balþs and Baldrs,[4] pald and
Paltar, is possible after all. On mythological grounds it is even
probable : Balder's wife *Nanna* is also the bold one, from nenna to
dare ; in Gothic she would have been *Nanþô* from nanþjan, in
OHG. *Nandâ* from gi-nendan. The Baldr of the Edda may not
distinguish himself by bold deeds, but in Saxo he fights most
valiantly ; and neither of these narratives pretends to give a
complete account of his life. Perhaps the Gothic *Balthae* (Jornandes 5, 29) traced their origin to a divine Balþs or Baldrs (see
Suppl.).

Yet even this meaning of the ' bold ' god or hero might be a
later one: the Lith. *baltas* and Lett. *balts* signify the white, the
good; and by the doctrine of consonant-change, baltas exactly
answers to the Goth. balþs and OHG. pald. Add to this, that the
AS. genealogies call Wôden's son not Bealdor, Baldor, but *Bœldæg*,
Beldeg, which would lead us to expect an OHG. Paltac, a form that
I confess I have nowhere read. But both dialects have plenty of
other proper names compounded with dæg and tac : OHG. Adaltac,

---

[1] Baldrs, Paltar, must be kept distinct from the compound *Baldheri*
(Schannat no. 420. 448), *Paldheri* (Trad. patav. no. 35), AS. *Baldhere.* This
Paldheri is the same as *Paldachar* (Trad. patav. no. 18).

[2]

	Goth.				
Goth.	kalds		vilþeis	hulþs	gulþ.
ON.	kaldr	but	villr	hollr	gull.
OHG.	chalt		wildi	hold	kold.

[3] Conf. Gothic alþan and alþs aldis, also aldrs ; Goth. falþan and OHG.
faldan, afterwards faltan. As þ degenerates into d, and d into t, any d put for
þ, or t for d, marks a later form : the Goth. fadr stands for faþr, as we see by
pater [the AS. ' fæder, môdor,' after a usurpation of 1000 years, must have
given place to the truer ' father, mother ' again]. In the ON. valda pret. olli,
we must regard the ll as older than the ld, in spite of the Goth. valdan and
OHG. waltan [some would prefer to call valda an archaism].

[4] Baldr may be related to balþ, as tîr to tý, and zior to zio.

Alptac, Ingatac, Kêrtac, Helmtac, Hruodtac, Regintac, Sigitac;
OS. Alacdag, Alfdag (Albdag, Pertz 1, 286), Hildidag, Liuddag,
Osdag, Wulfdag; AS. Wegdæg, Swefdæg; even the ON. has the
name Svipdagr. Now, either Bældæg simply stands for Bealdor,
and is synonymous with it (as *e.g.*, Regintac with Reginari, Sigitac
with Sigar, Sigheri)[1]; or else we must recognise in the word *dæg,
dag, tac* itself a personification, such as we found another root
undergoing (p. 194-5) in the words div, divan, dina, dies; and both
alike would express a shining one, a white one, a god. Prefixing to
this the Slavic *bièl, bèl*, we have no need to take Bældæg as standing
for Bealdor or anything else, *Bæl-dæg* itself is white-god, light-god,
he that shines as sky and light and day, the kindly *Bièlbôgh, Bèlbôgh* of the Slav system (see Suppl.). It is in perfect accord with
this explanation of Bæl-dæg, that the AS. tale of ancestry assigns
to him a son *Brond*, of whom the Edda is silent, brond, brand, ON.
brandr, signifying jubar, fax, titio. Bældæg therefore, as regards
his name, would agree with Berhta, the bright goddess.

We have to consider a few more circumstances bearing on this
point. Baldr's beauty is thus described in Sn. 26: ' Hann er svâ *fagr*
âlitum ok *biartr svâ at lysir af honum*, oc eitt gras er svâ hvitt, at
iafnat er til *Baldrs brâr*, þat er allra grasa *hvîtast* oc þar eptir mâttu
marka hans fegurð bæði â hâri ok lîki '; he is so fair of countenance
and bright that he shines of himself, there is a grass so white that it
is evened with Baldr's brows, it is of all grasses whitest, and thereby
mayest thou mark his fairness both in hair and body. This
plant, named *Baldrsbrâ* after the god's white eyebrow,[2] is either the
anthemis cotula, still called *Barbro* in Sweden, *Balsensbro, Ballensbra*
in Schonen, and *Barbrogräs* in Denmark, or the matricaria maritima
inodora, which retains the original name in Iceland (see Suppl.).[3]
In Skåne there is a *Baldursberg*, in the Öttingen country a
Baldern, and in the Vorarlberg, east of Bregenz, *Balderschwang;*
such names of places demand caution, as they may be taken from
men, Baldar or Baldheri, I therefore withhold the mention of
several more. But the heavenly abode of the god was called
Breiðablik, nom. pl. (Sæm. 41[b], Sn. 21-7), *i.e.* broad splendors,

---

[1] The cases are hardly analogous : Bæld-*æg* and Regin-*tac*.—TRANS.
[2] Homer emphasizes the dark brows of Zeus and Hera, ὀφρὺς κυανέα.
Conf. λευκόφρυς and Artemis λευκοφρύνη, white-browed Diana.
[3] Germ. names of the camomile : kuhauge, rindsauge, ochsenauge (ox-eye).
Dalecarl. hvitet-oja (white eye), in Båhuslän hvita-piga (white girl).

which may have reference to the streaks of the milky way ; a place near Lethra, not far from Roeskild, is said to have borne the name of *Bredeblick*.[1] This very expression re-appears in a poem of the twelfth century, though not in reference to a dwelling-place, but to a host of snow-white steeds and heroes advancing over the battle-field : Dô brâhte Dietherîches vane zvencik dûsint lossam in *breither blickin* uber lant, Roth. 2635. In Wh. 381, 16 : ' daz bluot über die *blicke* flôz, si wurdn almeistic rôtgevar,' did the blood flow over the paths of the field, or over the shining silks ?

If *Bœldœg* and *Brond* reveal to us that the worship of Balder had a definite form of its own even outside of Scandinavia, we may conclude from the general diffusion of all the most essential proper names entering into the main plot of the myth there, that this myth as a whole was known to all Teutons. The goddess *Hel*, as will be more fully shown in ch. XIII, answers to the Gothic im-personal noun halja, OHG. hella. *Höðr* (acc. Höð, gen. Haðar, dat. Heði), pictured as a blind god of tremendous strength (Sn. 31), who without malice discharges the fatal arrow at Baldr, is called *Hotherus* in Saxo, and implies a Goth. *Haþus*, AS. *Heaðo*, OHG. *Hadu*, OFrank. *Chado*, of which we have still undoubted traces in proper names and poetic compounds. OHG. Hadupraht, Hadufuns, Hadupald, Hadufrid, Hadumâr, Hadupurc, Hadulint, Haduwîc (Hedwig), &c., forms which abut close on the Catumêrus in Tacitus (Hadumâr, Hadamâr). In AS. poetry are still found the terms heaðorinc (vir egregius, nobilis), Cædm. 193, 4. Beow. 737. 4927 ; heaðowelm (belli impetus, fervor), Cædm. 21, 14. 147, 8. Beow. 164. 5633; heaðoswât (sudor bellicus), Beow. 2919. 3211. 3334; heaðowæd (vestis bellica), Beow. 78 ; heaðubyrne (lorica bellica), Cod. exon. 297, 7 ; heaðosigel and heaðogleám (egregium jubar), Cod. exon. 486, 17 and 438, 6 ; heaðolâc (pugnae ludus), Beow. 1862. 3943 ; heaðogrim (atrocissimus), Beow. 1090. 5378 ; heaðosioc (pugna vulneratus), Beow. 5504; heaðosteáp (celsus), Beow. 2490. 4301. In these words, except where the meaning is merely intensi-fied, the prevailing idea is plainly that of battle and strife, and the god or hero must have been thought of and honoured as a warrior. Therefore *Haþus*, *Höðr*, as well as Wuotan and Zio, expressed phenomena of war ; and he was imagined blind, because he dealt out at random good hap and ill (p. 207).—Then, beside Höðr, we have *Hermóðr* interweaving himself in the thread of Balder's history ; he is dispatched to Hel, to demand his beloved brother back from the underworld. In Saxo he is already forgotten ; the AS. genealogy places its *Heremóð* among Wôden's ancestors, and names as his son either Sceldwa or the Sceáf renowned in story, whereas in the North he and Balder alike are the offspring of Oðinn ; in the same way we saw (p. 219) Freyr taken for the father as well as the son of Niörðr. A later *Heremód* appears in Beow. 1795. 3417, but still in kinship with the old races ; he is perhaps that hero, named by the side of Sigmundr in Sæm. 113ᵃ, to whom Oðinn lends helm and hauberk. AS. title-deeds also contain the name; Kemb. 1, 232. 141 ; and in OHG. *Herimuot, Herimaot,* occurs very often (Graff 2, 699 anno 782, from MB. 7, 373. Neugart no. 170. 214. 244. 260. annis 809-22-30-34. Ried. no. 21 anno 821), but neither song nor story has a tale to tell of him (see Suppl.).

So much the more valuable are the revelations of the Merseburg discovery ; not only are we fully assured now of a divine Balder in Germany, but there emerges again a long-forgotten mythus, and with it a new name unknown even to the North.

When, says the lay, *Phol* (Balder) and *Wodan* were one day riding in the forest, one foot of Balder's foal, ' demo *Balderes* volon,' was wrenched out of joint, whereupon the heavenly habitants bestowed their best pains on setting it right again, but neither Sinngund and Sunna, nor yet Frûa and Folla could do any good, only Wodan the wizard himself could conjure and heal the limb (see Suppl.).

The whole incident is as little known to the Edda as to other Norse legends. Yet what was told in a heathen spell in Thuringia before the tenth century is still in its substance found lurking in conjuring formulas known to the country folk of Scotland and Denmark (conf. ch. XXXIII, Dislocation), except that they apply to Jesus what the heathen believed of Balder and Wodan. It is somewhat odd, that Cato (De re rust. 160) should give, likewise for a dislocated limb, an Old Roman or perhaps Sabine form of spell, which is unintelligible to us, but in which a god is evidently invoked: Luxum si quod est, hac cantione sanum fiet. Harundinem prende tibi viridem pedes IV aut V longam, mediam diffinde, et duo homines teneant ad coxendices. Incipe cantare in alio S.F motas vaeta daries dardaries astataries *Dissunapiter!* usque dum coeant. What follows is nothing to our purpose.

The horse of Balder, lamed and checked on his journey, acquires a full meaning the moment we think of him as the god of light or day, whose stoppage and detention must give rise to serious mischief on the earth. Probably the story in its context could have informed us of this; it was foreign to the purpose of the conjuring-spell.

The names of the four goddesses will be discussed in their proper place; what concerns us here is, that Balder is called by a second and hitherto unheard-of name, *Phol.* The eye for our antiquities often merely wants opening: a noticing of the unnoticed has resulted in clear footprints of such a god being brought to our hand, in several names of places.

In Bavaria there was a *Pholesauwa, Pholesouwa,* ten or twelve miles from Passau, which the Traditiones patavienses first mention in a document drawn up between 774 and 788 (MB. vol. 28, pars 2, p. 21, no. 23), and afterwards many later ones of the same district: it is the present village of Pfalsau. Its composition with *aue* quite fits in with the supposition of an old heathen worship. The gods were worshipped not only on mountains, but on 'eas' inclosed by brooks and rivers, where fertile meadows yielded pasture, and forests shade. Such was the castum nemus of Nerthus in an *insula* Oceani, such Fosetesland with its willows and well-springs, of which more presently. *Baldrshagi* (Balderi pascuum), mentioned in the Friðþiofssaga, was an enclosed sanctuary (griðastaðr), which none might damage. I find also that convents, for which time-hallowed venerable sites were preferred, were often situated in 'eas'; and of one nunnery the very word is used: 'in der megde *ouwe,*' in the maids' ea (Diut. 1, 357).[1] The ON. mythology supplies us with several eas named after the loftiest gods: Oðins*ey* (Odensee) in Fünen, another Oðins*ey* (Onsöe) in Norway, Fornm. sög. 12, 33, and Thôrs*ey,* 7, 234. 9, 17; Hlês*ey* (Lässöe) in the Kattegat, &c., &c. We do not know any OHG. Wuotanesouwa, Donaresouwa, but Pholesouwa is equally to the point.

Very similar must have been *Pholespiunt* (MB. 9, 404 circ. 1138.

[1] So the Old Bavarian convent of Chiemsee was called *ouwa* (MB. 28ᵃ, 103 an. 890), and afterwards the monastery there 'der herren *werd,*' and the nunnery 'der nunnen *werd*'. Stat 'zo gottes *ouwe*' in Lisch, mekl. jb. 7, 227, from a fragment belonging to Bertholds Crane. Demantin 242.

Pfalspiunt, 5, 399 anno 1290), now Pfalzpoint on the Altmühl, between Eichstädt and Kipfenberg, in a considerable forest. Piunt means an enclosed field or garden;[1] and if an ea could be consecrated to a god, so could a field. Graff 3, 342 has a place called Frawûn*piunt*, which, to judge by the circumstances, may with like reason be assigned to the goddess Frouwa; no doubt it also belongs to Bavaria (see Suppl.).

In the Fulda Traditions (Schannat p. 291, no. 85) occurs this remarkable passage: Widerolt comes tradidit sancto Bonifacio quicquid proprietatis habuit in *Pholesbrunnen* in provincia Thuringiae. To this Pholesbrunno, the village of *Phulsborn* has the first claim, lying not far from the Saale, equidistant from the towns Apolda, Dornburg and Sulza, and spelt in Mid. Age documents Phulsborn and Pfolczborn; there is however another village, *Falsbrunn* or Falsbronn, on the Rauhe Eberach in the Franconian Steigerwald. Now *Pfolesbrunno* all the more plainly suggests a divinity (and that, Balder), as there are also *Baldersbrunnen:* a Baldebrunno has been produced from the Eifel mts, and from the Rhine Palatinate,[2] and it has been shown that the form ought to be corrected into *Baldersbrunno* as well as the modern Baldenhain to *Baldershain* (Zeitschr. f. d. alt. 2, 256); and Bellstadt in the Klingen district of Schwarzburg-Sondershausen was formerly *Baldersteti*, Schannat dioec. Fuld. p. 244, anno 977 (see Suppl.). From the Norse mythus of Balder, as given by Saxo, we learn that Balder in the heat of battle opened a fountain for his languishing army: Victor Balderus, ut afflictum siti militem opportuni liquoris beneficio recrearet, *novos* humi *latices* terram altius rimatus aperuit, quorum erumpentes scatebras sitibundum agmen hianti passim ore captabat. Eorundem vestigia sempiterna firmata vocabulo, quamquam pristina admodum scaturigo desierit, nondum prorsus exolevisse creduntur. This spot is the present *Baldersbrönd* near Roeskild (note to Müller's Saxo, p. 120). But the legend may be the same as old German legends, which at a later time placed to king Charles's account (p. 117, and infra, Furious host) that which heathendom had told of

---

[1] A Salzburg doc. of the tenth cent., in Kleinmayrn p. 196: Curtilem locum cum duobus pratis, quod *piunti* dicimus.

[2] Conf. Schöpflin's Alsat. dipl. no. 748, anno 1285: in villa Baldeburne. A Westphal. doc. of 1203 (Falke trad. corb. p. 566) names a place *Balderbroc*, which might mean palus, campus Balderi.

Balder; in that case the still surviving name has itself proved a
fountain, whence the myth of Balder emerges anew.[1]

But the name of Phol is established more firmly still. A
Heinricus de *Pholing* frequently appears in the Altach records of
the 13th century, MB. part 11, a Rapoto de *Pholingen, Phaling*, in
MB. 12, 56. 60; this place is on the left bank of the Danube below
Straubingen, between the two convents of Altach. I doubt if the
Polling in other records (and there are several Pollings in the
Ammer country) can be the same word, as the aspirate is wanting
and the liquid doubled. Pfullendorf or Follendorf near Gotha is
in docs. of the 14th century *Phulsdorf.* A *Pholenheim* in Schannat,
Vind. lit. coll. 1, 48. 53. Not far from Scharzfeld, between the
Harz mts and Thuringia, is an old village named *Pölde,* called in
early records and writings *Polidi, Palidi, Palithi, Pholidi* (Gramm.
2, 248), the seat of a well-known convent, which again may have
been founded on the site of a heathen sanctuary. If a connexion
with the god can be established in this case, we at the same time
gather from it the true value of the varying consonant in his name.

Of Phol so many interpretations crowd upon us, that we should
be puzzled if they could all be made good. The Chaldaic *bel* or *bal*
seems to have been a mere title pertaining to several gods: bel=
Uranus, bel=Jupiter, bel=Mars. The Finnish *palo* means fire, the
ON. *bâl,* AS. *bael* rogus, and the Slav. *páliti* to burn, with which
connect Lat. *Pales* and the *Palilia.* Of *phallus* we have already
spoken. We must first make sure of the sounds in our native
names for a divinity of whom as yet we know nothing but the
bare name (see Suppl.). On the question as to the sense of the word
itself, I set aside the notion one might stumble on, that it is merely
a fondling form of Paltar, Balder, for such forms invariably preserve
the initial of the complete name; we should expect Palzo, Balzo,
but not Phol.[2] Nor does the OHG. Ph seem here to be equivalent

---

[1] Greek tradition tells of Herakles and Zeus: φασὶ τὸν Ἡρακλέα δίψει ποτὲ
καταχέντα εὔξασθαι τὸ Διὶ πατρὶ ἐπιδεῖξαι αὐτῷ μικρὰν λιβάδα. ὁ δὲ μὴ θέλων
αὐτὸν κατατρύχεσθαι, ῥίψας κεραυνὸν ἀνέδωκε μικρὰν λιβάδα, ἣν θεασάμενος ὁ
Ἡρακλῆς καὶ σκάψας εἰς τὸ πλουσιώτερον ἐποίησε φέρεσθαι (Scholia in Il. 20, 74).
This spring was Scamander, and the λιβὰς Ἡρακλῆος may be set by the side of
Pfolesbrunno as well as Pfolesouwa, λιβάδιον being both mead and ea; and
does not the Grecian demigod's pyre kindled on Oeta suggest that of Balder?

[2] So I explain the proper name *Folz* from Folbreht, Folrât, Folmâr, and
the like; it therefore stands apart from Phol. [The Suppl. qualifies the sweep-
ing assertion in the text; it also takes notice of several other solutions, as
Apollo, Pollux, foal, &c.]

to the ordinary F which corresponds to the Saxon F, but rather to be an aspirate which, answering to the Saxon tenuis P, represents an Old-Aryan media B. But we know that a Saxon initial P=OHG. Ph is found almost exclusively in foreign words[1] (porta, phorta ; putti, phuzi ; pêda, pheit) ; it follows that for *Phol*, in case the Sax. form *Pol* is really made out, we must either look for such a foreign P, or as a rare exception, in which the law of consonant-change does assert itself, an Old-Aryan B. I incline to this last hypothesis, and connect Phol and Pol (whose o may very well have sprung from a) with the Celtic *Beal, Beul, Bel, Belenus*, a divinity of light or fire, the Slav. *Bièlbôgh, Bèlbôgh* (white-god), the adj. bièl, bèl (albus), Lith. baltas, which last with its extension T makes it probable that Bældæg and Baldr are of the same root, but have not undergone consonant-change. *Phol* and *Paltar* therefore are in their beginning one, but reveal to us two divergent historical developments of the same word, and a not unimportant difference in the mythology of the several Teutonic races.[2]

So far as we can see, the god was worshipped under the name of *Phol* chiefly by the Thuringians and Bavarians, *i.e.* according to ancient nomenclature the Hermunduri and Marcomanni, yet they seem to have also known his other name *Paltar* or *Balder*, while

---

[1] That is, really *borrowed* words, as port, paternal, palace, in which the Low Germ. makes *no* change (like that in firth, father), and therefore the High Germ. stands only one stage instead of two in advance of Latin : Pforte, Pfalz, &c. Such words stand outside the rule of consonant-change.—TRANS.

[2] I have thus far gone on the assumption that *Phol* and *Balder* in the Merseberg spell designate one and the same divine being, which is strongly supported by the analogy I have pointed out between Pholesouwa and Baldrshagi, Pholesbrunno and Baldrsbrunnr ; and his cultus must have been very familiar to the people, for the poem to be able to name him by different names in succession, without fear of being misunderstood. Else one might suppose by the names, that Phol and Balder were two different gods, and there would be plenty of room left for the question, who can possibly be meant by Phol ? If PH could here represent V = W, which is contrary to all analogy, and is almost put out of court by the persistent PH, PF in all those names of places ; then we might try the ON. *Ullr*, Ollerus in Saxo, p. 45, which (like ull, OHG. wolla, wool) would be in OHG. *Wol*, so that 'Wol endi Wôdan (Ullr ok Oðinn)' made a perfect alliteration. And Ullr was connected with Baldr, who in Sæm. 93ᵃ is called 'Ullar sefi,' sib to U., Ulli cognatus (see Suppl.). But the gen. would have to be Wolles, and that is contradicted by the invariably single L in Pholes. The same reason is conclusive against Wackernagel's proposal to take *Fol* for the god of fulness and plenty, by the side of the goddess Follâ ; I think the weak form Follo would be demanded for it by an OHG. Pilnitis ; v. Haupts zeitschr. 2, 190. Still more does the internal consistency of the song itself require the identity of Phol and Balder ; it would be odd for Phol to be named at the beginning, and no further notice to be taken of him.

Baldag, Bœldœg prevailed among the Saxons and Westphalians, and the AS. bealdor had passed into a common noun. Now as the Bavarian Eor stood opposed to the Alamannic Zio, we ought to find out whether Phol was in like manner unknown to the Alamanns and the races most akin to them.[1]

Lastly, from eastern Germany we are transported to the north-west by a name appertaining closely to the Balder cultus, and again linking itself with the Edda. The Edda cites among the Ases a son of Baldr and Nanna, *Forseti*, who like his father dwelt in a shining hall *Glitnir* (glit, nitor, splendor, OHG. kliz) built of gold and silver, and who (as Baldr himself had been called the wisest, most eloquent and mildest god, whose verdicts are final, Sn. 27) passed among gods and men for the wisest of judges; he settled all disputed matters (Sæm. 42ª. Sn. 31. 103), and we are told no more about him (see Suppl.).

This Forseti is well entitled to be compared with the Frisian god *Fosite*, concerning whom some biographies composed in the ninth century gives us valuable information. The vita sancti Wilibrordi († 739), written by the famous Alcuin († 804), relates as follows, cap. 10 : Cum ergo pius verbi Dei praedicator iter agebat, pervenit in confinio Fresonum et Danorum ad quamdam insulam, quae *a quodam deo suo Fosite* ab accolis terrae *Fositesland* appella-tur, quia in ea *ejusdem dei fana* fuere constructa. qui locus a paganis in tanta veneratione habebatur, ut nil in ea, vel animalium ibi pascentium, vel aliarum quarumlibet rerum, gentilium quisquam *tangere* audebat, nec etiam a *fonte* qui ibi ebulliebat *aquam haurire nisi tacens* praesumebat. Quo cum vir Dei tempestate jactatus est, mansit ibidem aliquot dies, quousque sepositis tempestatibus opportunum navigandi tempus adveniret. sed parvipendens stultam

---

[1] The inquiry, how far these names reach back into antiquity, is far from exhausted yet. I have called attention to the *Pfol*graben (-ditch), the *Pfal*hecke (-hedge, -fence), for which devil's dyke is elsewhere used ; then the raising of the whirlwind is ascribed in some parts to the devil, in others to Herodias [meaning H.'s daughter the dancer], in others again to Pfol. Eastern Hesse on the Werra has a 'very queer' name for the whirlwind, beginning with *Bull-* or *Boil-* ; and in the neighbouring Eichsfeld *Pulloineke* is pronounced with shyness and reluctance (Münchner gel. anz. 1842, p. 762). A Niddawitz ordinance of the same district (3, 327) contains the family name *Boyls*perg (Polesberc ?), Pfoylsperg. The spelling Bull, Boil, would agree with the con-jecture hazarded above, but I do not connect with this the idol Biel in the Harz, for Bielstein leads back to bîlstein, *i.e.* beilstein. Schmid's westerw. id. 145 has *pollecker, bollecker* for spectre, bugbear (see Suppl.).

loci illius religionem, vel ferocissimum regis animum, qui violatores
sacrorum illius atrocissima morte damnare solebat; tres homines
in eo fonte cum invocatione sanctae Trinitatis baptizavit.   sed et
animalia in ea terra pascentia in cibaria suis mactare praecepit.
Quod pagani intuentes, arbitrabantur eos vel in furorem verti, vel
etiam veloci morte perire; quos cum nil mali cernebant pati,
stupore perterriti, regi tamen Radbodo quod viderant factum
retulerunt.   Qui nimio furore succensus in sacerdotem Dei vivi
suorum injurias *deorum* ulcisci cogitabat, et per tres dies semper
tribus vicibus sortes suo more *mittebat*, et nunquam damnatorum
sors, Deo vero defendente suos, super servum Dei aut aliquem ex
suis cadere potuit; nec nisi unus tantum ex sociis *sorte monstratus*
martyrio coronatus est.— Radbod feared king Pippin the Frank,
and let the evangelist go unhurt.[1]   What Wilibrord had left
unfinished, was accomplished some time after by another priest,
as the vita sancti Liudgeri, composed by Altfrid († 849), tells of
the year 785: Ipse vero (Liudgerus) . . . . studuit *fana* destruere,
et omnes erroris pristini abluere sordes.   curavit quoque ulterius
doctrinae derivare flumina, et consilio ab imperatore accepto, trans-
fretavit in confinio Fresonum atque Danorum ad quandam insulam,
quae a nomine *dei sui* falsi *Fosete Foseteslant* est appellata . . . .
Pervenientes autem ad eandem insulam, destruxerunt *omnia* ejusdem *Fosetis fana*, quae illic fuere constructa, et pro eis Christi
fabricaverunt ecclesias, cumque habitatores terrae illius fide Christi
imbueret, baptizavit eos cum invocatione sanctae Trinitatis in fonte,
qui ibi ebulliebat, in quo sanctus Willibrordus prius homines tres
baptizaverat, a quo etiam fonte nemo prius *haurire aquam nisi*
tacens praesumebat (Pertz 2, 410).—Altfrid evidently had the work
of Alcuin by him.   From that time the island took the name of
hélegland, Helgoland, which it bears to this day; here also the
evangelists were careful to conserve, in the interest of christianity,
the sense of sacredness already attaching to the site.   Adam of
Bremen, in his treatise De situ Daniae (Pertz 9, 369), describes
the island thus: Ordinavit (archiepiscopus episcopum) in Finne
(Fühnen) Eilbertum, quem tradunt conversum (l. captum) a piratis
Farriam insulam, quae in ostio fluminis Albiae longo secessu latet
in oceano, primum reperisse constructoque monasterio in ea fecisse
habitabilem.   haec insula contra Hadeloam sita est.   cujus longi-

[1] Acta sanctor. Bened., sec. 3. pars 1, p. 609.

tudo vix VIII milliaria panditur, latitudo quatuor; homines stramine fragmentisque navium pro igne utuntur. Sermo est piratas, si quando *praedam inde vel minimam tulerint, aut mox perisse nau-fragio, aut occisos ab aliquo, nullum redisse indempnem;* quapropter solent *heremitis ibi viventibus decimas praedarum offerre cum magna devotione.* est enim feracissima frugum, ditissima volucrum et pecudum nutrix, collem habet unicum, arborem nullam, scopulis includitur asperrimis, nullo aditu nisi uno, ubi et *aqua dulcis* (the spring whence they drew water in silence), *locus venerabilis omnibus nautis,* praecipue vero piratis, unde nomen accepit ut *Heiligeland* dicatur. hanc in vita sancti Willebrordi *Fosetisland* appellari dicimus, quae sita est in confinio Danorum et Fresonum. sunt et aliae insulae contra Fresiam et Daniam, sed nulla earum tam memo-rabilis.—The name Farria, appearing here for the first time, either arose from confounding the isle of Föhr with Helgoland, or we must emend the passage, and read ' a piratis Farrianis.' By the customs of these mariners and vikings even of christian times, we may assure ourselves how holy the place was accounted in the heathen time (see Suppl.).

In an island lying between Denmark, Friesland and Saxony, we might expect to find a heathen god who was common to all three. It would be strange if the Frisian *Fosite* were unknown to the Norsemen ; and stranger still if the Eddic *Forseti* were a totally different god. It is true, one would have expected a mention of this deity in particular from Saxo Gram., who is quite silent about it; but then he omits many others, and in his day Fosite's name may have died out amongst the Frisians.

There is some discrepancy between the two names, as was natural in the case of two nations : ON. *Forseti* gen. *Forseta,* Fris. *Fosite* gen. *Fosites.* The simplest supposition is, that from Forsite arose by assimilation Fossite, Fosite, or that the R dropt out, as in OHG. mosar for morsar, Low Germ. mösar; so in the Frisian Angeln, according to Hagerup p. 20, föst, föste = förste, primus. Besides, there is hardly any other way of explaining Fosite. In ON. *forseti* is praeses, princeps, apparently translatable into OHG. *forasizo,* a fitting name for the god who presides over judgment, and arranges all disputes. The Gothic *faúragaggja* bears almost the same sense, which I also find, even in much later writings, attached to our word *vorgänger* (now = predecessor). More complete AS.

genealogies would perhaps name a *Forseta* or *Forsete* as Bældæg's son.[1]

Forseti, Fosite are a proof of the extent of Balder's worship. If we may infer from Pholesouwa and Baldrshagi that the god loved isles and 'eas,' Helgoland is a case in point, where the flocks of his son grazed; and so is perhaps the worship of the Hercules-pillars. which, following Tacitus, we might fix on some other island near it.[2]

[1] Later writers have turned Fosete into a goddess Foseta, Phoseta, Fosta, to approximate her to the Roman Vesta; maps of Helgoland, in which are found marked a 'templum Fostae vel Phosetae' of the year 768, and a 'templum Vestae' of 692, were made up in Major's Cimbrien (Plön, 1692), conf. Wiebel's programm über Helgoland, Hamb. 1842. The god Foste and Fosteland could easily find their way into the spurious Vita Suiberti cap. 7.

[2] Another thought has struck my mind about *Fosete*. In the appendix to the Heldenbuch, *Ecke, Vasat, Abentrot* are styled brothers. The form *Fasat* instead of the usual *Fasolt* need not be a mistake; there are several OHG. men's names in -at, and OS. in -ad, -id, so that Fasat and Fasolt can hold their ground side by side. Now *Fasolt* (conf. ch. XX. Storm) and *Ecke* were known as god-giants of wind and water, *Abentrot* as a dæmon of light. As Ecke-Oegir was worshipped on the Eider and in Lässöe, so might Fosite be in Helgoland. The connexion with *Forseti* must not be let go, but its meaning as For-seti, Fora-sizo becomes dubious, and I feel inclined to explain it as Fors-eti from fors [a whirling stream, 'force' in Cumbld], Dan. fos, and to assume a dæmon of the whirlpool, a *Fossegrimm* (conf. ch. XVII. Nichus), with which *Fosite's* sacred spring would tally. Again, the Heldenbuch gives those three brothers a father Nentigêr (for so we must read for Mentiger) = OHG. *Nandgêr;* and does not he suggest Forseti's mother Nanna = *Nandâ?*

CHAPTER XII.

OTHER GODS.

In addition to the gods treated of thus far, who could with perfect distinctness be pointed out in all or most of the Teutonic races, the Norse mythology enumerates a series of others, whose track will be harder to pursue, if it does not die out altogether. To a great extent they are those of whom the North itself has little or nothing to tell in later times.

1. (HEIMDALL.)

Heimðallr, or in the later spelling Heimdallr, though no longer mentioned in Saxo, is, like Baldr, a bright and gracious god: *hvîtastr* âsa (whitest of âses, Sæm. 72ᵃ),[1] sverðâs *hvîta*, Sæm. 90ᵃ, *hvîti* âs, Sn. 104; he guards the heavenly bridge (the rainbow), and dwells in *Himinbiörg* (the heavenly hills). The heim in the first part of his name agrees in sound with himinn; þallr seems akin to þöll, gen. þallar (pinus), Swed. tall, Swiss däle, Engl. deal (Stald. 1, 259, conf. Schm. 2, 603-4 on mantala), but þöll also means a river, Sn. 43, and Freyja bears the by-name of Mardöll, gen. Mardallar, Sn. 37. 154. All this remains dark to us. No proper name in the other Teutonic tongues answers to Heimðallr; but with *Himinbiörg* (Sæm. 41ᵇ 92ᵇ) or the common noun himinfiöll (Sæm. 148ᵃ Yngl. saga cap. 39), we can connect the names of other hills: a *Himilînberg* (mons coelius) haunted by spirits, in the vita S. Galli, Pertz 2, 10; *Himelberc* in Lichtenstein's frauend. 199, 10; a *Himilesberg* in the Fulda country, Schannat Buchon. vet. 336; several in

---

[1] When this passage says further, 'vissi hann vel fram, *sem Vanir aðrir*,' liter. 'he foreknew well, like other Vanir,' his wisdom is merely likened to that of the Vanir (Gramm. 4, 456 on *ander*), it is not meant that he was one of them, a thing never asserted anywhere [so in Homer, 'Greeks and *other* Trojans' means 'and Trojans *as well*']. The Fornald. sög. 1, 373 calls him, I know not why, 'heimskastr allra âsa,' heimskr usually signifying ignorant, a greenhorn, what the MHG. poets mean by tump.

Hesse (Kuchenb. anal. 11, 137) near Iba and Waldkappel (Niederh. wochenbl. 1834 pp. 106, 2183); a *Himmelsberg* in Vestgötland, and one, alleged to be Heimdall's, in Halland. At the same time, *Himinvângar*, Sæm. 150[a], the OS. hebanwang, hebeneswang, a paradise (v. ch. XXV), the AS. *Heofenfeld* coelestis campus, Beda p. 158, and the like names, some individual, some general, deserve to be studied, but yield as yet no safe conclusion about the god.

Other points about him savour almost of the fairy-tale : he is made out to be the son of nine mothers, giantesses, Sæm. 118[a,b]. Sn. 106. Laxd. p. 392 ; he wants less sleep than a bird, sees a hundred miles off by night or day, and hears the grass grow on the ground and the wool on the sheep's back (Sn. 30).[1] His horse is *Gulltoppr*, gold-tuft, and he himself has golden teeth,[2] hence the by-names *Gullintanni* and *Hallinskîði*, ' tennur Hallinskîða,' Fornm. sög. 1, 52. It is worthy of remark, that Hallinskîði and Heimdali are quoted among the names for the ram, Sn. 221.

As watchman and warder of the gods (vörðr goða, Sæm. 41), Heimdall winds a powerful horn, *Giallarhorn*, which is kept under a sacred tree, Sæm. 5[b] 8[a]. Sn. 72-3. What the Völuspâ imparts, must be of a high antiquity (see Suppl.).

Now at the very outset of that poem, all created beings great and small are called *megir Heimðallar*, sons or children of the god ; he appears therefore to have had a hand in the creation of the world, and of men, and to have played a more exalted part than is assigned to him afterwards. As, in addition to Wuotan, Zio presided over war, and Frô over fruitfulness, so the creative faculty seems to have been divided between Oðinn and Heimðallr.

A song of suggestive design in the Edda makes the first arrangement of mankind in classes proceed from the same *Heimðallr*, who traverses the world under the name of *Rîgr* (see Suppl.). There is a much later German tradition, very prevalent in the last few centuries, which I have ventured to trace to this heathen one, its origin being difficult to explain otherwise.[3] As for the name *Rîgr*, it seems to me to have sprung, like dîs from idis, by aphæresis from an older form, which I cannot precisely determine, but would connect with the MHG. Irinc, as in ON. an n before g or k often

---

[1] Conf. KM. 3, 125.

[2] Li *diente d' oro*, Pentam. 3, 1. Of a certain Haraldr : tennr voru miklor ok *gulls litr á*, Fornald. sög. 1, 366.

[3] Zeitschrift f. d. alt. 2, 257—267. Conf. ch. XIX.

drops out (conf. stînga stack, þacka þanki), and, as will be shown later, Iringes strâza, Iringes wec answers to a Swedish Eriksgata.[1] The shining galaxy would suit extremely well the god who descends from heaven to earth, and whose habitation borders on Bifröst.

Norwegian names of places bear witness to his cultus: *Heimdallarvattn*, a lake in Guldbrandsdalen (Guðbrandsdalr), and *Heimdallshoug*, a hill in Nummedalen (Naumudalr); neither is mentioned in the ON. sagas.

2. (BRAGI, BREGO.)

Above any other god, one would like to see a more general veneration of the ON. *Bragi* revived, in whom was vested the gift of poetry and eloquence. He is called the best of all skalds, Sæm. 46[a]. Sn. 45, frumsmiðr bragar (auctor poeseos), and poetry itself is *bragr*.[2] In honour of him the *Braga*full or *bragar*full was given (p. 60); the form appears to waver between bragi gen. braga, and bragr gen. bragar, at all events the latter stands in the phrase '*bragr* karla' = vir facundus, praestans, in '*âsa bragr*' deorum princeps = Thôrr (Sæm. 85[b]. Sn. 211[a], but *Bragi* 211[b]), and even '*bragr* qvenna' femina praestantissima (Sæm. 218[a]).[3]

Then a poet and king of old renown, distinct from the god, himself bore the name of *Bragi hinn gamli*, and his descendants were styled Bragnîngar. A minstrel was pictured to the mind as old and long-bearded, sîðskeggi and skeggbragi, Sn. 105, which recalls Oðinn with his long beard, the inventor of poetry (p. 146), and Bragi is even said to be Oðin's son, Sn. 105 (see Suppl.).

In the AS. poems there occurs, always in the nom. sing., the term *brego* or *breogo*, in the sense of rex or princeps: bregostôl in Beow. 4387 and Andr. 209 is thronus regius; bregoweard in Cædm. 140, 26. 166, 13 is princeps.[4] Now, as gen. plurals are attached to

---

[1] Der gammel *Erik*, gammel *Erke* (old E.), has now come to mean old Nick in Swedish ; conf. supra p. 124, on *Erchtag*.

[2] Sæm. 113[b], of Oðinn : gefr hann brag skáldom (dat carmen poetis).

[3] Does not the Engl. *brag*, Germ. *prahlen* (gloriari) explain everything ? Showy high-flown speech would apply equally to boasting and to poetry. Then, for the other meaning, 'the boast, glory, master-piece (of men, gods, women, angels, bears),' we can either go back to the more primitive sense (gloria) in *prangen, prunk, pracht, bright*, or still keep to *brag*. 'Beauty is nature's *brag*, and must be shewn,' says Comus.—TRANS.

[4] In Beda 4, 23 (Stevens. p. 304) a woman's name Bregosuid, Bregoswið ; in Kemble 5, 48 (anno 749) *Bregeswiðestân*, and 1, 133-4 (anno 762), 5, 46 (anno 747), 5, 59 (anno 798) a man's name Bregowine. In Beow. 3847 bregoróf is clarissimus.

it : brego engla, Cædm. 12, 7.   60, 4.   62, 3 ; brego Dena, Beow.
848 ; hæleða brego, Beow. 3905 ; gumena brego, Andr. 61 ; beorna
brego, Andr. 305 (conf. brego moncynnes, Cod. exon. 457, 3) ; there
grows up an instructive analogy to the above-mentioned ' bragr
karla,' and to the genitives similarly connected with the divine
names Týr, Freá and Bealdor (pp. 196, 211, 220).   The AS. *brego*
equally seems to point to a veiled divinity, though the forms and
vowel-relations do not exactly harmonize.[1]

Their disagreement rather provokes one to hunt up the root
under which they could be reconciled : a verb briga brag would
suit the purpose.   The Saxon and Frisian languages, but not the
Scandinavian or High German, possess an unexplained term for
cerebrum : AS. brëgen (like rëgen pluvia, therefore better written
so than brægen), Engl. brain, Fris. brein, Low Sax. bregen ; I think
it answers to the notions ' understanding, cleverness, eloquence,
imitation,' and is connected with φρήν, φρενός, -φρων, -φρονος.   Now
the ON. bragr, beside poesis, means also mos, gestus, and ' braga
eftir einum' referre aliquem gestu, imitari.   OHG. has nothing like
it, nor any such proper name as Prako, Brago, Brëgo.

But, as we detected among the Saxons a faint trace of the god
or god's son, we may lay some stress on the fact that in an OS.
document of 1006 *Burnacker* occurs as the name of a place, v.
Lünzel's Hildesheim, p. 124, conf. pref. v. (see Suppl.).   Now Bragi
and his wife Iðunn dwelt in *Brunnakr*, Sn. 121ª, and she is called
' Brunnakrs beckjar gerðr,' Brunnakerinae sedis ornatrix, as Sk.
Thorlacius interprets it (Spec. 6, pp. 65-6).   A well or spring,
for more than one reason, suits a god of poetry ; at the same time a
name like ' springfield ' is so natural that it might arise without any
reference to gods.

Bragi appears to have stood in some pretty close relation to
Oegir, and if an analogy between them could be established, which
however is unsupported hitherto on other grounds, then by the
side of ' briga brag ' the root ' braga brôg ' would present itself, and
the AS. brôga (terror), OHG. pruoko, bruogo, be akin to it.   The
connexion of Bragi with Oegir may be seen by Bragi appearing
prominently in the poem Oegisdrecka, and by his sitting next to
Oegir in Sn. 80, so that in intimate converse with him he brings
out stories of the gods, which are thence called *Bragarœður*,

---

[1] The Irish breitheam, brethemb (judex) is said to be pronounced almost
as ' brehon,' Trans. of Irish acad. 14, 167.

speeches of Bragi. It is with great propriety, no doubt, that these narratives, during which Oegir often interrupts him with questions (Sn. 93), as Ganglêri does Hâr when holding forth in the first part of the Edda, were put in the mouth of the patron of poetry.

3. AKI, UOKI (OEGIR, HLÊR). FÎFEL, GEOFON.

This Oegir, an older god of the giant kind, not ranked among the Ases, but holding peaceable intercourse with them, bears the name of the terrible, the awful. The root ' aga ôg ' had given birth to plenty of derivatives in our ancient speech: Goth. agis $\phi\acute{o}\beta\sigma$, ôg $\phi\sigma\beta\acute{e}\sigma\mu\alpha\iota$, OHG. akiso, egiso, AS. egesa horror, OHG. akî, ekî, AS. ege (êge? awe) terror, ON. œgja terrori esse, which can only be spelt with œ, not æ. To the proper name *Oegir* would correspond a Goth. Ôgeis, AS. Êge, OHG. Uogi, instead of which I can only lay my hand on the weak form *Uogo, Oago*. But œgir also signifies the sea itself: sôl gengr î œginn, the sun goes into the sea, sets; œgi-siôr pelagus is like the Goth. mari-sáivs; the AS. eagor and êgor (mare) is related to êge, as sigor to sige. I attach weight to the agreement of the Greek $\dot{\omega}\kappa\epsilon\alpha\nu\acute{o}s$, $\text{'}\Omega\kappa\epsilon\alpha\nu\acute{o}s$ and $\text{'}\Omega\gamma\acute{\eta}\nu$, whence the Lat. oceanus, Oceanus was borrowed, but aequor (mare placidum) seems not cognate, being related to aequus, not to aqua and Goth. ahva (see Suppl.).[1]

The boisterous element awakened awe, and the sense of a god's immediate presence. As Wôden was also called Wôma (p. 144), and Oðinn Omi and Yggr, so the AS. poets use the terms wôma, swêg, brôga and egesa almost synonymously for ghostly and divine phenomena (Andr. and El. pp. xxx—xxxii). *Oegir* was therefore a highly appropriate name, and is in keeping with the notions of fear and horror developed on p. 207-8.

This interpretation is strikingly confirmed by other mythical conceptions. The Edda tells us of a fear-inspiring helmet, whose name is *Oegishialmr :* er öll qvikvendi brœðast at siâ, Sn. 137 ; such a one did Hreiðmar wear, and then Fafnir when he lay on the gold and seemed the more terrible to all that looked upon him, Sæm. 188[a] ; vera (to be) undir *Oegishialmi*, bera Oegishialm yfir

---

[1] Oegir is also called *Gymir*, Sæm. 59. *Gŭmir*, Sn. 125. 183 possibly epulator ? but I know no other meaning of the ON. gaumr than cura, attentio, though the OHG. gouma, OS. gôma means both cura and epulae, the AS. gŷming both cura and nuptiae.

einum, means to inspire with fear or reverence, Laxd. saga, p. 130.
Islend. sög. 2, 155 ; ek bar Oegishialm yfir alla folki, Fornald. sög.
1, 162 ; hafa Oegishialm î augum, ibid. 1, 406, denotes that terrible
piercing look of the eyes, which others cannot stand, and the
famous basilisk-glance, ormr î auga, was something similar.[1] Now
I find a clear trace of this Norse helmet in the OHG. man's name
Egihelm (Trad. fuld. 1, 97 ; in Schannat no. 126, p. 286 Eggihelm),
i.e. Agihelm, identical with the strengthened-vowel form *Uogihelm*,
which I am unable to produce. But in the Eckenlied itself Ecke's
costly magic helmet, and elsewhere even Ortnit's and Dietrich's,
are called *Hildegrîm, Hildegrîn ;* and the ON. *grîma* mask or
helmet (in Sæm. 51ª a name for night) has now turned up in a
Fulda gloss, Dronke p. 15 : ' scenici = *crîmûn* ' presupposes a sing.
krîmâ larva, persona, galea ; so we can now understand *Krîmhilt*
(Gramm. 1, 188) the name of a Walkurie armed with the helmet of
terror, and also why ' daemon ' in another gloss is rendered by
egisgrîmolt. The AS. *egesgrîme* is equally a mask, and in El. 260
the helmet that frightens by its figure of a boar is called a *grîmhelm*. I venture to guess, that the wolf in our ancient apologue
was imagined wearing such a helmet of dread, and hence his name
of *Isangrîm*, iron-mask, Reinh. ccxlii (see Suppl.). Nor have we
yet come to the end of fancies variously playing into one another :
as the god's or hero's helmet awakened terror, so must his shield
and sword ; and it looks significant, that a terrific sword fashioned
by dwarfs should likewise be named in the two forms, viz. in the
Vilkinasaga *Eckisax*, in Veldek's Eneit *Uokesahs* (not a letter may
we alter), in the Eckenlied *Ecken* sahs, as Hildegrîn was Ecken
helm, Eckes helm. In the Greek αἰγίς I do not look for any verbal
affinity, but this shield of Ζεὺς αἰγίοχος (Il. 15, 310. 17, 593),
wielded at times by Athena (2, 447. 5, 738) and Apollo (15, 229.
318. 361. 24, 20), spreads dismay around, like Oegishialmr,
Hildegrîm and Eckisahs ; Pluto's helmet too, which rendered
invisible, may be called to mind.—That ancient god of sea, Oceanus
and Oegir (see Suppl.), whose hall glittered with gold, Sæm. 59,[2]

---

[1] Fornm. sög. 9, 513 : gekk alvaldr und *Ŷgishialmi.* The spelling with ŷ
goes to confirm our œ, and refute æ, as an ŷ can only stand for the former, not
for the latter ; conf. môr and the deriv. mŷri = mœri, Gramm. 1, 473.

[2] In the great feast which he gave to the gods, the ale *came up of itself* (sialft
barsc þar öl, Sæm. 59), as Hephæstus's tripods ran αὐτόματοι in and out of the
θεῖον ἀγῶνα, Il. 18, 376. Even so Freyr had a sword *er sialft vegiz* (that swings
itself), Sæm. 82ª, and Thôr's Miölnir comes back of itself everytime it is thrown.

would of all others wear the glittering helmet which takes its
name from him. From all we can find, his name in OHG. must
have been *Aki* or *Uoki;* and it requires no great boldness to
suppose that in the *Ecke* of our heroic legend, a giant all over, we
see a precipitate of the heathen god. Ecke's mythical nature is
confirmed by that of his brothers Fasolt and Abentrôt, of whom
more hereafter. As the Greek Okeanos has rivers given him for
sons and daughters, the Norse Oegir has by Rân nine daughters,
whose names the Edda applies to waters and waves. We might
expect to find that similar relations to the seagod were of old
ascribed to our own rivers also, most of which were conceived of as
female [and still bear feminine names].

And there is one such local name in which he may be clearly
recognised. The *Eider*, a river which divides the Saxons from the
Northmen, is called by the Frankish annalists in the eighth and
ninth centuries *Egidora, Agadora, Aegidora* (Pertz 1, 355-70-86.
2, 620-31); Helmold 1, 12. 50 spells *Egdora.* The ON. writers
more plainly write *Oegisdyr* (Fornm. sög. 11, 28. 31, conf. Geogr. of
a Northman, ed. by Werlauff p. 15), *i.e.*, ocean's door, sea-outlet,
ostium, perhaps even here with a collateral sense of the awful.
Again, a place called *Oegisdyr* is mentioned in Iceland, Landn. 5,
2, where we also find 3, 1 an *Oegissîða*, latus oceani. Further, it
comes out that by the AS. name *Fîfeldor* in Cod. exon. 321, 8 and
by the *Wieglesdor* in Dietmar of Merseb. ad ann. 975, p. 760 is
meant the Eider again, still the aforesaid Oegisdyr; while a various
reading in Dietmar agrees with the annalist Saxo ad ann. 975 in
giving *Heggedor* = Eggedor, Egidor. Now, seeing that elsewhere
the AS. poems use Fîfelstreám, Fîfelwæg (Boeth. 26, 51. El. 237)
for the ocean, and Fîfelcynnes eard (Beow. 208) for the land of the
ocean-sprites, we may suppose *Fîfel* and its corruption *Wiegel* to be
another and an obsolete name of Oegir.

The same may hold good of the AS. *Geofon*, OS. *Geban*, a being
whose godhead is sufficiently manifest from the ON. *Gefjun*, who is
reckoned among the Asynior, though she bore sons to a giant.
The Saxon *Gëban* however was a god ; the Heliand shows only the
compound Gebenesstrôm 90, 7. 131, 22, but the AS. poets, in
addition to Geofenes begang, Beow. 721, Geofenes staδ, Cædm. 215,
8, and the less personal geofonhûs (navis), Cædm. 79, 34, geofonflôd,
Cod. exon. 193, 21, have also a *Geofon* standing independently in

the nom., Cædm. 206, 6, and gifen geotende, Beow. 3378. An OHG. *Këpan* is nowhere found, even in proper names, though Stählin 1, 598 gives a *Gebeneswîlare.* I know not whether to take for the root the verb giban to give, in which case *Gibika* (p. 137) and Wuotan's relation to Neptune (pp. 122, 148) would come in here ; or to look away to the Greek χιών fem. [χιϝών, hib-ernus ?] and the notion of snow and ice giants.

And the North itself furnishes some names which are synonymous with Oegir. In the Fundinn Noregr (Sn. 369. Fornald. sög. 2, 17) we read : Forniotr âtti 3 syni, hêtt einn *Hlér, er ver köllum Oegi* (one hight Hler, whom we call Oegir), annarr Logi, þridji Kari (Rask, afh. 1, 95 : Kâri). *Hlér*, gen. Hlês, appears from this to have been the older name, in use among the giants, by which Oegir is spoken of in Sn. 79, and after which his dwelling-place was named *Hlés-ey* (Sæm. 78ᵇ 159ᵇ 243ᵇ), now Lässöe in the Cattegat.

4. (FORNIOTR).

Of this *Hlér* I have nothing more to tell (see Suppl.), but his father *Forniotr* has left a notable trace of himself behind ; he belongs even less than Oegir to the circle of Ases, being one of the older demonic giants, and proving that even these demigods or personified powers of nature must also have borne sway among the Teutonic races outside of Scandinavia. Forniotr is to be explained, not as for-niotr primus occupans, but rather as forn-iotr, the ancient Iotr (Rask, afhand. 1, 78), a particularly apt expression for those giants, and closely connected with iötunn itself, AS. eoton, as will be shown further on. Now in the AS. Liber medicinalis, from which Wanley, pp. 176—80 gives insufficient extracts, there is according to Lye's dictionary a plant of healing virtue spoken of (twice apparently, from the various spelling) by the name of *Forneotes folme, Fornetes folme* (*i.e.* Forneoti manus). As none of the ON. writings allude to this herb, its name must be a remnant of the Saxon people's own mythology. In OHG. the giant may have been called Firnëz, and the plant Firnëzes folma. We remember how, in Beow. 1662, Grendel has torn off the hand of a water-sprite, and presents it as tâcen of his victory, just as Tristan chops off the giant Urgan's hand, and takes it with him to certify the deed, 16055-65-85. The amputation of the huge giant-hand seems therefore part of an ancient myth, and to have been fitly retained in the name of a broad-leaved vegetable; there is also a plant called *devil's-hand*, and in more than one legend the Evil one leaves the print of his hand on rocks and walls.

If these last allusions have led us away from the beneficent deities rather to hurtful demons and malignant spirits, we have here an easy transit to the only god whom the teaching of the Edda represents as wicked and malevolent, though it still reckons him among the Ases.

5. (Loki, Grendel), Saturn.

Logi, as we have seen, was a second son of Forniotr, and the three brothers *Hlér, Logi, Kari* on the whole seem to represent water, fire and air as elements. Now a striking narrative (Sn. 54. 60) places *Logi* by the side of *Loki*, a being from the giant province beside a kinsman and companion of the gods. This is no mere play upon words, the two really signify the same thing from different points of view, *Logi* the natural force of fire, and *Loki*, with a shifting of the sound, a shifting of the sense: of the burly giant has been made a sly seducing villain. The two may be compared to the Prometheus and the Hephæstus (Vulcan) of the Greeks; Okeanos was a friend and kinsman of the former. But the two get mixed up. In Loki, sâ er flestu illu ræðr (Sn. 46), who devises the most of ill, we see also the giant demon who, like Hephæstus, sets the gods a-laughing; his limping reminds us of Hephæstus and the lame fire (N. Cap. 76), his chaining of Prometheus's, for Loki is put in chains like his son Fenrir. As Hephæstus forges the net for Ares and Aphrodite, Loki too prepares a net (Sn. 69), in which he is caught himself. Most salient of all is the analogy between Hephæstus being hurled down from Olympus by Zeus (Il. 1, 591-3) and the devil being cast out of heaven into hell by God (ch. XXXIII, Devil), though the Edda neither relates such a fall of Loki, nor sets him forth as a cunning smith and master of dwarfs, probably the stories of Loki and Logi were much fuller once. Loki's former fellowship with Oðinn is clearly seen, both from Sæm. 61[b], and from the juxtaposition of three creative deities on their travels, *Oðinn, Hœnir, Loðr*, Sæm. 3[a], instead of which we have also *Oðinn, Hœnir, Loki*, Sæm. 180, or in a different order *Oðinn, Loki, Hœnir*, Sn. 80. 135 (conf. supra, p. 162). This trilogy I do not venture to identify with that of Hlêr, Logi, Kari above, strikingly as Oðinn corresponds to the ἲς ἀνέμοιο; and though from the creating Oðinn

proceed breath and spirit (önd), as from *Loðr* (blaze, glow) come
blood and colour (lâ ok litr), the connexion of Hœnir, who imparts
sense (ôð), with water is not so clear: this Hœnir is one of the
most unmanageable phenomena of the Norse mythology, and with
us in Germany he has vanished without leaving a trace. But the
fire-god too, who according to that gradation of sounds ought
either to be in Goth. Laúha and OHG. Loho, or in Goth. Luka and
OHG. Locho, seems with the loss of his name to have come up
again purely in the character of the later devil. He lasted longer
in Scandinavia, and myths everywhere show how nearly Loki the
âs approaches Logi the giant. Thorlacius (spec. 7, 43) has proved
that in the phrase ' *Loki* fer yfir akra ' (passes over the fields), and
in the Danish ' *Locke* dricker vand ' (drinks water), fire and the
burning sun are meant, just as we say the sun is drawing water,
when he shines through in bright streaks between two clouds.
Loka daun (Lokii odor) is Icelandic for the ignis fatuus exhaling
brimstone (ibid. 44); *Lokabrenna* (Lokii incendium) for Sirius;
Loka spœnir are chips for firing. In the north of Jutland, a weed
very noxious to cattle (polytrichum comm.) is called *Lokkens havre*,
and there is a proverb ' Nu saaer Lokken sin havre,' now Locke
sows his oats, *i.e.*, the devil his tares ; the Danish lexicon translates
Lokeshavre avena fatua, others make it the rhinanthus crista galli.
When the fire crackles, they say ' Lokje smacks his children,' Faye
p. 6.   Molbech's Dial. lex. p. 330 says, the Jutland phrase ' *Lokke*
saaer havre idag (to-day),' or what is equivalent ' *Lokke* driver idag
med sine geder (drives out his goats),' is spoken of vapours that
hang about the ground in the heat of the sun. When birds drop
their feathers in moulting time, people say they ' gaae i *Lokkis* arri
(pass under L.'s harrow?)'; 'at höre paa Lockens eventyr
(adventures)' means to listen to lies or idle tales (P. Syv's gamle
danske ordsprog 2, 72),   According to Sjöborg's Nomenklatur, there
is in Vestergötland a giant's grave named *Lokehall*. All of them
conceptions well deserving notice, which linger to this day among
the common people, and in which Loki is by turns taken for a beneficent and for a hurtful being, for sun, fire, giant or devil. Exactly
the same sort of harm is in Germany ascribed to the devil, and the
kindly god of light is thought of as a devastating flame (see Suppl.).

On this identity between Logi and Loki rests another vestige of the Norse dæmon, which is found among the other Teutonic races. If Logi comes from liuhan (lucere), *Loki* will apparently fall to the root lukan (claudere, conf. claudus lame); the ON. lok means finis, consummatio, and loka repagulum, because a bolt or bar closes. In Beowulf we come upon an odious devilish spirit, a thyrs (Beow. 846) named *Grendel*, and his mother, Grendeles môdor (4232-74), a veritable devil's mother and giant's mother. An AS. document of 931 in Kemble 2, 172 mentions a place called *Grendles* mêre (Grendeli palus). Now the AS. *grindel*, OHG. *krintil*, MHG. *grintel* is precisely repagulum, pessulus ; so the name *Grendel* seems related to grindel (obex) in the same way as Loki to loka ; the ON. grind is a grating, which shuts one in like bolt and bar. Gervase of Tilbury (in Leibn. 1, 980) tells of an English fire-demon named *Grant*. It is very remarkable, that we Germans have still in use a third synonymous expression for a diabolic being, its meaning heightened no doubt by composition with ' hell'; *höllriegel* vectis infernalis, hell-bar, a hell-brand, devil or the devil's own ; a shrewish old hag is styled höllriegel or the devil's grandmother; and Hugo von Langenstein (Martina 4[b]) already used this *hellerigel* as a term of abuse. Now hell was imagined as being tightly bolted and barred ; when Christ, says Fundgr. 1, 178, went down to Hades in the strength of a lion, he made ' die grintel brechen '. Lastly, we may even connect the OHG. *dremil* (pessulus, Graff 5, 531) with the ON. *trami* or *tremill*, which mean both cacodaemon and also, it seems, clathri, cancelli : ' tramar gneypa þik skulo ! ' Sæm. 85[a] ; and in the Swedish song of Torkar, *trolltram* is an epithet of the devil who stole the hammer. As this is the Thrymr of the Edda, one might guess that trami stands for þrami, with which our dremil would more exactly accord. Thus from several sides we see the mythical notions that prevailed on this subject joining hands, and the merging of Logi into Loki must be of high antiquity. Foersom (on Jutl. superstit. p. 32) alleges, that the devil is conceived of in the form of a lässeträ, *i.e.*, the pole with which a load is tied down.

Beside Loki the âs, Snorri sets another before us in the Edda, *Utgarðaloki*, as a king whose arts and power deceive even godlike Thôrr ; it was one of his household that outdid the other Loki himself, Sn. 54 seq.[1] Saxo, who in the whole of his work

---

[1] ' Thorlacius's theory, of an older nature-worship supplanted by the Ases, rests mainly on the antithesis of an Ökuþôrr to Asaþôrr, of Logi to Loki, and probably of Hlêr to Oegir, each pair respectively standing for thunder, fire,

never once names the Eddic Loki, tells wonderful things of this
' Ugarthilocus,' pp. 163-6 : he paints him as a gigantic semi-divine
monster, who dwells in a distant land, is invoked in a storm like
other gods, and grants his aid. A valiant hero, named Thorkill,
brooks the adventurous journey to Ugarthilocus: all this is but
legendary variation of the visit which, in Snorri, Thôrr pays to
Utgarðaloki. Still it is worth noticing, that Thorkill plucks out one
of Ugarthilocus's huge spear-like hairs, and takes it home with him
(Saxo 165-6). The *utgarðar* were the uttermost borders of the
habitable world, where antiquity fixed the abode of giants and
monsters, *i.e.*, hell; and here also may have been present that
notion of the bar, closing up as it were the entrance to that
inaccessible region of ghosts and demons.

Whether in very early times there was also a Saxon *Loko* and
an Alamannic *Lohho*, or only a *Grendil* and *Krentil*; what is of
capital importance is the agreement in the myths themselves. To
what was cited above, I will here add something more. Our
nursery-tales have made us familiar with the incident of the hair
plucked off the devil as he lay asleep in his grandmother's lap
(Kinderm. 29). The corresponding Norwegian tale makes three
feathers be pulled out of the dragon's tail, not while he sleeps, but
after he is dead.

Loki, in punishment of his misdeeds, is put in chains, like
Prometheus who brought fire to men; but he is to be released
again at the end of the world. One of his children, *Fenrir*,[1] *i.e.*,
himself in a second birth, pursues the moon in the *shape of a wolf*,
and threatens to swallow her. According to Sn. 12. 13, an old
giantess in the forest gave birth to these giants in wolfskin girdles,
the mightiest of them being *Mânagarmr* (lunae canis) who is to
devour the moon; but in another place, while *Sköll* chases the sun,
Hati, Hröðvitnis sonr (Sæm. 45ª) dogs the moon. Probably there
were fuller legends about them all, which were never written
down; an old Scotch story is still remembered about ' the tayl of

water. To the elder series must be added Sif = earth, and the miðgarðsormr
(world-snake). But what nature-god can Oðinn have taken the place of?
None? And was his being not one of the primeval ones ? ' &c. [Quoted from
Suppl., vol. iii.]

[1] Goth. Fanareis ? OHG. Fanari, Feniri ? can it be our fahnenträger,
pannifer? But the early Norse does not seem to have the word answering to
the Goth. fana, OHG. fano (flag). [Has the fox holding up his tail as a
standard, in the unrighteous war of beasts against birds, anything to do with
this ?]

the wolfe and the warldis end' (see Suppl.). But the popular belief seems to have extended generally, and that from the earliest times, all over Germany, and beyond it. We still say, when baneful and perilous disturbances arise, 'the *devil* is broke loose,' as in the North they used to say ' *Loki* er or böndum ' (ch. XXIII). In the Life of Göz von Berlichingen, p. 201 : ' the *devil* was every-where at large ' ; in Detmar's chronik 1, 298 : ' do was de *duvel* los geworden,' *i.e.*, disorder and violence prevailed. Of any one who threatened from a safe distance, the folk in Burgundy used the ironical phrase: ' Dieu garde *la lune des loups !* '¹ meaning, such threats would not be fulfilled till the end of the world ; in the same way the French popular song on Henry IV. expresses the far end of the future as the time when the wolf's teeth shall get at the moon : jusqu' à ce que l'on *prenne la lune avec les dents.*² Fischart in several places speaks of this ' *wolf des mons,*' and most fully in his Aller practik grossmutter : ' derhalben dörft ihr nicht mehr für ihn betten, dass ihn Gott *vor den wölfen wölle behüten,* denn sie werden ihn diss jahr nicht erhaschen ' (need not pray for the moon, they won't get her this year).³ In several places there circulate among the people rhymes about the twelve hours, the last two being thus distinguished: ' um elfe kommen die *wölfe,* um zwölfe bricht das *gewölbe,*' at 11 come the wolves, at 12 bursts the vault, *i.e.*, death out of the vault. Can there be an echo in this of the old belief in the appearing of the wolf or wolves at the destruction of the world and the bursting of heaven's vault ? In a lighted candle, if a piece of the wick gets half detached and makes it burn away too fast, they say ' a *wolf* (as well as thief) is in the candle ;' this too is like the wolf devouring the sun or moon. Eclipses of sun or moon have been a terror to many heathen nations ; the incipient and increasing obscuration of the luminous orb marks for them the moment when the gaping jaws of the wolf threaten to devour it, and they think by loud cries to bring it succour (ch. XXII, Eclipses). The breaking loose of the wolf and the ultimate enlargement of Loki from his chains, who at the time of the Ragnarökr will war against and overcome the gods, is in striking accord with the release of the chained Prometheus, by whom Zeus is then to be overthrown.

¹ Lamonnaye, glossaire to the noei bourguignon, Dijon 1776, p. 242.
² Conf. Ps. 72, 7 : donec auferetur luna.
³ May we in this connexion think of the fable of the *wolf* who goes down the well to eat up the *moon*, which he takes for a cheese ?

The formula, ' unz Loki verðr lauss ' (= unz riufaz regin, till the gods be destroyed), answers exactly to the Greek πρὶν ἂν ἐκ δεσμῶν χαλάσθῃ Προμηθεύς (Aesch. Prom. 176. 770. 991) ; the writhings of the fettered Loki make the earth to quake (Sæm. 69. Sn. 70), just as χθών σεσάλευται in the case of Prometheus (Aesch. 1081). Only the Greek Titan excites our noblest sympathy, while the Edda presents Loki as a hateful monster.

Loki was fair in form, evil in disposition ; his father, a giant, was named *Farbauti* (boatman ?), his mother *Laufey* (leaf-ea) and *Nál* (needle ; thin and insinuating, miô ok auðþreiflig, 355), all of them words easy to translate into OHG. as Farpôzo (remex), Loupouwa, Nâdala, though such names are nowhere found. He is never called Farbauta sonr, but always after his mother, Loki Laufeyjar sonr (Sæm. 67ᵃ 72ᵇ 73ᵃ), which had its origin in alliteration, but held its ground even in prose (Sn. 64) and in the Locke Löje, Loke Lovmand, Loke Lejemand of the later folk-songs. This Laufey (Swed. Löfö) is first of all the name of a place, which was personified, and here again there is doubtless reference to an element. By his wife *Sigyn* Loki had a son *Nari* or Narvi, and by a giantess *Angrboða* three children, the aforesaid *Fenrir*, the serpent *Iörmungandr* and a daughter *Hel*. It is worthy of notice, that he himself is also called *Loptr* (aërius), and one of his brothers *Helblindi*, which is likewise a name of Oðinn. I just throw out these names, mostly foreign to our German mythology, in the hope of enlisting for them future inquiry.

Once again we must turn our attention to a name already brought forward among the gods of the week (pp. 125-6), for which a rare concurrence of isolated facts seems almost to secure a place in our native antiquities. The High German week leaves two days, one in the middle and one at the end, not named after gods. But sambaztag for Saturday, as well as mittwoch for Wuotanstag, was a sheer innovation, which the church had achieved or gladly accepted for those two days at all events. The first six days were called after the sun, the moon, Zio, Wuotan, Donar and Fria ; what god was entitled to have the naming of the seventh day ? Four German deities were available for Mars, Mercury, Jupiter, Venus, but how was *Saturn* to be put into German ? The Mid. Ages went on explaining the seventh day by the Roman god : our Kaiserchronik,

which even for the third, fourth, fifth and sixth days names no
German gods, but only Mars, Mercury, Jupiter, Venus, expresses
itself thus clumsily :

An dem sameztage sâ	Then on the Saturday
einez heizet rotundâ,	Is a thing named rotunda
daz was ein hêrez betehûs,	That was a lofty temple,
der got hiez *Saturnûs*,	The god was named Saturnus,
darnâch was iz aller tiuvel êre.	Thereafter was it to all devils'
	honour.

Here the worship of Saturn is connected with the pantheon built
in honour of all the gods or devils, which Boniface converted into
a church of St. Mary.   The Anglo-Saxons, English, Frisians, Dutch
and Low Saxons have left to the ' dies Saturni' the god's very
name : *Sœteres*day or *Sœternes*dæg, *Satur*day, *Sater*dei, *Sater*dach,
*Saters*dag, and even the Irish have adopted dia *Satuirn* or Satarn ;
whereas the French samedi, Span. sabado, Ital. sabato, agrees with
our High Germ. samstag.   Here is identity, not only of idea, as in
the case of the other gods, but of name, and the absence of consonant-change seems to betray downright borrowing: or may the
resemblance have been accidental, and a genuine German name
have been modified in imitation of the foreign one ?   In OHG
neither a Sâtarnes- nor a Sâzarnestac can be found ; but in AS.
sœtere means insidiator (OHG. sâzari, conf. sâza, MHG. sâze insidiae,
a sitting in wait, as lâga, lâge is lying in wait) ; and what is still
more remarkable, a document of Edward the Confessor (chart.
antiq. rot. M. no. 1.   Kemble 4, 157) supplies us with the name of
a place *Sœteresbyrig*, quite on a par with Wôdnesbyrig ; further, the
plant gallicrus, our hahnenfuss, Engl. crowfoot, was in AS. *sâtorlâðe*
Saturni taedium as it were (-loathing, ON. leiði, OHG. leidi).[1]   I
call to mind, that even the ancient Franks spoke of *Saturnus* (p. 88)
as a heathen god, and of *Saturni* dolium, though that may have
referred to the mere planetary god (see Suppl.).

The last name for the ' sabbath ' brings us to the ON. laugar-

---

[1] In the AS. are preserved various dialogues between *Saturn* and Solomon,
similar to those between Solomon and Marculf in continental Germany, but
more antique and, apart from their christian setting or dressing up, not unlike
the questions and discourses carried on in the Edda between Oðinn and Vafþrûð-
nir, between Vîngþôrr and Alviss, between Hàr and Gàngleri.   Here also the
name Saturn seems to make for my point, and to designate a god of Teutonic
paganism.

dagr, Swed. lögerdag, Dan. löverdag, by which in later times no doubt washing or bathing day was meant, as the equivalent þvottdagr shows; but originally *Loga*dagr, *Loka*dagr may have been in use,[1] and Logi, Loki might answer to the Latin Saturnus,[2] as the idea of devil which lay in Loki was popularly transferred to the Jewish *Satan* and [what seemed to be the same thing] the heathen *Saturn*, and *Locki* in ON. is likewise seducer, tempter, trapper. We might even take into consideration a by-name of Oðinn in Sæm. 46ᵃ, *Saðr* or perhaps Sâðr, though I prefer to take the first form as equivalent to Sannr (true) and Sanngetall.

But that AS. *Sæteresbyrig* from the middle of the 11th century irresistibly recalls the 'burg' on the Harz mts, built (according to our hitherto despised accounts of the 15th century in Bothe's Sachsenchronik) to the idol *Saturn*, which Saturn, it is added, the common people called *Krodo*; to this we may add the name touched upon in p. 206 (Hrêðe, Hrêðemônað), for which an older *Hruodo, Chrôdo* was conjectured.[3] We are told of an image of this Saturn or Krodo, which represented the idol as a man standing on a great fish, holding a pot of flowers in his right hand, and a wheel erect in his left; the Roman Saturn was furnished with the sickle, not a wheel (see Suppl.).[4]

Here some Slav conceptions appear to overlap. Widukind (Pertz 5, 463) mentions a brazen *simulacrum Saturni* among the Slavs of the tenth century, without at all describing it; but Old Bohemian glosses in Hanka 14ᵃ and 17ᵃ carry us farther. In the first, Mercurius is called ' Radihost vnuk Kirtov ' (Radigast grandson of Kirt), in the second, Picus Saturni filius is glossed ' ztracec

---

[1] Conf. Finn Magnusen, lex. pp. 1041-2, dagens tider p. 7.

[2] I suppose the author had in his mind Homer's constant epithet, Κρόνος ἀγκυλομήτης wily, crooked-counselled Kronos.—TRANS.

[3] To *Hrôdo* might now be referred those names *Roysel* (later spelling Reusel) and *Roydach* in Gramaye, who understands them of Mars ; ancient documents must first place it beyond doubt, which day of the week is meant. There is an actual *Hruodtac*, a man's name in OHG. (Graff 5, 362), and an OS. *Hrôddag* is found in Trad. corb. § 424, ed. Wigand ; these may be related to Hruodo, Hrôdo as Baldag to Balder, and the contraction Roydag, Rodag would be like Roswith for Hrôdsuith. If Roydag should turn out to be the seventh day of the week, it would be a strong testimony to the worship of Chrodo ; if it remain the third, we have to add, that the third month also was sacred to Mars, and was called *Hrêðemonað* by the Anglo-Saxons.

[4] ' The Kaiserchr. 3750 says, to Saturn we offer quicksilver ; whereas now Saturn's symbol signifies lead. In Megenberg, Saturn is called *Satjâr*. The Saxon Saturn is supported by Hengest's reference to that god '. (Extracted from Suppl., vol. iii.)

Sitivratov zin' (woodpecker, Sitivrat's son); and in a third 20ᵃ, Saturn is again called Sitivrat. Who does not see that Sitivrat is the Slavic name for Saturn, which leads us at the first glance to sit = satur? Radigast = Mercury (p. 130n.) is the son of Stračec = Picus; and in fact Greek myths treat Picus (Πῖκος) as Zeus, making him give up the kingdom to his son Hermes. Picus is Jupiter, son of Saturn; but beside Sitivrat we have learnt another name for Saturn, namely *Kirt,* which certainly seems to be our *Krodo* and *Hruodo.* Sitivrat and Kirt confirm *Saturn* and *Krodo;* I do not know whether the Slavic word is to be connected with the Boh. krt, Pol. kret, Russ. krot, *i.e.,* the mole.[1] I should prefer to put into the other name Sitivrat the subordinate meaning of sito-vrat, sieve-turner, so that it would be almost the same as kolo-vrat, wheel-turner, and afford a solution of that wheel in Krodo's hand; both wheel (kolo) and sieve (sito) move round, and an ancient spell rested on sieve-turning. Slav mythologists have identified Sitivrat with the Hindu *Satyâvrata,* who in a great deluge is saved by Vishnu in the form of a fish. Krodo stands on a fish; and Vishnu is represented wearing wreaths of flowers about his neck, and holding a wheel (chakra) in his fourth hand.[2] All these coincidences are still meagre and insecure; but they suffice to establish the high antiquity of a Slavo-Teutonic myth, which starts up thus from more than one quarter.

[1] Hardly with Crete, where Kronos ruled and Zeus was born.
[2] Edw. Moore's Hindu Pantheon, Lond. 1810, tab. 13 and 23.—' Sitivrat, who corresponds to Saturn, *is* the Indian Satyâvrata, *i.e.,* according to Kuhn, he that hath veracious (fulfilled) vows; so Dhritavrata, he that hath kept-vows = Varunas, Ouranos.' (Quoted from Suppl., vol. iii.)

CHAPTER XIII.

GODDESSES.

In treating of gods, the course of our inquiry could aim at separating the several personalities; the goddesses[1] it seems advisable to take by themselves and all at one view, because there is a common idea underlying them, which will come out more clearly by that method. They are thought of chiefly as *divine mothers who travel round and visit houses*, from whom the human race learns the occupations and arts of housekeeping and husbandry: *spinning, weaving, tending the hearth, sowing and reaping*. These labours bring with them peace and quiet in the land, and the memory of them abides in charming traditions even more lastingly than that of wars and battles, from which most goddesses as well as women hold themselves aloof.

But as some goddesses also take kindly to war, so do gods on the other hand favour peace and agriculture; and there arises an interchange of names or offices between the sexes.

1. ERDA, NIRDU, GAUE, FIRGUNIA, HLUODANA.

In almost all languages the *Earth* is regarded as female, and (in contrast to the father sky encircling her) as the breeding, teeming fruit-bearing mother: Goth. *aírþa*, OHG. *ërada, ërda*, AS. *eorðe*, ON. *iörð*, Gr. *ἔρα* (inferred from *ἔραζε*); Lat. *terra, tellus, humus* = Slav. *země*, ziemia, zemlia, Lith. *zieme*, Gr. *χαμή* (? whence *χαμᾶζε*), *αἶα, γαῖα, γῆ*: the 'mother' subjoined in *Δημήτηρ*, Zema mate, indicates the goddess. The form aírþa, ërda (also herda) is itself a derivative; the simpler OHG. *ero* (in the Wessobr. prayer: ero noh ûfhimil, earth nor heaven) and *hero* (in a gloss, for solum,

---

[1] OHG. in Notker has only the strong form *gutin* gen. gutinno, MHG. *gotinne*, Trist. 4807. 15812. Barl. 246-7. seldomer *gütinne*, MS. 2, 65ᵇ; AS. *gyden* pl. gydena, but also weak *gydene* pl. gydenan, Mones gl. 4185 Proserpinam = to gidenan (1. tôgydenan, additional goddess); ON. *gyðja* (which might be dea or sacerdos fem.), better *âsynja* (see Suppl.).

Graff 4, 999) might be masc. (like herd = solum, Graff 4, 1026) or
fem. still.[1] The Goth. *mulda*, OHG. *molta*, AS. *molde*, ON. *mold*,
contain only the material sense of soil, dust ; equally impersonal is
the OS. *folda*, AS. *folde*, ON. *fold*, conf. feld, field, Finn. peldo
(campus), Hung. föld (terra). But the ON. *Iörð* appears in the
flesh, at once wife and daughter of Oðinn, and mother of Thôrr
(Sn. 11. 39. 123), who is often called Iarðar burr. Distinct from
her was *Rindr*, another wife of Oðinn, and mother of Vali (Sæm.
91[a] 95[a] 97[b]), called *Rinda* in Saxo, and more coarsely painted ; her
name is the OHG. *rinta*, AS. *rind* = cortex, hence crusta soli vel
terrae, and to *crusta* the AS. *hruse* (terra) is closely related. As
this literal sense is not found in the North, neither is the mythical
meaning in Germany (see Suppl.).

But neither in Iörð nor in Rindr has the Edda brought out in
clear relief her specially maternal character ; nowhere is this more
purely and simply expressed than in the very oldest account we
possess of the goddess. It is not to all the Germani that Tacitus
imputes the worship of *Nerthus*, only to the Langobardi (?), Reudigni,
Aviones, Angli, Varini, Eudoses, Suardones and Vuithones (Germ.
40): Nec quicquam notabile in singulis, nisi quod in commune
Nerthum,[2] id est *Terram matrem* colunt, eamque intervenire rebus
hominum, invehi populis, arbitrantur. Est in insula oceani castum
nemus, dicatumque in eo vehiculum, veste contectum, attingere uni
sacerdoti concessum. Is adesse penetrali *deam* intelligit, vectamque
bubus feminis multa cum veneratione prosequitur. Laeti tunc dies,
festa loca, quaecunque adventu hospitioque dignatur. Non bella
ineunt, non arma sumunt ; clausum omne ferrum : pax et quies
tunc tantum nota, tunc tantum amata : donec idem sacerdos satiatam conversatione mortalium *deam* templo reddat. Mox *vehiculum*
et vestes, et, si credere velis, *numen* ipsum *secreto lacu abluitur*.
Servi ministrant, quos statim idem lacus haurit.[3] Arcanus hinc

---

[1] The two forms ero and hero remind one of the name Eor, Cheru, attributed to Mars (supra, pp. 203-4).
[2] The MSS. collated have this reading, one has *nehertum* (Massmann in
Aufsess and Mones anzeiger, 1834, p. 216); I should prefer Nertus to Nerthus,
because no other German words in Tacitus have TH, except Gothini and
Vuithones. As for the conjectural Herthus, though the aspirate in herda
might seem to plead for it, the termination -us is against it, the Gothic having
aírþa, not aírþus. Besides, Aventin already (Frankf. 1580, p. 19[a]) spells *Nerth*.
[3] The lake swallows the slaves who had assisted at the secret bathing.
More than once this incident turns up, of putting to death the servants employed in any secret work ; as those who dug the river out of its bed for

terror sanctaque ignorantia, quid sit illud, quod tantum perituri vident (see Suppl.).[1]

This beautiful description agrees with what we find in other notices of the worship of a godhead to whom peace and fruitfulness were attributed. In Sweden it was *Freyr*, son of *Niörðr*, whose curtained car went round the country in spring, with the people all praying and holding feasts (p. 213) ; but Freyr is altogether like his father, and he again like his namesake the goddess *Nerthus*. The spring-truces, harvest-truces, plough-truces, fixed for certain seasons and implements of husbandry, have struck deep roots in our German law and land-usages. Wuotan and Donar also make their appearance in their wains, and are invoked for increase to the crops and kindly rain ; on p. 107, anent the car of a Gothic god whose name Sozomen withholds, I have hinted at Nerthus.

The interchange of male and female deities is, luckily for us here, set in a clear light, by the prayers and rhymes to Wuotan as god of harvest, which we have quoted above (p. 155 seq.), being in other Low German districts handed over straight to a goddess. When the cottagers, we are told, are mowing rye, they let some of the stalks stand, tie flowers among them, and when they have finished work, assemble round the clump left standing, take hold of the ears of rye, and shout three times over :

Fru Gaue, haltet ju fauer,	Lady Gaue, keep you some fodder,
düt jar up den wagen,	This year on the waggon,
dat ander jar up der kare ![2]	Next year on the wheelbarrow

Whereas Wode had better fodder promised him for the next year, Dame Gaue seems to receive notice of a falling off in the quantity of the gift presented. In both cases I see the shyness of the christians at retaining a heathen sacrifice : as far as words go, the old gods are to think no great things of themselves in future.

In the district about Hameln, it was the custom, when a reaper in binding sheaves passed one over, or left anything standing in the

---

Alaric's funeral (Jornand. cap. 29), or those who have hidden a treasure, Landn. 5, 12 (see Suppl.).

[1] Speaking of Nerthus, we ought to notice Ptolemy's *Nertereans*, though he places them in a very different locality from that occupied by the races who revere Nerthus in Tacitus.

[2] Braunschw. anz. 1751, p. 900. Hannov. gel. anz. 1751, p. 662 [is not ' haltet ' a mistake for ' hal ' and something else ?] In the Altenburg country they call this harvest-custom *building a barn*. Arch. des henneb. vereins 2, 91.

field, to jeer at him by calling out: 'scholl düt dei *gaue frue* (or, de *fru Gauen*) hebben (is that for dame G.) ?'[1]

In the Prignitz they say *fru Gode*, and call the bunch of ears left standing in each field *vergodendeelsstrûss*, *i.e.*, dame Gode's portion bunch.[2]   *Ver* is a common contraction for frau [as in jungfer]; but a dialect which says fauer instead of foer, foder, will equally have Gaue for *Gode*, *Guode*. This Guode can be no other than Gwode, Wode; and, explaining fru by the older fro, *fro Woden* or *fro Gaue* (conf. Gaunsdag for Wonsdag, p. 125) will denote a lord and god, not a goddess, so that the form of prayer completely coincides with those addressed to Wuotan, and the *fruh Wod* sub-joined in the note on p. 156 (see Suppl.). If one prefer the notion of a female divinity, which, later at all events, was undoubtedly attached to the term fru, we might perhaps bring in the ON. *Gôi* (Sn. 358. Fornald. sög. 2, 17), a mythic maiden, after whom February was named. The Greek Γαῖα or Γῆ is, I consider, out of the question here.

In an AS. formulary for restoring fertility to fields that have been bewitched, there occur two remarkable addresses; the first is '*erce, erce, erce, eorþan môdor!*' by which not the earth herself, but her mother seems to be meant; however, the expression is still enigmatical. Can there lie disguised in *erce* a proper name *Erce* gen. Ercan, connected with the OHG. adj. ërchan, simplex, genuinus, germanus? it would surely be more correct to write *Eorce?* ought it to suggest the lady *Erche*, *Herkja*, *Herche*, *Helche* renowned in our heroic legend? The distinct traces in Low Saxon districts of a divine dame, *Herke* or *Harke* by name, are significant. In Jessen, a little town on the Elster, not far from Wittenberg, they relate of *frau Herke* what in other places, as will be shown, holds good of Freke, Berhta and Holda. In the Mark she is called *frau Harke*, and is said to *fly through the country* between Christmas and Twelfth-day, dispensing earthly goods in abundance; by Epiphany the maids have to finish spinning their flax, else *frau Harke* gives

---

[1] Hannov. gel. anz. 1751, p. 726. More pleasing to the ear is the short prayer of the heathen Lithuanians, to their earth-goddess, when in drinking they spilt some of the ale on the ground : *Zemenyle* ziedekle, pakylek musu ranku darbus ! blooming Earth, bless the work of our hands.

[2] Adalb. Kuhns märkische sagen, pp. 337. 372, pref. p. vii. Conf. in ch. XXII the cry of the dwarfs : 'de *gaue fru* is nu dot (dead)'.

them a good scratching or soils their distaff (see Suppl.).[1] In
earlier times a simpler form of the name was current; we find in
Gobelinus Persona (Meibom 1, 235) the following account, which
therefore reaches back beyond 1418 : Quod autem *Hera* colebatur a
Saxonibus, videtur ex eo quod quidam vulgares recitant se audivisse
ab antiquis, prout et ego audivi, quod inter festum nativitatis Christi
ad festum epiphaniae Domini *domina Hera volat per aëra*, quoniam
apud gentiles Junoni aër deputabatur.   Et quod Juno quandoque
Hera appellabatur et depingebatur cum tintinnabulis et alis,
dicebant vulgares praedicto tempore : *vrowe Hera* seu corrupto
nomine *vro Here de vlughet*, et credebant illam sibi conferre rerum
temporalium abundantiam.   Have we here still extant the old *Ero*,
"*Eρα, Hero* meaning earth ? and does "*Hρα* belong to it ? If the
AS. *Erce* also contains the same, then even the diminutive form
Herke must be of high antiquity.

The second address in the same AS. ritual is a call to the earth :
' hâl wes thu *folde, fira môdor !* ' hale (whole) be thou earth, mother
of men ; which agrees with the expression *terra mater* in Tacitus.

The widely extended worship of the teeming nourishing earth
would no doubt give rise to a variety of names among our forefathers, just as the service of Gaia and her daughter Rhea mixed
itself up with that of Ops mater, Ceres and Cybele.[2] To me the
resemblance between the cultus of Nerthus and that of the Phrygian
mother of gods appears well worthy of notice.   Lucretius 2, 597—
641 describes the peregrination of the *magna deûm mater* in her
lion-drawn *car* through the lands of the earth :

> Quo nunc insigni per magnas praedita terras
> horrifice fertur divinae matris imago
> Ergo quom primum magnas invecta per urbeis
> munificat tacita mortaleis muta salute,
> aere atque argento sternunt iter omne viarum,
> largifica stipe ditantes, ninguntque rosarum
> floribus, umbrantes matrem comitumque catervam.

The Romans called the VI. kal. Apr. *lavatio matris deûm*, and kept
it as a feast, Ovid. fast. 4, 337 :

---

[1] Adalb. Kuhn in the Märkische forschungen 1, 123-4, and Märk. sagen
pp. 371-2 ; conf. Singularia magdeburg. 1740. 12, 768.
[2] Ops mater= *terra mater* ; Ceres= *Geres*, quod *gerit* fruges, antiquis enim
C quod nunc G ; Varro de ling. lat., ed. O. Müller p. 25.   Her Greek appellation Δημήτηρ seems also to lead to γῆ μήτηρ (see Suppl.).

Est locus, in Tiberin qua lubricus influit Almo,
    et nomen magno perdit ab amne minor ;
illic purpurea canus cum veste sacerdos
    Almonis dominam sacraque lavit aquis.

Ammian. Marcell. 23, 3 (Paris 1681, p. 355) : Ad Callinicum,—ubi
ante diem sextum kal. quo Romae matri deorum pompae celebrantur
annales, et *carpentum quo vehitur simulacrum* Almonis undis ablui
perhibetur.   Conf. Prudentius, hymn. 10, 154 :

Nudare plantas ante *carpentum* scio
proceres togatos *matris Idaeae* sacris.
Lapis nigellus evehendus essedo
muliebris oris clausus argento sedet,
quem dum ad lavacrum praeeundo ducitis
pedes remotis atterentes calceis
Almonis usque pervenitis rivulum.

Exactly in the same way Nerthus, after she has travelled round the
country, is bathed in the sacred lake in her waggon ; and I find it
noted, that the Indian *Bhavani*, wife of Shiva, is likewise driven
round on her feast-day, and *bathed in a secret lake* by the Brahmans
(see Suppl.).[1]

Nerthus's 'island in the ocean' has been supposed to mean
Rügen, in the middle of which there is actually a lake, called the
Schwarze see, or Burgsee.   What is told as a legend, that there in
ancient times the devil was adored, that a maiden was maintained
in his service, and that when he was *weary* of her, she was *drowned*

---

[1] Gregor. Turon. de glor. conf. cap. 77 compares or confounds with the
Phrygian *Cybele* some Gallic goddess, whose worship he describes as follows :—
'Ferunt etiam in hac urbe (Augustoduno) *simulachrum* fuisse *Berecynthiae,* sicut
sancti martyris Symphoriani passionis declarat historia.   Hanc cum *in
carpento, pro salvatione agrorum et vinearum suarum,* misero gentilitatis more
deferrent,* adfuit supradictus Simplicius episcopus, haud procul adspiciens
cantantes atque psallentes ante hoc simulachrum, gemitumque pro stultitia plebis
ad Deum emittens ait : illumina quaeso, Domine, oculos hujus populi, ut
cognoscat, quia simulachrum Berecynthiae nihil est ! et facto signo crucis contra
protinus simulachrum in terram ruit.   Ac defixa solo animalia, quae plaustrum
hoc quo vehebatur trahebant, moveri non poterant.   Stupet vulgus innumerum,
et *deam laesam* omnis caterva conclamat ; *immolantur victimae,* animalia
verberantur, sed moveri non possunt.   Tunc quadringenti de illa stulta
multitudine viri conjuncti simul ajunt ad invicem : si virtus est ulla deitatis,
erigatur sponte, jubeatque boves, qui telluri sunt stabiliti, procedere ; certe si
moveri nequit, nihil est deitatis in ea.   Tunc accedentes, et *immolantes unum
de pecoribus,* cum viderent deam suam nullatenus posse moveri, relicto
gentilitatis errore, inquisitoque antistite loci, conversi ad unitatem ecclesiae,
cognoscentes veri Dei magnitudinem, sancto sunt baptismate consecrati.'
Compare the Legenda aurea cap. 117, where a festum *Veneris* is mentioned.

in the black lake,[1] must have arisen, gross as the perversion may
be, out of the account in Tacitus, who makes the goddess, when
satiated with the converse of men, *disappear in the lake* with her
attendants. But there are no other local features to turn the scale
in its favour ;[2] and the Danish islands in the Baltic have at least
as good a claim to have been erewhile the sacred seat of the
goddess.

We have yet more names for the earth-goddess, that demand
investigation: partly Old Norse, partly to be gathered from the
Romans.   In the Skáldskaparmál, p. 178, she is named both
Fiörgyn and *Hlóðyn*.

Of *Fiörgyn* I have treated already, p. 172 ; if by the side
of this goddess there could stand a god *Fiörgynn* and a neuter
common noun *fairguni*, if the idea of Thôr's mother at the same
time passes into that of the thundergod, it exactly parallels and
confirms a female *Nerthus* (Goth. Naírþus, gen. Naírþáus) by the
side of the masculine *Niörðr* (Nerthus), just as Freyja goes with
Freyr.   If it was not wrong to infer from Perkunas a mountain-
god *Fairguneis*, Lithuanian mythology has equally a goddess
Perkunatele.

Hlóðyn is derived in the same way as Fiörgyn, so that we may
safely infer a Goth. *Hlôþunja* and OHG. *Hluodunia*.   In Völuspâ
56 Thôrr is called ' mögr *Hlóðynjar*,' which is son of earth again ;
and Fornald. sög. 1, 469 says : *î Hlóðynjar skaut*.   In the ON.
language *hlóð* is a hearth,[3] the goddess's name therefore means
protectress of the fireplace; and our OHG. *hërd* (p. 251), beside solum
or terra, also denotes precisely focus, arula, fornacula, the hearth
being to us the very basis of a human habitation, a paternal Lar, so
to speak, corresponding to the mother earth.   The Romans also
worshipped a goddess of earth and of fire under the common name
of *Fornax*, dea *fornacalis*.[4]   But what is still more important to us,
there was discovered on Low Rhenish ground a stone, first kept at
Cleve and afterwards at Xanten, with the remarkable inscription:

---

[1] Deutsche sagen, num. 132.

[2] Of Hertha a proverb is said to be current in Pomerania : ' de *Hertha* gift
gras, und füllt schün und fass (barn and vessel),' Hall. allg. lit. z. 1823, p. 375).
But the un-Saxon rhyme of gras with fass (for fat) sufficiently betrays the
workmanship.   It is clumsily made up after the well-known rule of the farmer :
' Mai kühl und nass füllt scheunen und fass ' (see Suppl.).

[3] Liter. strues, ara, from hlaðan hlóð, struere, Gramm. 2, 10, num. 83.

[4] Ovid. fast. 2, 513.

DEAE HLUDANAE SACRVM C. TIBERIVS VERVS. *Hludana* is neither a Roman nor a Celtic goddess, but her name answers perfectly to that of the Norse divinity, and Sk. Thorlacius has the merit of having recognised and learnedly proved the identity of the two.[1] In this inscription I see striking evidence of the oneness of Norse and German mythology. Thorlacius, not without reason, compares the name with *Λητώ* and *Latona*. Might not *Hlôrriði*, an epithet of Thôrr the son of Hlôðyn, be explained as *Hlôðriði*?

2. TANFANA. NEHALENNIA.

Another goddéss stands wrapt in thicker darkness, whom Tacitus calls *Tanfana*, and a stone inscription *Tamfana* (TAMFANAE SACRUM, p. 80). We are sure of her name, and the termination *-ana* is the same as in Hludana and other fem. proper names, Bertana, Rapana, Madana. The sense of the word, and with it any sure insight into the significance of her being, are locked up from us.

We must also allude briefly to the Belgian or Frisian dea *Nehalennia*, about whose name several inscriptions of like import[2] remove all doubt; but the word has also given rise to forced and unsatisfying interpretations. In other inscriptions found on the lower part of the Rhine there occur compounds, whose termination (*-nehis, -nehabus*, dat. plurals fem.) seems to contain the same word that forms the first half of Nehalennia; their plural number appears to indicate nymphs rather than a goddess, yet there also hangs about them the notion of a mother (see ch. XVI, the Walachuriun).

3. (ISIS).

The account in Tacitus of the goddess *Isis* carries us much farther, because it can be linked with living traditions of a cultus that still lingered in the Mid. Ages. Immediately after mentioning the worship of Mercurius, Hercules, and Mars, he adds (cap. 9): Pars Suevorum et *Isidi* sacrificat. Unde causa et origo peregrino

---

[1] Antiq. bor. spec. 3, Hafn. 1782. Conf. Fiedler, gesch. und alt. des untern Germaniens, 1, 226. Steiner's cod. inscr. Rheni no. 632. Gotfr. Schütze, in his essay De dea Hludana, Lips. 1748, perceived the value of the stone, but could not discern the bearings of the matter.

[2] Montfaucon ant. expl. 2, 443. Vredii hist. Flandr. 1, xliv. Mém. de l'acad. celt. 1, 199—245. Mone, heidenth. 2, 346.

sacro, parum comperi, nisi quod *signum* ipsum, *in modum liburnae figuratum*, docet advectam religionem. The importation from abroad can hardly consist in the name *Isis*, seeing that Mercury, Mars, Hercules, names that must have sounded equally un-German, raised no difficulty ; what looked foreign was the symbol, the figure of a *ship*, reminding the writer of the Roman *navigium Isidis.*

When spring had set in, and the sea, untraversed during winter, was once more navigable, the Greeks and Romans used to hold a solemn procession, and present a *ship* to Isis. This was done on the fifth of March (III non. Mart.), and the day is marked in the kalendarium rusticum as *Isidis navigium.*[1] The principal evidence is found in Apuleius and Lactantius,[2] two writers who are later than Tacitus, but the custom must have reached back to a much older date. On Alexandrian coins Isis appears walking by the side of Pharus, unfurling a sail.

Say that from Egypt the worship of Isis had penetrated to Greece, to Rome, how are we to imagine, that in the first century, or before, it had got itself conveyed to one particular race inhabiting the heart of Germany? It must have been a similar cultus, not the same, and perhaps long established amongst other Germans as well.

I will here draw attention to a strange custom of a much later time, which appears to me to be connected with this. About the year 1133, in a forest near Inda (in Ripuaria), a *ship* was built, set upon wheels, and *drawn about the country* by men who were yoked to it, first to Aachen (Aix), then to Maestricht, where mast and sail were added, and up the river to Tongres, Looz and so on, every-where with crowds of people assembling and escorting it. Where-ever it halted, there were *joyful shouts, songs of triumph and dancing*

---

[1] Gesner, script. rei rust., ed. Lips. 1773. 1, 886 ; so also in the Calend. vallense, and in the Cal. lambec. (Graevii thes. 8, 98).

[2] Apuleii met. lib. 11 (Ruhnken p. 764-5) : Diem, qui dies ex ista nocte nascetur, aeterna mihi nuncupavit religio ; quo sedatis hibernis tempestatibus et lenitis maris procellosis fluctibus, navigabili jam pelago *rudem dedicantes carinam* primitias commeatus libant mei sacerdotes. Id sacrum sollicita nec profana mente debebis operiri ; nam meo monitu sacerdos in ipso procinctu pompae roseam manu dextra sistro (Egyptian timbrel) cohaerentem gestabit coronam. Incontanter ergo dimotis turbulis alacer continuare pompam meam, volentia fretus ; et de proximo dementer velut manum sacerdotis deosculabundus rosis decerptis, pessimae mihique detestabilis dudum belluae istius corio te protinus exue. Lactantius, instit. 1, 27 : Certus dies habetur in fastis, quo *Isidis navigium* celebratur, quae res docet illam non tranasse, sed navigasse.

round the ship kept up till far into the night. The approach of the ship was notified to the towns, which opened their gates and went out to meet it.

We have a detailed, yet not complete, report of it in Rodulfi chronicon abbatiae S. Trudonis, lib. xi., which on account of its importance I will here insert, from Pertz 12, 309 seq.:

Est genus mercenariorum, quorum officium est ex lino et lana texere telas, hoc procax et superbum super alios mercenarios vulgo reputatur, ad quorum procacitatem et superbiam humiliandam et propriam injuriam de eis ulciscendam pauper quidam rusticus ex villa nomine Inda[1] hanc diabolicam excogitavit technam. Accepta a judicibus fiducia et a levibus hominibus auxilio, qui gaudent jocis et novitatibus, *in proxima silva navem composuit*, et eam *rotis suppositis affigens vehibilem super terram effecit*, obtinuit quoque a potestatibus, ut *injectis funibus textorum humeris* ex Inda Aquisgranum traheretur.[2] Aquis suscepta cum *utriusque sexus grandi hominum processione:* nihilominus a textoribus Trajectum [Maestricht] est provecta, ibi emendata, *malo veloque insignita* Tungris [Tongres] est inducta, de Tungris Los [Looz]. Audiens abbas (sancti Trudonis)[3] Rodulfus *navim* illam *infausto omine compactam* malaque solutam alite cum *hujusmodi gentilitatis studio* nostro oppido adventare, praesago spiritu hominibus praedicabat, ut ejus susceptione abstinerent, quia *maligni spiritus* sub hac ludificatione in ea traherentur, in proximoque seditio per eam moveretur, unde caedes, incendia rapinaeque fierent, et humanus sanguis multus funderetur. Quem ista declamantem omnibus diebus, quibus *malignorum spirituum* illud *simulacrum* loci morabatur, oppidani nostri audire noluerunt, sed eo studio et gaudio excipientes, quo perituri Trojani fatalem equum in medio fori sui dedicaverunt, statimque *proscriptionis sententiam* accipiunt villae textores, qui *ad profanas hujus simulacri excubias venirent tardiores.* Pape! Quis vidit unquam tantam (ut ita liceat latinisare) in rationalibus animalibus brutitatem? quis tantam in renatis in Christo *gentili-*

---

[1] Inden in the Jülich country, afterwards Cornelimünster, not far from Aix; conf. Pertz 1, 394. 488. 514. 592. 2, 299. 489.

[2] This of ships being built in a wood and *carried on men's shoulders* reminds one of Saxo Gram. p. 93, and of the 'Argo humeris travecta Alpes' (Pliny N.H. 3, 18; their being set on wheels, of Nestor's story about Oleg; conf. the ship of Frô above. [An inadvertence on the author's part : the ship is not 'carried,' but 'drawn by ropes thrown over the weavers' shoulders'.]

[3] St. Tron between Liège and Louvain.

tatem ? Cogebant sententia proscriptionis textores, nocte et die *navim stipare omni armaturae genere,* solicitasque ei excubias nocte et die continuare. Mirumque fuit, quod non cogebant eos ante navim *Neptuno* hostias immolare, de cujus naves esse solent regione, sed *Neptunus* eas *Marti* reservabat, quod postea multipliciter factum est.

Textores interim occulto sed praecordiali gemitu Deum justum judicem super eos vindicem invocabant, qui ad hanc ignominiam eos detrudebant, cum juxta rectam vitam antiquorum Christianorum et apostolicorum virorum manuum suarum laboribus viverent, nocte et die operantes, unde alerentur et vestirentur, liberisque suis idipsum providerent. Quaerebant et conquerebantur ad invicem lacrymabiliter, unde illis magis quam aliis mercenariis haec ignominia et vis contumeliosa, cum inter Christianos alia plura essent officia suo multum aspernabiliora, cum tamen nullum dicerent aspernabile, de quo Christianus posset se sine peccato conducere, illudque solum esset vitabile et ignobile quod immunditiam peccati contraheret animae, meliorque sit rusticus textor et pauper, quam exactor orphanorum et spoliator viduarum urbanus et nobilis judex. Cumque haec et eorum similia secum, ut dixi, lacrymabiliter conquererentur, concrepabant ante illud, nescio cujus potius dicam, *Bacchi* an *Veneris, Neptuni* sive *Martis,* sed ut verius dicam ante omnium *malignorum spirituum* execrabile domicilium genera diversorum *musicorum, turpia cantica* et religioni Christianae indigna *concinentium. Sancitum quoque erat a judicibus,* ut *praeter textores, quicumque ad tactum navi appropinquarent, pignus de collo eorum ereptum textoribus* relinquerent, nisi se ad libitum redimerent. Sed quid faciam ? loquarne an sileam ? utinam spiritus mendacii stillaret de labiis meis : sub fugitiva adhuc luce diei imminente luna *matronarum catervae* abjecto femineo pudore *audientes strepitum hujus vanitatis, passis capillis de stratis suis exiliebant, aliae seminudae, aliae simplice to͡ntum clamide circumdatae, chorosque ducentibus circa navim impudenter irrumpendo se admiscebant.* Videres ibi aliquando mille hominum animas sexus utriusque *prodigiosum et infaustum celeusma usque ad noctis medium* celebrare. Quando vero execrabilis illa chorea rumpebatur, emisso *ingenti clamore vocum inconditarum* sexus uterque hac illacque bacchando ferebatur ; quae tunc videres agere, nostrum est tacere et deflere, quibus modo contingit graviter luere. Istis tam nefandis factis *plus quam duo-*

decim diebus supradicto ritu celebratis, conferebant simul oppidani quid agerent amodo de *deducenda a se navi.*

Qui sanioris erant consilii, et qui eam *susceptam* fuisse dolebant, timentes Deum pro his quae facta viderant et audierant, et sibi pro his futura conjiciebant, *hortabantur ut comburatur* (combureretur) aut isto vel illo modo de medio tolleretur ; sed stulta quorundam coecitas huic salubri consilio contumeliose renitebatur. Nam *maligni spiritus, qui in illa ferebantur,* disseminaverant in populo, quod locus ille et inhabitantes *probroso nomine amplius notarentur, apud quos remansisse inveniretur.* Deducendam igitur eam ad villam, quae juxta nos est, Leugues decreverunt. Interea Lovaniensis dominus audiens de *daemonioso navis* illius *ridiculo,* instructusque a religiosis viris terrae suae de illo vitando et terrae suae arcendo *monstro,* gratiam suam et amicitiam mandat oppidanis nostris, commonefaciens eos humiliter, ut pacem illam quae inter illos et se erat reformata et sacramentis confirmata non infringerent, et inde praecipue illud *diaboli ludibrium* viciniae suae inferrent; quod si *ludum* esse dicerent, quaererent alium cum quo inde luderent. Quod si ultra hoc mandatum committerent, pacem praedictam in eum infringerent et ipse vindictam in eos ferro et igne exsequeretur. Id ipsum mandaverat Durachiensibus dominis, qui et homines ejus fuerant manuatim, et interpositis sacramentis et obsidibus datis sibi confoederati. Hoc cum jam tertio fecisset, spretus est tam ab oppidanis nostris quam Durachiensibus dominis. Nam propter peccata inhabitantium volebat Dominus mittere super locum nostrum ignem et arma Lovaniensium. Ad hanc igitur *plebeiam fatuitatem* adjunxit se dominus Gislebertus (advocatus abbatiae S. Trudonis) contra generis sui nobilitatem, *trahendamque* decrevit *navem* illam *terream* usque Leugues ultra Durachiensem villam, quod et fecit malo nostro omine cum omni oppidanorum nostrorum multitudine et ingenti *debacchantium vociferatione.* Leuguenses, oppidanis nostris prudentiores et Lovaniensis domini mandatis obsequentes, portas suas clauserunt et *infausti ominis monstrum intrare non permiserunt.*

Lovaniensis autem dominus precum suarum et mandatorum contemptum nolens esse inultum, diem constituit comitibus tanquam suis hominibus, qui neque ad primum, neque ad secundum, sed nec ad tertium venire voluerunt. Eduxit ergo contra eos et contra nos multorum multitudinis exercitum armatorum tam peditum quam militum. Nostro igitur oppido seposito, tanquam firmius munito et bellicosorum hominum pleno, primum impetum in Durachienses fecit, quibus viriliter resistentibus castellum, nescio quare, cum posset non obsedit, sed inter Leugues et Durachium pernoctavit. Cumque sequenti die exercitum applicare disponeret et ex quatuor partibus assultum faceret, habebat enim ingentem multitudinem, supervenit Adelbero Metensium primicerius filiorum Lovaniensis domini avunculus, cujus interventu, quia comitissa Durachiensis erat soror ejus, et Durachiense erat castellum sancti Lamberti, Lovaniensis dominus ab impugnatione cessavit et ab obsidione se amovit, promisso ei quod Durachienses paulo post ei ad justitiam suam educerentur. Et cum ista et alia de dominis et inter dominos tractarentur, pedites et milites per omnia nostra circumjacentia se diffuderunt, villas nostras, ecclesias, molendina et quaecumque occurrebant combustioni et perditioni tradentes, recedentes vero quae longe a nobis fuerant prout cuique adjacebant inter se diviserunt.

Obviously, throughout the narrative everything is put in an odious light; but the proceeding derives its full significance from this very fact, that it was so utterly repugnant to the clergy, and that they tried in every way to suppress it as a sinful and heathenish piece of work. On the other hand, the secular power had authorized the procession, and was protecting it; it rested with the several townships, whether to grant admission to the approaching ship, and the popular feeling seems to have ruled that it would be shabby *not to forward it on its way.*

Mere dancing and singing, common as they must have been on all sorts of occasions with the people of that time, could not have so exasperated the clergy. They call the ship 'malignorum spirituum simulacrum' and 'diaboli ludibrium,' take for granted it was knocked together 'infausto omine' and 'gentilitatis studio,' that 'maligni spiritus' travel inside it, nay, that it may well be called a ship of Neptune or Mars, of Bacchus or Venus; they must burn it, or make away with it somehow.

Probably among the common people of that region there still survived some recollections of an ancient heathen worship, which, though checked and circumscribed for centuries, had never yet been entirely uprooted. I consider this ship, travelling about the country, welcomed by streaming multitudes, and honoured with festive song and dance, to be the car of the god, or rather of that goddess whom Tacitus identifies with Isis, and who (like Nerthus) brought peace and fertility to mortals. As the car was covered up, so entrance to the interior of the ship seems to have been denied to men; there need not have been an image of the divinity inside. Her name the people had long ago forgotten, it was only the learned monks that still fancied something about Neptune or Mars, Bacchus or Venus: but to the externals of the old festivity the people's appetite kept returning from time to time. How should that 'pauper rusticus' in the wood at Inden have lighted on the thought of building a ship, had there not been floating in his mind recollections of former processions, perhaps of some in neighbouring districts?

It is worthy of note, that the *weavers*, a numerous and arrogant craft in the Netherlands, but hateful to the common herd, were compelled to draw the ship by ropes tied to their shoulders, and to guard it; in return, they could keep the rest of the people from coming too near it, and fine or take pledges from those who did so.[1]

Rodulf does not say what became at last of the 'terrea navis,' after it had made that circuit; it is enough for him to relate, how, on a reception being demanded for it and refused, heats and quarrels arose, which could only be cooled in open war. This proves the warm interest taken by contemporaries, fanned as it was to a flame for or against the festival by the secular and the clerical party.

There are traces to be found of similar *ship-processions* at the beginning of spring in other parts of Germany, especially in Swabia, which had then become the seat of those very Suevi of Tacitus (see Suppl.). A minute of the town-council of Ulm, dated St. Nicholas' eve, 1530, contains this prohibition: 'Item, there shall none, by day nor night, trick or disguise him, nor put on any carnival raiment, moreover shall keep him from the *going about* of the *plough* and *with ships* on pain of 1 gulden'.[2] The custom of *drawing the plough about* seems to have been the more widely spread, having

---

[1] Does the author imply that the favour of the peasantry, as opposed to artizans, makes it likely that this was a relic of the worship of Earth? Supposing even that the procession was that of the German Isis; Tacitus nowhere tells us what the functions of this Isis were, or that she 'brought peace and fertility'.—TRANS.

[2] Carl Jäger, Schwäb. städtewesen des MA. (Mid. Ages), 1, 525.

originally no doubt been performed in honour of the divinity from
whom a fruitful year and the thriving of crops was looked for.
Like the ship-procession, it was accompanied by dances and bonfires. Sebast. Frank, p. 51ᵃ of his Weltbuch: 'On the Rhine,
Franconia and divers other places, the young men do gather all the
dance-maidens and *put them in a plough*, and draw their piper, who
sitteth on the plough piping, into the water; in other parts they
draw a *fiery plough* kindled with a fire very artificial made thereon,
until it fall to wrack.' Enoch Wiedemann's chronik von Hof tells
how 'On Shrove-Tuesday evil-minded lads *drove a plough about*,
yoking to it such damsels as did not pay ransom; others went
behind them sprinkling chopped straw and sawdust.' (Sächs.
provinz. bl. 8, 347.) Pfeiffer, chron. lips. lib. 2, § 53: 'Mos erat
antiquitus Lipsiae, ut liberalibus (feast of Liber or Bacchus, *i.e.*,
carnival) personati juvenes per vicos oppidi *aratrum circum
ducerent*, puellas obvias per lasciviam ad illius jugum accedere
etiam repugnantes cogerent, hoc veluti ludicro poenam expetentes
ab iis quae *innuptae* ad eum usque diem mansissent'.[1] On these
and similar processions, more details will be given hereafter; I only
wish at present to shew that the driving of the *plough* and that of
the *ship* over the country seem both to rest on the same old-
heathen idea, which after the dislodgement of the gods by christianity could only maintain itself in unintelligible customs of the
people, and so by degrees evaporate: namely, on the visible manifestation of a beneficent benign divinity among men, who everywhere approached it with demonstrations of joy, when in springtime
the soil was loose again and the rivers released from ice, so that
agriculture and navigation could begin anew.[2] In this way the

[1] Scheffer's Haltaus, 202. Hans Sachs also relates I. 5, 508ᵃ, how the
maids who *had not taken men*, were forced *into the plough* (see Suppl.).

[2] To this day, in the churches of some villages of Holstein, largely inhabited by seamen, there hang *little ships*, which in springtime, when navigation
re-opens, are decorated with ribbons and flowers: quite the Roman custom in
the case of Isis (p. 258). We also find at times *silver ships* hung up in churches,
which voyagers in stress of weather have vowed in case of a safe arrival home;
an old instance of this I will borrow from the Vita Godehardi Hildesiensis:
Fuit tunc temporis in Trajectensi episcopatu vir quidam arti mercatoriae dedi-
tus, qui frequenter mare transiret; hic quodam tempore maxima tempestate in
medio mari deprehenditur, ab omnibus conclamatur, et nil nisi ultimus vitae
terminus timetur. Tandem finito aliquanto tempore auxilium beati Godehardi
implorabant, et *argenteam navim* delaturos, si evaderent, devoverunt. Hos in
ecclesia nostra *navim argenteam* deferentes postea vidimus (in King Lothair's
time). In a storm at sea, sailors take vows: E chi dice, *una nave vo far fare*, e
poi portarla in Vienna al gran barone; Buovo d'Antona 5, 32. The Lapps at

Sueves of Tacitus's time must have done honour to their goddess by carrying her ship about. The forcing of unmarried young women to take part in the festival is like the constraint put upon the weavers in Ripuaria, and seems to indicate that the divine mother in her progress at once looked kindly on the bond of *love* and *wedlock*, and punished the backward ; in this sense she might fairly stand for Dame Venus, Holda and Frecke.

The Greeks dedicated a ship not only to Isis, but to *Athene*. At the Panathenæa her sacred peplos was conveyed by ship to the Acropolis : the *ship*, to whose mast it was suspended as a sail, was built on the Kerameikos, and moved on dry land by an underground mechanism, first to the temple of Demeter and all round it, past the Pelasgian to the Pythian, and lastly to the citadel. The people followed in solemnly ordered procession.[1]

We must not omit to mention, that Aventin, after transforming the Tacitean Isis into a *frau Eisen*, and making iron (eisen) take its name from her, expands the account of her worship, and in addition to the little ship, states further, that on the death of her father (Hercules) she travelled through all countries, came to the German king Schwab, and staid for a time with him ; that she taught him the forging of iron, the sowing of seed, reaping, grinding, kneading and baking, the cultivation of flax and hemp, spinning, weaving and needle work, and that the people esteemed her a holy woman.[2] We shall in due time investigate a goddess *Zisa*, and her claims to a connexion with Isis.

4. HOLDA, HOLLE.

Can the name under which the Suevi worshipped that goddess

yule-tide offer to their jauloherra small *ships* smeared with reindeer's blood, and hang them on trees ; Högström, efterretninger om Lapland, p. 511. These votive gifts to saints fill the place of older ones of the heathen time to gods, as the voyagers to Helgoland continued long to respect Fosete's sanctuary (p. 231). Now, as *silver ploughs* too were placed in churches, and later in the Mid. Ages were even demanded as dues, these *ships* and *ploughs* together lend a welcome support to the ancient worship of a maternal deity (see Suppl.).

[1] Philostr. de vitis sophist. lib. 2 cap. 1, ed. Paris. 1608, p. 549.

[2] So Jean le Maire de Belges in his Illustrations de Gaule, Paris, 1548, bk. 3 p. xxviii : 'Au temps duquel (Hercules Allemannus) la deesse *Isis*, royne d'Egypte, veint en Allemaigne et montra au rude peuple l'usaige de mouldre la farine et faire du pain.' J. le Maire finished his work in 1512, Aventin not till 1522 ; did they both borrow from the spurious Berosus that came out in the 15th century ? Hunibald makes a queen *Cambra*, who may be compared with the Langobardic Gambara, introduce the arts of building, sowing and weaving (see Suppl.).

whom the Romans identified with Isis—may not at least one of her secondary names—have been *Holda?* The name has a purely Teutonic meaning, and is firmly grounded in the living traditions of our people to this day.

Holdâ is the kind, benignant, merciful goddess or lady, from hold (propitius), Goth. hulþs (Luke 18, 13; root, hilþan halþ hulþun, to bend, bow), ON. hollr; the Gothic form of it would be *Hulþô.* For the opposite notion of a malignant diabolic being, Ulphilas employs both the fem. *unhulþô* and the masc. *unhulþa,* from which I infer a *hulþa* by the side of *hulþô :* one more confirmation of the double sex running through the idea of these divinities. It is true, such a by-name could be shared by several gods or spirits. Notker in the Capella 81 renders verus genius by 'mîn wâre *holdo'.* And in MHG. parlance, *holde* (fem. and masc.) must have been known and commonly used for ghostly beings. Albrecht of Halberstadt, in translating Ovid's Metamorphoses, uses *wazzerholde* (gen. -en) for nymph; rhyme has protected the exact words from corruption in Wikram's poetic paraphrase.[1] In the largely expanded Low German version of the Ship of Fools (Narragonia, Rostock 1519; 96ᵃ) we find the following passage which is wanting in the HG. text: 'Mannich narre lövet (believeth) an vogelgeschrei, und der *guden hollen* (bonorum geniorum) gunst'. Of more frequent occurrence is the MHG. *unholde* (fem.), our modern *unhold* (masc.), in the sense of a dark, malign, yet mighty being.

The earliest example of the more restricted use of the name *Holda* is furnished by Burchard, bp. of Worms, p. 194ᵃ:[2] Credidisti

---

[1] Frankf. 1631; 4, 171ᵃ von einer wazzerholden, rh. solden; 176ᵃ wazzerholde, rh. solde.

[2] If, in the inscription 'deae *Hludanae'* quoted p. 257, we might by a slight transposition substitute *Huldanae,* this would be even more welcome than the analogy to ON. Hlôðyn, it would be the most ancient evidence for *Hulda,* supported as she already is by the Goth. *unhulþô* and the OHG. female name *Holda,* a rare one, yet forthcoming in Schannat, trad. fuld. no. 445; also *Holdasind* in Graff 4, 915. Schütze's treatise De dea Hludana first appeared Lips. 1741; and when Wolf (in Wodana, p. 50) mentions a Dutch one De dea *Huldea,* Trajecti 1746, if that be really the title, this can be no other than a very tempting conjecture by Cannegieter founded on our 'Hulda' which occurs in Eccard. A Latin dative *Huldanae* would mean our weak form, OHG. Holdûn, AS. Holdan, just as Berta, Hildegarda are in Latin docs. inflected Bertanae, Hildegardanae; though there may also have sprung up a nom. Bertana, Huldana. So the dat. Tanfanae too would lead us to at all events a German nom. *Tanfa,* and cut short all the attempts to make out of -fana a Celtic word or the Latin fanum. *Tanfa* suggests an ON. man's name *Danpr,* or the OHG.

ut aliqua femina sit, quae hoc facere possit, quod quaedam a diabolo deceptae se affirmant necessario et ex praecepto facere debere, id est cum daemonum turba in similitudinem mulierum transformata, quam vulgaris stultitia *Holdam* (al. *unholdam*) vocat, certis noctibus equitare debere super quasdam bestias, et in eorum se consortio annumeratam esse. The remarkable varia lectio '*unholda*' is taken from the Cod. vindob. univ. 633. Burchard has here put the German word in the place of the more usual ' *Diana* paganorum dea,' who in other passages is named in a like sense and in the same connexion. [A still earlier notice of Holda is found in Walafrid Strabo, see Suppl.]

In popular legends and nursery-tales, *frau Holda* (Hulda, Holle,[1] Hulle, frau Holl) appears as a superior being, who manifests a kind and helpful disposition towards men, and is never cross except when she notices 'disorder in household affairs. None of the German races appear to have cherished these oral traditions so extensively as the Hessians and Thuringians (that Worms bishop was a native of Hesse). At the same time, dame Holle is found as far as the Voigtland,[2] past the Rhön mts in northern Franconia,[3] in the Wetterau up to the Westerwald,[4] and from Thuringia she crosses the frontier of Lower Saxony. Swabia, Switzerland, Bavaria, Austria, North Saxony and Friesland do not know her by that name.

From what tradition has still preserved for us,[5] we gather the following characteristics. *Frau Holle* is represented as a being *of the sky*, begirdling the earth : when it snows, she is making her

root damph ; granted a change of F into CH or TH [*f* has become *ch* in sachte, nichte, achter, ruchtbar or ruchbar, &c.], there would arise yet further possibilities, *e.g.* a female name *Tancha* (grata) would correspond to the OHG. masc. Dancho (gratus) Graff 5, 169 ; conf. Dankrât = Gibicho, Haupt's zeitschr. 1, 573.—I am not convinced of Huldana, and confess that *Hludana* may also maintain itself, and be explained as *Hlûda* (clara, praeclara) ; the weight of other arguments must turn the scale. Among these however, the use of gute *holden* and *hollar* vættir (Saem. 240[b]) for spirits, and of *holl* regin (Saem. 60[a]) for gods, is especially worthy of notice. In ON. the adj. hollr had undergone assimilation (Goth. hulþs, OHG. hold), while the proper name *Huldr* retained the old form ; for to me the explanation huldr = occultus, celatus, looks very dubious.

[1] Holle from Hulda, as Folle from Fulda.
[2] Jul. Schmidt's Reichenfels p. 152.
[3] Reinwald, Henneb. id. 1, 68. 2, 62. Schmeller 2, 174.
[4] Schmidt's Westerwäld. idiot. 73. 341.
[5] Kinderm. no. 24. Deutsche sagen, nos. 4—8. Falkenstein's Thur. chronica 1, 165-6 (see Suppl.).

bed, and the feathers of it fly.[1] She stirs up *snow*, as Donar does
rain: the Greeks ascribed the production of snow and rain to their
Zeus: Διὸς ὄμβρος, Il. 5, 91. 11, 493 as well as νιφάδες Διός, Il. 19,
357; so that Holda comes before us as a goddess of no mean rank.[2]
The comparison of snowflakes to feathers is very old; the Scythians
pronounced the regions north of them inaccessible, because they
were filled with feathers (Herod. 4, 7. conf. 31). Holda then must
be able to move through the air, like dame Herke.

She loves to haunt the *lake* and *fountain ;* at the hour of noon
she may be seen, a fair white lady, *bathing* in the flood and
disappearing ; a trait in which she resembles Nerthus. Mortals,
to reach her dwelling, pass through the well ; conf. the name
wazzerholde.[3]

Another point of resemblance is, that she *drives about in a
waggon.* She had a linchpin put in ít by a peasant whom she
met ; when he picked up the chips, they were gold.[4] Her annual
progress, which, like those of Herke and Berhta, is made to fall
between Christmas and Twelfth-day, when the supernatural has
sway,[5] and wild beasts like the wolf are not mentioned by their
names, brings *fertility* to the land. Not otherwise does ' Derk with
the boar,' that Freyr of the Netherlands (p. 214), appear to *go his
rounds* and look after the ploughs. At the same time Holda, like
Wuotan, can also ride on the winds, clothed in terror, and she, like
the god, belongs to the ' wütende heer '. From this arose the
fancy, that *witches* ride in Holla's company (ch. XXXIV, snow-

---

[1] Dame Holle shakes her bed, Modejourn. 1816, p. 283. They say in
Scotland, when the first flakes fall : The men o' the East are pyking their
geese, and sending their feathers here awa' there awa'. In Prussian Samland,
when it snows : The angels shake their little bed ; the flakes are the down-
feathers, but many drop past, and get down to our earth.

[2] As other attributes of Holda have passed to Mary, we may here also
bring into comparison the *Maria ad nives,* notre dame *aux neiges,* whose feast was
held on Aug. 5 ; on that day the lace-makers of Brussels pray to her, that their
work may keep as white as snow. In a folk-song of Bretagne : Notre dame
Marie, sur votre trône de *neige !* (Barzas breiz 1, 27). May not the otherwise
unintelligible Hildesheim legend of Hillesnee (DS. no. 456) have arisen out of
a *Holde snî ?*

[3] If the name *brunnenhold* in the Märchenbuch of Alb. Ludw. Grimm 1,
221 is a genuine piece of tradition, it signifies a fountain-sprite. [Newborn
babes are fetched by the nurse out of *dame Holle's pond ;* Suppl.]

[4] A similar legend in Jul. Schmidt's Reichenfels p. 152.

[5] This must be a purely heathen view. I suppose the christian sentiment
was that expressed by Marcellus in Hamlet i. 1 : ' no spirit dares stir abroad,
the nights are wholesome, &c. '.—TRANS.

wives); it was already known to Burchard, and now in Upper Hesse and the Westerwald, *Holle-riding, to ride with Holle*, is equivalent to a witches' ride.[1] Into the same 'furious host,' according to a wide-spread popular belief, were adopted the souls of *infants dying unbaptized*; not having been christian'd, they remained heathen, and fell to heathen gods, to Wuotan or to Hulda.

The next step is, that Hulda, instead of her divine shape, assumes the appearance of an *ugly old woman*, long-nosed, big-toothed, with bristling and thick-matted hair. ' He's had a jaunt with Holle,' they say of a man whose hair sticks up in tangled disorder; so *children* are frightened with her or her equally hideous train:[2] 'hush, there's *Hulle-betz* (-bruin), *Hulle-pöpel* (-bogie) coming.' *Holle-peter*, as well as Hersche, Harsche, Hescheklas, Ruprecht, Rupper (ch. XVII, house-sprites), is among the names given to the muffled servitor who goes about in Holle's train at the time of the winter solstice. In a nursery-tale (Märchen no. 24) she is depicted as an *old witch* with *long teeth ;* according to the difference of story, her kind and gracious aspect is exchanged for a dark and dreadful one.

Again, *Holla* is set before us as a *spinning*-wife; the cultivation of flax is assigned to her. Industrious maids she presents with *spindles*, and spins their reels full for them over night; a slothful spinner's distaff she *sets on fire*, or *soils* it.[3] The girl whose spindle dropt into her fountain, she rewarded bountifully. When she

[1] Estor's oberh. idiot., sub v.

[2] Erasm. Alberus, fable 16 : ' Es kamen auch zu diesem heer Viel weiber die sich forchten sehr (were sore afraid), Und trugen *sicheln* in der hand, *Fraw Hulda* hat sie ausgesandt.' Luther's Expos. of the Epistles, Basel 1522 fol. 69[a] : ' Here cometh up *dame Hulde* with the *snout* (potznase, botch-nose), to wit, nature, and goeth about to gainsay her God and give him the lie, hangeth her old ragfair about her, the *straw-harness* (stroharnss); then falls to work, and scrapes it featly on her *fiddle*.' He compares nature rebelling against God to the heathenish Hulda with the frightful nose (Oberlin, sub v. potzmänn-chen), as she enters, muffled up in straw and frippery, to the fiddle's playing.

[3] Brückner, Contrib. to the Henneberg idioticon, p. 9, mentions a popular belief in that part of Franconia : ' On the high day comes the *Hollefrau* (Hollefra, Hullefra), and *throws in reels ;* whoever does not spin them full, she breaks their necks,' (conf. infra *Berhta* and *Berhtolt* and the *Devil*). ' On the high day she is *burnt*,' which reminds one of ' Carrying Death out' in Teutonic and Slav countries, and ' Sawing the old woman' in Italy and Spain. By the addition of -frau after the name (conf. gaue fru, p. 253) we perceive its originally adjective character. Cod. pal. 355[b] : ' ich wen, kain *schusel in kaim rocken* wart nie als hesslich als du bist,' I ween no scare-crow on a distaff was ever as ugly as thou.

enters the land at Christmas, all the *distaffs* are well stocked, and
left standing for her; by Carnival, when she turns homeward, all
spinning must be finished off, and the *staffs* are now kept out of
her sight (Superst. 683) ; if she finds everything as it should be,
she pronounces her blessing, and contrariwise her curse; the
formulas 'so many hairs, so many good years!' and 'so many
hairs, so many bad years!' have an oldworld sound. Apparently
two things have been run into one, when we are also told, that
during the 'twelve-nights' no flax must be left in the *diesse*, or
dame Holla will come.[1] The concealment of the implements
shows at the same time the sacredness of her holiday, which ought
to be a time of rest.[2] In the Rhön mts, they do no farm-work on
Hulla's Saturday, neither hoe, nor manure, nor 'drive the team a-
field '. In the North too, from Yule-day to New-year's day, neither
wheel nor windlass must go round (see Superst., Danish, 134; Suppl.).

This superintendence of agriculture and of strict order in the
household marks exactly the office of a *motherly deity*, such as we
got acquainted with in Nerthus and Isis. Then her special care of
flax and *spinning* (the main business of German housewives, who
are named after spindle and distaff,[3] as men are after sword and
spear), leads us directly to the ON. *Frigg*, Oðin's wife, whose being
melts into the notion of an earth-goddess, and after whom a
constellation in the sky, Orion's belt, is called *Friggjar rockr*,
Friggae colus. Though Icelandic writings do not contain this
name, it has remained in use among the Swedish country-folk
(Ihre, sub v. *Friggerock*). The constellation is however called
Mariärock, Dan. *Marirock* (Magnusen, gloss. 361. 376), the
christians having passed the same old idea on to Mary the
heavenly mother. The Greeks put spindle and distaff in the hands
of several goddesses, especially Artemis (χρυσηλάκατος, Il. 20, 70)
and her mother Leto, but also Athene, Amphitrite and the Nereids.
All this fits in with Holda, who is a goddess of the chase (the wild
host), and of water-springs.

---

[1] Braunschw. anz. 1760, no. 86 ; the *diesse* is the bundle of flax on the
dis-staff.
[2] This makes one think of Gertrude. The peasants' almanacks in
Carniola represent that *saint* by two little mice nibbling at the thread on a
spindle (vretenò), as a sign that there ought to be *no spinning* on her day. The
same holds good of the Russian *piatnitsa*, Friday (Kopitars rec. von Strahls
gel. Russland).
[3] RA. 163-8. 470. Women are called in AS. friðowebban, peace-weavers.

One might be tempted to derive dame Holda from a character in the Old Testament. In 2 Kings 22, 14 and 2 Chron. 34, 22 we read of a prophetess חֻלְדָּה Huleddah, Huldah, for which Luther puts *Hulda;* the Septuagint has 'Ολδά, the Vulgate *Olda,* but the Lat. Bible Viteb. 1529 (and probably others since) *Hulda,* following Luther, who, with the German Holda in his mind, thus domesticated the Jewish prophetess among his countrymen. Several times in his writings he brings up the old heathen life ; we had an instance a page or two back.[1] I do not know if any one before him had put the two names together; but certainly the whole conception of a dame Holda was not first drawn from the 'Olda' of the Vulgate, which stands there without any special significance; this is proved by the deep-rootedness of the name in our language, by its general application [as adj. and com. noun] to several kinds of spirits, and by the very ancient negative unholda.

Were it only for the kinship of the Norse traditions with our own, we should bid adieu to such a notion as that. True, the Eddic mythology has not a Holla answering to our Holda; but Snorri (Yngl. saga c. 16. 17) speaks of a wise woman (völva, seiðkona) named *Huldr,* and a later Icelandic saga composed in the 14th century gives a circumstantial account of the enchantress *Hulda,* beloved of Oðinn, and mother of the well-known half-goddesses Thorgerðr and Irpa.[2] Of still more weight perhaps are some Norwegian and Danish folk-tales about a wood or mountain wife *Hulla, Huldra, Huldre,* whom they set forth, now as young and lovely, then again as old and gloomy. In a blue garment and white veil she visits the pasture-grounds of herdsmen, and mingles in the dances of men ; but her shape is disfigured by a tail, which she takes great pains to conceal. Some accounts make her beautiful in front and ugly behind. She loves music and song, her lay has a doleful melody and is called *huldreslaat.* In the forests you see *Huldra* as an old woman clothed in gray, marching at the head of her flock, milkpail in hand. She is said to carry off people's unchristened infants from them. Often she appears, not alone, but as mistress or queen of the mountain-sprites, who are

---

[1] I believe Luther followed the Hebrew, merely dropping the final *h,* as he does in Jehova, Juda, &c.—TRANS.

[2] Müller's sagabibl. 1, 363—6.

called *huldrefolk*.[1] In Iceland too they know of this *Huldufôlk*, of
the *Huldumenn;* and here we find another point of agreement
with the popular faith of Germany, namely, that by the side of our
dame Holde there are also *holden, i.e.*, friendly spirits, a silent
subterranean people, of whom dame Holde, so to speak, is the
princess (see Suppl.). For this reason, if no other, it must be more
correct to explain the Norse name *Hulla, Huldra* from the ON.
hollr (fidus, fidelis, propitius) which is huld in Dan. and Swed., and
not from the ON. hulda (obscuritas) as referring to the subterranean
abode of the mountain-sprites. In Swedish folk-songs I find
' huldmoder, hulda moder' said of one's real mother in the same
sense as kära (dear) moder (Sv. vis. 1, 2, 9); so that huld must
have quite the meaning of our German word. It is likely that the
term huldufôlk was imported into the Icelandic tongue from the
Danish or Norwegian. It is harder to explain the R inserted in
the forms *Huldra, Huldre;* did it spring out of the plural form
hulder (boni genii, hollar vættir) ? or result from composition ?

The German *Holda* presides over spinning and agriculture, the
Norse *Hulle* over cattle-grazing and milking.

5. PERAHTA, BERCHTE.

A being similar to Holda, or the same under another name,
makes her appearance precisely in those Upper German regions
where Holda leaves off, in Swabia, in Alsace, in Switzerland, in
Bavaria and Austria.[2] She is called *frau Berchte, i.e.*, in OHG.
Perahta, the bright,[3] luminous, glorious (as Holda produces the
glittering snow): by the very meaning of the word a benign and
gladdening influence, yet she is now rarely represented as such ; as
a rule, the awe-inspiring side is brought into prominence, and she

---

[1] Details to be found in Müller's sagab. 1, 367-8. Hallager p. 48. Faye
pp. 39-43 and 10. 15. 25. 26. 36. Frigge, nytaarsgave for 1813, p. 85. Ström's
Söndmör 1, 538-59. Vilses Spydeberg 2, 419. Villes Sillejord. p. 230.
Asbiörnsen, passim.

[2] A portion of Franconia and Thuringia knows both *Berchta* and *Holda*,
there at all events is the boundary between the two. Matthesius, in his
Exposition of the gospels for feastdays, p. 22, names dame Hulda and *old*
Berchte side by side.

[3] Among the celebrated maidens of Menglöð is a *Biört* (Sæm. 111a),
Menglöð herself is called 'sû in sôlbiarta' (111b), and the father of her
betrothed Svipdagr Sôlbiartr (sun-bright, 112a). A Menglöð in a later story
appears to some one in a dream (Fornm. sög. 3, 222-3), and leaves him a
marvellous pair of gloves.

appears as a grim bugbear to frighten children with. In the stories of *dame Berchta* the bad meaning predominates, as the good one does in those of dame Holda; that is to say, the popular christian view had degraded Berchta lower than Holda. But she too is evidently one with Herke, Freke and some others (see Suppl.).

Where their identity comes out most plainly is in the fact that they all go their rounds at the same time, in the so-called 'twelfths' between Christmas and New-year. Berchta however has a particular day assigned her at the end of that period, which I never find named after Holda. And no less similar are their functions.

Berchta, like Holda, has the oversight of *spinners;* whatever spinning she finds unfinished the last day of the year, she spoils (Superst. 512). Her festival has to be kept with a certain traditional food, *gruel and fish.* Thôrr says he has had *sîldr* ok *hafra* (herrings and oats) for supper, Sæm. 75[a]; our *white lady* has prescribed the country folk a dish of *fish* and *oat-grits* for evermore, and is angry whenever it is omitted (Deutsche sagen, no. 267). The Thuringians in the Saalfeld country wind up the last day of the year with *dumplings* and *herrings.* Fish and farinaceous food were considered by christians the proper thing for a fast.[1]

The revenge taken by the wrathful *Berchta*, when she misses the fish and dumplings, has a quaint and primitive sound: whoever has partaken of other food on her day, she cuts his belly open, fills it with chopped straw, and sews up the gash with a *ploughshare* for a needle and an *iron chain* by way of thread (Superst. 525).[2]

---

[1] The Braunschw. anz. 1760, p. 1392, says *no leguminous plants* are to be eaten when dame Holla is going round in the 'twelve-nights'. Either a mistake, or to be understood of particular kinds of pulse.

[2] Almost the same is told in the Voigtland of the *Werre* or *dame Holle.* The *Werre*, on the holy eve of the high New-year, holds a strict inquiry whether all the *distaffs are spun off;* if they are not, she defiles the flax. And on that evening you must eat *polse*, a thick pap of flour and water prepared in a peculiar way; if any one omits it, she *rips his body open*, Jul. Schmidt, Reichenfels, p. 152. The name *Werra* (from her 'gewirrt,' tangled shaggy hair?) is found in Thom. Reinesius, Lect. var., Altenbg 1640, p. 579 (in the critical notes on Rhyakinus's, *i.e.* Andr. Rivinus or Bachmann's Liber Kiranidum Kirani, Lips. 1638): Nostrates hodieque petulantioribus et refractariis manducum aliquem cum ore hiante frendentem dentibus, aut furibundam silvescente coma, facie lurida, et cetero habitu terribilem cum comitatu maenadum *Werram* interminantur. Reinesius (1587-1667) came from Gotha, but lived at Hof in the Voigtland. A *werre* is also a noisome chirping insect of the cricket kind (Popowitsch 620). In MHG.: 'sæjet diu *Werre* (Discordia) ir sâmen dar,' sows her seed, Ms. 2, 251[b], conf. Troj. 385 (see Suppl.); and in

And the same threat is held out in other districts also (see Suppl.).

Börner's Folk-tales of the Orlagau (between the Saale and the Orle) furnish abundant details. At p. 153 : The night before Twelfthday, *Perchtha* always examines the spinning-rooms of the whole neighbourhood, she brings the spinners empty reels, with directions to spin them full within a very brief time, and if all she demands cannot be delivered, she punishes them by tangling and befouling the flax. On the same occasion she cuts open any one's body, that has not eaten *zemmede* [1] that day, takes out any other food he has had, and fills the empty space with hay or straw wisps and bricks, and at last sews his body up again, using a *ploughshare* for a needle, and for thread a *röhm chain*.—P. 159 : At Oppurg, the same night of the year, *Perchtha* found the spinning-room full of merrymaking guests, and *in a towering rage she handed in through the window twelve empty reels*, which were to be spun full to the rim within an hour, when she would come back ; one quarter of an hour had passed after another in fearful expectation, when a saucy girl ran up to the garret, reached down a roll of tow, and wrapped it round the empty reels, then they spun two or three thicknesses of thread over the tow, so that the reels looked full. Perchtha came, they handed over to her their finished work, and she walked off with it, shaking her head. (Conf. the similar story of the *white manikin* in Bader, p. 369).—P. 167 : At Langendembach lived an old spinning-wife, who swiftly wound the thread all the winter through, and did not so much as leave off on Twelfthday-eve, though son and daughter-in-law warned her : ' If Perchtha comes, it will go hard with you '. ' Heyday ! ' was her answer, ' Perchtha brings me no shirts, I must spin them myself.' After a while *the window is pushed open, Perchtha looks into the room*, and throws some empty

---

Selphartes regel (Wackernagel's lb. 903), there is exhibited, together with bruoder Zornli and bruoder Ergerli, a bruoder *Werra*, ' der sîn herze mit weltlichen dingen also *beworren* hat (has so entangled his heart with worldly things), daz da niht mê in mag '. And that notion of *tangled thread and hair*, which prevails about Bertha and Holda, may after all be akin to this. On L. Zurich she is called de *Chlungere*, because she puts chlungel (knots, lumps) in the unfinished yarn of slothful maidens, Alb. Schott, Deutsche colonien in Piedmont, p. 282. In Bavaria and German Bohemia, *Berhta* is often represented by St. *Lucia*, though her day comes on Dec. 13. Frau *Lutz* cuts the belly open, Schmeller 2, 532. Jos. Rank, Böhmerwald, p. 137. Conf. the *Lusse* in Sweden, Wieselgren. 386-7.

[1] Made of flour and milk or water, and baked in a pan : fasting fare, evidently.

spools to her, which she must have back, spun full, in an hour's time. The spinner took heart of grace, spun a few rounds on each spool for dear life, and *threw* them, one and all, *into the brook* that ran past the house (and by that, Perchtha seems to have been appeased).—P. 173 : As a miner was returning from Bucha to Könitz on Perchtha's night, she came up to him at the cross-roads, and demanded with threats, that he should *put a wedge in her waggon.* He took his knife, cut the wedge as well as he could, and fitted it into Perchtha's waggon, who made him a present of the *fallen chips.* He picked them up, and at home he drew gold out of every pocket in which he had put Perchtha's gifts.—P. 182 : Two peasants of Jüdewein, after stopping at the alehouse in Köstriz till late on Perchtha's eve, had gone but a little way, when *Perchtha* came driving in a waggon, and called to them to put a peg in the pole of her waggon. One of the men had a knife, and Perchtha supplied him with wood, the peg was let in, and the handy man carried home several pieces of money in his shoe as a reward.— P. 113 : Between Bucha and Wilhelmsdorf in the fruitful vale of the Saale, Perchtha queen of the *heimchen* had her dwelling of old ; at her command the heimchen had to water the fields of men, while she worked underground with her plough. At last the people fell out with her, and she determined to quit the country ; on Perchtha's eve the ferryman at Altar village received notice to be ready late in the night, and when he came to the Saale bank, his eyes beheld a *tall stately dame* surrounded by weeping children, and demanding to be *ferried over.* She stept into the craft, the little ones dragged a *plough* and a number of other tools in, loudly lamenting that they had to leave that lovely region. Arrived at the other side, Perchtha bade the boatman cross once more and fetch the heimchen that had been left behind, which under compulsion he did. She in the meantime had been *mending the plough,* she pointed to the *chips,* and said to the ferryman, ' There, take that to reward thy trouble '. Grumbling, he pocketed three of the chips, and at home flung them on the window-shelf, and himself, ill at ease, into bed. In the morning, three gold-pieces lay where he had thrown the chips. The memory of *Perchtha's passage* is also preserved at Kaulsdorf on the Saale, and at Köstriz on the Elster, not far from Gera.—P. 126 : Late one night, the master wheel-wright at Colba was coming home from Oppurg, where he had been to work; it was the eve of the Three-kings (Twelfthday), and on the bank of the rivulet Orla he came upon *Perchtha*, her *broken plough* surrounded by weeping *heimchen*. 'Hast thou a hatchet with thee, so help me mend!' she cried to the terrified traveller. He gave what help he could, but the *fallen chips* offered him for wages he would not touch: 'I have plenty of them at home,' says he. When he got home, he told what had happened to him, and while his people shook their heads incredulously, he pulled off one of his shoes, which something had got into, that hurt his foot, and out rolled a bright new gold-piece. A twelvemonth passed, and one of his men, who had heard him tell the tale, set out on Perchtha's night, and waited by the Orla, just where his master had met Perchtha; in a little while, on she came with her *infant train*: 'What seekest thou here at this hour?' she cried in anger, and when he stammered out an answer, she continued: 'I am better provided with tools this time, so take thou thy due!' and with those words she dug her hatchet into the fellow's shoulder. The same story is repeated near Kaulsdorf at a part of the brook which is called the water over the way, at Presswitz near the Saal-house, and on the sandhill between Pössneck and the forester's lodge of Reichenbach. Below the Gleitsch, a curiously shaped rock near Tischdorf, the story varies in so far, that there *Perchtha along with the heimchen was driving a waggon,* and had just broken the axle, when she fell in with a countryman, who helped her out with a makeshift axle, and was paid in chips, which however he disdained, and only carried a piece home in his shoe.—P. 133 : A spinning-girl walked over from the Neidenberg during that night, she had done every bit of her spinning, and was in high spirits, when *Perchtha* came marching up the hill towards her, with a great troop of the *heimchen-folk,* all children of one sort and size, one set of them toiling to push a heavy *plough,* another party loaded with farming-tools; they loudly complained that they had no longer a home. At this singular procession the spinner began to laugh out loud, *Perchtha enraged* stept up to the giddy thing, *blew upon her,* and struck her blind on the spot. The poor girl had a trouble to find her way into the village, she led a wretched life, could no longer work, but sat mournful by the wayside begging. When the year was past and Perchtha visited Altar again, the blind one, not knowing one from another, asked an alms of the high dame as she

swept by ; Perchtha spoke graciously : ' Here last year I blew a
pair of lights out, this year I will blow them in again'. With these
words she blew into the maid's eyes, which immediately began to
see again. The same legend is found in the so-called Sorge, near
Neustadt on the Orla. Touching stories of the weeping children,
who tramp along in Perchtha's great troop, will be given when we
come to treat minutely of the ' wütende heer '. (See Suppl.).

To these significant traditions of Thuringia, others can be added
from Bavaria and Austria. In the mountain district about Trauen-
stein (Up. Bavaria, opposite Salzburg) they tell the children on the
eve of Epiphany, that if they are naughty, *Berche* will come and cut
their bellies open. *Greasy cakes* are baked that day, and the
workmen say you must grease your stomach well with them, so
that *dame Berche's knife* may glance off (Schm. 1, 194). Is that the
reason why she is called *wild Bertha, iron Bertha ?* Crusius, Ann.
Suev. p. 2, lib. 8, cap. 7, p. 266, relates, as his explanation of the
origin of the name, that Henry IV. bestowed privileges on the city
of Padua : Inde, in signa libertatis, armato carrocio uti coeperunt in
bello, *Bertha* nominato. Hinc dictum ortum puto, quo terrentur
inquieti pueri, ' Schweig, oder die *eiserne Bertha* kommt ! ' [1] In
other places, Franconian and Swabian, she is named *Hildaberta*
(apparently a combination of the two names Holda and Berta), and
Bildaberta ; with hair all shaggy she walks round the houses at
night, and tears the bad boys to pieces (see Suppl.).[2]

Dame Precht with the long nose is what Vintler calls her: and
even a MHG. poem, which in one MS. is entitled ' daz mære von
der Stempen,' has in another the heading ' von *Berchten mit der
langen nas* ' (Haupt's Altd. bl. 1, 105). It is only from the former
(with corrected spelling) that I am able to extract what has a
bearing on our subject :

nu merket reht waz (ich) iu sage :	Now mark aright what I you tell:
nâch wîhennaht am zwelften tage,	after Christmas the twelfth day,
nâch dem heilgen ebenwîhe [3]	after the holy New-year's day
(gotgeb, daz er uns gedîhe),	(God grant we prosper in it),
dô man ezzen solt ze nahte,	when they should eat supper

---

[1] Conf. Crusius p. 1, lib. 12, cap. 6, p. 329, where Bertha the mother of
Charles is meant. The Lombards called a carrocium *Berta* and *Berteciola*
(Ducange sub v.), perhaps the carriage of the travelling goddess or queen ?
[2] Joach. Camerarius, chronol. Nicephori, p. 129.
[3] Even-holy, equally-holy day, Scheffer's Haltaus, p. 68.

und man ze tische brâhte	and had to table brought
allez daz man ezzen solde,	all that they should eat,
swaz der wirt geben wolde	whatso the master would give,
dô sprach er zem gesinde	then spake he to his men
und zuo sîn selbes kinde :	and to his own child :
' ezzet hînte fast durch mîn bete,	' eat fast (hard) to night, I pray,
daz iuch die Stempe niht entrete.'	that the Stempe tread you not.'
daz kintlîn dô von forhten az,	The child then ate from fear,
er sprach: 'veterlîn, waz ist daz,	he said : ' father, what is this
daz du die *Stempen* nennest ?	that thou the Stempe callest ?
sag mir, ob dus erkennest.'	tell me, if thou it knowest.'
der vater sprach : 'daz sag ich dir,	The father said : ' this tell I thee,
du solt ez wol gelouben mir,	thou mayest well believe me,
ez ist so griuwelîch getân,	there is a thing so gruesome done,
daz ich dirz niht gesagen kan :	that I cannot tell it thee :
wan swer des vergizzet,	for whoso forgets this,
daz er nicht fast izzet,	so that he eats not fast,
ûf den kumt ez und trit in.'	on him it comes, and treads him.'

Here also children and servants are warned by the master of the
house to eat up clean all that is brought on the table, and are
threatened with a trampling from *Stempe*. This cognomen of
Berchte must have come from stamping (step, tap, thump, &c.), and
perhaps it ought to be spelt *Stempfe* (German stampfen, to stamp) ;
but in Bavaria there is a proper name *Stempo* (MB. 2, 280, anno
1130), not Stempho, and both stampen and stampfen seem to be
correct for trampling and squeezing, Ital. stampare : she is the
night hag, similar to alp and schrat [old scratch ?]. Add to this,
that in the Nordgau of Franconia, dame Holda is called the *Trempe*
(Döderlein, Antiq. nordg. 41), *i.e.*, the trampling racketing one ;
Stalder defines trämpeln as walking with short, measured steps
(tripping), and the Drut (night-goblin) approaches with soft foot-
fall ; at the same time, trampel, trampelthier, is a heavy clumsy
woman. Now, as S is occasionally added before an initial T, it is
surely not going too far, to connect Stempe with the more ancient
Tamfana, Tanfana, p. 257 (see Suppl.).

Martin of Amberg [1] calls her *Percht mit der eisnen nasen* (with

---

[1] His Gewissensspiegel (mid. of 14th cent.) is in two MSS. at Vienna
(Hoffm. pp. 335-6) ; conf. Schm. 4, 188. 216, and the Jahrb. der Berliner
gesellsch. für deutsche spr. 2, 63—65.

iron nose), and says that people leave meat and drink standing for her; which means a downright sacrifice.

In the mountains of Salzburg there is kept up to this day, in honour of the terrible *Perchtel*, a so called *Perchta-running, Perchta-leaping* at the time of the rauchnächte [incense-nights ?][1] In the Pinzgau, from 100 to 300 young fellows (styled the *Berchten)* will roam about in broad daylight in the oddest disguises, carrying cows' bells, and cracking whips.[2] In the Gastein valley the procession, headed by from 50 or 100 to 300 stout fellows, goes hopping and skipping from village to village, from house to house, all through the valley (Muchar, Gastein pp. 145-7). In the north of Switzerland, where in addition to *Berchtli* the softened form *Bechtli* or *Bechteli* is in use, *Bechteli's day* is the 2nd (or, if New-year's day falls on a Saturday, the 3rd) of January, and is honoured by the young people in general with social merrymakings ; they call the practice *berchteln, bechteln.* In the 16th century it was still the custom at Zürich, for men to intercept and press one another to take wine ; this was called ' conducting to *Berchtold* ' (Stald. 1, 150-6). There was thus a masculine *Bercht* or *Berchtolt,* related to Wuotan, as Berhta was to Freke ; and from this again there arose in Swabia a new feminine, *Brechtölterin, Prechtölterin* (Schmid, Schwäb. wtb. 93). In Alsace the *bechten* was performed by prentices and journeymen running from one house or room to another, and keeping up a racket (see passages in Oberlin, sub. v. Bechten). Cunrat of Dankrozheim says in his Namenbuch, composed 1435 : [3]

> darnauch so komet die milde *Behte,*
>
> die noch hat ein gar gross geslehte (great kindred).

He describes her as the *mild,* gracious to men, not as the terrible. *Berchtolt* however is in Swabian legend the *white mannikin,* who brings spools to be filled with spinning (Mone's anz. 8, 179), exactly like Berchta, p. 274 (see Suppl.).

And as a kind benevolent being she appears in many other descriptions, which undoubtedly reach far back into the Mid. Ages. The *white lady,* by her very name, has altogether the same meaning,

---

[1] This *Perchtenspringen* is like the *hexentusch* in the Böhmerwald, which, Jos. Rank p. 76-7 says, is performed at Whitsuntide, when young men and boys provide themselves with loud cracking whips, and chase all the witches out of houses, stables and barns.

[2] Journey through Upper Germany, p. 243. Schm. 1, 195.

[3] Ad. Walt. Strobel's beitr., Strasb. 1827, p. 123.

for peraht, berht or brecht, signifies bright, light, white.   This
white lady usually attaches herself to particular families, but even
then she keeps the name of *Berta, e.g.*, Berta of Rosenberg.   In
snow-white garments she shows herself by night in princely houses,
she rocks or dandles the babies, while their nurses sleep: she acts
the old *grandmother* or *ancestress* of the family (see Suppl.).

There is a good deal in the fact, that several women of that
name, who are famed in our national traditions, stand connected
with the ghostly *Berhta ;* they have been adopted out of the divine
legend into the heroic legend.   In Italy and France, a far distant
past is expressed by the phrase : 'nel tempo ove *Berta filava,*' when
B. span (Pentamerone.   Liebrecht 2, 259), 'au tems que la reine
Berthe filait :' the same idea still, of the spinning matron.[1]   *Berta,*
the daughter of king Flower and of Whiteflower, afterwards the
wife of king Pippin and mother of the great hero Charles,
she who in the MLG. poem of Flos is called both *Vredeling* and
Brehte (1555. 7825), does not belie her mythic origin.[2]   She is
called Berhte *mit dem fuoze* (foot), Flore 309; in French, Berthe *au
grand pied ;* and acc. to the Reali di Franza 6, 1 : ' Berta *del gran
pie,* perche ella aveva un pie un poco maggior dell altro, e quello
era il pie destro,' had the right foot larger.   The French poet Adenez
tries apparently to extenuate the deformity by making both her
feet large, he calls her 'Berte *as grans pies*' (Paris ed. LII. 78. 104);
so the Mid. Dutch, ' Baerte *met ten breden voeten,*' Florîs 3966.
But the one big foot is more genuine, as may be seen by the far

[1] I can produce another *spinning Bertha.*   The Vita S. Berthae Avenna-
censis in diœcesi Remensi (conf. Flodoardus 4, 47) says (Acta Sanctor., Maii p.
114[b]) : Quae dum lustraret situs loci illius, pervenit ad quendam hortum, in
quo erat fons mirae pulcritudinis.   Quem ut vidit Deo devota femina, minime
concupivit, sed possessoribus ipsius praedii sic locuta est : O fratres, hunc
fontem praedii vestri vendite mihi, et accepta digna pecunia cedite usibus
nostris.   Cui sic aiunt : En praesto sumus, si tamen detur pretium a nobis
taxatum.   Sancta autem, videntibus qui aderant, libram unam denariorum
posuit super lapidem qui erat super os ejusdem fontis, domini vero ac vendi-
tores receperunt aes.   Tunc sancta mater, Deo plena, *colo* quam manu tenebat
coepit *terram fodere,* et in modum sulci *rigam facere,* orans ac dicens : Ostende
nobis, Domine, misericordiam tuam, et salutare tuum da nobis ! Revertens
namque monasterium, colum eadem post se trahebat, tantaque abundantia
aquae eam sequebatur, ut ad usus omnes hominibus pertinentes sufficeret, sicut
usque hodie apparet.   Nomen quoque sancta mater fluviolo ipsi composuit
dicens : *Libra* vocaberis, quia una libra pro emptione tua data est.
[2] How firmly she is rooted, may be seen by her being the link that joins
the Carolingian legend to the Langobardic : she is mother of Carl, wife of
Pippin the son of Rother (4789), and daughter of Flore and Blancheflor, whose
name again contains the notion of whiteness.

more ancient tradition of a ' reine *Pédauque,* regina *pede aucae,*'
whose figure stands carved in stone on old churches.[1] It is apparently a *swan-maiden's* foot, which as a mark of her higher nature
she cannot lay aside (any more than Huldra her tail, or the devil
his horse hoof) ; and at the same time the spinning-woman's splay-
foot that worked the treadle, and that of the trampling dame
Stempe or Trempe. If we had older and minuter descriptions of
' frau Berhta ' in Germany, perhaps this foot would also be
mentioned in them (see Suppl.).

It still remains for us to explain her precise connexion with a
particular day of the year. It is either on Dec. 25 (dies natalis), or
twelve days after Christmas, on Jan. 6, when the star appeared to
the Three Kings (magi), that the christian church celebrates the
feast of the manifestation of Christ under the name of *epiphania*
(v. Ducange, sub v.), *bethphania* or *theophania* (O. Fr. tiephaine,
tiphagne). In an OHG. gloss (Emm. 394), theophania is rendered
giperahta naht, the bright night of the heavenly vision that
appeared to the shepherds in the field.[2] Documents of the Mid.
Ages give dates in the dative case: ' perchtentag, perhtennaht '
(for OHG. zi demo perahtin taga, zi deru Perahtûn naht) ; again,
' an der berechtnaht,' M. Beham (Mone, anz. 4, 451) ; ' ze perh-
nahten,' MB. 8, 540 (an. 1302); ' unze an den ahtodin tac nâh der
Perhtage,' till the eighth day after the Perht's (fem.) day, Fundgr.
110, 22 ; ' von dem nehsten Berhtag,' MB. 9, 138 (an. 1317) ; ' an
dem Prehentag,' MB. 7, 256 (an. 1349);—these and other contracted
forms are cited with references in Scheffer's Haltaus p. 75, and
Schm. 1, 194.[3] Now from this there might very easily grow up a
personification, *Perchten*tac, *Perchten*naht, the bright day becoming
Bright's, *i.e.,* dame Bright's, day. (Conrad of Dankrotsheim, p. 123,
puts his *milde Behte* down a week earlier, on Dec. 30.)[4]

Two hypotheses present themselves. Either the entire fabulous
existence of a Perhta *first arose* accidentally and by misunderstand-
ing, out of such personification ; or the analogy of the ' bright ' day
was tacked on to a *previously existing* Perhta. Now it is true we

---

[1] Altd. w. 3, 47-8 ; Paris too connects this Pédauque with Berte, iii. iv.
198 ; *reine Pedauque,* Michelet hist. de France 1, 496-8. 2, 152.
[2] Luke 2, 9. O. i. 12, 3. 4. Hel. 12, 8. Maria 182.
[3] The OHG. '*pherintac* = parasceve (Graff 5, 360) is Good Friday, and
distinct from Prehentag, Perchtentag.
[4] Dec. 28 is Innocents', 29 St. Thomas's, 31 St. Silvester's.

cannot point out a dame Perhta before the 15th or 14th century, or at earliest the 13th; but the first supposition need not break down, even if we did manage to hunt up her personal name in older authorities: even in the 9th century the expression 'perahtûn naht' might have developed into 'Perahtûn naht'. Still the characteristics we have specified of a mythical Berta, and above all, her identity with Holda, seem to me to decide the matter the other way. If, independently of the christian calendar, there was a Holda, then neither can Perahta be purely a product of it; on the contrary, both of these adjective names lead up to a heathen deity, who made her peregrination at that very season of yule, and whom therefore the christians readily connected with the sacredness of Christmas and New-year.

I will here group together the features which unmistakably make Holda and Bertha appear in this light. They drive about in *waggons*, like mother Earth, and promote agriculture and navigation among men; a *plough*, from which there fall chips of gold, is their sacred implement. This too is like the gods, that they appear *suddenly*, and Berhta especially hands her gifts *in at the window*. Both have spinning and weaving at heart, they insist on diligence and the keeping of festivals holy, on the transgressor grim penalties are executed. The souls of *infant children* are found in their host, as they likewise rule over *elves* and *dwarfs*, but *night-hags* and *enchantresses* also follow in their train:— all this savours of heathenism.

It is very remarkable, that the Italians too have a mis-shapen fairy *Befana*, a terror to children, who has sprung out of epiphania (befania): on that day the women and children set a doll made of old rags in the window; she is black and ugly, and brings presents. Some say, she is *Herod's daughter*; Ranke's hist. zeitschr. 1, 717. 'La *Befania*' (Pulci's Morg. 5, 42). Berni says: 'il di di Befania vo porla per *Befana* alla fenestra, perche qualcun le dia d' una ballestra'.[1] It would be astonishing, if twice over, in two different nations, a name in the calendar had caused the invention of a supernatural being; it is more likely that, both in Italy, and among us, older traditions of the people have sought to blend themselves with the christian name of the day.

[1] Franc. Berni, rime 105.   Crusca sub v. befana.

6. (HERODIAS. DIANA. ABUNDIA).

Herodias, of whom we have just been reminded by Befana, will illustrate this even better. The story of Herod's daughter, whose dancing brought about the beheading of John the Baptist, must have produced a peculiarly deep impression in the early part of the Mid. Ages, and in more than one way got mixed up with fables. Religious poets treat the subject in full, and with relish (Hel. 83-5); Otfried seems to leave it out designedly. It was imagined, that on account of her thoughtless rather than malicious act (for the proposal came from her revengeful mother), *Herodias* (the daughter) was condemned to roam about in company with evil and devilish spirits. She is placed at the head of the 'furious host' or of witches' nightly expeditions, together with Diana, with Holda and Perahta, or in their stead. In Burcard of Worms 10, 1 we read: Illud etiam non omittendum, quod quaedam sceleratae mulieres retro post Satanam conversae, daemonum illusionibus et phantasmatibus seductae, credunt se et profitentur nocturnis horis cum *Diana* paganorum dea vel cum *Herodiade* et innumera multitudine mulierum equitare super quasdam bestias, et multa terrarum spatia intempestae noctis silentio pertransire, ejusque jussionibus *velut dominae* obedire, et certis noctibus ad ejus servitium evocari.— Joh. Salisberiensis († 1182) in Polycr. 2, 17: Quale est, quod noctilucam quandam, vel *Herodiadem* vel praesidem noctis dominam, concilia et conventus de nocte asserunt convocare, varia celebrari convivia, &c.—Angerius, episcopus Conseranus (an. 1280): Nulla mulier de nocturnis equitare cum Diana dea paganorum vel cum *Herodiade* seu Bensozia[1] et innumera mulierum multitudine profiteatur.—Similar statements have passed into later writings, such as those of Martin von Amberg, and Vintler. It is worth noticing, that to the worship of this *Herodias, one third of the whole world* is ceded, and so a most respectable diffusion allowed. Ratherius (bishop of Verona, but a Frank, b. at Lobi near Cambray, d. 974) in his Praeloquia (Martene and Durand 9, 798. opp. edit. Ballerini pp. 20. 21): Quis enim eorum, qui hodie in talibus usque ad perditionem animae in tantum decipiuntur, ut etiam eis, quas (Ball.

---

[1] Ducange sub v. Diana spells Benzoria, but has the true meaning under Bensozia itself; it seems to mean bona socia, friendly propitious being. Bona dea, Dio Cass. 37, 35. 45. Conf. ch. XXVIII, dobra sretia, bona Fortuna; ch. XVI, good wife, under Wood-women.

de quibus) ait Gen.[1], *Herodiam* illam baptistae Christi interfectricem, quasi *reginam* imo *deam* proponant; asserentes, *tertiam totius mundi partem* illi traditam : quasi haec merces fuerit prophetae occisi, cum potius sint daemones, talibus praestigiis infelices mulierculas, hisque multum vituperabiliores viros, quia perditissimos, decipientes.—A full and remarkable account of the medieval tradition, that was tacked on to Herodias, is contained in the Reinardus 1, 1139—1164 :

> Praecipue *sidus* celebrant, ope cujus, ubi omnes
>   defuerant testes, est data Roma Petro,
> traditaque injusto *Pharaildis* virgo labori ;
>   sed sanctifaciunt qualiacunque volunt.
> Hac famosus erat felixque fuisset *Herodes*
>   prole, sed infelix hanc quoque laesit amor :
> haec virgo, thalamos *Baptistae* solius ardens,
>   voverat hoc demto nullius esse viri.
> Offensus genitor, comperto prolis amore,
>   insontem sanctum decapitavit atrox.
> Postulat afferri virgo sibi tristis, et affert
>   regius in disco tempora trunca cliens.
> Mollibus allatum stringens caput illa lacertis
>   perfundit lacrimis, osculaque addere avet ;
> oscula captantem *caput aufugit* atque *resufflat*,
>   illa per impluvium turbine flantis abit.
> Ex illo nimium memor ira *Johannis* eandem
>   *per vacuum coeli* flabilis urget iter :
> mortuus infestat miseram, nec vivus amarat,
>   non tamen hanc penitus fata perisse sinunt.
> Lenit *honor* luctum, minuit *reverentia* poenam,
>   *pars hominum moestae tertia servit herae.*
> *Quercubus et corylis a noctis parte secunda*
>   *usque nigri ad galli carmina prima sedet.*
> Nunc ea nomen habet *Pharaildis, Herodias* ante
>   saltria, nec subiens nec subeunda pari.

Conf. Aelfrici homiliae 1, 486. Here we have Herodias described as *moesta hera* cui *pars tertia hominum* servit, the reverential homage she receives assuages her bitter lot; only from midnight

---

[1] Ballerini cannot understand this Gen. ; is it Gennadius (Massiliensis), a writer at the end of the fifth century ?

till first cockcrow she sits on oaks and hazel-trees, the rest of her
time she floats through the empty air. She was inflamed by love
for John, which he did not return; when his head is brought in on
a charger, she would fain have covered it with tears and kisses, but
it draws back, and begins to blow hard at her; the hapless maid is
whirled into empty space, and there she hangs for ever.[1] Why she
was afterwards (in the twelfth century) called *Pharaildis*, is not
explained by the life of a saint of that name in Flanders (Acta
sanct. 4 Jan.); nor does anything that the church tells of John the
Baptist and Herodias (Acta sanct. 24 Jun.) at all resemble the
contents of the above story : Herodias is Herod's wife, and the
daughter is named Salome. *Pharaildis* on the contrary, M. Dutch
Verelde,[2] leads us to ver Elde = *frau Hilde* or *frau Hulde*, as in a
doc. of 1213 (Bodmanns Rheing. alterth. p. 94) there occurs a
'miles dictus *Verhildeburg*,' and in a Frisian doc. of the 14th
century a *Ferhildema*, evidently referring to the mythic Hildburg.
Still more remarkable seems a M. Dutch name for the milky way,
Vroneldenstraet = frauen Hilde or Hulde strasse (street, highway).
So that the poet of the Reinardus is entirely in the right, when
Herodias sets him thinking of *Pharaildis*, and she again of the
milky way, the *sidus* in his first line.

There is no doubt whatever, that quite early in the Mid. Ages
the christian mythus of *Herodias* got mixed up with our native
heathen fables : those notions about dame *Holda* and the ' furious
host ' and the nightly jaunts of sorceresses were grafted on it, the
Jewish king's daughter had the part of a *heathen goddess* assigned
her (Ratherius says expressly : imo *dea*), and her worship found
numerous adherents. In the same circle moves *Diana*, the lunar
deity of night, the wild huntress; Diana, Herodias and Holda

---

[1] This reference to the *turbo* (the whirlwind of his blast), looks mythical
and of high antiquity. Not only did *Ziu* or *Zio*, once a deity, become with the
christians a name for the whirlwind, p. 203 (and Pulloineken too may have to
do with *Phol*, p. 229) ; but to this day such a wind is accounted for in Lower
Saxony (about Celle) by the dancing *Herodias* whirling about in the air. Elsewhere the raising of it is ascribed to the *devil*, and offensive epithets are
hurled at him, as in the Saalfeld country : ' Schweinezahl fähret,' there goes
swine-tail (Praetorius, Rübezahl 3, 120), and on the Rhön mts. : ' Säuzagel,'
sow-tail (Schm. 4, 110), to shew contempt for the demon, and abate his fury
(see Suppl.). I shall bring in some other stories, when treating of the wind-
sprites.

[2] Canneart, strafrecht 153-5. Belg. mus. 6, 319. Conf. *Vergode* for frau
Gaude.

stand for one another, or side by side. *Diana* is denounced by
Eligius (Superst. A); the passage in the decrees of councils
(Superst. C) has found its way into many later writings (Superst.
D, G): like Herodias, she appears as *domina* and *hera*. The life of
St. Caesarius Arelatensis mentions a 'daemonium, quod rustici
Dianam vocant,' so that the name was familiar to the common
people; that statue of Diana in Greg. Tur. 8, 15 I have spoken of
on p. 110. But the strongest testimony to the wide diffusion of
Diana's cultus seems to be a passage in the life of St. Kilian, the
apostle of the East Franks († 689): Gozbertus dux Franciae . . .
volens crebra apud se tractare inquisitione, utrum Ejus quem
(Kilianus) praedicabat, vel *Dianae* potius cultus praeferendus esset.
Diana namque apud illum in summa veneratione habebatur
(Surius 4, 133; Acta sanct. Bolland. 8 Jul. (p. 616). As it is
principally in Thuringia, Franconia and Hesse that *frau Holda*
survives, it is not incredible that by *Diana* in the neighbourhood
of Würzburg, so far back as the 7th century, was meant no other
than she.

Lastly, the retrospective connexion of this Herodias or Diana
with personages in the native paganism, whether of Celtic or
Teutonic nations, receives a welcome confirmation from the legend
of a *domina Abundia* or *dame Habonde*, supplied by French
authorities of the Mid. Ages. A bishop of Paris, Guilielmus
Alvernus (Guillaume d' Auvergne), who died 1248, speaks thus of
nymphs and lamiae (opera, Par. 1674, fol. I. 1036): 'Sic et daemon,
qui praetextu mulieris, cum aliis de nocte domos et cellaria dicitur
frequentare, et vocant eam *Satiam* a satietate, et *dominam
Abundiam* pro abundantia,[1] quam eam praestare dicunt domibus,
quas frequentaverit: hujusmodi etiam daemones, quas *dominas*
vocant vetulae, penes quas error iste remansit, et a quibus solis
creditur et somniatur. Dicunt has *dominas* edere et bibere de escis
et potibus, quos in domibus inveniunt, nec tamen consumptionem
aut imminutionem eas facere escarum et potuum, maxime si vasa
escarum sint discooperta et vasa poculorum non obstructa
eis in nocte relinquantur. Si vero operta vel clausa inveniunt
seu obstructa, inde nec comedunt nec bibunt, propter quod
infaustas et infortunatas relinquunt, nec *satietatem* nec *abun-*

---

[1] The Romans also personified *Abundantia* as a superior being, but she
only appears on coins, she had neither temples nor altars.

dantiam eis praestantes.' The like is repeated on p. 1068, but on p. 1066 we read: ' Sunt et aliae ludificationes malignorum spirituum, quas faciunt interdum in nemoribus et locis amoenis et frondosis arboribus, ubi apparent in similitudine *puellarum* aut *matronarum* ornatu muliebri et *candido,* interdum etiam in stabulis, cum luminaribus cereis, ex quibus apparent distillationes in comis et collis equorum, et comae ipsorum diligenter tricatae, et audies eos, qui talia se vidisse fatentur, dicentes veram ceram esse, quae de luminaribus hujusmodi stillaverat.[1] De illis vero substantiis, quae apparent in domibus, quas *dominas nocturnas,* et *principem* earum vocant *dominam Abundiam,* pro eo quod domibus, quas frequentant, abundantiam bonorum temporalium praestare putantur, non aliter tibi sentiendum est, neque aliter quam quemadmodum de illis audivisti. Quapropter eo usque invaluit stultitia hominum et insania vetularum, ut vasa vini et receptacula ciborum discooperta relinquant, et omnino nec obstruant neque claudant eis noctibus, quibus ad domos suas eas credunt adventuras, ea de causa videlicet, ut cibos et potus quasi paratos inveniant et eos absque difficultate apparitionis pro beneplacito sumant.

The Roman de la rose (Méon 18622 seq.) informs us:

> qui les cinc sens ainsinc deçoit
> par les fantosmes, quil reçoit,
> dont maintes gens par lor folie
> cuident estre par nuit estries
> *errans* auecques *dame Habonde,*
> et dient, que par tout le monde
> *li tiers enfant* de nacion
> *sunt de ceste condicion.*
>
> qu'il vont trois fois en la semaine.
> si cum destinee les maine,
> et par tous ces ostex se boutent,
> ne cles ne barres ne redoutent,
> ains sen entrent par les fendaces,
> par chatieres et par crevaces,
> et se partent des cors les ames
> et vont avec les *bonnes dames*
> par leus forains et par maisons,
> et le pruevent par tiex raisons:

[1] Conf. Deutsche sagen, no. 122.

que les diversités veues
ne sunt pas en lor liz venues,
ains sunt lor ames qui laborent
et par le monde ainsinc sen corent, &c

18686. Dautre part, que *li tiers du monde*
aille ainsinc *avec dame Habonde,*
si cum voles vielles le pruevent
par les visions que truevent,
dont convient il sans nule faille
que trestous li mondes i aille.

As Ratherius and the Reinardus represent a third part of the world
as given up to the service of Herodias, the same statement is here
applied to dame Habonde; *Herodias* and *Abundia* are therefore
one. A connexion between Abundia and our native *Folla, Fulla*
(fulness) will presently be made apparent. The term *enfans* may
refer either to the *unchristened babes* above, or to the great
multitude of heathen, who remained shut out of the christian
community. It had long been the custom to divide the known
world into three parts.[1] The domina *clothed in white* reminds one
of Perahta the bright, the *bona domina* or *bona socia*[2] of Holda the
gracious, and Herodias haunting the oaks by night of the Old
German tree-worship. They are originally benignant beings all,
whose presence brings prosperity and plenty to mankind; hence to
them, as to friendly spirits or gods, meat and drink are set for a
sacrifice in the night season. Holda, Berhta and Werra seem to
love a particular kind of food, and look for it on their feast-day.

7. HRUODA (HREDE). OSTARA (EASTRE).

Thus far we have got acquainted with the names and worship
of several goddesses, who were honoured under different names by
particular tribes of Teutondom (Nerdu, Hludana, Tanfana, Holda,
Berhta), and others resembling them have only become known to
us under foreign appellations (Isis, Diana, Herodias, Abundia): of
all these (so long as I consider still doubtful the connexion of

---

[1] Agitur pars tertia mundi, Ovid. met. 5, 372 ; tertia pars mundi fumans
perit Africa flammis, Coripp. 1, 47 : tertia pars orbis Europa vocatur, Walthar. 1.

[2] Is the name *socia* connected with the *Satia* in Guilielmus Alvernus ?

'Erce' with our Herke) *not one* is to be found among the Anglo-Saxons.

On the other hand, the Anglo-Saxon historian tells us the names of two beings, whom he expressly calls ancient goddesses of his people, but of whose existence not a trace is left amongst other Germans. A clear proof, that here as well as there, heathenism was crowded with divinities of various shape and varying name, but who in their characteristics and cultus corresponded to one another. Why this multiplicity of form should prevail more in the case of the female deities than of the male, can be fairly explained, I think, by the greater respect paid to the chief masculine divinities: they were too famous and too highly thought of, for their principal names not to have penetrated all branches of the nation.

The two goddesses, whom Beda (De temporum ratione cap. 13) cites very briefly, without any description, merely to explain the months named after them, are *Hrede* and *Eástre*, March taking its Saxon name from the first, and April from the second: ' *Rhedmonath* a *dea* illorum *Rheda*, cui in illo sacrificabant, nominatur.'— ' Antiqui Anglorum populi, gens mea . . . apud eos Aprilis *Esturmonath*, qui nunc paschalis mensis interpretatur, quondam a *dea* illorum, quae *Eostra* vocabatur et cui in illo festa celebrantur (?), nomen habuit ; a cujus nomine nunc paschale tempus cognominant, consueto *antiquae observationis* vocabulo gaudia novae solennitatis vocantes.'[1]

It would be uncritical to saddle this father of the church, who everywhere keeps heathenism at a distance, and tells us less of it than he knows, with the invention of these goddesses. There is nothing improbable in them, nay the first of them is justified by clear traces in the vocabularies of other German tribes. March is in OHG. lenzinmânôt, named after the season lenzo, lengizo [lengthening of days];[2] but it may have borne other names as well. Oberlin quotes, from Chorion's Ehrenkranz der teutschen sprach, Strassb. 1644, p. 91, *Retmonat* for March; and a doc. of 1404

---

[1] One MS. (Kolmesen opusc. p. 287 ; this ref. given in Rathlef's Hoya and Diepholz 3, 16) reads : Veteres Anglicani populi vocant Estormonath paschalem mensem, idque a *dea quadam* cui *Teutonici* populi in paganismo sacrificia fecerunt tempore mensis Aprilis, quae Eostra est appellata.

[2] Gramm. 2, 510. Langez. Diut. 3, 88.

(Weisth. 1, 175) has *Redtmonet*, it is not clear for what month. When we find in the Appenzeller reimchronik p. 174 :

> In dem *Redimonet*
> die puren kamen donet,
> do der merzenmonat gieng herzu
> an ainem morgen fru
> do zundentz Rorschach an ;

here *Redimonet* seems, by the displacement so common in the names of months, to be the month before March, as Chorion uses his *Retmonat* for February as well. Von Arx explains the word quite differently, and I think untenably, by a mountain. Apart from the Swiss term altogether, I believe the AS. name was really *Hrêð* or *Hrêðe* = OHG. *Hruod* or *Hruodâ*, and derived, as I said on p. 206, from hruod gloria, fama ; so that we get the meaning of a shining and renownful goddess. The Trad. fuld. 2, 196, furnish a female name Hruadâ, gen. Hruadûn, and in 1, 42. 2, 26, another nom. Hruadun, this last apparently formed like ON. Fiörgyn and Hlôdyn. The AS. adj. hrêð or hrêðe means crudelis (Cædm. 136, 21. 198, 2), perhaps victoriosus ? I am in doubt about hrêð, sigehrêð, guðhrêð, Beow. 5146. 974. 1631; they waver between an adj. and a subst. sense, and in the last passage, ' Beowulfe wearð guðhrêð gifeðe,' victoria is evidently meant. When the AS. Menologue, line 70, translates Martius by reðe, this may stand for hrêðe.

We Germans to this day call April *ostermonat*, and *ôstarmânoth* is found as early as Eginhart (temp. Car. Mag.). The great christian festival, which usually falls in April or the end of March, bears in the oldest of OHG. remains the name *ôstarâ* gen. -ûn ;[1] it is mostly found in the plural, because two days (ôstartagâ, aostortagâ, Diut. 1, 266ᵃ) were kept at Easter. This *Ostarâ*, like the AS. *Eástre*, must in the heathen religion have denoted a higher being, whose worship was so firmly rooted, that the christian teachers tolerated the name, and applied it to one of their own grandest anniversaries.[2] All the nations bordering on us have retained the Biblical ' pascha '; even Ulphilas writes paska, not

---

[1] T. 157, 1. 3. 5. O. i. 22, 8. iii. 6, 16. iv. 9, 8. Hymn. 21, 4. Fragm. theol. xiv. 17.

[2] Conf. Ideler's chronologie 1, 516.

áustrô, though he must have known the word; [1] the Norse tongue
also has imported its pâskir, Swed. påsk, Dan. paaske. The OHG.
adv. *ôstar* expresses movement toward the rising sun (Gramm. 3,
205), likewise the ON. *austr*, and probably an AS. eástor and Goth.
áustr. In Latin the identical *auster* has been pushed round to the
noonday quarter, the South. In the Edda a male being, a spirit of
light, bears the name of *Austri*, so a female one might have been
called *Austra ;* the High German and Saxon tribes seem on the
contrary to have formed only an *Ostarâ, Eástre* (fem.), not Ostaro,
Eástra (masc.).[2] And that may be the reason why the Norsemen
said pâskir and not austrur : they had never worshipped a goddess
Austra, or her cultus was already extinct.

Ostara, Eástre seems therefore to have been the divinity of the
radiant dawn, of upspringing light, a spectacle that brings joy and
blessing,[3] whose meaning could be easily adapted to the resurrec-
tion-day of the christian's God. *Bonfires* were lighted at Easter,
and according to a popular belief of long standing, the moment the
sun rises on Easter Sunday morning, he gives *three joyful leaps,* he
dances for joy (Superst. 813). Water drawn on the Easter
morning is, like that at Christmas, holy and healing (Superst. 775.
804) ; here also heathen notions seems to have grafted themselves
on great christian festivals. Maidens clothed in white, who at
Easter, at the season of returning spring, show themselves in clefts
of the rock and on mountains, are suggestive of the ancient goddess
(see Suppl.).

8. ZISA.

Beda's account of Hrede and Eástre[4] shall be followed now by
a statement reaching back to the 11th century, and deserving
attention if only for its great age, concerning a goddess *Zisa*
worshipped at Augsburg in the heathen time.

---

[1] For oriens he chooses urruns, for occidens sagqs, *i.e.*, rising and sinking of
the sun, not that he did not know vistr (versus occidentem), root vis (repose,
stillness, evening).

[2] Composite proper names : Ostroberht, Austroberta, Austregisil, Ostro-
gotha (like Visigotha, Vistrimund, Westeralap, Sundarolt, Nordberaht, &c. &c.)

[3] In the Basque language *ostara* means May, the budding leafing time,
from ostoa, leaf, foliage : a mere accidental resemblance.

[4] I might introduce into the text an AS. *Ricen*, if I knew any more about
her than what Lye's glossary quotes from Cod. Cot. 65, 87 : *Ricenne* Diana. It
is formed like þinen (ancilla), wylpen (bellona), &c.

The Cod. Monach. Lat. 2 (of 1135), and the Cod. Emmeran. F.
IX. fol. 4ᵃ (of 12-13th cent.) contain identic 'Excerpta ex Gallica
historia'.[1]

'Dum hec circa *renum* geruntur, in *noricorum* (interlined
bawariorum, Cod. Vind. CII. pauwariorum) finibus grave vulnus
romanus populus accepit. quippe *germanorum* gentes (interlined
suevi), que *retias* occupaverant, non longe ab alpibus tractu pari
patentibus campis, ubi duo rapidissimi amnes [interlined *licus* et
werthaha (CII vuerdaha)] inter se confluunt, in ipsis *noricis* finibus
(interlined terminis *bawariorum* et *suevorum*) civitatem non quidem
muro sed vallo fossaque cinxerant, quam appellabant *zizarim* (CII.
cizarim) ex nomine dee *cize*,[2] quam religiosissime colebant. cujus
templum quoque ex lignis *barbarico* ritu constrictum, postquam eo[3]
colonia *romana* deducta est, inviolatum permansit, ac vetustate
collapsum nomen[4] colli servavit. hanc urbem *titus annius* pretor
ad arcendas barbarorum excursiones kal. sextilibus (interlined
exacta jam estate) exercitu circumvenit. ad meridianam oppidi
partem, que sola a continenti (interlined littoribus) erat, pretor ipse
cum *legione martia* castra operosissime communivit. ad occidentem vero, qua barbarorum adventus erat, *ávar*, *bôgudis* regis filius,
cum equitatu omni et auxiliaribus *macedonum* copiis inter flumen et
vallum loco castris parum amplo infelici temeritate extra flumen
(interlined *werthaha*) consedit. pulchra indoles, non minus *romanis*
quam *grecis* disciplinis instructa. igitur quinquagesimo nono die,
qua eo ventum est, cum is dies *dee cize* (CII. deę cizę) apud *barboros*
celeberrimus, ludum et lasciviam magis quam formidinem ostentaret,
immanis *barbarorum* (interlined *suevorum*, CII. svivorum) multitudo,
ex proximis silvis repente erumpens ex improviso castra irrupit,
equitatum omnem, et quod miserius erat, auxilia sociorum delevit.
avar,[5] cum in hostium potestatem regio habitu vivus venisset, [sed

---

[1] I owe their communication to Schmeller's kindness. The same piece is
found at Vienna in two forms : in the Cod. Lat. CII (olim hist. prof. 652) sec.
xi. ineuntis fol. 79. 80 ; and in the Cod. CCXXVI (olim univ 237) sec. xii.
In both it stands between Jorn. De reb. get. and De regn. succ. CII has
interlinear glosses and marginal notes (exactly like the Munich MSS.) by a
scarcely later hand, which also writes the heading 'Excerptum ex Gallica
historia'. CCXXVI adopts the interlinears into the text, but otherwise agrees.

[2] On margin : 'Quem male polluerat cultura nefaria dudum
           gallus monticulum hunc tibi *ciza* tulit'.

[3] On margin : 'post conditam urbem *augustam* a *romanis*'.

[4] Marg. note : 'ut usque hodie ab incolis *cizunberc* nominetur'.

[5] Marg. note : 'ex cujus vocabulo, quia ibi mactatus et tumulatus est
chrikesaveron (CII chrekasaver) nomen accepit. *grecus* enim erat'.

que apud *barbaros* reverentia ?] more pecudis ibidem mactatur.[1]
oppidani vero non minori fortuna sed maiori virtute pretorem in
auxilium sociis properantem adoriuntur. *romani* haud segniter
resistunt. duo principes oppidanorum *habino*[2] et *caccus*[3] in primis
pugnantes cadunt. et inclinata jam res oppidanorum esset, ni
maturassent auxilium ferre socii in altera ripa jam victoria potiti.
denique coadunatis viribus castra irrumpunt, pretorem, qui paulo
altiorem tumulum (interlined *perleih*) frustra ceperat, *romana* vi
resistentem obtruncant. legionem[4] divinam (interlined *martiam*),
ut ne nuncius cladis superesset, funditus delent. *Verres* solus
tribunus militum amne transmisso in proximis paludibus se
occultans[5] honestam mortem subterfugit. nec multo post *sicilie*
proconsul immani avaricia turpem mortem promeruit. nam cum se
magistratu abdicaret, judicio civium damnatus est.'

The same fragment, only without the interlined words and
without marginal additions, stands in Goldast's Rerum suev. script.
aliquot veteres, Ulm 1727 fol. p. 3 under the rubric : ' *Velleii Galli*
fragmentum de victoria Suevorum contra Romanos' (conf. Haupts
zeitschr. 10, 291). It has the readings ' dea *Cisa*' and ' *Cisara,*'
and for Caccus ' *Cacus,*' but agrees in the other names. Further,
for loco parum *amplo*, I find the better reading *apto*. The paren-
thesis ' sed—reverentia' is wanting, so is the concluding sentence
' nam—damnatus est'. I should believe that Goldast had borrowed
it all from Wolfg. Lazius's Reip. Rom. libri xii. Francof. 1591 p.
52, if this copy had not some variations too ; the heading runs :
' Velleii excerpta ex Gallica historia ' ; it has *Cisara,* but *Cizę,* also
' Habbino, Caccus, amplo,' and concludes with promeruit. Lazius

---

[1] On margin :
    ' Hoc nomen terris *bogudis* dat regia proles
      grecavar (CII grecus auar), pecudis de suevis more litatus.'
[2] On margin :
      ' Prefectus *habeno* se victum hicque sepultum
        perpetuo montis nomine notificat.
qui juxta montem occisus et sepultus nomen monti *habenonberch* dedit, quem
rustici havenenberch (CII havenonperch) dicunt.'
[3] CII : ' a cujus nomine putamus *iekingen* nominari.'
[4] On margin : ' de hac ibi perdita legione adhuc *perleich* nominatur.'
Then in smaller but contemporaneous writing :
      ' Indicat hic collis *romanam* nomine cladem
      martia quo legio tota simul periit.
      subdidit hunc *rome* prepes victoria *petro*,
      hoc sibimet templum qui modo constituit.'
[5] On margin : ' hic quia in paludibus adjacentibus latuit, lacui *uerisse* huc
usque nomen dedit'.

says : 'quam nos historiam in pervetusto codice membran. literis antiquissimis scriptam reperimus'; that would be the sixth MS. known hitherto, and copies must have been pretty numerous in the 11-12th centuries. The one that Goldast had before him may probably have been the oldest.

Either one or the other of them, both Otto von Freisingen and the author (or continuator) of the Auersberg chronicle seem to have had before them. The former tries to connect the story with Quintilius Varus (instead of Verres), and after relating his over-throw, adds (chron. 3, 4) : 'Tradunt Augustenses hanc caedem ibi factam, ostenduntque in argumentum collem ex ossibus mortuorum compactum, quem in vulgari *perleich* (Mone, anz. 1, 256), eo quod legio ibi perierit, usque hodie vocant, vicumque ex nomine Vari ap-pellatum monstrant'. The Auersberg chronicler's account, though he almost verbally adopts the older fragment, I hold it needful to insert here, because the marginal glosses are curiously interwoven with the text, and referred to ' discovered·inscriptions on stone '.[1]

De Augusta Vindelicorum vel Rhetiae. sicut ex scriptis veterum colligitur haec civitas tria nomina accepit. Germanorum quippe gentes primum considentes in partibus Rhetiae, quae nunc est pars Sueviae, non longe ab alpibus in planitie, loco tamen munito propter concursum duorum rapidorum fluminum, hanc urbem construxerunt, et non muris sed fossatis eam firmaverunt, et ex nomine *deae Zizae*, quam religiosissime colebant, *Zizerim* eam nominabant. hujus quoque deae templum ex lignis barbarico ritu constructum, etiam postquam Romani eam incolere coeperunt, inviolatum permansit. at vetustate collapsum nomen colli servavit, in quo postmodum in lapide exsculpti hi versus sunt reperti :

> quem male polluerat cultura nefaria dudum
> gallus monticulum hunc tibi *Ziza* tulit.

unde usque in praesens ab incolis idem monticulus *Zizenberg* no-minatur. apud hanc urbem Romani deleti sunt magna caede. nam *Titus Annius* praetor ad arcendas barbarorum excursiones cum exercitu in kal. Augusti eam circundedit, ipseque ad meri-dianam oppidi partem, quae sola patebat, castra sua cum legione Martia operosissime communivit. ad occidentem vero ultra fluvium, ubi Suevis aut barbaris aditus patebat, *Avar Bogudis* regis

---

[1] Chron. Conradi ursperg. Argent. 1532, p. 308. ed. 1609, p. 225.

filius cum omni equitatu et auxilio *macedonico* consedit. igitur quinquagesimo nono die, quam eo ventum est, cum is dies *deae Zizֶ* apud barbaros celeberrimus esset, ludum et lasciviam magis quam formidinem cives ostentarunt. tunc etiam immanis barbarorum multitudo, quae de partibus Sueviae illuc convenerat, de proximis silvis repente erumpens ex improviso castra irrupit et *Avaris* exercitum delevit. ipsum quoque *Avar* regio habitu indutum vivum comprehendentes crudeliter in modum pecoris mactaverunt. a quo in loco, ubi mactatus est, vicus usque hodie appellatus est *Criechesaveron*, in quo hi versus reperti sunt :

> his nomen terris *Bogudis* dat regia proles
> *Graecus Avar*, pecudis de *Suevis* more litatus.

oppidani vero non minori fortuna sed majori virtute praetorem in auxilium sociis properantem invadunt, quibus Romani haud segniter resistunt. in quo conflictu duo principes oppidanorum *Habino* et *Caccus* in primis pugnantes cadunt, et inclinata jam res esset oppidanorum, ni maturassent auxilium ferre *Suevi* in altera ripa victoria jam potiti. de nominibus autem illorum principum interfectorum exstant adhuc loca denominata, nam rustici de *Habinone* vocant monticulum *Habinoberg*, in quo hi versus reperti sunt :

> praefectus *Habino* se victum atque sepultum
> perpetuo montis nomine notificat.

a *Cacco* vero dicunt *Gegginen* denominari. denique coadunatis *Suevis* et oppidanis castra irrumpunt, et praetorem, qui paulo altiorem tumulum frustra ceperat, romana vi resistentem obtruncant, legionemque divinam, ut nec nuncius cladis superesset, funditus delent. de hac perdita legione adhuc *perlaich*, quasi perdita legio, nominatur, ubi postmodum hi versus sunt reperti :

> indicat hic collis romanam nomine cladem,
> martia quo legio tota simul periit.

solus *Verres* tribunus militum amne transmisso in proximis paludibus se occultans honestam mortem subterfugit, lacui *Vernse* hucusque nomen dedit. versus :

> das nomen lacui *Verres* quo tu latuisti.

hic tamen non multo post Siciliae proconsul effectus turpem mortem promeruit. nam cum se magistratu abdicaret judicio civium damnatus est. propter hunc *Verrem* tradunt Augustenses hanc caedem fuisse eandem, quam sub Augusto factam quidam describunt, sed *Varum* illum nominant his verbis : ea tempestate *Varus,* romano more, superbe et avare erga subditos se gerens a Germanis deletus est.

Some later writers also mention the tradition. About 1373— 91, an ecclesiastic, Küchlin, composed in rhyme a history of Augsburg [1] for the burgomaster Peter Egen the Young, who wished to have his house painted with illustrations from it. Cap. 2, fol. 99 says of the Swabians :

> Sie bawten einen tempel gross darein
> zu eren (in honour of) *Zise* der abgöttin,
> die sie nach heidnischen sitten (after heathen ways)
> anbetten zu denselben zeiten (adored in those days).
> Die stat ward genennt (city got named) auch *Zisaris*
> nach der abgöttin (after the goddess), das was der pris.
> Der tempel als lang stůnd unversert (stood uninjured),
> bis im von alter was der val beschert (its fall decreed),
> und da er von alter abgieng (as from age it passed away),
> der berg namen von im empfieng (the hill took name),
> daruf gestanden was (whereon had stood) das werck,
> und haist noch hüt (hight still to-day) der *Zisenberck.*

Conf. Keller's Fastn. sp., p. 1361. Sigism. Meisterlin, in his Augsburg chronicle [2] (which is in print from the 8th chap. of bk 1), treats of this *Cisa* in chaps. 5-6 of bk 2. In the unprinted chap. 4 of bk 1, he unmistakably refers to Küchlin, and again at the end of chap. 7 : ' das er auch melt (tells) von der göttin *Cisa,* die auch genent wird *Cizais,* das sy geert habend (they honoured her) die doch aus Asia warend ; dawider seind die andern, die von *Cysa* schreibent, die sprechent, das sy die Vindelici habend nach schwebischen sitten angebettet. von der göttin wirst du hernach mer haben, ob got wil (buch 3. cap. 5. 6).'   (See Suppl.)

Hopeless contradictions lie on the face of that fragment. Bogud, a Punic ship's-captain, who lived in the year 494 of Rome, or 260 B.C.,[3] is here turned into a Macedonian king ; and his son Avar is made contemporary with the Ciceronian Verres of 200 years after, or even of the still later Varus. Yet Bogudes and Varus do occur as contemporaries of Pompey in Dio Cassius 41, 42.

---

[1] Cod. Monach. Lat. 61 ; likewise sent me by Schmeller.
[2] Augsb. 1522 fol.   Meisterlin wrote it in 1456, and died about 1484.
[3] Niebuhr's Rom. Hist. 3, 677.

What Titus Annius was meant by the 'praetor,' I cannot guess ; there is a consul of that name A.U.C. 601 and 626, or B.C. 153, 128. Velleius Paterculus can never have written this sort of thing.[1]

But all the rubbish it contains does not destroy the value of the remarkable story to us. The comparatively pure Latinity is enough to show that it was not composed so late as the twelfth century ; Lazius and Velser [2] are inclined to place it in the Carolingian period, and it looks like the work of a foreigner, to whom the Germans are heathens and barbarians. The glosses confirm the local connexion of the whole tradition with Augsburg and its neighbourhood ; and not only the Latin verses, but the German forms werthaha (R. Wertach), cizûnberc, habino, habinonberc, look too old for the 12th century. Habino (Hepino), Habinolf, is an authentic OHG. man's name : Cacus is unknown to me, Cacan, Cagan would seem more vernacular, and the derived local name Geginen leads up to it. Some of the names quoted are preserved to this day : the eminence in the middle of the city, next the senate-house, is still called *Perlach,* on which the monastery and church of *St. Peter* were founded in 1064 ; so the verse 'subdidit hunc (collem) Romae praepes victoria *Petro*' was composed after that ? The name *perleih,* which the legend derives from periens or perdita legio, suggests the OHG. eikileihi, aigilaihi (phalanx), Gl. ker. 124. Diut. 1, 223 ; and in other compounds we find leih in a variety of senses.[3] Zisenberg and Havenenberg are names no longer heard, while *Pfersen* (Veris-sê) MB. 33[b], 108 an. 1343, and *Kriegshaber* are well known villages. Whatever may be the explanation of the older and correcter form Criechesaveron, it is very plain that the name of the place *Criahhes* (graeci) *avarâ* (imago, conf. pp. 86, 95, yet also *avaro* proles) first suggested 'Graecus Avar,' as well as *Habinonberc* the hero 'Habino '. The Auersberg chronicler's statement, that the Latin verses were found carved in all those places, must be rejected.

We find then, that tradition, true to her wont, has mixed up

---

[1] G. Jo. Vossius, De hist. Lat. 1, 24.

[2] Marci Velseri rer. Augustanar. libri 8. 1594 fol. p. 45.

[3] Henisch p. 293 explains 'berlach' at Augsburg 'ab ursis in publica cavea ibi altis.' a thing which was done in other towns, *e.g.* Bern. On the Perlach tower there was fixed a figure of St. Michael, which came into view every time the clock struck on Michaelmas-day ; in earlier times a wooden temple of Isis (p. 294, ex lignis) is said to have stood on the spot ; Fischart's geschichtkl. 30[b] : 'der amazonischen Augspurger japetisch fraw *Eysen*'.

fact and fiction; the great point is, that she brings us tidings of a Suevic goddess. *Cisa* seems the older and better spelling, and *Ciza* would be harder to explain. Now from this name of the goddess we can hardly derive that of the town *Cisara*, supposing it to be a purely German derivative; names of places are never formed with such a termination from male or female proper names. It seems more likely that Cisara = *Cisae ara*, from the altar and temple of the goddess: and later writers might corrupt Cisaram into Zizarim, Zizerim. We read that she was most devoutly (religiosissime) honoured by the Suevi, her anniversary is a grand festival devoted to games and merrymaking, the day is precisely defined as the fifty-ninth after Aug. 1, it fell therefore on Sept. 28. At such a season might be held a feast of the divinity who had prospered the harvest just gathered in. On Sept. 29 the christians kept one of their grandest days, that of St. Michael, who often had to replace a heathen god of war and victory. It seems worthy of notice, that the Saxons had their great feast of victory about the same time, viz., the beginning of October; Widukind pp. 423-4. With the first Sunday after Michaelmas the *holy common-week* was considered in the Mid. Ages to begin; Scheffer's Haltaus, pp. 141-2. *na der hilligen meinweken*, Weisth. 3, 240. In the handing down of a precise and doubtless genuine date, I feel the credibility of the story confirmed.

Now who is *Cisa?* One naturally thinks first of that Suevic *Isis* (p. 257) in Tacitus, whose name even is not unlike Cisa, Zisa, if we make allowance for the mere dropping of the initial, an omission which the Roman might be prompted to make by the similarity of the Isis that he knew. But even if Zisa be totally different from Isis, she can with all the better right be placed by the side of our *Zio*, in whom also was displayed a thoroughly Swabian deity (p. 199); nay, together with our supposed feminine *Ziu* (p. 203) there may have been a collateral form *Zisâ*, so that her *Zisûnberg* would exactly correspond to the god's Ziewesberg, Zisberg (see Suppl.). Shall I bring forward a reason for this guess, which shall be anything but far-fetched? The Mid. Dutch name for the third day of the week had the curious form Disendach (p. 125), which being of course a corruption of *Tisendach* brings us at once to *Tise* = Zisa. It is a matter for further researches to demonstrate,[1] but

[1] Down in the Riess between the rivers Lech and Wertach, in the midst of Sueves, at a time supposed to be before even the Romans settled in the region,

that three divinities, Zio, Zisa and Isis, are assigned to the Suevi, is already abundantly clear.

8. FRIKKA (FRIGG). FROUWA (FREYJA).

Our inquiry turns at length to the goddesses of the Norse religious system, of whom unequivocal traces are forthcoming in the rest of Teutondom.

Foremost of these are *Frigg* the wife of Oðinn, and *Freyja* the sister of Freyr, a pair easy to confound and often confounded because of their similar names. I mean to try if a stricter etymology can part them and keep them asunder.

The name of *Freyja* seems the easier : it is motived no doubt by the masculine Freyr (Gramm. 3, 335). Now as we recognised Freyr in the Gothic fráuja (p. 209), Freyja leads us to expect a Gothic fráujô, gen. fráujons, both in the general sense of domina mistress, and in the special one of a proper name *Fráujô*. The notion of mistress, lady, never occurs in Ulphilas. To make up for it, our OHG. remains express it very frequently, by *fruwâ, frôwâ;* the MHG. *frouwe, frou* and our modern *frau* have preserved themselves purely as common nouns, while the masc. *frô* has vanished altogether. In meaning, frouwe and frau correspond exactly to hêrre, herr, and are used like it both in addressing and otherwise.[1] Our minnesängers are divided as to the respective superiority of frouwe (domina) and wîp (femina),[2] wîp expressing more the sex, and frouwe the dignity ; to this day we feel frau to be nobler than weib, though the French femme includes a good deal of what is in our frau. It seems worthy of notice, that the poets

no Slav gods need be looked for ; neither does the Slav mythology know anything at all certain about a Ziza, alleged to be Ceres mammosa (Boh. cic, cec, Pol. cyc, Russ. titi, mamma), in support of whom forsooth our Cisa must be wronged ; see Hanusch 278. It were better to think of the MHG. name for the zeisig (zeis-chen, siskin) diu *zîse,* ein kleiniu *zîse,* Ms. 1, 191b. Wh. 275, 30 ; which can scarcely have arisen from cicindela (glow-worm, Graff 5, 711) ; however, no connexion has come to light between the goddess and the form of a bird, though some little birds, the woodpecker, the titmouse, were held sacred.

[1] Like our *frô,* the O Fr. *dame* (dominus) is now lost ; *dame* (domina) remains, like our *frau.* The Span. keeps both *don* and *doña,* the Ital. only *donna.* The Romance tongues express the masc. notion by two other words, *sire, sieur* (p. 27) and *seigneur, signore, señor, i.e.,* senior, out of which an Ital. *signora,* a Span. *señora* have sprouted, but no Fr. feminine.

[2] Walth. 48-9. 57. Amgb. 45b 46a. Ms. 2, 182b 216a. Docen misc. 2, 278-9. frouwe unde wîp, Parz. 302, 7 (see Suppl.).

harp on the connexion of *frau* with *froh* glad (fro-lic) and *freude*
joy ; conf. Frîdank 106, 5—8. Tit. 15, 35.

The AS. and OS. languages have done the very reverse : while
their masc. freá, fraho is used far more freely than the OHG.
frouwo, they have developed no fem. by its side. The M. Dutch
dialect has *vrauwe, vrouwe* in addressing and as title (Huyd. op St.
1, 52. 356. Rein. 297. 731. 803. 1365. 1655. 2129. 2288. 2510-
32-57-64, &c.), seldomer in other positions, Rein 2291 ; the modern
vrouw has extended its meaning even beyond the limits of our
frau.

All the above languages appear to lack the fem. proper name,
in contrast to the ON. which possesses *Freyja* almost solely as the
goddess's name, and no freyja = hera. Yet we find *húsfreyja* house-
wife, Saem. 212[b], and Snorri is still able to say that *freyja* is a
tignarnafn (name of honour) derived from the goddess,[1] that grand
ladies, ríkiskonur, are *freyjur*, Sn. 29. Yngl. saga c. 13. The
readings frûr, fruvor here are corrupt, for the Icel. form *frú* has
evidently slipped in from the Dan. *frue*, Swed. *fru,* and these from
Germany. The goddess should be in Swed. *Fröa*, Dan. *Fröe*, which
I have never met with ; the Swed. folk-song of Thor's hammer
calls Freyja *Fröijenborg* (the Dan. Fridlefsborg), a Danish one has
already the foreign *Fru.* Saxo is silent about this goddess and
her father altogether ; he would no doubt have named her Fröa.
Our Merseburg poem has now at last presented us with *Frûâ* =
Frôwâ, as the proper name of the goddess.[2]

Frigg gen. Friggjar, daughter of Fiörgynn and wife of Oðinn, is
kept strictly apart from *Freyja*, gen. Freyju : in the Vafþrudnismâl
and the beginning of the Grîmnismâl, *Oðinn* and *Frigg* are plainly
presented as husband and wife ; and as Hroptr and Svâfnir are
also names of Oðinn, ' Hroptr ok *Frigg*, Svâfnir ok *Frigg* ' in Saem.

[1] As fráujô from Fráujô, and freyja from Freyja, a song of Frauenlob's,
Ettm. p. 112 makes *wîp* come from a Frankish king *Wippeo.* Is this an echo
of a mythical Wippo, Wibba (geneal. of Mercia, end of ch. VII) ? The explanation is as false as when the Edda derives vîf from vefa, for all a woman's
being practically a weaver and a peace-weaver ; we should have to assume two
roots, viban and veiban, side by side. The ON. proper name *Vefreyja* is also
worthy of note, Fornald. sög. 2, 459. 3, 250. 594.

[2] The reasons why we may not take *frûâ* here for a mere title (and so a
noun com.) are set forth in the Zeitschr. f. d. a. 2, 189. As for the *u* in the
MS., it looks to me quite plain, else Wackernagel's proposal to read *Friia* =
Frija, Friga, Frîa, would be acceptable (friiu does occur in T. 93, 3). Frûa
and Frîa are alike welcome and suitable for my explanation.

91[b] 93[a] express the same relation. Saxo Gram., p. 13, has correctly ' *Frigga* Othini conjux '. In prayers the two goddesses even stand side by side : ' svâ hialpi ther hollar vættir, *Frigg* ok *Freyja*, ok fleiri goð (more gods), sem þû feldir mer fâr af höndom !' Sæm. 240[b]. So they do at the burning of Baldr's body, Sn. 66, conf. 37. And that Danish folk-song has likewise ' *Frigge, Fru* og Thor '.

The ON. usually has *gg* where the AS. has *cg* and OHG. *cc* or *kk*, namely, where a suffix *i* had stood after *g* or *k :* thus, ON. egg (acies), AS. ecg, OHG. ekki ; ON. bryggja (pons), AS. brycge, OHG. prukkâ ; ON. hryggr (dorsum), AS. hrycg, OHG. hrukki. In the same way we get an AS. *Fricg*, OHG. *Frikka, Frikkia,* even farther away from *Frouwâ* than Frigg from Freyja.

It is the confounding of these two beings that will explain how Adam of Bremen came to put *Fricco* instead of Frô for Freyr (supra, p. 212) ; he would equally have said *Fricca* for Freyja. Fricco, Friccho, Friccolf were in use as proper names in OHG.

And now it seems possible to explain, what is otherwise unaccountable, why the sixth day of the week, dies Veneris, should be called in ON. both *Freyju*dagr and also *Friâ*dagr, in OHG. never Frouwûntac, but *Friâ*tac, *Frîge*tac, now *Freitag*, in AS. *Frige*dæg (for Fricgedæg ?), v. supra, pp. 123-6, and in Faröese *Frujggja*deâ (Lyngbye 532).

Among these forms the AS. presents no difficulty : in the OHG. and ON. names we are puzzled by the absence of the guttural. I believe a solution is offered by that most important passage in Paulus Diac. 1, 8 where Wodan's consort is named *Frea,* which can only mean Frigg, not Freyja, as Saxo Gram. too, while expressly grounding on Paulus, makes use of the form *Frig :* ' Paulo teste auctore *Frig* dea '.[1]

This Langob. *Frea* accords with the OHG. *Frîa*, I take it to be not only identical with *Frigg*, but the original form of the name ; it has less to do with Freyja and the AS. masc. freá. As an ON. brû (pons) stands related to bryggia, so will frî to frigg. The Langob. *Frea* is = Fräa, Fria, Frija, Frêa. Its root is suggested by

---

[1] The AS. chroniclers (p. 128) borrow *Frea* from Paulus. With *Frea* we must above all connect the *frea* of the Laws of Liutprand 6, 40 and 67, and this means uxor, domina, not libera, ingenua. Paulus therefore, in assigning Frea to Wodan as his wife, has put her in the place of the Norse Frigg. The substitution is often made : thus, when Fornald. sög. 2, 25-6 has ' heita â *Freyju* ok â Hött (Oðinn),' it is Frigg that should have been associated with Oðinn, as is done in the Grímnismâl (see Suppl.).

such words as: Goth. freis, frijis (liber), OHG. frî; Goth. frijôn (amare), OHG. frîôn; especially may we take into account the OS. neut. frî (mulier), Hel. 9, 21. 13, 16. 171, 21. 172, 1, the AS. freo (mulier), Cædm. 29, 28. freolîc cwên (pulcra femina), Beow. 1275. freolîcu meowle, Cod. exon. 479, 2. freolîc wîf, Beow. 1222. freolîc fæmne, Cædm. 12, 12. 54, 28.[1] Now, as frî (liber) and our frech, ON. frekr (protervus, impudens), frî (mulier formosa) and ON. frîðr (formosus), friðr (pax) seem to be all related, even the adjectival forms betray the shifting sense of the substantival.[2]

We gather from all this, that the forms and even the meanings of the two names border closely on one another. *Freyja* means the gladsome, gladdening, sweet, gracious goddess, *Frigg* the free, beautiful, loveable; to the former attaches the general notion of frau (mistress), to the latter that of frî (woman). *Holda*, from hold (sweet, kind), and *Berhta* from berht (bright, beautiful) resemble them both. The Swedish folk-song, in naming Froijenborg, calls her 'den väna solen,' the beautiful sun.

Hence the mingling of their myths becomes the more conceivable. Saxo, p. 13, relates how *Frigga*, to obtain gold for her ornaments, violated conjugal fidelity; more minutely told, and differing much in the details, the tale about *Freyja* in Sn. 356 appears to be the same adventure. On quite another ground however the like offence is imputed to Frigg too (Sæm. 63. Yngl. saga cap. 3). In Sn. 81 the valshamr of *Freyja* is spoken of, but in 113-9 that of *Frigg*; the former is supported by Sæm. 70.

Hence the variations in the name for the day of the week. The OHG. *Frîa*tac ought clearly to be Friggjardagr in ON., and the ON. *Freyju*dagr should be Frouwûntac in OHG. Hence too the uncertainty in the naming of a constellation and of several plants. Orion's belt, elsewhere named Jacob's staff and also spindle (colus ἠλακάτη), is called by the Swedish people *Friggerock* (colus Friggae, Ihre, p. 663) or *Frejerock* (Finn Magnusen 361ᵃ), as we noticed before, or *Fröjas rock* (Wieselgren. 383). The orchis odoratissima, satyrium albidum, a plant from which love-potions are brewed, Icel. *Friggjargras*, otherwise hionagras (herba conjugalis); the later

---

[1] Conf. the MHG. wîplich wîp, Parz. 10, 17. MS. 1, 50ᵃ 202ᵃ. 2, 42ᵇ 182ᵇ 258ᵃ. wîbîn wîp, MsH. 1, 359ᵇ; similarly θηλύτεραι γυναῖκες, Od. 11, 386. 434. 15, 422. Hesiod scut. 4.

[2] We might connect Venus with the Goth. qinô, qêns, as venire with qiman; the Wel. *gwen* would answer to Gvenus for Venus; the Ir. dia beine, Friday, from *bean, ben* (lady) = Venus = AS. cwên.

christian way of thinking has substituted *Mary* for the heathen goddess. And the labouring man in Zealand speaks of the above constellation also by the name of *Mariärok, Marirok*. Several kinds of fern, adiantum, polypodium, asplenium, are named lady's hair, maidenhair, *Mariengras,* capillus *Veneris,* Icel. *Freyjuhâr,* Dan. *Fruehaar, Venusstraa, Venusgräs,* Norweg. *Marigras,* &c. Even if the Norse names here have sprung out of Latin ones, they show how *Venus* was translated both by Frigg and Freyja and Mary. As for *Mary,* not only was the highest conception of beauty carried over to her, (frîo scôniôsta, idiso scôniôst, Hel. 61, 13. 62, 1), but she was pre-eminently *our lady, frau, domina, donna.* Conf. infra *frau*achueli, *lady*cow, Marienkälblein. In the nursery-tales she sets the girls *sewing* and *spinning* like Holda and Berhta, and Holda's snow appears to mean the same as Mary's snow (p. 268).

Before so close a contact of the two names I pause, doubting with which of them to connect the strong and incontestable similarity of certain divine names in the non-Teutonic [Aryan] languages. First of all, an OBoh. gloss gives *Priye* for Aphrodite; taking into account the Goth. frijôn, the OHG. friudil (lover), MHG. vriedel, and the Slav. priyátel (friend), Boh. přjtel, Pol. przyiáciel, it must have meant either Freyja the goddess of love and fruitfulness, or Frigg the divine mother and patroness of marriage. In Sanskrit also prî is to love, priyas a friend, Ramâpriya dear-to-Lakshmi = lotus, Yamapriya pleasing-to-Yama = ficus indica, priya in names of gods = husband or wife, Pott's forsch. 2, 424-7. Then *prithivî* is the earth, and *mâtâ Prithvî* Terra mater, from whom comes fruit and increase (conf. Wel. *pridd* terra, Bopp's gloss. 223[b]); and the word, though next of kin to prithus (πλατύς latus), the earth being named the broad and wide, seems nevertheless connected with Fria, Frigg and fridu.

Frigg the daughter of Fiörgynn (p. 172), as consort of the highest god,[1] takes rank above all other goddesses : she knows the fates of men (Sæm. 63[b]. Sn. 23. 64), is consulted by Oðinn (Sæm. 31[a]), administers oaths, handmaids fulfil her hest, she presides over

---

[1] Some of the AS. genealogies have ' Wôden et *Freáláf ejus uxor,*' so that Frigg = Freáláf (OHG. Frôleip?) which fits in with that *Fridlefsborg* in the Danish song, p. 300 ; others make Freáláf Wôden's father. But in lieu of him we have also *Friðu*lâf and *Friðu*wulf, a fresh confirmation of the connexion between frið and the goddess's name.

marriages, and her aid is implored by the childless (Fornald. sög. 1, 117) ; hence hionagras is also *Friggjargras.* We may remember those maidens yet unmarried (p. 264) being yoked to the plough of the goddess whose commands they had too long defied. In some parts of northern England, in Yorkshire, especially Hallamshire, popular customs show remnants of the worship of Fricg. In the neighbourhood of Dent, at certain seasons of the year, especially autumn, the country folk hold a procession and perform old dances, one called the giant's dance : the leading giant they name *Woden,* and his wife *Frigga,* the principal action of the play consisting in two swords being swung and clashed together about the neck of a boy without hurting him.[1] Still more remarkable is the clear vestige of the goddess in Lower Saxony, where to the common people she is *fru Freke,*[2] and plays the very parts which we saw assigned to *frau Holle* (pp. 267-8): a strong argument, by the way, for the divine nature of this latter. Then in Westphalia, legend may derive the name of the old convent *Freckenhorst, Frickenhorst,* from a shepherd Frickio, to whom a light appeared in the night (like the fall of snow by night at Hildesheim, p. 268) on the spot where the church was to be built ; the name really points to a sacred hurst or grove of *Frecka* fem., or of *Fricko* masc., whose site christianity was perhaps eager to appropriate ; conf. *Fræcinghyrst,* Kemble 1, 248. 2, 265. There is a *Vrekeleve, Fricksleben,* not far from Magdeburg (see Suppl.).

Freya is the goddess most honoured after or along with Frigg ; her worship seems to have been even the more prevalent and important of the two, she is styled 'agætuz af Asynjum,' Sn. 28, and ' blôtgyðja,' Yngl. saga cap. 4, to whom frequent sacrifices were offered. Heiðrekr sacrificed a boar to her, as elsewhere to Freyr, and honoured her above all other gods.[3] She was wedded to a

---

[1] Communicated by J. M. Kemble, from the mouth of an 'old Yorkshireman '. I account for the *sword* by the ancient use of that weapon at weddings ; conf. R.A. 426-7. 431 ; esp. the old Frisian custom pp. 167-8, conf. Heimreich's Nordfries. chron. 1, 53-4. In Swabia, as late as the 18th century, the bridesmen carried large swords with fluttering ribbons before the bride ; and there is a striking similarity in the Esthonian custom (Superst. M. 13).

[2] Eccard de orig. Germ. p. 398 : Celebratur in plebe Saxonica *fru Freke,* cui eadem munia tribuuntur, quae superiores Saxones Holdae suae adscribunt. Fru Freke has just been unearthed again by Ad. Kuhn, namely in the Ukermark, where she is called Fruike, and answers to fru Harke in the Mittelmark and fru Gode in the Prignitz.

[3] Hervararsaga, ed. Verel. p. 138, ed. 1785 p. 124. By the editors of the Fornald. sög. 1, 463 the passage is banished into the notes as an unsupported reading.

man (not a god, at least not an As), named *Oðr*, but he forsook her, and she sought him all over the world, among strange peoples, shedding tears. Her name *Sŷr* (Sn. 37) would perhaps be Saúrs in Gothic: Wilh. Müller has detected the very same in the *Syritha* of Saxo Gram. p. 125, who likewise goes in search of *Othar*. Freyja's tears were golden, gold is named after them, and she herself is 'grâtfagr,' fair in greeting (weeping), Sn. 37. 119. 133; in our nursery-tales pearls and flowers are wept or laughed out, and dame Holla bestows the gift of weeping such tears. But the oldest authorities make her warlike also; in a *waggon* drawn by two cats (as Thôrr drives two goats)[1] she rides to the battlefield, 'ríðr til vîgs,' and goes shares with Oðinn in the slain (supra p. 133, conf. Sæm. 42ᵃ. Sn. 28. 57). She is called 'eigandi valfalls' (quae sortitur caesos in pugna), Sn. 119; *valfreyja*, mistress of the chosen, Nialss. p. 118, and of the valkyrs in general; this seems to be in striking accord with Holda or Berhta (as well as Wuotan) adopting the *babes that die unchristened* into their host, heathen goddesses the heathen souls. Freyja's dwelling is named *Fôlk-vângr* or *Fôlkvângar*, the plains on which the (dead?) folk troop together; this imparts new credibility to the connexion of St. *Gertrude*, whose minne is drunk, with Frowa, for the souls of the departed were supposed to *lodge with Gertrude the first night* (p. 61). Freyja's hall is Sessrymnir, the seat-roomy, capacious of much *folk;* dying women expect to find themselves in her company after death. Thôrgerðr in the Egilss., p. 103, refuses earthly nourishment, she thinks to feast with Freyja soon: 'ok engan (nâttverð) mun ek fyrr enn at *Freyju*'. Yet love-songs please her too, and lovers do well to call upon her: 'henni lîkaði vel mansöngr, â hana er gott at heita til âsta,' Sn. 29. That the *cat* was sacred to her, as the wolf to Wuotan, will perhaps explain why this creature is given to night-hags and witches, and is called *donneraas, wetteraas* (-carrion). When a bride goes to the wedding in fine weather, they say 'she has fed the cat well,' not offended the favourite of the love-goddess. The meaning of a phrase in Walther 82, 17 is dark to me: 'weder rîtest gerner *eine guldîn katze*, ald einen wunderlîchen Gêrhart Atzen?' In Westphalia, however, the *weasel* was named froie,

---

[1] Freyja has a *waggon* like Nerthus (mother of Freyr?), like Holda and Freyr himself, Wuotan and Donar (pp. 105-7, 251-2-4, 275); the kingly waggon is proper only to great exalted deities.

Reinh. clxxii, which I suppose means frau, fräulein (froiken), as that ghostly creature was elsewhere called *mühmlein* (aunty), *fräulein, donna, donnola,* titles sure to be connected with myths, and these would doubtless point in the first place to our goddess and her worship. The Greeks said Galinthias was turned into a weasel or cat (γαλέη), Ovid. metam. 9, 306 (see Suppl.).

In so far as such comparisons are allowable, *Frigg* would stand on a line with Here or Juno, especially the pronuba, Jupiter's spouse; and *Freyja* with Venus,[1] but also with Isis who seeks Osiris. *Freyr* and his sister *Freyja* are suggestive of Liber and Libera (Dionysus and Proserpina, or even her mother Demeter; of sun and moon). *Mary* could replace the divine mother and the goddess of beauty; verbally *Frigg* agrees better with Libera, and Adam of Bremen's *Fricco,* if he was god of love, answers in name to Liber, in character to Freyr.

The passage quoted from Paul Diac. is one of the clearest and most convincing testimonies to the harmony between the German and Norse mythologies. An author of Charles the Great's time tells us that the Langobards named Wodan's wife *Frea,* and she is called *Frigg* in the Edda. He cannot have drawn this from Norse tradition, much less can his narrative through Saxo's intermediacy have become the source of the northern faith.

But in favour of Freyja too we possess a weighty piece of external evidence. The Edda makes her the owner of a costly necklace named *Brîsînga men* (Brisingorum monile); she is called 'eigandi Brîsîngamens,' Sn. 37. 119. How she acquired this jewel from the dwarfs, how it was cunningly stolen from her by Loki, is fully narrated in a tale by itself, Sn. 354—357. In the poets therefore Loki is Brîsîngs þiofr (Thorl. obs. 6, 41. 63); a lost lay of the Edda related how Heimdallr fought with Loki for this ornament, Sn. 105. When Freyja pants with rage, the necklace starts from her breast (stauk þat it micla men Brîsînga), Sæm. 71[b]. When Thôrr, to get his hammer back, dresses up in Freyja's garments, he does not forget to put her famous necklace on: 'hafi

---

[1] In the Tanhäuser, as sung in Switzerland (Aufsess. anz. 1832, 240-2; Uhland's volksl. p. 771), instead of the usual dame *Venus* we find precisely *frau Frene,* and acc. to Stald. 1, 395 *frein* is there a collateral form of *frei* free. A woman's name Vreneli is known from Hebel. Vrene may be Verena the martyr, or Veronica, v. Vréne, Ben. 328.

hann (have he) it mikla *men Brîsînga !'* Sæm. 72.—Now this very
trinket is evidently known to the AS. poet of Beowulf 2399, he
names it *Brosinga mene*, without any allusion to the goddess; I
would read ' Brîsinga mene,' and derive the word in general from a
verb which is in MHG. brîsen, breis (nodare, nodis constringere,
Gr. κεντεῖν to pierce), namely, it was a chain strung together of
bored links. Yet conf. ch. XX, *brising* St. John's fire: perhaps
the dwarfs that forged it were called *Brîsîngar?* The jewel is so
closely interwoven with the myth of Freyja, that from its mention
in AS. poetry we may safely infer the familiarity of the Saxon race
with the story itself; and if the Goths worshipped a goddess
Fráujô, they too would doubtless know of a Breisiggê mani.[1]
Conf. ch. XX, *Iarðar men*, Earth's necklace, *i.e.*, turf in the ON.
legal language.

We cannot but feel it significant, that where the gospel simply
speaks of τὸ ἅγιον sacrum (Matt. 7, 6), the OS. poet makes it a
hêlag *halsmeni* (holy necklace), Hel. 52, 7; an old heathen reminiscence came over him, as once before about doves perching on
shoulders (p. 148). At the same time, as he names only the swine,
not the dogs, it is possible that he meant *halsmeni* to be a mere
amplification of ' merigrioton,' pearls.

But this legend of the goddess's necklace gains yet more in importance, when we place it by the side of Greek myths. Brîsînga
men is no other than Aphrodite's ὅρμος (Hymn to Venus 88), and
the chain is her girdle, the κεστὸς ἱμὰς ποικίλος which she wears
on her bosom, and whose witchery subdues all gods and mortals.
How she loosens it off her neck (ἀπὸ στήθεσφιν) and lends it to
Here to charm her Zeus with, is told in a lay that teems with
world-old myths, Il. 14, 214-8. As the ἱμάς is worn in turn by
Here and by Aphrodite, the Norse fable gives the jewel now to
Frigg and now to Freyja, for that ' gold of Frigg ' in Saxo is the
same as Brîsînga men. Then there is another similarity: the same
narrative makes Freyja possess a beautiful chamber, so strong that,
when the door is locked, no one can enter against her will: ' hun

---

[1] Just as from Freyja proceeded the general notion of a freyja frouwà, so
necklace-wearing serves to describe a beautiful wife or maiden. In Sæm. 97ᵃ
menglöð (monili laeta, rejoicing in a necklace) means simply femina, but in
108ᵃ 111ᵃ *Menglöð* is a proper name (see p. 272 note); in 222ᵃ *menskögul* is
used of Brynhildr. Women are commonly named from their ornaments of
gold or precious stones, Sn. 128 (see Suppl.).

âtti ser eina skemmu, er var bæði fögr ok sterk, svâ at þat segja menn, ef hurðin var læst, at eingi mâtti komast î skemmuna ân (without) vilja Freyju,' Sn. 354. We are told the trick by which Loki after all got in, and robbed her of the necklace;[1] Homer says nothing about that, but (Il. 14, 165-8) he knows of Here's θάλαμος,

τόν οἱ φίλος υἱὸς ἔτευξεν
"Ηφαιστος, πυκινὰς δὲ θύρας σταθμοῖσιν ἐπῆρσε
κληῖδι κρυπτῇ, τὴν δ' οὐ θεὸς ἄλλος ἀνῷγεν.

What can be more exactly in accordance with that inaccessible apartment of Freyja, especially as the ἱμάς is spoken of directly after? Hephaistos (Vulcan), who built his mother the curiously contrived bedchamber, answers to the dwarfs who forged the necklace for Freyja. The identity of Frigg and Freyja with Here and Aphrodite must after this mythus be as plain as day.

10. FOLLA. SINDGUND.

Another thing that betrays the confusion of Frigg with Freyja is, that the goddess *Follâ*, now proved by the Merseburg poem to belong to our German mythology, is according to it a sister of Frûâ, while the ON. *Fulla* again is handmaid to Frigg, though she takes rank and order among the Asynjor themselves (Sn. 36-7).[2] Her office and duties are sufficiently expressed in her name; she justifies our reception of the above-mentioned *Abundia* or *dame Habonde* into German mythology, and. corresponds to the masculine god of plenty *Pilnitis, Pilnitus,* whom the Lettons and Prussians adored. Like dame Herke on p. 253, she bestowed prosperity and abundance on mortals, to her keeping was intrusted the divine mother's chest (eski), out of which gifts were showered upon them.

It may be, that Fullâ or Follâ was at the same time thought of as the full-moon (Goth. fulliþs, Lith. Pilnatis, masc.), as another heavenly body, Orion, was referred to Frigg or Freyja: in the Merseburg MS. she is immediately followed by *Sunnâ* with a sister *Sindgund*, whose name again suggests the path of a constellation. The Eddic *Sôl* ranks with the Asynjor, but Sindgund (ON. Sinn-

---

[1] He bored a hole and crept through as a fly, then as a flea he stung the sleeping goddess till she shook off the ornament: an incident still retained in nursery-tales. Conf. the stinging fly at the forging, Sn. 131.

[2] If we read Frîa for Frûa, then Folla would stand nearer to her as in the Norse, whether as attendant goddess or as sister. Yet, considering the instability of those goddesses' names, she may keep her place by Frouwa too.

gunnr ?) is unknown to the Edda. In ch. XXII. on the constellations I shall come back to these divinities (see Suppl.).

11. GART. SIPPIA. SUNIA. WARA. SAGA. NANDA.

From surviving proper names or even impersonal terms, more
rarely from extant myths, we may gather that several more
goddesses of the North were in earlier times common to the rest of
Teutondom.

Frey's beloved, afterwards his wife, was named *Gerðr*, she
came of the giant breed, yet in Sn. 79 she is reckoned among the
Asynjor. The Edda paints her beauty by a charming trait : when
Freyr looked from heaven, he saw her go into a house and close the
door, and then air and water shone with the brightness of her arms
(Sæm. 81. Sn. 39). His wooing was much thwarted, and was
only brought to a happy issue by the dexterity of his faithful
servant Skîrnir. The form of her name *Gerðr*, gen. Gerðar, acc.
Gerði (Sæm. 117ᵇ), points to a Goth. Gardi or Gardja, gen. Gardjôs,
acc. Gardja, and an OHG. Gart or Garta, which often occurs in the
compounds Hildigart, Irmingart, Liutkart, &c., but no longer alone.
The Latin forms Hildegardis, Liudgardis have better preserved the
terminal *i*, which must have worked the vowel-change in Gerðr,
Thôrgerðr, Valgerðr, Hrîmgerðr. The meaning seems to be cingens,
muniens [Gurth ?], Lat. Cinxia as a name of Juno (see Suppl.).

The Goth. *sibja*, OHG. *sippia, sippa*, AS. *sib* gen. sibbe, denote
peace, friendship, kindred; from these I infer a divinity *Sibja, Sippia,
Sib*, corresponding to the ON. *Sif* gen. Sifjar, the wife of Thôrr, for
the ON. too has a pl. sifjar meaning cognatio, sifi amicus (OHG.
sippio, sippo), sift genus, cognatio. By this sense of the word, *Sif*
would appear to be, like Frigg and Freyja, a goddess of loveliness
and love ; as attributes of Oðinn and Thôr agree, their wives Frigg
and Sif have also a common signification. Sif in the Edda is called
the fair-haired, ʻ it hârfagra goð,' and gold is *Sifjar haddr* (Sifae
peplum), because, when Loki cut off her hair, a new and finer crop
was afterwards forged of gold (Sn. 119. 130). Also a herb, polytrichum aureum, bears the name *haddr Sifjar*. Expositors see in
this the golden fruits of the Earth burnt up by fire and growing up
again, they liken Sif to Ceres, the ξανθὴ Δημήτηρ (Il. 5, 500) ; and
with it agrees the fact that the O Slav. *Siva* is a gloss on ʻCeres dea

frumenti' (Hanka's glosses 5ᵃ 6ᵃ,ᵇ) ; only the S in the word seems
to be the Slav. zhivète = Zh, and V does not answer to the Teut.
F, B, P. The earth was Thôr's mother, not his wife, yet in Sn.
220 we do find the simple *Sif* standing for earth. To decide, we
ought to have fuller details about Sif, and these are wholly wanting in our mythology. Nowhere amongst us is the mystic relation
of seed-corn to Demeter, whose poignant grief for her daughter
threatens to bring famine on mankind (Hymn to Cer. 305—315), nor
anything like it, recorded.

The Gothic language draws a subtle distinction between *sunja*
(veritas) and *sunjô* (defensio, probatio veritatis); in OHG. law,
sunna, sunnis means excusatio and impedimentum. The ON. law
likewise has this *syn* gen. synjar, for excusatio, defensio, negatio,
impedimentum, but the Edda at the same time exhibits a personified *Syn*, who was to the heathen a goddess of truth and justice,
and protected the accused (Sn. 38). To the same class belongs *Vör*
gen. Varar, goddess of plighted faith and covenants, a dea foederis
(Sn. 37-8), just as the Romans deified Tutela. The phrase ' vîgja
saman *Varar hendi*,' consecrare Tutelae manu (Saem. 74ᵇ), is like
the passages about Wish's hands, p. 140. As in addition to the
abstract wish we saw a Wish endowed with life, so by the side of
the OHG. wara foedus there may have been a goddess *Wara*, and
beside sunia a *Suniâ* (see Suppl.).

In the same way or *sage* (saw, tale) is intensified into a heathen
goddess *Sagâ*, daughter of Wuotan; like Zeus's daughter the Muse,
she instructs mankind in that divine art which Wuotan himself
invented. I have argued in a separate treatise (Kleine schr. 1, 83—
112), that the *frou Aventiure* of the Mid. Ages is a relic of the
same.

Nanna the wife of Baldr would be in Goth. *Nanþô*, OHG.
Nandâ, AS. *Nôðe*, the bold, courageous (p. 221), but, except in ON.,
the simple female name is lost; Procopius 1, 8 has Gothic Θευδε-
νάνθα, ON. Thioðnanna (see Suppl.).

Inferences like these, from dying words to dead divinities,
could be multiplied; to attempt them is not unprofitable, for they
sharpen the eye to look in fresh quarters [for confirmation or con-

futation]. The discovery from legend or elsewhere of a harmony between myths may raise our guesses into demonstrations.[1]

12. RAHANA (RAN). HELLIA (HEL).

My survey of the gods closed with Oegir and Loki; and the goddesses akin to these shall be the last mentioned here.

To correspond to the ON. *Gefjon* the Old Saxons had, as far as we know, not a female but a male being, *Geban, Geofon* (sea, p. 239). With four giant oxen, according to Sn. 1, Gefjon ploughs Zealand out of the Swedish soil, and a lake arises, whose inward bend exactly fits the projecting coast of Zealand. She is described as a virgin, and all maidens who die virgins wait upon her, Sn. 36. Her name is called upon when oaths are taken: sver ek við *Gefjon*, F. Magn. lex. 386 (see Suppl.). *Gefn*, a name of Freyja (Sn. 37 and Viga- glumss. cap. 27) reminds one of Gefjon.

Rán was the wife of the seagod Oegir, they had nine daughters who are cited by name in the Edda, and called *Ránar* (or *Oegis*) *dœtr*.[2] Men who are drowned fall to the share of *Rán*, which of itself attests her divinity: *fara til Ránar* is to get drowned at sea, Fornald. sög. 2, 78; and *sitja at Ránar* to be drowned, Fornm. sög. 6, 376. Those who were drowned she drew to her in a *net*, and

---

[1] It seems almost as if the MHG. poets recognised a female personage *frô Fuoge* or *Gefuoge* (fitness), similar in plastic power to the masc. Wish, a personified compages or ἁρμονία. Lachmann directs me to instances in point. Er. 7534-40 (conf. Iwein, p. 400):

So hete des meisters sin	So had the master's thought
geprüevet ditz gereite	turned out this riding-gear
mit grôzer wîsheite ;	with great wisdom ;
er gap dem helfenbeine	he gave the ivory
und dâ bî dem gesteine	and withal the jewelry
sîn gevellige stat,	each its proper place,
als in diu *Gevuoge* bat.	as him dame Fitness bade.

(Conf. Er. 1246 : als in mîn wâre schulde bat).—Parz. 121, 11 :

Wer in den zwein landen wirt,	Whoso in the two lands thrives,
Gefuoge ein wunder an im birt ;	Fitness a wonder in him bears ;

he is a miraculous birth of Fitness, her child, her darling.—Conversely, Walther 64, 38 :

Frô Unfuoge, ir habt gesiget.	Dame Unfitness, thou hast triumphed.

And 65, 25 :

Swer *Ungefuoge* swîgen hieze	Whoso bade Indecorum hush,
und sie abe den bürgen stieze !	and hurled her from her strongholds.

It is true, the prefixes ge-, un-, argue a later and colder allegory. And the weak fem. form (acc. in -en) would be preferable, OHG. Fuogâ, gen. Fuogûn, as in N. cap. 135 hîfuogûn, sotigenam (see Suppl.).

[2] Sæm. 79[b] 144[a] 153[b] 180. Sn. 124-9. 185. Eyrbygg. saga p. 274, and index sub v. Rán. Egilssaga p. 616.

carried them off, whence the explanation of her name : *rán* neut. is rapina, ræna rapere, spoliare (see Suppl.).

On the discovery of the rare word *rahanen* (spoliare) in the Hildebr. lied 57, I build the supposition that other Teutonic lands had also a subst. rahan (rapina, spolium) and a goddess *Rahana* (conf. Tanfana, Hluodana), as well as an Uogi = Oegir.[1]

As we passed from Oegir (through Forniot and Logi) to Loki, so we may from Rân to *Hel*, who is no other than Loki's daughter, and like him a dreadful divinity. Rân receives the souls that die by water, Hel those on land, and Freyja those that fall in battle.

The ON. *Hel* gen. Heljar shows itself in the other Teutonic tongues even less doubtfully than Frigg and Freyja or any of the above-mentioned goddesses : Goth. *Halja* gen. Haljôs, OHG. *Hellia, Hella* gen. Hellia, Hella, AS. *Hell* gen. Helle ; only, the personal notion has dropt away, and reduced itself to the local one of halja, hellia, hell, the nether world and place of punishment. Originally Hellia is not death nor any evil being, she neither kills nor torments ; she takes the souls of the departed and holds them with inexorable grip. The idea of a place evolved itself, as that of œgir oceanus out of Oegir, and that of gëban mare from Gëban ; the converted heathen without any ado applied it to the christian underworld, the abode of the damned ; all Teutonic nations have done this, from the first baptized Goths down to the Northmen, because that local notion already existed under heathenism, perhaps also because the church was not sorry to associate lost spirits with a heathen and fiendish divinity.[2] Thus hellia can be explained from Hellia even more readily than ôstara from Ostara.

In the Edda, Hel is Loki's daughter by a giantess, she is sister to the wolf Fenrir and to a monstrous snake. She is *half black* and half of human colour (*blá* hâlf, en hâlf með hörundar lit), Sn. 33, after the manner of the pied people of the Mid. Ages ; in other

---

[1] The Trad. patav. pp. 60-2 assure us of a man's name Raan, Rhaan (Rahan ?). An OHG. Rahana rests on a very slender foundation.

[2] Hel has no affinity at all with ON. hella petra, hellir antrum, as the Goth. hallus petra shows (from hillan sonare, because a rock resounds) : a likelier connexion is that with our höle antrum, OHG. holî, more frequent in neut. hol, for which we should expect a Gothic hul, as in fact a fem. hulundi is caverna, for a cave covers, and so does the nether world (both therefore from hilan celare). Only, the vowels in höle (= huli) and hölle (= halja) do not agree.

passages her *blackness* alone is made a subject of comparison : *blár* sem *Hel*, Nialss. 117. Fornm. sög. 3, 188 ; conf. *Heljarskinn* for complexion of deathly hue, Landnámab. 2, 19. Nialss. cap. 96. Fornald. sög. 2, 59. 60 ;[1] death is black and gloomy. Her dwelling is deep down in the darkness of the ground, under a root of the tree Yggdrasill, in Niflheim, the innermost part of which is there-fore called *Niflhel*, there is her court (rann), there her halls, Sæm. 6ᵇ 44ᵃ 94ᵃ. Sn. 4. Her platter is named *húngr*, her knife *sultr*, synonymous terms to denote her insatiable greed. The dead go down to her, *fara til Heljar*, strictly those only that have died of sickness or old age, not those fallen in fight, who people Valhalla. Her personality has pretty well disappeared in such phrases as *í hel slâ*, drepa, berja *í hel*, to smite into hell, send to Hades ; *í helju vera*, be in Hades, be dead, Fornald. sög. 1, 233. Out of this has arisen in the modern dialects an altogether impersonal and distorted term, Swed. *ihjäl*, Dan. *ihiel*, to death.[2] These languages now express the notion of the nether world only by a compound, Swed. *helvete*, Dan. *helvede*, *i.e.*, the ON. *helvíti* (supplicium infernale), OHG. *hellawîzi*, MHG. *hellewîze*. One who is drawing his last breath is said in ON. liggja milli heims oc heljar (to lie betwixt home and hell), to be on his way from this world to the other. The unpitying nature of the Eddic *Hel* is expressly emphasized ; what she once has, she never gives back : haldi Hel því er *hefir*, Sn. 68 , *hefir* nu Hel, Sæm. 257ᵃ, like the *wolf* in the apologue (Rein-hart xxxvi), for she is of wolfish nature and extraction ; to the wolf on the other hand a *hellish throat* is attributed (see Suppl.).

Two lays in the Edda describe the way to the lower world, the

[1] The ancients also painted Demeter, as the wrathful earth-goddess, *black* (Paus. 8, 42. O. Müller's Eumenides 168, conf. Archæol. p. 509 the black Demeter at Phigalia), and sometimes even her daughter Persephone, the fair maid doomed to the underworld : '*furva* Proserpina,' Hor. Od. 2, 13 (Censorin. De die nat. c. 17). *Black* Aphrodite (Melanis) is spoken of by Pausanias 2, 2. 8, 6. 9, 27 and by Athenæus bk. 13 ; we know the *black* Diana of Ephesus, and that in the Mid. Ages *black* Madonnas were both painted and carved, the Holy Virgin appearing then as a sorrowing goddess of earth or night ; such at Loretto, Naples, Einsiedeln, Würzburg (Altd. W. 2, 209. 286), at Oettingen (Goethe's Corresp. with a child 2, 184), at Puy (Büsching's Nachr. 2, 312-333). Marseilles and elsewhere. I think it specially significant, that the Erinnys or Furia dwelling in Tartarus is also represented both as black and as *half white half black*.

[2] O Swed. has more correctly ihæl, *i.e.*, ihäl (Fred. af Normandie 1299. 1356. 1400. 1414). In Östgötalagen p. 8, one reading has already ihiæll for ihæl ; they no longer grasped the meaning of the term.

Helreið Brynhildar and the Vegtamsqviða; in the latter, Oðin's
ride on Sleipnir for Baldr's sake seems to prefigure that which
Hermôðr afterwards undertakes on the same steed in Sn. 65-7.
But the incidents in the poem are more thrilling, and the dialogue
between Vegtamr[1] and the vala, who says of herself:

>   var ek snifin sniôfi (by snow), ok slegin regni,
>
>   ok drifin döggo (by dew), dauð (dead) var ek leingi,

is among the sublimest things the Edda has to shew. This vala
must stand in close relationship to Hel herself.

Saxo Gram. p. 43 very aptly uses for Hel the Latin *Proserpina*,
he makes her give notice of Balder's death. In the Danish popular
belief *Hel* is a three-legged horse, that goes round the country,
a harbinger of plague and pestilence; of this I shall treat further
on. Originally it was no other than the *steed* on which the goddess
posted over land, picking up the dead that were her due; there is
also a *waggon* ascribed to her, in which she made her journeys.

A passage in Beowulf shows how the Anglo-Saxons retained
perfectly the old meaning of the word. It says of the expiring
Grendel 1698: 'feorh âlegde, hæðene sâwle (vitam deposuit,
animam gentilem), þær hine *Hel onféng*,' the old-heathen goddess
took possession of him.

In Germany too the Mid. Ages still cherished the conception of
a voracious, hungry, insatiable Hell, an *Orcus esuriens, i.e.*, the man-
devouring ogre: 'diu *Helle ferslindet* al daz ter lebet, si *ne wirdet
niomer sat*,' N. Cap. 72. 'diu *Helle* und der arge wân werdent
niemer sat,' Welsch. gast. It sounds still more personal, when she
has *gaping yawning jaws* ascribed to her, like the wolf; pictures in
the MS. of Cædmon represent her simply by a wide open mouth.

Der tobende wuoterîch	The raging tyrant
der was der *Hellen* gelîch,	he was like the Hell
diu daz abgrunde	who the chasm (steep descent)
begenit mit ir munde	be-yawneth with her mouth
unde den himel zuo der erden.	from heaven down[2] to earth.
unde ir doch niht ne mac werden,	And yet to her it cannot hap

----

[1] Oðinn calls himself *Vegtamr* (way-tame, broken-in to the road, gnarus
viae), son of *Valtamr* (assuetus caedibus), as in other places gângtamr (itineri
assuetus) is used of the horse, Sæm. 265ᵇ, but Oðinn himself is Gângrâðr or
Gângleri. Vegtamr reminds one of the holy priest and minstrel *Wechtam* in
Hunibald.

[2] I have supposed that 'unde den' is a slip for 'abe dem'.—TRANS.

daz si imer werde vol;	that she ever become full;
si ist daz *ungesatlîche* hol,	she is the insatiable cavern,
daz weder nu noch nie ne sprah	: that neither now nor ever said
'diz ist des ih niht ne mac.'	'this is what I cannot (manage).'

Lampr. Alex. 6671-80. Old poems have frequent allusions to the abgrund (chasm, abyss) and the doors of hell: helligruoba, hellagrunt, helliporta, &c. Gramm. 2, 458; der abgrunde tunc, der tiefen helle tunc (the deep hell's dinge, darkness), Mart. 88ᵇ 99ᶜ.

Of course there are Bible texts that would in the first instance suggest much of this, *e.g.*, about the insatiableness of hell, Prov. 27, 20. 30, 16 (conf. Freidank lxxiv), her being uncovered, Job 26, 6, her opening her mouth, Isaiah 5, 14. But we are to bear in mind, that all these have the masc. $\H{a}\delta\eta\varsigma$ or infernus, with which the idea of the Latin Orcus also agrees, and to observe how the German language, true to its idiosyncrasy, was obliged to make use of a feminine word. The images of a door, abyss, wide gaping throat, strength and invincibility (fortis tanquam orcus, Petron. cap. 62), appear so natural and necessary to the notion of a nether world, that they will keep recurring in a similar way among different nations (see Suppl.).

The essential thing is, the image of a greedy, unrestoring, female deity.[1]

But the higher we are allowed to penetrate into our antiquities, the less hellish and the more godlike may *Halja* appear. Of this we have a particularly strong guarantee in her affinity to the Indian Bhavani, who travels about and bathes like Nerthus and Holda (p. 268), but is likewise called *Kâlî* or *Mahakâlî*, the great *black* goddess. In the underworld she is supposed to sit in judgment on souls. This office, the similar name and the black hue (kâla niger, conf. câligo and $\kappa\epsilon\lambda\alpha\iota\nu\acute{o}\varsigma$) make her exceedingly like Halja. And Halja is one of the oldest and commonest conceptions of our heathenism.

---

[1] In the south of Holland, where the Meuse falls into the sea, is a place named *Helvoetsluis*. I do not know if any forms in old documents confirm the idea contained in the name, of Hell-foot, foot of Hell. The Romans have a Helium here : Inter Helium ac Flevum, ita appellantur ostia, in quae effusus Rhenus, ab septentrione in lacus, ab occidente in amnem Mosam se spargit, medio inter haec *ore* modicum nomine suo custodiens alveum, Plin. 4, 29. Tac. also says 2, 6 : immenso *ore*. Conf. supra p. 198 on *Oegisdyr* (see Suppl.).

CHAPTER XIV.

CONDITION OF GODS.

Now that we have collected all that could be found concerning the several divinities of our distant past, I will endeavour to survey their nature as a whole; in doing which however, we must be allowed to take more frequent notice of foreign and especially Greek mythology, than we have done in other sections of this work: it is the only way we can find connecting points for many a thread that otherwise hangs loose.

All nations have clothed their gods in human shape, and only by way of exception in those of animals; on this fact are founded both their appearances to men, or incarnation, their twofold sex, their intermarrying with mankind, and also the deification of certain men, *i.e.*, their adoption into the circle of the gods. It follows moreover, that gods are begotten and born, experience pain and sorrow, are subject to sleep, sickness and even death, that like men they speak a language, feel passions, transact affairs, are clothed and armed, possess dwellings and utensils. The only difference is, that to these attributes and states there is attached a higher scale than the human, that all the advantages of the gods are more perfect and abiding, all their ills more slight or transient.

This appears to me a fundamental feature in the faith of the heathen, that they allowed to their gods not an unlimited and unconditional duration, but only a term of life far exceeding that of men. All that is born must also die, and as the omnipotence of gods is checked by a fate standing higher than even they, so their eternal dominion is liable at last to termination. And this reveals itself not only by single incidents in the lives of gods, but in the general notion of a coming and inevitable ruin, which the Edda expresses quite distinctly, and which the Greek system has in the background: the day will come when Zeus's reign shall end.

But this opinion, firmly held even by the Stoics,[1] finds utterance only now and then, particularly in the story of Prometheus, which I have compared to the Norse ragnarökr, p. 245-6.

In the common way of thinking, the gods are supposed to be *immortal* and *eternal*. They are called θεοὶ αἰὲν ἐόντες, Il. 1, 290. 494, αἰειγενέται 2, 400, ἀθάνατοι 2, 814, ἀθάνατος Ζεύς 14, 434; and therefore μάκαρες 1, 339. 599 in contrast to mortal man. They have a special right to the name ἄμβροτοι immortales, while men are βροτοί mortales; ἄμβροτος is explained by the Sansk. amrita immortalis, the negative of mrita mortalis (conf. Pers. merd, homo mortalis); in fact both amrita and ἀμβρόσιος, next neighbour to ἄμβροτος, contain a reference to the food, by partaking of which the gods keep up their immortality. They taste not the fruits of the earth, whereby the βροτοί live, οἳ ἀρούρης καρπὸν ἔδουσιν, Il. 6, 142. With βροτός again is connected βρότος thick mortal blood, whereas in the veins of the gods flows ἰχώρ (Il. 5, 340. 416), a light thin liquid, in virtue of which they seem to be called ἄβροτοι = ἄμβροτοι.

Indian legend gives a full account of the way amrita, the elixir of immortality, was brewed out of water clear of milk, the juice of herbs, liquid gold and dissolved precious-stones ;[2] no Greek poem tells us the ingredients of ambrosia, but it was an ἀμβροσιὴ τροφή (food), and there was a divine drink besides, γλυκὺ νέκταρ, Il. 1, 598, of a red colour 19, 38, its name being derived either from νη and κτᾶσθαι, or better from νεκ-ταρ necem avertens. Where men take bread and wine, the gods take ambrosia and nectar, Od. 5, 195, and hence comes the

ἄμβροτον αἷμα θεοῖο,
ἰχώρ, οἷός πέρ τε ῥέει μακάρεσσι θεοῖσιν·
οὐ γὰρ σῖτον ἔδουσ᾽, οὐ πίνουσ᾽ αἴθοπα οἶνον·
τοὔνεκ᾽ ἀναίμονές εἰσι καὶ ἀθάνατοι καλέονται.

—Il. 5, 339.

Theirs is no thick glutinous αἷμα (conf. our seim, ON. seimr, slime), nor according to the Indians do they sweat ; and this ἀναίμων (bloodless) agrees with the above explanation of ἄβροτος. The

---

[1] Atque omnes pariter deos perdet mors aliqua et chaos. Seneca in Herc. 1014.
[2] Cleopatra had costly pearls melted in her wine, and it is said to be still a custom with Indian princes ; conf. Sueton. Calig. 37.

adjectives ἄβροτος, ἄμβροτος, ἀμβρόσιος, νεκτάρεος are passed on
from the food to other divine things[1] (see Suppl.). Plainly then
the gods were not immortal by their nature, they only acquired and
secured this quality by abstaining from the food and drink of men,
and feasting on heavenly fare. And hence the idea of death is not
always nor as a matter of course kept at a distance from them;
Kronos used to kill his new born children, no doubt before nectar
and ambrosia had been given them,[2] and Zeus alone could be saved
from him by being brought up secretly. Another way in which
the mortality of certain gods is expressed is, that they fall a prey
to Hades, whose meaning borders on that of death, e.g., Persephone.

If a belief in the eternity of the gods is the dominant one
among the Greeks, and only scattered hints are introduced of their
final overthrow; with our ancestors on the contrary, the thought of
the gods being immortal seems to retire into the background.
The Edda never calls them eylifir or ôdauðligir, and their death is
spoken of without disguise : þâ er regin deyja, Sæm. 37[a], or more
frequently : regin riufaz (solvuntur), 36[b] 40[a] 108[b]. One of the
finest and oldest myths describes the death of Balder, the burning
of his body, and his entrance into the lower world, like that of
Proserpine ; Oðin's destined fall is mentioned in the Völuspâ 9[a],
Oðins bani (bane), Sn. 73, where also Thôrr falls dead on the
ground ; Hrûngnir, a giant, threatens to slay all the gods (drepa
guð öll), Sn. 107. Yet at the same time we can point to clear
traces of that prolongation of life by particular kinds of food and
drink. While the einherjar admitted into Valhöll feast on the
boiled flesh of a boar, we are nowhere told of the Ases sharing in
such diet (Sæm. 36. 42. Sn. 42) ; it is even said expressly, that
Oðinn needs no food (önga vist þarf hann), and only drinks wine
(vîn er honum bæði dryckr ok matr, both meat and drink) ;
with the viands set before him he feeds his two wolves Geri and
Freki. Við vîn eitt vâpngöfugr Oðinn æ lifir (vino solo armipotens
semper vivit), Sæm. 42[b] ; æ lifir can be rendered ' semper vescitur,

---

[1] Both nectar and ambrosia, like the holy grail of the Mid. Ages, have
miraculous powers : poured into the nose of a corpse, they prevent decay, Il.
19, 38 ; they ward off hunger, Il. 19, 347. 353.

[2] As human infants may only be exposed before milk and honey have
moistened their lips, conf. RA. pp. 458-9. When Zeus first receives in the
assembly of the gods the son whom Leto bore him, he hands him nectar in a
golden bowl : by this act he recognised him for his child.

nutritur,' or 'immortalitatem nanciscitur,' and then the cause of his
immortality would be found in his partaking of the wine.   Evidently this wine of the Norse gods is to the beer and ale (ölr) of
men, what the nectar of the Greek gods was to the wine of mortals.
Other passages are not so particular about their language;[1] in
Sæm. 59 the gods at Oegir's hall have ale set before them, conf. öl
giöra, 68ᵇ; Heimdall gladly drinks the good mead, 41ᵇ; verðar
nema oc sumbl (cibum capere et symposium) 52, leaves the exact
nature of the food undefined, but earthly fare is often ascribed to
the gods in so many words.[2] But may not the costly Oðhrœris
dreckr, compounded of the divine Qvâsir's blood and honey, be
likened to amrita and ambrosia ?[3] Dwarfs and giants get hold of
it first, as amrita fell into the hands of the giants; at last the
gods take possession of both.   Oðhrœris dreckr confers the gift of
poesy, and by that very fact immortality: Oðinn and Saga, goddess
of poetic art, have surely drunk it out of golden goblets, gladly and
evermore (um alla daga, Sæm. 41ᵃ). We must also take into
account the creation of the wise Qvâsir (conf. Slav. kvas, convivium,
potus) ; that at the making of a covenant between the Aesir and
Vanir, he was formed out of their spittle (hraki); the refining of
his blood into a drink for gods seems a very ancient and far-
reaching myth.   But beside this drink, we have also notices of a
special food for gods : Iðunn has in her keeping certain apples, by
eating of which the aging gods make themselves young again (er
goðin skulo âbîta, þâ er þau eldaz, oc verða þâ allir ungir, Sn. 30ᵃ).
This reminds one of the apples of Paradise and the Hesperides, of the
guarded golden apples in the Kindermärchen no. 57, of the apples
in the stories of Fortunatus and of Merlin, on the eating or biting
of which depend life, death and metamorphosis, as elsewhere on a
draught of holy water.   According to the Eddic view, the gods have
a means, it is true, of preserving perpetual freshness and youth,

[1] As Homer too makes Ganymede οἰνοχοεύειν, Il. 20, 234, and of Hebe it is
even said, νέκταρ ἐῳνοχόει 4, 3.
[2] Zeus goes to banquet (κατὰ δαῖτα) with the Ethiopians, Il. 1, 423 ; ὅταν
πρὸς δαῖτα καὶ ἐπὶ θοίνην ἴωσι, Plato's Phædr. 247, as Thôrr does with the Norwegians ; even when disguised as a bride, he does not refuse the giants' dishes,
Sæm. 73ᵇ ; and the Ases boiled an ox on their journey, Sn. 80.
[3] In Sanskrit, sudha nectar is distinguished from amrita ambrosia.   Everywhere there is an eagle in the business : Garuda is called sudhâhara, or amritâ-
harana, nectar-thief or ambrosia-thief (Pott, forsch. 2, 451); it is in the shape of
an eagle that Oðinn carries off Oðhrœrir, and Zeus his cupbearer Ganymede
(see ch. XXXV and XXX, Path-crossing and Poetry).

but, for all that, they are regarded as subject to the encroach-
ments of age, so that there are always some *young* and some *old*
gods ; in particular, Odinn or Wuotan is pictured everywhere as an
old greybeard (conf. the old god, p. 21), Thôrr as in the full
strength of manhood, Balder as a blooming youth. The gods grow
hárir ok *gamlir* (hoar and old), Sn. 81. Freyr has ' at tannfê '
(tooth-fee) presented him at his teething, he is therefore imagined
as *growing up*. In like manner Uranos and Kronos appear as old,
Zeus (like our Donar) and Poseidon as middle aged, Apollo, Hermes and Ares as in the bloom of youth. Growth and age, the
increase and decline of a power, exclude the notion of a strictly
eternal, immutable, immortal being ; and mortality, the termination,
however long delayed, of gods with such attributes, is a necessity
(see Suppl.).

Epithets expressing the power, the omnipotence, of the reigning
gods have been specified, pp. 21-2. A term peculiar to ON. poetry
is *gin*regin, Sæm. 28[a] 50[a] 51[a] 52[b], *gin*heilög goð 1[a] ; it is of
the same root as gîna, OHG. kînan, hiare, and denotes numina
ampla, late dominantia, conf. AS. ginne grund, Beow. 3101. Jud.
131, 2. ginne rîce, Cædm. 15, 8. ginfæst, firmissimus 176, 29.
ginfæsten god, terrae dominus 211, 10. gârsecges gin, oceani
amplitudo 205, 3.

The Homeric ῥεῖα (= ῥᾳδίως, Goth. raþizô) beautifully expresses the power of the gods ; whatever they do or undertake
comes easy to them, their life glides along free from toil, while
mortal men labour and are heavy laden : θεοὶ ῥεῖα ζώοντες, Il. 6,
138. Od. 4, 805. 5, 122. When Aphrodite wishes to remove her
favourite Alexander from the perils of battle, τὸν δ' ἐξήρπαξ'
Ἀφροδίτη ῥεῖα μάλ', ὥστε θεός, Il. 3, 381 ; the same words are
applied to Apollo, when he snatches Hector away from Achilles 20,
443. The wall so laboriously built by the Greeks he overturns ῥεῖα
μάλα, as a boy at play would a sand-heap 15, 362. With a mere
breath (πνοιῇ), blowing a little (ἦκα μάλα ψύξασα), Athene turns
away from Achilles the spear that Hector had thrown 20, 440 (see
Suppl.). Berhta also blows (p. 276), and the elves breathe (ch.
XVII), on people.

The sons of men grow up slowly and gradually, gods attain
their full size and strength *directly after birth*. No sooner had

Themis presented nectar and ambrosia (ἀμβροσίην ἐρατεινήν) to the newborn Apollo, than he leapt, κατέβρως ἄμβροτον, out of his swathings, sat down among the goddesses, began to speak, and, unshorn as he was, to roam through the country (Hymn. in Ap. Del. 123—133). Not unlike Vali, whom Rindr bore to Oðinn; when only *one night old* (einnættr), unwashen and unkempt, he sallies forth to avenge Baldr's death on Höðr, Sæm. 6ᵇ 95ᵇ. Here the coincidence of ἀκερσεκόμης with the Edda's ' ne höfuð kembr ' is not to be disregarded. Hermes, born at early morn, plays the lute at mid-day, and at eve drives oxen away (Hymn. in Merc. 17 seq.). And Zeus, who is often exhibited as a child among the Kuretes, grew up *rapidly* (καρπαλίμως μένος καὶ φαίδιμα γυῖα ηὔξετο τοῖο ἄνακτος), and in his first years had strength enough to enter the lists with Kronos (Hes. theog. 492). The Norse mythology offers another example in Magni, Thôr's son by the giantess Iarnsaxa: when three nights old (þrínættr), he flung the giant Hrûngni's enormous foot, under whose weight Thôrr lay on the ground, off his father, and said he would have beaten the said giant dead with his fist, Sn. 110 (see Suppl.).

The *shape* of the gods is like the human (p. 105), only vaster, often exceeding even the gigantic. When Ares is felled to the ground by the stone which Athene flings, his body covers seven roods of land (ἑπτά δ' ἐπέσχε πέλεθρα πεσών, Il. 21, 407), a size that with a slight addition the Od. 11, 577 puts upon the titan Tityos. When Here takes a solemn oath, she grasps the earth with one hand and the sea with the other (Il. 14, 272). A cry that breaks from Poseidon's breast sounds like that of nine or even ten thousand warriors in battle (14, 147), and the same is said of Ares when he roars (5, 859); Here contents herself with the voice of Stentor, which only equals those of fifty men (5, 786). By the side of this we may put some features in the Edda, which have to do with Thôrr especially: he devours at a wedding one ox and eight salmon, and drinks three casks of mead, Sæm. 73ᵇ; another time, through a horn, the end of which reaches to the sea, he drinks a good portion of this, he lifts the snake that encircles the whole world off one of its feet, and with his hammer he strikes three deep valleys in the rocky mountain, Sn. 59, 60. Again, Teutonic mythology agrees with the Greek in never imputing to its gods the deformity of *many heads, arms* or *legs;* they are only bestowed

on a few heroes and animals, as some of the Greek giants are
ἑκατόγχειρες. Such forms are quite common in the Hindu and
Slav systems: Vishnu is represented with four arms, Brahma with
four heads, Svantovit the same, while Porevit has five heads and
Rugevit seven faces. Yet Hecate too is said to have been three-
headed, as the Roman Janus was two-faced, and a Lacedæmonian
Apollo four-armed.[1] Khuvera, the Indian god of wealth, is a
hideous figure with three legs and eight teeth. Some of the Norse
gods, on the contrary, have not a superfluity, but a deficiency of
members: Oðinn is one-eyed, Týr one-handed, Höðr blind, and
Logi or Loki was perhaps portrayed as lame or limping, like
Hephæstus and the devil. Hel alone has a dreadful shape, black
and white; the rest of the gods and goddesses, not excepting Loki,
are to be imagined as of beautiful and noble figure (see Suppl.).

In the Homeric epos this ideally perfect human shape, to which
Greek art also keeps true, is described in standing epithets for gods
and especially goddesses, with which our ruder poetry has only a
few to set in comparison, and yet the similarity of these is significant. Some epithets have to serve two or three divinities by
turns, but most are confined to individuals, as characteristic of
them. Thus Here is λευκώλενος or βοῶπις (the former used also
of Helen, Il. 3, 121,[2] the latter of a Nereid 18, 40), Athene γλαυκῶ-
πις or ἠΰκομος (which again does for Here), Thetis ἀργυρόπεζα,
Iris ἀελλόπος, ποδήνεμος, χρυσόπτερος, Eos ῥοδοδάκτυλος, Demeter
(Ceres) ξανθή 5, 500, and καλλιπλόκαμος 14, 326, just as Sif is
hârfögr (p. 309), in allusion to the yellow colour of the waving
corn. As the sea rolls its dark waves, Poseidon bears the name
κυανοχαίτις, Il. 14, 390. 15, 174. 20, 144. Zeus could either be
called the same, or κυανόφρυς (a contrast to Baldr brâhvítr, brow-
white p. 222), because to him belong ἀμβρόσιαι χαῖται Il. 1, 528, the
hair and locks of Wish (p. 142), and because with his dark brows
he makes signs. This confirmatory lowering of the brows or
nodding with the head (νεύειν, κατανεύειν κυανέῃσιν ἐπ' ὀφρύσι Il.
1, 527. 17, 209) is the regular expression of Zeus's will: κεφαλῇ
κατανεύσομαι, ἀθανάτοισι μέγιστον τέκμωρ, Il. 1, 524. In refusing,
he draws the head back (ἀνανεύει). Thôr's indignant rage is shown
by sinking the eyebrows over the eyes (sîga brýnnar ofan fyrir

---

[1] O. Müller's archæol. p. 515.
[2] And Aphrodite throws her πήχεε λευκώ round Æneas.—TRANS.

augun, Sn. 50), displaying gloomy brows and shaking the beard. Obviously the two gods, Zeus and Donar, have identical gestures ascribed to them for expressing favour or anger. They are the glowering deities, who have the avenging thunder at their command; this was shown of Donar, p. 177, and to Zeus is given the grim louring look (δεινὰ δ' ὑπόδρα ἰδών, Il. 15, 13), he above all is the μέγ' ὀχθήσας (1, 517. 4, 30), and next to him Poseidon of the dingy locks (8, 208. 15, 184). Zeus again is distinguished by beaming eyes (τρέπεν ὄσσε φαεινώ 13, 3. 7. 14, 236. 16, 645), which belong to none else save his own great-hearted daughter 21, 415; Aphrodite has ὄμματα μαρμαίροντα, 3, 397, twinkling, shimmering eyes (see Suppl.).

Figures of Greek divinities show a *circle of rays* and a *nimbus* round the head;[1] on Indo-Grecian coins Mithras has commonly a circular nimbus with pointed rays,[2] in other representations the rays are wanting. Mao (deus Lunus) has a halfmoon behind his shoulders; Aesculapius too had rays about his head. In what century was the halo, the *aureole*, first put round the heads of christian saints? And we have also to take into account the crowns and diadems of kings. Ammian. Marc. 16, 12 mentions Chnodomarius, cujus vertici flammeus torulus aptabatur. N. Cap. 63 translates the honorati capitis radios of the Sol auratus by *houbetskîmo* (head-sheen), and to portray the sun's head surrounded with flames is extremely natural. In ON. I find the term *rôða* for caput radiatum sancti, which I suppose to be the OHG. *ruota* rod, since virga also goes off into the sense of flagellum, radius, ON. geisli. A likening of the gods to radiant luminaries of heaven would at once suggest such a nimbus, and blond locks do shine like rays. It is in connexion with the setting sun that Tac. Germ. 45 brings in formas deorum and *radios capitis*. Around Thôr's head was put, latterly at all events, a ring of stars (Stephanii not. ad Saxon. Gram. p. 139). According to a story told in the Galien restoré, a beam came out of Charles the Great's mouth and illumined his head.[3] What seems more to the purpose, among the Prilwitz figures, certain Slavic idols, especially Perun, Podaga and Nemis, have rays about their

[1] O. Müller's archæol. p. 481.
[2] Götting. anz. 1838, 229.
[3] This beam from Charles's mouth is like the one that shines into his beloved's mouth and lights up the gold inside (see ch. XVI., Menni).

heads ; and a head in Hagenow, fig. 6, 12 is encircled with rays, so
is even the rune R when it stands for Radegast. Did rays originally
express the highest conception of divine and lustrous beauty ?
There is nothing in the Homeric epos at all pointing that way (see
Suppl.).

It is a part of that insouciance and light blood of the gods, that
they are *merry*, and *laugh*. Hence they are called blî∂ regin
(p. 26), as we find ' froh' in the sense of gracious applied to gods
and kings,[1] and the spark of joy is conveyed from gods to men.
Fráuja, lord, is next of kin to *froh* glad (p. 210). It is said of the
Ases, *teitir* vâro, Sæm. 2ᵃ ; and of Heimdall, dreckr *gla∂r* hinn gô∂a
miö∂ 41ᵇ. And ' in *sváso* gu∂ ' 33ᵃ contains a similar notion. In
this light the passages quoted (pp. 17-8) on the *blithe* and *cheerful*
God gather a new importance : it is the old heathen notion still
lurking in poetry. When Zeus in divine repose sits on Olympus
and looks down on men, he is moved to mirth (ὁρόων φρένα τέρψο-
μαι, Il. 20, 23), then laughs the blessed heart of him (ἐγέλασσε δέ
οἱ φίλον ἦτορ, 21, 389) ; which is exactly the Eddic ' hlô honum
hugr î briosti, hlô Hlôrri∂a hugr î briosti,' laughed the mind in his
breast : a fresh confirmation of the essential oneness of Zeus and
Thôrr. But it is also said of heroes : ' hlô þâ Atla hugr î briosti,'
Sæm. 238ᵇ. ' hlô þâ Brynhildr af öllum hug,' with all her heart
220ᵃ. OS. ' hugi ward frômôd,' Hel. 109, 7. AS. ' môd âhlôh,'
Andr. 454. Later, in the Rudlieb 2, 174. 203. 3, 17 the king in
his speech is said *subridere ;* in the Nibel. 423, 2 of Brunhild :
' mit *smielinden munde* si über ahsel sah,' looked over her shoulder.
Often in the song of the Cid : ' *sonrisose* de la boca,' and ' alegre era'.[2]
Θυμὸς ἰάνθη, Il. 23, 600 ; conf. θυμὸν ἴαινον, Hymn. in Cer. 435.
Half in displeasure Here laughs with her lips, not her brows :
ἐγέλασσε χείλεσιν, οὐδὲ μέτωπον ἐπ' ὀφρύσι κυανέῃσιν ἰάνθη, Il.
15, 102 ; but Zeus feels joy in sending out his lightnings, he is
called τερπικέραυνος 2, 781. 8, 2. 773. 20, 144. So Artemis
(Diana) is ἰοχέαιρα, rejoicing in arrows, 6, 428. 21, 480. Od. 11,
198. At the limping of Hephæstus, the assembly of gods bursts
into ἄσβεστος γέλως, uncontrolled laughter, Il. 1, 599 ; but a gentle
smile (μειδᾶν) is peculiar to Zeus, Here and Aphrodite. As

---

[1] Andreas and Elene p. xxxvii.
[2] Helbl. 7, 518 : diu wârheit des *erlachet*, truth laughs at that.

Aphrodite's beauty is expressed by φιλομμειδής, smile-loving (Il. 4, 10. 5, 375), so is Freyja's on the contrary by 'grâtfögr,' fair in weeping (see Suppl.).

We have to consider next the manner in which the gods put themselves in motion and become visible to the eyes of mortals. We find they have a *gait* and *step* like the human, only far mightier and swifter. The usual expressions are βῆ, βῆ ἴμεν, βῆ ἰέναι, Il. 1, 44. 2, 14. 14, 188. 24, 347, βεβήκει 1, 221, ἔβη 14, 224, βάτην 5, 778, βήτην 14, 281, ποσὶ προβιβάς 13, 18, προσεβήσετο 2, 48. 14, 292, κατεβήσετο 13, 17, ἀπεβήσετο 2, 35 ; and in the Edda *gengr*, Sæm. 9ᵃ, gêk 100ᵃ, gêngo 70ᵃ 71ᵇ, gengêngo 1ᵃ 5ᵃ, or else *fôr* 31ᵃ 31ᵇ 53ᵃ 75ᵃ, this fara meaning no more than ire, proficisci, and Oðinn was even called Gângleri, Sæm. 32. Sn. 24, *i.e.*, the walker, traveller ; the AS. poets use *gewât* (evasit, abiit) or *siðôde* of God returning to heaven, Andr. 118. 225. 977. El. 94-5. But how enormously the walk of the gods differs from the common, we see in the instance of Poseidon, who goes an immense distance in three steps, Il. 13, 20, or that of the Indian Vishnu, who in three paces traverses earth, air and sky. From such swiftness there follows next the *sudden appearance* and *disappearance* of the gods ; for which our older speech seems to have used Goth. hvaírban, OHG. huerban, AS. hweorfan (verti, ferri, rotari): ' *hwearf* him tô heofenum hâlig dryhten ' says Cædm. 16, 8 ; and ' Oðinn *hvarf* þâ,' vanished, Sæm. 47. Homer employs, to express the same thing, either the verb ἀΐσσω (impetu feror), or the adverbs καρπαλίμως (as if ἁρπαλίμως raptim) and κραιπνῶς raptim. Thus Athene or Here comes ἀΐξασα, Od. 1, 102. Il. 2, 167. 4, 74. 19, 114. 22, 187 ; Thetis, the dream, Athene, Here, all appear καρπαλίμως, Il. 1, 359. 2, 17. 168. 5, 868. 19, 115. Od. 2, 406 ; Poseidon and Here κραιπνά, κραιπνῶς, Il. 13, 18. 14. 292 ; even Zeus, when he rises from his throne to look on the earth, στῆ ἀναΐξας 15, 6. So Holda and Berhta *suddenly* stand at the window (p. 274). Much in the same way I understand the expression used in Sæm. 53ᵃ of Thôrr and Týr : fôro *driugom* (ibant tractim, raptim, ἑλκηδόν), for driugr is from driuga, Goth. driugan trahere, whence also Goth. draúhts, OHG. truht turba, agmen, ON. draugr larva, phantasma, OHG. gitroc fallacia, because a spectre appears and vanishes quickly in the air. At the same time it means the rush and din

that betoken the god's approach, the wôma and ômi above, from
which Oðinn took a name (p. 144-5). The rapid movement of
descending gods is sometimes likened to a shooting star, or the
flight of birds, Il. 4, 75.   15, 93. 237 ; hence they often take even
the form of some bird, as Tharapila the Osilian god flew (p. 77).
Athene flies away in the shape of a ἄρπη (falcon ?), Il. 19, 350, an
ὄρνις bird, Od. 1, 320, or a φήνη osprey, 3, 372 ; as a swallow she
perches (ἕζετ' ἀναΐξασα) on the house's μέλαθρον 22, 239.   The
exchange of the human form for that of a bird, when the gods are
departing and no longer need to conceal their wondrous being,
tallies exactly with Oðin's taking his flight as a falcon, after he
had in the shape of Gestr conversed and quarrelled with Heiðreckr:
viðbrast î *vals* líki, Fornald. sög. 1, 487 ; but it is also retained in
many stories of the devil, who assumes at departure the body of a
raven or a fly (exit tanquam corvus, egressus est in muscae
similitudine).   At other times, and this is the prettier touch of the
two, the gods allow the man to whom they have appeared as his
equals, suddenly as they are going, to become aware of their divine
proportions : heel, calf, neck or shoulder betrays the god.   When
Poseidon leaves the two Ajaxes, one of them says, Il. 13, 71 :

> ἴχνια γὰρ μετόπισθε ποδῶν ἠδὲ κνημάων
> ῥεῖ' ἔγνων ἀπιόντος· ἀρίγνωτοι δὲ θεοί περ.

So, when Venus leaves Aeneas, Virg. 1, 402 :

> Dixit, et *avertens* rosea cervice refulsit
> et vera incessu patuit dea.   Ille ubi matrem
> agnovit, tali *fugientem* est voce secutus.

So, Il. 3, 396, Alexander recognises the

> θεᾶς περικαλλέα δειρήν,
> στήθεά θ' ἱμερόεντα καὶ ὄμματα μαρμαίροντα.

And in ON. legend, Hallbiörn on awaking sees the shoulder of a
figure in his dream before it vanishes : þykist siâ â herðar honum,
Fornald. sög. 3, 103 ; as is likewise said in Olaf the saint's saga
cap. 199. ed. Holm., while the Fornm. sög. 5, 38 has it : siâ svip
mannsins er â brutt gekk ; conf. os humerosque deo similis, Aen. 1,
589. This also lingers in our devil-stories : at the Evil one's
departure his cloven hoof suddenly becomes visible, the ἴχνια of
the ancient god.

As the incessus of Venus declared the goddess, the motion (ἴθμα)
of Here and Athene is likened to that of timorous doves, Il. 5, 778.

But the gliding of the gods over such immense distances must have seemed from first to last like flying, especially as their departure was expressly prepared for by the assumption of a bird's form. It is therefore easy to comprehend why two several deities, Hermes and Athene, are provided with peculiar *sandals* (πέδιλα), whose motive power conveys them over sea and land with the speed of wind, Il. 24, 341. Od. 1, 97. 5, 45; we are expressly told that Hermes *flew* with them (πέτετο, Il. 24, 345. Od. 5, 49); plastic art represents them as winged shoes, and at a later time adds a pair of wings to the head of Hermes.[1] These winged sandals then have a perfect right to be placed side by side with the *feather-shift* (fiaðrhamr) which Freyja possessed, and which at Thôr's request she lent to Loki for his flight to Iötunheim, Sæm. 70[a.b]; but as Freyja is more than once confounded with Frigg (p. 302), other legends tell us that Loki flew off in the 'valsham Friggjar,' Sn. 113. I shall come back to these falcon or swan coats in another connexion, but their resemblance to the Greek pedīla is unmistakable; as Loki is here sent as a messenger from the gods to the giants, he is so far one with Hermes, and Freyja's feather-shift suggests the sandals of Athene. Sn. 132-7: 'Loki átti *skúa, er hann rann á lopt ok lög*,' had shoes in which he ran through air and fire. It was an easy matter, in a myth, for the investiture with winged hamr or sandals to glide insensibly into an actual assumption of a bird's form: Geirröðr catches the flying Loki as a veritable bird, Sn. 113, and when Athene starts to fly, she is a swallow (see Suppl.).

The mighty gods would doubtless have moved whithersoever it pleased them, without wings or sandals, but simple antiquity was not content with even these: the human race used *carriages* and *horses*, and the gods cannot do without them either. On this point a sensible difference is to be found between the Greek and German mythologies.

All the higher divinities of the Greeks have a *chariot and pair* ascribed to them, as their kings and heroes in battle also fight in chariots. An ὄχημα for the god of thunder would at once be suggested by the natural phenomenon itself; and the conception of the sun-chariot driven by Helios must also be very ancient. The

[1] O. Müller's archæol. 559.

car of Here, and how she harnesses her steeds to it, mounts it in company with Athene, and guides it, is gorgeously depicted in Il. 5, 720-76; so likewise Demeter and Kora appear seated in a carriage. Hermes is drawn by rams,[1] as the Norse Thôrr [by he-goats]. The Okeanides too have their vehicle, Aesch. Prom. 135. But never are Zeus, Apollo, Hermes or any of the most ancient gods imagined riding *on horseback;* it is Dionysos, belonging to a different order of deities, that first rides a panther, as Silenus does the ass, and godlike heroes such as Perseus, Theseus, and above all, the Dioscuri are mounted on horses. Okeanos bestrides a winged steed, Prom. 395. It seems worth remarking, that modern Greek legend represents even Charon as mounted.

In Teutonic mythology the *riding* of gods is a far commoner thing. In the Merseburg poem both Wuotan and Phol ride in the forest, which is not at all inconsistent with the word used, 'faran'; for it is neither conceivable that Wuotan drove while Balder rode, nor that Balder drove a one-horse carriage. Even Hartmann von Aue still imagines God riding a horse, and contented with Enit for his groom (p. 18). Among those that ride in the Edda are Oðinn (who saddles his Sleipnir for himself, Sæm. 93[a]), Baldr and Hermôðr; in Sæm. 44[a] and Sn. 18 are given the names of ten other horses as well, on which the Ases daily ride to council, one of them being Heimdall's Gulltoppr, Sn. 30. 66; the owners of the rest are not specified, but, as there were twelve Ases and only eleven horses are named, it follows that each of those gods had his mount, except Thôrr, who is invariably introduced either driving or walking (p. 167), and when he gets Gullfaxi as spoil from Hrûngnir, gives him away to his son Magni, Sn. 110. Oðin's horse leaps a hedge seven ells high, Fornm. sög. 10, 56. 175. Even the women of the gods are mounted: the valkyrs, like Oðinn, ride through air and water, Sn. 107, Freyja and Hyndla on a boar and a wolf, as enchantresses and witches are imagined riding a wolf, a he-goat or a cat. Night (fem.) had a steed Hrîmfaxi, rimy-mane, as Day (masc.) had Skînfaxi, shiny-mane.

At the same time *carriages* are mentioned too, especially for goddesses (p. 107). The sacred car of Nerthus was drawn by cows, that of Freyja by cats, Holda and Berhta are commonly found driving waggons which they get mended, the fairies in our nursery-

[1] O. Müller's archæol. 563.

tales travel through the air in coaches, and Brynhildr drives in her waggon to the nether world, Sæm. 227. The image of a Gothic deity in a waggon was alluded to on p. 107; among the gods, Freyr is expressly described as mounted on his car, while Thôrr has a waggon drawn by he-goats: on Wôden's waggon, conf. p. 151 (see Suppl.).

When we consider, that waggons were proper to the oldest kings also, especially the Frankish kings, and that their riding on horseback is nowhere mentioned; it seems probable that originally a similar equipage was alone deemed suitable to the gods, and their riding crept in only gradually in the coarser representations of later times. From heroes it was transferred to gods, though this must have been done pretty early too, as we may venture to allow a considerable antiquity to the story of Sleipnir and that of Balder's horse or foal. The Slavs also generally furnished their god Svantovit with a horse to ride on.

Some few divinities made use of a *ship*, as may be seen by the stories of Athene's ship and that of Isis, and Frey's Skîðblaðnir, the best of all ships, Sæm. 45ᵇ.

But whichever way the gods might move, on earth, through air or in water, their walk and tread, their riding and driving is represented as so *vehement*, that it produces a loud noise, and the din of the elements is explained by it. The driving of Zeus or Thôrr awakens thunder in the clouds; mountains and forests tremble beneath Poseidon's tread, Il. 13, 18; when Apollo lets himself down from the heights of Olympus, arrows and bow clatter (ἔκλαγξαν) on his shoulder 1, 44, δεινὴ δὲ κλαγγὴ γένετ᾽ ἀργυρέοιο βιοῖο, dreadful was the twang of his silver bow 1, 49. In the lays of the Edda this *stirring up of nature* is described in exactly the same way, while the AS. and OHG. writings, owing to the earlier extinction of heathen notions, have preserved no traces of it: 'framm reið Oðinn, foldvegr dundi,' forth rode O., earth's way thundered, Sæm. 94ᵃ; 'biörg brotnoðo, brann iörð loga, ôk Oðins sonr î Iötunheima,' mountains crumbled, earth blazed, when rode, &c. 73ᵃ; 'flô Loki, fiaðrhamr dundi,' the wing-coat whirred, 70ᵃ 71ᵃ; 'iörð bifaz (quaked), enn allir for sciâlfa garðar Gymis' when Skîrnir came riding 83ᵃ. The rage and writhing of gods who were bound produced equally tremendous effects (p. 246).

On the other hand, delightful and salutary *products of nature* are also traced to the immediate influence of the gods. Flowers spring up where their feet have strayed; on the spot where Zeus clasped Here in his arms, shot up a thick growth of sweet herbs and flowers, and glittering dewdrops trickled down, Il. 14, 346—51. So, when the valkyrs rode through the air, their horses' manes shook fruitful dew on the deep vales below, Sæm. 145[b]; or it falls nightly from the bit of Hrîmfaxi's bridle 32[b] (see Suppl.).

Of one thing there is scarcely a trace in our mythology, though it occurs so often in the Greek: that the gods, to screen themselves from sight, *shed a mist* round themselves or their favourites who are to be withdrawn from the enemy's eye, Il. 3, 381. 5, 776. 18, 205. 21, 549. 597. It is called ἠέρι καλύπτειν, ἠέρα χεῖν, ἀχλὺν or νέφος στέφειν, and the contrary ἀχλὺν σκεδάζειν to scatter, chase away, the mist. We might indeed take this into account, that the same valkyrs who, like the Servian vîly, favour and shield their beloved heroes in battle, were able to produce clouds and hail in the air; or throw into the reckoning our tarnkappes and helidhelms, whose effect was the same as that of the mist. And the Norse gods do take part with or against certain heroes, as much as the Greek gods before Ilion. In the battle of Brâvîk, Oðinn mingled with the combatants, and assumed the figure of a charioteer Brûni; Saxo Gram., p. 146. Fornald. sög. 1, 380. The Grîmnismâl makes Geirröðr the protégé (föstri) of Oðinn, Agnarr that of Frigg, and the two deities take counsel together concerning them, Sæm. 39; in the Völs. saga cap. 42, Oðinn suggests the plan for slaying the sons of Ionakr. The Greek gods also, when they drew nigh to counsel or defend, appeared in the form of a human warrior, a herald, an old man, or they made themselves known to their hero himself, but not to others. In such a case they *stand before, beside* or *behind* him (παρά, Il. 2, 279. ἐγγύθι, Od. 1, 120. ἀγχοῦ, Il. 2, 172. 3, 129. 4, 92. 5, 123. πρόσθεν 4, 129. ὄπιθεν 1, 197); Athene leads by the hand through the battle, and wards the arrows off 4, 52; she throws the dreadful ægis round Achilles 18, 204; Aphrodite shields Aeneas by holding her veil before him 5, 315; and other heroes are removed from the midst of the fray by protecting deities (p. 320). Venus makes herself visible to Hippomenes alone, Ovid Met. 10, 650. Now they appear in friendly guise, Od. 7, 201 seq.; now clothed in terror: χαλεποὶ δὲ θεοὶ φαίνεσθαι ἐναργεῖς, Il. 20, 131 (see Suppl.).

The Iliad, 14, 286 seq., relates how Ὕπνος (sleep), sitting in the shape of a song-bird on the boughs of a fir-tree on Mt. Ida, overpowers the highest of all the gods; other passages show that the gods went to their beds every night, and partook like men of the benefit of sleep, Il. 1, 609. 2, 2. 24, 677. Still less can it be doubted of the Norse gods, that they too slept at night: Thôrr on his journeys looks out for night-lodging, Sn. 50; of Heimdall alone is it said, that he needs less sleep than a bird, Sn. 30. And from this sway of *sleep* over the gods follows again, what was maintained above, that of death: Death is the brother of Sleep. Besides, the gods fell a prey to *diseases*. Freyr was sick with love, and his great hugsôtt (mind-sickness) awakened the pity of all the gods. Oðinn, Niörðr and Freyr, according to the Yngl. saga 10. 11. 12, all sink under sicknesses (sôttdauðir). Aphrodite and Ares receive wounds, Il. 5, 330. 858; these are quickly healed [yet not without medical aid]. A curious story tells how the Lord God, having fallen sick, descends from heaven to earth to get cured, and comes to Arras; there minstrels and merryandrews receive commands to amuse him, and one manages so cleverly, that the Lord *bursts out laughing* and finds himself rid of his distemper.[1] This may be very ancient; for in the same way, sick daughters of kings in nurserytales are *made to laugh* by beggars and fiddlers, and so is the goddess Skaði in the Edda by Loki's juggling tricks, when mourning the death of her father, Sn. 82. Iambe cheered the sorrowing Demeter, and caused her, πολλὰ παρασκώπτουσα, μειδῆσαι γελάσαι τε, καὶ ἵλαον σχεῖν θυμόν, Hymn. in Cer. 203 (see Suppl.).

Important above all are the similar accounts, given by Greek antiquity and by our own, of the *language* of the gods. Thus, passages in the Iliad and the Odyssey distinguish between the divine and human names for the same object:

> ὃν Βριάρεων καλέουσι θεοί, ἄνδρες δέ τε πάντες
> Αἰγαίων'. Il. 1, 403.
> τὴν ἦτοι ἄνδρες Βατίειαν κικλήσκουσιν,

[1] De la venue de Dieu à Arras, in Jubinal's Nouveau recueil de contes 2, 377-8.

ἀθάνατοι δέ τε σῆμα πολυσκάρθμοιο Μυρίνης. 2, 813.
χαλκίδα κικλήσκουσι θεοί, ἄνδρες δὲ κύμινδιν. 14, 291.
ὃν Ξάνθον καλέουσι θεοί, ἄνδρες δὲ Σκάμανδρον. 20, 74.[1]
μῶλυ δέ μιν καλέουσι θεοί. Od. 10, 305.

A whole song in the Edda is taken up with comparing the languages, not only of gods and men, but of Vanir, elves, dwarfs, giants and subterraneans, and that not in a few proper names and rare words, but in a whole string of names for the commonest objects. At the very outset it surprises us, that while goð and æsir are treated as synonymous, a distinction is drawn between goð and ginregin. In 13 strophes are given 78 terms in all: on examining these, it soon appears that the variety of names (six) for each thing simply comes of the richness of the Teutonic tongue, and cannot possibly be ascribed to old remnants or later borrowings from any Finnic, Celtic or Slavic languages. They are synonyms or poetic names, which are distributed among six or eight orders of beings endowed with speech, according to the exigencies of alliteration, not from their belonging to the same class, such as poetical or prose. I will illustrate this by quoting the strophe on the names for a cloud:

scý heitir með mönnom, en scúrván með goðom,
kalla *vindflot* Vanir,
úrván iötnar, âlfar *veðrmegin*;
kalla î heljo *hiálm huliz*.

Everything here is Teutonic, and still the resources of our language are not exhausted by a long way, to say nothing of what it may have borrowed from others. The only simple word is skŷ, still used in the Scandinavian dialects, and connected with skuggi umbra, AS. scuwa, scua, OHG. scuwo. The rest are all appropriate and intelligible periphrases. Scûrvân [shower-weening] pluviae expectatio, from skûr imber, Germ. schauer; ûrvân just the same, from ûr pluvia, with which compare the literal meaning of Sanskr. abhra nubes, viz. aquam gerens.[2] Vindflot is apparently navigium venti, because the winds sail through the air on clouds. Veðrmegin transposed is exactly the OHG. maganwetar turbo; and hiâlmr

---

[1] Perhaps we ought also to reckon αἰετός and περκνός 24, 316, which is no mere ἐπίκλησις as in 7, 138. 18, 487 (Od. 5, 273). 22, 29. 506, though 'Αστυάναξ in this last passage happens to have Σκαμάνδριος (6, 402) answering to it, as Ξάνθος has Σκάμανδρος.

[2] Bopp, gloss. sanskr. 16ᵃ 209ᵃ.

huliz appears elsewhere as hulizhiâlmr, OS. helith-helm, a tarn-helmet, grîma, mask, which wraps one in like a mist or cloud. Of course the Teutonic tongue could offer several other words to stand for cloud, beside those six; e.g., nifl, OHG. nebal, Lat. nebula, Gr. νεφέλη; Goth. milhma, Swed. moln, Dan. mulm; Sansk. mêgha, Gr. ὀμίχλη, ὀμίχλη, Slav. megla; OHG. wolchan, AS. wolcen, which is to Slav. oblako as miluk, milk, to Slav. mleko; ON. þoka nebula, Dan. taage; M.Dut. swerk nubes, OS. gisuerc, caligo, nimbus; AS. hoðma nubes, Beow. 4911. And so it is with the other twelve objects whose names are discussed in the Alvismâl. Where simple words, like sôl and sunna, mâni and skîn, or iörd and fold, are named together, one might attempt to refer them to different dialects: the periphrases in themselves show no reason (unless mythology found one for them), why they should be assigned in particular to gods or men, giants or dwarfs. The whole poem brings before us an acceptable list of pretty synonyms, but throws no light on the primitive affinities of our language.

Plato in the Cratylus tries hard to understand that division of Greek words into divine and human. A duality of proper names, like Briareos and Aigaion, reminds us of the double forms Hlêr and Oegir (p. 240), Ymir and Oergelmir, which last Sn. 6 attributes to the Hrîmþurses; Iðunn would seem by Sæm. 89[a] to be an Elvish word, but we do not hear of any other name for the goddess. In the same way Xanthus and Skamander, Batieia and Myrina might be the different names of a thing in different dialects. More interesting are the double names for two birds, the χαλκίς or κύμινδις (conf. Plin. 10, 10), and the αἰετός and περκνός. Χαλκίς is supposed to signify some bird of prey, a hawk or owl, which does not answer to the description ὄρνις λιγυρά (piping), and the myth requires a bird that in sweet and silvery tones sings one to sleep, like the nightingale. Περκνός means dark-coloured, which suits the eagle; to imagine it the bird of the thundergod Perkun, would be too daring. Poetic periphrases there are none among these Greek words.

The principal point seems to be, that the popular beliefs of Greeks and Teutons agree in tracing obscure words and those departing from common usage to a distinction between divine and human speech. The Greek scholiasts suppose that the poet, holding converse with the Muses, is initiated into the language of

gods,[1] and where he finds a twofold nomenclature, he ascribes the
older, nobler, more euphonious (τὸ κρεῖττον, εὔφωνον, προγενέσ-
τερον ὄνομα) to the gods, the later and meaner (τὸ ἔλαττον, μετα-
γενέστερον) to men.   But the four or five instances in Homer are
even less instructive than the more numerous ones of the Norse
lay.   Evidently the opinion was firmly held, that the gods, though
of one and the same race with mortals, so far surpassed living men
in age and dignity, that they still made use of words which had
latterly died out or suffered change.   As the line of a king's
ancestors was traced up to a divine stock, so the language of gods
was held to be of the same kind as that of men, but right feeling
would assign to the former such words as had gradually disappeared
among men.   The Alvismâl, as we have seen, goes farther, and
reserves particular words for yet other beings beside the gods ;
what I maintained on p. 218 about the impossibility of denying the
Vanir a Teutonic origin, is confirmed by our present inquiry.—That
any other nation, beside Greeks and Teutons, believed in a separate
language of gods, is unknown to me, and the agreement of these
two is the more significant.   When Ovid in Met. 11, 640 says :
Hunc Icelon *superi, mortale* Phobetora *vulgus* nominat, this is
imitated from the Greeks, as the very names show (see Suppl.).
The Indians trace nothing but their alphabet (dêvanâgarî, dêva-
writing), as our forefathers did the mystery of runes (p. 149), to a
divine origin, and the use of the symbol may be connected with
that of the sound itself ; with the earliest signs, why should not
the purest and oldest expressions too be attributed to gods ?
Homer's ἔπεα πτερόεντα (winged words) belong to heroes and other
men as well as to gods, else we might interpret them strictly of the
ease and nimbleness with which the gods wield the gift of speech.

Beside language, the gods have *customs* in common with men.
They love song and play, take delight in hunting, war and banquets,
and the goddesses in ploughing, weaving, spinning ; both of them
keep *servants* and *messengers*.   Zeus causes all the other gods to be
summoned to the assembly (ἀγορή, Il. 8, 2. 20, 4), just as the Ases

---

[1] ὡς μουσοτραφὴς καὶ τὰς παρὰ θεοῖς ἐπίσταται λέξεις, οἶδε τὴν τῶν θεῶν
διάλεκτον, οἶδε τὰ τῶν θεῶν (ὀνόματα), ὡς ὑπὸ μουσῶν καταπνεόμενος. θέλων ὁ
ποιητὴς δεῖξαι ὅτι μουσόληπτός ἐστιν, οὐ μόνον τὰ τῶν ἀνθρώπων ὀνόματα ἐπαγ-
γέλλεται εἰδέναι, ἀλλ᾽ ὥσπερ καὶ οἱ θεοὶ λέγουσι.

attend at the þíng (Sæm. 93ᵃ), on the rökstôla, and by the Yggdrasill (Sæm. 1ᵇ 2ᵃ 44ᵃ), to counsel and to judge. Hebe, youth, is
cupbearer of the gods and handmaid to Here (Il. 5, 722), as Fulla
is to Frigg (Sn. 36); the youth Ganymede is cupbearer too, and so
is Beyla at the feast of the Ases (Sæm. 67ᵃ); Skîrnir is Frey's
shoemaker (81) and messenger, Beyggvir and Beyla are also called
his servants (59). These services do no detriment to their own
divine nature. Beside Hermes, the goddess Iris goes on errands
for the Greek gods (see Suppl.).

Among the gods themselves there is a difference of *rank*. Three
sons of Kronos have the world divided among them, the sky is
allotted to Zeus, the sea to Poseidon, hell to Hades, and the earth
they are supposed to share between them (Il. 15, 193). These
three tower above all the rest, like Hâr, Iafnhâr and Thriði in the
Norse religion, the triad spoken of on p. 162. This is not the same
thing as 'Wuotan, Donar, Ziu,' if only because the last two are not
brothers but sons of Wuotan, although these pass for the three
mightiest gods. Then, together with this triad, we become aware
of a circle of twelve (p. 26), a close circle from which some of the
gods are excluded. Another division, that into *old* and *new* gods,
does not by any means coincide with this: not only Oðinn and his
Ases, but also Zeus and his colleagues, appear as upstarts[1] to have
supplanted older gods of nature (see Suppl.).

All the divinities, Greek and Norse, have *offices* and *functions*
assigned them, which define their dominion, and have had a marked
influence on their pictorial representation. In Sn. 27—29 these
offices are specified, each with the words: 'hann ræðr fyrir (he
looks after),' or 'â hann skal heita til, er gott at heita til (to him
you shall pray for, it is good to pray for)'. Now, as any remnants
of Greek or Teutonic paganism in the Mid. Ages were sure to
connect themselves with some christian saints, to whom the
protection of certain classes or the healing of certain diseases was
carried over, it is evident that a careful classification of these
guardian saints according to the offices assigned them, on the
strength of which they are good to pray to,[2] would be of advantage to our antiquities. And the animals dedicated to each

---

[1] Aesch. Prom. 439 θεοῖσι τοῖς νέοις, 955 νέον νέοι κρατεῖτε, 960 τοὺς νέους
θεούς. Eumen. 156. 748. 799 οἱ νεώτεροι θεοί. Conf. Otfr. Müller, p. 181.

[2] Conf. Haupt's zeitschr. für d. alt. 1, 143-4.

deified saint (as once they were to gods) would have to be specified too.

The favourite *residence* of each god is particularly pointed out in the Grîmnismâl; mountains especially were consecrated to the Teutonic, as to the Greek deities: Sigtýsberg, Himinbiörg, &c. Olympus was peculiarly the house of Zeus ($\Delta\iota\grave{o}\varsigma$ $\delta\hat{\omega}\mu\alpha$), to which the other gods assembled (Il. 1, 494); on the highest peak of the range he would sit apart ($\mathring{\alpha}\tau\epsilon\rho$ $\mathring{\alpha}\lambda\lambda\omega\nu$ 1, 498. 5, 753), loving to take counsel alone ($\mathring{\alpha}\pi\mathring{\alpha}\nu\epsilon\upsilon\theta\epsilon$ $\theta\epsilon\hat{\omega}\nu$ 8, 10). He had another seat on Ida (11, 183. 336), whence he looked down to survey the doings of men, as Oðinn did from Hliðsciâlf. Poseidon sat on a height in the wooded range of Samos (13, 12). Valhöll and Bilskirnir, the dwellings of Oðinn and Thôrr, are renowned for their enormous size; the one is said to have 540 doors, through any one of which 800 einheriar can go out at once, and Bilskirnir has likewise 540 'golfe' [ON. gôlfr, floor] (see Suppl.).

If now we take in one view the relations of *gods and men*, we find they meet and touch at all points. As the created being is filled with a childlike sense of its dependence on the creator, and prayers and offerings implore his favour, so deity too delights in its creations, and takes in them a fatherly interest. Man's longing goes forth towards heaven; the gods fix their gaze on the earth, to watch and direct the doings of mortals. The blessed gods do commune with each other in their heavenly abodes, where feasts and revels go on as in earthly fashion; but they are more drawn to men, whose destinies enlist their liveliest sympathy. It is not true, what Mart. Cap. says 2, 9: ipsi dicuntur dii, et caelites alias perhibentur . . . nec admodum eos mortalium curarum vota sollicitant, $\mathring{\alpha}\pi\alpha\theta\epsilon\hat{\iota}\varsigma$que perhibentur. Not content with making their will known by signs and messengers, they resolve to come down themselves and appear to men. Such appearance is in the Hindu mythology marked by a special name: *avatâra, i.e.*, descensus.[1]

Under this head come first the solemn *car-processions* of deities heralding peace and fruitfulness or war and mischief, which for the most part recur at stated seasons, and are associated with popular festivals; on the fall of heathenism, only motherly wise-women

---

[1] Bopp's gloss. sansk. 21[a].

still go their rounds, and heroes ride through field or air. More rarely, and not at regular intervals, there take place *journeys* of gods through the world, singly or in twos or threes, to inspect the race of man, and punish the crimes they have noticed. Thus Mercury and Oðinn appeared on earth, or Heimdall to found the three orders, and Thôrr visited at weddings; Oðinn, Hœnir and Loki travelled in company; medieval legend makes God the Father seek a lodging, or the Saviour and St. Peter, or merely three angels (as the Servian song does, Vuk 4, no. 3). Most frequent however are the *solitary appearances* of gods, who, invoked or uninvoked, suddenly bring succour to their favoured ones in every time of need; the Greek epos is quite full of this. Athene, Poseidon, Ares, Aphrodite mingle with the warriors, warning, advising, covering; and just as often do Mary and saints from heaven appear in christian legends. The Lithuanian Perkunos also walks on earth (see Suppl.).

But when they descend, they are *not* always *visible;* you may hear the car of the god rush by, and not get sight of him bodily; like ghosts the blessed gods flit past the human eye unnoticed, till the obstructive mist be removed from it. Athene seizes Achilles by the hair, only by him and no other is she seen, Il. 1, 197; to make the succouring deities visible to Diomed, she has 'taken the mist from his eyes, that was on them before' 5, 127:

> ἀχλὺν δ' αὖ τοι ἀπ' ὀφθαλμῶν ἕλον, ἢ πρὶν ἐπῆεν,
> ὄφρ' εὖ γιγνώσκῃς ἠμὲν θεὸν ἠδὲ καὶ ἄνδρα.

Just so Biarco, in Saxo Gram., p. 37, is unable to spy Othin riding a white steed and aiding the Swedes, till he peeps through the ring formed by the arm of a spirit-seeing woman: a medium that elsewhere makes the elfin race visible to the bleared eyes of man. In another way the gods, even when they showed themselves bodily, concealed their divine nature, by assuming the form of a *human* acquaintance, or of an *animal*. Poseidon stept into the host, disguised as Kalchas, Il. 13, 45, Hermes escorted Priam as a Myrmidon warrior 24, 397, and Athene the young Telemachus as Mentor. In the same way Othin appeared as the chariot-driver Bruno (p. 330), or as a one-eyed old man. *Metamorphoses* of gods into *animals* in Teutonic mythology take place only for a definite momentary purpose, to which the character of the animal supplies the key; *e.g.*, Oðinn takes the shape of a snake, to slip through a hole he has bored (Sn. 86), and of an eagle, to fly away in haste (86), Loki that of a fly, in order to sting (131), or to creep through a keyhole (356) ; no larger designs are ever compassed by such means. So, when Athene flies away as a bird, it expresses the divinity of her nature and the suddenness of her departure. But the swan or bull, into which Zeus transformed himself, can only be explained on the supposition that Leda too, and Io and Europa, whom he was wooing, were thought of as swan-maidens or kine. The form of animal would then be determined by the mythus, and the egg-birth of the Dioscuri can be best understood in this way (see Suppl.).

In the Asiatic legends, it seems to me, the manifestations of deity are conceived deeply and purely in comparison, and nowhere more profoundly than in those of India. The god comes down and abides in the flesh for a season, for the salvation of mankind. Wherever the doctrine of metempsychosis prevailed, the bodies of animals even were eligible for the avatâra; and of Vishnu's ten successive incarnations, the earlier ones are animal, it was in the later ones that he truly 'became man' (see Suppl.). The Greek and Teutonic mythologies steer clear of all such notions; in both of them the story of the gods was too sensuously conceived to have invested their transformations with the seriousness and duration of an avatâra, although a belief in such incarnation is in itself so nearly akin to that of the heroes being bodily descended from the gods.

I think that on all these lines of research, which could be extended to many other points as well, I have brought forward a series of undeniable resemblances between the Teutonic mythology and the Greek. Here, as in the relation between the Greek and Teutonic languages, there is no question of borrowing or choice, nothing but unconscious affinity, allowing room (and that inevitably) for considerable divergences. But who can fail to recognise, or who invalidate, the surprising similarity of opinions on the immortality of gods, their divine food, their growing up overnight, their journeyings and transformations, their epithets, their anger and their mirth, their suddenness in appearing and recognition at parting, their use of carriages and horses, their performance of all natural functions, their illnesses, their language, their servants and

messengers, offices and dwellings ? To conclude, I think I see a
further analogy in the circumstance, that out of the names of living
gods, as Týr, Freyr, Baldr, Bragi, Zeus, grew up the common nouns
týr, fráuja, baldor, bragi, deus, or they bordered close upon
them (see Suppl.).

CHAPTER XV.

HEROES.

Between God and man there is a step on which the one leads into the other, where we see the Divine Being brought nearer to things of earth, and human strength glorified. The older the epos, the more does it require gods visible in the flesh; even the younger cannot do without heroes, in whom a divine spark still burns, or who come to be partakers of it.

Heroism must not be made to consist in anything but battle and victory: a *hero* is a man that in fighting against evil achieves immortal deeds, and attains divine honours. As in the gradation of ranks the noble stands between the king and the freeman, so does the hero between God and man. From nobles come forth kings, from heroes gods. ἥρως ἐστὶν ἐξ ἀνθρώπου τι καὶ θεοῦ σύνθετον, ὃ μήτε ἄνθρωπός ἐστι, μήτε θεὸς, καὶ συναμφότερόν ἐστι (Lucian in Dial. mortuor. 3), yet so that the human predominates: 'ita tamen ut plus ab homine habeat,' says Servius on Aen. 1, 200. The hero succumbs to pains, wounds, death, from which even the gods, according to the view of antiquity, were not exempt (p. 318). In the hero, man attains the half of deity, becomes a *demigod*, semideus: ἡμιθέων γένος ἀνδρῶν, Il. 12, 23; ἀνδρῶν ἡρώων θεῖον ᾽γένος, οἳ καλέονται ἡμίθεοι, Hes. ἔργ. 159. Jornandes applies *semidei* to the anses (supra p. 25), as Saxo Gram. pronounces Balder a *semideum,* arcano superûm semine procreatum. Otherwise in ON. writings we meet with neither hâlfgoð nor hâlfâs ;[1] but N. Cap. 141 renders hemithei heroesque by '*halbkota* unde *erdkota* (earthgods)'.

Heroes are distinct from dæmonic beings, such as angels, elves, giants, who fill indeed the gap between God and man, but have not a human origin. Under paganism, messengers of the gods were

---

[1] Hâlftröll, hâlfrisi are similar, and the OHG. halpdurinc, halpwalah, halpteni (ON. hâlfdan) as opposed to altdurinc, altwalah.

gods themselves;[1] the Judeo-christian angel is a dæmon. Rather may the hero be compared to the christian saint, who through spiritual strife and sorrow earns a place in heaven (see Suppl.).

This human nature of heroes is implied in nearly all the titles given to them. For the definite notion of a divine glorified hero, the Latin language has borrowed *heros* from the Greek, though its own *vir* (=Goth. vaír ON. ver,[2] AS. OHG. wer, Lett. wihrs, Lith. wyras) in the sense of vir fortis (Tac. Germ. 3) so nearly comes up to the Sanskr. *vîra* heros. Hērōs, ἥρως, which originally means a mere fighter, has been identified with rather too many things: hĕrus, ῞Ηρη, ῾Ηρακλῆς, even ῎Αρης and ἀρετή = virtus, so that the Goth. áirus, ON. âr, âri=nuntius, minister, might come in too, or the supposed digamma make a connexion with the aforesaid vîra look plausible. More undeniably, our *held* is a prolongation[3] of the simple ON. halr, AS. hæle vir: the name Halidegastes (like Leudogastes) is found so early as in Vopiscus; and a Goth. *haliþs*, OHG. *halid*, helid may be safely inferred from the proper names Helidperaht, Helidcrim, Helidgund, Helidniu, Helidberga,[4] though it is only from the 12th century that our memorials furnish an actual *helit* pl. helide; the MHG. *helet*, helt, pl. helde, occurs often enough. Of the AS. *hæleð* I remark that it makes its pl. both hæleðas and hæleð (*e.g.*, Beow. 103), the latter archaic like the Goth. mênôþs, whence we may infer that the Gothic also had a pl. haliþs, and OHG. a pl. helid as well as helidâ, and this is confirmed by a MHG. pl. held, Wh. 44, 20. In OS. I find only the pl. helidôs, helithôs; in the Heliand, helithcunni, helithocunni mean simply genus humanum. M.Dut. has *helet* pl. helde. The ON. *höldr* pl. höldar (Sæm. 114[b] 115[a]. Sn. 171) implies an older höluðr (like mânuðr = Goth. mênôþs); it appears to mean nothing but miles, vir, and höldborit (höld-born) in the first passage to be something lower than hersborit, the höldar being free peasants, bûendr. The Dan. *helt*, Swed. *hjelte* (OSwed. hälad) show an anomalous *t* instead of *d*, and are perhaps to be traced to the

---

[1] At most, we might feel some doubt about *Skírnir*, Frey's messenger and servant ; but he seems more a bright angel than a hero.

[2] With this we should have to identify even the veorr used of Thôrr (p. 187) in so far as it stood for viörr.

[3] Fortbildung : thus staff, stack, stall, stem, stare, &c. may be called prolongations of the root sta.—TRANS.

[4] In early docs. the town of Heldburg in Thuringia is already called *Helidiberga*, MB. 28[a] 33.

German rather than the ON. form. If we prefer to see both in halr and in haliþs the verb haljan occulere, defendere, tueri, the transition from tutor to vir and miles is easily made; even the Lat. cĕler is not far from cēlo to conceal.

Beside this principal term, the defining of which was not to be avoided here, there are several others to be considered. Notker, who singularly avoids heleda, supplies us in Cap. 141 with: 'heroes, taz chît, *hertinga* alde *chueniga*'. This *hertinga* suggests the AS. *heardingas*, Elene 25. 130, whether it be a particular line, or heroes in general that are meant by it; and we might put up with the derivation from herti, heard (hard), viri duri, fortes, exercitati, as hartunga in N. ps. 9, 1 means exercitatio. But as we actually find a Gothic line of heroes Azdingi, Astingi, and also an ON. of Haddîngjar, and as the Goth. *zd*, ON. *dd*, AS. *rd*, OHG. *rt* correspond to one another, there is more to be said for the Gothic word having dropt an *h* in the course of transmission, and the forms hazdiggs, haddîngr, hearding, hartinc being all one word.[1] Now, if the ON. haddr means a lock of hair (conf. p. 309), we may find in *haddîngr, hazdiggs*, &c. a meaning suitable enough for a freeman and hero, that of crinitus, capillatus, cincinnatus; and it would be remarkable that the meaning heros should be still surviving in the tenth century. No less valuable to us is the other term *chuenig*, which can hardly be connected with chuning rex, as N. always spells it; it seems rather to be = chuonig, derived either from chuoni audax, fortis (as fizusig from fizus callidus), or from its still unexplained root.[2] Other terms with a meaning immediately bordering on that of hero are: OHG. *dëgan* (miles, minister); *wîgant* (pugil); *chamfio*, chempho (pugil), AS. cempa, ON. kappi; the ON. *hetja* (bellator), perhaps conn. with hatr odium, bellum; and *skati*, better *skaði*, AS. sceaða, scaða, properly nocivus, then prædator, latro, and passing from this meaning, honourable in ancient times, into that of heros; even in the Mid. Ages, Landscado, scather of the land, was a name borne by noble families. That *heri* (exercitus), Goth. *harjis*, also meant miles, is shown by OHG.

---

[1] The polypt. Irminon 170b has a proper name *Ardingus* standing for Hardingus.

[2] Graff 4, 447 places chuoni, as well as chuninc and chunni, under the all-devouring root chan; but as kruoni, AS. grêne viridis, comes from kruoan, AS. grôwan, so may chuoni, AS. cêne, from a lost chuoan, AS. côwan pollere ? vigere ?

glosses, Graff 4, 983, and by names of individual men compounded with heri; conf. ch. XXV, einheri. The OHG. *wrecchio*, hrecchio, reccho, had also in a peculiar way grown out of the sense of exsul, profugus, advena, which predominates in the AS. wrecca, OS. wrekio, into that of a hero fighting far from home, and the MHG. *recke*, ON. *reckr* is simply a hero in general.[1] Similar developments of meaning can doubtless be shown in many other words; what we have to keep a firm hold of is, that the very simplest words for man (vir) and even for man (homo) adapted themselves to the notion of hero; as our *mann* does now, so the ON. *halr*, the OHG. *gomo* (homo), ON. *gumi* served to express the idea of heros. In Diut. 2, 314[b], heros is glossed by gomo, and gumnar in the Edda has the same force as skatnar (see Suppl.).

Now, what is the reason of this exaltation of human nature? Always in the first instance, as far as I can see, a relation of bodily kinship between a god and the race of man. The heroes are epigoni of the gods, their line is descended from the gods: ættir guma er frâ goðom kômo, Sæm. 114[a].

Greek mythology affords an abundance of proofs; it is by virtue of all heroes being directly or indirectly produced by gods and goddesses in conjunction with man, that the oldest kingly families connect themselves with heaven. But evidently most of these mixed births proceed from Zeus, who places himself at the head of gods and men, and to whom all the glories of ancestors are traced. Thus, by Leda he had Castor and Pollux, who were called after him Dios-curi, Hercules by Alcmena, Perseus by Danaë, Epaphus by Io, Pelasgus by Niobe, Minos and Sarpedon by Europa; other heroes touch him only through their forefathers: Agamemnon was the son of Atreus, he of Pelops, he of Tantalus, and he of Zeus; Ajax was sprung from Telamon, he from Aeacus, he from Zeus and Aegina. Next to Zeus, the most heroes seem to proceed from Ares, Hermes and Poseidon: Meleager, Diomedes and Cycnus were sons of Ares, Autolycus and Cephalus of Hermes, while Theseus was a son of Aegeus, and Nestor of Neleus, but both Aegeus and Neleus

---

[1] Some Slavic expressions for hero are worthy of notice: Russ. *vítiaz*, Serv. *vitez;* Russ. *boghatyr*, Pol. *bohater*, Boh. *bohatyr*, not conn. either with bôgh deus, or boghât dives, but the same as the Pers. *behâdir*, Turk. *bahadyr*, Mongol. *baghâtor*, Hung. *bátor*, Manju *bátura*, and derivable from *b'adra* lively, merry; Schott in Erman's zeitschr. 4, 531 [Mongol. *baghâ* is force, βία, and *-tor*, *-tur* an adj. suffix].

were Poseidon's children by Aethra and Tyro. Achilles was the son of Peleus and Thetis, Aeneas of Anchises and Venus.[1] These examples serve as a standard for the conditions of our own heroic legend (see Suppl.).

Tacitus, following ancient lays, places at the head of our race as its prime progenitor *Tuisco*, who is not a hero, but himself a god, as the author expressly names him ' *deum* terra editum'. Now, as Gaia of herself gave birth to Uranos and Pontos, that is to say, sky and sea sprang from the lap of earth, so Tuisco seems derivable from the word tiv, in which we found (pp. 193-4) the primary meaning to be sky; and Tuisco, *i.e.*, Tvisco, could easily spring out of the fuller form Tivisco [as Tuesday from Tiwesdæg]. Tvisco may either mean coelestis, or the actual offspring of another divine being Tiv, whom we afterwards find appearing among the gods : Tiv and Tivisco to a certain degree are and signify one thing. Tvisco then is in sense and station Uranos, but in name Zeus, whom the Greek myth makes proceed from Uranos not directly, but through Kronos, pretty much as our Tiv or Zio is made a son of Wuotan, while another son Donar takes upon him the best part of the office that the Greeks assigned to Zeus. Donar too was son of Earth as well as of Wuotan, even as Gaia brought forth the great mountain-ranges (οὔρεα μακρά, Hes. theog. 129 = Goth. faírgunja mikila), and Donar himself was called mountain and faírguneis (pp. 169. 172), so that οὐρανός sky stands connected with οὖρος ὄρος mountain, the idea of deus with that of ans (pp. 25. 188). Gaia, Tellus, Terra come round again in our goddesses Fiörgyn, Iörð and Rindr (p. 251) ; so the names of gods and goddesses here cross one another, but in a similar direction.

This earth-born Tvisco's son was *Mannus*, and no name could sound more Teutonic, though Norse mythology has as little to say of him as of Tvisco (ON. Týski ?). No doubt a deeper meaning once resided in the word ; by the addition of the suffix -isk, as in Tiv Tivisco, there arose out of mann a *mannisko* = homo, the

---

[1] In the Roman legend, Romulus and Remus were connected through Silvia with Mars, and through Amulius with Venus ; and Romulus was taken up to heaven. The later apotheosis of the emperors differs from the genuine heroic, almost as canonization does from primitive sainthood ; yet even Augustus, being deified, passed in legend for a son of Apollo, whom the god in the shape of a dragon had by Atia ; Sueton. Octav. 94.

thinking self-conscious being (see p. 59); both forms, the simple and the derived, have (like tiv and tivisko) the same import, and may be set by the side of the Sanskr. Manus and manushya. Mannus however is the first hero, son of the god, and father of all men. Traditions of this forefather of the whole Teutonic race seem to have filtered down even to the latter end of the Mid. Ages: in a poem of meister Frauenlob (Ettm. p. 112), the same in which the mythical king Wippo is spoken of (see p. 300), we read:

Mennor der êrste was genant,	Mennor the first man was named
dem diutische rede got tet	to whom Dutch language God
bekant.	made known.

This is not taken from Tacitus direct, as the proper name, though similar, is not the same (see Suppl.).

As all Teutons come of Tvisco and Mannus, so from the three (or by some accounts five) sons of Mannus are descended the three, five or seven main branches of the race. From the names of nations furnished by the Romans may be inferred those of their patriarchal progenitors.

1. INGUIO. ISCIO. IRMINO.

The threefold division of all the Germani into Ingaevones, Iscaevones and Herminones[1] is based on the names of three heroes, *Ingo, Isco, Hermino,* each of whom admits of being fixed on yet surer authority.

Ing, or *Ingo, Inguio* has kept his place longest in the memory of the Saxon and Scandinavian tribes. Runic alphabets in OHG. spell *Inc,* in AS. *Ing,* and an echo of his legend seems still to ring in the Lay of Runes:

> *Ing* wæs ærest mid Eástdenum
> gesewen secgum, oð he siððan eást
> ofer wæg gewât. wæn æfter ran.
> þus Heardingas þone hæle nemdon.

Ing first dwelt with the East Danes (conf. Beow. 779. 1225. 1650), then he went eastward over the sea,[2] his wain ran after. The wain

---

[1] Proximi oceano Ingaevones, medii Herminones, ceteri Istaevones vocantur, Tac. Germ. 2.

[2] Cædm. 88, 8 says of the raven let out of Noah's ark: gewât ofer wonne wæg sigan.

is a distinctive mark of ancient gods, but also of heroes and kings ;
its being specially put forward here in connexion with a sea-
voyage, appears to indicate some feature of the legend that is
unknown to us (see Suppl.). Ing's residence in the east is
strikingly in harmony with a pedigree of the Ynglings given in the
Islendîngabôk (Isl. sög. 1, 19). Here at the head of all stands
' *Yngvi* Tyrkja konungr,' immediately succeeded by divine beings,
Niörðr, Freyr, Fiölnir (a byname of Oðinn), Svegdir, &c. In the
same way Oðinn was called Tyrkja konungr (Sn. 368) from his
residing at Byzantium (p. 163 note).[1] The Ynglînga saga on the
other hand begins the line with Niörðr, after whom come Freyr,
Fiölnir and the rest; but of Freyr, whom the wain would have
suited exactly, it is stated that he had another name *Yngvi* or
Yngvifreyr (p. 211-2), and the whole race of *Ynglingar* were named
after him.[2] *Ingîngar* or *Ingvîngar* would be more exact, as is
shown by the OHG. and AS. spelling, and confirmed by a host of
very ancient names compounded with Ing or Ingo : Inguiomêrus
(Ingimârus, Ingumâr, or with asp. Hincmarus), Inguram, Ingimund,
Ingiburc, Inginolt, &c. Even Saxo Gram. writes Ingo, Ingimarus.
As for Ynglîngar, standing for Inglîngar, it may be formed from
the prolongation Ingil in Ingelwin, Ingelram, Ingelberga and the
Norse Ingellus, unless it is a mere confusion of the word with
ŷnglîngr juvenis, OHG. jungilinc, AS. geongling, from the root
ûng, junc, geong, which has no business here at all (?).—The main
point is, that the first genealogy puts Ingvi before Niörðr, so that
he would be Frey's grandfather, while the other version makes him
be born again as it were in Freyr, and even fuses his name with
Frey's, of which there lurks a trace likewise in the AS. ' freá
Ingwina' (p. 211). This Ingwina appears to be the gen. pl. of
Ingwine, OHG. Inguwini, and 'dominus Ingwinorum' need not
necessarily refer to the god, any hero might be so called. But with
perfect right may an Ingvi, Inguio be the patriarch of a race that

---

[1] Snorri sends him to Turkland, Saxo only as far as Byzantium.—TRANS.
[2] As the ON. genealogies have Yngvi, Niörðr, Freyr, the Old Swedish
tables in Geijer (häfder 118. 121. 475) give *Inge, Neorch, Fro* ; some have
Neoroch for Neorch, both being corruptions of Neorth. Now, was it by
running Ingvi and Freyr into one, that the combination *Ingvifreyr* (transposed
into AS. freá Ingwina) arose, or was he cut in two to make an additional
link ? The Skâldskaparmâl in Sn. 211ᵃ calls *Yngvifreyr* Oðin's son, and from
the enumeration of the twelve or thirteen Ases in Sn. 211ᵇ it cannot be doubted
that *Yngvifreyr* was regarded as equivalent to the simple *Freyr*.

bears the name of *Ingvíngar* = Ynglîngar. And then, what the
Norse genealogy is unable to carry farther up than to Ingvi, Tacitus
kindly completes for us, by informing us that Inguio is the son of
Mannus, and he of Tvisco; and his *Ingaevones* are one of two
things, either the OHG. pl. *Inguion* (from sing. Inguio), or *Ingwini*
after the AS. Ingwine.

Thus pieced out, the line of gods and heroes would run:
Tvisco, Mannus, Ingvio, Nerthus, Fravio (or whatever shape the
Gothic Fráuja would have taken in the mouth of a Roman). The
earth-born Tvisco's mother repeats herself after three intermediate
links in Nerthus the god or hero, as a Norse Ingui stands now
before Niörðr, now after; and those Vanir, who have been moved
away to the east, and to whom Niörðr and his son Freyr were held
mainly to belong (pp. 218-9), would have a claim to count as one
and the same race with the Ingaevones, although this association with Mannus and Tvisco appears to vindicate their Teutonic
character.

But these bonds draw themselves yet tighter. The AS. lay
informed us, that Ing bore that name among the *Heardings*, had
received it from them. This *Heardingas* must either mean heroes
and men generally, as we saw on p. 342, or a particular people.
Hartung is still remembered in our Heldenbuch as king of the
Reussen (Rûs, Russians), the same probably as 'Hartnît' or
'Hertnît von Reussen'; in the Alphart he is one of the Wölfing
heroes.[1] *Hartunc* and his father Immunc (Rudlieb 17, 8) remain
dark to us. The *Heardingas* appear to be a nation situated east of
the Danes and Swedes, among whom Ing is said to have lived for
a time; and this his sojourn is helped out both by the Turkish
king Yngui and the Russian Hartung. It has been shown that to
Hartunc, Hearding, would correspond the ON. form *Haddíngr*.
Now, whereas the Danish line of heroes beginning with Oðinn
arrives at Fróði in no more than three generations, Oðinn being
followed by Skiöldr, Friðleifr, Fróði; the series given in Saxo
Gram. stands thus: Humbl, Dan, Lother, Skiold, Gram, Hading,
Frotho. But Hading stands for *Hadding*, as is clear from the
spelling of 'duo Haddingi' in Saxo p. 93, who are the Haddîngjar
often mentioned in the Edda; it is said of him, p. 12: 'orientalium

---

[1] Hernit = Harding in the Swedish tale of Dietrich (Iduna 10, 253-4.
284).

robore debellato, Suetiam reversus,' which orientals again are Rutheni; but what is most remarkable is, that Saxo p. 17-8 puts in the mouth of this Danish king and his wife Regnilda a song which in the Edda is sung by *Niörðr* and *Skaði* (Sn. 27-8).[1] We may accordingly take Hadding to be identical with Niörðr, *i.e.*, a second birth of that god, which is further confirmed by Friðleifr (= Freálâf, whom we have already identified with the simple Freá, p. 219) appearing in the same line, exactly as Freyr is a son of Niörðr, and Saxo says expressly, p. 16, that Hadding offered a Fröblôt, a sacrifice in honour of Freyr. Whether in *Fróði* (OHG. Fruoto, MHG. Fruote), the hero of the Danish story, who makes himself into three, and whose rule is praised as peaceful and blissful, we are to look for Freyr over again, is another question.

In the god-hero of Tacitus then there lingers, still recognisable, a Norse god; and the links I have produced must, if I mistake not, set the final seal on the reading ' Nerthus '. If we will not admit the goddess into the ranks of a race which already has a Terra mater standing at its very head, it is at all events no great stretch to suppose that certain nations transferred her name to the god or hero who formed one of the succeeding links in the race.

There are more of these Norse myths which probably have to do with this subject, lights that skim the deep darkness of our olden time, but cannot light it up, and often die away in a dubious flicker. The Formâli of the Edda, p. 15, calls Oðinn father of Yngvi, and puts him at the head of the Ynglîngar : once again we see ourselves entitled to identify Oðinn with Mannus or Tvisco. Nay, with all this interlacing and interchange of members, we could almost bear to see Oðinn made the same as Niörðr, which is done in one manuscript. But the narrative ' frâ Forníoti ok hans ættmönnum ' in Fornald. sög. 2, 12 carries us farther: at the top stands *Burri*, like the king of Tyrkland, followed by *Burr, Oðinn, Freyr, Niörðr, Freyr, Fiölnir ;* here then is a double *Freyr*, the first one taking Yngvi's place, *i.e.*, the Yngvifreyr we had before ; but also a manifold *Oðinn*, Fiölnir being one of his names (Sæm. 10ᵃ 46ᵇ 184ᵃ. Sn. 3). *Burri* and *Burr*, names closely related to

---

[1] So Wh. Müller (Haupt's zeitschr. 3, 48-9) has justly pointed out, that Skaði's choice of the muffled bridegroom, whose feet alone were visible (Sn. 82), agrees with Saxo's ' eligendi mariti libertas curiosiore corporum attrectatione,' but here to find a ring that the flesh has healed over. Skaði and Ragnhild necessarily fall into one.

each other like Folkvaldi and Folkvaldr, and given in another list
as *Burri* and *Bors*, seem clearly to be the *Buri* and *Börr* cited by
Sn. 7. 8 as forefathers of the three brothers Oðinn, Vili, Ve (see p.
162). Now, *Buri* is that first man or human being, who was
licked out of the rocks by the cow, hence the êristporo (erst-born),
an OHG. *Poro,* Goth. *Baúra ;* Börr might be OHG. *Paru,* Goth.
Barus or whatever form we choose to adopt, anyhow it comes from
baíran, a root evidently well chosen in a genealogical tale, to denote
the first-born, first-created men.[1] Yet we may think of Byr too,
the wish-wind (see Oskabyrr, p. 144). Must not *Buri, Börr, Oðinn*
be parallel, though under other names, to *Tvisco, Mannus, Inguio ?*
Inguio has two brothers at his side, Iscio and Hermino, as Oðinn
has Vili and Ve; we should then see the reason why the names
Týski and Maðr[2] are absent from the Edda, because Buri and Börr
are their substitutes ; and several other things would become
intelligible. Tvisco is ' terra editus,' and Buri is produced out of
stone ; when we see Oðinn heading the Ynglîngar as well as
Inguio the Ingaevones, we may find in that a confirmation of the
hypothesis that Saxons and Cheruscans, preeminently worshippers
of Wôdan, formed the flower of the Ingaevones. These gods and
demigods may appear to be all running into one another, but always
there emerges from among them the real supreme divinity,
Wuotan.

I go on expounding Tacitus. Everything confirms me in the
conjecture that Inguio's or Ingo's brother must have been named
Iscio, Isco, and not Istio, Isto. There is not so much weight to be
laid on the fact that sundry MSS. even of Tacitus actually read
Iscaevones : we ought to examine more narrowly, whether the *st*
in Pliny's Istaevones be everywhere a matter of certainty ; and
even that need not compel us to give up our *sc ;* Iscaevo was
perhaps liable to be corrupted by the Romans themselves into Istaevo,
as Vistula crept in by the side of the truer Viscula (Weichsel). But
what seem irrefragable proofs are the *Escio* and *Hisicion*[3] of

---

[1] So in the Rigsmâl 105[a], *Burr* is called the first, *Barn* the second, and *Ioð*
(conf. AS. eáden) the third child of Faðir and Môðir.

[2] ON. for man: sing. maðr, mannis, manni, mann ; pl. menn, manna,
mönnum, menn.

[3] In Nennius § 17, Stevenson and Sanmarte (pp. 39. 40) have adopted the
very worst reading *Hisitio.*

Nennius, in a tradition of the Mid. Ages not adopted from Tacitus, and the *Isiocon*[1] in a Gaelic poem of the 11th century (see Suppl.). If this will not serve, let internal evidence speak: in Tuisco and Mannisco we have been giving the suffix -isc its due, and Tuisto, a spelling which likewise occurs, is proof against all attempt at explanation. Now *Isco*, as the third name in the same genealogy, would agree with these two. For Tvisco and Mannus the Norse legend substitutes two other names, but Inguio it has preserved in Ingvi; ought not his brother Iscio to be discoverable too? I fancy I am on his track in the Eddic *Askr*, a name that is given to the first-created man again (Sæm. 3. Sn. 10), and means an ash-tree. It seems strange enough, that we also come across this *ask* (let interpretation understand it of the tree or not) among the Runic names, side by side with 'inc, ziu, er,' all heroes and gods; and among the ON. names for the earth is *Eskja*, Sn. 220[b]. And even the vowel-change in the two forms of name, Iscio and Askr, holds equally good of the suffix *-isk, -ask*.

Here let me give vent to a daring fancy. In our language the relation of lineal descent is mainly expressed by two suffixes, ING and ISK. Manning means a son the offspring of man, and mannisko almost the same. I do not say that the two divine ancestors were borrowed from the grammatical form, still less that the grammatical form originated in the heroes' names. I leave the vital connexion of the two things unexplained, I simply indicate it. But if the Ingaevones living ' proximi oceano' were Saxon races, which to this day are addicted to deriving with -ing, it may be remarked that *Asciburg*, a sacred seat of the Iscaevones who dwelt ' proximi Rheno,' stood on the Rhine.[2] Of *Askr*, and the relation of the name to the tree, I shall treat in ch. XIX; of the Iscaevones it remains to be added, that the Anglo-Saxons also knew a hero *Oesc*, and consequently *Oescingas*.

Zeuss, p. 73, gives the preference to the reading *Istaevones*, connecting them with the Astingi, Azdingi, whom I (p. 342) took for Hazdingi, and identified with the ON. Haddîngjar, AS. Heardingas, OHG. Hertingâ. The hypothesis of Istaevones = Izdaevones would require that the Goth. *zd* = AS. rd, OHG. rt, should in the time of

---

[1] Pointed out by Leo in the zeitschr. f. d. alt. 2, 534.
[2] Conf. Askitûn (Ascha near Amberg), Askiprunno (Eschborn near Frankfort), Askipah (Eschbach, Eschenbach) in various parts; Ascarîh, a man's name (see Suppl.).

Tacitus have prevailed even among the Rhine Germans; I have never yet heard of an OHG. Artingâ, Ertingâ, nor of an ON. Addîngar, Eddîngar. According to this conjecture, ingenious anyhow and worth examining further, the ancestral hero would be called *Istio*= *Izdio*, Izdvio, OHG. *Erto*, ON. *Eddi*, with which the celebrated term *edda* proavia would agree, its Gothic form being **izdô,** OHG. ertâ. Izdo, Izdio proavus would seem in itself an apt name for the founder of a race. The fluctuation between *i* and *a* would be common to both interpretations, 'Iscaevones = Askingâ' and 'Istaevones= Artingâ'.

The third son of Mannus will occupy us even longer than his brothers. Ermino's posterity completes the cycle of the three main races of Germany: *Ingaevones, Iscaevones, Herminones.* The order in which they stand seems immaterial, in Tacitus it merely follows their geographical position; the initial vowel common to them leads us to suppose an alliterative juxtaposition of the ancestral heroes in German songs. The aspirate given by the Romans to Herminones, as to Hermunduri, is strictly no part of the German word, but is also very commonly retained by Latin writers of the Mid. Ages in proper names compounded with Irmin. In the name of the historical Arminius Tacitus leaves it out.

As with Inguio and Iscio, we must assign to the hero's name the otherwise demonstrable weak form *Irmino,*[1] *Ermino,* Goth. *Aírmana*: it is supported by the derivative Herminones, and even by the corruptions 'Hisicion, Armenon, Negno' in Nennius (see Suppl.). Possibly the strong-formed Irman, Irmin, Armin may even be a separate root. But what occurs far more frequently than the simple word, is a host of compounds with irman-, irmin-, not only proper names, but other expressions concrete and abstract: Goth. Ermanaricus (Aírmanareiks), OHG. Irmanrîh, AS. Eormenrîc, ON. Iörmunrekr, where the *u* agrees with that in the national name Hermundurus; OHG. Irmandegan, Irmandeo, Irmanperaht, Irmanfrit, Irminolt, Irmandrût, Irmangart, Irmansuint, &c. Attention is claimed by the names of certain animals and plants: the ON. Iörmungandr is a snake, and Iörmunrekr a bull, the AS. Eormenwyrt and Eormenleáf is said to be a mallow, which I also

---

[1] Pertz 1, 200. 300. 2, 290. 463. 481; the abbas Irmino of Charles the Great's time is known well enough now; and a female name *Iarmin* is met with in deeds.

find written geormenwyrt, geormenleáf. Authorities for irmangot, irmandiot, OS. irminthiod, irminman, irmansûl, &c., &c., have been given above, p. 118. A villa *Irmenlô, i.e.*, a wood (in illa silva scaras sexaginta) is named in a deed of 855, Bondam's charterbook, p. 32. silva Irminlô, Lacombl. 1, 31.

In these compounds, especially those last named, irman seems to have but a general intensifying power, without any distinct reference to a god or hero (conf. Woeste, mittheil. p. 44); it is like some other words, especially got and diot, regin and megin, which we find used in exactly the same way. If it did contain such reference, Eormenleáf would be Eormenes leáf, like Forneotes folme, Wuotanes wec. Irmandeo then is much the same as Gotadeo, Irmanrîh as Diotrîh; and as irmangot means the great god, irmandiot the great people, iörmungrund the great wide earth, so irmansûl cannot mean more than the great pillar, the very sense caught by Rudolf in his translation universalis columna (p. 117).

This is all very true, but there is nothing to prevent *Irmino* or *Irmin* having had a personal reference in previous centuries : have we not seen, side by side with *Zeus* and *Týr*, the common noun deus and the prefix tý-, tîr- (p. 195-6) ? conf. p. 339. If Sæteresdæg has got rubbed down to Saturday, Saterdach (p. 125), so may Eritac point to a former Erestac (p. 202), Eormenleáf to Eormenes leáf, Irmansûl to Irmanessûl; we also met with Donnerbühel for Donnersbühel (p. 170), Woenlet for Woenslet, and we say Frankfurt for Frankenfurt [Oxford for Oxenaford, &c.]. The more the sense of the name faded out, the more readily did the genitive form drop away; the OHG. godes hûs iş more literal, the Goth. guþhûs more abstract, yet both are used, as the OS. regano giscapu and regangiscapu, metodo giscapu and metodgiscapu held their ground simultaneously. As for geormen = eormen, it suggests Germanus (Gramm. 1, 11).

It is true, Tacitus keeps the *Hermino* that lies latent in his Herminones apart from Arminius with whom the Romans waged war ; yet his famous ' canitur adhuc barbaras apud gentes,' applied to the destroyer of Varus, might easily arise through simply misinterpreting such accounts as reached the Roman ear of German songs about the mythical hero. Granted that irmansûl expressed word for word no more than ' huge pillar,' yet to the people that worshipped it it must have been a divine image, standing for

a particular god. To discover who this was, we can only choose
one of two ways : either he was one of the three great divinities,
Wôdan, Thonar, Tiu, or some being distinct from them.

But here we must, above all things, ponder the passage partly
quoted on p. 111 from Widukind, himself a Saxon ; it says, a
heathen god was worshipped, whose name suggested *Mars*, his
pillar-statue *Hercules*, and the place where he was set up the sun
or *Apollo*. After that, he continues : ' Ex hoc apparet, aestima-
tionem illorum utcumque probabilem, qui Saxones originem duxisse
putant de Graecis, quia *Hirmin* vel *Hermes* graece *Mars* dicitur,
quo vocabulo ad laudem vel ad vituperationem usque hodie etiam
ignorantes utimur '. From this it follows, that the god to whom
the Saxons sacrificed after their victory over the Thuringians was
called *Hirmin, Irmin*, and in the 10th century the name was still
affixed in praise or blame to very eminent or very desperate
characters.[1] Apollo is brought in by the monk, because the altar
was built ad orientalem portam, and Hercules, because his pillar
called up that of the native god ; no other idol can have been
meant, than precisely the *irminsûl* (pp. 115—118), and the true form
of this name must have been *Irmines, Irmanes* or *Hirmines sûl*.
The Saxons had set up a pillar to their *Irmin* on the banks of the
Unstrut, as they did in their own home.

The way Hirmin, Hermes and Mars are put together seems a
perfect muddle, though Widukind sees in it a confirmation of the
story about the Saxons being sprung from Alexander's army
(Widuk. 1, 2. Sachsensp. 3, 45). We ought to remember, first,
that Wôdan was occasionally translated Mars instead of Mercurius
(pp. 121. 133), and had all the appearance of the Roman Mars
given him (p. 133) ; then further, how easily Irmin or Hirmin in
this case would lead to Hermes, and Ares to Mars, for the Irminsûl
itself is connected with Eres-burg (p. 116). What the Corvei
annalist kept distinct (p. 111), the two images of Ares and of
Hermes, are confounded by Widukind. But now, which has the
better claim to be Irmin, *Mars* or *Mercury?* On p. 197 I have
pronounced rather in favour of Mars, as Müllenhoff too (Haupt 7,
384) identifies Irmin with Ziu ; one might even be inclined to see

---

[1] Much as we say now : he is a regular *devil*, or in Lower Saxony *hamer*
(p. 182). The prefix *irmin-* likewise intensifies in a good or bad sense ; like
'irmingod, irminthiod,' there may have been an irminthiob = 'meginthiob,
reginthiob '.

in it the name of the war-god brought out on p. 202, 'Eru, Heru,' and to dissect Irman, Erman into Ir-man, Er-man, though, to judge by the forms Irmin, Eormen, Ermun, Iörmun, this is far from probable, the word being derivative indeed, yet simple, not compound; we never find, in place of Ertag, dies Martis, any such form as Ermintac, Irminestac. On behalf of Mercury there would speak the accidental,[1] yet striking similarity of the name Irmansûl or Hirmensûl to ʿΕρμῆς and ἕρμα = prop, stake, pole, pillar (p. 118), and that it was precisely Hermes's image or head that used to be set up on such ἕρματα, and further, that the Mid. Ages referred the irmen-pillars to Mercury (p. 116). In Hirmin the Saxons appear to have worshipped a *Wôdan imaged as a warrior*.

If this view be well grounded, we have Wôdan wedging himself into the ancient line of heroes; but the question is, whether *Irmin* is not to be regarded as a second birth or son of the god, whether even an ancestral hero *Irmino* is not to be distinguished from this god *Irmin*, as Hermino in Tacitus is from Arminius? So from thiod, regin, were formed the names Thiodo, Regino. It would be harder to show any such relation between Ing and Ingo, Isc and Isco; but I think I can suggest another principle which will decide this point: when races name themselves after a famous ancestor, this may be a deified man, a demigod, but never a purely divine being. There are Ingaevones, Iscaevones, Herminones, Oescingas, Scilfingas, Ynglîngar (for Ingîngar), Völsûngar, Skiöldûngar, Niflûngar,[2] as there were Heracleidae and Pelopidae, but no Wôdeningas or Thunoringas, though *a* Wôdening and *a* Kronides. The Anglo-Saxons, with Wôden always appearing at their head, would surely have borne the name of Wôdeningas, had it been customary to take name from the god himself. Nations do descend from the god, but through the medium of a demigod, and after him they name themselves. A national name taken from the highest god would have been impious arrogance, and alien to human feeling.

As Lower Saxony, especially Westphalia, was a chief seat of the Irmin-worship, we may put by the side of Widukind's account of *Hirmin* a few other traces of his name, which is not even yet

---

[1] To the Greek aspirate corresponds a Teutonic S, not H: ὁ, ἡ sa, sô; ἑπτά sibun; ἅλς salt. [There are exceptions: ὁ, ἡ, οἱ he, her, hig; ὅλος whole, hela; ἑλῶ haul, holen].

[2] A patronymic suffix is not necessary: the Gáutôs, Gevissi, Suâpâ take name from Gáuts, Gevis, Suâp, divine heroes.

entirely extinct in that part of Germany. Strodtmann has noted down the following phrases in Osnabrück : 'he ment, use herre gott heet *Herm* (he thinks our Lord is called H., *i.e.* is never angry); use herre gott heet nich *Herm*, he heet leve herre, un weet wal tó-te-gripen (knows how to fall on) '. Here there seems unconcealed a slight longing for the mild rule of the old heathen god, in contrast to the strictly judging and punishing christian God. In Saxon Hesse (on the Diemel), in the districts of Paderborn, Ravensberg and Münster, in the bishopric of Minden and the duchy of Westphalia,[1] the people have kept alive the rhyme :

> *Hermen*, sla dermen,
> sla pipen, sla trummen,
> de kaiser wil kummen
> met hamer un stangen,[2]
> wil *Hermen* uphangen.

Hermen is challenged, as it were, to strike up his war-music, to sound the catgut, pipe and drum ; but the foe draws nigh with maces and staves, and will hang up Hermen (see Suppl.). It is not impossible that in these rude words, which have travelled down the long tradition of centuries, are preserved the fragments of a lay that was first heard when Charles destroyed the Irmensûl. They cannot so well be interpreted of the elder Arminius and the Romans.[3] The striking and the staves suggest the ceremony of carrying out the Summer.

In a part of Hesse that lies on the Werra, is a village named Ermschwerd, which in early documents is called Ermeswerder, Armeswerd,[4] *Ermeneswerde* (Dronke's trad. fuld. p. 123), *Ermeneswerethe* (Vita Meinwerci an. 1022. Leibn. 1, 551), = Irmineswerid, insula Irmini, as other gods have their isles or eas. This interpretation seems placed beyond a doubt by other such names of places. Leibn. scr. 1, 9 and Eccard, Fr. or. 1, 883, De orig. Germ. 397

---

[1] Rommel's Hessen 1. p. 66 note. Westphalia (Minden 1830) i. 4, 52 The tune is given in Schumann's Musical. zeitung for 1836.

[2] Variants : mit stangen und prangen (which also means staves) ; mit hamer un tangen (tongs).

[3] This explanation has of course been tried : some have put *Hermann* for Hermen, others add a narrative verse, which I do not suppose is found in the people's mouth : 'un *Hermen* slaug dermen, slaug pipen, slaug trummen, de fürsten sind kummen met all eren mannen, hebt *Varus* uphangen '.

[4] The same vowel-change is seen in *Ermensulen* (deed of 1298 in Baring's Clavis dipl. p. 493 no. 15), a Westphalian village, now called *Armenseul*.

give *Irmineswagen* for the constellation arctus, plaustrum coeleste, I do not know on what authority : this wain would stand beside Wuotanswagen, Donnerswagen, and even Ingswagen.

Some of the later AS. and several O. Engl. authorities, in specifying four great highways that traverse England, name amongst them *Ermingestrete*, running from south to north of the island.[2] But we may safely assume the pure AS. form to have been Eormenstræt or Eormenes-stræt, as another of the four ways, *Wætlingastrœt*, occurs in the Saxon Chron. (Ingr. 190. Thorpe's anal. p. 38), and in the Treaty of Ælfred and Guthrun (Thorpe, p. 66), and 'andlang *Waetlinga* straet' in Kemble **2, 250** (an. 944). Lye has *Irmingstrœt* together with *Irmingsûl*, both without references. The conjectural Eormenstræt would lead to an OHG. Irmanstrâza, and Eormenesstræt to Irmanesstrâza, with the meanings via publica and via Irmani.

Now it is not unimportant to the course of our inquiry, that one of the four highways, Wætlingastræt, is at the same time translated to the sky, and gets to look quite mythical. A plain enough road, extending from Dover to Cardigan, is the *milky way* in the heavens, *i.e.*, it is travelled by the car of some heathen god.

Chaucer (House of Fame 2, 427), describing that part of the sky, says :

> Lo there, quod he, cast up thine eye,
> se yondir, lo, the galaxie,
> the whiche men clepe the milky way
> for it is white, and some parfay
> ycallin it han *Watlingestrete*,
> that onis was brente with the hete,
> whan that the sunnis sonne the rede,
> which hite Phaeton, wolde lede
> algate his fathirs carte and gie.

In the Complaint of Scotland, p. 90, it is said of the comet : ' it aperis oft in the quhyt circle callit circulus lacteus, the quhilk the marynalis callis *Vatlanstreit* '. In Douglas's Virgil, p. 85 :

---

[2] IIII cheminii Watlingestrete, Fosse, Hickenildestrete, *Ermingestrete* (Thorpe's Anc. laws, p. 192) ; conf. Henry of Hunt. (Erningestreet), Rob. of Glouc., Oxf. 1742, p. 299 (also Erning., after the preceding). Ranulph Highden's Polychr., ed. Oxon. p. 196. Leland's Itinerary, Oxf. 1744. 6, 108—140. Gibson in App. chron. Sax. p. 47. Camden's Britannia, ed. Gibson, Lond. 1753, p. lxxix. In the map to Lappenberg's Hist. of Engl., the direction of the four roads is indicated.

Of every sterne the twynkling notis he
that in the still hevin move cours we se,
Arthurys house, and Hyades betaikning rane,
Watlingestrete, the Horne and the Charlewane,
the feirs Orion with his goldin glave.

Wætlinga is plainly a gen. pl.; who the Wætlings were, and how they came to give their name to an earthly and a heavenly street, we do not know. Chaucer perhaps could still have told us, but he prefers to harp at the Greek mythus. Phaëthon, also the son of a god, when he presumed to guide his father's sun-chariot, burnt a broad streak in the sky, and that is the track we call the milky way. The more common view was, that Here, indignant at the bantling Hermes or Herakles being put to her breast, spilt her milk along the sky, and hence the bright phenomenon. No doubt, among other nations also, fancy and fable have let the names of earthly and heavenly roads run into one another.[1]

A remarkable instance of this is found in one of our national traditions; and that will bring us round to Irmin again, whom we almost seem to have lost sight of.

[1] I limit myself to briefly quoting some other names for the *milky way*. In Arabic it is *tarik al thibn* (via straminis); Syriac *schevil tevno* (via paleae); Mod. Hebrew *netibat theben* (semita paleae); Pers. *rah kah keshan* (via stramen trahentis); Copt. *pimoit ende pitoh* (via straminis); Ethiop. *hasare zamanegade* (stipula viae); Arab. again *derb ettübenin* (path of the chopped-straw carriers); Turk. *saman ughrisi* (paleam rapiens, paleae fur); Armen. *hartacol* or *hartacogh* (paleae fur); all these names run upon scattered chaff, which a thief dropt in his flight. More simple is the Arabic *majerra* (tractus), *nahr al majerra* (flumen tractus), and the Roman conception of *path of the gods* or *to the gods*; also Iroq. *path of souls*, Turk. *hadjiler juli* (pilgrims' path), hadji is a pilgrim to Mecca and Medina. Very similar is the christian term used in the Mid. Ages, ' galaxias *via sancti Jacobi* ' already in John of Genoa's Catholicon (13th cent.); *camino di Santiago, chemin de saint Jaques, Jacobsstrasse*, Slov. *zesta v' Rim* (road to Rome), from the pilgrimages to Galicia or Rome, which led to heaven [was there no thought of Jacob's ladder?] This James's road too, or pilgrim's road, was at once on earth and in heaven; in Lacomblet, docs. 184 and 185 (an. 1051) name a *Jacobswech* together with the via regia. ON. *vetrarbraut* (winterway). Welsh *caer Gwydion* (p. 150), and *Arianrod* (silver street? which comes near Argentoratum). Finn. *linnunrata* (birdway), Lith. *paukszcziú kielés*, perhaps because souls and spirits flit in the shape of birds; Hung. *Hadakuttya* (via belli), because the Hungarians in migrating from Asia followed this constellation (see Suppl.). *Vroneldenstraet* (p. 285) and *Pharaildis* fit intelligibly enough with *frau Holda* and Herodias, whose airy voyages easily account for their giving a name to the milky way, the more so, as Wuotan, who joins Holda in the nightly hunt, shows himself here also in the Welsh appellation caer *Gwydion*. Even the fact of *Diana* being mixed up with that chase, and *Juno* with the milky way, is in keeping; and gods or spirits sweep along the heavenly road as well as in the heavenly hunt.

Widukind of Corvei is the first who gives us out of old songs the beautiful and truly epic story of the Saxons' victory over the Thuringians,[1] which Ruodolf before him (Pertz 2, 674) had barely touched. Irmenfried, king of the Thuringians, being oppressed by Dieterich, king of the Franks, called the Saxons to his aid : they appeared, and fought valiantly. But he began to waver in his mind, he secretly negotiated a treaty with the Franks, and the two nations were about to unite against the formidable Saxon host. But the Saxons, becoming aware of the treachery, were beforehand ; led by the aged Hathugât, they burst into the castle of the Thuringians, and slew them all ; the Franks stood still, and applauded the warlike renown of the Saxons. Irmenfried fled, but, enticed by a stratagem, returned to Dieterich's camp. In this camp was staying Irmenfried's counsellor *Iring*, whose prudent plans had previously rendered him great services. When Irmenfried knelt before Dieterich, Iring stood by, and having been won by Dieterich, slew his own lord. After this deed of horror, the Frankish king banished him from his sight, but Iring said, ' Before I go, I will avenge my master,' drew his sword, stabbed Dieterich dead, laid his lord's body over that of the Frank, so that the vanquished in life might be the victor in death, *opened a way* for himself with the sword (viam ferro faciens), and escaped. ' Mirari tamen non possumus ' adds Widukind, ' in tantum famam praevaluisse, ut *Iringi* nomine, quem ita vocitant, lacteus coeli circulus usque in praesens sit notatus.' Or, with the Auersberg chronicler : ' famam in tantum praevaluisse, ut lacteus coeli circulus Iringis nomine *Iringesstrâza* usque in praesens sit vocatus ' (sit notatus in Pertz 8, 178).

In confirmation, AS. glosses collected by Junius (Symb. 372) give ' via secta : *Iringes uuec*,' from which Somner and Lye borrow their ' *Iringes weg*, via secta '. Conf. via sexta *iringesuuec*, Haupts zeitschr. 5, 195. Unpubl. glosses of the Amplonian libr. at Erfurt (10-11th cent. bl. 14[a]) have ' via secta : *Iuuâringes uueg* ' ; which Iuwaring agrees very remarkably with the later form Euring in *Euringsstrass*, Aventin 102[b] 103[a].

---

[1] Conf. the differing but likewise old version, from a H. German district, in Goldast's Script. rer. Suev. pp. 1—3, where Swabians take the place of the Saxons. The Auersberg chron. (ed. Argent. 1609, pp. 146-8) copies Widukind. Eckehard, in Pertz 8, 176-8.

In the Nibelungenlied 1285. 1965—2009, these heroes appear again, they are the same, but differently conceived, and more akin to the H. German version in Goldast:[1] *Irnvrit* of Düringen and *Irinc* of Tenemarke, one a landgraf, the other a markgraf, both vassals of Etzel (Attila). The Lied von der klage (threnody) adds, that they had fallen under the ban of the empire, and fled to Hunland; here we see a trace of the banishment that Dieterich pronounced on Iring. In the poems of the 13th century, however, Iring is not a counsellor, still less a traitor and a murderer of Irmenfried: the two are sworn friends, and both fall before the irresistible Hagene and Volker.

Add to all this, that the Vilk. saga cap. 360, though silent on Irnfried, tells of *Irung's* last combat with Hogni, and makes him sink against a stone wall, which is still called *Irûngs veggr* in memory of the hero. The Norse redactor confounded vegr (via) with veggr (murus); his German source must have had *Iringes vec*, in allusion to the 'cutting his way in Widukind.

So now the road is paved to the conclusions we desire to draw: German legend knew of an *Iringes wec on earth and in heaven*, so did AS. legend of a double Wætlinga-stræt, and so was the road to Rome and St. James set in the firmament as well. These fancies about *ways* and *wains*, we know, are pagan, and indicate god-myths. The Thuringian *Irnvrit*, originally *Irmanfrit*, it is reasonable to suppose, is the same as *Irman, Irmin* (conf. Sigfrit, Sigmunt, Sigi), and the *Hermunduri* = Irman-duri are plainly connected with the *Durings* (Thuringians): so that Irman assumes a peculiar significance in Thuringian tradition. If this would but tell us of an *Irmines wec*, all would come right.

It does tell, however, in three or four places, of an *Iringes wec*. The names *Irinc* and *Irmin*, apart from the alliteration which doubtless operated in the ancient lay, have nothing in common; the first has a long *î*,[2] and of themselves they cannot have represented

---

[1] As already quoted, Deutsch. heldens. p. 117.

[2] Or *iu*, as some roots shift from the fourth to the fifth vowel-series (like hîrât and hiurât, now both heirat and heurat; or tîr and tŷr, p. 196), so *Iurinc* (expanded into Iuwarinc, as the OHG. poss. pron. iur into iuwar); so in the 16-17th cent. *Eiring* alternates with *Euring*. A few MSS. read Hiring for Iring, like Hirmin for Irmin, but I have never seen a Heuring for Euring, or it might have suggested a Saxon *hevenring*, as the rainbow is called the ring of heaven. An old AS. name for Orion, *Eburðrung, Ebirðring*, seems somehow connected, especially with the *Iuwaring* above.

one another. Now, either the legend has made the two friends change places, and transferred *Irmin's way* to Iring, or *Iring* (not uncommon as a man's name too, *e.g.*, Trad. Fuld. 1, 79) is of himself a demigod grown dim, who had a way and wain of his own, as well as Irmin. Only, Irmin's worship seems to have had the deeper foundations, as the image of the *Irmansûl* sufficiently shows. As the name of a place I find *Iringes purc* (burg), MB. 7, 47. 157. 138. 231. *Iringisperc* (berg) 29, 58.

Up to this point I have refrained from mentioning some Norse traditions, which have a manifest reference to the earthly heropath. It had been the custom from of old, for a new king, on assuming the government, to travel the great highway across the country, confirming the people in their privileges (RA. 237-8). This is called in the O. Swed. laws ' *Eriksgatu* ridha,' riding Eric's road.[1] Sweden numbers a host of kings named *Erik* (ON. Eirîkr), but they are all quite historical, and to none of them can be traced this custom of the *Eriksgata*. With the royal name of Erik the Swedes must from very early times have associated the idea of a god or deified king ; the vita Anskarii written by his pupil Rimbert, has a remarkable passage on it (Pertz 2, 711). When the adoption of christianity was proposed to king Olef about 860, a man of heathen sentiments alleged, ' Se in *conventu deorum*, qui ipsam terram possidere credebantur, et ab eis missum, ut haec regi et populis nunciaret : Vos, inquam,[2] nos vobis propitios diu habuistis, et terram incolatus vestri cum multa abundantia nostro adjutorio in pace et prosperitate longo tempore tenuistis, vos quoque nobis sacrificia et vota debita persolvistis, grataque nobis vestra fuerunt obsequia. At nunc et sacrificia solita subtrahitis, et vota spontanea segnius offertis,[3] et, quod magis nobis displicet, alienum deum super nos intro ducitis. Si itaque nos vobis propitios habere vultis, sacrificia omissa augete et vota majora persolvite, alterius quoque dei culturam, qui contraria nobis docet, ne apud vos recipiatis et ejus servitio ne intendatis. Porro, si etiam plures deos

---

[1] The venerable custom still prevailed in the 15-16th cent. : ' statuta provincialium generose confirmavit et sigillavit in equitatu qui dicitur *Eriksgata*,' Diarium Vazstenense ad an. 1441 (ed. Benzel, Ups. 1721) p. 86. ' Rex Christoferus Sueciae et Daciae equitatum fecit qui dicitur *Eriksgata* secundum leges patriae,' ibid. ad an. 1442. Even Gustavus Vasa rode his Eriksgata.

[2] For inquimus, as elsewhere inquit for inquiunt.

[3] Votum, what an individual offers, as opposed to the sacrificium presented publicly and jointly : conf. supra, p. 57.

habere desideratis, et nos vobis non sufficimus, *Ericum*, quondam regem vestrum, nos unanimes *in collegium nostrum asciscimus*,[1] ut sit *unus de numero deorum*.'—I have transcribed the whole passage, because it aptly expresses the attitude of the pagan party, and the lukewarmness already prevailing towards their religion: the heathen priests thought of adding a fresh hero to their throng of gods.[2] This seems to exclude all later Erics from any claim to the Eriksgata; probably there were mixed up even then, at least in Rimbert's mind, traditions of a divine Erik.

It can no longer remain doubtful now, what god or divine hero lies hidden in this Erik. I had at one time thought of Er (Mars), because the form Erctag is met with a few times for Ertag (p. 124), but the short vowel in Er, and the long one in Irinc, Eirîkr, are enough to warn us off. Instead of Eriksgata we also meet with *Riksgata*, and this points decidedly to *Rîgr*, the earthly name of the god Heimdallr, who in the Edda walks the *green roads* (grœnar brautir) of earth, to beget the three races of men. In the green earthly roads are mirrored the white and shining paths of heaven.[3] Then the problem started on p. 234, whether the ON. form *Rîgr* arose out of *Irîngr* by aphæresis and syncope, now finds a solution approaching to certainty. Heimdallr dwells in Himinbiörg on the quaking roost (Bifröst), the rainbow, which is the bridge or path by which the gods descend from heaven to earth. The rainbow is the celestial ring, as the galaxy is the celestial road, and Heimdallr keeper of that road, Heimdallr is Rîgr = Iring, walking the earth and translated to the skies; now we comprehend, why there lived among the nations many a various tale of *Eriksgata, Iringeswec, Iringesstrâza*, and was shifted now to one and now to the other celestial phenomenon. Iring, through *Iuwaring*, borders on *Eburðrung* the old name of Orion (see Suppl.). And if our heroic legend associates Irmenfrit, *i.e.*, Irmin with Iring, and Irmin-street alternates with Iring-street, then in the god-myth also, there must have existed points of contact between Irmin = Oðinn and Iring = Heimdallr: well, Heimdallr was a son of Oðinn, and the Welsh milky way was actually named after Gwydion, *i.e.*, Wôden. From the Irminsûl four roads branched out across the country, Eriksgata

---

[1] So king Hâkon is admitted into the society of gods, Hermôðr and Bragi go to meet him : ' siti Hâkon með heiðin goð' (Hâkonarmâl).

[2] Dahlmann guesses it may be the Upsal Erik (d. 804).

[3] Altd. blätter 1, 372-3.

extended in four directions, four such highways are likewise known
to English tradition, though it gives the name of Ermingestret to
only one, and bestows other mythic titles on the rest. Of Irmin
and of Iring, both the divine personality and the lapse into hero-
nature seem to be made out.

2. MARSO. GAMBARO. SUAPO.

Now that I have expounded the primeval triad of Germanic
races, I have to offer some conjectures on the sevenfold division.
Pliny's quintuple arrangement seems not so true to fact, his Vindili
are Tacitus's Vandilii, his Peucini not referable to any founder of a
race. But Tacitus to his first three adds four other leading races,
the Marsi, Gambrivii, Suevi and Vandilii, in whose names there
exists neither alliteration nor the weak form as a mark of derivation.

The Marsi between Rhine and Weser, an early race which soon
disappears, in whose country the Tanfana sanctuary stood, lead up
to a hero *Marso*, whom we must not mix up with the Roman Mars
gen. Martis, nor with Marsus the son of Circe (who in like manner
gives name to an Italian people, Gellius 16, 11. Pliny 7, 2.
Augustine in Ps. 57). The Marsigni = Marsingi, a Suevic people,
acknowledged the same name and origin. The proper name *Marso*
occurs in Mabillon no. 18, in a deed of 692, also in the polypt.
Irminonis p. 158[a] 163[b], but seldom elsewhere. *Mersi*burg and
*Marse*burg, Pertz 8, 537. 540, seem to belong here, while some
other names given above, p. 201, are open to doubt; I do not
know if a MHG. phrase, obscure in itself, is at all relevant: ' zuo
allen *marsen* varn,' MS. 1, 25[a], which may signify, to go to all the
devils, expose oneself to every danger; conf. ' einen *marsen* man,'
Crane 2865. The Gothic marzjan (impedire, offendere) might seem
allied to the root, but that would have been merrian, merran
in OHG.

The name of the Gambrivii I assign to the root gambar,
kambar strenuus, from which also is derived the name of *Gambara*,
ancestress of the Langobards. There may have been likewise a
hero Gambaro. And the forest of Gambreta (instead of Gabreta)
is worth considering. Gambara's two sons are called *Ibor* = OHG.
Epur, AS. Eofor, ON. Iöfur, *i.e.* aper, boar, and *Ajo :* all the three
names appear to be corrupt in Saxo Gram.

Ought we to assume for the Suevi, OHG. Suâpâ, an eponymous hero *Suevo*, Suâpo, and perhaps connect with him an old legend of a mountain ? Pliny 4, 13 places in the land of the 'gens Ingaevonum, quae est prima Germaniae,' a certain '*Sevo* mons immensus' reaching to the Sinus Codanus ; and Solinus, following him, says 22, 1 : ' Mons *Sevo* ipse ingens . . . initium Germaniae facit, hunc Inguaeones tenent ;' but Isidor (Orig. 10, 2) makes out of it : ' dicti autem Suevi putantur a monte *Suevo*, qui ab ortu initium Germaniae facit'. From this evidently is taken the account of the immigrating Swâben in the Lay of Anno 284 : 'si sluogen iri gecelte (pitched their tents) ane dem berge *Suebo* (so several read for Suedo), dannin wurdin si geheizin Suâbo '.[1] In the Low German psalms 57, 17 mons coagulatus is rendered ' berg *sueuot*,' which is perhaps to be explained by the legend of the lebirmer [liver-sea, Tacitus's mare pigrum ? Germ. 45. Agr. 10]. It seems more to the point, that in Sæm. 164-8 the *Sefa* fiöll (fells, mountains, of the Sevs) are mentioned in those very Helga-songs, one of which sings of *Svafa*land, king *Svafnir* and the valkyr *Svava*. A *v* after *s* is frequently dropped, and the readings Sevo, Suevo can thus be reconciled. Suâpo then would be a counterpart to Etzel and Faírguns (pp. 169, 172) ? The AS. Sweppa, or rather Swæfdæg, can hardly be brought in here.

Tacitus's Vandilii and Pliny's Vindili stand in the same relation to each other as Arminius and Irmin, Angrivarii and Inguiones ; both forms come from winding and wending, out of which so many mythic meanings flow. Wuotan is described under several names as the wender, wanderer [Germ. wandeln ambulare, mutare].

On the slight foundation of these national names, Marsi, Gambrivii, Suevi and Vandilii, it is unsafe as yet to build. Tacitus connects these with Mannus, but the heroes themselves he does not even name, let alone giving any particulars of them.

3. (HERCULES). (ULYSSES). ALCIS.

Clear and definite on the other hand are the historian's notices of another famous hero : Fuisse apud eos et *Herculem* memorant, primumque omnium virorum fortium ituri in proelia canunt, Germ.

---

[1] Kaiserchr. 285 : sîn gecelt hiez er slahen dô ûf einin berc der heizit *Swero*, von dem berge *Swero* sint sie alle geheizen Swâbo. For Swero read *Swevo* (see Suppl.).

3. Speaking of sacrifices in cap. 9, after mentioning Mercurius first, he immediately adds : *Herculem* ac Martem concessis animalibus placant, the demigod being purposely put before even Mars. Chapter 34 tells us of the ocean on the coast of the Frisians, then says : Et superesse adhuc *Herculis columnas* fama vulgavit, sive adiit *Hercules,* seu quidquid ubique magnificum est, in claritatem ejus referre consensimus. Nec defuit audentia Druso Germanico, sed obstitit oceanus in se simul atque in *Herculem* inquiri. Mox nemo tentavit, sanctiusque ac reverentius visum de actis deorum credere quam scire. The Annals 2, 12 name a ' silva *Herculi* sacra,' between the Weser and Elbe in the land of the Cheruscans ; while the Peutinger Table puts a ' castra *Herculis* ' near Noviomagus (Nimwegen). All this means something, it all points to some demigod who is identified, not unadvisedly, with that of the Romans. Hercules, whose deeds were accomplished in countries widely remote, is thought to have visited Germany also, and the Gaditanian pillars at one end of Europe have a counterpart in the Frisian ocean on another side of it. In the German battle-song the praise of Hercules is sounded first, victims are slain to him as to the highest gods, to him a wood is consecrated. Of pillars, even Widukind still knows something, by his speaking of Hirmin's effigies columnarum (pl.), not columnae. Was the plural irmansûlî (p. 115) more exact than irmansûl, and had the image several pillars ? Did the Roman in his Hermin and Herminones think of Herakles and Hercules, whose name bore plainly on its face the root "Ηρα, Hera ? was that why he retained the aspirate in Herminones and Hermunduri, and not in Arminius ? An approximation of sound in the names of the two heroes, Roman and German, may surely be presupposed. The position of Herculis silva and columnae does not indeed agree with that of the Herminones, but the worship of such a hero was sure to spread far and not to be confined to the particular race to which he gave his name. In the German Irman, Irmin, it seems correct for the aspirate to be wanting, as in Arminius ; in Cherusci it is indispensable, and therefore the Romans never wrote Herusci.

If in this ' Hercules ' we wish to see one of the great gods themselves, we must apparently exclude Mercury and Mars, from whom he is distinguished in cap. 9, *i.e.,* Wuotan and Zio. And for supposing him to mean Donar, *i.e.,* Jupiter (as Zeuss does, p. 25), I see no other ground than that the Norse Thôrr, like Hercules, performs innumerable heroic deeds, but these may equally be placed to the credit of Irmin, and Irmin and the thundergod have nothing else in common. Yet, in favour of 'Hercules' being Donar, we ought perhaps to weigh the AS. sentences quoted on p. 161, note ; also, that Herakles was a son of Zeus, and a foe to giants.

I had thought at one time that Hercules might stand for Sahsnôt, Seaxneát, whom the formula of renunciation exalts by the side of Thunar and Wôdan ; I thought so on the strength of 'Hercules Saxanus,' whose surname might be explained by saxum = sahs. But the inscriptions in which we meet with this Hercules Saxanus extend beyond the bounds of Germany, and belong rather to the Roman religion. Our Sahsnôt has with more justice been assigned to Zio (p. 203), with whom Hercules cannot be connected. I now think the claims of Irmin are better founded: as Hercules was Jupiter's son, Irmin seems to have been Wôdan's ; and he must have been the subject of the battle-songs (ituri in proelia canunt), even of those which Tacitus understood of Arminius (canitur adhuc) ; though they would have suited Mars too, p. 207 (see Suppl.).

It is a harder matter to form an opinion about the ' Ulysses ' : Ceterum et *Ulixem* quidam opinantur longo illo et fabuloso errore in hunc oceanum delatum adisse Germaniae terras, Asciburgium-que, quod in ripa Rheni situm hodieque incolitur, ab illo consti-tutum nominatumque ; aram quin etiam *Ulixi* consecratam, adjecto Laertae patris nomine, eodem loco olim repertam ; Tac. Germ. 3. In Odysseus people have seen Oðinn, in Asciburg Asburg ; but if Wôden stood for the god Mercury, it cannot here mean the hero, still less can Askiburg be traced to the âses, a purely Norse form, which in these regions would have been anses. When Tacitus makes Ulixes the founder of *Asciburg*, nothing is simpler than to suppose him to have been *Isco, Escio, Asko* (p. 350) ; and if it was *Isco* that set the Romans thinking of Ul-ixes, how it helps to esta-blish the *sc* in Iscaevones ! *Mannus* the father of Isco may have suggested *Laertes*, inasmuch as λαός people, and λᾶος stone, are mixed up in the creation of the first *man* (the origo gentis) out of *stone* or rock (see ch. XIX) ; in the same way *Asco* grew up out of the tree (ash), and δρῦς and πέτρη stand together in the mythus not without meaning. As liut from liotan, λαός seems to come from the same root as λᾶος, λᾶας.[1]

The interpretatio Romana went more upon analogies of sense than of sound; so, in dealing with *Castor* and *Pollux*, I will not take them for the brothers Hadu and Phol = Baldr (see Suppl.). These Gemini, however, are the very hardest to interpret; the passage about them was given on p. 66, and an attempt was made to show that *alx* referred to the place where the godlike twins were worshipped : I confess it does not satisfy me. Our antiquity has plenty of hero brothers to show, but no twins with a name like *Alci*, if this plural of Alcus is the true form. It occurs to me, that one of Oðin's names is *Iálkr* (Sæm. 46ᵇ 47ᵇ), and *jolk* in the Vermland dialect means a boy.[2] This comes more home to us than the Samogitic *Algir* (angelus est summorum deorum, Lasicz, p. 47), towards which the dictionaries offer nothing but alga, reward. Utterly untrustworthy is any comparison with the Slav deities Lel and Polel, themselves as yet unsupported by authority (see Suppl.).[3]

4. BEOWULF, SIGFRIT, AMALO, ERMENRICH, DIETERICH, &c.

From the above specimens in Tacitus we may conclude that all the Teutonic races had a pretty fully developed Heroology ; and if our ancient stores of native literature had been still accessible to us, we might have gained a much closer insight into its nature and its connexion as a whole. As it is, we are thrown upon dry *genealogies*, dating from many centuries after, and touching only certain races, namely the Goths, Langobards, Burgundians, but above all, the Anglo-Saxons and Scandinavians. We may learn from them the connexion of the later kings with the ancient gods and heroes, but not the living details of their myths. Yet we could be content, if even such pedigrees had also been preserved of the Franks and other nations of continental Germany.

The Anglo-Saxon genealogies seem the most important, and the

---

[1] " Ulixes = Loki, Sn. 78. For Laertes, whose name Pott 1, 222 explains as protector of the people, conf. Ptolemy's Λακιβούργιον." Extr. from Suppl., vol. iii.

[2] Almqvist, Svensk språklära, Stockh. 1840, p. 385ᵃ.

[3] In Lith. lele is pupa, akies lele pupilla, leilas butterfly.

Appendix gives them in full [but see above, p. 165]. All the families branch out from *Wôden*, as most of the Greek do from Zeus ; it was a proud feeling to have one's root in the highest of all gods. Prominent among his sons are *Saxneât* and *Bœldœg*, who were themselves accounted divine; but several other names can claim a place among the earliest heroes, *e.g., Sigegeât* and *Wôdelgeât*[1] (both akin to the Gothic *Gâuts*), *Freâwine, Wuscfreâ, Sœfugel, Westerfalcna*; and many are fallen dim to us. *Câsere*, which in other AS. writings is used for cyning,[2] seems to be a mere appellative, and to have acquired the character of a proper name after the analogy of the Roman ⌐sar (?). All these genealogies give us barely the names of the god's sons and grandsons, never those of their mothers or grandmothers; and the legend, which ought like the Greek ones to give life to the relationship, is the very thing we miss.

Some of the Norse traditions gain in value, by being taken with the genealogies. The Völsûngasaga sets out with Oðin's being the father of *Sigi*, but all particulars of the relationship are withheld ; *Rerir* the son of Sigi is in the immediate keeping of the highest gods, and so on. Another time, on the contrary, we are informed, Sn. 84—86, how Oðinn under the name of *Bölverkr* (OHG. Palowurcho ?) became servant to the giant Baugi, in order to get at the divine drink, which the giant's brother Suttûngr kept, guarded by his daughter *Gunnlöð;* between her and the god took place sundry passages of love, dimly hinted at by Sæmund also 12[b] 23[a,b] 24[a], but we are nowhere told what heroes were begotten in the three nights that Oðinn passed with the giant's daughter. *Gunnlöð* belongs to the race of giants, not of men, which is also the case with *Gerðr* whom Freyr wooed, and perhaps with others, who are not reckoned among the âsynjor. The Greeks also held that from the union of gods with titans' daughters might spring a hero, or even a god (like Týr, p. 208).—Only Saxo, p. 66, and no other authority, tells us of a Norwegian king and hero ' *Frogerus*, ut quidam ferunt, Othino patre natus,' to whom the gods gave to be invincible in fight, unless his adversary could grasp the dust from

[1] OHG. *Wuotilgôz* (Zeitschr. f. d. alt. 1, 577), conf. wüeteln above, p. 132, and Wodel-beer, p. 156 (see Suppl.).

[2] In Boëth. 38, 1 Agamemnon is styled câsere, and Ulysses cyning [in the Pref., Rædgot, Ealleric, Theodric are cyningas, the emperor always câsere] ; in a doc. in Kemble 2, 304 Eádred is ' cyning and câsere '.

under his feet,[1] which the Danish king Frotho by fraud contrived to
do. Can this *Froger* be the AS. Freoðegâr, Freðegâr in the Wessex
genealogy, who had Brond for father, Bældæg for grandfather,
Wôden for great-grandfather ?   The ON. table of lineage seems to
mix up Frioðegar with Froði, his adversary.[2]   According to the
Formâli of the Edda, p. 15, and the Yngl. saga c. 9, Norway traced
her eldest line of kings to *Sœmíngr*, the son of Oðinn by Skaði,
previously the wife of Niörðr ; some write *Semíngr*, which means
pacificator, and would lead to Friðgeir again.   Skaði was daughter
to the iötunn Thiassi, and the Sigurðardrâpa (-killing) calls
Sigurðr Laðaiarl ' afspríngr Thiassa,' (Th. progenies).—The Her-
rauðssaga cap. 1 makes Hrîngr spring from *Gauti*, and him from
Oðinn : this *Gautr* or *Gauti* (conf. Ing and Ingo, Irmin and Irmino),
Goth. Gáuts, OHG. Kôz, AS. Geát, whether surname, son or
ancestor of Oðinn, cannot belie his divinity (conf. p. 367) ; and his
son Godwulf too, confounded by some with Folcwalda (p. 165, last
table), looks mythical.   It is from *Gáuts* that the Gáutôs (Kôzâ, Γαυ-
τοί) professed to be descended, these being other than the Guþans
(Tac. Gothones, Γότθοι), but related to them nevertheless, for the
Gothic genealogy starts with the same Gáuts at the head of it.—
Again, *Sigrlami* is called Oðin's son, Fornald. sög. 1, 413.   But who
can ' *Bous* (gen. Boi), Othini ex Rinda filius ' be in Saxo Gram. 46 ?
Possibly *Biar*, Biaf, Beav = Beowulf, to whom we are coming (see
Suppl.).[3]

Another Oðinsson, *Skiöldr*, is the famed ancestral hero of the
Danes, from whom are derived all the Skiöldûngar (Sn. 146); he
may have been most nearly related to the people of Schonen, as in
the Fornm. sög. 5, 239 he is expressly called Skânûnga goð (see p.
161), and was probably worshipped as a god.   In Saxo Gram. he
does not take the lead, but follows after Humblus, Dan[4] and
Lother ; *Skiold* himself has a son Gram,[5] from whom come Hadding

---

[1] A token of victory? as the vanquished had to present such dust (RA.
111-2).

[2] The AS. name Frôdheri stands yet farther away (Beda 2, 9 § 113).

[3] Saxo 122 mentions one hero begotten by Thôrr : *Haldanus Biarggrammus*
apud Sueones *magni Thor filius* existimatur.   And I know of no other but this
one.

[4] *Dan*, in Saxo's view the true ancestor of the Danes, is called in the
Rîgsmâl *Danr*, and placed together with *Danpr*, Sæm. 106[b].

[5] Elsewhere *Gramr* is the proper name of a particular sword, while the
appellative *gramr* denotes king.

and then Frotho; but the AS. genealogy places its Scild after *Sceáf*, and singularly makes them both ancestors of Oðinn. From *Sceáf* descends *Sceldwa*, from him consecutively *Beaw*, *Tœtwa*, *Geát*, and after several more generations comes *Wóden* last. The ON. version of the lineage is in harmony with this; and even in the Gothic pedigree, which only begins with *Gáuts*, we may suppose a Skáufs, Skildva, Táitva to have preceded, to whom the OHG. names Scoup, Scilto, Zeizo would correspond.—None however is so interesting as Sceldwa's son, the Anglo-Saxon *Beaw*, called by the Scandinavians *Biar*, *Biaf*, but in the living AS. epos *Beowulf*. It is true, the remarkable poem of that name is about a second and younger Beowulf, in whom his forefather's name repeats itself; but fortunately the opening lines allude to the elder Beowulf, and call his father *Scild* (Goth. Skildus, agreeing with Skiöldr) a Scêfing, *i.e.*, son of *Sceáf*. Beaw is a corruption of Beow, and Beow an abbreviation of *Beowulf*: it is the complete name that first opens to us a wider horizon. *Beowulf* signifies bee-wolf (OHG. *Piawolf?*), and that is a name for the *woodpecker*, a bird of gay plumage that hunts after bees, of whom antiquity has many a tale to tell.[1] Strange to say, the classical mythus (above, pp. 206, 249) makes this *Picus* a son of *Saturn*, inasmuch as it either identifies him with *Zeus* who is succeeded by a *Hermes*, or makes him nourisher of *Mars's* sons and father of *Faunus*. We see Picus (Picumnus) interwoven into the race of Kronos, Zeus, Hermes and Ares, the old Bohemian Stračec = picus into that of Sitivrat, Kirt and Radigost, as *Beowulf* is into that of *Geát* and *Wóden*. If the groups differ in the details of their combination, their agreement as wholes is the more trustworthy and less open to suspicion. And just as the footprints of Saturn were traceable from the Slavs to the Saxons and to England, but were less known to the Northmen, so those of the divine bird in Stračec and Beowulf seem to take the same course, and never properly to reach Scandinavia. The central Germans stood nearer to Roman legend, although no actual borrowing need have taken place.

What a deep hold this group of heroes had taken, is evidenced by another legend. *Sceáf* (*i.e.*, manipulus frumenti) takes his name

[1] Can the name in Upper Germany for the turdus or oriolus galbula, *Birolf*, Pirolf, brother Pirolf (Frisch 1, 161), possibly stand for *Biewolf* (or Biterolf)? The Serbs call it *Urosh*, and curiously this again is a hero's name. Conf. the Finn. uros [with heros?], p. 341.

from the circumstance, that when a boy he was conveyed to the country he was destined to succour, while *asleep*[1] on a sheaf of corn in the boat. The poetry of the Lower Rhine and Netherlands in the Mid. Ages is full of a similar story of the *sleeping* youth whom a swan conducts in his ship to the afflicted land; and this swan-knight is pictured approaching out of paradise, from the grave, as *Helias*, whose divine origin is beyond question. Helias, Gerhart or Loherangrin of the thirteenth century is identical then with a *Scôf* or *Scoup* of the seventh and eighth, different as the surroundings may have been, for the song of Beowulf appears to have transferred to *Scild* what belonged of right to his father *Sceáf*. The beautiful story of the swan is founded on the miraculous origin of the swan-brothers, which I connect with that of the Welfs; both however seem to be antique lineage-legends of the Franks and Swabians, to which the proper names are mostly wanting. Had they been preserved, many another tie between the heroes and the gods would come to light.[2]—Further, to *Sceldwa* or *Skiöldr* belongs obviously the name *Schiltunc* in the Tirol and Parzival,[3] as the name *Schil-bunc*, Nib. 88, 3, points to a race of *Scilpungâ*, corresponding to the AS. *Scilfingas*, ON. *Scilfingar*, of whom Skelfir, Scilfe, Scilpi is to be regarded as the ancestor. This *Skelfir* the Fornald. sög. 2, 9 makes the father of Skiöldr, so that the *Skilfinga* and *Skiöldinga* ætt fall into one. Either Scelf is here confounded with Scêf, or Scêf must be altered to Scelf, but the frequent occurrence of the form Sceáf, and its interpretation (from sheaf), seem alike to forbid this (see Suppl.).

As the Skiöldûngar descend from Skiöldr, so do the Giukûngar from *Giuki = Gibika, Kipicho*, with whom the Burgundian line begins : if not a god himself (p. 137), he is a divine hero that carries us back very near to Wuotan. The *Gibichensteine* (-stones) moreover bear witness to him, and it is to the two most eminent women of this race that Grimhildensteine, Brunhildensteine are allotted.[4]

---

[1] Umborwesende ? Beow. 92.

[2] The ship that brought Sceáf and the swan-knight carries them away again at last, but the reason is disclosed only in later legend : it was forbidden to inquire into their origin, Parz. 825, 19. Conr., Schwanritter 1144-73.

[3] Zeitschr. für deut. alterth. 1, 7.

[4] Brunehildestein, lectulus Brunihilde, Kriemhiltenstein, Criemildespil (Heldensage p. 155) ; Krimhilte graben (Weisth. 1, 48); in loco Grimhiltaperg nominato (Juvavia p. 137) ; de Crimhilteperc, MB. 7. 498.

Frau *Uote* however appears as ancestress of the stock.[1] It has not
been so much noticed as it ought, that in the Lex Burg. *Gislahari*
precedes *Gundahari* by a whole generation, whilst our epic
(Nibelungen) makes Gîselhere Gunthere's younger brother, and the
Edda never names him at all. The Law makes no mention of any
brothers, and Gîselher the young has merely the name of his elder
kinsman. *Gêrnôt* (from gér = gáis) and *Gîselher* seem to be
identical (conf. Gramm. 2, 46). But the Norse Guttormr can
hardly be a distortion of Godomar, for we meet with him outside of
the legend, *e.g.*, in Landn. 1, 18. 20, where the spelling Guðormr
(Guntwurm) would lead us to identify him with Gunthere, and in
Saxo Gram. are found several Guthormi (see Suppl.). Then *Hagano*
the one-eyed, named from hagan (spinosus, Waltharius 1421), is
' more than heroic '.[2]

Even deeper reaching roots must be allowed to the Welisungs,
their name brings us to a divine *Valis* who has disappeared (conf.
the ON. Vali, p. 163), but the mere continuance of an OHG.
Welisunc is a proof of the immemorial diffusion of the Völsûngasaga itself (see Suppl.). How, beginning with Wuotan, it goes on
to *Sigi, Sigimunt, Sigifrit, Sintarfizilo*, has been alluded to on p
367, and has already been treated of elsewhere.[3] With Sigfri
stands connected *Helfrich*, Chilpericus, ON. Hialprekr. It i;
worthy of note, that the AS. Beowulf calls Sigfrit *Sigemund*, and
Sigmundr is a surname of Oðinn besides.[4] Such a flood of
splendour falls on Siegfried in the poems, that we need not stick at
trifles; his whole nature has evident traces of the superhuman
brought up by an elf Regino, beloved by a valkyr Brunhild,
instructed in his destiny by the wise man Grîpir, he wears the
helmet of invisibility, is vulnerable only on one spot in his body,
as Achilles was in the heel, and he achieves the rich hoard of the
Nibelungs. His slaying of the dragon Fâfnir reminds us of $\Pi \acute{v} \theta \omega v$[5]

---

[1] Haupts zeitschr. 1, 21.

[2] Lachmann's examination of the whole Nibelung legend, p. 22.

[3] Haupts zeitschr. 1, 2—6.

[4] In the Copenh. ed. of the Edda, Sæm. 2, 889 *Sigemon*, and in Finn
Magn. lex. 643 *Segemon*, is said to have been a name of the Celtic Mars ;
I suppose on the ground of the inscriptt. in Gruter lviii. 5 : *Marti Segomoni*
sacrum . . . in civitate Sequanorum ; and ii. 2 : Diis deabus omnibus
Veturius L.L. Securius (al. *Segomanus*) pro se quisque (see Suppl.).

[5] Almost the same, granting a change of *th* into *f* (as in $\theta \acute{\eta} \rho$, $\phi \acute{\eta} \rho$) ; of our
â standing for Greek *ῡ* there are more examples : fnâsu, blâsu = $\pi \nu \epsilon \acute{v} \omega$, $\phi \lambda \acute{v} \omega$.

whom Apollo overcame, and as Python guarded the Delphic oracle,
the dying Fâfnir prophesies.[1] We must take into account *Loðfáfnir*
Sæm. 24, 30. Sinfiötli, who, when a boy, kneads snakes into the
dough, is comparable to the infant Hercules tested by serpents.

Through Siegfried the Frankish Welisungs get linked to the
Burgundian Gibichungs, and then both are called Nibelungs.

Among Gothic heroes we are attracted by the *Ovida* and
Cnivida in Jornandes cap. 22, perhaps the same as *Offa* and
Cnebba in the Mercian line. But of far more consequence is the
great Gothic family of Amals or Amalungs, many of whose names
in the Jornandean genealogy seem corrupt. The head of them all
was Gapt, which I emend to *Gaut* (Gáuts), and so obtain an allusion
to the divine office of casting [giessen, ein-guss, in-got] and meting
(pp. 22. 142) ; he was a god, or son of a god (p. 164), and is even
imported into the Saxon lines as *Geát*, Wôdelgeát, Sigegeát (p. 367).
In this Gothic genealogy the weak forms Amala, Isarna, Ostro-
gotha, Ansila, confirm what we have observed in Tuisco, Inguio,
Iscio, Irmino ; but those best worth noting are *Amala,* after
whom the most powerful branch of the nation is named, *Ermanaricus* and *Theodericus.* Ermanaricus must be linked with Irmino
and the Herminones, as there is altogether a closer tie between
Goths and Saxons (Ingaevones and Herminones) as opposed to the
Franks (Iscaevones), and this shows itself even in the later epics.—
Amongst the Amalungs occur many names compounded with
vulf, which reminds us of their side-branch, the Wülfings ; if it be
not too bold, I would even connect *Isarna* (Goth. Eisarna) with
Isangrim. To me the four sons of Achiulf seem worthy of
particular notice : Ansila, Ediulf, Vuldulf, and Hermenrich. Of
the last we have just spoken, and Ansila means the divine ; our
present concern is with *Ediulf* and *Vuldulf.* I find that Jornandes,
cap. 54, ascribes to the Scyrians also two heroes *Edica* and *Vulf ;*
the Rugian *Odoacer* has a father *Eticho* and a brother *Aonulf ;* and

---

[1] The epithet *sveinn* (Sw. sven, Dan. svend) given to the Norse *Sigurðr*
appears already in Fâfnir's address ' *sveinn* ok *sveinn !* ' and in the headings to
ch. 142-4 of the Vilk. saga. The same hero then is meant by the *Sivard
snaresvend* (fortis puer) of the Danish folk-song, who, riding on Grani,
accompanies to Askereia (see ch. XXXI), and by *Svend Felding* or *Fälling* of
the Danish folk-tale (Thiele 2, 64-7. Müller's sagabibl. 2, 417-9). He drank
out of a horn handed to him by elvish beings, and thereby acquired the strength
of twelve men. Swedish songs call him *Sven Färling* or *Fotling ;* Arvidsson
1, 129. 415.

the legend on the origin of the Welfs has the proper names *Isenbart, Irmentrud, Welf* and *Etico* constantly recurring. Now, welf is strictly catulus (huelf, whelp, ON. hvelpr), and distinct from wolf; natural history tells us of several strong courageous animals that are brought into the world blind; the Langobardic and Swabian genealogies play upon dogs and wolves being exposed; and as *Odoacer, Otacher* (a thing that has never till now been accounted for) is in some versions called Sipicho, ON. Bicki, and this means dog (bitch), I suspect a similar meaning in Edica, Eticho, Ediulf, Odacar, which probably affords a solution of the fable about the ' blind Schwaben and Hessen': their lineage goes back to the blind Welfs. In the genealogy Ediulf is described as brother to Ermenrich, in later sagas Bicki is counsellor to Iörmunrekr; the Hildebrandslied has but too little to say of Otacher. Then Vuldulf also (perhaps Vuldr-ulf) will signify a glorious beaming wolf (see Suppl.).—As Siegfried eclipsed all other Welisungs, so did *Dieterich* all the Amalungs; and where the epos sets them one against the other, each stands in his might, unconquered, unapproachable. Dieterich's divine herohood comes out in more than one feature, *e.g.*, his fiery breath, and his taking the place of Wuotan or Frô (p. 213-4) at the head of the wild host, as *Dietrichbern* or *Bernhard.* The fiery breath brings him nearer to Donar, with whom he can be compared in another point also: Dieterich is wounded in the forehead by an arrow, and a piece of it is left inside him, for which reason he is called the deathless;[1] not otherwise did the half of Hrûngnir's hein (stone wedge) remain in Thor's head, and as Grôa's magic could not loosen it, it sticks there still, and none shall aim with the like stones, for it makes the piece in the god's forehead stir (Sn. 109—111).[2] This horn-like stone was very likely shown in images, and enhanced their godlike appearance.

The renowned race of the *Billings* or *Billungs*, whose mythic roots and relations are no longer discoverable, was still flourishing in North Germany in the 10-11th centuries. The first historically certain Billing died in 967, and another, above a hundred years older, is mentioned.[3] The Cod. Exon. 320, 7 says: ' *Billing* weold

[1] Simon Keza, chron. Hungaror. 1, 11. 12. Heinr. von Müglein (in Kovachich p. 8); conf. Deutsche heldensage p. 164.

[2] Hence the proverb: seint losnar hein î höfði Thôrs.

[3] Wedekind's Hermann duke of Saxony, Lüneb. 1817, p. 60. Conf. the miles Billinc, comes Billingus in docs. of 961-8 in Höfers zeitschr. 2, 239. 344, and the OHG. form Billungus in Zeuss, Trad. wizenb. pp. 274. 287. 305.

Wernum,' he belongs therefore to the stock of Werina, who were near of kin to the Angles. There was a *Billinga* hæð (heath) near Whalley, and London has to this day a Billingsgate. In OHG. we find a man's name *Billunc* (Ried nos. 14. 21-3, A.D. 808. 821-2). If we take into account, that a dwarf *Billingr* occurs in the Edda, Sæm. 2ᵃ 23ᵃ, a hero *Pillunc* in Rol. 175, 1, and *Billunc* and Nîdunc coupled together in the Renner 14126-647, the name acquires a respectable degree of importance (see Suppl.). The derivative Billinc implies a simple bil or bili (lenitas, placiditas), from which directly [and not from our adj. billig, fair] are formed the OHG. names Pilidrût, Pilihilt, Pilikart, Pilihelm; to which add the almost personified *Billich* (equity) in Trist. 9374. 10062. 17887. 18027, and the ON. goddess *Bil*, Sn. 39 ; the *ll* in Billung could be explained through Biliung. Just as Oðinn in Sæm. 46ᵇ is called both Bileygr (mild-eyed) and Baleygr (of baleful eye), so in Saxo Gram. 130 a Bilvisus (æquus) stands opposed to Bölvisus (iniquus).

5. ORENTIL. WIELANT. MIMI. TELL, &c.

In addition to the heroes ascertained thus far, who form part of the main pedigree of whole nations, and thence derive weight and durability, there is another class of more isolated heroes ; I can only put forward a few of them here.

We have still remaining a somewhat rude poem, certainly founded on very ancient epic material, about a king *Orendel* or *Erentel*, whom the appendix to the Heldenbuch pronounces the first of all heroes that were ever born. He suffers shipwreck on a voyage, takes shelter with a master fisherman *Eisen*,[1] earns the seamless coat of his master, and afterwards wins frau *Breide*, the fairest of women : king *Eigel* of Trier was his father's name. The whole tissue of the fable puts one in mind of the Odyssey : the ship-wrecked man clings to the plank, digs himself a hole, holds a bough before him ; even the seamless coat may be compared to Ino's veil, and the fisher to the swineherd, dame Breide's templars would be Penelope's suitors, and angels are sent often, like Zeus's messengers. Yet many things take a different turn, more in German fashion, and incidents are added, such as the laying of a naked sword between the newly married couple, which the Greek story knows nothing of. The hero's name is found even in OHG. documents :

---

[1] Who is also found apparently in a version of the Lay of king Oswald.

Orendil, Meichelb. 61; *Orentil,* Trad. fuld. 2, 24. 2, 109 (Schannat
308); *Orendil* a Bavarian count (an. 843 in.Eccard's Fr. or. 2, 367);
a village *Orendelsal,* now Orendensall, in Hohenlohe, v. Haupts
zeitschr. 7, 558.—But the Edda has another myth, which was
alluded to in speaking of the stone in Thôr's head. Grôa is busy
conning her magic spell, when Thôrr, to requite her for the
approaching cure, imparts the welcome news, that in coming from
Iötunheim in the North he has carried her husband the bold
Örvandill in a basket on his back, and he is sure to be home soon ;
he adds by way of token, that as Örvandil's toe had stuck out of the
basket and got frozen, he broke it off and flung it at the sky, and
made a star of it, which is called *Örvandils-tâ.* But Grôa in her
joy at the tidings forgot her spell, so the stone in the god's head
never got loose, Sn. 110-1. Grôa, the growing, the grass-green, is
equivalent to Breide, *i.e.,* Berhta (p. 272) the bright, it is only
another part of his history that is related here : Örvandill must
have set out on his travels again, and on this second adventure
forfeited the toe which Thôrr set in the sky, though what he had
to do with the god we are not clearly told. Beyond a doubt, the
name of the glittering star-group is referred to, when AS. glosses
render 'jubar' by *earendel,* and a hymn to the virgin Mary in Cod.
Exon. 7, 20 presents the following passage :

> Eala *Earendel,* engla beorhtast,
> ofer middangeard monnum sended,
> and sôðfæsta sunnan leoma
> torht ofer tunglas, þu tîda gehwane
> of sylfum þe symle inlîhtes !

i.e., O jubar, angelorum splendidissime, super orbem terrarum
hominibus misse, radie vere solis, supra stellas lucide, qui omni
tempore ex te ipso luces ! Mary or Christ is here addressed under
the heathen name of the constellation. I am only in doubt as to
the right spelling and interpretation of the word ; an OHG. *ôrentil*
implies AS. eárendel, and the two would demand ON. aurvendill,
eyrvendill ; but if we start with ON. örvendill, then AS. earendel,
OHG. erentil would seem preferable. The latter part of the
compound certainly contains entil = wentil.[1] The first part should

---

[1] Whence did Matthesius (in Frisch 2, 439[a]) get his " Pan is the heathens'
Wendel and head bagpiper " ? Can the word refer to the metamorphoses of the
flute-playing demigod ? In trials of witches, Wendel is a name for the devil,
Mones anz. 8, 124.

be either ôra, eáre (auris), or else ON. ör, gen. örvar (sagitta).
Now, as there occurs in a tale in Saxo Gram., p. 48, a Horvendilus
filius Gervendili, and in OHG. a name Kêrwentil (Schm. 2, 334)
and Gêrentil (Trad. fuld. 2, 106), and as geir (hasta) agrees better
with ör than with eyra (auris), the second interpretation may command our assent ;[1] a sight of the complete legend would explain the
reason of the name. I think Orentil's father deserves attention
too : *Eigil* is another old and obscure name, borne for instance by
an abbot of Fulda who died in 822 (Pertz 1, 95. 356. 2, 366.
Trad. fuld. 1, 77-8. 122). In the Rhine-Moselle country are the
singular *Eigelsteine*, Weisth. 2, 744 (see Suppl.).[2] In AS. we find
the names *Aegles* burg (Aylesbury), *Aegles* ford (Aylesford), *Aegles*
þorp; but I shall come back to Eigil presently. Possibly Orentil
was the thundergod's companion in expeditions against giants.
Can the story of Orentil's wanderings possibly be so old amongst
us, that in Orentil and Eigil of Trier we are to look for that Ulysses
and Laertes whom Tacitus places on our Rhine (p. 365) ? The
names shew nothing in common.[3]

Far-famed heroes were *Wieland* and *Wittich*,[4] whose rich
legend is second to none in age or celebrity. *Vidigoia* (Vidugáuja)
of whom the Goths already sang, OHG. *Witugouwo* as well as
Witicho, MHG. *Witegouwe* and *Witege*, AS. *Wudga*, in either form
silvicola, from the Goth. vidus, OHG. witu, AS. wudu (lignum,
silva), leads us to suppose a being passing the bounds of human
nature, a forest-god. Frau Wâchilt, a mermaid, is his ancestress,
with whom he takes refuge in her lake. At the head of the whole
race is placed king *Vilkinus*, named after Vulcanus as the Latin
termination shews, a god or demigod, who must have had another
and German name, and who begets with the merwoman a gigantic
son *Vadi*, AS. *Wada* (Cod. Exon. 323, 1), OHG. *Wato*, so named I
suppose because, like another Christopher, he *waded* with his child
on his shoulder through the Grœnasund where it is nine yards

---

[1] And so Uhland (On Thor, p. 47 seq.) expounds it : in Grôa he sees the
growth of the crop, in Örvandill the sprouting of the blade. Even the tale in
Saxo he brings in.

[2] The false spelling Eichelstein (acorn-stone) has given rise to spurious
legends, Mones anz. 7, 368.

[3] I have hardly the face to mention, that some make the right shifty Ulysses
father to Pan, our Wendel above.

[4] The still unprinted M.Dutch poem, De kinderen van Limburg, likewise
mentions *Wilant*, *Wedege* and *Mimminc*.

deep (between Zealand, Falster and Moen) ; the Danish hero *Wate* in Gudrun is identical with him; the AS. *Wada* is placed toward Helsingen. Old English poetry had much to tell of him, that is now lost : Chaucer names ' *Wades* boot Guingelot,' and a place in Northumberland is called *Wade's* gap ; Wætlingestrêt could only be brought into connexion with him, if such a spelling as Wædling could be made good.—Now, that son, whom Vadi carried through the sea to apprentice him to those cunning smiths the dwarfs, was *Wielant*, AS. *Weland, Welond,* ON. *Völundr,* but in the Vilk. saga *Velint,* master of all smiths, and wedded to a swan-maiden Hervör alvitr. The rightful owner of the boat, which English tradition ascribes to Wada, seems to have been *Wieland ;* the Vilk. saga tells how he timbered a boat out of the trunk of a tree, and sailed over seas. Lamed in the sinews of his foot, he forged for himself a winged garment, and took his flight through the air. His skill is praised on all occasions, and his name coupled with every costly jewel, Vilk. saga cap. 24. Witeche, the son he had by Baduhilt, bore a hammer and tongs in his scutcheon in honour of his father ; during the Mid. Ages his memory lasted among smiths, whose workshops were styled *Wieland's* houses,[1] and perhaps his likeness was set up or painted outside them; the ON. ' Völundar hûs ' translates the Latin labyrinth ; a host of similar associations must in olden times have been generally diffused, as we learn from the names of places : *Welantes* gruoba (pit), MB. 13, 59 ; *Wielantes* heim, MB. 28ᵃ, 93 (an. 889) ; *Wielantis* dorf, MB. 29, 54 (an. 1246) ; *Wielantes* tanna (firs), MB. 28ᵇ, 188. 471 (an. 1280) ; *Wielandes* brunne, MB. 31, 41 (an. 817). The multiplication of such names during long centuries does not admit of their being derived from human inhabitants. The Dan. *Velands*urt (-wort), Icel. *Velants*urt, is the valerian, and according to Stald. 2, 450 *Wieland*beere the daphne cneorum. Tradition would doubtless extend Wieland's dexterity to Wittich and to Wate, who also gets the credit of the boat, and in the Gudrun-lay of the healing art. In Sæm. 270ᵃ, ' bœkur ofnar *völundom* ' are stragula artificiose contexta, and any artist might be called a völundr or wielant. A gorgeous coat of mail (hrægel, OHG. hregil) is in Beow. 904 *Welandes* geweorc. Ælfred in Boëth. 2, 7 translates fidelis

---

[1] Juxta domum *Welandi* fabri, Ch. ad ann. 1262 in Lang's reg. 3, 181 : conf. Haupts zeitschr. 2, 248. I find also *Witigo* faber, MB. 7, 122.

ossa Fabricii 'þæs wîsan goldsmiðes bân *Welondes*' (metrically :
Welandes bân) ; evidently the idea of faber which lay in Fabricius
brought to his mind the similar meaning of the Teutonic name,
Weland being a cunning smith in general. For the name itself
appears to contain the ON. vél = viel (ars, τέχνη, OHG. list),
Gramm. 1, 462, and smiðvélar meant artes fabriles ; the AS. form
is wîl, or better wil, Engl. wile, Fr. guile; the OHG. wiol, wiel (with
broken vowel) is no longer to be found. But further, we must pre-
suppose a verb wielan, AS. wëlan (fabrefacere), whose pres. part. wielant, wëland, exactly forms our proper name, on a par with wîgant,
werdant, druoant, &c. ; Graff 2, 234 commits the error of citing
Wielant under the root lant, with which it has no more to do than
heilant (healer, saviour). The OFr. *Galans* (Heldens. 42) seems
to favour the ON. form *Völundr* [root val] since Veland would
rather have led to a Fr. Guilans , possibly even the ON. vala
(nympha) is a kindred word ? An OHG. name Wieldrûd seems
the very thing for a wise-woman.—This development of an intrinsic
significance in the hero's name finds an unexpected confirmation
in the striking similarity of the Greek fables of Hephæstus,
Erichthonius and Dædalus. As Weland offers violence to
Beadohild (Völundr to Böðvildr), so Hephæstus lays a snare for
Athene, when she comes to order weapons of him ; both Hephæstus
and Völundr are punished with lameness, Erichthonius too is lame,
and therefore invents the four-horse chariot, as Völundr does the
boat and wings. One with Erichthonius are the later Erechtheus
and his descendant Dædalus, who invented various arts, a ring-
dance, building, &c., and on whose wings his son Icarus was soaring
when he fell from the clouds. But Δαίδαλος [1] is δαίδαλος, δαιδάλ-
εος, cunningly wrought, δαίδαλμα (like ἄγαλμα) a work of art, and
δαιδάλλειν the same as our lost wielan. As our list [like the Engl.
cunning and craft] has degenerated from its original sense of scientia
to that of calliditas and fraus, and vél has both meanings, it is not
surprising that from the skill-endowed god and hero has proceeded
a deformed deceitful devil (p. 241). The whole group of Wate,
Wielant, Wittich are heroes, but also ghostly beings and demigods
(see SuppL).

The Vilkinasaga brings before us yet another smith, *Mîmir*, by

---

[1] A reduplication like παίπαλος, παιπαλόεις tortus, arduus, παιπάλλειν tor-
quere ; conf. λαῖλαψ, μαῖμαξ, &c.

whom not only is Velint instructed in his art, but Sigfrit is brought up—another smith's-apprentice. He is occasionally mentioned in the later poem of Biterolf, as *Mîme* the old (Heldensage, pp. 146-8); an OHG. *Mimi* must have grown even more deeply into our language as well as legend: it has formed a diminutive *Mîmilo* (MB. 28, 87-9, annis 983-5), and *Mîmâ*, *Mîmidrût*, *Mîmihilt* are women's names (Trad. fuld. 489. Cod. lauresh. 211); the old name of Münster in Westphalia was *Mîmi*gardiford, *Mîmi*gerneford (Indices to Pertz 1. 2), conf. *Mîmi*gerdeford in Richthofen 335; the Westphalian Minden was originally *Mîmi*dun (Pertz 1, 368), and Memleben on the Unstrut *Mîmi*leba. The great number of these proper names indicates a mythic being, to which *Memerolt* (Morolt 111) may also be related.—The elder Norse tradition names him just as often, and in several different connexions. In one place, Saxo, p. 40,[1] interweaves a *Mimingus*, a 'silvarum satyrus' and possessor of a sword and jewels, into the myth of Balder and Hother, and this, to my thinking, throws fresh light on the vidugáuja (wood-god) above. The Edda however gives a higher position to its *Mîmir:* he has a fountain, in which wisdom and understanding lie hidden; drinking of it every morning, he is the wisest, most intelligent of men, and this again reminds us of 'Wielandes brunne'. To *Mîmis*brunnr came Oðinn and desired a drink, but did not receive it till he had given one of his eyes in pledge, and hidden it in the fountain (Sæm. 4ᵃ. Sn. 17); this accounts for Oðinn being one-eyed (p. 146). In the Yngl. saga cap. 4, the Ases send *Mîmir*, their wisest man, to the Vanir, who cut his head off and send it back to the Ases. But Oðinn spake his spells over the head, that it decayed not, nor ceased to utter speech; and Oðinn holds conversation with it, whenever he needs advice, conf. Yngl. saga cap. 7, and Sæm. 8ᵃ 195ᵇ. I do not exactly know whom the Völuspâ means by *Mîmis* synir (sons), Sæm. 8ᵃ; *Mîma*meidr 109ᵃ implies a nom. *Mîmi* gen. *Mîma*, and may be distinct from *Mîmir* (conf. Bragr and Bragi, p. 235).—Mîmir is no As, but an exalted being with whom the Ases hold converse, of whom they make use, the sum-total of wisdom, possibly an older nature-god; later fables degraded him into a wood-sprite or clever smith. His oneness with heroes tends to throw a divine splendour

---

[1] P. E. Müller's ed., p. 114, following which I have set aside the reading Mimringus, in spite of the Danish song of Mimering tand.

on them. Swedish folk-song has not yet forgotten *Mimes* å (Arvidsson 2, 316-7), and in Konga härad and Tingås socken in Småland there lies a *Mimes* sjö, inhabited according to the legend by neckar (nixies), ibid. p. 319. Perhaps some of the forms quoted have by rights a short *i*, as have indisputably the AS. mimor, meomor, gemimor (memoriter notus), mimerian (memoria tenere), our Low German mimeren (day-dreaming), Brem. wtb. 3, 161, and the Memerolt, Memleben above ; so that we might assume a verb meima, máim, mimum. Then the analogy of the Latin memor and Gr. μιμέομαι allows us to bring in the giant and centaur *Μίμας*, *i.e.*, the wood-sprite again (see Suppl.).

According to the Edda (Sæm. 133), Völundr had two brothers Slagfiðr and Egill, all three ' synir Finnakonûngs,' sons of a Finnish king, whereas the saga transplanted to the North from Germany makes its Vilkinus a king of Vilkinaland. Or can Finna be taken as the gen. of *Finni*, and identified with that Finn Folcwaldansunu on p. 219 ? Slagfiðr might seem = Slagfinnr, but is better explained as Slagfiöðr (flap-wing, see ch. XVI, Walachuriun). All three brothers married valkyrs, and *Egill*, the one that chiefly concerns us here, took Ölrûn (Aliorûna). The Vilk. saga, cap. 27, likewise calls Velint's younger brother *Eigill*: ' ok þenna kalla menn *Ölrûnar Eigil*,'[1] but the bride is not otherwise alluded to ; this form Eigill agrees with the OHG. Eigil on p. 376, not with the ON. Egill, dat. Agli, for the dat. of Eigill would have been Eigli. Well, this Eigill was a famous archer ; at Nidung's command he shot an apple off the head of his own little son, and when the king asked him what the other two arrows were for, replied that they were intended for him, in case the first had hit the child. The tale of this daring shot must have been extremely rife in our remotest antiquity, it turns up in so many places, and always with features of its own. As the Vilkinasaga was imported into Scandinavia in the 13th century, the story of Eigill was certainly diffused in Lower Germany before that date. But Saxo Grammaticus in Denmark knew it in the 12th century, as told of *Toko* and king Harald Gormsson, with the addition, wanting in Eigill, that Toko

---

[1] Peringskiöld translates ' Egillus sagittarius,' and Rafn ' Egil den träffende,' but this was merely guessed from the incidents of the story. Arrow is not öl, but ör ; Orentil on the contrary, Eigil's son, does seem to have been named from the arrow.

after the shot behaved like a hero in the sea-storm. The Icelanders too, particularly the Iomsvîkînga saga, relate the deeds of this *Pálnatôki*, but not the shot from the bow, though they agree with Saxo in making Harald fall at last by Tôki's shaft. The king's death by the marksman's hand is historical (A.D. 992), the shot at the apple mythical, having gathered round the narrative out of an older tradition, which we must presume to have been in existence in the 10-11th centuries. To the Norwegian saga of Olaf the Saint (†1030), it has attached itself another way : Olaf wishing to convert a heathen man, Eindriði, essayed his skill against him in athletic arts, first swimming, then shooting; after a few successful shots, the king required that Eindriði's boy should be placed at the butts, and a writing-tablet be shot off his head without hurting the child. Eindriði declared himself willing, but also ready to avenge any injury. Olaf sped the first shaft, and narrowly missed the tablet, when Eindriði, at his mother's and sister's prayer, declined the shot (Fornm. sög. 2, 272). Just so king Haraldr Sigurðarson (Harðráða, † 1066) measured himself against an archer Hemîngr, and bade him shoot a hazelnut off his Biörn's head, and Hemîngr accomplished the feat (Müller's sagabibl. 3, 359. Tháttr af Hemingi cap. 6, ed. Reykjavik p. 55). Long afterwards, the legend was transferred to a Hemming Wolf, or von Wulfen, of Wewelsflet in the Wilstermarsch of Holstein, where the Elbe empties itself into the sea. Hemming Wolf had sided with count Gerhard in 1472, and was banished by king Christian. The folk-tale makes the king do the same as Harald, and Hemming as Toko; an old painting of Wewelsflet church represents the archer on a meadow with bow unbent, in the distance a boy with the apple on his head, the arrow passes through the middle of the apple, but the archer has a second between his teeth, and betwixt him and the boy stands a wolf, perhaps to express that Hemming after his bold answer was declared a wolf's head.[1] Most appropriately did the mythus rear its head on the emancipated soil of Switzerland : In 1307, it is said, Wilhelm *Tell*, compelled by Gessler, achieved the same old master-shot, and made the courageous speech ; but the evidence of chroniclers does not begin till toward the 16th century,[2]

---

[1] Schleswigholst. prov. berichte 1798, vol. 2, p. 39 seq.   Müllenhof, Schleswigholst. sagen no. 66.

[2] I suspect the genuineness of the verses, alleged to be by Heinrich von

shortly before the first printed edition of Saxo, 1514. Of the unhistorical character of the event there cannot be the slightest doubt. The mythic substratum of the *Tell* fable shews itself in an Upper Rhine legend of the 15th century (in Malleus malef. pars 2 cap. 16, de sagittariis maleficis) which immediately preceded the first written record of that of Tell : Fertur de ipso *(Punchero)*, quod quidam de optimatibus, cum artis sue experientiam capere voluisset, eidem *proprium filium parvulum ad metam posuit*, et pro signo *super birretum pueri denarium*, sibique mandavit, ut *denarium sine birreto per sagittam amoveret*. Cum autem maleficus id se facturum sed cum difficultate assereret, libentius abstinere, ne per diabolum seduceretur in sui interitum; verbis tamen principis inductus, sagittam unam collari suo circa collum immisit, et alteram balistae supponens *denarium a birreto* pueri sine omni nocumento *excussit*. Quo viso, dum ille maleficum interrogasset, 'cur sagittam collari imposuisset?' respondit, 'si deceptus per diabolum puerum occidissem, cum me mori necesse fuisset, subito *cum sagitta altera vos transfixissem*, ut vel sic mortem meam vindicassem'. This shot must have taken place somewhere about 1420, and the story have got about in the middle part of the 15th century.—Beside the above-mentioned narratives, Norse and German, we have also an Old English one to shew in the Northumbrian ballad of the three merry men, Adam *Bell*, Clym of the Clough, and *William* of Cloudesle ; this last, whose christian name, like the surname of the first, reminds one of Tell, offers in the king's presence to set an apple on the head of his son, seven years old, and shoot it off at 120 paces. The arrow sped from the bow, and cleft the apple. I suppose that *Aegel's* skill in archery would be known to the Anglo-Saxons ; and if we may push Wada, Weland and Wudga far up into our heathen time, *Aegel* seems to have an equal claim. The whole myth shows signs of having deep and widely extended

Hünenberg of 1315, which Carl Zay has made known in his book on Goldau, Zurich 1807, p. 41 :

> Dum pater in puerum telum crudele coruscat
> Tellius ex jussu, saeve tyranne, tuo,
> pomum, non natum, figit fatalis arundo :
> altera mox ultrix te, periture, petet.

H. von Hünenberg is the same who, before the battle of Morgarten, shot a warning billet over to the Swiss on his arrow (Joh. Müller 2, 37), he was therefore a bowman himself. Justinger and Johann von Winterthur are silent about Tell ; Melchior Russ († 1499) and Petermann Etterlin (completed 1507) were the first who committed the story to writing.

roots. It partly agrees even with what Eustathius on Il. 12, 292
tells us, that Sarpedon, a hero of the blood of Zeus, was made
when a child to stand up and have a ring shot off his breast
without injury to him, an action which entailed the acquisition of
the Lycian kingdom (see Suppl.).[1]

With these specimens of particular heroes—crumbs from the
richly furnished table of our antiquities—I will content myself, as
there are still some reflections of a more general kind to be made.

I started with saying, that in the heroic is contained an exalting
and refining of human nature into divine, originally however
founded on the affinity of some god with the human race. Now
as procreation is a repetition, and the son is a copy of the father
(for which reason our language with a profound meaning has avarâ
for image and avaro for child); so in every hero we may assume
to a certain extent an incarnation of the god, and a revival of at
least some of the qualities that distinguish the god. In this sense
the hero appears as a sublimate of man in general, who, created
after the image of God, cannot but be like him. But since the
gods, even amongst one another, reproduce themselves, *i.e.*, their
plurality has radiated out of the primary force of a single
One (p. 164), it follows, that the origin of heroes must be very
similar to that of polytheism altogether, and it must be a difficult
matter in any particular case to distinguish between the full-bred
divinity and the half-blood. If heroes, viewed on one side, are
deified men, they may on the other hand be also regarded as
humanized gods; and it comes to the same thing, whether we say
that the son or grandson begotten by the god has attained a semi-
divine nature, or that the god born again in him retains but a part
of his pristine power. We are entitled to see in individual heroes
a *precipitate of former gods*, and a mere continued extension, in a
wider circle, of the same divine essence which had already branched
out into a number of gods (see Suppl.).

This proposition can the more readily be demonstrated from the
popular faiths of Greece and Germany, which commit themselves
to no systematic doctrine of emanation and avatâra, as in these

[1] Similar legends seem to live in the East. In a MS. of the Cassel library
containing a journey in Turkey, I saw the representation of an archer taking
aim at a child with an apple on its head.

religions the full-blooded animalism of herohood developed itself
the more richly for that very reason.   While the Indian heroes are
in the end reabsorbed into the god, *e.g.*, Krishna becomes Vishnu,
there remains in Greek and German heroes an irreducible dross of
humanism, which brings them more into harmony with the
historical ingredients of their story.   Our hero-legend has this long
while had no consciousness remaining of such a thing as incarnation, but has very largely that of an apotheosis of human though
god-descended virtue.

Herakles can never become one with Zeus, yet his deeds remind
us of those of his divine sire.   Some traits in Theseus allow of his
being compared to Herakles, others to Apollo.   Hermes was the
son of Zeus by Maia, Amphion by Antiope, and the two brothers,
the full and the half-bred, have something in common.

In Teutonic hero-legend, I think, echoes of the divine nature
can be distinguished still more frequently ; the Greek gods stood
unshaken to the last, and heroes could be developed by the side of
them.   But when once the Teutonic deities encountered christianity,
there remained only one of two ways open to the fading figures
of the heathen faith, either to pass into evil diabolic beings, or
dwindle into good ones conceived as human.   The Greek heroes
all belong to the flowering time of paganism ; of the Teutonic a
part at least might well seem a poverty-stricken attenuation and
fainter reproduction of the former gods, such as could still dare to
shew its face after the downfall of the heathen system.   Christian
opinion in the Mid. Ages guided matters into this channel ; unable
to credit the gods any longer with godhood, where it did not
transform them into devils, it did into demigods.   In the Edda the
æsir are still veritable gods ; Jornandes too, when he says, cap. 6 :
' mortuum (Taunasem regem) Gothi *inter numina populi sui*
coluerunt '—be this Taunasis Gothic or Getic—assumes that there
were Gothic gods, but the anses he regards as only victorious
heroes exalted into demigods ; and in Saxo, following the same line
of thought, we find that Balder (who exhibits some Heraklean
features, v. supra p. 226-7), and Hother, and Othin himself, have
sunk into mere heroes.[1]   This capitis deminutio of the gods brought

---

[1] In the AS. Ethelwerd p. 833 we read : ' Hengest et Horsa, hi nepotes
fuere *Woddan* regis barbarorum, quem post infanda dignitate *ut deum honorantes*,
sacrificium obtulerunt pagani victoriae causa sive virtutis, ut humanitas saepe
credit hoc quod videt '.   Wm. of Malmesbury's similar words were quoted

them nearer to heroes, while the heroes were cut off from absolute deification; how much the two must have got mixed up in the mist of legend! Yet in every case where bodily descent from the gods is alleged of a hero, his herohood is the more ancient, and really of heathen origin.

Among the heroes themselves there occur second births, of which a fuller account will be given further on, and which shew a certain resemblance to the incarnations of gods. As a god renews himself in a hero, so does an elder hero in a younger.

Beings of the giant brood, uniting themselves now to gods and now to heroes, bring about various approximations between these two.

We have seen how in the genealogy of Inguio, first Oðinn, then Niörðr and Freyr interweave themselves: Niörðr and Hadding seem identical, as do Heimdall and Rîgr, but in Niörðr and Heimdall the god is made prominent, in Hadding and Rîgr the hero. Irmin appears connected with Wuotan and Zio, just as Ares and Herakles approach each other, and Odysseus resembles Hermes. Baldr is conceived of as divine, Bældæg as heroic. In Siegfried is

---

above, p. 128 ; he also says '*deum esse delirantes*'. Albericus tr. font. 1, 23 (after A.D. 274) expresses himself thus : ' In hac generatione decima ab incarnatione Domini regnasse invenitur *quidam Mercurius* in Gottlandia insula, quae est inter Daciam et Russiam extra Romanum imperium, a quo Mercurio, qui Woden dictus est, descendit genealogia Anglorum et multorum aliorum '. Much in the same way Snorri in the Yngl. saga and Form. 13. 14 represents Oðinn as a *höfðingi* and *hermaðr* come from Asia, who by policy secured the worship of the nations ; and Saxo p. 12 professes a like opinion : ' ea tempestate cum *Othinus quidam*, Europa tota, *falso divinitatis titulo* censeretur,' &c. conf. what he says p. 45. What other idea could orthodox christians at that time form of the false god of their forefathers ? To idolatry they could not but impute wilful deceit or presumption, being unable to comprehend that something very different from falsified history lies at the bottom of heathenism. As little did there ever exist a real man and king Oðinn (let alone two or three), as a real Jupiter or Mercury.—But the affinity of the hero nature with the divine is clearly distinct from a *deification* arising out of human pride and deceit. Those heathen, who trusted mainly their inner strength (p. 6), like the Homeric heroes πεποιθότες βιήφι (Il. 12, 256), were yet far from setting themselves up for gods. Similar to the stories of *Nebucadnezar* (er wolte selbe sîn ein got, would himself be god, Parz. 102, 7. Barl. 60, 35), of *Kosroes* (Massmann on Eracl. p. 502), of the Greek *Salmoneus* (conf. N. Cap. 146), and the Byzantine *Eraclius*, was our Mid. Age story of *Imelôt* aus wüester Babilônie, ' der wolde selve wesen got ' (Rother 2568) = *Nibelôt* ze Barîse ' der machet himele guldîn, selber wolt er got sin ' (Bit. 299), just as Salmoneus imitated the lightning and thunder of Zeus. Imelôt and Nibelôt here seem to mean the same thing, as do elsewhere Imelunge and Nibelunge (Heldens. 162) ; I do not know what allusion there might be in it to a Nibelunc or Amelunc (see Suppl.).

an echo of Baldr and Freyr, perhaps of Oðinn, in Dietrich of Thôrr and Freyr. Ecke oscillates between the giant and the hero. Even Charles and Roland are in some of their features to be regarded as new-births of Wuotan and Donar, or of Siegfried and Dietrich. As for Geát, Sceáf, Sceldwa, for lack of their legends, it is difficult to separate their divine nature from their heroic.

One badge of distinction I find in this, that the names of gods are in themselves descriptive, *i.e.*, indicating from the first their inmost nature;[1] to the names of half-gods and heroes this significance will often be wanting, even when the human original has carried his name over with him. Then, as a rule, the names of gods are simple, those of heroes often compound or visibly derived. Donar therefore is a god from the first, not a deified man : his appellation expresses also his character. The same reason is decisive against that notion of Wuotan having made his way out of the ranks of men into those of the gods.

Demigods have the advantage of a certain familiarness to the people : bred in the midst of us, admitted to our fellowship, it is they to whom reverence, prayers and oaths prefer to address themselves : they procure and facilitate intercourse with the higher-standing god. As it came natural to a Roman to swear ' mehercle ! mecastor ! ecastor ! edepol !' the christians even in the Mid. Ages swore more habitually by particular saints than by God himself.

We are badly off for information as to the points in which the *Hero-worship* of our forefathers shaped itself differently from divine worship proper ; even the Norse authorities have nothing on the subject. The Grecian sacrifices to heroes differed from those offered to gods : a god had only the viscera and fat of the beast presented to him, and was content with the mounting odour; a deified hero must have the very flesh and blood to consume. Thus the einherjar admitted into Valhöll feast on the boiled flesh of the boar Sæhrîmnir, and drink with the Ases ; it is never said that the Ases shared in the food, Sæm. 36. 42. Sn. 42 ; conf. supra, p. 317. Are we to infer from this a difference in the sacrifices offered to gods and to demigods ?

Else, in the other conditions of their existence, we can perceive many resemblances to that of the gods.

Thus, their *stature* is enormous. As Ares covered seven roods,

[1] Something like the names of the characters in the Beast-apologue.

Herakles has also a body of gigantic mould. When the godlike
Sigurðr strode through the full-grown field of corn, the dew-shoe [1]
of his seven-span sword was even with the upright ears (Völs. saga
cap. 22. Vilk. saga cap. 166); a hair out of his horse's tail was
seven yards long (Nornag. saga cap. 8).—One thing hardly to be
found in Teutonic gods, *many-handedness*, does occur in an ancient
hero. Wudga and Hâma, Witege and Heime, are always named
together. This *Heimo* is said to have been by rights called Studas,
like his father (whom some traditions however name Adelgêr,
Madelgêr); not till he had slain the worm Heima,[2] did he adopt its
name (Vilk. saga cap. 17). To him are expressly attributed *three
hands* and *four elbows*, or else *two hands* with *three elbows* (Heldens.
257. Roseng. p. xx, conf. lxxiv); the extra limbs are no exaggera-
tion (Heldens. 391), rather their omission is a toning down, of the
original story. And *Asprian* comes out with *four hands* (Roseng.
p. xii). Starkaðr, a famous godlike hero of the North, has *three
pairs of arms*, and Thor cuts four of his hands off (Saxo Gram., p.
103); the Hervararsaga (Rafn p. 412, 513) bestows *eight hands* on
him, and the ability to fight with four swords at once: *átta handa*,
Fornald. sög. 1, 412. 3, 37. In the Swedish folk-song of Alf, originally heathen, there is a hero Torgnejer (roaring like thunder ?),
'han hade *otta* händer (Arvidss. 1, 12).[3] Such cumulation of limbs
is also a mark of the giant race, and some of the heroes mentioned
do overlap these; in the Servian songs I find a *three headed* hero
Balatchko (Vuk 2, no. 6, line 608); Pégam too in the Carniolan
lay has three heads (tri glave).—*Deficiency of members* is to be
found in heroes as well as gods: Oðinn is one-eyed, Týr one-
handed, Loki (=Hephæstus ?) lame, Höðr blind, and Viðar dumb;[4]

[1] Döggskôr, Sw. doppsko, the heel of the sword's sheath, which usually
brushes the dew : so the Alamanns called a lame foot, that dragged through
the dewy grass, toudregil. This ride through the corn has something in it
highly mythic and suggestive of a god.

[2] *Heimo* appears to mean worm originally, though used elsewhere of the
cricket or cicada (Reinh. cxxv), for which our present heimchen (little worm)
is better suited. A renowned Karling hero was also named *Heimo* (Reinh.
cciv). We find again, that *Madelgêr* is in Morolt 3921 a dwarf, son of a mermaid, and in Rol. 58, 17 a smith.

[3] In the prophecies of the North Frisian Hertje (A.D. 1400) the tradition of
such monstrosities is applied to the future : 'Wehe den minschen, de den
leven, wen de lüde 4 arme kriegen und 2 par schö över de vöte dragen und 2
höde up den kop hebben !' Heimreichs chron., Tondern 1819 ; 2, 341. It
may however refer merely to costume.

[4] Goth. háihs, hanfs, halts, blinds, dumbs.

so is Hagano one-eyed, Walthari one-handed, Gunthari and Wielant lame, of blind and dumb heroes there are plenty.

One thing seems peculiar to heroes, that their early years should be clouded by some defect, and that out of this darkness the bright revelation, the reserved force as it were, should suddenly break forth. Under this head we may even place the blind birth of the Welfs, and the vulgar belief about Hessians and Swabians (p. 373). In Saxo Gram., p. 63, *Uffo* is dumb, and his father *Vermund* blind ; to him corresponds the double *Offa* in the line of Mercia, and both of these Offas are lame and dumb and blind. According to the ' vita *Offae* primi, Varmundi filii,' he was of handsome figure, but continued blind till his seventh year, and dumb till his thirtieth ; when the aged Varmund was threatened with war, all at once in the assembly Offa began to speak. The ' vita *Offae* secundi' says,[1] the hero was at first called Vinered (so we must emend Pineredus), and was blind, lame and deaf, but when he came into possession of all his senses, he was named Offa secundus. Exactly so, in Sæm. 142ª, Hiörvarðr and Sigurlinn have a tall handsome son, but ' hann var þögull, ecki nafn festiz við hann '. Only after a valkyrja has greeted him by the name of *Helgi*, does he begin to speak, and is content to answer to that name. *Starkaðr* too was þögull in his youth (Fornald. sög. 3, 36), and *Halfdan* was reckoned stupid (Saxo, p. 134) ; just as slow was the heroism of *Dietleib* in unfolding itself (Vilk. saga cap. 91), and that of *Iliya* in the Russian tales. Our nursery-tales take up the character as *äscherling, aschenbrodel, askefis* (cinderel) : the hero-youth lives inactive and despised by the kitchen-hearth or in the cattle-stall, out of whose squalor he emerges when the right time comes. I do not recollect any instance in Greek mythology of this exceedingly favourite feature of our folk-lore.

Unborn children, namely those that have been cut out of the womb, usually grow up heroes. Such was the famous Persian Rustem in Ferdusi, as well as Tristan according to the old story in Eilhart, or the Russian hero Dobrunä Nikititch, and the Scotch Macduff. But Völsûngr concerns us more, who spoke and made vows while yet *unborn*, who, after being cut out, had time to kiss his mother before she died (Völsûngas. cap. 2. 5). An obscure

---

[1] These remarkable vitae Offae primi et secundi are printed after Watts's Matth. Paris, pp. 8, 9.

passage in Fâfnismâl (Sæm. 187ᵃ) seems to designate Sigurðr also an *óborinn;* and in one as difficult (Beow. 92), may not the 'umbor-wesende' which I took in a different sense on p. 370, stand for *unbor*-wesende, to intimate that Sceáf passed for an unborn ?   The Landnâmabôk 4, 4 has an Uni hinn *óborni* (m.), and 1, 10 an Ulfrûn in *óborna* (f.) ; for wise-women, prophetesses, also come into the world the same way.¹   Our Mid: Ages tell of an *unborn* hero Hoyer (Benecke's Wigalois, p. 452) ; in Hesse, Reinhart of Dalwig was known as the *unborn,* being, after the cæsarian operation, brought to maturity in the stomachs of newly slaughtered swine.²
As early as the tenth century, Eckhart of St. Gall informs us : Infans excisus et arvinae porci recens erutae, ubi incutesceret, involutus, bonae indolis cum in brevi apparuisset, baptizatur et Purchardus nominatur (Pertz 2, 120) ; this is the Burchardus *ingenitus,* afterwards abbot of St Gall.   One Gebehardus, ex defunctae matris Dietpurgae utero excisus, is mentioned in the Chron. Petershus. p. 302, with the remark : De talibus excisis literae testantur quod, si vita comes fuerit, felices in mundo habeantur. To such the common standard cannot be applied, their extraordinary manner of coming into the world gives presage of a higher and mysterious destiny.   Not unlike is the Greek myth of Metis and Tritogeneia : the virgin goddess springs out of the forehead of Zeus.   The phrase about ' Hlöðr being *born with helmet, sword and horse* ' (above, p. 76), is explained by the Hervararsaga, p. 490, to mean, that the arms and animals which accompany the hero were forged and born at the time of his birth.   Schröter's Finnish Runes speak of a child that was born *armed :* this reminds us of the superstition about lucky children being born with hood and helmet (see ch. XXVIII).

It was noticed about the gods (p. 321), that Balder's brother, when scarcely born, when but one night old, rushed to vengeance, unwashed and uncombed.   This is like the children born of liten Kerstin after long gestation : the newborn son gets up directly and combs his hair, the new born daughter knows at once how to sew silk.   Another version makes her give birth to two sons, one of whom combs his yellow locks, the other draws his sword, both equipped for swift revenge (Svenska fornsånger 2, 254-6).   Here

¹ Heimreich's Nordfries. chr. 2, 341.
² Zeitschrift für Hess. gesch. 1, 97.

combing and not combing seem to be the same characteristic. A new born child speaks ; Norske eventyr 1, 139.

As the *birth* of beloved kings is announced to their people by joyful phenomena, and their death by terrible, the same holds good of heroes. Their generosity founds peace and prosperity in the land. *Fróði's* reign in Denmark was a period of bliss; in the year of *Hakon's* election the birds bred twice, and trees bore twice, about which beautiful songs may be gleaned out of his saga, cap. 24. On the night that *Helgi* was born, eagles cried, and holy waters streamed from the mountains, Sæm. 149ᵃ.

Sigurð's walk and manner of appearing was impetuous, like that of a god ; when he first approached the burg of Brynhildr, ' iörð dûsaði ok opphimin,' earth shook and heaven, Sæm. 241ᵇ ; and of Brynhild's laughing, as of that of the gods (p. 324), we are told : ' hlô, bœr allr dundi,' she laughed and all the castle dinned, Sæm. 208ᵃ. A divine strength reveals itself in many deeds and movements of heroes. *Dietrich's* fiery breath may be suggestive of Donar, or perhaps only of a dragon : ' ob sîn âtem gæbe fiur als eines wilden trachen,' (Parz. 137, 18).

A widely prevalent mark of the hero race is their being *suckled by beasts*, or *fed by birds*. A *hind* offers her milk to Sigurðr when exposed, Vilk. saga 142 ; a *she-wolf* gives suck to the infant Dieterich (like Romulus and Remus) together with her four blind whelps, hence his name of Wolfdieterich. The same fellowship with whelps seems imputed to the beginnings of the Goths and Swabians, as to those of the Romans (p. 373) ; but the *woodpecker* also, that Bee-wolf, brought food to the sons of Mars, and we have come to know the Swabians as special devotees of Zio (p. 199). The Servian hero Milosh Kobilitch was suckled by a *mare* (kobila), Vuk 2, 101 ; does that throw light on the OHG. term of abuse merihûnsun, zâgûnsun (RA. 643) ? A like offensive meaning lurked in the Latin lupa.[1] But it is not only to sucklings that the god-sent animals appear ; in distress and danger also, swans, ravens, wolves, stags, bears, lions will join the heroes, to render them assistance ; and that is how animal figures in the scutcheons and helmet-insignia of heroes are in many cases to be accounted for, though they may arise from other causes too, *e.g.*, the ability of certain heroes to transform themselves at will into wolf or swan.

[1] Fils de truie ; Garin 2, 229.

The *swan's wing*, the swan's coat, betokens another supernatural quality which heroes share with the gods (p. 326), the power of flying. As Wieland ties on his swan-wings, the Greek Perseus has *winged shoes*, talaria, Ov. met. 4, 667. 729, and the Servian Relia is called krilát (winged), being in possession of krilo and okrilie (wing and wing-cover), Vuk 2, 88. 90. 100. A piece of the wing remaining, or in women a swan's foot, will at times betray the higher nature.

The superhuman quality of heroes shines out of their *eyes* (luminum vibratus, oculorum micatus, Saxo Gram. 23): *ormr í auga*. The *golden teeth* of gods and heroes have been spoken of, p. 234. In the märchen sons are born with a *star* on the forehead, Kinderm. 96. Straparola 4, 3 ; or a golden star falls on the forehead, Pentam. 3, 10. The Dioscuri had a star or flame shining on their heads and helmets : this may have reference to the rays encircling the head (p. 323), or to constellations being set in the sky. In some cases the heroic form is disfigured by animal peculiarities, as Siegfried's by his horny skin, and others by a scaly ; the märchen have heroes with *hedgehog spikes*. The legend of the *Merovings*, imperfectly handed down to us, must be founded on something of the kind. When Clodio the son of Faramund with his queen went down to the shore, to cool themselves from the sultry summer heat, there came up a monster (sea-hog ?) out of the waves, which seized and overpowered the bathing queen. She then bore a son of singular appearance, who was therefore named Merovig, and his descendants, who inherited the peculiarity, Merovings.[1] Theophanes expressly declares, that the Merovings were called κριστάται and τριχοραχάται, because all the kings of that house had bristles down the backbone (ῥάχις), like swine. We still find in Rol. 273, 29, where it is true they are enumerated among heathens,

> di helde von *Meres ;*
> vil gewis sît ir des,
> daz niht kuoners mac sîn :
> *an dem rucke tragent si borsten sam swîn.*

The derivation of the name is altogether unknown. Can it possibly have some connexion with the boar-worship of Frô, which may

---

[1] Fredegar's epitome (Bouquet 2, 396), and Conradus Ursperg., Arg. 1609, p. 92. Per contra, Müllenhoff in Haupt's zeitschr. 6, 432.

have been especially prevalent among the Franks ? Lampr. Alex.
5368 also has : sîn hût was ime bevangen al mit *swînes bursten* (see
Suppl.).

One principal mark to know heroes by, is their possessing
intelligent horses, and conversing with them. A succeeding chapter
will shew more fully, how heathendom saw something sacred and
divine in horses, and often endowed them with consciousness and
sympathy with the destiny of men. But to heroes they were indispensable for riding or driving, and a necessary intimacy sprang up
between the two, as appears by the mere fact of the horses having
proper names given them. The touching conversation of Achilles
with his *Xanthos* and *Balios* (Il. 19, 400—421) finds a complete
parallel in the beautiful Karling legend of *Bayard ;* compare also
Wilhelm's dialogue with *Puzzât* (58, 21—59, 8), in the French
original with *Baucent* (Garin 2, 230-1), and Begon's with the same
Baucent (p. 230). In the Edda we have Skîrnir talking with his
horse (Sæm. 82ᵇ) ; and Goðrûn, after Sigurð's murder, with *Grani*
(231ᵇ) :

        hnipnaði Grani þâ, drap î gras höfði.

Well might Grani mourn, for the hero had bestridden him ever
since he led him out of Hialprek's stable (180), had ridden him
through the flames (202ᵃ), and carried off the great treasure.
Swedish and Danish folk-songs bring in a sagacious steed *Black*,
with whom conversation is carried on (Sv. vis. 2, 194. Sv. forns.
2, 257. Danske vis. 1, 323). In the poems on Artus the horses
are less attractively painted ; but how naïvely in the Servian,
when Mila shoes the steed (Vuk 1, 5), or Marko before his death
talks with his faithful *Sharats* (2, 243 seq. Danitza 1, 109). In
Mod. Greek songs there is a dialogue of Liakos with his horse
(Fauriel 1, 138), and similar ones in the Lithuanian dainos (Rhesa
p. 224). The Persian Rustem's fairy steed is well-known (see
Suppl.).[1]

If many heroes are carried off in the bloom of life, like Achilles
or Siegfried, others attain a *great age*, beyond the limit of the
human. Our native legend allows Hildebrand the years of Nestor

---

[1] A Mongolian warrior's dying song has :

My poor cream-coloured trotter, you will get home alive.
Then tell my mother, pray : ' full fifteen wounds had he '.
And tell my father, pray : 'shot through the back was he,' &c.—TRANS.

with undiminished strength, and to the Scandinavian Starkaðr is measured out a life that runs through several generations; the divinely honoured Goðmundr is said to have numbered near five hundred years, Fornald. sög. 1, 411. 442. In the genealogies that have come down to us, great length of life is given to the first ancestors, as it is in the Bible also. *Snaerr hinn gamli*, sprung from Kâri and Jökull, is said to have attained 300 years, and *Hálfdan gamli* as many, Fornald. sög. 2, 8. The MHG. poem of Dietrich's ancestors (1869—2506) gives *Dietwart* and *Sigeher* 400 years of life each, *Wolfdieterich* 503, *Hugdieterich* 450, and *Dietmar* 340; Dietrich of Bern is the first that reaches only the ordinary limit, Otnit the son of Sigeher was killed when young.[1] The Servian Marko was three hundred years old, almost like the giants of old. On the other hand, the life of heroes is enfeebled by union with goddesses and superhuman females. Examples will be given, when the valkyrs are discussed; the belief of the Greeks is expressed in a remarkable passage of the Hymn to Venus 190, where Anchises, after he has embraced Aphrodite, fears that he shall lead a stricken life (ἀμενηνός) among men:

ἐπεὶ οὐ βιοθάλμιος ἀνὴρ
γίγνεται, ὅστε θεαῖς εὐνάζεται ἀθανάτῃσι.

The goddess does not conceal, that age will come on him apace, and that Zeus's thunderbolt will maim him if he boast of her favours. The story of Staufenberger and the sea-fairy is founded on similar notions.

Another thing in which the condition of heroes resembles that of gods is, that particular local *haunts* and *dwellings* are assigned them. Such abodes seem by preference to bear the name of *stone*, as Gibichenstein, Brunhildenstein, Kriemhildenstein, Eigelstein, Waskenstein; which points to sacred rocks uninhabited by men,

---

[1] These are undoubtedly genuine myths, that lose themselves in the deeps of time, however distorted and misplaced they may be. *Sigeher* (OHG. Siguhari) is plainly the ON. *Sigarr*, from whom the Siglîngar or Siklîngar take their name; Sigeher's daughter is called *Sigelint*, Sigar's daughter *Signŷ*, but the two are identical. *Hugdieterich*, who in woman's clothing woos *Hilde-burg*, is one with *Hagbarðr* (Sw. Habor, Dan. Hafbur), who likewise succeeds in his suit for Signŷ (Sw. Signil, Dan. Signild), though here the story has a tragic end, and the names disagree; but hug and hag, both from one root, support each other. *Sigeminne* too, the wife of Wolfdieterich, who in the Hel-denbuch is the son of Hugdieterich, comes near to Signŷ. The part about Hugdieterich in the Heldenbuch is throughout uncommonly sweet, and cer-tainly very ancient.

and a primeval, firmly rooted worship. More rarely we find *castle* or *hall* connected with a hero (Iringes burc, Orendelsal), a few times *ea* and *burn*, oftener *way* or *street ;* now, as the notion of a highway lies close to that of a conspicuous *column* to which the roads led up, we may well connect the ' Herculis columnae,' the Irmansuli, with the *Roland-pillars,* which we come upon just in those northern parts of Germany where heathenism prevailed latest. As king Charles occupies Wuotan's place in certain legends, especially that of the ' furious host,' Roland, the noblest hero of his court, who is to him almost exactly what Donar is to Wuotan, seems to replace the divine vanquisher of giants. *Æthelstân-pillars* have been mentioned, p. 119. It is worthy of note, that, while Scandinavia offers nothing else that can be likened to the Irmen-pillars, yet at Skeningen, a town of Östergötland, there stood erected in the marketplace, just where Roland-pillars do stand, the figure of a giant or hero, which the people called *Thore* lång (Thuro longus), and at which idolatry was practised in former times.[1] This figure appears far more likely to belong to the heathen god than to any hero or king; and probably the column in the market place of Bavais in Hainault, from which seven roads branched off, and which is said to have been reared in honour of a king Bavo, had a similar meaning (see Suppl.).

According to a widely accepted popular belief, examined more minutely in ch. XXXII on Spiriting away, certain heroes have sunk from the rocks and fortresses they once inhabited, into *clefts* and *caverns* of the mountains, or into subterranean *springs,* and are there held wrapt in a seldom interrupted slumber, from which they issue in times of need, and bring deliverance to the land. That here again, not only Wuotan, Arminius, Dieterich and Siegfried, but such modern heroes as Charles, Frederick Barbarossa and even Tell are named, may assure us of the mystic light of myth which has settled on them. It was a Norse custom, for aged heroes, dead to the world and dissatisfied with the new order of things, to shut themselves up in a hill : thus Herlaugr with twelve others goes into the haugr (Egilss. p. 7), and in like manner Eticho the Welf, accompanied by twelve nobles, retires into a mountain in the Scherenzerwald, where no one could find him again (Deutsche

---

[1] Olaus Magnus 14, 15. Stjernhöök, De jure Sveon. vet., p. 326. Broocmans beskrifn. öfver Östergötland, Norrköping 1760. 1, 190.

sagen, no. 518).   Siegfried, Charles and Frederick, like King
Arthur of the Britons, abide in mountains with their host.

Be it be remarked lastly, that the heroic legend, like the divine,
is fond of running into triads.   Hence, as Oðin, Vili, Ve, or Hâr,
Iafnhâr and Thriði stand together, there appear times without
number three heroic brothers together, and then also it commonly
happens, that to the third one is ascribed the greatest faculty of
success.   So in the Scythian story of the three brothers Leipoxais,
Arpoxais and Kolaxais (Herod. 4, 5) : a golden plough, yoke and
sword having fallen from heaven, when the eldest son and the
second tried to seize them, the gold burned, but the third carried
them off.   The same thing occurs in many märchen.

CHAPTER XVI.

WISE WOMEN.

The relation of women to the gods is very different from that of men, because men alone can found famous houses, while a woman's family dies with her. The tale of ancestry contains the names of heroes only; king's daughters are either not named in it at all, or disappear again as soon as they have been introduced as brides. For the same reason we hear of deified sons, but not of deified daughters; nay, the marriage of mortals with immortals issues almost always in the birth of sons. There are therefore no women to be placed by the side of the heroes, whom in the preceding chapter we have regarded as a mixture of the heavenly and earthly natures : the distaff establishes no claim to immortality, like the sword. To the woman and the bondman, idle in battle, busy in the house, the Anglo-Saxons very expressively assigned the occupation of weaving peace : heroic labours suited men.

But that which women forfeit here, is amply made up to them in another sphere. In lieu of that distinct individuality of parts given to heroes, which often falls without effect in the story, they have general duties assigned them of momentous and lasting influence. A long range of charming or awful half-goddesses mediates between men and deity : their authority is manifestly greater, their worship more impressive, than any reverence paid to heroes. There are not, strictly speaking, any heroines, but whatever among women answers to heroes appears more elevated and spiritual. Brunhild towers above Siegfried, and the swan-maid above the hero to whom she unites herself (see Suppl.).

In other mythologies also it is observable, that in the second rank of deities female beings predominate, while the first is reserved almost exclusively for the male, but the divine heroes we have spoken of come only in the third rank. I have on p. 250 partly accounted for the longer duration of the tradition of several goddesses by its having left more abiding, because more endearing, impressions on the mind of the people.

There is no harder problem in these investigations, than to distinguish between goddesses and half-goddesses. Every god's wife must ipso facto pass for a real goddess ; but then there are unmarried goddesses ; *e.g.*, Hel. One who cannot be shown to be either wife or daughter of a god, and who stands in a dependent relation to higher divinities, is a half-goddess. Yet such a test will not always serve, where a mythology has been imperfectly preserved ; for the very reason that half-goddesses stand higher than half-gods, the boundary-line between them and the class of great gods is harder to hit. The line may be disturbed, by particular races promoting divine beings of lower rank, whose worship got the upper hand among them, to a higher ; it is true the same thing seems to occur in hero-worship, but not so often.

The mission and functions of half-goddesses then may be roughly defined thus : to the upper gods they are *handmaids*, to men *revealers*.

It is a significant feature in our heathenism, that women, not men, are selected for this office. Here the Jewish and christian view presents a contrast : prophets foretell, angels or saints from heaven announce and execute the commands of God ; but Greek and Teutonic gods employ both male and female messengers. To the German way of thinking, the decrees of destiny assume a greater sacredness in the mouth of woman, soothsaying and sorcery in a good as well as bad sense is peculiarly a women's gift, and it may even be a part of the same thing, that our language personifies virtues and vices as females. If human nature in general shews a tendency to pay a higher respect and deference to the female sex, this has always been specially characteristic of Teutonic nations. Men earn deification by their deeds, women by their wisdom : ' *Fatidicae*, augescente superstitione *deae*,' p. 95 (see Suppl.).

This Germanic *reverence for woman*, already emphasized by Tacitus, is markedly expressed in our old systems of law, especially the Alamannian and Bavarian, by doubling the composition for injury (RA. 404) : the defenceless one thereby receives protection and consecration, nay, she is to forfeit the privilege the moment she takes up man's weapons. And not only does a worship of woman shew itself in the minne-songs of our Mid. Ages, but in a remarkable formula of chivalry occurring both in folk-songs and in court-poems : 'durch *aller frouwen êre*,' by all women's honour, Wolfdiet. 104. Morolt 855. 888. 2834. Morolf 1542. Ecke 105. 117. **174**. Roseng. 2037. MsH. 3, 200ª ; 'durch reiner (pure) frouwen êre,' Ecke 112 ; 'durch *willen* (for the sake) *aller frouwen*;' thus one hero cries to another 'nu beite (stay), durch *willen aller meide !*' Rab. 922-4 ; 'durch *willen schœner* wîbe,' Ecke 61 ; 'durch *ander maget* (other maids') *êre*,' Gudr. 4863 ; 'durch *elliu wîp*,' in the name of all women, Parz. 13, 16 ; '*êre* an mir *elliu wîp*,' respect in me all women, Erec 957 ; '*êret* an mir *elliu wîp !*' says a woman in Parz. 88, 27, to ensure attention to her prayer ; '*allen meiden* tuot ez ze *êren* (do it in honour of),' Gudr. 1214, 3; '*êre* und minne *elliu wîp !*' is the injunction on giving a sword, Trist. 5032 ; 'tuon allez daz *frouwen wille* sî,' do all that may be woman's will, Bit. 7132 ; 'als liep iu alle *frouwen* sîn,' as all women are dear to you, Laurin 984. Their worship was placed on a par with that of God : 'êret *Got* und *diu wîp*,' Iw. 6054 ; 'durch *Got* und durch der *wîbe* lôn (guerdon)' Wh. 381, 21 ; 'wart sô mit riterschaft getân, dês *Got* sol danken und diu *wîp*,' may God and the ladies requite it, Wh. 370, 5 ; 'dienen *Got* und alle *frouwen êren*,' Ms. 2,99ᵇ ; of Parzivâl it is even said : 'er getrûwete *wîben baz* (better) *dan Gote*,' Parz. 370, 18. These modes of speech, this faith, can be traced up to a much earlier age, as in O. i. 5, 13 : 'dô sprah er *êrlîcho* ubaral, sô man *zi frowûn* skal'; and v. 8, 58 : 'ni sît irbolgan *wîbe*,' ye shall not bully a woman, Etzels hofhalt. 92-3; 'sprich wîben übel mit nihte' says the poem of the Stete ampten 286. The very word frau is the name of a goddess, conf. p. 299 on the meanings of frau and weib (see Suppl.).

But more than that, when the hero in stress of battle *looked upon his love* (OHG. trûtin, trûtinna, MHG. triutinne), *thought of* her, *named* her name, he increased thereby his strength, and was sure of the victory. We might even bring under this head the declaration of Tacitus : memoriae proditur, quasdam acies inclinatas jam et labantes a feminis restitutas constantia precum et objectu pectorum. From the poems of the 13th century I will quote the principal passages only :

und als er dar zuo *an sach* (on-saw, looked at)
die schœnen frowen Enîten,
daz half (holp) im vaste strîten (fight hard). Er. 933.
swenne mich *der muot iwer ermant* (the thought of you mans),

sô ist sigesælic (victorious) mîn hant:
wand (for) iwer guote minne
die sterkent mîne sinne (nerve my senses),
daz mir den vil langen tac (all the long day)
niht wider gewesen mac (nought can vex). Er. 8867.
diu dâ *gegenwurtic saz* (who there present sat),
diu gehalf ir manne baz (she holp her man better).
ob im dehein zwîvel (if ever a doubt) geschach,
swenn (whenever) er si danne wider (again) *an sach,*
ir schœne gap im niwe kraft (strength),
sô daz er unzagehaft (undismayed)
sîne sterke wider gewan (his strength regained)
und vaht (fought) als ein geruowet (rested) man. Er. 9171.
der *gedanc* (thinking) *an sîn schœne wîp*
der kreftigete im den lîp (life, body). Er. 9229.
swenne im diu muoze (opportunity) geschach
daz er die maget (maid) reht *ersach,*
daz gap ir gesellen (to her fellow, lover)
Gâwâne manlîch ellen (élan). Parz. 409, 13. 410, 5.
nu *sach* er daz si umb in was in sorgen (in fear for him),
alrêst er niuwe kraft enpfant (felt). Lohengr. p. 54-5.
den Heiden *minne* nie verdrôz (never wearied),
des (therefore) was sîn herze in strîte grôz. Parz. 740, 7.
ern welle (if he do not) *an minne denken,*
sone mag er niht entwenken (cannot escape). Parz. 740, 15.
wes sûmest (wherefore delayest) du dich, Parzivâl,
daz du *an die kiuschen* liehtgemâl (pure-one so bright)
niht *denkest,* ich mein dîn wîp,
wiltu behalten (save) hie den lîp? Parz. 742, 27.
der getoufte nam (the christian gained) an kreften zuo,
er *dâht* (thought), des was im niht ze fruo (none too soon),
an sîn wîp die küniginne
unt an ir werden (worthy) minne. Parz. 743, 23.
swâ ich sider (after) kom in nôt (difficulty),
ze hant sô ich (the moment I) *an si dâhte,*
ir minne helfe brâhte. Parz. 768, 27.
müede was ir bêder lîp (weary were both their bodies),
niuwan daz sie (had they not) *dâhten an diu wîp*
sie wæren bêdesamt gelegen (both together fallen). Alt. bl. 1,340.

In the Carmen de Phyllide et Flora it is said 31, 4 : 'Ille *me commemorat* inter ipsas caedes,' my beloved in the battle breathes my name, to issue therefrom victorious.[1]　This sounds altogether heathen, for the gods too were at your side the moment you uttered their *names.* Snorri, in Yngl. saga cap. 2, says of Oðinn : 'svâ var oc um hans menn, hvar sem þeir urðu î nauðum staddir, â siâ eða â landi, þâ *kölluðu* þeir *á nafn* hans, oc þôttiz iafnan fâ af þvî frô,' so was it also with his men, wherever they were in trouble, on sea or on land, then called they on his name, and immediately were gladdened by it.　When Hrûngnir became intolerable to the Ases, 'þâ nefna þeir Thôr, þvî næst kom Thôrr î höllina,' Sn. 108.　Kraka, a semi-divine being, admonished Erich : si suprema necessitatis violentia postularet, *nominis* sui *nuncupatione* remedium celerius esse quaerendum, affirmans se divina partim virtute subnixam et quasi consortem coelitus insitam numinis gestare potentiam, Saxo Gram., p. 72.　So the valkyrja comes to the rescue of her chosen hero, when he calls out her name ; she is become his guardian, as if sent by the gods to bring him aid (see Suppl.).

The mission of such women then is to announce and prepare good or ill, victory or death to mortal men ; and we have seen that the popular faith retained longest its connexion with fighting and victory.　Their own being itself, like that of the heroes, rests on human nature, they seem for the most part to have sprung from kingly and heroic families, and probably an admixture of divine ancestors is to be presumed in their case too.　But to perform their office, they must have wisdom and supernatural powers at their command : their wisdom spies out, nay, guides and arranges complications in our destiny, warns of danger, advises in difficulty.　At the birth of man they shew themselves predicting and endowing, in perils of war giving help and granting victory.　Therefore they are called *wise women*, ON. *spâkonor* (conf. spâkr, OHG. spâhi, prudens), Scot. *spae wife*, MHG. *wîsiu wîp*, Nib. 1473. 3.　1483, 4 (see Suppl.).

1. ITIS, IDES (Dîs).

But I will first take an older word, which appears to me to yield

---

[1] Philander of Sittewald 2,727, Soldatenl. p. 241, still mentions the practice in time of danger ' of commending oneself to the loved one's grace and favour '.

exactly the meaning we have just unravelled, and in its generalness
to comprehend all the particular beings to be studied more minutely
by and by. The OHG. *itis* pl. itisî, OS. ides, pl. idisî, AS. ides, pl.
idesa, denotes femina in general, and can be used of maids or matrons,
rich or poor.[1] Yet, like the Greek νύμφη, it seems even in the
earliest times to have been specially applied to superhuman beings,
who, being considered lower than goddesses and higher than earthly
women, occupy precisely that middle rank which is here in
question. Tacitus informs us, that a famous battle-field on the
Weser was called by the Cheruscans *Idisia*viso (so I emend Idis-
taviso), *i.e.*, nympharum pratum, women's meadow; it matters not
whether the spot bore that name before the fight with the Romans,
or only acquired it afterwards (v. Haupt's zeitschr. 9, 248). There
at one time or another a victory was won under the lead of these
exalted dames. The Merseburg poem sets the *idisî* before us in
full action:

> sumâ hapt heptidun, sumâ heri lezidun,
> sumâ clûbôdun umbi cuniowidi;

Some put a check (on the fighting), as we read in Renner 20132:

> dez muoz (therefore must) ich *heften* einen *haft*
> an dirre materie ân mînen danc (against my will),
> wan ich fürhte (for I fear) sie werde ze lanc.

Others letted the host (hinder, make late, Goth. hari latidêdun);
others again grasped (clawed) at chains or wreaths, *i.e.*, withs and
twigs with which to twist shackles, or to twine garlands for the
victor. Here then their business was to bind and check, which is
also demanded by the very object of the conjuring-spell; in striking
harmony with this are the names of two Norse valkyrs, mentioned
together in Sæm. 45[a], *Hlöck* = OHG. Hlancha, *i.e.*, catena, and
Herfiötr = OHG. Herifezzara, exercitum vinciens. But it must
have been as much in their power to set free and help on, as to
shackle and hamper. Compounded with itis we have the female
names *Itispuruc* (Meichelb. no. 162), Itisburg (Trad. fuld. Schannat
181), Idisburg (Lacombl. no. 87), and *Itislant* (Graff 1, 159); which,
like Hiltipurc, Sigipurc, Sigilant (MB. 14, 362), are proper to such
women of our olden time (see Suppl.).[2]

---

[1] Freolicu meowle = ides, Cod. exon. 479,2. 'Weras and idesa,' or 'eorlas
and idesa' are contrasted, ibid. 176, 5. 432, 2.

[2] Here the local meaning coincides with the personal; we may therefore

But we obtain much fuller information as to their nature from the Norse authorities. It has been overlooked hitherto, that the OHG. itis, AS. ides, is the same as the ON. *dis* pl. dîsir; similar instances of aphæresis are the Rîgr for Iring on p. 234, and Sangrim, Singrim for Isangrim, Isingrim (Reinh. ccviii). Any remaining doubt disappears on comparing the Eddic ' *dis* Skiöldûnga,' Sæm. 169ᵃ 209ᵃ with the AS. '*ides* Scildinga,' Beow. 2337. The Norse dîsir likewise are sometimes kind protecting beings, sometimes hostile and hindering, Sæm. 185ᵃ 195ᵃ 254ᵇ 273ᵃ. An instance of the latter sort is found in the story of Thiðrandi, whom *dîsir* destroyed, 'thann er sagt at *dîsir* vaegi,' quem deas interfecisse dicunt (Nialss. cap. 97), though the full narrative (Fornm. sög. 2, 195) calls them simply *konur*, women; so *Spâdîsir*, nymphae vaticinantes, Völs. saga cap. 19, means just the same as *spâkonur;* and the phrase ' ecki eru allar *dîsir* dauðar enn ' in Alfs saga cap. 15, means in the most general sense, all good spirits are not dead yet; 'yðr munu dauðar *dîsir* allar,' to you all spirits are dead, Fornald. sög. 2, 47. But the Norse people worshipped them, and offered them sacrifice : the mention of *dîsablôt* is very frequent, Egilss. cap. 44 p. 205; Vigagl. saga cap. 6 p. 30; 'blôta kumla *dîsir,*' deabus tumulatis sacrificare, Egilss. p. 207. This passage implíes a connexion between dîsir and ghosts, departed spirits, whose reappearance portends something : ' *konor* hugðak dauðar koma î nôtt,' dead women, *i.e.*, dîsir, come at night, Sæm. 254ᵃ. Herjans *dîs* (Sæm. 213ᵇ) is nympha Odini, a maiden dwelling at Valhöll in the service of Oðinn; *dîs* Skiöldûnga (Sæm. 169ᵃ 209ᵃ), divine maid sprung from the Skiöldung stock, is an epithet both of Sigrûn and of Brynhild, conf. AS. *ides* Scyldinga, *ides* Helminga, Beow. 1234. But Freyja herself is called *Vanadîs*, nympha Vanorum, Sn. 37; and another goddess, Skaði *öndurdîs* (walking in wooden shoes), Sn. 28, which is equivalent to öndur*guð*. Several proper names of women are compounded with *dîs* : Thôrdîs, Hiördîs, Asdîs, Vigdîs, Halldîs, Freydîs (to which might have corresponded an OHG. Donaritis, &c.) : they prove the pretty high antiquity of the monosyllabic form dîs, which even in the Edda invariably alliterates with D. With the orginal form *idis* the

compare Magadaburg with Idisaburg, Idisoburg, and Islant with Itislant, Itisolant. The Frankish Dispargum on the contrary seems not to be Idisberg, but Tiesberg, fanum Martis (Herm. Müller, Salic law, p. 33-4).

name of the goddess Idunn may possibly be connected (see Suppl.).

2. VELEDA. GANNA. ALARÛN.

If, as I suppose, the generic term *idis* was already current in the time of Tacitus, he gives us other more specific appellations as mere proper names, though still a certain general meaning seems to belong to them too. His statements about *Veleda, Ganna,* and *Aurinia* I have already quoted in ch. V, where the connexion between prophetesses and the priestly office was pointed out. *Veleda* appears to be almost an appellative, and akin to the Norse Vala, Völva (p. 97-8), or even to the masc. Völundr (p. 378), perhaps also to the name valkyrja.[1] She lives on a *tower*, like Jetha (p. 96) and Brynhildr (Völs. saga cap. 24). Treaties were ratified in her presence ; she not only prophesied, but had to settle disputes among the people, and carry out plans. In Sæm. 4ᵇ 5ᵃ the *Vala*, after whom the famous lay Völuspâ is named, is also called *Heiðr* and *Gullveig;* and as our female names Adalheid, Alpheid, &c., are formed with -heid, Finn Magnusen p. 416ᵇ would derive Veleda from a supposed Valaheid, which however is nowhere found (see Suppl.). The description given of her is an attractive one : where-ever in the land this vala velspâ (fatidica) came, she worked witchery, she was believed to travel about aud make *visitations to houses.* This ' til hûsa koma ' reminds us of the ' *drepa â vett* sem *völur,*' pulsare aedes sicut fatidicae, Sæm. 63ᵃ, as in other cases also prophesying, inspiring and boon-bestowing women were always supposed to pass through the country, knocking at the houses of those whom they would bless.

Ganna (p. 95-6) could be explained with more certainty, if the real meaning of its root ginnan were disclosed to us : a MHG. ginnen is secare, the ON. ginna allicere, seducere ; and in Sæm. 21ᵃ we are warned not to trust the wheedling words of valas, ' völo vilmæli trûi engi maðr ' ; we shall see presently, how the AS. poets use similar expressions about Wyrd.

When Drusus had crossed the Weser and was nearing the Elbe,

---

[1] I find *Walade*ricus in Trad. corb. p. 364, § 213 ; a wild woman is called in Wolfdieterich 514 ' die wilde *waldin,*' and 735 ' diu übel *walledein* '; but this seems a corruption of vâlandinne, she-devil.

there met him in the land of the Cheruscans a superhuman female, γυνή τις μείζων ἢ κατὰ ἀνθρώπου φύσιν, who forbade his farther advance, and foretold his approaching end (Dio Cass. 55, 1). Species *barbarae mulieris*, humana amplior, victorem tendere ultra, sermone Latino, prohibuit (Sueton. in Claudio 1).[1] There may have been German folk-tales about this, which became known to the Romans. Wise-women of the fatherland, as well as heroes, rose up in their country's need, and by their appearance terrified the foe.

Aurinia is said (p. 95) to have been famous in Germany before Veleda ; copyists may easily have corrupted *ali* into 'au,' and *runa* into 'rinia' : we should then have *Aliruna*, though it would be still more handy if Tacitus had written *Alioruna*. But anyhow we cannot fail to recognise the agreement (which many have noted) with Jornandes cap. 24, who, in accounting for the origin of the Huns, relates of the Gothic king Filimer : Repperit in populo suo quasdam *magas mulieres*, quas patrio sermone *aliorumnas* (al. alyrumnas, aliorunas, aliuruncas) is ipse cognominat, easque habens suspectas de medio sui proturbat, longeque ab exercitu suo fugatas in solitudine coegit errare. Quas silvestres homines, quos faunos ficarios vocant, per eremum vagantes dum vidissent, et earum se complexibus in coitu miscuissent, genus hoc ferocissimum edidere.' Many names of women are formed with -*rûn*, -*rûna* (Gramm. 2, 517), and OHG. documents even offer, though sparingly, *Alarûn Alerûna*, MB. 3, 416 (an. 1140); 'Gosprecht der *Alraunyn* sun,' MB. 27, 80 (an. 1309). I have never seen Elirûn, the form we should expect from ali-.[2] But it is significant, that the ON. name *Ölrûn*, Sæm. 133-4, belongs precisely to a *wise-woman* ; and *alrûna* (Graff 2, 523), now *alraun*, from its old sense of a prophetic and diabolic spirit, has at length passed into that of the root (mandragora,

---

[1] A similar tale about Alexander Severus : *Mulier Druias* eunti exclamavit Gallico sermone, 'vadas, nec victoriam speres, nec te militi tuo credas !' Ael. Lampridius in Alex. Sev. cap. 60. And Attila at the passage of the Lech is said to have been scared away by a rune-maiden calling out three times 'back, Attila !' Paul of Stetten's Erl. aus der gesch. Augsburgs, p. 25. Of still more weight is the agreement of an ON. tradition in Saxo Gram. p. 15 : 'Hadingum (our mythic Harding, Hartung) *obvia femina* hac voce compellat :

　　Seu pede rura teras, seu ponto carbasa tendas,
　　infestos patiere deos, totumque per orbem
　　propositis inimica tuis elementa videbis.

[2] It throws some light on the meaning of -rûn, that in AS. also *burgrûna* or *burgrûnan* stands for parcae and furiae (Lye sub v., and Gl. épinal. 617).

mandrake) out of which he is cut. We now turn to some other
names, about which the fountain of tradition flows more freely (see
Suppl.).

3. NORNI (FATAE).

The three Fates are the subject of an independent and profound
myth in the Edda. Collectively they are called the *nornir*, and
singly, *Urðr*, *Verðandi*, *Skuld*, Sæm. 4ᵃ. Sn. 18. The term *norn*
(parca) has not been discovered hitherto in any other dialect,[1]
though undoubtedly it belongs to a genuine Teutonic root, and is
formed like thorn, corn, horn, &c., and would have been in OHG.
norn, pl. nornî; but even Swedish and Danish know it no longer
(see Suppl.). In the three proper names it is impossible to mistake
the forms of verbal nouns or adjectives: *Urðr* is taken from the
pret. pl. of verða (varð, urðum), to become, *Verðandi* is the pres.
part. of the same word, and *Skuld* the past part. of skula, shall, the
auxiliary by which the future tense is formed. Hence we have
what was, what is, and what shall be, or the past, present and
future, very aptly designated, and a Fate presiding over each.[2] At
the same time the very names prove that the doctrine of norns was
originally not foreign to any of the Teutonic nations. A Gothic
Vaúrþs, Vaírðandei, Skulds, an OHG. Wurt, Werdandi, Scult, and
so on, must have been known once as personal beings; in the OS.

---

[1] Nürnberg (mons Noricus) has nothing to do with it, it is no very old
town either (in Böhmers regest. first in 1050, no. 1607; conf. MB. 29, 102).
In the fields at Dauernheim near Nidda is a well called *Nörnborn*, *Nornborn*,
and its spring is said to flow only when there is war. But I should like to see
the name authenticated by an old document. The AS. gen. pl. neorxena, which
only occurs in ' neorxena wong' = paradisus, has been proposed, but the abbreviation would be something unheard of, and even the nom. sing. neorxe or
neorxu at variance with norn; besides, the Parcae are nowhere found connected
with paradise. May we trace *norn* to niosan (sternutare), whose past part. is in
OHG. *noran*, MHG. *norn*, because of the prophetic virtue there is in sneezing
(ch. XXXV)? But the special meaning in this verb [conn. with nose] seems
older than any such general meaning, and its ON. form hniosa stands opposed.

[2] ' *Fatum* dicunt esse quicquid dii effantur. Fatum igitur dictum a fando,
i.e., loquendo. *Tria* autem *fata* finguntur in colo, in fuso, digitisque fila ex
lana torquentibus, propter trina tempora : *praeteritum*, quod in fuso jam
netum atque involutum est, *praesens*, quod inter digitos nentis trahitur, *futur-
um* in lana quae colo implicata est, et quod adhuc per digitos nentis ad fusum
tanquam praesens ad praeteritum trajiciendum est,' Isidori etym. 8, 11 § 92, a
passage pretty extensively circulated in the Mid. Ages (v. Gl. Jun. 398), yet
no proof of the Teutonic notion being borrowed from the classical. In § 93
Isidore adds : ' quas (parcas) tres esse voluerunt, unam quae vitam hominis
ordiatur, alteram quae contexat, tertiam quae rumpat '.

and AS. poetry we are able to lay our finger on the personality of
the first norn : 'thiu *Wurdh* is at handun' says the Heliand 146,
2, just as 'dôd is at hendi,' 92, 2 : the Fate, or death, stands so
near, that she can grasp with her hand [1] the man who is fallen due
to her; we should say just as concretely 'is at hand, is at the
door'. Again : 'thiu *Wurth* nâhida thuo,' drew nigh then, Hel.
163, 16. ' *Wurth* ina benam,' the death-goddess took him away
66, 18. 111, 4. Not so living is the term as used in the Hildebr.
lied 48, '*wêwurt* skihit,' or perhaps separately 'wê! *wurt* skihit,'
because 'geschehen' to happen is used more of abstract inanimate
things. An OHG. gloss also has *wurt* for fatum (Graff 1, 992).
Far more vivid are the AS. phrases : 'me þæt *Wyrd* [2] gewâf,'
parca hoc mihi texuit, Cod. exon. 355 ; ' *Wyrd* oft nereð unfægne
eorl, þonne his ellen deáh,' parca saepe servat virum, donec virtus
ejus viget (ellan taoc, Hildeb.), Beow. 1139 ; 'him wæs *Wyrd* ungemete neah, se þone gomelan grêtan sceolde, sêcean sâwlehord,
sundur gedælan lîf wið lîce,' 4836 (so, 'deáð ungemete neah' 5453) ;
' swâ him *Wyrd* ne gescrâf,' ita ei fatum non ordinavit, decrevit,
Beow. 5145. El. 1047. conf. Boëth. ed. Rawl. p. 151 ; 'ealle
Wyrd forsweop,' [3] swept all away, Beow. 5624; 'hie seo *Wyrd*
beswâc, forlêolc and forlærde,' eos parca decepit, allexit, seduxit,
Andr. 613 ; ' us seo *Wyrd* sceðeð,' nos fatum laedit, Andr. 1561.
The instances in Cædmon are less concrete, yet in 61, 12 the *Wyrd*
is called 'wälgrim,' bloodthirsty.—Of the *Wyrd* then are predicated :
grêtan (excitare, OHG. cruozan), scrîfan (ordinare, OHG. scrîpan),[4]
wefan (texere, OHG. wepan), beswîcan (decipere, OHG. pisuîchan),
forlæcan (fallere, OHG. farleichan), forlæran (seducere, male
informare), sceðan (nocere). She is painted powerful, but often
cruel and warlike (see Suppl.). We cannot in the same way point
out a personal application of the other two names, though the

---

[1] MHG. 'er hât den tôt an der hant,' Reinh. 1480. 1806. Nib. 1480, 4.
Morolt. 29ᵇ. Dietr. 29ᵃ. Pf. Chuonrât 3860. Karl 52ᵃ.

[2] With D, not Th, because the pret. of weorðan is wearð, pl. wurdon,
which supports the derivation I proposed ; so the OHG. Wurt, because werdan
has pret. pl. wurtum.

[3] So I read for the 'forsweof' of the editions, conf. forswâpen, Cædm. 25, 9.

[4] Conf. note to Elene p. 161, on a similar use of the MHG. *schrîben*, and
Klausen in Zeitschr. für alterth. 1840 p. 226 on the Roman notion of the
Parcae keeping a *written record*. N. Cap. 50. 55 renders parca by *brievara*, the
recorder. Tertullian, De anima cap. 39, informs us that on the last day of the
first week of a child's life they used to pray to the *fata Scribunda*. Fleming
479 calls the three Fates ' des verhängnis *schreiberinnen* '.

third, *Skuld*, OHG. *Scult*, AS. *Scyld*, continued in constant use as an abstract fem. skuld, scult, scyld, in the sense of debitum, delictum.[1] When christianity had banished the heathen notions, one name alone was found sufficient, and soon even that died out, giving place to new fangled terms such as schicksal, verhängnis (destiny) and the like, far more cumbrous and unwieldy than the old simple words. The English and especially the Scotch dialect seems to have harboured the old word longest : we all know the *weird-sisters* in Macbeth, which Shakspeare took from Hollinshed; they are also in Douglas's Virgil 80, 48, and the Complaynt of Scotland (written 1548) mentions, among other fabulous stories, that ' of the *thre weïrdsystirs*,' (Leyden's ed. Edinb. 1801, p. 99); in Warner's Albions England (first printed 1616) we have ' the *weirdelves*,' probably meaning the Parcae of the ancients. More native apparently is ' the *weïrd lady of the woods*,' who, when asked for advice, prophesies out of her cave, Percy's Reliques 3, 220-2.[2]

Even in the North, *Urðr* must have been of more consequence than the other two, for the fountain by the sacred ash is named after her, *Urðarbrunnr*,[3] and beside it stands the hall from which the three norns issue; it is also ' *Urðar* orð,' word (Sæm. 112ᵃ) that is chiefly spoken of, and once ' grimmar *urðir* ' dira fata, is used impersonally, Sæm. 216ᵇ.—These three virgins allot to every man his term of life, ' *skapa* mönnum aldr; *sköp* î ârdaga (year-days),' Sn. 18. Sæm. 181ᵃ. I have elsewhere (R.A. 750) shown the technical pertinence of the term *skapa* to the judicial office of the norns,[4] to whom for the same reason are ascribed *dômr* and

---

[1] Fornald. sög. 1, 32 *Skuld*, daughter of an âlfkona ; also in Saxo Gram. p. 31, Sculda, n. prop.

[2] Conf. Jamieson sub v. *weird* (weerd, weard). Chaucer already substitutes *fatal sustrin* for weirdsysters (Troil. 3, 733. Leg. of gd wom. 2619). In Engl. dictionaries we find *wayward sisters* explained by parcae and furiae ; *wardsisters* would create no difficulty, but *wayward* means capricious, and was once *way-warden*, in which the warden suggests the Dan. vorren, vorn (Gramm. 2, 675). What AS. form can there be at the bottom of it? [wá = woe is the usual etym.]

[3] This *brunnr* deserves attention, for the wayfaring wives and fays of the Mid. Ages also appear habitually at fountains, as the muses and goddesses of song haunted the same, and particular goddesses, esp. Holda, loved wells and springs (p. 268). Altogether it is hard often to tell which dame Holda resembles more, an ancient goddess or a wise-woman.

[4] Conf. AS. wyrda *gesceaft*, Cædm. 224, 6. wyrda *gesceapu*, Cod. exon. 420, 25. OS. *wurdhgiscapu* (decreta fati), Hel. 113, 7 ; and the OHG. term *scephentâ*, MHG. *schepfe* (Ottoc. 119ᵇ) and *schepfer;* the poet, also a vates, was in

qviðr, Sæm. 273^b; '*liotar nornir* skôpo oss lânga þrâ,' dirae parcae creaverunt nobis longum moerorem 217^a; '*nornir* heita þær er nauð *skapa*, Skâldskaparmâl p. 212.^{a} In the same sense '*nornir visa*,' Sæm. 88^b, they give us to *wit* judgment, and are *wise*. Hence to them, as to judges, a *seat* is given: 'â *norna stôli* sat ek niu daga' 127^a. They approach every new born child, and utter his doom; at Helgi's birth, it is said in Sæm. 149:

> nôtt var î bœ, *nornir* qvâmo,
> þœr er öðlîngi *aldr* um *skôpo*:
> þann bâðo fylki frœgstan verða,
> ok Buðlûnga beztan þyckja.
> *snero* þœr af afli *örlögþâtto*,
> þâ er borgir braut î Brâlundi:
> þœr um *greiddo gullinsîmo*,
> ok und mânasal miðjan *festo*.
> þœr austr ok vestr enda fâlo,
> þar âtti lofðûngr land â milli:
> brâ *nipt Nera* â norðrvega
> einni *festi*. ey bað hon halda.

This important passage tells us, that norns entering the castle at night spun for the hero the threads of his fate, and stretched the golden *cord (þâttr* = dâht, docht, = *sîmi)* in the midst of heaven; one norn hid an end of the thread eastward, another westward, a third fastened it northward; this third one is called 'sister of Neri'.[1] Their number, though not expressly stated, is to be gathered from the threefold action. All the region between the eastern and western ends of the line was to fall to the young hero's lot; did the third norn diminish this gift, when she flung a band northward, and bade it hold for aye? (see Suppl.).

It seems the regular thing in tales of norns and fays, for the advantages promised in preceding benefactions to be partly neutralized by a succeeding one.

The Nornagestssaga cap. 11 says: There travelled about in the

OHG. *scuof*, OS. *scôp*, from the same root. The AS. word *metten* I connect with *metod* (creator, see p. 22). In Boëth. p. 101 (Rawlinson) a varia lectio has 'þâ graman *mettena*,' the unkind fates; the '*metodo* giscapu' in Hel. 66, 19. 67, 11 answer to those '*wyrda* gesceapu,' and the gen. plurals '*metodo*, *wyrda*' imply that not one creator, but several are spoken of. Vintler calls them '*diernen*,' die dem menschen *erteilen*,' maids that dole out to man.

[1] Conf. *nipt Nara*, Egilssaga p. 440.

land ' *völvur*,' who are called ' *spákonur*,' who foretold to men their
fate, ' spáðu mönnum aldr ' or ' örlög '. People invited them to
their houses, gave them good cheer and gifts. One day they came
to Nornagest's father, the babe lay in the cradle, and two tapers were
burning over him. When the first two women had gifted him, and
assured him of happiness beyond all others of his race, the third
or youngest norn, ' hin yngsta *nornin*,' who in the crowd had been
pushed off her seat and fallen to the ground, rose up in anger, and
cried 'I cause that the child shall only live till the lighted taper beside
him has burnt out '. The eldest *völva* quickly seized the taper, put
it out, and gave it to the mother with the warning not to kindle it
again till the last day of her son's life, who received from this the
name of *Norn's-guest*. Here *völva, spákona* and *norn* are perfectly
synonymous ; as we saw before (p. 403) that the *völur* passed
through the land and *knocked at the houses*,[1] the *nornir* do the very
same. A kind disposition is attributed to the first two norns, an
evil one to the third. This third, consequently *Skuld*, is called
'the youngest,' they were of different ages therefore, *Urðr* being considered the oldest. Such tales of travelling gifting sorceresses
were much in vogue all through the Mid. Ages (see Suppl.).[2]

[1] I have elsewhere shown in detail, that the journeying house-visiting Muse
dame Aventiure is an inspiring and prophetic norn, and agrees to a feature
with the ancient conception ; see my Kleine schriften 1, 102.

[2] Nigellus Wirekere, in his Speculum stultorum (comp. about 1200), relates
a fable (exemplum) :

<blockquote>
Ibant *tres* hominum curas relevare *sorores*,
quas nos *fatales* dicimus esse *deas*.
</blockquote>

They *travel through the land*, to remedy the oversights of nature. Two of the
sisters, soft-hearted and impulsive, want to rush in and help at the first appearance of distress, but are restrained by the third and more intelligent one,
whom they address as *domina*, and revere as a higher power. First they fall
in with a beautiful noble maiden, who has all good things at her command, and
yet complains ; she is not helped, for she can help herself. Then they find in
the forest a modest maid laid up in bed, because sore feet and hips hinder her
from walking ; she too obtains no help from the goddesses ; excellently
endowed in mind and body, she must bear her misfortune patiently. At last
in the neighbourhood of a town the sisters come upon a poor rough peasant
lass :

<blockquote>
Exiit in bivium ventrem purgare puella
rustica, nil reverens inverecunda deas,
vestibus elatis retro nimiumque rejectis,
poplite deflexo crure resedit humi,
una manus foenum, panis tenet altera frustum ;
</blockquote>

this one, at the suggestion of the third sister, when the first two have turned
away, is heaped with the gifts of fortune by the goddesses :

<blockquote>
Haec mea multotiens genitrix narrare solebat,
cujus me certe non meminisse pudet.
</blockquote>

The Edda expressly teaches that there are *good* and *bad* norns (gôðar ok illar, grimmar, liotar), and though it names only three, that there are more of them : some are descended from gods, others from elves, others from dwarfs, Sn. 18. 19. Sæm. 187-8. Why should the norns be furnished with dogs ? *grey* norna, Sæm. 273ᵃ.

We see, throughout this Eddic description, things and persons are kept clearly apart. Destiny itself is called *örlög*, or else *nauðr* (necessitas), *aldr* (aevum) ; the norns have to manage it, espy it, decree it, pronounce it (see Suppl.). And the other dialects too had possessed the same term : OHG. *urlac*, AS. *orlæg*, MHG. *urlouc* (Gramm. 2, 7. 87. 789. 790), OS. *orlag, orlegi, aldarlagu* (Hel. 103, 8. 113, 11. 125, 15) ;[1] it was only when the heathen goddesses had been cast off, that the meanings of the words came to be confounded, and the old flesh-and-blood *wurt, wurð, wyrd* to pale into a mere impersonal *urlac*.

In the same relation as *norn* to *örlög*, stands *parca* to *fatum* (from fari, like qviðr from qveða qvað, quoth), and also αἶσα, μοῖρα to ἀνάγκη (nauðr) or εἱμαρμένη. But when once the parcae had vanished from the people's imagination, the Romance language (by a process the reverse of that just noticed amongst us) formed out of the abstract noun a new and personal one, out of *fatum* an Ital. *fata*, Span. *hada*, Prov. *fada* (Rayn. sub v.), Fr. *fée*.[2] I do not know if this was prompted by a faint remembrance of some female beings in the Celtic faith, or the influence of the Germanic norns. But these *fays*, so called at first from their announcing destiny, soon came to be ghostly wives in general, altogether the same as our idisî and völur.[3] How very early the name was current in Italy, is proved by Ausonius, who in his Gryphus ternarii numeri brings forward the 'tres Charites, *tria Fata*,' and by Procopius, who

---

[1] From legan (to lay down, constituere), like the AS. lage, ON. lög (lex) ; therefore urlac, fundamental law. The forms urlouc, urliuge have significantly been twisted round to the root liugan, louc (celare).

[2] Conf. nata, née ; amata, aimée ; lata, lée. Some MHG. poets say *feie* (Hartm. Wolfr.), sîne *feie*, Haupt's zeitschr. 2, 182-3, others *feine* (Gotfr. Conr.).

[3] OFr. poems call them, in addition to fées, *divesses* (Marie de Fr. 2, 385), *duesses* (Méon 4, 158. 165). *duesse* and *fée* (Wolf, lais 51) ; *puceles bien eurées* (Méon 3, 418), *franches puceles senées* (3, 419) ; *sapaudes* (wise-women, from sapere ?), Marie de Fr. 2, 385. Enchanting beauty is ascribed to them all : 'plus bela que *fada*,' Ferabras 2767 ; conf. 16434. A book of H. Schreiber (Die feen in Europa, Freib. 1842) throws much light on the antiquities of fay-worship. Houses, castles and hills of the fays remind us of the wise-women's towers, of the Venus-hill and Holla-hill, and of giant's houses. In Irish, *siabrog, sighbrog*, is first a fays' house, then the fay community.

mentions (De bello Goth. 1, 25, ed. Bonn. 2, 122) a building in the Roman Forum called τὰ τρία φᾶτα (supra p. 405, note) with the remark: οὕτω γὰρ Ῥωμαῖοι τὰς μοίρας νενομίκασι καλεῖν.[1] At that time therefore still neuter; but everywhere the number *three*, in norns, moirai, parcae and fays (see Suppl.).[2]

About the Romance fays there is a multitude of stories, and they coincide with the popular beliefs of Germany. Folquet de Romans sings:

> Aissim *fadero tres serors*
> en aquella ora qu'ieu sui natz,
> que totz temps fos enamoratz.

Guilhdei. Poitou:

> Assi fuy de nueitz *fadatz* sobr'un puegau.
> (so was I gifted by night on a mount).

Marcabrus:

> *Gentil fada*
> vos adastret, quan fas nada
> d'una beutat esmerada.

Tre fate go past, laughing, and give good gifts, Pentam. 1, 10. 4, 4; the first *fate* bestow blessings, the last one curses 2, 8; Pervonto builds a bower for *three* sleeping *fate*, and is then gifted 1, 3; *tre fate* live down in a rocky hollow, and dower the children who descend 2, 3. 3, 10; *fate* appear at the birth of children, and lay them on their breast 5, 5; Cervantes names 'los siete castillos de las *siete fadas*,' Don Quix. 4, 50; ' *siete fadas* me *fadaron* en brazos de una ama mia,' Rom. de la infantina; there are *seven fays* in the land, they are asked to stand godmothers, and seats of honour are prepared at the table: six take their places, but the seventh was forgotten, she now appears, and while the others endow with good things, she murmurs her malison (La belle au bois dormant); in the German kindermärchen (Dornröschen) it is *twelve wise women*, the *thirteenth* had been overlooked. So in the famed forest of

---

[1] Accordingly I do not derive *fata* from φάτις (speech), or φατός spoken, though the Latin verb is of course the same word as φημί. Conf. Ducange sub v. Fadus, and Lobeck's Aglaoph. 816. Fatuus and fatua are also connected.

[2] Lersch in the Bonner jb. 1843. 2,129—131 separates the three parcae from the three fata, because in sculptures they have different adjuncts: the Roman parcae are represented writing (p. 406), the Grecian moirai weaving, the tria fata simply as women with horns of plenty. But almost everything in the doctrine of fays points to a common nature with our idises and norns, and works of art fall into the background before the fulness of literature.

Brezeliande, by the fontaine de Barendon, *dames faées* in white apparel shew themselves, and begift a child, but one is spiteful and bestows calamity (San Marte, Leg. of Arthur p. 157-8. 160). At Olger's birth *six wise women* appear, and endow; the last is named *Morgue.* In the Children of Limburg (Mones anzeiger 1835, 169), when Ectrites falls asleep in a meadow beside a fountain and a lime-tree, *three wayfaring wives* approach, and foretell the future. The OFr. romance of Guillaume au court nez describes how Renoart falls asleep in a boat, and *three fays* come and carry him off. In Burchard of Worms they are still spoken of as *three sisters* or *parcae,* for whom the people of the house spread the table with three plates and three knives; conf. the ' praeparare mensas cum lapidibus vel epulis in domo'. In the watches of the night the fatuae come to children, wash them and lay them down by the fire (see Suppl.). In most of the tales there appear *three* fays, as well as *three* norns and *three* parcae; occasionally *seven* and *thirteen;* but they also come singly, like that ' weirdlady of the wood,' and with proper names of their own.[1] French

---

[1] *La fata* in Guerino meschino p. m. 223. 234—8 ; *Morganda fatata, fata Morgana, Morghe la fee* (Nouv. Renart 4810) ; 'diu frouwe *de la rosche bîse* (black rock), die gesach nieman, er schiede dan vrô, rîche unde wîse,' whom none saw but he went away glad, rich and wise, Ben. 144. MsH. 1, 118ᵃ. Monnier's Culte des esprits dans la Séquanie tells of a fée *Arie* in Franche-comté, who appears at country (esp. harvest) feasts, and rewards diligent spinners ; she makes the fruit fall off the trees for good children, and distributes nuts and cakes to them at Christmas, just like Holda and Berhta. I believe her to be identical with the Welsh *Arianrod,* daughter of Don and sister of Gwydion (Woden), in Croker 3, 195 ; her name contains arian (argentum), so that she is a shining one, and it is also used of the milky way. A jeu composed in the latter half of the 13th century by Adam de la Halle of Arras (publ. in Théatre franç. au moyen âge, Paris 1839, p. 55 seq.) gives a pretty full account of *dame Morgue* et sa *compaignie.* They are beautiful women (beles dames parées), who at a fixed time of the year seek a night's lodging at a house, where dishes are set on the table for them ; men that look on must not speak a word. Beside *Morgue la sage* there appear (p. 76-7) two other fays, *Arsile* and *Maglore,* and the last, on sitting down, notices that *no knife* has been laid for her, while the others praise the beauty of theirs. Maglore cries out in anger : ' Suije li pire ? peu me prisa qui estavli, ni avisa que toute seule à coutel faille '. Arsile tries to pacify her, and says, it is fitting that we give a present to those who have arranged this place so prettily. Morgue endows one with riches, Arsile with the poetic art, but Maglore says :

De mi certes naront il nient :
bien doivent falir à don bel,
puisque jai fali à coutel
honni soit qui riens leur donra !

Morgue however insisting on a gift, Maglore bestows on one fellow a bald head, and on the other a calamitous journey :

tradition brings to light a close connexion between fays and our
giant-maidens : the fays carry enormous blocks of stone on their
heads or in their aprons, while the free hand plies the spindle ;
when the fay who was doing the building part had finished her
task, she called out to her sisters not to bring any more, and these,
though two miles off, heard the cry and dropped their stones, which
buried themselves deep in the ground ; when the fays were not
spinning, they carried four stones at once. They were good-
natured, and took special care of the children whose fates they
foretold. They went in and out of the neighbours' houses by the
chimney, so that one day the most careless one among them burnt
herself, and uttered a loud wail, at which all the fays of the
neighbourhood came running up. You never could deceive them :
once, when a man put his wife's clothes on and nursed the baby,
the fay walked in and said directly : ' non, tu n'es point la belle
d'hier au soir, tu ne files, ni ne vogues, ni ton fuseau n'enveloppes '.
To punish him, she contented herself with making the apples that
were baking on the hearth shrink into peas.

Of such stories there are plenty ; but nowhere in Romance or
German folk-tales do we meet, as far as I know, with the Norse
conception of *twining* and *fastening* the *cord*, or the Greek one of
spinning and *cutting* the *thread of life*. Only one poet of the Mid.
Ages, Marner, has it 2, 173[b] :

> zwô schepfer flâhten mir ein *seil*,
> dâ bî *diu dritte* saz (the third sat by) ;
> diu *zerbrachz* (broke it) : daz was mîn unheil.

But this seems borrowed from the Roman view of breaking off the
thread (rumpat, **p.** 406, note).   Ottokar makes the *schepfen*

ains comperront chier le coutel
qu'il ouvlierent chi à metre.
Then before daybreak the fays depart to a meadow, their place of meeting, for
they shun to meet the eyes of men by day. Here we see plainly enough the
close resemblance of these three fays to the three norns. The French editor
wrongly understands coutel of a cloth spread for the fay ; the passage in
Burchard of Worms removes all doubt. If Maglore be a corruption of
Mandaglore, Mandagloire, as the mandragora is elsewhere called, a close
connexion may be established with Alrûne, Ölrûn. Morgue is shortened from
Morgan, which is the Breton for merwoman (from mor, the sea, and gwen,
splendens femina). One might be tempted to connect Morgan with that
inexplicable ' norn,' as the ON. morni stands for morgni ; but the norn has
nothing to do with the morning or the sea (see Suppl.).
[1] H. Schreiber, Feen in Europa pp. 11. 12. 16. 17.   Michelet 2, 17.

(creating) impart all success in good or evil. The 'banun festan' in Hild. lied is hardly to be explained by the fastening of a thread of death.

If we compare the Norse mythus with the Greek, each has taken shape in its own independent way. In Homer it is the personified *Aἶσα*[1] that spins the thread for the newborn:

ἄσσα οἱ Αἶσα

γεινομένῳ ἐπένησε λίνῳ, ὅτε μιν τέκε μήτηρ.   Il. 20, 127;

'what things Aisa span for him at birth with her thread'. But in Od. 7, 197 other spinners (two) are associated with her:

ἄσσα οἱ Αἶσα Κατακλῶθές τε βαρεῖαι

γεινομένῳ νήσαντο λίνῳ, ὅτε μιν τέκε μήτηρ·

'what Aisa and the Kataklothes unkind span'. Hesiod (ἀσπ. 258) makes three goddesses stand beside the combatants, **Κλωθώ, Λάχεσις, Ἄτροπος**, the last small of stature, but eldest and most exalted of all. But in Theog. 218 he names them as

Κλωθώ τε Λάχεσίν τε καὶ Ἄτροπον, αἵτε βροτοῖσιν

γεινομένοισι διδοῦσιν ἔχειν ἀγαθόν τε κακόν τε·

'who give to mortals at birth to have both good and ill;' and in almost the same words at 905. The most detailed description is given by Plato (De republ. **617** Steph. **508** Bekk.): The three μοῖραι are daughters of Ἀνάγκη (necessity), on whose knees the spindle (ἄτρακτος) turns; they sit clothed in white and garlanded, singing the destiny, Lachĕsis τὰ γεγονότα, Klotho τὰ ὄντα, Atrŏpos τὰ μέλλοντα: just the same relation to past, present and future as the norns have, though the Greek proper names do not themselves express it. Κλωθώ (formed like Αὐξώ, Θαλλώ, Λητώ, Μορμώ, Γοργώ) spins (from κλώδω spin, twine), Lachesis allots (from λαχεῖν), Ἄτροπος, the unturnable, cuts the thread. It must not be overlooked, that Hesiod sets up the last, Atropos, as the mightiest, while with us Wurt the eldest produces the most powerful impression. Latin writers distribute the offices of the parcae somewhat differently, as Apuleius (De mundo p. 280): Clotho *praesentis temporis habet curam, quia quod torquetur in digitis, momenti*

---

[1] I think *aἶσα* is the OHG. êra, our ehre, for which we should expect a Gothic áiza, áisa (as áistan is aestimare): êra = honor, decus, dignitas, what is fair and fitting, what is any one's due; κατ' αἶσαν, ex dignitate, to each his meed. If this etymology holds, we understand why *frau Ere* was personified (see Suppl.).

praesentis indicat spatia ; Atropos *praeteriti* fatum est, quia quod
in fuso perfectum est, praeteriti temporis habet speciem ; Lachesis
futuri, quod etiam illis quae futura sunt finem suum deus dederit
(see Suppl.). Isidore's opinion was quoted on p. 405.[1] The Nornagestssaga bears a striking resemblance to that of Meleager, at
whose birth three moirai tell his fortune: Atropos destines him to
live only till the billet then burning on the hearth be burnt out ;
his mother Althaea plucks it out of the fire.[2] Our modern tales
here exchange the norns or fates for *death*, Kinderm. no. 44.
Another tale, that of the *three spinners* (no. 14), depicts them as
ugly old women, who come to help, but no longer to predict ; they
desire to be bidden to the marriage and to be called *cousins*.
Elsewhere *three old women* foretell, but do not spin.[3] A folk-tale
(Deutsche sagen no. 9) introduces *two maidens spinning* in a cave
of the mountain, and under their table is the Evil one (I suppose
the third norn) chained up ; again we are told of the roof-beam on
which a *spinning wife* sits at midnight.[4] We must not forget the
AS. term which describes a norn as *weaving*, ' Wyrd *gewâf* '
(p. 406); and when it is said in Beow. 1386 : ' ac him Dryhten
forgeaf wîgspêda *gewiofu* ' (ei Dominus largitus est successuum
bellicorum texturas), this is quite heathen phraseology, only
putting God in the place of Wyrd. Gottfried (Trist. 4698), in
describing Blicker of Steinach's purity of mind, expresses himself
thus :

> ich wæne, daz in *feinen*
> ze wunder haben *gespunnen*
> und haben in in ir *brunnen*
> geliutert und gereinet ;

' I ween that fays spun him as a wonder, and cleansed him in their
fountain '.

Saxo Gram. p. 102 uses the Latin words *parca, nympha*, but
unmistakably he is describing norns : ' Mos erat antiquis, super

---

[1] The Hymn to Mercury 550-561 names individually some other μοῖραι,
still three in number, winged maidens dwelling on Parnassus, their heads
besprinkled with white meal, who prophesy when they have eaten fresh divine
food (ἡδεῖαν ἐδωδὴν) of honey. Otherwise they are called θριαί.
[2] Apollodorus i. 8, 2.
[3] Altd. wb. 1, 107-8-9-10. Norske eventyr no. 13. Rob. Chambers p.
54-5. Müllenhoff's Schleswigh. s. p. 410. Pentamer. 4, 4.
[4] Jul. Schmidt, Reichenfels p. 140.

futuris liberorum eventibus *parcarum* oracula consultare. Quo
ritu Fridlevus Olavi filii fortunam exploraturus, nuncupatis
solenniter votis, deorum aedes precabundus accedit, ubi introspecto
sacello[1] *ternas* sedes totidem *nymphis* occupari cognoscit. Quarum
prima indulgentioris animi liberalem puero formam, uberemque
humani favoris copiam erogabat. Eidem *secunda* beneficii loco
liberalitatis excellentiam condonavit. *Tertia* vero, protervioris
ingenii invidentiorisque studii femina, *sororum* indulgentiorem
aspernata consensum, ideoque earum donis officere cupiens, futuris
pueri moribus parsimoniae crimen affixit.' Here they are called
sisters, which I have found nowhere else in ON. authorities; and
the third nymph is again the illnatured one, who lessens the boons
of the first two. The only difference is, that the norns do not
come to the infant, but the father seeks out their dwelling, their
temple (see Suppl.).[2]

The weaving of the norns and the spindle of the fays give us
to recognise *domestic motherly* divinities; and we have already
remarked, that their appearing suddenly, their haunting of wells
and springs accord with the notions of antiquity about frau Holda,
Berhta and the like goddesses, who devote themselves to spinning,
and bestow boons on babes and children.[3]   Among Celts especially,

---

[1] They had a *temple* then, in which their oracle was consulted.

[2] The Lettish *Laima*, at the birth of a child, lays the sheet under it, and
determines its fortune. And on other occasions in life they say, ' taip *Laima*
leme,' so Fate ordained it ; no doubt Laima is closely connected with lemti
(ordinare, disponere). She runs barefooted over the hills (see ch. XVII,
Watersprites). There is also mentioned a *Dehkla* (nursing-mother, from deht
to suckle). A trinity of parcae, and their spinning a thread, are unknown to
the Lettons ; conf. Stender's Gramm. p. 264. Rhesas dainos pp. 272. 309.
310.—The Lithuanians do know a *Werpeya* (spinner). The Ausland for 1839,
no. 278 has a pretty Lithuanian legend : The *dieves valditoyes* were seven
goddesses, the first one spun the lives of men out of a distaff given her by the
highest god, the second set up the warp, the third wove in the woof, the fourth
told tales to tempt the workers to leave off, for a cessation of labour spoilt the
web, the fifth exhorted them to industry, and added length to the life, the sixth
cut the threads, the seventh washed the garment and gave it to the most high
god, and it became the man's winding-sheet. Of the seven, only *three* spin or
weave.

[3] Not a few times have Holda and Berhta passed into Mary ; and in the
three Marys of a Swiss nursery-rhyme I think I can recognise the heathen norns
or idisî :

rite. rite rösli,	ride, ride a-cock horse,
ze Bade stot e schlössli,	at Baden stands a little castle,
ze Bade stot e güldi hus,	at Baden stands a golden house,
es lüeged *drei Mareie* drus.	there look three Marys out of it :
die eint spinnt side,	the one spins silk,

the fatae seem apt to run into that sense of *matres* and *matronae*,[1] which among Teutons we find attaching more to divine than to semi-divine beings. In this respect the fays have something higher in them than our idises and norns, who in lieu of it stand out more warlike.

4. WALACHURIUN (VALKYRJOR).

Yet, as the fatae are closely bound up with fatum—the pronouncing of destiny, vaticination—the kinship of the fays to the norns asserts itself all the same. Now there was no sort of destiny that stirred the spirit of antiquity more strongly than the issue of battles and wars: it is significant, that the same urlac, urlouc expresses both fatum and bellum also (Graff 2, 96. Gramm. 2, 790), and the idisî forward or hinder the fight. This their office we have to look into more narrowly.

From Caesar (De B. Gall. 1, 50) we already learn the practice of the Germani, 'ut *matresfamilias* eorum *sortibus* et *vaticinationibus* declararent, utrum proelium committi ex usu esset, necne'. Mistresses of families practised augury, perhaps women selected for the purpose, of superior and godlike repute like Veleda.

Let us bear in mind, which gods chiefly concerned themselves with the event of a battle: *Oðinn* and *Freyja* draw to themselves all those who fall in fight, and Oðinn admits them to his heavenly abode (pp. 133, 305). This hope, of becoming after death members of the divine community, pervades the religion of the heathen. Now the ON. *valr*, AS. *wœl*, OHG. *wal*, denotes the carnage of the battle-field, the sum of the slain : to take possession of this val, to gather it in, was denominated *kiosa*, kiesen, to choose ; this verb seems a general technical term for the acceptance of any sacrifice made to a higher being.[2] But Oðinn, who has the *siges kür* (choosing

die ander schnätzelt chride,	the other cards . . . . ?
die drit schnit haberstrau.	the third cuts oaten straw.
bhüet mer Gott mis chindli au !	God keep my childie too !

Schnätzeln is, I suppose, to wind ? [snast = wick ? snood ? In the märchen of the Goosemaid, schnatzen is apparently to comb]. The seventh line sometimes runs : di dritte *schneidt den faden* (cuts the thread). Conf. Vonbun p. 66. Firmenich 2, 665[b]. Mannhardt pp. 388. 392. The nursery-song in the Wunderhorn p. 70-1 has *three spinning tocken, i.e.* nymphs, fays.

[1] Lersch in the Bonn Annual 1843, pp. 124—7.

[2] Chief passage, Sæm. 141[a]. Conf. Gramm. 4, 608, and AS. **wîg** *curon*, Cædm. 193, 9 ; MHG. sige kiesen, Iw. 7069, sig erkiesen, Wh. 355, 15. So, den tôt kiesen.

of victory, p. 133, note), is served in Valhöll by maidens, and them he sends out into every battle, to choose the slain, Sn. 39; '*kiosa* er liðnir ero,' Sæm. 164ᵇ; vildi þik *kiosa*, Sæm. 254ᵃ.

Hence such a maiden, half divine, is called *valkyrja* ; and it is another most welcome coincidence, that the AS. language has retained the very same term *wælcyrie* (wælcyrge, wælcyrre) to English such Latin words as bellona, erinnys, Alecto, Tisiphone, and employs it even for parca and venefica. The Cott. MS. Vitell. A. 15 has a gloss 'wælcyrigean eágan, gorgoneus': this is translating the Greek idea into an AS. one ; did the eyes of the wælcyrigean instil horror like the Gorgons' heads? I am quite safe in assuming an OHG. *walachuriâ* (walachurrâ) ; *valakusjô* would be the Gothic form. At the end of the Langobardian genealogy we find a man's name *Walcausus*.[1]

Another name of the *valkyrjur* is ON. *valmeyjar* (battle-maids), perhaps also the present Norw. *valdöger*, which Hallager 140ᵇ says is guardian-spirit. Again, they are called *skialdmeyjar, hialmmeyjar*, because they go forth armed, under shield and helmet (vera und hialmi, Sæm. 151ᵃ 192ᵇ) ; *nonnor Herjans*, nuns of Oðinn 4ᵇ. The Edda bestows on the valkyrja the epithets: *hvît* 168ᵇ, *hvît und hialmi* (alba sub galea) 145ᵇ, *biört* 174ᵇ, *sôlbiört*, sunbright 167ᵇ, *biartlituð* 142ᵃ, *hialmvitr* 157ᵃ, *gullvari
ð* 167ᵇ, *margullin* mær 145ᵃ, *alvitr* 164ᵃ, all descriptive of beauty or helmet-ornaments. Helm and shield distinguish these helm and shield women as much as heroes, they ride on shield-service, under shield-roof, Sæm. 250ᵇ, and are called *skialdmeyjar* aldrstamar, or young shield-maidens of Atli's court. The legend of the *Amazons* (Herod. 4, 110—117. Jorn. cap. 6.7.8. Paul. Diac. 1, 15) seems to rest on similar yet different notions. A valkyr in Sæm. 167ᵇ is named *suðrœn* (australis), apparently in the sense of biört, sôlbiört ? Again at 151ᵇ, dîsir suðrœnar (see Suppl.).[2]

---

[1] Of *valr, wal* itself we might seek the root in velja, valjan (eligere), so that it should from the first have contained the notion of choosing, but being applied to strages, and its sense getting blurred, it had to be helped out by a second verb of the same meaning. Our Tit. 105, 4 has a striking juxtaposition : 'Sigûn diu sigehaft ûf dem *wal*, da man *welt* magede kiusche und ir stieze'. It is only in Dietr. 91ᵇ and Rab. 536. 635. 811. 850. 923 that *welrecke* occurs ; can it have any relationship to walküre ?

[2] Oðinn has Frigg, the *valkyrjur* and the ravens in the waggon with him, Sn. 66. For valkyrja I also find the name *skörûngr*, derivable either from skar superbia, or skari agmen. Brynhildr is called in Völs. saga cap. 24 'mestr skörûngr' (see Suppl.).

One name is particularly attractive : *ôskmeyjar*, wish-maidens (Sæm. 212. Völs. saga cap. 2), given them, I think, because they are in Oðin's service, and Oðinn is called *Oski*, *Wunsc*. But there is something more : I find a confirmation of my opinion that Wuotan bore the name of *Wunsc* in his identity with *Mercury*, for Mercury carries the magic wand (caduceus), which is like our *wishing-rod*, OHG. *wunsciligerta* (-yerde, yard). The likeness will come out more distinctly from a closer inspection of the two rods, which is yet to come ; but if Wuotan and *Wunsc*, Oðinn and *Oski* are one, we may suppose that the thorn, the sleeping-thorn, which Oðinn put into the dress of the valkyrja Brynhildr (Sæm. 192ᵃ), was likewise a *wishing-thorn*. It throws light on the nature of Brunhild and Chrimhild, that rocks are named after them, one called *spilstein*, Chriemhilde*spil* (p. 370), which does not find a meaning so well from spil (ludus) as from spille (spindle, fusus). For other stones have the name *kunkel* (distaff), and in French fairy-tales *quenouille* à la bonne dame ;[1] Dornröschen (thorn-rosekin) pricked her finger with the spindle and fell into a dead sleep, as Brunhild did with the wishing-thorn. Spindles are an essential characteristic of all the wise-women of antiquity among Teutons, Celts and Greeks.[2] The walküre is a *wunsch-kint*, *Wunsches kint*, pp. 139, 142 (see Suppl.).

The name *wünschelweib*, which lasted down to a late time, shall be produced hereafter; here I call up from the poem of the Staufenberger a being by whom the connexion of valkyrs with fays is placed beyond doubt. To the knight there shews herself a maiden in *white apparel* (the hvît and biört above), sitting on a stone (line 224) ; she has *watched over him in danger and war from his youth up*, she *was about him unseen* (332—364) ; now she becomes his love, and is with him *whenever he wishes for her* (swenne du einest wünschest nâch mir, sô bin ich endelîchen bî dir 474). By super-human power she moves swiftly whither she lists (wâr ich wil, dâ bin ich, den *wunsch* hât mir Got gegeben 497). Staufenberger, after being united to her in love, may do anything except take a wedded wife, else he will die in three days.

> ' er *wünschte* nâch der frouwen sîn,
> bî im sô war diu schœne fîn.'

---

[1] H. Schreiber pp. 20. 21.
[2] I like also Schreiber's derivation, pp. 65—67, of the name *Nehaea*, *Nehalennia* (supra p. 257) from the root nere, neza to spin.

When he notwithstanding resolves on another marriage, she *drives her foot through the floor*, and he has to die (1016. 1066). According to this remarkable story, *wunschweib* or *wünschelweib* is one whose presence her lover can procure, by wishing it, whenever he longs for her, 'names her name' as it were (p. 398): this is, though not a false, yet a later meaning substituted for the original one, which had reference to the god of wishing, the divine Wish. Old Norse legend will unfold to us more precisely the nature of these women.

In Valhöll the occupation of the *óskmeyjar* or *valkyrjur* was to *hand the drinking-horn* to the gods and einherjar, and to furnish the table. Here comes out their peculiar relation to *Freyja*, who 'chooses val' like them, is called *Valfreyja* (p. 305),[1] and pours out at the banquet of the Ases (at gildi Asa), Sn. 108. Exactly in the same way did *Göndul*, sitting on a stôl î rioðrinu (in the niuriute, clearing), offer the comers *drink out of a horn* (Fornald. sög. 1, 398. 400); and with this agree the deep draughts of the modern folk-tale: a beautifully dressed and garlanded maiden from the Osenberg offers the count of Oldenburg a *draught* in a silver *horn*, while uttering predictions (Deutsche sagen, no. 541). Svend Fälling drank out of the horn handed him by elf-women, and in doing so, spilt some on his horse, as in the preceding story (Thiele 2, 67); I have touched (p. 372) on the identity of Svend Fälling with Siegfried, whose relation to the valkyr Brunhild comes out clearly in the Danish story. In a Swedish folk-song in Arvidsson 2, 301, three mountain-maids hold out silver *tankards* in their *white hands*. Quite in harmony are some Norwegian traditions in Faye p. 26-8-9. 30; and additional Danish ones in Thiele 1, 49.55. 3,44 (see Suppl.).

Still more to the purpose is the office of the valkyrs in war. Not only 'kiosa val, kiosa feigð,'[2] but 'râða vîgum' or 'sigri,' therefore the deciding of battle and victory, is placed in their hands, Sn. 39. They are said to be 'görvar (alert) at rîða grund,' 'görvar

---

[1] So, in a Faröese song, *Valvfrygv* (Finn Magn. lex. p. 805).

[2] The *taking possession of souls* at the moment of death by Oðinn and Freyja, or by their messengers the valkyrs, appears to me so deep-rooted a feature of our heathenism, that we may well find it lingering even in christian traditions. Of this sort is the scramble of *angels* and *devils* for the soul, described in the poem Muspilli, which Schmeller has hunted up, Georg 1235-44. 6082—86. and Méon 1, 239. 4, 114-5; and a striking passage in the Morolt I shall quote in ch. XVII. Will any one think of tracing this idea to the Epistle of Jude 9, or the apocryphal Book of Enoch?

at ríða til goðþioðar,' Sæm. 4ᵇ. Rooted in their being is an irresistible *longing* for this warlike occupation; hence the Edda expresses their most characteristic passion by the verb 'þrá' (desiderant), Sæm. 88ᵇ, 'þráðo' (desiderabant) or 'fýstoz' (cupiebant), 134ᵃ: it is their own longing, striving and wishing that has swung itself round into that wishing for them. Usually *nine* valkyrjur ride out together, Sæm. 142, 162; their lances, helmets and shields glitter 151ᵃ. This *nineness* is also found in the story of Thiðrandi (see p. 402), to whom nine dîsir appear first in white raiment, then nine others in black. Sæm. 44-5, and after him Sn. 39, enumerate *thirteen* of them: *Hrist, Mist, Skeggöld, Skögul, Hildr, Thrûðr, Hlöck, Herfiötr, Göll, Geirahöð* (al. Geirölul), *Randgríð, Râdgríð, Reginleif;* but Sæm. 4ᵇ only *six*: *Skuld, Skögul, Gunnr, Hildr, Göndul, Geirskögul.*[1] The prose of Sn. 39 distinguishes *three* as strictly val-choosers and mistresses of victory: *Guðr, Rota* and *Skuld* 'norn en ŷngzta'. The celebrated battle-weaving song of the Nialssaga names the following: *Hildr, Hiörþrimul, Sangríðr* (l. Rangríðr), *Svipul, Gunnr, Göndul;* the Hâkonarmâl: *Göndol, Skögol, Geirskögol;* the Krâkumâl (ed. Rafn, p. 121) only *Hlöck* and *Hildr.* Several of these names are of extraordinary and immediate value to our investigation, and not one of the remainder ought to be left out of sight in future study (see Suppl.).

Skuld, for instance: we gather from it the affinity of norns and valkyrs, and at the same time the distinction between them. A dîs can be both norn and valkyr, but the functions are separate, and usually the persons. The norns have to pronounce the fatum, they sit on their chairs, or they roam through the country among mortals, fastening their threads. Nowhere is it said that they ride. The valkyrs *ride* to war, decide the issue of the fighting, and conduct the fallen to heaven; their riding is like that of heroes and gods (pp. 327. 392), mention is made of their horses: skalf Mistar *marr* (tremuit Mistae equus), Sæm. 156ᵃ; *mar*gullin mær (aureo equo vecta virgo), 145ᵃ; when the steeds of the valkyrs shake themselves, dew drips from their manes into the valleys, and fertilizing hail falls on trees 145ᵃˏᵇ, with which compare the ' destillationes in comis et collis equorum ' of the wise-women (p. 287); the name Mist, which elsewhere means mist, may have indicated

[1] Unpublished passages in the skâlds supply 29 or 30 names (Finn Magn. lex. p. 803).

a like phenomenon. Of the norns, none but *Skuld the youngest* (p. 405) can be a valkyrja too : were Urðr and Verðandi imagined as too aged or too dignified for the work of war ? did the cutting, breaking, of the thread (if such an idea can be detected in the North) better become the maiden practised in arms ?

Two other valkyrs, *Hlöck* and *Herfiötr*, have been claimed above (p. 401) as idisî, and interpreted as restrainers of the fight. In the Kormakssaga there also occurs *Hlökk* gen. Hlakkar, for bellona.

Hildr, Gunnr, Thrûðr deserve to be studied the more closely, because their personality turns up in other Teutonic tongues as well, and the presence there of some walachuriun argues that of the whole sisterhood.   Even in ONorse, *Hildr* and *Gunnr* (=Guðr) got generalized into *hildr* and *gunnr* (pugna, proelium) ; of bellona was made bellum : '*hildr* hefir þû oss verit,' bellona nobis fuisti, Sæm. 164ᵇ.   Conversely, beside the AS. *hild* and *gûð* we still find a personal *Hild* and *Gûð:* gif mec *Hild* nime (if H. take me), Beow. 899. 2962 ; *Gûð* nimeð 5069 ; *Gûð* fornam (carried off) 2240 ; as elsewhere we have 'gif mec deáð nimeð,' Beow. 889, wîg ealle fornam 2154, gûðdeáð fornam 4494, Wyrd fornam 2411 (conf. OS. Wurd farnimid, Hel. 111, 11), swylt fornam 2872, Wyrd forsweop (supra p. 406) ; conf. '*Hilde* grâp' 5009.   And as other beings that do us good or harm are by turns aroused and quieted, it is said picturesquely : *Hildi* vekja (bellonam excitare), Sæm. 160ᵃ 246ᵃ ; elsewhere merely vîg vekja (bellum excitare) 105ᵃ.   The valkyrs, like Oðinn (p. 147), are accompanied by *eagles* and *ravens,* who alight on the battlefield,[1] and the waging of war is poetically expressed as *ala gögl gunna systra* (aves alere sororum belli), Sæm. 160ᵃ.   The forms in OHG. were *Hiltia* and *Gundia* (Gûdea), both found in the Hild. lied 6. 60, though already as mere common nouns ; composite proper names have -hilt, -gunt.[2]   The legend of *Hildr,* who goes to the val at night, and by her magic wakes the fallen warriors into life again, is preserved both in the Edda (Sn. 164-5) and also in the OHG. poem of Gûdrûn, where she is called *Hilde.*[3]—Lastly, *Thrûðr,* which likewise sinks into a mere appella-

---

[1] Andr. and El. p. xxvi. xxvii. Conf. Luke 17, 37 : ὅπου τὸ σῶμα, ἐκεῖ συναχθήσονται καὶ οἱ ἀετοί.

[2] The Trad. fuld., in Schannat no. 443, have preserved the name, well suited to a valkyr, of *Themarhilt* (from dëmar, crepusculum).

[3] Deutsche heldensage p. 327 seq. Conf. supra p. 285, on Hilde and Hildburg.

tive *þrúðr* virgo, and in OHG. occurs in a great many female
names (*e.g.* Alpdrûd [Ælfþryð, Elfrida], Wolchandrûd, Himildrûd,
Plîddrût, Plihdrût = Plectrud, Kêrdrûd = Gertrude, Mîmidrûd,
Sigidrûd, which naturally suggest ghostly beings), has assumed
the general meaning of witch, sorceress, hobgoblin.[1] Hans Sachs
several times uses ' alte *trute* ' for old witch, and noisy children are
quieted with the words : ' hush, the *drut* will come ! ' [2] so that here
she exactly fills the place of frau Holla or Berhta, and can
the more appropriately be the ancient valkyr. An AS. wood-
maiden, named *Dhryð*, comes up in the Vita Offae secundi (supra,
p. 388) : she is from France, where she had been sentenced to
death for her crimes, exposed in a ship, and cast on the shore of
Mercia. Here Offa saw the maiden passing fair, and married her,
but she soon committed new transgressions. She is called 9ª Drida,
9ᵇ Petronilla, 15ᵇ Qvendrida (*i.e.*,cwên Thryð ; conf. Kemble's preface to Beow. pp. xxxv. xxxvi, and Bäckström 1, 220 (see Suppl.).

Beside the valkyrs named, there must have been many others,
and the second section of the Sæmundaredda names several as
lovers or wives of heroes. Such are *Svava, Sigrlinn, Kâra, Sigrûn,
Sigrdrîfa*, who are expressly called valkyrjur, Sæm. 142ᵇ 145ᵇ 157,
169. 194. It also comes out, that they were of human origin,
being daughters of kings, Svava of Eylimi, Sigrlinn of Svafnir,
Sigrûn of Högni, Kâra of Hâlfdan, Sigrdrîfa of Buðli ; Svava was
the lover of Helgi Hiörvarðsson, Sigrlinn of Hiörvarðr, Sigrûn of
Helgi Hundîngsbani, Kâra of Helgi Haddîngskaði, and Sigrdrîfa,
who is no other than Brynhildr, of Sigurðr. *Grîmhildr* (helmet-
maiden, p. 238), and above all *Brynhildr, Prunhilt*, whose very
name betokens the mail-clad Hildr, is superhuman: her inaccessible
hall stands on a mountain, like those of Veleda and Jetha (pp. 95-
6) ; it was a *schildburg* (skialdborg), where she herself, bound by
the spell, slept under her shield, till Sigurðr released her. Then
she prophesied to him, Sæm. 194ᵇ, and before her death she
prophesies again, 224 226ᵇ. Her hall was encircled with *flickering
flame, ' oc var um sal hennar vafrlogi,' Sn. 139 (see Suppl.), as was
also that of *Menglöð* (OHG. Maniklata, *i.e.*, monili laetabunda),
another valkyr: salr er slûnginn er vîsom vafrloga (Sæm. 110ª, conf.

---

[1] Some people think Gerdrut, Gerdraut, an unchristian name. Frau *Trude*
(Kinderm. 43).

[2] Flögel, gesch. des groteskekom. p. 23.

107[a, b]). Before this Menglöð, nine virgins kneel, sit, and sing; sacrifice is offered to them all (111[a]); conf. ch. XXXVI. Then *Vebiörg skialdmœr* appears in Fornald. sög. 1, 384. And *vrð Babehilt*, whom Dietrich finds at a fountain, *asleep* (as Sigurd found Brynhild), and who gives him healing salves, and foretells his fate (Ecke 151—160), must also be reckoned among norns or valkyrs. The valkyrs bestowed on their favourites, as Staufenberger's lover did on him (p. 419), victory and protection in battle (Sigrûn hlífði honom opt síðan î orrostom, Sæm. 142[b]); this relation is technically expressed by *verja* (tueri 134[a]); they hide their heroes' ships (Svava 145[a, b], Sigrûn 153[b]). The above-mentioned Hildr too, the daughter of king Högni (Hagene), was Heðin's betrothed. The memory of these shield-maidens has filtered down even into modern folksongs: in Arvidsson 1, 189, *Kerstin sköldmö* with her 8000 maids redeems her betrothed from captivity; at other times it is a sister that rescues her brother, by which is not meant a sister by birth, but a valkyr again, for these higher beings are everywhere called *sisters*, and fraternize with their protégés (Arvidsson 2, 120-1-2. Nyerup 4, 38-9). Now those women in our medieval poetry, the sight of whom nerves to victory, whose name need only be uttered to bring them to one's side as quickly as a wish can be formed and accomplished, are evidently shield-women of this kind (see Suppl.).

Oðinn then admitted into his band of valkyrs mortal maidens of kingly race, deified women standing by the side of the deified heroes; yet I do not suppose that all valkyrs were of such lineage, but that the oldest and most famous were, like the norns, descended from gods or elves. It is also worth noting, that Kâra and her Helgi were looked upon as a *second birth* of Svava and the elder Helgi, Sæm. 148[b] 169. In the Völundarqviða *three* other valkyrs make their appearance together: *Hlaðguðr svanhvît, Hervör alvitr*, and *Ölrûn*, the first two being daughters of king Löðver, the third of Kiâr; they unite themselves to Slagfiðr, Völundr and Egill, live with them seven years, and then escape, 'at vitja vîga,' to pursue their old trade of war again. On the whole, it seems the union of these half-goddesses with heroes turned out detrimentally to both parties: the heroes came to an early death or other harm, as Staufenberger's example teaches; and 'Sigrûn varð skammlîf,' she grew scant of life, Sæm. 169[a]. Perhaps we should be right in assuming that promotion to the valkyr's office took place under an obligation of *virginity*,[1] which again reminds one of the Amazons. At all events, when Oðinn was angry with Sigrdrîfa for letting his favourite fall in battle,[2] he decreed that now she should be given in marriage, ' qvað hana giptaz scyldo,' Sæm. 194ᵃ. Hlaðguðr, Hervör and Ölrûn had been carried off by the men forcibly and against their will (see Suppl.).[3] All these female names are descriptive. *Ölrûn* was discussed on p. 404. *Hlaðguðr* is literally bellona stragis; *Hervör*, like the kindred Gunnvör, alludes to hosts and battles, the adj. *alvitr* to the gift of prophecy, and *svanhvît* to the swan-shape. Saxo Gram. 22-3 names another *Svanhvita*, who has likewise much of the valkyr, is a seer of spirits, and presents a sword to Regner to seal their covenant. As for *Slagfiðr* (see p. 380), I prefer to explain it not as Slagfinnr, though he is called a son of the Finnakonûngr, but as *Slagfiöðr* = alatus, pennatus, which goes better with Svanhvît his lover, and is supported by the OHG. word slagifëdara, penna.

How little we are entitled to separate the *norns* and *valkyrs* totally from one another, is taught by the tale of these three maidens also. Not to mention the prevalence among valkyrs as well as norns of the number three and sisterly companionship, nor Hervör's having the epithet *alvitr* (omniscia), which better fits a norn than a valkyr ; it is said of all three, that they sat on the sea-beach *spinning* costly *flax*, nay, of the same ' all-witting ' one (who is repeatedly called *ûnga*, as Skuld is in other places), that she was about to ' *örlög drÿgja*,' to dree a weird, Sæm. 133ᵃ 134ᵃ.

[1] Pompon. Mela 3, 8 : ' Oraculi numinis Gallici antistites, *perpetua virginitate* sanctae, numero *novem* esse traduntur. *Gallicenas* vocant, putantque ingeniis singularibus praeditas maria ac ventos concitare, seque in quae velint animalia vertere, sanare quae apud alios insanabilia sunt, *scire ventura et praedicare*, sed non nisi deditas navigantibus, et in id tantum ut se consulerent profectas [l. profectis ?] '. The similarity of these nine sooth-telling gallicenae is unmistakable. Some read Galli Cenas, others Barrigenas, conf. Tzschucke, Not. crit. pp. 159—163.

[2] N.B. against Oðin's will, who could therefore be outwitted : destiny stood above the god.

[3] On p. 406 we saw wise-women represented as acquainted with *writing*, and as actually writing ; it will be for similar reasons that valkyrs *embroider* and *paint*. The Völs. saga cap. 24 says of Brynhild : ' hun sat î einni skemmu við meyjar sînar, hun kunni meira hagleik enn aðrar konur, hun lagði sinn borða með gulli, ok saumaði â þau stôrmerki, er Sigurðr hafði giört '. And in this chamber Sigurð comes to her. I place beside this the opening lines of a Swedish song :

Sven Färling han rider till jungfruns gård,
som *stickade* på silket det hvita.
And this hero is identical with Sigurð.

The award of battle is one part of destiny; not only norns, but valkyrs also were imagined *spinning* and *weaving*. This is placed in the clearest light by the fearfully exciting poem in cap. 158 of the Nialssaga. Through a crevice in the rock Dörruðr sees women sit singing over a *web*, at which human heads serve them for weights, entrails for warp and weft, swords for spools, and arrows for a comb: in their weird song they describe themselves as *valkyrjur*, and their web as intended for the spectator Dörruðr.[1] At length they tear up their work, mount their steeds, and *six* of them ride to the south, *six* to the north. Compare with this the *weaving* Wyrd of the AS. poet (p. 415). The parting of the maidens into two bands that ride in opposite directions, is like those nine in white and nine in black, who came riding up in succession (p. 421).

I have set norns and μοῖραι side by side; with equal aptness a comparison can be drawn between valkyrs and κῆρες (without any verbal affinity, for no doubt the likeness is only an apparent one): the κήρ too might be seen on the battlefield in bloody garments, tending the wounded, dragging away the dead. A κήρ is allotted to the child as soon as it is born; Achilles had two κῆρες between whom he might choose, and Zeus put two in the balance, to decide the death of Hector or Achilles.[2] Hesiod (scut. 249—254) makes the dingy white-toothed κῆρες contend *over the fallen warriors*, each throws her talons round the wounded man, eager to drink his blood, just as he ascribes talons and a thirst for blood to the moirai (p. 414): a fresh confirmation of the identity of norns and valkyrs. The claws of the moirai and kêres, the wings of the thriai, point to their possession of a *bird's shape*. The later view [Hesiod's] brings into prominence the sinister side of the kêres.

5. SWAN-MAIDENS.

But we have now to make out a new aspect of the valkyrs. We are told that they travel *through air and water*, ' ríða lopt ok lög,' Sæm. 142[b] 159[b]; theirs is the power to fly and to swim, in other words, they can assume the body of a *swan*, they love to

---

[1] So at least we may understand ' vindum, vindum vef *Darraðar*,' even if the name and the whole story first arose out of a ' vef darraðar,' web of the dart, conf. AS. deoreð (jaculum). We know that the Sturlûngasaga contains a very similar narrative.

[2] Il. 8, 70. 9, 411. 18, 535—540. 22, 210. 23, 79. 24, 82.

linger on the sea-shore; and the swan was considered a bird of *augury*.[1] The Völundarqviða relates: Three women sat on the shore, *spinning flax*, and had their *álptarhamir* (swan-shifts) by them, so that any moment they could fly away again as swans: 'meyjar *flugo*,' and 'settuz at hvílaz â sævarströnd'; one of them has even the surname of *svanhvít* (swanwhite), and wears swan's feathers (svanfiaðrar drô). In the Hrômundarsaga (Fornald. sög. 2, 375-6), the same *Kára*, who the Edda says was a second birth of Svava, appears as an enchantress in *swan-shift*, (fiölkýngiskona î âlftarham), and hovers above the hero, singing.[2] By her assistance Helgi had always conquered, but it happened in one fight, that he swung his sword too high in the air, and hewed off his lover's foot, she fell to the ground, aud his luck was spent. In Saxo Gram., p. 100, Fridlevus hears up in the air at night 'sonum *trium olorum* superne clangentium,' who prophesy to him, and drop a girdle with runes on it. Brynhildr is 'like the swan on the wave' (Fornald. sög. 1, 186): the simile betrays at the same time, that she had really the power of changing into the bird. Many tales of *swan-wives* still live among the Norse people. A young man saw *three swans* alight on the shore, lay their white bird-shifts in the grass, turn into beautiful maidens, and bathe in the water, then take their shifts again, and fly away in the shape of swans. He lay in wait for them another time, and abstracted the garment of the youngest; she fell on her knees before him, and begged for it, but he took her home with him, and married her. When seven years were gone by, he shewed her the shift he had kept concealed; she no sooner had it in her hand, than she *flew out as a swan* through the open window, and the sorrowing husband died soon after. Afzelius 2, 143-5. On the other hand, the swan-hero forsakes his wife the moment she asks the forbidden question. A peasant had a field, in which whatever he set was trampled down every year on St. John's night. Two years in succession he set his two eldest sons to watch in the field; at midnight they heard a hurtling in the air, which sent them into a deep sleep. The next year the third son watched, and he saw *three maidens* come flying,

---

[1] Es *schwant* mir, it swans me = I have a boding. The reference to the bird seems undeniable, for we also say in the same sense: es wachsen (there grow) mir *schwansfedern*' (so already in Zesen's Simson). Conf. the Eddic 'svanfiaðrar drô (wore)'.

[2] Rafn has chosen the reading *Lara*.

who laid their wings aside, and then danced up and down the field. He jumped up, fetched the wings away, and laid them under the stone on which he sat. When the maidens had danced till they were tired, they came to him, and asked for their wings; he declared, if one of them would stay and be his wife, the other two should have their wings back. From this point the story takes a turn, which is less within the province of the swan-wife myth; but it is worth noting, that one of the maidens offers her lover a drink of water out of a *golden pitcher*, exactly as elfins and wish-wives do elsewhere (pp. 420, 326). Molbech no. 49.

These lovely swan-maidens must have been long known to German tradition. When they bathe in the cooling flood, they lay down on the bank the *swan-ring*, the *swan-shift*; who takes it from them, has them in his power.[1] Though we are not expressly told so, yet the *three prophetic merwomen* whose garments Hagene took away, are precisely such; it is said (Nib. 1476, 1) by way of simile again:

> sie swebten *sam die vogele* ûf der fluot.

It is true, our epic names only two of them (the Danish story only one), the *wîsiu wîp, Hadburc* and *Sigelint*,[2] but one of them begins to prophesy, and their garments are described as 'wunderlich,' 1478, 3. The myth of Völundr we meet with again in an OHG. poem, which puts *doves* in the place of swans : three doves fly to a fountain, but when they touch the ground they turn into maidens, Wielant removes their clothes, and will not give them up till one of them consents to take him for her husband. In other tales as widely diffused, young men throw the shift, ring or chain over them, which turns them into *swans*.[3] When the resumption of human shape cannot be effected completely, the hero retains a *swan-wing*; evidence of the high antiquity of this detail lies in its connexion with the heroic legend of Scoup or Sceáf (p. 370); and it has found its way into modern pedigrees.[4] Especially impor-

---

[1] Musæus, Volksmärchen vol. 3 : The stolen veil.

[2] There is a plant named, I suppose, from this Sigelint; Sumerl. 22, 28 (conf. 23, 19) has *cigelinta* fel draconis, and 53, 48 *cigelinde;* Graff 6, 145 has *sigeline;* see Sigel, Siglander in Schm. 3, 214.

[3] Kinderm. no. 49. Deutsche sagen 2, 292-5. Adalb. Kuhn p. 164, the swan-chain.

[4] Conf. Deutsche sagen no. 540 : 'the *Schwanrings* of Plesse,' who carry a *swan's wing* and *ring* on their scutcheon. A doc. of 1441 (Wolf's Nörten no. 48) names a Johannes *Swaneflügel*, decretorum doctor, decanus ecclesiae majoris Hildesemensis. In a pamphlet of 1617 occurs the phrase : 'to tear the *ring* and *mask* off this pseudonym'.

tant, as placing in a clear light the exact relation of these swan-wives to the walküren, is a statement about them in Altd. bl. 1 128: A nobleman hunting in a wild forest saw a maiden bathing in the river, he crept up and took away the gold chain on her hand, then she could not escape. There was peculiar virtue in this chain: 'dor ümme (on account of it) werden sülche frowen *wünschelwybere* genant'. He married her, and she had seven children at a birth, they all had gold rings about their necks, *i.e.*, like their mother, the power of assuming a swan-shape. Swan-children then are *wish-children*. In Gudrun, the prophetic angel comes over the sea-wave in the shape of a wild bird singing, *i.e.*, of a *swan*, and in Lohengrin a talking *swan* escorts the hero in his ship; in AS. poetry *swanrâd* (-road) passed current for the sea itself, and alpiz, ælfet, âlpt (cygnus) is akin to the name of the ghostly alp, ælf (see Suppl.).

We hear tell of a *swan* that swims on the lake in a hollow mountain, holding a *ring* in his bill: if he lets it fall, the earth comes to an end.[1] On the Urðarbrunnr itself two *swans* are maintained (Sn. 20); another story of a soothsaying *swan* is communicated by Kuhn, p. 67, from the Mittelmark. A young man metamorphosed into a swan is implied in the familiar Westphalian nursery-rhyme:

> swane, swane, pek up de nesen,
>
> wannehr bistu krieger wesen (wast a warrior)?

Another, of Achen, says:

> krune krane, wisse schwane,
>
> we wel met noh Engeland fahre?

And the name Sæfugel in the AS. genealogies seems to indicate a swan-hero.

The spinner Berhta, the *goose-footed*[2] queen, may fairly suggest swan-maidens (p. 280).[3] If those prophetic 'gallicenae' were able

---

[1] Gottschalk's Sagen, Halle 1814, p. 227.

[2] The pentagram was a Pythagorean symbol, but also a Druidic; as it goes by the name of elf's foot, elf's cross, goblin-foot, and resembles a pair of goose-feet or swan-feet, semi-divine and elvish beings are again brought together in this emblem; the valkyr Thruð is next door to a swan-maiden, and Staufenberger's lover likewise had such a foot.

[3] The beautiful story of the Good Woman, publ. in Haupt's zeitschr. 2, 350, is very acceptable as shewing yet another way in which this fairy being got linked with the hero-legend of the Karlings. The two children born on one day at paske flourie, and brought up in mutual love (77—87), are clearly identical with *Flore* and *Blanchefleur*, for these also are not real names, but

to assume what animal shapes they pleased, why, then the Celts
too seem to have known about swan-metamorphosis in very early
times, so that in French fay-legends we may supply the omissions;
e.g., in Méon 3, 412:

> en la fontaine se baignoient
> *trois puceles* preuz et *senées,*
> qui de biaute sembloient *fées:*
> lor robes a tout lor *chemises*
> orent desoz une arbre mises
> du bout de la fontaine en haut.

puceles senées 3, 419. bien eurées 418. la plus mestre 413-5.
The shifts were stolen, and the maidens detained. In the Lai du
Desiré the knight espies in the forest a swan-maiden without her
wimple (sans guimple). The wimple of the white-robed fay
answers to the swan-shift.

6. Wood-Wives.

We have seen that the wish-wives appear on pools and lakes
in the *depth of the forest:* it is because they are likewise *wood-wives,*
and under this character they suggest further reflections. The old
sacred forest seems their favourite abode: as the gods sat throned
in the groves, on the trees, the wise-women of their train and
escort would seek the same haunts. Did not the Gothic aliorunas
dwell in the woodland among wood-sprites? Was not Veleda's
tower placed on a rock, that is, in the woods? The Völundarqviða
opens with the words:

> meyjar flugo sunnan *Myrkvið* igögnom,

invented in fairy-tale fashion, to suit the name of their daughter *Berhta*, the
bright, white. Berhta marries Pepin, and gives birth to *Charlemagne;* in the
Garin le Loherain, Pepin's wife is said to be *Blanchefleur* of Moriane, but in the
story now in question she is the unnamed daughter of count Ruprecht of
Barria (Robert of Berry), spoken of simply as *diu guote frouwe* (162. 1130), *diu
guote* (1575), *la bone dame* (3022), conf. bonadea. bonasocia, p. 283; her
husband, who steps into the place of the childless last king (Merovingian), is
Karelman (3020), and the only name that can suit herself is *Berte*, already
contained in that of her father Ruodbert. The children of this pair are
' *Pippîn* der kleine (little)' and ' *Karle* der mêrre (greater)'. The events in the
middle part of the story are quite other (more fully unfolded, if not more
pleasing) than those told of Flore and Blanchefleur; but we plainly perceive
how on the new Karling race in the freshness of its bloom were grafted older
heathen myths of the swan-wife, of the good wife (p. 253), of the mild woman
(p. 280), of the bona socia (p. 283), and of the bonne dame (p 287); Conf.
Sommer's pref. to Flore xxvi. xxvii. xxxii.

maids flew from south through murky wood to the seashore, there they tarried seven years, till they grew homesick:

>meyjar fŷstoz â *myrkvan viđ,*

they could resist no longer, and returned to the sombre wood. Almost all swan-maidens are met with *in the forest.* The *seven years* agree with those of the Swedish story on p. 427.[1]

As *Sigrûn, Sigrdrîfa, Sigrlinn* are names of valkyrs, and our epic still calls one of the wise-women *Sigelint,* I believe that the OHG. *siguwîp,* AS. *sigewîf,* ON. *sigrvîf,* was a general designation of all wise-women, for which I can produce an AS. spell communicated to me by Kemble:

>sitte ge *sigewîf,* sîgađ tô eorđan!
>næfre ge wilde (l. wille) *tô wuda fleogan!*
>beo ge swâ gemyndige mînes gôdes,
>swâ bîđ manna-gehwylc metes and êđeles.[2]

Like norns, they are invited to the house with promise of gifts.

On this point we will consider a passage in Saxo, where he is unmistakably speaking of valkyrs, though, as his manner is, he avoids the vernacular term. In his account of Hother and Balder, which altogether differs so much from that of the Edda, he says, p. 39: Hotherus inter venandum errore nebulae perductus in quoddam *silvestrium virginum conclave* incidit, a quibus proprio nomine salutatus, 'quaenam essent' perquirit. Illae *suis ductibus auspiciisque* maxime *bellorum fortunam* gubernari testantur: saepe enim se *nemini conspicuas proeliis interesse, clandestinisque subsidiis optatos amicis praebere successus:* quippe conciliare prospera, adversa infligere posse pro libitu memorabant. After bestowing their advice on him, the maidens with their house (aedes, conclave) vanish before Hother's eyes (see Suppl.). Further on, p. 42: At Hotherus extrema locorum devia pervagatus, insuetumque mortalibus *nemus* emensus, *ignotis forte virginibus* habitatum reperit *specum:* easdem esse constabat, quae eum insecabili veste quondam donaverant. They now give him more counsel, and are called *nymphae.*[3]

---

[1] In the Wallachian märchen 201, three wood-wives bathing have their crowns taken from them.

[2] Sedete bellonae, descendite ad terram, nolite in silvam volare! Tam memores estote fortunae meae, quam est hominum quilibet cibi atque patriae.

[3] Three *other* nymphs appear directly after, and prepare enchanted food for Balder with the spittle of snakes, p. 43. A '*femina silvestris* et immanis' is also mentioned by Saxo p. 125.

This seems no modern distorted view, to imagine the maids of war, that dwelt in Oðin's heavenly company, that traversed air and flood, as likewise haunting the *woodland cave ;* therefore Saxo was right to call them *silvestres*, and to place their chamber, their cave, in the forest.

The older stages of our language supply some similar expressions, in which I recognise the idea of *wise wood-wives*, not of mere elvish wood-sprites. They are called *wildiu wîp*, and the Trad. fuld., p. 544, speak of a place 'ad domum *wildero wîbo*'. Burcard of Worms, p. 198[d], mentions '*agrestes feminas* quas *silvaticas* vocant, et quando voluerint ostendunt se suis amatoribus, et cum eis dicunt se oblectasse, et item quando voluerint abscondunt se et evanescunt'. This 'quando voluerint' seems to express the notion of wish-life. Meister Alexander, a poet of the 13th century, sings (str. 139, p. 143[b]): 'nû gênt si vür in (go they before him) über gras in *wilder wîbe* wæte (weeds)'. So: 'von einem *wilden wîbe* ist Wate arzet,' is (*i.e.* has learnt to be) physician, Gudr. 2117; 'das *wilde fröuwelîn*,' Ecke 189. In the Gl. monst. 335, *wildaz wîp* stands for lamia, and 333 *wildiu wîp* for ululae, funereal birds, death-boding wives, still called in later times *klagefrauen, klagemütter*, and resembling the prophetic Berhta (p. 280). In groves, on trees, there appeared *dominae, matronae, puellae* clothed in white (pp. 287-8), distinguishable from the more elvish tree-wife or dryad, whose life is bound up with that of the tree. The Vicentina Germans worship a *wood-wife*, chiefly between Christmas and Twelfthday: the women spin flax from the distaff, and *throw it in the fire* to propitiate her:[1] she is every bit like Holda and Berhta. As three bunches of corn are left standing at harvest-time for Wuotan and frau Gaue, so to this day in the Frankenwald they leave *three handfuls of flax lying on the field* for the *holzweibel* (wood-wives, Jul. Schmidt's Reichenfels, p. 147), a remnant of older higher worship. Between Leidhecken and Dauernheim in the Wetterau stands the high mountain, and on it a stone, *der welle fra gestoil* (the wild woman's chairs); there is an impression on the rock, as of the limbs of human sitters. The people say the *wild folk* lived there 'wei di schtan noch mell warn,' while the stones were still soft; afterwards, being persecuted, the man ran away, the wife and child remained in custody at Dauernheim until they died. Folk-songs

---

[1] Deutsche sagen no 150.

make the huntsman in the wood start a dark-brown maid, and hail
her: 'whither away, *wild beast?*' (Wunderhorn 2, 154), but his
mother did not take to the bride, just as in the tale of the swan-
children. We find a more pleasing description in the Spanish
ballad De la infantina (Silva p. 259): a huntsman stands under a
lofty oak:

En una rama mas alta viera estar una *infantina,*
cabellos de su cabeza todo aquel roble cobrian:
'*siete fadas* (7 fays) me fadaron en brazos de una ama mia,
que andasse los siete años sola en esta montina'.

But the knight wants first to take his mother's opinion, and she
refuses her consent. When Wolfdieterich sits by a fire in the
forest at night, *rauhe Els* comes up, the *shaggy woman,* and carries
off the hero to her own country,[1] where she is a queen and lives on
a high rock: at length, bathing in the jungbrunnen, she lays aside
her hairy covering, and is named *Sigeminne,* 'the fairest above all
lands'.[2]—Synonymous with 'wildaz wîp' the glosses have *holzmuoja*
(lamia and ulula), she who wails or moos in the wood; *holzfrowe*
(lamia) Altd. bl. 2, 195; *holzrûna* (Gl. mons. 335. Doc. 219ᵇ)
meaning the same, but suggestive of that Gothic aliorumna, AS.
burgrûne, and the ON. *Sigrûn* (see Suppl.).[3]

7. MENNI, MERIMANNI.

One general name for such beings must from very early times
have been *menni, minni*; it is connected with *man* (homo), and
with the ON. *man* (virgo), but it occurs only in compounds: *meri-
manni* (neut.), pl. merimanniu, translates sirena or scylla (Reda umbe
diu tier, in Hoffm. fundgr. 19, 18), *meriminni,* Gl. Doc. 225ᵃ mons.
333. In the 13th century poets, *merminne* is equivalent to
merwîp, merfrouwe, yet also to *wildez wîp*: 'diu wîse *merminne,*'
Diut. 1, 38. 'gottinne oder *merminne,* die sterben niht enmohten
(could not die),' Eneit. 8860. In the Wîgamûr 112. 200. 227 seq.,

---

[1] Called *Troje,* conf. Ecke 81; and *Elsentroje,* Deutsche heldensage 198.
211 (see Suppl.).
[2] In the Wolfdietr. (Dresd. MS. 290—7), *twelve goddesses* go to a mountain,
fetch the hero to them, and tend him; the loveliest wants him for a husband.
These beings are more wise-women than elfins.
[3] As the Χάριτες (Graces) and fays *spin* and *weave,* so do the wild women
also: 'mit *wilder wîbe* henden geworht,' Ulr. Lanz. 4826; πέπλος ὃν χάριτες
λάμον αὐταί, Il. 5, 338 (see Suppl.).

there appears a *wildez wíp*, who dwells in a hollow rock of the sea, and is indifferently termed *merwíp* 168. 338, *merfrouwe* 134, and *merminne* 350. AS. *merewíf*, Beow. 3037. M. Dutch *maerminne*. Those three *wísiu wíp* of the Nibelungen are also called *merwíp* 1475, 1. 1479, 1 ; they foretell and forewarn ; their having individual names would of itself put them on a par with the Norse valkyrs : *Hadburc, Sigelint.* The third, whose name the poem omits (p. 428), is addressed by Hagne as ' aller wîseste wîp !' 1483, 4. Wittich's ancestress (p. 376) is named frouwe *Wâchilt*, as if Wave-Hilde, she is a *merminne*, and says sooth to the hero, Râb. 964—974. Morolt also has an aunt a *merminne* who lives in mount *Elsabé* and rules over dwarfs ; her name is not given, but that of her son is Madelgêr, and she likewise gives wise advice to Morolt ; Mor. 40[b] 41[a]. The *merminne* in Ulrich's Lanzelet (lines 196 seq.) is said to be *wís* (5751. 6182), she has under her 10,000 *unmarried* women (dern keiniu bekande man noch mannes gezoc), they dwell on a mountain by the sea, in an ever-blooming land. In the Apollonius, a benevolent *merminne* is queen of the sea (lines 5160. 5294) ; here the poet had in his mind a siren in the classical sense, but the Germans must have had a *merminne* before they ever heard of sirens. The Danish name is *maremind* (Danske viser 1, 118. 125). Norse legend has preserved for us a precisely corresponding male being, the taciturn prophetic *marmennill* (al. marmendill, marbendill), who is fished up out of the sea, and requires to be let go into it again ; Hâlfssaga c. 7 (Fornald. sög. 2, 31—33), and Isl. sög. 1, 33 (Landn. 2, 5).[1] From him coral is named *marmennils smíði*, he cunningly wrought it in the sea. At a later time the word *merfei* was used in Germany : that lover of Staufenberger, whom he found in the forest, and the Fair Melusina (possibly even a tradition of ancient Gaul), are precisely the fairy being that had previously been called *merimenni*.[2] —But, similar to the merminne, there was also a *waltminne*, which word equally stands for lamia in old glosses (Diut. 3, 276). *Sigeminne*, whether the baptized Rauch-els, Wolfdieterich's lover (p. 433), or the wife of Hugdieterich,[3] may with perfect right be

---

[1] Marmennill is extremely like the Greek Proteus, who is also reluctant at first to prophesy, Od. 4, 385 seq. There may have been Proteus-like stories current of our Baldander and Vilander, p. 172 (see Suppl.).

[2] Yet *merfeine* occurs already in Diut. 1, 38 ; *wazzerfeine* (Oberl. sub v.), and even *merfêîn*, MS. 2, 63[a].

[3] Deutsche heldensage pp. 185. 200-1.

regarded as a *waltminne* or *merminne*.[1] In the Vilk. saga cap. 17
I find *sœkona* used of the woman whom Vilkinus found *in the wood*,
and who bore him Vadi. Saxo Gram., p. 15, speaks of a tugurium
silvestris immanisque feminae (see Suppl.).

By this array of authorities it is proved to satisfaction, that the
wildaz wîp or *menni, minni* was thought of as a higher, superhuman
being, such as can be placed at the side of the Scandinavian *norn*
and *valkyr*. But in the scanty remains of our tradition the names
stand wofully bare, finer distinctions are inevitably lost, and in
more than one place the boundary-lines between gods, demigods,
elves and giants cross one another. Equally with norns and valkyrs
(pp. 413-9. 425), we have goddesses spinning and weaving, as
Holda, Berhta, Freyja, and even giantesses, as we shall see by and
by.

Among the figures in the Greek and Teutonic mythologies, we
have placed side by side the νύμφαι and idisî, the μοῖραι and nornir,
the κῆρες and valkyrior. But several isolated names might be
compared in the same way, as for instance, Νίκη or Victoria with
some Sigrûn or Sigrdrîfa, Ἔρις and Ἐννώ or Bellona with a Hildr
and Gunnr. Eris, like Iris, is sent forth on an errand by Zeus
(Il. 11, 3), as Skögul or Göndul by Oðinn. I often find these
Grecian figures in attendance on individual gods: in Il. 5, 333
πτολίπορθος Ἐννώ goes with Athene; in 5, 592 πότνι' Ἐννώ with

---

[1] A Leyden parchm. MS. of the 13th century contains the following legend
of Charles the Great : *Aquisgrani* dicitur Ays (Aix), et dicitur eo quod Karolus
tenebat ibi quandam *mulierem fatatam*, sive quandam *fatam*, que alio nomine
nimpha vel *dea* vel adriades (l. *dryas*) appellatur, et ad hanc consuetudinem
habebat et eam cognoscebat, et ita erat, quod ipso accedente ad eam vivebat
ipsa, ipso Karolo recedente moriebatur. Contigit, dum quadam vice ad ipsam
accessisset et cum ea delectaretur, radius solis intravit os ejus, et tunc Karolus
vidit *granum auri* linguae ejus affixum, quod fecit abscindi, et contingenti (l. in
continenti) mortua est, nec postea revixit. The grain of gold, on which the spell
hung, is evidently to explain the name of the city : later tradition (Petrarcha
epist. fam. 1, 3. Aretin's legend of Charlem. p. 89) has instead of it a ring,
which archbishop Turpin removes from the mouth of the corpse, and throws
into a lake near Aachen ; this lake then attracts the king, and that is why he
made the town his favourite residence. There is no further mention of the
maiden's fairy existence. It was a popular belief (applied to the Frankish
king and gradually distorted) about the union of a wild-woman or mermaid
with a christian hero. Not very differently was Charles's ancestress Berhta, as
we saw above (p. 430), made into a 'good woman,' *i.e.* a fay. [The similarity
of names in the heroic line: Pepin of Herstal, Charles Martel, Pepin the Little,
Charles the Great, seems to have made it doubtful whether Berhta was Charlemagne's mother or his great-grandmother.]

Ares; in 4, 440 and 5, 518 Ἔρις ἄμοτον μεμαυῖα with Ares, who is also followed by Δεῖμος and Φόβος (p. 207-8). And lastly, the Charites are nearly allied; and there was supposed to be a special Charis of victory. Still nearer to our wood-wives stand particular classes of nymphs, especially those whom Theocritus 5, 17 names τὰς λιμνάδας νύμφας, or those called νύμφαι ἀκοίμητοι, δειναὶ θεαὶ ἀγροιώταις 13, 44. The graceful myth of swan-wives appears indeed to be unknown to the Greeks and Romans, while we Teutons have it in common with the Celts; yet a trace of it remains in the story of Zeus and Leda (p. 338), and in the swan's prophetic song, as in the Indian Nalus too the gold-bedizened swan (hansa = anser, goose) finds human speech (Bopp's ed. pp. 6. 7).

The Slavs have not developed any idea of goddesses of fate.[1] The beautiful fiction of the *vila* is peculiar to Servian mythology: she is a being half fay, half elf, whose name even resembles that of the vala. The relation of valkyrs to christian heroes is suggested by the *fraternal bond* between the vila and Marko (Vuk 2, 98. 232. Danitza for 1826, p. 108), as also by the vilas appearing singly, having proper names, and prophesying. In some things they come nearer the German elfins of our next chapter: they live on hills, love the song and the round dance (Ir. elfenm. lxxxii), they mount up in the air and discharge fatal arrows at men: 'ustrièlila ga vila,' the vila has shot him with her shaft. Their cry in the wood is like the sound of the woodpecker hacking, and is expressed by the word 'kliktati'. The vila has a right to the child whom his mother in heedless language (diavo ye odniyo!) has consigned to the devil (Vuk no. 394), as in similar cases the wolf or bear fetches him away. Vile te odnele! (vilae te auferant) is a curse (Vuks sprichw. p. 36); 'kad dot'u vile k otchim' (quando vilae ante oculos veniunt) signifies the moment of extreme distress and danger (ibid. 117). The vila rides a seven-year old stag, and bridles him with snakes, like the Norse enchantresses (see Suppl.).[2]

[1] The Bohem. sudice translates parca, but it simply means judge (fem.): the Russians even adopt the word parka. We must at least notice the *lichoplezi* in Hanka's Glosses 21ᵃ, who are said to be *three*, like the sirens and mermaids.

[2] The Bulgarian *samodíva* or *samovíla* corresponds to the Servian vila. When the wounded Pomák cries to his 'sister' samodíva, she comes and cures him. The samodívy carry off children; and mischief wrought by the

elements, by storms, &c., is ascribed to them. Like the Fates, they begift the newborn : three samodívy visit the infant Jesus, one sews him a shirt, another knits him a band, and the third trims a cap for him. Some stories about them closely resemble those of the swan-maids. Stoyán finds three samodívy bathing, removes their clothes, restores those of the two eldest, but takes the youngest (Maríyka) home, and marries her. St. John christens her first child, and asks her to dance as do the samodívy. But she cannot without her 'samodívski drékhi,' Stoyán produces them, she flies away, bathes in the móminski fountain, and recovers her móminstvo (virginity).—TRANS.

END OF VOL. I.